THE ARCHITECTURAL DRAWINGS OF ANTONIO DA SANGALLO THE YOUNGER AND HIS CIRCLE

THE ARCHITECTURAL DRAWINGS OF

ANTONIO DA SANGALLO THE YOUNGER

AND HIS CIRCLE

VOLUME III·A

Antiquity and Theory

TEXT

Christoph Luitpold Frommel | Georg Schelbert

HARVEY MILLER PUBLISHERS

HARVEY MILLER PUBLISHERS
An Imprint of Brepols Publishers
London/Turnhout

British Library Cataloguing in Publication Data
A catalogue record for this book
is available from the British Library
ISBN 978-1-912554-37-9 (Text)
ISBN 978-1-912554-38-6 (Plates)
ISBN 978-1-912554-39-3 (2 volumes)

This book was produced in collaboration with and with funding by Bibliotheca Hertziana – Max Planck Institute for Art History, department II Prof. Tristan Weddigen: *Art of the Modern Age in a Global Context* (project number BH-P-19-25)

D/2022/0095/96

Printed in the EU on acid-free paper.

Contents

Acknowledgments

Twenty years after the publication of the second volume of the corpus of drawings of Antonio da Sangallo, we are delighted at last to be able to follow up with the two outstanding volumes. One of the many reasons for the long delay was the departure of the co-editor, Nick Adams, who for health reasons was no longer able to continue the work, which was taken over by Georg Schelbert. The Architectural History Foundation in New York and its president Victoria Newhouse have continued to support the preparation of these volumes in every possible way, while the Tristan Weddigen Department of the Bibliotheca Hertziana – Max Planck Institute for Art History provided the final funding to complete the project. In Harvey Miller publishers (an imprint of Brepols) we have found a new publishing house that that has shown continuous dedication toward the final realization and distribution of the work.

The surviving drawings of Antonio da Sangallo and his circle are the first substantially complete archive of drawings by a modern architect. Sangallo was Raphael's deputy as papal architect from 1516–20 and his successor from 1520 until his death in 1546. His drawings provide an overview of the entire field of activity of an architect of the High Renaissance. The corpus is arranged according to the objects in the drawings. Following the first two volumes which were dedicated to military architecture and machinery, and to sacred architecture and villas, the third volume is devoted to antique drawings and theoretical studies, and the fourth to designs for palaces and houses. As in the previous volumes, a sharp separation of subjects is not always possible, if only because on many sheets drawings on different themes are placed next to each other. In allocating the drawing sheets to the respective volumes, a decision was made according to the main subject. In some cases, the recto and verso sides of a sheet were assigned to different volumes.

The majority of the texts in the catalogue date back to the 1980s and 1990s, a heyday of research into Renaissance architecture that no longer exists in this form in the academic world today. After the publication of the second volume, at the beginning of the new millennium, catalogue entries still awaiting publication were written by younger researchers, some of them students of the original contributors. In 2004 Ian Campbell was able to attribute the Codex Rootstein Hopkins, the only major group of drawings not in the Gabinetto Disegni e Stampe of the Uffizi Gallery, to Giovanni Battista Sangallo and to prepare the catalogue entries.

Not all contributors were able to update the entries in their entirety. However, attempts were made to take into account relevant new publications. The Sangallo circle's drawings of antiquities have received some attention in recent decades. This can be attributed also to the The Census of Antique Works of Art and Architecture Known in the Renaissance, although this outstanding database focuses rather less on Sangallo the artist than on the signifiance of ancient monuments for the Renaissance. The reference numbers to the database are noted in our entries.

The original versions of the two essays preceding volumes three and four also date from the beginning of the millennium. However, the authors have made every effort to bring them into line with the current scholarship.

Enzo Bentivoglio and Ian Campbell wrote or completed missing catalogue entries and deciphered the often difficult to read captions on the original drawings. The editors are grateful to Ian Campbell, Sabine Eiche, Caroline Elam, Renata Franciscono, Deborah Howard, Bridget Mason and Peter Spring for translations and reviews of the texts. The Gabinetto dei Disegni e delle Stampe delle Gallerie degli Uffizi supported this fundamental project both through generous access to the original works and through reproduction permission. We would like to thank the director Johannes Röll and Regine Schallert of the photo library of the Bibliotheca Hertziana – Max-Planck Institute for Art History, who were a great help in managing the image material.Until 2016 the editing was in the hands of Liz Allen, Karen Banks and Mary Gladue. The final phase was taken over by the editors themselves.

Sangallo and Antiquity

CHRISTOPH LUITPOLD FROMMEL

I The Study of Ancient Monuments before 1513

BRUNELLESCHI AND ALBERTI

Since the fourteenth century, and probably even earlier, artists had drawn and measured ancient monuments, and in so doing prepared the ground for the renewal of architecture.[1] But the first artist reported to have measured Roman monuments systematically was Filippo Brunelleschi (1377–1446): "... levassono [together with the young Donatello] grossamente in disegno quasi tuttj gli edificj di Roma e in molti luoghi circustanti di fuorj colle misure delle largheze e alteze...."[2] For Brunelleschi the architecture of the ancients was the only legitimate kind—it was architecture true and pure. He went to great efforts to secure a translation of the most important chapters of Vitruvius's treatise, the only surviving text to present a systematic idea of ancient architecture, so that he might understand better the character, vocabulary, and syntax of ancient architecture.[3] In Leon Battista Alberti (1404–72) he found someone of equal stature, someone with similar humanistic and artistic convictions, who would lay the theoretical foundation for the future development of architecture.[4] Even though architecture did not become Alberti's main interest until the 1440s, his humanistic education and intensive study of the ancient monuments equipped him to understand Vitruvius fully for the first time since antiquity. He began collecting every available text on architecture; studied the monuments of imperial Rome, which Vitruvius could not yet have known; and in a systematic Aristotelian fashion developed his findings into his own treatise *De re aedificatoria*, which he presented to pope Nicolas V in 1452. In this work he sketched out the ideal image of an ancient city, which he and many another longed to revive, and by comparing Vitruvius's theory with the actual monuments, laid the foundation for the studies of Francesco del Borgo, Giuliano da Sangallo, Francesco di Giorgio, Bramante, Raphael, Peruzzi, Palladio and, last but not least, Antonio da Sangallo the Younger.

Alberti criticised Vitruvius's language and obscurities and did not hesitate to modify his norms whenever the monuments or other writers offered something more convincing. His persistent goal, in practice as well as in theory, was to assist in the rebirth of antiquity and thus to establish the preconditions for a new kind of life in the style of the ancients. His few buildings demonstrate that he was able to do this because he brought the habits and functions that had developed in the course of the Middle Ages into harmony with ancient types and forms. He found compromises that could, on the one hand, satisfy patrons and accommodate the changed artistic practices of his time and, on the other, transform these habits as far as possible into more antique ones.

Alberti's drawing of a bath complex, probably a fragment of a villa project, already shows an attempt at such a compromise (Fig. 1).[5] It corresponds only partially to the "balinearum dispositionum demonstrationes" in the tenth chapter of Vitruvius's fifth book, but the archaic manner of the drawing, the many parallels with the *De re aedificatoria* and the shallow niches at the end of the ambulatory, which recall Brunelleschi, argue for an early date around 1450. Evidently, Alberti was trying to reawaken the appetite of his wealthy contemporaries for the benefits of bathing, sweating, massaging, and anointing by incorporating a few functional rooms in villas or palaces with open views and loggias suitable for all seasons.[6] It was the start of a new bathing culture, which would afterwards be revived about 1480 in the Palazzo Ducale in Urbino and a little later at the Rocca of Ostia, and which would culminate in Bramante's project for the Cortile del Belvedere and Raphael's design for the Villa Madama.[7] At the same time, shortly before 1450, Alberti started to win over to his ideals some of the most important architectural patrons in Italy. The result was the onset of an age that gave

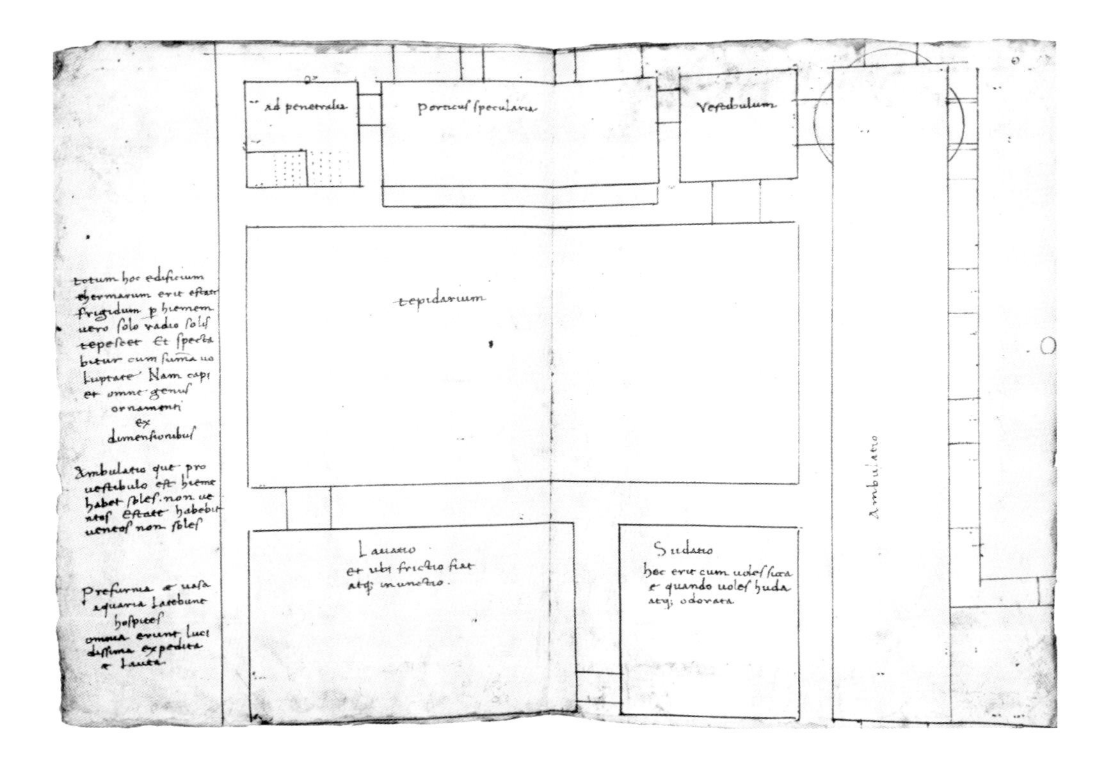

FIG. 1
LEON BATTISTA ALBERTI.
Fragment of a design for a villa with bath complex (Florence, Biblioteca Laurenziana, Codex Ashburnham 1828, App., fol. 56 v.f., photo: Bibliotheca-Hertziana – Max Planck Institute for Art History)

itself as unreservedly as possible to the promptings of ancient art, trying wherever feasible to emulate it. As heir to Alberti and Bramante, as colleague of Raphael and as Palladio's most important precursor, Antonio da Sangallo the Younger occupies a central place in this development. His rich store of almost two thousand architectural drawings affords perhaps the most complete idea that we have of the goals and problems of Renaissance architects and the astonishingly rapid changes that occurred in their understanding of antiquity.[8]

CHOICE AND MANNER OF REPRESENTATION BEFORE SANGALLO

The representation of architecture in plan, elevation, cross-section, and perspective views can be traced back as far as Villard de Honnecourt's pattern book of around 1230 and is ultimately of antique origin.[9] Brunelleschi learned these representational methods, which in the meantime had been perfected in the builders' guilds, probably in the workshop of Florence Cathedral, and from him they were picked up by the young Alberti. Jacopo della Quercia's project for the *Fonte Gaia* in Siena shows how far perspective had arrived in 1408,[10] while Ghiberti's drawing for the niche of St Stephen for Orsanmichele in Florence indicates that the combination of orthogonal elevation and perspective was already in use at the time.[11] The drawings of the somewhat amateurish Ciriaco da Ancona, which we know primarily from copies and which must have been inspired by the more professional drawings of Brunelleschi, Alberti, Donatello or Ghiberti, convey an idea of how ancient

FIG. 2 LEON BATTISTA ALBERTI.
Project for the high altar of S. Lorenzo in Damaso in Rome (London, British Museum, 1860,0616.38, photo: British Museum)

buildings were drawn in the first half of the century.[12] The use of wash for contrasts of light and shade, the employment of perspective, and the delight in such details as the figural elements and fragments of architecture in the foreground of his drawings all prepare the way for Mantegna, Bramante's Prevedari engraving and Giuliano da Sangallo's late drawings.

Although Alberti restricts himself in the plan of the bathing complex to a simple outline of the walls and omits all decoration, he works to scale and shows a professional knowledge of the proportions and wall thicknesses required for rooms undoubtedly meant to be vaulted (cf. Fig. 1). Alberti would eventually develop his graphic capabilities to such an extent that even from a distance he could direct building sites in detail. Filarete's treatise from the early 1460s is also evidence that even before Alberti's death Florentine architects were using highly sophisticated methods of representation, such as the perspective cross-section.[13]

Elevation drawings by Alberti from these years were probably similar to that of the project for cardinal Scarampi's funeral altar in San Lorenzo in Damaso in Rome, which may be autograph (Fig. 2).[14] Since Scarampi died in 1465, the drawing is datable to Alberti's time and we do not know of any comparable example of the preceding decades. The drawing is orthogonal and drawn with ruler and compass. Only the altar table, the central opening with coffered vault, the lateral shell niches, and some pilasters are foreshortened. Though this combination of orthogonal and perspective drawing does not fully correspond to Alberti's own principles of pure orthogonality, it goes far beyond Ghiberti's niche for St Stephen. Both architecture and ornament are of the calibre of Alberti's last years, and the drawings of his late projects may not have been very different.

Some of the few preserved drawings of this early period, and perhaps even some by Brunelleschi, could have ended up in the library of Piero de' Medici, who already in 1456 had sent draughtsmen to Rome and owned three volumes of drawings after the antique.[15]

THE "LIBRO PICCOLO" AND THE "TACCUINO SENESE" OF GIULIANO DA SANGALLO

One of Alberti's first direct followers in architecture was undoubtedly Giuliano da Sangallo (ca. 1445–1516).[16] During his training as a carpenter and woodcarver, he had witnessed the completion of some of Brunelleschi's and Alberti's Florentine buildings. It is likely that the Medici took an interest in furthering the education of the young artist, who was to become the most talented Florentine architect of his generation. They may even have sent him to Rome to meet Alberti, with whom they had close connections and who had already inspired so many artists. Giuliano profited more than anyone else from Alberti's understanding of ancient monuments, his methods of representation and his reconstructions. By his own testimony, Giuliano began surveying the monuments of Rome as early as 1465, and the studies of capitals, bases and cornices in the "Libro Piccolo" of the Codex Barberini, which are still similar to the drawings of the circle of Benozzo Gozzoli, may go back to these early years (Fig. 3).[17] To most Quattrocento painters and sculptors such details of antique architecture were more important than surveys of entire monuments. In the "Taccuino Senese," which is datable only after the late 1490s, Giuliano dedicated attention to entire surveys, such as those of ancient centralized buildings, above all mausolea in the environs of Rome and Naples, some of which Brunelleschi and Alberti had already discovered as important sources of inspiration and which Giuliano may have visited when presenting a model to the king of Naples in 1489, or even earlier (Fig. 4).[18]

The city-view panels in Berlin, Urbino and Baltimore from about 1480–1510 are probably Giuliano's invention and demonstrate the evolution of his virtuosity, not only in representing architecture in convincing perspective and lighting, but also in combining the language and typology of antiquity with that of his own time in an urban context.[19]

FIG. 3 GIULIANO DA SANGALLO.
Views of antique capitals (Biblioteca Vaticana, Codex Barberini 4424, fol. 14 v., "libro piccolo"; photo: Biblioteca Apostolica Vaticana)

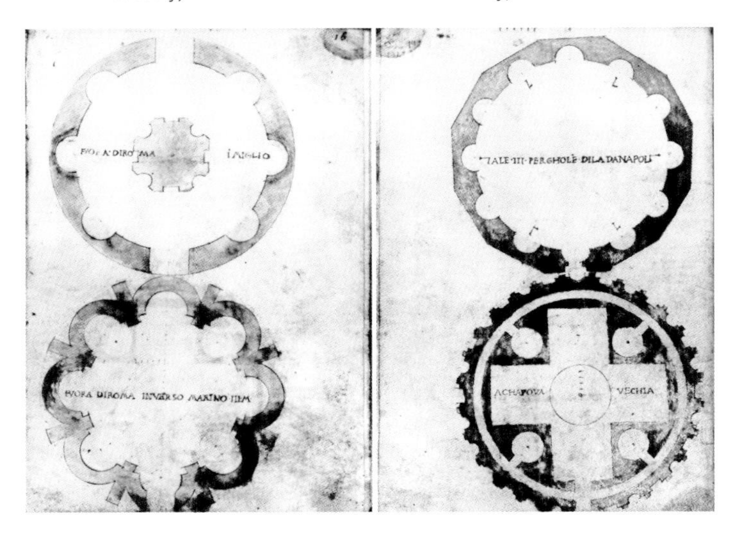

FIG. 4 GIULIANO DA SANGALLO. Ground plans of antique mausoleums (Siena, Biblioteca Comunale, S.IV.8, fols 16 r. and v; photo: Bibliotheca-Hertziana – Max Planck Institute for Art History)

FIG. 5 ANDREA MANTEGNA. Padua, Eremitani Church, Ovetari chapel, frescoes with the history of St James 1448–57, Detail (photo: Bibliotheca-Hertziana – Max Planck Institute for Art History)

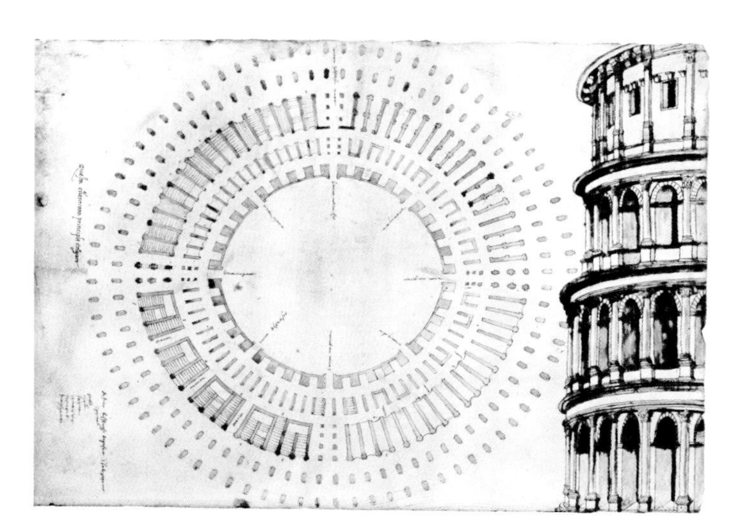

FIG. 6 GIULIANO DA SANGALLO. Groundplan and perspective view of the exterior of the Colosseum (Biblioteca Vaticana, Codex Barberini 4424, fol. 12 v., "libro piccolo"). (photo: Biblioteca Apostolica Vaticana)

FIG. 7 GIULIANO DA SANGALLO. Elevation of the three orders (Siena, Biblioteca Comunale, *Taccuino*, Codex S.IV.8, fol. 6 r.). (photo: Bibliotheca-Hertziana – Max Planck Institute for Art History)

As he did with wooden models, Lorenzo de' Medici may have ordered them as gifts for prominent princes whom he wanted to encourage to build in the new classical style. In the Baltimore panel the plan of the Colosseum is already oval[20] and the perspective is centred on one of Giuliano's magnificent triumphal arches which appear only in his Taccuino Senese.[21] Its rhythm seems to be inspired by the arch of Gallienus[22] and is more complex than that of the arches which Botticelli and Perugino had painted in the early 1480s in the background of their Sistine Chapel frescoes.

Alberti must have already measured some triumphal arches when he designed the facade of the Tempio Malatestiano in around 1450, and some years later he probably also studied the triumphal centrepiece of the Castel Nuovo at Naples.[23] In the interior of S. Andrea in Mantua he used the triumphal motif for the first time in sequence, the so-called "rhythmic travée," and made it one of the most successful articulating devices in post-medieval architecture. Reflections of the rediscovery of the triumphal arch can be seen also in the young Mantegna's frescoes in the Ovetari chapel at Padua, and in the work of Jacopo Bellini and Bonfili and others (Fig. 5).[24] In the first two decades of the sixteenth century Giuliano, Gian Cristoforo Romano, Bernardo della Volpaia and Peruzzi strove to make increasingly precise drawings of triumphal arches.[25] In the drawings of Bramante and Antonio da Sangallo the Younger, however, they play a relatively minor role.[26]

Giuliano's Taccuino Senese includes small surveys of his projects for the Piccolomini chapel of Siena cathedral (1481), the villa at Poggio a Caiano (1485), Santa Maria delle Carceri (1485) and the palace of the king of Naples (1489), which he must have copied from earlier drawings.[27] On the last page of the Taccuino he mentions the completion of the dome of Loreto in 1500 and the death of a certain "Lorenzo di Pietro" in 1503, and as late as 1513 he added a measurement to the plan of the Colosseum.[28] In view of these dates, the Taccuino thus provides what is probably the most concrete idea of the state of knowledge of antiquity at the time when Antonio da Sangallo moved to Rome. As in the earlier "Libro Piccolo" (Fig. 6) the methods of representation range from ground plans and orthogonal elevations with some perspective detail (Fig. 7), to perspective cross-sections and perspective exterior and interior views such as those of the Piccolomini chapel, the Colosseum or the "bagno di Viterbo."[29] Drawing the Doric, Ionic, and Corinthian orders Giuliano also demonstrated a solid knowledge of Vitruvius and Alberti (Fig. 8). There he noted Vitruvius's various intercolumniations, the tapering of the entasis, and the enlargement of the architrave with the increasing height of the orders.[30] Like Alberti, he gave the Doric order a proportion of 1:8 and devoted special care to the Ionic order,

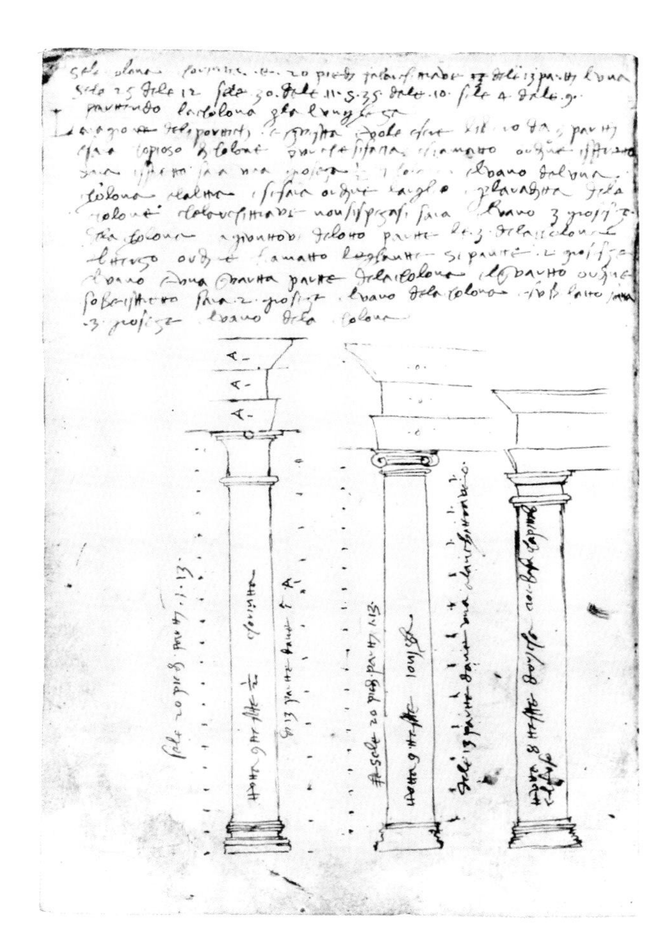

FIG. 8 GIULIANO DA SANGALLO.
Reconstruction of the Vitruvian orders.
(Siena, Biblioteca Comunale, *Taccuino*, Codex S.IV.8. fol. 31 v.).
(photo: Bibliotheca-Hertziana – Max Planck Institute for Art History)

whose proportions, as in Vitruvius, fluctuate between 1:8 and 1:9. He reconstructed its capital, base, and entablature; and like Francesco di Giorgio in the same years, noted the translation into Italian of the Vitruvian terms.

According to Vasari, Giuliano's pupil Simone Pollaiuolo, known as il Cronaca (1457–1508), was one of the most competent draughtsmen of ancient buildings.[31] He started as a stonemason and may have collaborated in the eighties with Andrea Bregno at the Piccolomini chapel of Siena cathedral. Drawings of many details of Bregno's executed work in the co-called Codex Strozzi by a hitherto unidentified draughtsman may have been copied after lost drawings of Cronaca.[32] Only active as an architect in his own right from about 1490, Cronaca collaborated with Giuliano in 1493 on the vestibule for the sacristy of S. Spirito in Florence—perhaps the most classical building before Bramante's Tempietto. In San Salvatore al Monte and the comparable church of San Pietro in Scrigno he was, however, more inspired by the detail of ancient prototypes than by their typology. The majority of his drawings after the antique are, in fact, limited to details and are clearly more akin to those in the Taccuino Senese of Giuliano, with whom he may have exchanged surveys, than to the mature parts of the Codex Barberini.[33] Whatever the case, Cronaca was one of the pioneers of orthogonal drawing after ancient monuments. Thus, in his studies of capitals, like Giuliano in the Taccuino, he occasionally combines an orthogonal front view with a ground plan or side view (Fig. 9, Fig. 10).[34] Orthogonal elevations of the Theatre of Marcellus and the Septizonium, and elevations of the Basilica Aemilia and the Arch of Constantine with perspective details in the Codex Strozzi and Raffaello da Montelupo's sketchbook in Lille, have been also interpreted as copies after Cronaca. The latter was, however, much less able to follow Vitruvius's more complex descriptions than Giuliano, as is shown by his reconstruction of the Doric portal.[35]

For a long time, the early architectural drawings of Peruzzi[36] were attributed to Cronaca, whom he must have admired not only as both connoisseur and draughtsman of the antique, but also as architect.[37] Peruzzi was however already inspired by Bramante not only in the orthogonal elevations with perspective details and strong chiaroscuro, which go far beyond Giuliano's Taccuino, but also in wide-angle interiors such as the imposing drawing of S. Stefano Rotondo (Fig. 11).[38] The fact that the influence of Giuliano and Cronaca as well as Bramante can be felt in Peruzzi's Farnesina, designed around 1505, also speaks in favor of dating these sheets to the beginning of Julius II's pontificate.[39]

The surveys of the Roman sculptor Gian Cristoforo Romano (ca. 1460–1512), such as those of the arches of Constantine and Septimius Severus, are only known through copies.[40] They are purely orthogonal and their combination with the plan, not drawn to scale, and their details without any perspective section recall Giuliano's Taccuino. Gian Cristoforo was the son of Jesaia da Pisa, a sculptor who had been in contact with Alberti, trained in Rome and worked there until 1491. After having lived for many years in Milan and Mantua, Gian Cristoforo Romano was perhaps one of the sculptors—like Andrea Sansovino and Domenico Aimo da Varignana—brought to Rome by Bramante to fill the numerous niches in the Cortile del Belvedere with statues.[41] When he was entrusted in 1510 with the execution of Bramante's project for the basilica in Loreto, he must already have absorbed his method and vision.

In the 1480s, when Giuliano was at the height of his career, his brother Antonio the Elder (1460–1534) collaborated closely with him, and after Lorenzo il Magnifico's death in 1492, when Giuliano had entered the service of Cardinal Giuliano della Rovere, Antonio the Elder became the preferred architect of the Borgias.[42] In 1499 at the latest, he was commissioned to build the Rocca in Civita Castellana and

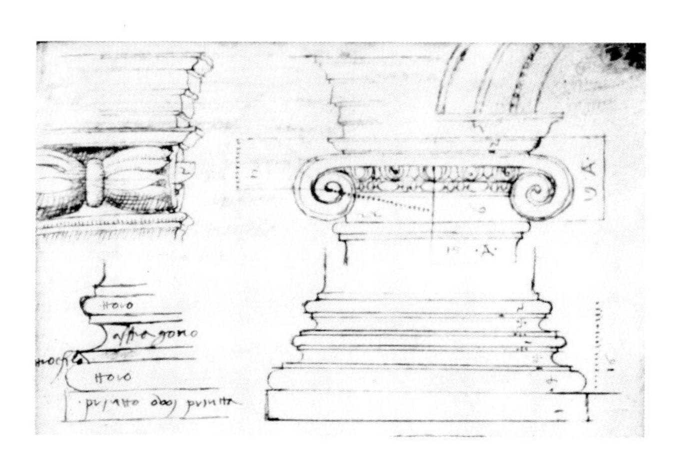

FIG. 9 GIULIANO DA SANGALLO. Ionic capital (Siena, Biblioteca Comunale, *Taccuino*, Codex S.IV.8, fol. 34 r., detail; photo: Bibliotheca-Hertziana – Max Planck Institute for Art History)

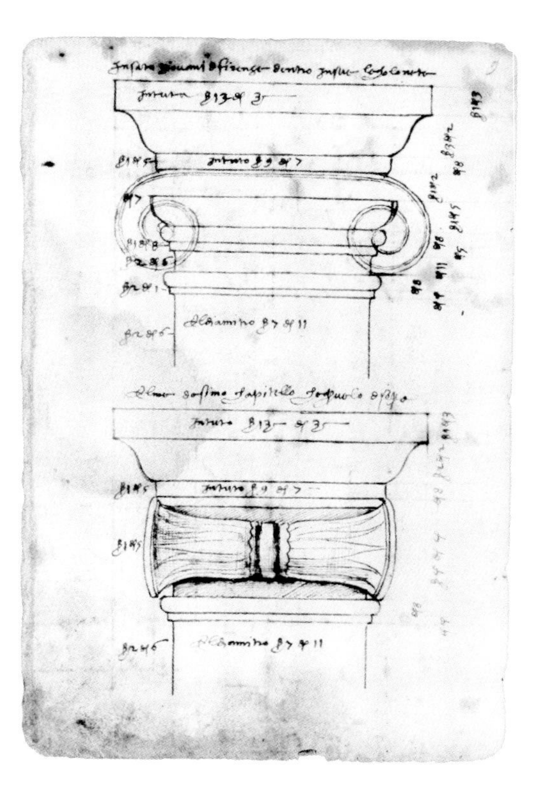

FIG. 10 SIMONE POLLAIUOLO, called IL CRONACA. Ionic capital of the Baptistry, Florence (Montreal, The Canadian Center for Architecture, Castellino Group, fol. 5 r.). (photo: Bibliotheca-Hertziana – Max Planck Institute for Art History)

must have gone there a number of times until the summer of 1503.[43] He may sometimes have taken with him his promising nephew, Antonio the Younger, who would later direct the work after 1510 or even earlier. Antonio the Elder's drawings of two castles, which may date from as early as the beginning of the 1490s, differ from Giuliano's contemporaneous sheets, both in their less convincing bird's-eye perspective and in their finely hatched modelling in ink.[44] The orthogonal survey of the Hadrianeum on U 1407A r with the solemn signature "... O DA SANGALLO ARCHITET." is again reminiscent of Giuliano's Taccuino and may be a copy after Antonio the Elder.[45]

BRAMANTE'S DRAWINGS

In the pontificate of Julius II the influence of Antonio the Elder, Giuliano and Cronaca on Antonio the Younger's development was increasingly superseded by that of Bramante. When Bramante (1444–1514) moved to Rome late in 1499, he not only knew all the methods of representing

FIG. 11 BALDASSARRE PERUZZI. *Interno* of Santo Stefano Rotondo (Florence, U Santarelli 161 r.) (photo: Gabinetto dei Disegni e delle Stampe degli Uffizi)

FIG. 12 BERNARDO DELLA VOLPAIA (after BRAMANTE?). Elevation of the Cortile del Belvedere (London, John Soane's Museum, Codex Coner, fol. 43r.; photo from Ashby 1904)

FIG. 13 Anonymous early sixteenth century. Copies after Bramante's projects for the choir and the exterior of St Peters (Florence, U 5A r.; photo: Gabinette dei Disegni e delle Stampe degli Uffizi)

architecture, but had already proved that he was superior to his contemporaries in representing interior spaces using all the stratagems of perspective and chiaroscuro.[46] He had learned not only from Fra Carnevale, Piero della Francesca, Mantegna and Melozzo, but also from masters of his own generation like Giuliano and Leonardo. Already in his first Roman years he surpassed Alberti's knowledge of ancient architecture and revolutionised the methods of presenting and reconstructing a monument.

In his drawings, some of which are known only through a copyist who is apparently directly connected to him, Bramante increased the spatial effect of the orthogonal elevations and sections through partial perspective and chiaroscuro.[47] Bernardo della Volpaia, one of Bramante's presumed pupils,[48] could have copied the outline of the Cortile del Belvedere in the Codex Coner,[49] which is combined with a perspective view into the loggia and perspective details of the orders and wall openings of the two upper floors, from Bramante's designs from the years 1503–06 (Fig. 12).[50] In his sketches for St Peter's from 1505–06 Bramante accompanies the ground plans with half-perspective sketches. As in the half-perspective view in the foundation medal, in the sketch on sheet U 5A r. the volumes are staggered in depth and culminate in the dome (Fig. 13).[51]

At the same time, in the technical construction drawings for the pendentives of St Peter's, which he delegated to his collaborator Antonio di Pellegrino, Bramante made use of the purely orthogonal section, related to the corresponding ground plan, a method that had already been used in the Florentine cathedral building workshop.[52] Finally, his detailed planning of the choir is attested by his own sketches (U 43A); indeed the differences between these drawings and Antonio's ground plan of the choir (U 44A) made eight years later only become apparent upon closer examination.[53]

Bramante may have drawn the survey of the tomb of Theodoric in Ravenna during his stay in Bologna in 1505–06.[54] (Fig 14) It anticipates the combination of ground plan and elevation drawn to scale in Bramante's late design for the dome of St Peter's, which is known from Serlio's woodcut (Fig. 15, S. Serlio, *Il Terzo Libro*, 1540, fol. 65 v.));[55] in both cases, the strictly orthogonal elevation gains plasticity through the use of intense chiaroscuro. U 1563A r. differs from the contemporary drawings of the young Antonio, to whom it was previously ascribed, not only in characteristic cyphers such as the more elegant "3" or the longer "9," which Antonio tried to imitate a little later, but also in the masterly certainty and intensity of the stroke and the carefree irregular hatching (cf. Fig. 14). Moreover, Bramante's survey may have been the starting point for Giuliano's more fantastic reconstruction of the tomb in the third part of the Codex Barberini, which would confirm its dating to the period after 1507.[56] On the

FIG. 14 DONATO BRAMANTE. Elevation ot the tomb of Theoderic in Ravenna (Florence, U 1563 A r.; photo: Gabinetto dei Disegni e delle Stampe degli Uffizi)

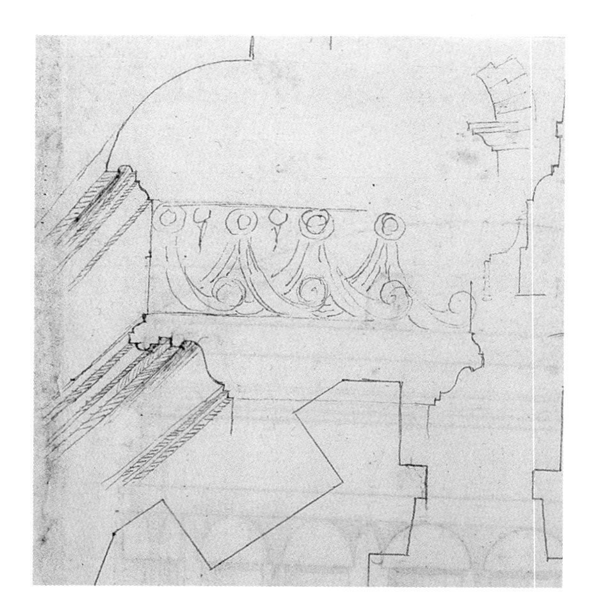

FIG. 16 DONATO BRAMANTE. Cornice of the monolithic vault of the tomb of Theoderic in Ravenna, detail (Florence, U 1563A v.; photo Gabinetto dei Disegni e delle Stampe degli Uffizi)

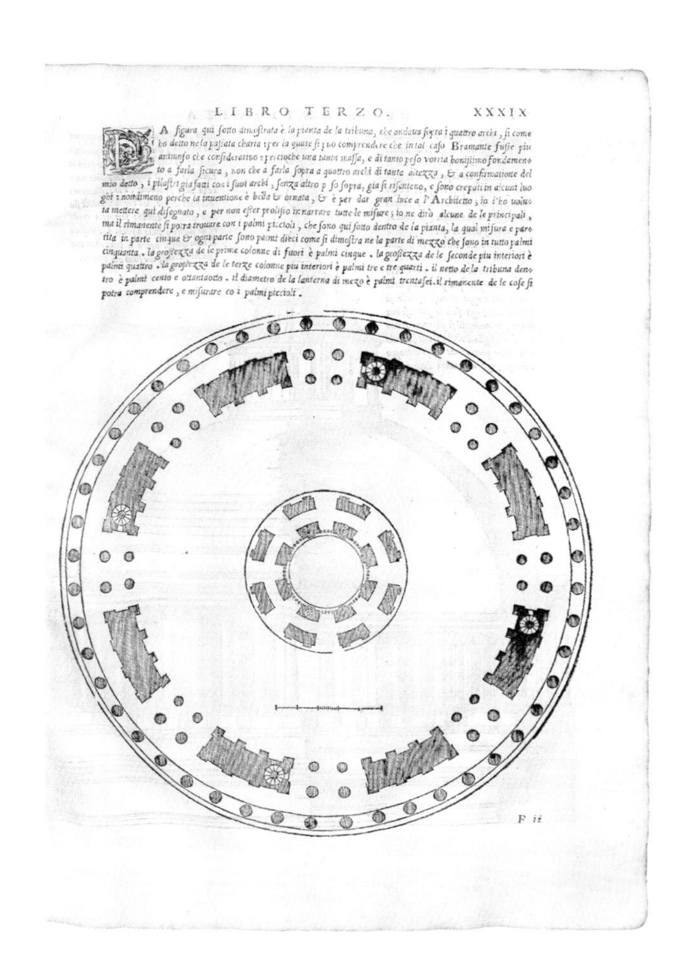

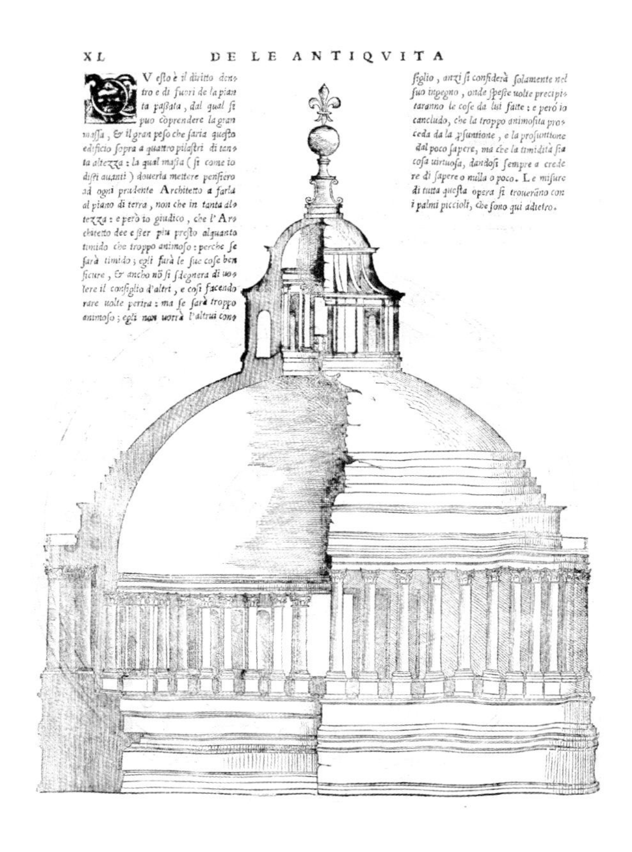

FIG. 15A–B SEBASTIANO SERLIO.
Ground plan, elevation, and cross section of Bramante's project for the dome of St Peter's (S. Serlio, *Il Terzo Libro*, 1544, 39–40.). (photo: Universitätsbibliothek Heidelberg)

verso of Bramante's drawing, in addition to the ground plan of the tomb, an early example of an axonometric section of a cornice is found—a method of representation that would soon enjoy great popularity, as in the Codex Coner, for example (Fig. 16, Bramante, Cornice of the monolithic vault of the tomb of Theodoric in Ravenna, U 1653A r, detail).[57]

Bramante must have started to measure the imperial *thermae* even before he accompanied the pope to Bologna (U 104A r, Fig. 17).[58] The cursory ground plan by Francesco di Giorgio and the drawing by the young Peruzzi, a Quattrocento-style reconstruction with the inscription "termini," no longer met the requirements.[59] But when Bramante planned the Tempietto in 1502 and excavated it with niches both outside and inside, the design already showed the influence of imperial architecture. His parchment plan for St Peter's of spring 1505 with its multiform rooms covered by groin and barrel vaults and domes and separated by masses of wall and screens of columns, shows the particular inspiration of the baths of Diocletian. Bramante measured its interior in *palmi* to make a freehand plan without compass and ruler. He probably took the plan, together with Giuliano in whose hand a measurement is corrected, and noted every irregularity and even the measurements of symmetrically recurring spaces and walls, in order to gain an accurate picture of this type of architecture that would be so decisive for his Roman projects. The small red chalk sketch of a plan on the verso shows the direct influence of the *thermae* on Bramante (Fig. 18).[60]

The date of 1507 on Peruzzi's fragmentary sketch of part of the surrounding walls of the Baths of Diocletian, which is measured in *palmi* and complementary to Bramante's plan, may also be a valid dating for some of Bramante's other drawings of the baths of Diocletian.[61] The semi-perspectival reconstruction of the elevation measured in *braccia* and wrongly attributed to Antonio the Elder may be have been copied from the same lost original as that designed by a

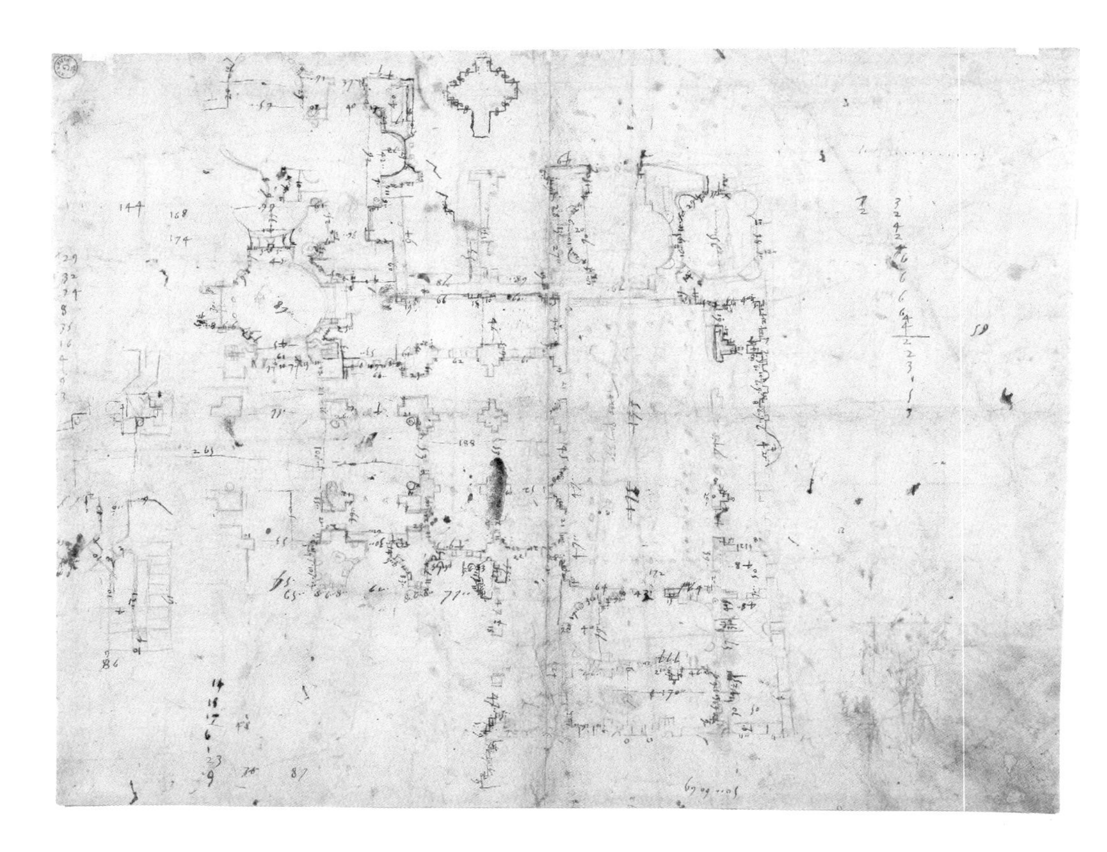

FIG. 17
DONATO BRAMANTE. Survey of the ground plan of the Baths of Diocletian (Florence, U 104A r.). (photo Gabinetto dei Disegni e delle Stampe degli Uffizi)

follower of Raphael in the sketchbook of Fossombrone.[62] Other plans of the Baths of Diocletian, such as those by Bernardo della Volpaia in the Codex Coner of around 1515, the two by Giovani Battista da Sangallo (U 2163A) and Giuliano's son Francesco (U 284A), the latter dated 1518, Peruzzi's plan (U 476A r.), measured in *braccia,* and Riniero Neruccio da Pisa's plan (Vienna, Albertina), measured in ancient feet, seem to be based on Bramante's survey, though not every detail is identical.[63]

Bramante's facade sketches for SS. Celso e Giuliano from 1508 are by far the most vivid testimony to his spontaneous and eminently three-dimensional design method, which Antonio was never able to achieve, even later.[64] Bramante knows how to evoke the effect of depth in the entrance bay with rapid feather strokes and hatching. In his roughly contemporary design for San Biagio della Pagnotta, known only from a copy (München, Staatliche Graphische Sammlung 35343), he develops the perspective of the choir out of the plan of the circular dome.[65] Here, too, he suggests spatial width and depth with the help of a wide angle and strong chiaroscuro contrasts, without attempting a completely coherent perspective.

Raphael's famous views of the interior and the porch of the Pantheon also seem to go back to an original by Bramante (Fig. 19).[66] None other than the master of the Prevedari

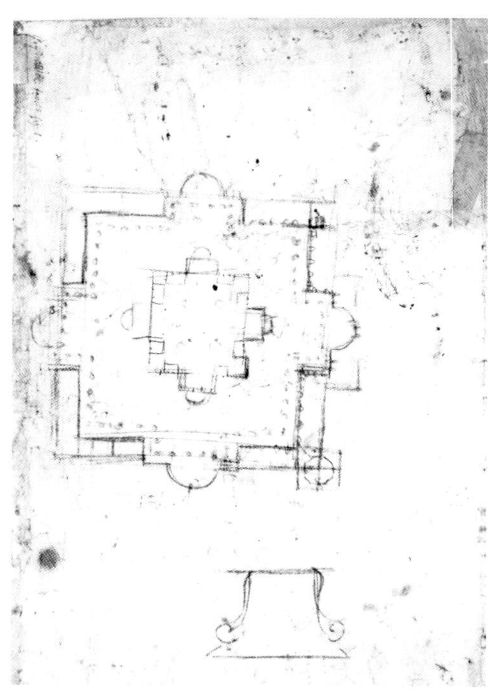

FIG. 18 DONATO BRAMANTE. Project for plan of a centralized building (Palazzo dei Tribunali?) (Florence, U 104A v.), detail. (photo Gabinetto dei Disegni e delle Stampe degli Uffizi)

FIG. 19 RAPHAEL after BRAMANTE (?).
Interior of the Pantheon (Florence, U 164A r.; photo: Gabinetto dei Disegni e delle Stampe degli Uffizi)

engraving could have succeeded in providing such a three-dimensional interior enlivened by chiaroscuro contrasts. The formulaic simplifications of the Corinthian capitals, the irregular hatching of the cornices and the deeply shaded wall openings in the Pantheon drawing are directly reminiscent of the drawing of the tomb of Theodoric and the sketches for SS. Celso e Giuliano, but are without parallel in the work of Raphael or other masters. In particular, the stretching of the two middle bays to make them almost orthogonal, the elimination of two bays to allow the inclusion of both the exedra and the entrance bay, and the sudden transition to a forced perspective at both sides of the representation are characteristic of Bramante, and resemble the presumed copies of Bramante's other drawings such as U 4 and 5A r.[67] Since Raphael is not documented in Rome before 1509, he may have met Bramante during his stay in Bologna in 1506/07 and copied the drawing. In any case, Raphael seems to have benefited from it as early as the spring of 1508 in the exedra of the "Madonna del Baldacchino," and during an encounter with Raphael Bramante himself may have added the darker hatching, a technique also adopted in the copies in the Codex Escurialensis and in Salzburg.[68] Again, before his move to Rome, Raphael may have copied the similarly half-perspective details of the porch of the Pantheon, which likewise do not accurately reflect the building.[69]

Bramante's sketches for the wooden scaffolding for the arches of the crossing of St Peter's probably date back to the years 1509/10, shortly before their execution.[70] Only the later orthogonal project for the dome, transmitted by Serlio, can be dated with some probability to Bramante's last year (cf. Fig. 15). Here his earlier concessions to perspective are eliminated in favor of a completely orthogonal view, and this may have been true for other drawings of his late period.

This significant development was played out chiefly in the dialogue between Florentine masters and Bramante. Surprisingly little was contributed to these developments by the Sienese Francesco di Giorgio (1439–1501), even though after about 1476 he was the most important of those who made Urbino a centre of European architecture and was celebrated as one of the greatest architects and connoisseurs of antiquity of his time.[71] He had begun as a sculptor and painter in his native Siena and was probably introduced to architecture there by Bernardo Rossellino. At any rate, he was familiar with such representational devices as perspective sections, wide-angle interior views, and bird's eye-perspectives; but his often purely linear ground plans, his simplified representations and reconstructions of ancient monuments, and his faulty interpretations of the Vitruvian orders show that he lacked the training and erudition of Giuliano da Sangallo. As a result his famous pupil

Baldassarre Peruzzi in his first Roman years was much less prepared than Antonio da Sangallo the Younger in his understanding of antique architecture.[72]

ANTONIO'S BEGINNINGS

When Antonio wrote his autobiographical remarks in 1531, he kept silent about his initial training under the two uncles who had ceased to be exemplary for him, and declared only his allegiance to Bramante and Raphael: "... abiamo consumato li nostri studi in Roma dalla eta nostra di anni XVIII al principio del pontificato di papa Julio ... e sempre stato alli servitii de' detti pontefici in le loro fabriche al tempo di papa Julio sotto Bramante sino a l'anno ... [secondo] del pontificato di Leone X, dipoi in compagnia di Rafaelo da Urbino...."[73] Vasari knew Antonio personally and mentions the architect's uncles in his biography, but confuses Antonio the Elder's activity under Alexander VI with that of Giuliano under Julius II: "... ed avendo (Antonio the Younger) nella sua fanciullezza imparato l'arte del legnaiolo, si partì di Fiorenza, che Giuliano da Sangallo suo zio era in faccende a Roma insieme con Antonio suo fratello: perché da bonissimo animo volto alle faccende dell'arte dell'architettura, e seguitando quelli, prometteva di sé quei fini, che nell'età matura cumulatamente veggiamo per tutta l'Italia in tante cose fatte da lui. Ora avenne che essendo Giuliano, per l'impedimento che ebbe di quel suo mal di pietra, sforzato ritornare a Fiorenza, Antonio venne in cognizione di Bramante di Castel Durante ...."[74]

Born in Florence on 12 April 1484, the son of a cooper, Antonio was just eight years old, when Lorenzo de' Medici died and Giuliano left Florence for longer periods.[75] Thus, he had only a vague recollection of the period of Medicean glory, and Antonio the Elder was probably one of his first teachers. While Giuliano had difficulty with Latin, Antonio the Younger learned it, in addition to mathematics and geometry. He boasts of his knowledge of Latin in the autobiographical remarks and it was, in fact, to be indispensable for his study of Vitruvius and the ancient monuments.[76]

The few drawings that survive from before 1514 transmit a clear idea of his evolution from the Quattrocentesque style of his uncles to that of Bramante. The earliest drawings could have been similar to Antonio the Elder's project for a poorhouse with the proud signature "A fatto questo disen(i)o m(aestr)o antonjo dasangallo."[77] Its handwriting differs from that of Antonio the Younger's drawings in the following years mainly in the letter "d," and the drawing style is still similar to that of Giuliano. Antonio may have assisted his uncle Antonio the Elder at Civita Castellana and returned with him to Florence in the summer of 1503. Already before the election of Julius II he must have sensed that Bramante was going to understand Vitruvius and ancient architecture even better than his uncles had done, and recognised how much he could learn from him in all respects. After Giuliano's appointment as second papal architect in the spring of 1504 Antonio seems to have followed him to Rome, where he worked for the next four years as a high-level carpenter and probably also as Giuliano's assistant. With pen and ink on parchment he started a similar codex to Giuliano's "Libro Piccolo," which is now dismembered into single sheets. On the recto and verso of one of the earliest pages (U 2045A), he copied six ground plans of ancient centralized buildings from the Taccuino Senese (and not from the "Piccolo Libro") (cf. Fig. 4).[78] The plan of a centralized ruin in Capua Vetere—"A CAPUA VECIA U(N) TENPIO"—is probably copied from another drawing by Giuliano, and only the plan—octagonal on the exterior and circular in the interior—is copied from the "Libro Piccolo," from Giuliano's "TEMPIO DI SIBILLA CUMANA" on fol. 8 v. By reconstructing the elevation and section of the latter, Antonio creates a semi-perspectival triad which in its language and proportions differs from Giuliano and already seems characteristic of Antonio's early style.[79] Evidently the high attic and the lantern of the exterior—"FURA"—are inspired by the Florentine Baptistery and the steep interior—"DI DRENTO"—by Brunelleschi.

When Giuliano, probably before 1500, had drawn in the "Piccolo Libro" the complex plan and the perspective section of the Colosseum, with its five concentric rings, two outer rows of piers, four axial entrances to the inner platform and numerous stairs, he was already far ahead of Francesco di Giorgio, though he had drawn the oval almost as a circle (cf. Fig. 6).[80] He repeated both plan and section in the Taccuino and accompanied them with an elevation of the exterior and a perspective section. Even in the latter drawing, however, Giuliano still did not depict the architectural framework and the shaded corridors with the same mastery of depth as the view on fol. 24 v. of the Codex Escurialensis.[81]

In the six early drawings dedicated to the Colosseum Antonio still followed Giuliano's way of representation, but tried to supersede his surveys and probably also the lost surveys of Antonio the Elder. From Giuliano's Taccuino he appears to have taken plan details as the formula for the stairs, which do not quite correspond to those of the existing building, but in the oval format, the measurements and the form of the piers and their counter piers he achieved a far more reliable reconstruction. In the later, only partially preserved inscription at the lower edge of the ground plan, he mentioned dividing the total length into seven parts—probably to ascertain that the total width corresponds to six parts, and that the plan therefore has a proportion of 6:7. In a note from the years before about 1517, in which he listed the lengths of the Pantheon, the Baths of Diocletian, and the Colosseum, he retained the same length of 333 *braccia* and height of 85 7/24 *braccia* for the Colosseum that he had ascertained in these early drawings and may therefore have added the inscription to the plan only at that time.[82] Later, but before 1514 while he was still using his more archaic "3," he recalculated a width of circa 267 *braccia* and a length of 323 *braccia*[83]—measurements which do not correspond to the 263 1/3 × 315.5 *braccia* taken by Giuliano at about the same time.[84] It is unlikely that Antonio used a compass, as he and Raphael would do in Leo X's pontificate.[85] He seems to have found the centres and radii of the four circle segments that make up the oval with the help of a rope and constructed the ovals of both plans with four centres and two radii, by mean of several rhombuses.[86] It was probably before 1514 that he set down five alternatives to this method of constructing the Colosseum.

Antonio's analytical intelligence is even more in evidence in the cross-section. Still following Giuliano with a semi-perspectival representation he reproduced the building and its complex connecting passages again in a much more precise and detailed manner. The combination of the four ascending orders and the innumerable staircases must have been valuable to Bramante, who at that time was in the process of building the Cortile del Belvedere.[87] Unlike Giuliano, Antonio added two upper tiers with pier arcades. In another drawing, however, he sketched only a single tier, albeit a much higher one, opening it with arches on columns.[88]

From Giuliano's Taccuino Senese (cf. Fig. 9 Siena, Biblioteca Comunale, *Taccuino*, Codex S.IV.8, fol. 6 r) Antonio also set out his elevation of the exterior on the parchment sheet, which was probably also part of a *taccuino*, but included the measurements of the arcades, piers, and individual storeys, and tried to make the proportions more exact (U 2043A r).[89] On the verso he placed the perspective views of the bases, capitals and entablatures of the four exterior orders side by side, from the "primo cornicione" on the far right to the fourth, with its console frieze, on the left. Evidently he had not yet had much experience in representing capitals and followed Giuliano's Taccuino Senese in representing the cornices without the Bramantesque section. This is also true of his drawing of the detail of Pontelli's Vatican portal and antique cornices (U 2044A r.).[90] The perspective view of a pier arcade on U 1576A verso and in the upper edge of U 2043A v. and the deep perspective view of one of the fauces and its stuccoing on the recto of U 1576A,[91] however, already show a strong influence of Bramante. The

FIG. 20 GIULIANO DA SANGALLO. Project for the loggia of the papal winds (Florence, U 283A r.; photo: Gabinetto dei Disegni e delle Stampe degli Uffizi)

FIG. 21 GIULIANO DA SANGALLO. Design for a façade (Florence, U 279A r.; photo Gabinetto dei Disegni e delle Stampe degli Uffizi).

archaic use of "ch," "d," "z" and "3" favors a dating for these drawings in the years 1504–06. At about the same time the young Peruzzi measured or copied the exterior piers of the ground floor and the elevation of the Colosseum and started a never-finished perspective view.[92]

Antonio's drawings of the years 1504–06 are still influenced by the four drawings of triumphal arches in Giuliano's Taccuino Senese, but not yet by the perspective representations in the "Libro degli Archi" and the later parts of the Codex Barberini.[93] Giuliano must have changed style soon after his project for the Loggia of the Papal Winds which is dated before November 1505 and not yet influenced by Bramante (Fig. 20).[94] Shortly afterwards Giuliano drew a façade project with triglyphs and other Bramantesque forms and in about 1507–09 two church façades with even stronger contrasts of light and shadow (Fig. 21).[95] Moreover the emphatically deep perspectives, picturesque plants and ruinous elements in the later parts of the Codex Barberini seem to be drawn under Bramante's direct influence and were already in about 1506/07 imitated by the young Peruzzi in his picturesque view of the "Spoglia Christi," a part of the Forum of Nerva.[96]

Antonio's first axonometric and perspective sections of details may be dated to the time of the measuring campaign in the Baths of Diocletian, or soon afterwards, when he started to become Bramante's direct pupil.[97] At the upper edge of U 2049Ar. (cf. entry in vol. IV), the rather pre-Bramantesque doorway of cardinal Cesarini, he indicated the four Vitruvian orders: "tuschicj / dorjchj / ionjchj / chorjntj," which at just this time were being deployed in exemplary fashion by Bramante in the Cortile del Belvedere and its circular staircase.[98] In the relation of plan and elevation of the project for a sort of Janus Quadrifrons and its strange barrel vault on the recto one still feels Antonio's recognition of Giuliano's legacy; and in the project for the tomb of a bishop he combines the system of the tomb of Pius II with a Bramantesque giant order. The coat of arms framed by volutes is inspired by Cronaca's fireplace in the Palazzo Strozzi, which was under construction in 1504.[99] Here his strokes are closer to those of Filippino Lippi, who may also have been one of his teachers and models.[100] Antonio has now given up the inscriptions in capital letters of the earlier sheets. The loose and hasty pen strokes seem influenced by Bramante and the sure ability to characterise form without straight-edge or compass are signs of his future mastery of draughtsmanship.

The high attic of the project for a centralized building on U 2046Ar. recalls his reconstruction of the tempietto in Capua Vetere on U 2045Ar., but the drawing style is now more dynamic and the Leonardesque rider on top of the lantern shows Antonio's considerable capacities as a figural draughtsman. The plan of a circular mausoleum, the view of a tomb crowned by five pyramids near S. Sebastiano, and the mausoleum of Romulus on the Via Appia demonstrate that after 1505 his interest in centralised funerary structures remained undiminished.[101]

One of the most characteristic drawings from the years shortly before becoming Bramante's assistant is his survey of the Temple of Portunus in Ostia, with explanations in both his contemporary and later hands.[102] It is the earliest combination of the plans of two storeys so characteristic of his later years. The two plans are drawn with a ruler and compasses and measured in *braccia*, but the perspective section above them is sketched freehand. Antonio reconstructed a balustrade as in Bramante's Tempietto, and one can perceive his familiarity with the wide-angled views of interior spaces of Bramante, who himself had been inspired by the crypt, the high plinth, the peristyle and the diagonal circular niches of the temple when designing the Tempietto in 1502. Antonio is now able to represent an interior space more skilfully than in his detail studies of the Colosseum or those of Giuliano in the "Bagno di Viterbo" of the Taccuino Senese, but does not fully succeed in imitating Bramante's dynamic strokes, chiaroscuro hatching and three-dimensional depth; here the columns look flat and the rotunda polygonal.[103] At this time Peruzzi came even closer to Bramante; his drawing (or copy from his drawing) for the portico of the Piazza del Campo in Siena of 1508[104] seems immediately influenced by the project for the lower loggia of the Cortile del Belvedere known through the copy in the Codex Coner (cf. Fig. 12, Codex Coner).[105]

ANTONIO'S YEARS AS BRAMANTE'S ASSISTANT (1509–13)

Not only Giuliano but also Antonio may have accompanied Bramante to Bologna and participated in the measurement of the two Ravenna monuments.[106] On this occasion he could have designed the plan of San Vitale (U 992A v.),[107] which in many ways differs from his survey of around 1526 (U 1413A r.) not only in its lesser precision but in the rear chapels, whose columns are shown as corresponding with those of the exedras.[108] Antonio is documented in Rome for the first time on 7 July 1507 when working together with another carpenter originating from the same Florentine quarter, Sebastiano di Marco de Giano da Sangallo.[109] They had to pay monthly rates for the wood used for the triumphal arch they had erected after Julius's return from Bologna in March, probably the huge arch on St Peter's square which imitated the Arch of Constantine, perhaps designed by Giuliano or Bramante himself.[110] These architects may already have designed and constructed some of the triumphal arches for the pope's entry into Bologna in November 1506.[111] Their workshop was then situated at "Lavinium near the papal palace," probably the fortress of Neptune, which had been begun by Antonio the Elder for Alexander VI and was continued under Julius II—possibly now under the direction of Giuliano, who in December 1508 signed a guarantee that enabled Antonio the younger to accept commissions.[112] The carpenter Sebastiano and the "architect" Raffaello Berti de Sarto, so far unidentified, may also have been members of Giuliano's team. We find Antonio's handwriting of these years on the drawing for the Rocca of Civitavecchia datable to 1509 where he still used his archaic "h."[113] This drawing is more developed than his copies of Francesco di Giorgio's machines.[114]

Antonio seems to have become Bramante's assistant only after March 1509 when Giuliano had turned his back on Rome for the second time, sickly and disappointed, as Vasari tells us.[115] Only then did Antonio fully follow Bramante's methods. Together with the older Antonio di Pellegrino, who was also trained as a carpenter, he was now not only the head of an immense building site and jointly responsible for the centring of the groin and barrel vaults of the choir of St Peter's but also, according to Vasari, to an increasing extent a draughtsman and designer for the gout-plagued Bramante.[116]

Only a few of Antonio's drawings can be dated with any certainty to the four years of intense collaboration with Bramante before the latter's death in 1514.[117] One of the first may be the elevation of the "zecha anticha."[118] In one of the windows of the otherwise purely orthogonal elevation he adopted not only Bramante's partial perspective but also—for the first time—his fine hatching. In about 1509/10 Antonio must also have drawn the beautiful axonometric section of the entablature of the Basilica Aemilia—one of the drawings which at first glance seem to be drawn by Bramante himself.[119] Nearly all archaic elements of the handwriting have disappeared and only the "h" in "da chapo" recalls the drawings of the preceding years. The straight lines are drawn with the ruler and at least some of the curved profiles are drawn with a compass. The axonometric section is similar to the detail of the cornice on Bramante's measurements of the tomb of Theodoric, and the fine hatching resembles the shading on Bramante's roughly contemporary design for the scaffolding of St Peter's.[120] On the recto Antonio repeats the entablature in orthogonal view and the capital in elevation with perspective details—certainly in order to obtain as objective an image of the forms as possible. This, his earliest known depiction of a Doric order, not only shows how closely he had approached Bramante but also anticipates his future projects.

In his sketch for the centring of the crossing arches of St Peter's, which could date from about 1510[121] and in the remarks on Labacco's sketch for the hall of the Lateran palace from 1512, the antiquated "ch" has definitively disappeared.[122] In the survey of the Temple of the Dio Redicolo on U 1168A r. which may date from 1510–13, Antonio is primarily interested in the Ionic portal, which he himself would reconstruct a short time later according to Vitruvian rules.[123] After 1520 he would re-use it with an outer frame for his own Ionic doors and windows. The columns embedded in the wall (*colonne alveolate*) were imitated at the time by Bramante in his altar house of St Peter's (cf. Fig. 22) and by Raphael in the portal of the Chigi stables.[124] But Antonio was also attracted to the temple's broken pediments and the refined ornament of its complex details.

The contemporary diagonal bird's-eye perspective of a mausoleum near the Porta del Popolo (U 1168A r.) still recalls a design in Giuliano's Codex Barberini, but the drawing

FIG. 22 Anonymous Dutch, Interior of St Peter's (Stockholm, Nationalmuseum, Anckarvärd collection n. 637 / NMH Anck 637), detail with lateral view of Bramante's altar-house (photo: Cecilia Heisser / Nationalmuseum CC PD)

technique is Bramantesque and the representation much more precise, for the first time attesting to Antonio's skill in reconstruction.[125] He provides the rectangular exterior, which evidently survived only in fragments, with the tripartite entablature and two pediments of a temple, and tries to incorporate the chapel-like annex within this system, much as he would do in about 1513 with the apse of S. Egidio in Cellere.[126] Unlike any of his earlier drawings, one senses here his native Florentine ability to give three-dimensional form to a building and his tendency, which he would fully develop in the Palazzo Farnese, to unite all the parts organically. On the same sheet the courtyard of an ancient house is surrounded by loggias and preceded by an atrium with three bays, a typology Antonio would use in 1514 for the Palazzo Farnese.[127] Here again is the same close relationship to contemporary projects as that found in Bramante's surveys of the Baths of Diocletian (cf. Fig. 17). In all of this one senses how much more direct and analytical his understanding of antiquity became during their collaboration. The two ground plans of ancient mausolea "fuora di roma I miglio" (U 575A r.) show the sureness of the experienced master who knew the vestibule of S. Costanza, the Lateran Baptistery and Bramante's project for SS. Celso e Giuliano.[128] The decorative character and the unusually slender order in the red chalk sketch on the verso, one of his few projects from this time, also favor a date before 1513.

II Sangallo's conquest of classical language (1513–20)

THE DORIC ORDER IN ALBERTI, GIULIANO DA SANGALLO AND BRAMANTE

Soon after the election of his compatriot Leo X in March 1513, Antonio rose to become one of the leading architects of Italy. He built the Farnese Church of S. Egidio in Cellere and articulated its exterior with four pedimented facades, which make reference, as in Alberti's S. Sebastiano, to the open portico of a temple.[129] In the Palazzo Farnese he tried to reconstruct the ancient house with atrium, peristyle and cavaedium,[130] and only now did he start to study the Vitruvian orders systematically. These accomplishments were also guided by Alberti's treatise, by his masters and by the intensive training of Antonio's eye.

Brunelleschi and Alberti had revived the column orders of Vitruvius and the monuments of the ancients as the basic element of the language of architecture.[131] In his fourth book, Vitruvius had described only the Doric and Ionic orders in detail. His Tuscan order was a simplified Doric (IV, ch. 7), and his Corinthian, which Brunelleschi preferred, differed from the Ionic only in its higher and richer capital (IV, ch. 5). According to Vitruvius, the Doric order was originally given a proportion of 1:6 and the Ionic 1:8. Both, however, had later been made more elegant by lengthening the Doric by two modules to 1:7 and the Ionic by 1.5 modules to 1:8.75. The brief descriptions by Pliny the Elder—according to which the Ionic, Doric, and Tuscan have the proportions respectively of 1:9, 1:6, and 1:7, while the Corinthian differs from the Ionic only in its higher capital—differ from those recommended by Vitruvius, and Pliny made it clear that there was no complete agreement in Roman antiquity about the proportions of the orders.[132] In the Old Sacristy, Brunelleschi came surprisingly close to Vitruvius's Corinthian norm, but in his later buildings he preferred somewhat more slender proportions. Alberti too, in his *De re aedificatoria* (VIII, ch. 7), favored a 1:9 ratio for the Ionic order and assigned a correspondingly slimmer one to the Corinthian of 1:9.5. In his description of the Doric entablature, with an architrave and triglyphs of one module and square metopes of one and a half modules, Alberti follows Vitruvius precisely. He combined the Doric order, however, with Attic bases and in giving it the slender proportion of 1:8, he no doubt felt himself justified by Vitruvius, who had already given licence to the "posteriores" of his own time to make the orders more elegant.[133] In both the proportions and the vocabulary of his executed buildings Alberti was much freer than in his treatise and never used the Doric with triglyphs.

While Giuliano da Sangallo's points of departure were Brunelleschi's and Alberti's buildings and Alberti's treatise, Bramante in his first Milanese works was guided by Alberti's S. Andrea in Mantua, and by prototypes in Urbino and Lombardy.[134] But although before 1498 he had only used variations on the Corinthian order, already on the exterior of S. Maria presso S. Satiro and in the interior of S. Maria delle Grazie, he tried to articulate the frieze with vertical elements that recalled the Doric triglyph or with projections of the entablature. Not until after 1490—possibly under the influence of Giuliano himself—did he begin to approach Vitruvius by using colonnades with straight entablatures, and by making one of the two cloisters in S. Ambrogio Doric, the other Ionic. After moving to Rome in the fall of 1499, he combined the intense study of Vitruvius and Alberti with that of the ancient monuments.

In 1501 he used a Doric order with triglyphs for the first time in the *piano nobile* of the Palazzo Caprini. He followed Alberti in the 1:9 order, the Attic base and an architrave slightly higher than one module and did so again a year later in the Tempietto.[135] As in the Theatre of Marcellus and

FIG. 23 JAN SCOREL (?). Bramante's choir of St Peter's (Rome, Biblioteca Vaticana, Collezione Ashby nr. 329), detail (photo: Biblioteca Apostolica Vaticana)

FIG. 24 BRAMANTE. Project for St Peter's (Florence, U 43A r.; photo Gabinetto dei Disegni e delle Stampe degli Uffizi)

the Temple of Cori, each bay of the Palazzo Caprini comprised three triglyphs and four metopes and thus the centre was marked by a triglyph. At the corners Bramante doubled the columns as in the Basilica Aemilia and thus could put a triglyph at the end of the frieze, thereby avoiding the problems in the articulation of the Doric corner that Vitruvius had warned against.[136] In the Tempietto of 1502 Bramante reconstructed a Doric *tholos* with the intercolumniations of the Vitruvian diastyle and a modular Doric entablature.[137] In 1503/04 he made the pilasters of the loggia of the Cortile del Belvedere even more slender than the columns of the Tempietto and put them on high pedestals. He reduced the width of the triglyphs by thirty per cent and the height of the square metopes by about eleven per cent in order to increase their number and to accelerate their rhythm. Base, capital, architrave and cornice are higher than the Vitruvian norm and the mutules, which appear here for the first time in his work, come closer to Alberti and the Basilica Aemilia than to Vitruvius.[138] In about 1505 he used a succession of Tuscan, Doric, Ionic, and Corinthian orders in the spiral staircase of the Vatican Belvedere.[139] Following Vitruvius's description of how the Doric and Ionic orders had developed, the eight columns of each order become progressively more slender within the margin of two modules. Thus the Tuscan changes from 1:5 to 1:6, the Doric from 1:6 to 1:7, and the Ionic from 1:7 to 1:8. Bramante probably intended to continue this system with a Composite variant of the Corinthian in the proportion of 1:9 up to the thirty-second column. Thus he attempted for the first time to organize the proportions of the Vitruvian orders by means of a continuous series of whole numbers, but did not make a rigid canon out of the proportions of his orders and felt free to change them from building to building.[140] The Ionic orders of the Cortile del Belvedere and of the drum of the cupola of the Torre Borgia are substantially squatter than the Tuscan order of Genazzano or the orders on most of his Doric buildings (cf. Fig. 12).

In 1506, in his project for St Peter's, Bramante integrated the existing choir, which had been begun more than fifty years before and had arrived at a height of several meters (cf. Fig. 13, Fig. 23). When he drew the two studies for the interior of the choir, which are only known through copies, he probably wanted to transform the polygonal pillars of Rossellino's exterior in a similar sequence of single and bent pilasters as that on the choir of S. Maria presso S. Celso in Milan and as sketched on U 43Ar.[141] Its measurements and rhythm are, however, hardly compatible with trigylphs and metopes. On the sketch for the façade, the Doric order of the lateral bays is, in fact, not yet provided with triglyphs (cf. Fig. 13, U 5A r.). Bramante must then have realised that the piers of the apse were too fragile. On the little plan of U 43Ar., which has always been attributed to Antonio but must be dated in 1505/06 and seems to be drawn by Bramante himself (Fig. 24, U 43Ar.), he reduces the three apse windows by about a third and on the detail sketches of the same sheet from 30 to 20 *palmi*. Here he has already doubled the pilasters in the interior of the apse, but many measurements and details still differ from the executed building. This change of project inspired him to propose a much more complex articulation of the exterior: In a continuous crescendo the simple corners between the choir and the transept are elaborated to form a conglomerate of fragments of four quadrangular columns and this crescendo culminates in the triumphal arch of the central bay of the apse where the quadrangular columns are separated by niches. In execution he provided each quadrangular column with corner triglyphs and a central metope. The double pilasters were connected by an obtuse angle and above their join a single triglyph one glyph deep was bent.[142] Bramante succeeded in combining these double, projecting and fragmentary quadrangular columns and their dynamic rhythm with the Doric frieze, reducing the width of the triglyphs by about nine per cent and aligning their outer edges with those of the protruding capitals—and not with the shafts.[143] Belonging to partly hidden quadrangular columns the corner triglyphs were complete on both sides. Strangely enough the eastern sides of the double columns continued in half-columns with corner triglyphs, which answered to the opposite corner, where the choir joined the transept. Both corners were adorned by a bent metope. The western side of the compound piers was only 3 2/3 *palmi* long but continued after the bend in a fragment of 7.5 *palmi*, thus making clear, that it could not be interpreted as an overlapping pilaster. The width of the metopes changed from 7.2 *palmi* above the pilasters to 11.5 and 12 *palmi* in the large intercolumniations. The cluster of four partly visible quadrangular columns is without precedent. It can only be understood as their intersection and is characteristic of Bramante's undogmatic design. As in ancient architecture the width of the triglyphs is constant but that of the metopes flexible. Only three elongated metopes correspond to the large intercolumniations above the windows, and these slow down the dynamic rhythm and the forces concentrated in the area of the columns. As in all his later Doric orders, and as in Antonio's project for the façade of St Peter's of about 1518, Bramante would probably have put rectangular mutules on the unfinished cornice.[144] The brackets of the projections would have turned around the corner and touched each other. In the copies of Bramante's project (U 4 and 5A r) the inner pilasters are provided with pedestals (cf. Fig. 13). Evidently he delayed the execution of those on the exterior until the height of the interior pedestals was decided, and thus the reproach in Antonio's memorial of 1518 that he gave the order a proportion of 1:12 probably does not do justice to Bramante's intentions. Both the dynamic rhythm of the order and the combination of the projection of the entablature with the Doric frieze have no precedent in antiquity and are unique even in Bramante's own work. He has no scruples in deviating from Vitruvius' canon and the ancient prototypes, but feels free to change the height and width of triglyphs and metopes or to bend them and integrate them into his playful use of a flexible vocabulary.

Bramante must also have made the first project for the exterior of Palazzo Fieschi. The vigorous wall relief of the ground floor, the classicising detail and the perfect proportions of its north-western projection are much more mature than those of the Cortile del Belvedere, and so similar to the choir of St Peter's that this project can hardly be dated earlier (Fig. 25).[145] After Bramante's death the project was

FIG. 25 Rome, Palazzo Fieschi, facade, groundfloor of north-western corner projection, detail (photo: Bibliotheca-Hertziana – Max Planck Institute for Art History)

changed by a more traditionalist architect—perhaps even Antonio himself—who increased the height and the windows of the *piano nobile*, substituted Bramante's smooth shafts in the portal with those of the Cancelleria windows and changed the entablature of the portal.[146] Before the construction of the Corso Vittorio Emanuele, when the southwestern façade was added, the eleven bays of the west wing were unfinished and overlooked a little square. The quadrangular column on the left corner still projects beyond the neighbouring house.

The second and eleventh of the thirteen triglyphs of the north-western projection are centred above the pilasters, so that the seventh stands in its centre. On the corners the full triglyphs continue in a fragmentary metope and a triglyph reduced to one diagonal glyph. In order to divide the two corner triglyphs by at least a fragmentary metope Bramante diminished the size of the triglyphs and with them the height of the frieze. On both sides a further gutta is added to the diagonal gutta of the corner glyph, while the corresponding mutules of the protruding cornice are unreduced. The rhythm of the side view of the left corner is symmetrical to that of the main front. The order then disappears in the wall, as if the projection were part of a quadrangular tower, and so it looks on a late nineteenth-century plan.[147] Bramante may, in fact, have planned four towers on the corners and four equal facades, which would have been even more symmetrical than the Cancelleria.

The right-hand corner of the projection overlaps a receding pilaster. There the diagonal corner glyph continues at the side in a triglyph with four guttae, which is repeated on the front side of the overlapped pilaster. The entablature then continues towards the portal in a less protruding cyma with short brackets, which is even more reduced than those of the secondary fronts of the Cancelleria. The long bracket of the receding pilaster and the first of the short ones form a single piece. Thus, for the sake of a symmetrical design, the two corners of the same bay differ from each other in a tectonically inconsequential way. The analogous windows of the ground-floor also reflect Bramante's authorship. They are not part of three-dimensional entities and did not need corner triglyphs. The triglyphs are modular but the metopes are much narrower than square and thus the number of triglyphs is greater than in a strictly modular system.

In the portal Bramante's successor renounced the diagonal position of the corner triglyph and provided its front side instead with a narrow and uncanonical slit, while its lateral face continues in a fragmentary triglyph with one glyph. The same rhythm returns in the receding entablature and thus the cornice is much less protruding. Both lateral brackets are fragmentary and those of the receding pilasters are not connected with the small ones of the reduced entablature. Evidently the attempt to be more consistent than Bramante led to an inferior design.

The many triglyphs of Palazzo Fieschi are as unique in Bramante's oeuvre as the small number on the altar-house of St Peter's, his last Doric building, which again is only known from a series of drawings (cf. Fig. 22).[148] There he probably had to use the shafts and Attic bases of the 4 *palmi* wide columns of the side aisles of Old St Peter's, which with their capitals again reached a proportion of about 1:9. The detail of the Doric order was even more similar to that of the Basilica Aemilia than in his earlier works. He centred the triglyphs above the columns, and though the pairs of corner columns would have permitted a solution similar to that of the Palazzo Caprini, he did not attempt corner triglyphs. The drawings agree that there were only three triglyphs on the wide bays and that the metopes were nearly three times wider than the triglyphs and decorated with similar religious motifs to those at the Tempietto. As on the choir of St Peter's and Palazzo Fieschi Bramante is not only interested in the precise reconstruction of the antique order but uses the Doric frieze for his sophisticated play of vertical and horizontal forces, with slow and quick rhythms. In conclusion one can say that Bramante was one of the very few Renaissance architects interested in corner triglyphs, although his usage contradicted the Vitruvian derivation of the triglyph from the wooden roof.

Giuliano da Sangallo followed neither Vitruvius and Alberti nor any particular ancient prototype when he designed his first known Doric frieze in about 1506/07 (cf. Fig. 21).[149] The width of the triglyphs corresponds nearly to their height and to the width of the metopes and the columns, and their cornice is provided with *ovoli* instead of mutules. About nine or ten years later Giuliano would use the Vitruvian module in his projects for the façade of S. Lorenzo and would make the entablature much lower, but even then his triglyphs were neither very well-articulated nor much smaller than the metopes, nor were they accompanied by mutules.[150]

PALAZZO BALDASSINI (1513/14)

Since about 1509 Antonio had collaborated with Bramante and profited from his profound knowledge of antiquity, but until about 1512 in his first buildings he used the language and the Cancelleria windows of his uncle Antonio the Elder. As late as 1512/13 in his project for Palazzo Baldassini he combined columns and arcades as authorised by Alberti but not by Vitruvius.[151] Already in the castle of Capodimonte he had decorated the pier arcades of the courtyard with stocky pilasters of a Doric order on high pedestals (Fig. 26), but in

FIG. 26 Capodimonte, courtyard of the the Farnese castle (photo Gabinetto Fotografico Nazionale)

FIG. 28 Rome, Vatican Palace, Ground floor of the Cortile del Belvedere, detail (photo: Bibliotheca-Hertziana – Max Planck Institute for Art History)

FIG. 27 Rome, Palazzo Baldassini, courtyard, detail (photo: Oscar Savio, Bibliotheca Hertziana – Max Planck Institute for Art History)

FIG. 29 Rome, Palazzo Baldassini, portal, detail (photo: Bibliotheca-Hertziana – Max Planck Institute for Art History)

the realized version of Palazzo Baldassini he provided them for the first time with the classicising language of Bramante's Cortile del Belvedere and a modular system (Fig. 27, Fig. 28). However, he made the arcades more slender, and the pedestals higher than those of Bramante. Moreover, he reduced the proportion of the pilasters to about 1:6.4 and made the triglyphs half as wide as the shafts of the pilasters, so that each bay comprised only six triglyphs. As on the Palazzo Fieschi the metopes are narrower than their height, the centre of each bay is accentuated by a triglyph and these are accompanied by rectangular mutules.

The influence of Palazzo Fieschi is even more evident in the portal of Palazzo Baldassini (cf. Fig. 25, Fig. 29). The related project on U 1000A looks more mature than the Doric order of the courtyard and was probably not designed until 1514.[152] On the right half of the verso Antonio reduces the three-bay elevation of a preliminary sketch to one bay with receding pilasters and studies three alternatives for its mutules. Two of them are provided with diagonal corner brackets, which had been already used on the Cancelleria and in the cloister of S. Maria della Pace. On the drawing Antonio indicates not only the alternation of brackets and lozenges but also the guttae corresponding to the triglyphs. In the elaborated elevation of the portal on the left half of the verso he considers two possibilities. In the left-hand alternative the triglyph, as in the Palazzo Fieschi, is centred on the column and accompanied by a reduced corner triglyph with corresponding mutules. In the right-hand alternative the module is slightly smaller and neither triglyphs nor metopes are reduced, but none of them is centred on the columns. The cornice on the recto is only provided with square brackets but still differs from the executed building: Both sides of the corner triglyph as well as the triglyph of the receding pilaster are complete, and in the corner next to the latter the triglyph is reduced to one glyph.

The realized portal corresponds largely to the right-hand alternative on the left half of the verso, but now its system and measurements almost exactly follow the arcades of the court and their smaller module. The brackets are still square, and thus one and the same serves as the lateral mutule of the corner triglyph and as the frontal mutule of the overlapped entablature. The cyma projects by an equal amount and the centre of the frieze is accentuated by a metope. The corner triglyphs are bent but reduced to the width of four guttae and the corners between the projecting and receding parts are filled with a bent metope like the choir of St Peter's. As on the corner projection of Palazzo Fieschi Antonio enlarged the lateral faces of the corner triglyphs, but reduced the depth of the receding entablature and its brackets in the manner of the portal of Palazzo Fieschi, thus arriving at a similarly problematic result.

PALAZZO FARNESE (1513–15)

Antonio started Palazzo Farnese at about the same time as Palazzo Baldassini but changed the project several times during the following thirty-three years.[153] He adopted the typology of Bramante's project for the Palazzo dei Tribunali with a square court, three loggias and the superposition of three orders of engaged columns. In his first project U 627A r. the language is still similar to that of the contemporary courtyard of Palazzo Baldassini.[154] The 1:8 proportions of the Doric and Composite orders and the 1:6 ¾ proportion of the Ionic order in the left half of the two upper stories are still reminiscent of Bramante's undogmatic freedom.[155] Because they do not stand on pedestals, the columns of the Doric order are now much more dominant than in the Palazzo Baldassini. Thus the module is greater, the entablature heavier and the number of triglyphs and metopes reduced to five. The architrave is higher than Vitruvius's norm of one module and composed of two fascias instead of the three recommended by Alberti (VII, ch. 9). The square metopes are smaller than 1 ½ modules and slightly higher than they are wide. As in the left-hand alternative of the project for the portal of Palazzo Baldassini the triglyphs are accompanied by rectangular mutules, a metope remains in the centre of each bay and hardly any distance separates the two corner triglyphs.

After Bramante's death in April 1514 Raphael and Fra Giocondo were appointed architects of St Peter's. After he arrived in the summer of 1514 the latter must have had a direct impact on Antonio, though his illustrations of the Doric order correspond much less closely to the Vitruvian canon and ancient prototypes than those of Palazzo Baldassini.[156] Antonio now began to intensify his Vitruvian studies and changed the Doric order to the canonical proportion of 1:7.[157] Perhaps it was only at this point that he changed the upper stories of the courtyard project on the right half of U 627 to give the Ionic and the Corinthian/Composite orders the equally Vitruvian proportions of 1:8 and 1:9.3.

In the atrium of Palazzo Farnese Antonio followed Fra Giocondo's reconstruction of the Roman atrium with two rows of six columns (Fig. 30).[158] He must have had more intense contact with Fra Giocondo, whose editions of Vitruvius remained his most important theoretical support even after the Sack of Rome, but who on his part must also have learned from Antonio's unique experience and knowledge.[159] The atrium was conditioned by the dimensions and proportions of the tower of the preceding Quattrocento palace. Antonio sketched its plan on the drawing for the portal of Palazzo Baldassini on U 1000A v with a narrower side aisle than in the executed building and with longitudinally aligned rather than transverse coffers.[160]

FIG. 30 Rome, Palazzo Farnese, Vestibule (photo: Oscar Savio, Bibliotheca Hertziana – Max Planck Institute for Art History)

FIG. 31 Rome, Palazzo Farnese, courtyard, corner ground floor (photo: Bibliotheca-Hertziana – Max Planck Institute for Art History)

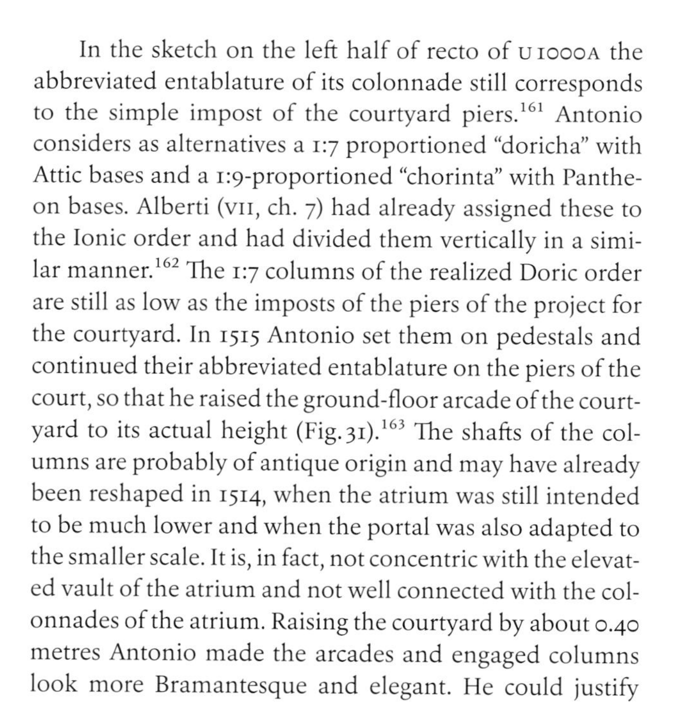

In the sketch on the left half of recto of U 1000A the abbreviated entablature of its colonnade still corresponds to the simple impost of the courtyard piers.[161] Antonio considers as alternatives a 1:7 proportioned "doricha" with Attic bases and a 1:9-proportioned "chorinta" with Pantheon bases. Alberti (VII, ch. 7) had already assigned these to the Ionic order and had divided them vertically in a similar manner.[162] The 1:7 columns of the realized Doric order are still as low as the imposts of the piers of the project for the courtyard. In 1515 Antonio set them on pedestals and continued their abbreviated entablature on the piers of the court, so that he raised the ground-floor arcade of the courtyard to its actual height (Fig. 31).[163] The shafts of the columns are probably of antique origin and may have already been reshaped in 1514, when the atrium was still intended to be much lower and when the portal was also adapted to the smaller scale. It is, in fact, not concentric with the elevated vault of the atrium and not well connected with the colonnades of the atrium. Raising the courtyard by about 0.40 metres Antonio made the arcades and engaged columns look more Bramantesque and elegant. He could justify the 1:8.3 proportion of the engaged columns by reference to Vitruvius (IX, 5), according to whom a theatre required more slender orders than a dignified temple, as illustrated by Antonio in the drawing U 1409A r., which can be dated before the Sack of Rome.[164] Palace courtyards were intended for theatrical performances among other uses, and not by chance Antonio now followed both the slender proportions and the cornice with dentils and mutules without brackets of the Theatre of Marcellus.[165] The proportions of the columns did not depend only on their respective orders and intercolumniations but also on the hierarchical function of the building.

The measurements and proportions of the orders of the ground floor of Palazzo Farnese have now become more similar to those of the Tempietto than in the project (U 627A v.). The heights of the bases, capitals, architraves and metopes and the width of the triglyphs and metopes of the courtyard correspond almost exactly to the Vitruvian canon and only the cornice is much higher: Antonio had come even closer to antiquity than his master. The distance between the corner columns is now increased so that the metope between them is square. The frieze above the quadrangular corner column, as at the portal of Palazzo Baldassini, is decorated with fragments of a metope. The plasticity of the columns and the decoration of the capitals and metopes are inspired by the Basilica Aemilia and Bramante's altar-house. Thus under the spell of Bramante and the ancient monuments, by about 1515 Antonio had acquired a more classicising language than any earlier Renaissance architect. Antonio's study of the architecture of antiquity was inseparable from the planning and execution of his first great projects. It is only in these designs that we see his remarkable approach to Vitruvius and to ancient architecture. The combination of orthogonal and perspective representation, of section and elevation and the fine hatching reveal him once more to be Bramante's master pupil and differ fundamentally from the drawings of Giuliano and others. He probably learned axonometry from Bramante, as did Bernardo della Volpaia (cf. Fig. 16 U 1563A v.). If Bernardo refers several times to Antonio but never to Bramante he probably also copied from the former.[166]

Only after Fra Giocondo's arrival Antonio may have reconstructed the Doric entablatures of the pycnostyle, diastyle, sistyle and distyle temples of Vitruvius (III, 3, 70–75) with changing widths of the metopes.[167] In the uppermost row he compares Fra Giocondo's reconstruction with that of "lo vechio," probably Antonio the Elder da Sangallo, who in his Madonna di San Biagio of about 1518 still used extremely large triglyphs and high, narrow metopes.[168]

THE COLLABORATION WITH RAPHAEL (1516–20)

After Giuliano's death, in the autumn of 1516, Antonio the Younger succeeded him as second architect of St Peter's and Raphael's deputy. As such he shared responsibility for all official construction projects of the Papal States and the planning of Rome in particular.

Raphael was Bramante's most creative pupil and had succeeded him in 1514 as the chief papal architect.[169] Under his influence, and in order to find his way back to the "belle forme de gli edifici antichi," he devoted himself simultaneously to Vitruvius and to the ancient monuments, following Alberti more directly and more competently than either Francesco di Giorgio or Giuliano da Sangallo, but he confessed: "Me ne porge una gran luce Vitruvio: ma non tanto che basti...."[170] To understand Vitruvius better, he brought into his household the learned Fabio Calvo, who translated the text for him, explained it and provided reconstructions of the different types of temples and the Greek and Roman forums.[171] Antonio's marginal notes in Calvo's translation show that he paid critical attention to its important passages.

Raphael followed Bramante's less rigid attitude to Vitruvius when adorning the projecting sections of the Doric friezes of palazzo Jacopo da Brescia and of the church of Sant'Eligio with nothing but a metope.[172] Sangallo meanwhile used the Vitruvian corner triglyph, and even bent it as Bramante had done, as in the right-hand alternative of his project for the Torre del Monte of about 1517 and in his designs for the façade and transept of St Peter's of 1519.[173] The latter example shows his Vitruvian approach to proportions, as the Doric order of the transept is exactly 1:7, the architrave and triglyphs correspond precisely to one module and the metopes are exactly square.

Only after having become the best expert in the Doric order, did Sangallo concentrate on the Ionic as well. In the Palazzo Baldassini, on 627A and in the ground floor rooms of Palazzo Farnese he had used Bramante's Ionic capitals with the diagonal volutes, but after the Sack of Rome in 1527 he preferred the straight volutes recommended by Vitruvius.

Raphael was the chief papal architect, but until 1518 the Medici commissioned members of the Sangallo family or other Florentine masters to design their private buildings in Florence as well as in Rome. Giuliano proposed the projects for the Palazzi Madama and Lante and Antonio the Younger made an alternative project for Palazzo Madama as well as the first projects for Villa Madama. Leo X had acquired the site on the slope above the Milvian Bridge as early as 1516, but only after having nominated his cousin Giulio vice-chancellor in spring 1517 did he conceive of a huge villa which would also serve as a guesthouse for his prominent foreign visitors.

Sangallo's U 1054A is evidently the earliest of all the surviving drawings for Villa Madama (Fig. 32).[174] Not only

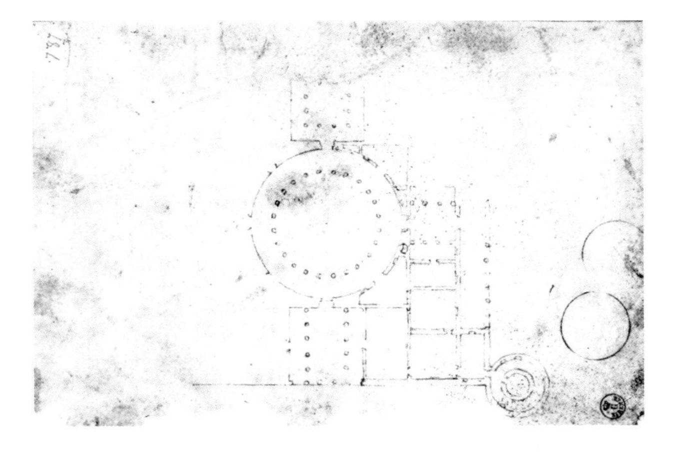

FIG. 32 ANTONIO DA SANGALLO THE YOUNGER. First project for Villa Madama (Florence, U 1054A r., detail; photo Gabinetto dei Disegni e delle Stampe degli Uffizi)

his pre-1527 handwriting on the verso, but also the way the columns and wall openings are drawn, are similar to U 259A recto and there is no doubt that the sheet is autograph. The fragmentary plan was evidently made for cardinal Giulio de' Medici's villa: The circular courtyard, the rectangular entrance porch and its colonnade, as well as the lateral atrium and the fortified tower re-appear in similar scale and form in Sangallo's succeeding drawings for the villa: U 179A and 1518A.[175] On the rear of the sheet Sangallo notes:"columela la villa sia partita in tre parte urbana rustica fruttuaria," a citation from Columella's treatise on agriculture.[176] The Villa Madama was however a villa suburbana and the cardinal and his architect possibly wanted only flower gardens and orchards. While Sangallo's more mature projects 179A and 1518A were already made for the actual site, the early plan must have been intended for a position at the foot of the hill. The Vitruvian entrance sequence of vestibulum, atrium, peristyle and the circular courtyard, and the central arch of the entrance colonnade are clearly inspired by Antonio's uncle Giuliano, to whom the project has erroneously been attributed. The atrium of the side entrance, however, is Antonio's invention, and is nearly identical to those of Palazzo Farnese and project U 259A.

The atrium of the main entrance, which connects the vestibule with the peristyle, is more Vitruvian in having only four columns, and more classicising than in earlier projects. Even more classicising is the colonnade of the circular courtyard, the direct forerunner of the court of the palace of Charles V in Granada.[177]

When Sangallo had to shift the villa to the upper part of the hill, he added a ground floor, large staircases and hanging gardens, but changed the individual rooms only slightly and does not seem to have added the many functions of an ancient villa at this stage. This must have been one of the main reasons why, in the spring or summer 1518, he was substituted by Raphael. Since Raphael retained large parts of the villa's layout, the terracing seems to have been begun before his arrival. On U 273A he substituted the circular court by a rectangular one, the centre of three axially connected rectangular courtyards. Introducing exedras and niches he animated the rooms dynamically and prepared them for rich decoration. Even more dynamic is the valley façade with its giant order and huge thermal windows.

The comparison between the projects shows Sangallo's artistic limits. His understanding of antiquity was concentrated on language and typology, but failed to create comparable beauty. Raphael not only changed the articulation of the walls but made the villa a truly *all'antica* complex by adding the open theatre, the hippodrome, the tripartite bath, the swimming pool, dining halls, *diaetae* and nymphaeums, which Sangallo had not foreseen. In his description of the theatre of Villa Madama, which Raphael probably wrote in the spring of 1519, he quoted verbatim from Calvo's translation of Vitruvius.[178]

Construction began in the summer of 1518, but already in the early autumn the unstable ground forced the cardinal to ask for help from the more experienced Sangallo. The latter succeeded in returning to the structurally safer circular courtyard but Raphael remained the responsible architect and adapted his ingenious system to the new circumstances. He added the huge exedras of the garden loggia planned to decorated them with stuccoes and paintings—the first case of coherent stucco decoration in the antique manner which he had pioneered in the second loggia of the Vatican palace. Sangallo, who had so far been a rival rather than an assistant, now became a real collaborator and under Raphael's influence his language changed, as can already be seen in his projects 254 and 252A for St Peter's of the autumn of 1518.[179]

But he himself also exerted influence on Raphael. Thus on U 70A he succeeded in substituting Raphael's 5 *palmi* order on the exterior of St Peter's by the more monumental and functional one of 9 *palmi*. In the following projects he introduced the aedicules from the Pantheon that he had already used on the *piano nobile* of Palazzo Farnese. In the drawings of 1519 for the exterior of the transept of St Peter's these are flanked by engaged columns of the order—a system he also used on the exterior of S. Giovanni dei Fiorentini. Since this arrangement appears on the contemporary projects of both St Peter's and the circular courtyard of Villa Madama, Sangallo and Raphael must have agreed. Already on the façade of Palazzo Branconio Raphael had been inspired by Sangallo's Pantheon aedicules. The approximately contemporary design for the Doric order of the rear wall of the palace's courtyard, which Giulio Romano drew for Raphael, is, however, less Vitruvian than those of Sangallo's preceding palaces, with the proportion of 1:8, the triglyphs greater than a module, and correspondingly enlarged square metopes.[180] Yet Raphael here is unmistakably under Sangallo's influence, just as the latter had to look to Raphael's dynamism for the rhythm of his facade project for St Peter's.[181] When Sangallo drew U 314A, the collaboration between the two must already have been intense and creative.

RAPHAEL'S PROJECT FOR RECONSTRUCTING ANCIENT ROME

Since 1514 Raphael had been responsible for Rome's urban planning and since 1515 he had also been in charge of the protection of the ancient monuments. Already in the fresco of the *Fire in the Borgo* of 1514 he transmitted his vision

FIG. 33 RAFFAEL AND GIULIO ROMANO, Vatican Palace, Sala di Costantino. *Adlocutio of Constantine*, detail (1520) (photo: Bibliotheca-Hertziana – Max Planck Institute for Art History)

of the appearance of the Borgo in antiquity. By and by, the idea of building the papal capital on the remnants of imperial Rome became more concrete, and in his projects of 1518/19 for St Peter's, S. Giovanni dei Fiorentini and the Sala di Costantino it is already dominant. Raphael must have understood that the ruins could be saved from increasing vandalism only if they became part of buildings with important functions.

In order to realize his ideas, Raphael needed precise surveys of what had survived. He started to prepare these and wanted to publish them with a preface dedicated to the pope, which he formulated, with the help of his friend Baldassare Castiglione, in the last two years of his life.[182] The project was to include plans, elevations, sections, and occasional perspective views. In the choice of the monuments, the representational method and the topographical classification, he went far beyond the existing collections of famous ancient *exempla* to be found in the Codex Coner and other sketchbooks.

According to contemporary sources work on the first *rione* was complete by the time Raphael died. It was not the *prima regio* of ancient Rome—located between the Caelian Hill and the Palatine—but rather the first of all to be finished, probably the area between Tiber and the Vatican, where Raphael was mainly active as an architect. In the background of the *Adlocutio of Constantine* in the Sala di Costantino Giulio Romano and G.F. Penni show reconstructions of the Mausoleum of Hadrian, the Ponte Sant'Angelo, the Vatican circus and the Meta Romuli which can be attributed to Raphael rather than to his pupils (Fig. 33). So far, however, no drawings for these reconstructions have been discovered. It is, in any case, difficult to understand how, in these years when so many gifted artists lived in Rome, not one single concrete document of Raphael's great project has yet been found. We do not even know which artists assisted Raphael in his ambitious enterprise or whether he was able to start excavations of any importance.

Sangallo must have followed these efforts with the utmost interest, but before he started his collaboration with Raphael in the winter of 1518/19, he probably did not contribute to the project, and after Raphael's death, he did not pursue it. He was interested in the precise knowledge of individual prototypes and forms, but hardly believed in the reconstruction of the whole imperial city.

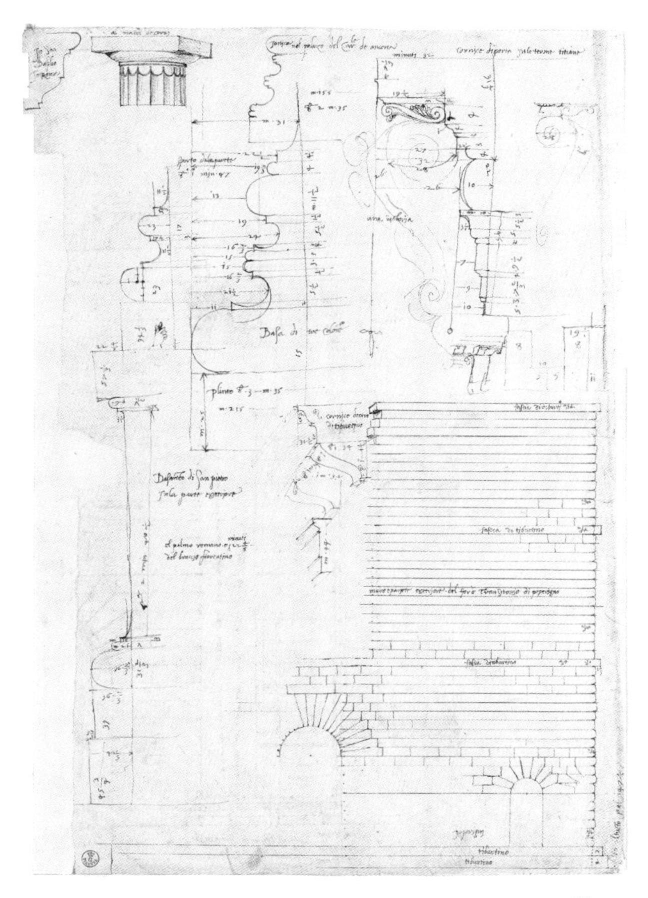

FIG. 34 BALDASSARRE PERUZZI AFTER ANTONIO DA SANGALLO (?). Elevation detail of the Temple of Mars Ultor (Florence, U 632A r.; photo: Gabinetto dei Disegni e delle Stampe degli Uffizi)

A sketch, which he may have made in 1519, when his collaboration with Raphael had intensified, gives an idea of the measures taken by the two papal architects in their attempt to incorporate the ancient monuments more effectively into the new city plan.[183] The present Via Canova, a side street of the newly laid-out Via Ripetta, leads alongside the Ospedale San Giacomo in Augusta to the slope of the Pincio, where it finds a focal point in the two-storey exedra of the Horti Aciliorum (U 915A r.).

One could assume that Antonio made his surveys of the Forum of Augustus—the only measurements in his hand that can be securely dated to those years—available to Raphael's project for Rome.[184] In 1518, the Prior of Rome had renewed Antonio Cosciari's lease on the Forum of Augustus, allowing him to make some structural changes there, but requiring him to preserve the three great columns of the Temple of Mars Ultor.[185] Sangallo measured the ground with the greatest exactitude[186] and then proposed four grand alternatives for the staircase of Cosciari's Suburbanum, which did not correspond to the ancient walls or to the idea of rebuilding the papal city on the remnants of ancient Rome—and thus can hardly been seen as part of Raphael's project.[187]

His reconstruction of the ancient ground plan of the Forum of Augustus (U 1141, 1139, 1123A) was copied several times. Sallustio Peruzzi attributed the reconstruction, however, wrongly, to his father, Baldassarre: "Hoc templum in lucem restitutum fuit opus Balthassaris Peruzziis."[188]

In contrast to most of his own surveys, Peruzzi's celebrated elevation of the Temple of Mars Ultor (U 632A v.) is likewise measured in *braccia* divided into 60 *minuti*, and it is drawn in a purely orthogonal manner (Fig. 34 [U 632 v]).[189] It seems, therefore, that he copied it, as did Serlio and Labacco, from Sangallo's surveys, which had not been restricted to the ground plan.[190]

Sangallo measured the often irregular fragments of the Forum of Augustus, recorded their position, and reconstructed their presumed context.[191] He took note of open questions, listed the finds, even sketched the arm of a caryatid, and with all this information achieved an exactitude far superior to earlier measurements. Sangallo's surveys of the Forum of Augustus are still acknowledged today to be unsurpassed; they differ from those of his earlier years in the same way that his contemporary designs for St Peter's differ from those for the Palazzo Farnese.

It is the first datable survey of a large monument to have been systematically measured after Bramante's death and continues the series of drawings of the Pantheon, the Colosseum and the imperial baths, although it is much less regular than these. The symmetry helped reconstruction and shows that Sangallo wanted to know, as well as understand, the centre of the ancient city. Although he did not indicate a precise orientation, he must have worked with a compass, as he would continue to do before 1524 on the survey of Forum of Nerva.[192] The use of the compass is already evident in a sketch for the Palazzo Farnese of about 1514, and he would use it again in 1519 in the planning of the Piazza Nicosia.[193] The compass had aided Leonardo da Vinci as early as 1501, when he measured Imola,[194] and it was certainly known to Leonardo's friend Bramante. Raphael described it as the most important aid in his Rome project, and his collaborators employed it about 1518–19 in their measurements of the Palazzo Alberini.[195]

At any rate, no survey can be attributed to Sangallo for the years between 1509 and 1520 that is not directly connected with one of his building projects. Designs by other artists working in the period 1518–20 show, too, how drawing from antiquity was changing under the influence of Raphael and Sangallo.[196]

III Sangallo as chief papal architect (1520–46)

THE YEARS BEFORE THE SACK OF ROME (1520–27)

As the pupil of his uncles Giuliano and Antonio the Elder, and above all of Bramante, Antonio had grown up with Vitruvius and Alberti. The important passages concerning temples and the orders had been constantly under discussion since the time of Brunelleschi and Alberti, and partial translations were available from Francesco di Giorgio and Raphael among others.[197] Although he knew some Latin, Antonio undoubtedly read these texts only with difficulty, but there were many clerics and humanists in Rome who could provide help. Neither the Quattrocento manuscripts of Vitruvius and Alberti nor the first printings of the two treatises from the 1480s were illustrated, and most of Alberti's drawings are lost. Even such leading masters of the next generation as Francesco di Giorgio and Giuliano da Sangallo had difficulty in producing competent illustrations of Vitruvius. Fra Giocondo corrected and cleaned up Vitruvius's text, and his illustrated editions of 1511 and 1513 made it accessible and better known to a still wider circle, but many of his illustrations were already rendered obsolete at the time of their appearance by the researches of Alberti, Bramante and the Sangallos. The tradition that Bramante had planned a treatise of his own, which would even have included the "lavoro tedesco" (Gothic style) so important to him, may not be entirely without foundation.[198] In 1520 there was no edition of Vitruvius commensurate with the state of knowledge of the Roman architects, and this void was not filled by Cesare Cesariano's 1521 Vitruvius, for his commentary and numerous illustrations still in many respects reflect the understanding current in Bramante's Milan, that is, in the time before 1500.[199]

In spring 1520 Antonio succeeded Raphael as chief papal architect and himself became the most prominent and influential architect of Christianity. After many years of intense collaboration with Bramante and Raphael he was well prepared for his new duties and responsibilities. In contrast to Raphael he was more interested in antique architecture in general than in ancient Rome. After his appointment evidence grows of an even more thorough study of Vitruvius, as had been the case with Raphael after Bramante's death. He noted his appointment on the three surviving title pages of his four copies of Fra Giocondo's edition of Vitruvius,[200] and his marginal comments in the recently discovered 1511 Prague Vitruvius are still written in his pre-1527 handwriting (Fig. 35).[201] He annotated what

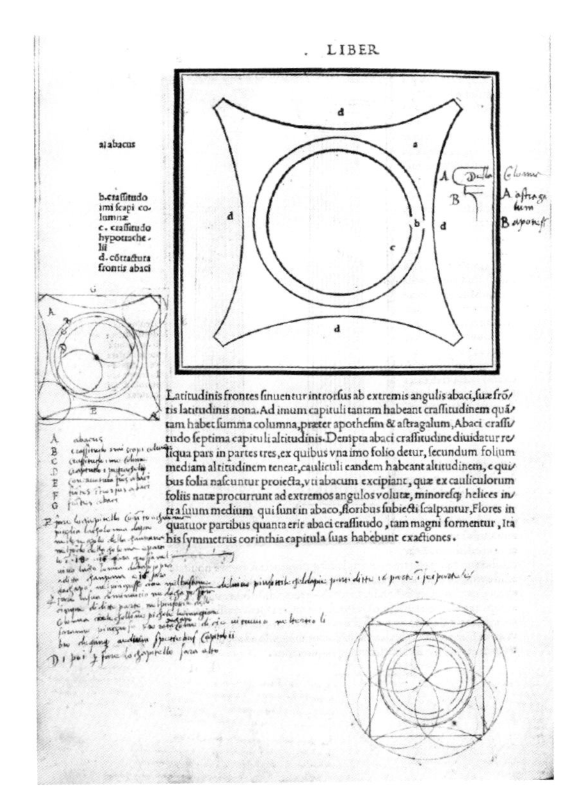
LIBER

a; abacus

b. crassitudo imi scapi columnæ
c. crassitudo hypotrachelii
d. cõtractura frontis abaci

Latitudinis frontes sinuentur introrsus ab extremis angulis abaci, suæ frõtis latitudinis nona. Ad imum capituli tantam habeant crassitudinem quãtam habet summa columna, præter apothesim & astragalum, Abaci crassitudo septima capituli altitudinis. Dempta abaci crassitudine diuidatur reliqua pars in partes tres, ex quibus vna imo folio detur, secundum folium mediam altitudinem teneat, cauliculi eandem habeant altitudinem, e quibus folia nascuntur proiecta, vti abacum excipiant, quæ ex cauliculorum foliis natæ procurrunt ad extremos angulos volutæ, minoresq; helices intra suum medium qui sunt in abaco, floribus subiecti scalpantur, Flores in quatuor partibus quanta erit abaci crassitudo, tam magni formentur, Ita his symmetriis corinthia capitula suas habebunt exactiones.

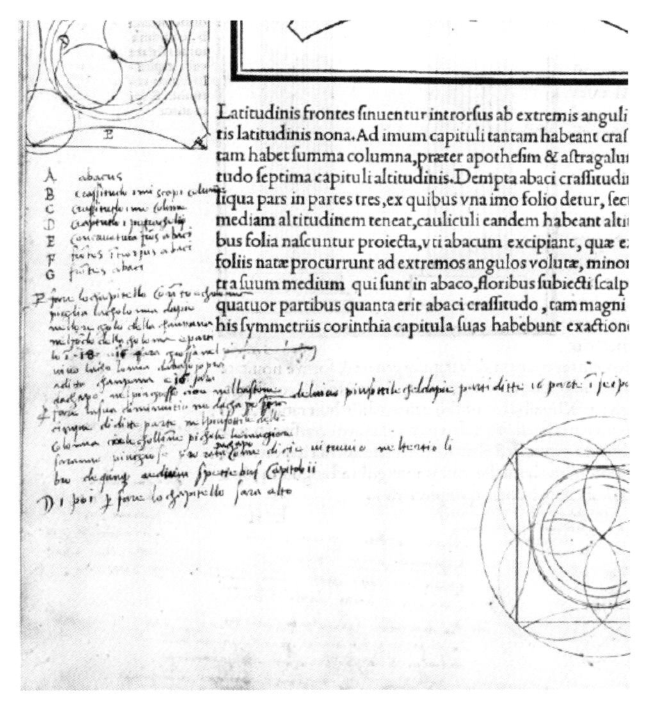

FIG. 35 ANTONIO DA SANGALLO THE YOUNGER. Marginal notes in his Vitruvius edition of 1511 (Prague, Stravov Library; photo: Juren 2004).

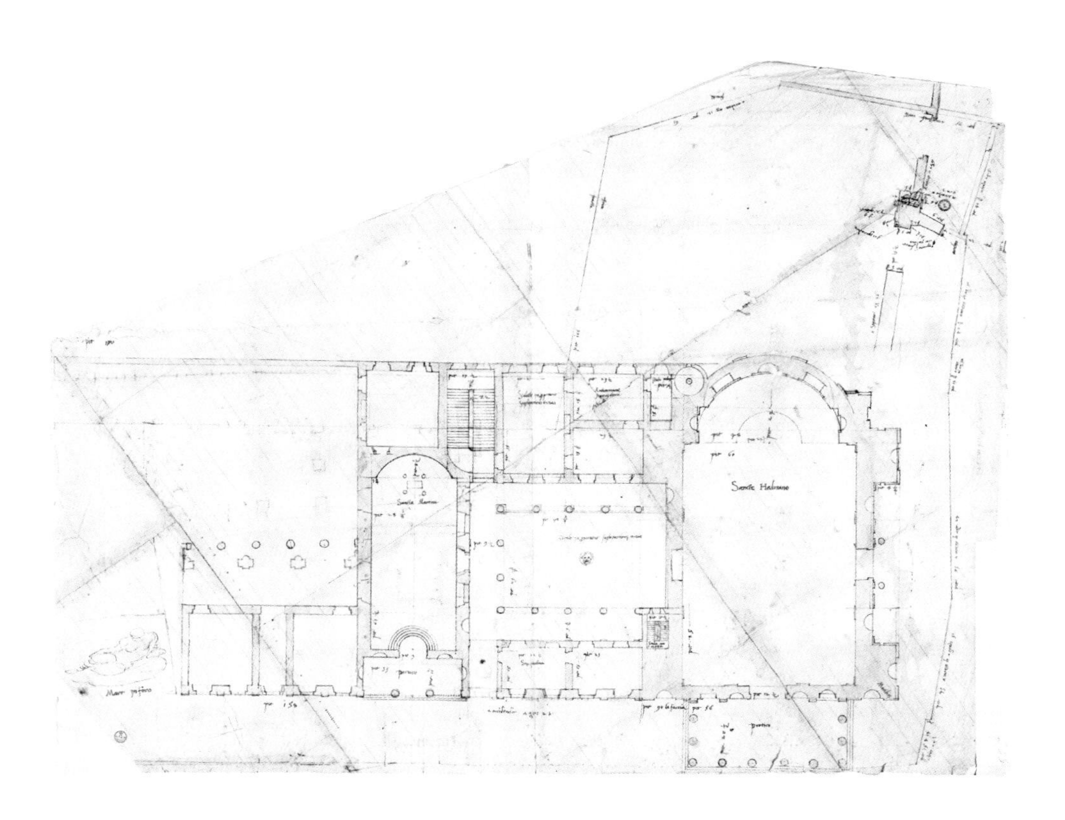

FIG. 36
BALDASSARE PERUZZI.
Survey and project for S. Adriano (Florence, U 625A r.; photo Gabinetto dei Disegni e delle Stampe degli Uffizi)

were for him the important passages of the Latin text and corrected some of Fra Giocondo's illustrations—a block and tackle, for example (fol. 96 v.)—but also went more deeply into the complicated system of modules, on which the perfection of the Greek temple depended, but which Alberti had simplified considerably in order to ease a return to the language of antiquity. Thus, on fol. 29 v., Antonio corrected Fra Giocondo's illustration of the base and capital of the Ionic order, and on fols 34 r.f. and 40 r. reconstructed the Corinthian capital and the Ionic portal, which Fra Giocondo had illustrated inadequately. He also came to the conclusion that the enlargement of the architrave with the increasing height of an order should be calculated by subdividing only the column shaft (fol. 30 v.).

Antonio continued the surveys of the imperial fora and also measured the ground plans of the area of the Curia using a compass.[202] These are so closely tied up with Peruzzi's project for its reconstruction as a church (Fig. 36) that they can only stem from the period of the collaboration between the two architects and, conceivably, it was Pope Hadrian VI (1522–23) who commissioned the rebuilding of his patron saint's church. It was also during Hadrian's pontificate that Antonio planned the church of S. Maria di Loreto.[203] At the same time he may have measured the neighbouring Column of Trajan and intended to give it a similar visual role to that of the obelisk on Piazza del Popolo or the exedra of the Horti Aciliorum. Under Hadrian VI he also drew the ground plan of an exedra of the Baths of Nero, which was made in connection with the planning of S. Luigi dei Francesi, and mentioned the palace then being planned there by Cardinal Enckenvoirt, one of Hadrian's confidants.[204]

In the years before the Sack of Rome his cousin Giovan Francesco da Sangallo was Antonio's most important collaborator. He was about the same age (1484–1530) and probably had also come to Rome in 1503–04.[205] He was three years younger than the painter Aristotele, his more renowned brother. Antonio's mother and his own mother were sisters of Giuliano and Antonio the Elder. In Rome he was less active as a creative architect than as a building contractor, but he was also one of the most careful draughtsmen of the ancient orders and their details. There is evidence that he was commissioned by his relatives to draw column orders and details of ancient buildings and to compare them with the norms of Vitruvius. Giovan Francesco's drawings both of Cardinal Cesarini's portal, and of the entablature of the Basilica Aemilia correspond with Antonio's[206]—evidence that the cousins had collaborated since before 1509. In about 1513 Antonio had recourse to a list of seven orders that Giovan Francesco had probably compiled earlier.[207] Besides the four Vitruvian orders noted in his early Taccuino, the list included the "Antiqua latina," "frisia," and "Siracusana," to which Pliny had assigned the capitals of the Pantheon. Like Bernardo dalla Volpiaia, Giovan Francesco used Bramante's axonometric section. Characteristically, however, most of Antonio's own drawings of the ancient orders stem only from the time after Gianfrancesco's death in 1530.

In his Palazzo Balami-Galitzin begun in about 1519, Giovan Francesco already followed the Ionic bases described by Vitruvius.[208] By and by, he developed such outstanding knowledge of Vitruvius that at the beginning of the 1520s Michelangelo and a number of Florentine patricians asked his advice.[209] He not only criticized Antonio's Ionic portal for Johannes Gorizius but also occasionally preferred ancient buildings over Vitruvius's rules, praising, for example, the Ionic capital of the Theatre of Marcellus even though it "sta male malissimo secondo Vitruvio."[210]

How minutely the Sangallos discussed each detail at the time is indicated by Giovan Francesco's suggested corrections for the façade of the papal Zecca in about 1524–25.[211] They show that Antonio entrusted the learned Vitruvian with the task of checking the details of his projects. In this facade, with its *opus pseudo-isodomum*, the decorative design of its low pedestal zone, and its triumphal arch on the dominant *piano nobile*, all the achievements and experiences of Antonio's previous years coalesce, and it was for good reason that he would return over and over again to this same system, even after the Sack of Rome. He evidently understood the Composite capital, which Alberti had already praised as a splendid combination of the Ionic and Corinthian orders and as a genuinely Italian invention, to be a variation if the Corinthian.[212] He may have preferred it in its simplified form to the Corinthian mainly because it was considerably easier and cheaper to execute in travertine.[213] After the death of Giovan Francesco, Antonio seems to have kept primarily those of his drawings that showed the great richness of invention from antiquity endangered by destruction. The parallel efforts of the Sangallo family indicate their growing need to understand the laws of ancient architecture with greater precision, to discover its norms, and to give its language—with its expanding vocabulary inspired by discoveries and excavations—an effective, generally comprehensible system.

In about 1523/24 Antonio changed the abbreviation for the *palmo* from a "p" with the crossed lower bar which resembles the abbreviation of the Latin *pro* and which he had still used in the project for the cathedral of Foligno of 1523,[214] to a "p" overlined, similar to the abbreviation of the Latin *per.* He had already used this form in his projects for the staircase of Palazzo Farnese, S. Giacomo Scossacavalli and S. Maria di Montemoro, which because of the early "h" can be dated before the Sack of Rome.[215] He did not, however, change the abbreviation of the *braccio*, which he still used for most of his surveys of ancient monuments until 1527—probably because it corresponded approximately to 2 ancient feet. In these years he used the ancient foot rarely and there are only a few drawings after the antique with the pre-1524 abbreviation of the *palmo.*[216] He now relied more and more on collaborators and started to annotate his drawings more extensively than before, as for instance in the project for the staircase of Palazzo Farnese.[217] The majority of the around 50 drawings after the antique which can be dated to the period of 1520–27 are dedicated to the theatre, in which he had been interested since his projects for Villa Madama,[218] to the Roman Fora which he had investigated since 1518,[219] and to the Pantheon.[220] Only a few are devoted to triumphal arches, baths, or temples, and just one to theory, where he compares the different proportions of the orders that Vitruvius had recommended for temples and theatres—a problem he must already have dealt with when designing the courtyard of Palazzo Farnese.[221]

THE TRIP TO NORTHERN ITALY IN 1526

A welcome opportunity for Antonio to expand his knowledge of ancient monuments—and the ancient theatre in particular—beyond the borders of central Italy came during his spring 1526 tour of inspection. After the victory of Charles V over the French in Pavia in 1524, when the political situation in the Papal States and their close ally Florence had become increasingly threatening, the papal architect was charged with inspecting the fortifications of Emilia and Romagna.[222] Antonio took Giovan Francesco, Sanmicheli, and perhaps Labacco and his brother Giovanbattista with him, and not only visited Florence, Piacenza, Parma, Ravenna, and Ancona but also found time for an excursion to Verona to see its ancient monuments, possibly encouraged by Sanmicheli's enthusiasm for them. His perspective views convey a strikingly three-dimensional impression of the amphitheatre. He rendered its rusticated surface and its rows of ashlar blocks, which almost overwhelm the tripartite entablature, and drew a detail of one of the portals.[223] Giovan Francesco did something similar in his complementary cross-section, which, like Antonio's view, was already measured in ancient *piedi.*[224] The details of the elaborate stairs demonstrate how much interest in complex stairways had been aroused by the projects of Bramante and Michelangelo.[225] Giovan Francesco also drew the Porta dei Leoni in Verona and even the ground plan of the Santo in Padua.[226]

Antonio's interest in late antique and medieval monuments is further confirmed by new surveys of S. Vitale in Ravenna.[227] In the commentary on his ground plan, which Giovan Francesco copied almost verbatim, he complains about the "mala composizione" but praises its "bella

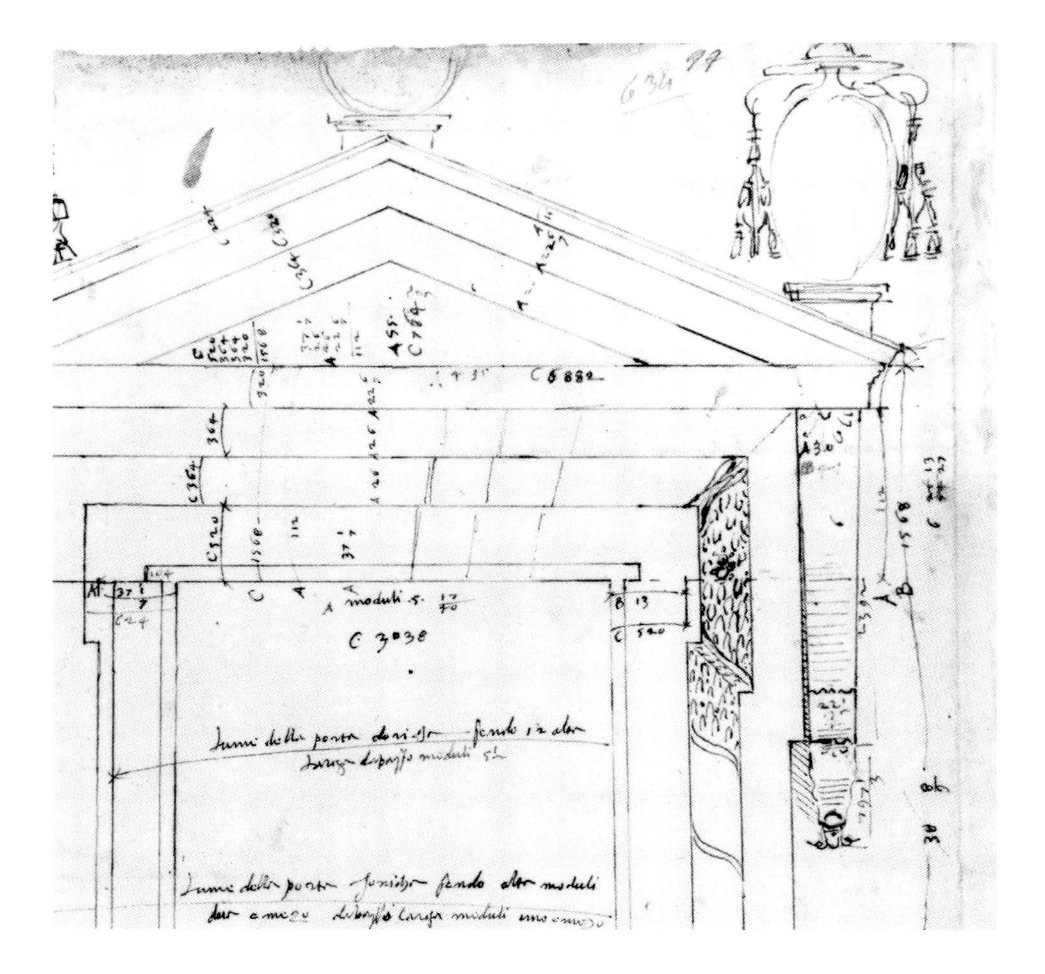

FIG. 37
ANTONIO DA SANGALLO THE YOUNGER. Portal for Loreto (Gabinetto dei Disegni e delle Stampe degli Uffizi 948A r.), detail with measures in moduli. (photo: Gabinetto dei Disegni e delle Stampe degli Uffizi)

fantasia," the variety of marbles used, and the floor mosaic. Behind an exedra, he indicated how he would have connected the piers by means of transverse arches and the columns by means of groined vaults with the corresponding articulations on the rear wall—a proposed improvement fundamentally different from that in his earlier ground plan.[228] It reveals his familiarity with the ambulatories of the new St Peter's.

At the same time, Sangallo also improved on Bramante's survey of the Tomb of Theodoric.[229] As in his project for the Medici chapel in Montecassino,[230] the elevation is placed directly above the ground plans of both storeys and the lower ground floor is now also articulated internally. The scale in ancient feet at the lower right is augmented by numerous individual measurements. The foreshortening of the side openings is more correct than in the earlier drawing, and the hatched shading is restricted to the arches over the upper niches. One senses everywhere how much Antonio had perfected his measuring technique and his method of representation over the past twenty years.

SANGALLO'S DEVELOPING APPROACH TO THEORY AND THE BEGINNING OF THE TREATISE (1527–34)

After escaping the Sack of Rome and following Clement VII into exile in Orvieto, Antonio spent an extended period of time in Florence, where he must have continued his study of Vitruvius. Immediately after the Sack of Rome, he had changed the "h" in his handwriting which had been easy to confuse with his "g," because he had written it with a short upper loop since the mid-1520s.[231] His drawings after the Sack of Rome are thus easily distinguished from those of the previous years. After Giovan Francesco's death in 1530 Antonio's younger brother Giovanbattista became his most important collaborator, especially in the measurement of ancient monuments and in his Vitruvian studies, and may then have begun to illustrate and annotate his copy of the *Editio Princeps*.[232] The brothers replaced the *braccio fiorentino* with the ancient foot (0.296 m.), which Bramante and Peruzzi had occasionally used before and which Antonio himself had used, for example, in Verona.[233] In more detailed projects and measurements of orders, portals or windows he subdivided the foot into 16 *digiti* or *dita* and 90 *minuti*.[234] One *minuto* thus corresponded to about 0.0033 m. and consequently to one third of the *digito* of a *braccio*. Even in complicated calculations with ancient modules, this enabled him to dispense with fractions most of the time, but in his last years he resorted, when necessary, to even smaller sub-units (Fig. 37).[235] This is all the more noteworthy as many architects were still using fractions of the *braccio* or *palmo*, including Peruzzi in his 1532–35 designs for the Ionic portal of the Palazzo Massimo alle Colonne.[236] At this point Antonio must have resumed checking his Vitruvian studies against the Roman monuments. Indeed, during his many years away from Rome he seems to have been waiting for just this opportunity. He drew upon Pliny's description of the Temple of Diana in Ephesus,[237] as he had done before the Sack of Rome.[238] As one the first specialised architects since antiquity, he was now penetrating some of the secrets of ancient architecture that had remained hidden from most of his contemporaries. He sharpened his eye and enriched his store of forms.

His project to produce an illustrated Vitruvius commentary, which may have been maturing since the last years before the Sack, solidified over the next few years, and for the time being his building activity was restricted primarily to fortifications. His plan to write a treatise was already far advanced in 1531 when he drafted its foreword.[239] In it he complained how poorly Vitruvius had been understood and proposed seven reasons for this: (i) until now architects had had neither the learning nor the professionalism to deal with him adequately; (ii) his frequently employed Greek terms were no longer comprehensible, and his text had been badly transmitted and poorly edited, so that Antonio had had to consult the oldest surviving copies and published editions; (iii) since in Vitruvius's day the general rules of architecture were well known, and no one could imagine they would ever be forgotten, he could limit himself to brief allusions; (iv) the indispensable illustrations promised by Vitruvius were lacking, either because they were lost or because he held them back out of anger that Augustus had given the commissions to ignorant architects instead; (v) to arrive at a better understanding of Vitruvius's text one had to study the literary sources as well as the buildings of ancient Greece and Rome;[240] (vi) most of the sources in the ancient libraries had disappeared, so that Antonio had had to rely primarily on the surviving buildings; and finally, (vii) since most of these were built "nei tempi buoni [...] della felicita dello imperio"—that is, after the composition of Vitruvius' treatise—they corresponded with some likelihood to his rules, and if in his turn he, Antonio, wanted to demonstrate this with examples, he should not be accused of arrogance, for he had a certain command of Latin as well as Italian—"qualche parte in le lettere latine e volgare"—and experience as an architect going back to the beginning of Julius II's pontificate. If, according to his commentary, much remained to be done, it was because, he explained, he had had to rely for his Latin and Greek on the help of friends, who had never let him down.

The illustrations in Antonio's commentary were not meant to be purely theoretical, like Fra Giocondo's or Cesariano's, but to present suitable prototypes of ancient and probably also modern architecture that corresponded to Vitruvius's norms. Neither Serlio nor Vignola—not even Alberti and Palladio—pursued such exacting goals in their treatises. Vignola was concerned primarily with codifying the orders, and Serlio in his third book of 1540 focused on exempla worth imitating. Even so, Serlio illustrated the best-known of the ancient buildings and arranged them hierarchically according to type as Alberti had done and as Antonio himself seems to have planned to do before 1513.[241] Only Daniele Barbaro and Palladio, in their Vitruvius commentary of 1556, followed Antonio's lead. But once again the ancient author retained the upper hand, and such thorny problems as the Ionic portal and the corner triglyphs remained unresolved.[242] Neither Serlio nor Palladio analysed ancient architecture with Vitruvius's eyes or annotated him with a similarly detailed knowledge of the ancient monuments. Both avoided typological series of the sort Antonio had prepared, say, for temples.[243] Not for nothing did Philandrier, in his Vitruvius commentary of 1544, still praise Antonio and his brother Giovanbattista as profound connoisseurs of the ancient monuments.[244] Had Antonio completed his ambitious treatise, there is no doubt that it would have had a decisive influence on later developments; but it is little wonder that he never did so.

THE TEMPLE, THE PANTHEON CORRECTION AND ANOTHER IDEAL PROJECT

Since about 1518 Antonio had been interested, above all, in the temple as the noblest task in architecture, and he concentrated, significantly, on a group of Roman peripteral temples whose closeness to Vitruvius seemed confirmed by the latter's own words. Antonio mistakenly believed that in two of the three temples on the Forum Holitorium he had rediscovered the Temple of Jupiter Stator and the Temple of Honor and Virtue, which Vitruvius presented as exempla in the second chapter of Book III.[245] Like the Temple of Honor and Virtue, the third temple in fact possessed no *opisthodomos*, and so, written in the hand Antonio used prior to the Sack of Rome, we find the following: "...li tre templi lì achanto [al Teatro di Marcello] sono questi secondo Vetruvio nello libro tertio capitolo primo nel peritteros:

lo dorico achanto santo Nichola era di Giove Statoris, lo ionicho dove è santo Nichola proprio edificati si era di Hermodi, la dove era le carciere pare ionicho senza posticho si era di Mariana Onore e Virtute facto da Mutio, e non aveva lo posticho perche le logie della sciena dello teatro di Marcello le toglieva lo locho che non ci era spatio che si potessi fare."[246] Thus, when he analysed two temples that Vitruvius himself had called exemplary, he could hope for normative proportions and complete agreement with the treatise.

In his numerous drawings and sketches of these three temples, which were measured primarily by Giovanbattista, Antonio was attempting the difficult reconstruction of one Doric and two Ionic variants of the peripteral temple, from the ground plan and the proportions of the orders to the intercolumniations, the rhythm of the Doric frieze, and the problem of the corner triglyphs. His reconstruction of the Doric frieze of the Temple of Jupiter Stator differs only marginally from the existing structure and Vitruvius's norm:[247] the triglyphs are one module wide, the metopes 1.55 modules wide, the centre bay is wider by a triglyph and a metope, and the corner bay is two-fifths of a module narrower.

Like Antonio's reconstruction of the Temple of Mars Ultor, the final result—the most complete and precise reconstruction of an ancient temple up to that time—survives only in copies by Peruzzi, Serlio, and Labacco. Labacco's commentary in the *Libro appartenente all'architettura* agrees even in its wording with Antonio's remarks and attests to the source of his material.[248] Peruzzi's drawings, measured in *braccia* of 60 *minuti*, are also recognizable as copies after Antonio's pre-1527 drawings.[249] He must have had the opportunity to inspect Antonio's documents when he was preparing his own treatise,[250] even though Antonio had not yet abandoned his plan of writing one himself. Antonio was still busy with it in the late 1530s when he moved up the date of his foreword to 1539.[251] Serlio in turn could have seen the drawing of the Temple of Mars Ultor among Peruzzi's personal effects or at Giovanbattista's when he began putting together his third book around 1536.

Antonio also worked on other types of temples described in the third book of Vitruvius—"L III."[252] Next to two temples in antis and a prostyle temple, he drew, as an example of a *dipteros*, the Temple of Diana of Ephesus, which according to Vitruvius had 127 columns.[253] He reconstructed an octostyle *amphiprostylos* and a hexastyle *peripteros* with the intercolumniation of the "Eustylo," but in the process, he widened the central bay of the hexastyle temple to the intercolumniation of a "Diastylo," as Vitruvius had recommended.[254] It is likely that he planned to include both ground plans in his treatise as illustrations of Vitruvius's norms.

How intensively he occupied himself with the different forms of the temple in the 1530s is demonstrated by another series of surveys. His masterly and economical sketch of the Temple of Antoninus and Faustina, probably drawn soon after the Sack of Rome, is measured in ancient feet and includes all essential architectural and figural details.[255] His survey of the Temple of Hercules in Cori is less detailed.[256] In October 1535, he added the words "dicto di Vitruvio peripteros" to the building survey of this temple that Riniero da Pisa had measured in ancient feet of 32 *minuti*.[257] Three years later, when he had already turned to the study of the orders, a visit of Paul III to Tivoli gave him the opportunity to measure the temple more precisely with his own hand.[258] In order to understand the numerous types of temples, soon after 1530 he even drew the *prostylos* in the background of one of the historical reliefs of Marcus Aurelius on the Capitol—"nelle storie di campidoglio."[259] He obviously planned to reproduce systematically and analyse the various types of temples described by Vitruvius. Only Barbaro and Palladio succeeded in doing this in their Vitruvius commentary of 1556, which would hardly have been possible without Antonio's preliminary work.

In his reflections on temples Antonio included Vitruvius's description of the basilica in Book V —"L V"—and he reconstructed it on U 2056A r. very much like a temple, not least because Alberti had associated it with temples, not with a forum, and because he himself had in mind the sacred function of late antique basilicas.[260] On the upper portion of the sheet, he opened one of the sides of the basilica by means of a portico to the "foro" and reduced the height of the upper story to a 3:4 proportion such as Vitruvius had recommended for market basilicas; but he furnished the interior with a barrel vault. Below, he reconstructed the ground plan and elevation, in several variants, of the Basilica at Fano, which Vitruvius himself had erected and described in detail in his fifth book, where we learn that it was lit by open metopes. Giovan Francesco's sketch of the basilica's entablature on U 1378A v. is identical to Antonio's, but it remains an open question as to who copied whom.[261]

Only a few years before the Sack of Rome Antonio began a systematic study of the Pantheon,[262] that most admired and—in particular for the architects of St Peter's—most important of all temples.[263] At that time, he also listed those elements, for the most part elevation measurements, which still lacked the precision he desired.[264] Out of this detailed study would seem to have come the drawing of a longitudinal section—still in *braccia* and therefore from before the Sack—that we know only from Peruzzi's drawing in Ferrara, probably copied from Sangallo (Fig. 38).[265]

Even then, Antonio must have reflected on the many inconsistencies of the Pantheon. As heirs to the Gothic,

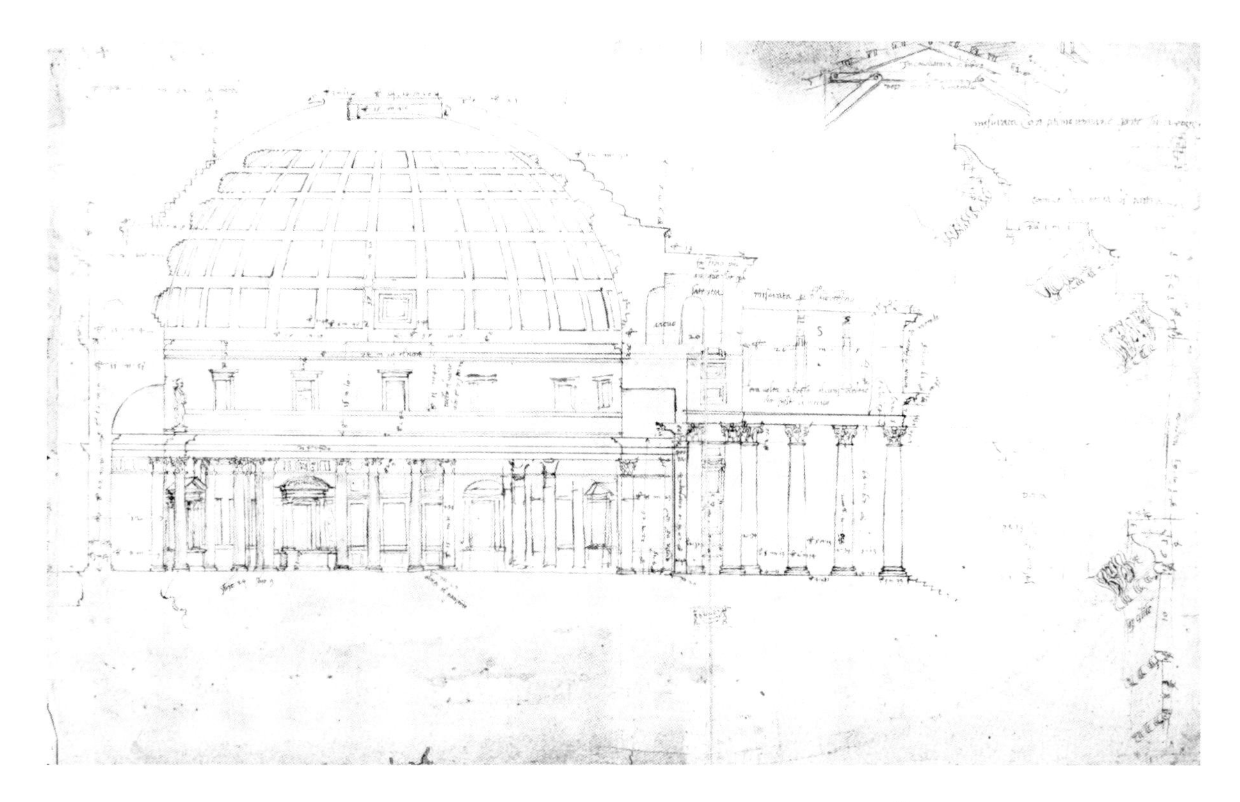

FIG. 38 BALDASSARE PERUZZI AFTER ANTONIO DA SANGALLO (?).
Longitudinal section of the Pantheon (Ferrara, Biblioteca Comunale, Ms Classe I, N.217 r.; photo: Wurm 1984, pl. 473)

architects from Brunelleschi onwards had observed a systematic coherence. They could study the vertical continuity of axes and the horizontal continuity of the cornices on the exterior of ancient temples, theatres and other buildings. Hence, every experienced eye must have observed how inorganically the portico was attached to the rotunda of the Pantheon, how the cornices jumped, how the view of the niches of the portico was blocked by its columns, and how behind the stone pediment of the portico there loomed a second pediment in brick and mortar. Worst of all, however, the interior could not be read by means of continuous vertical axes. According to Vasari, Michelangelo, who was anything but orthodox, went so far as to maintain that the Pantheon was the work of three different architects. But if few masters possessed Raphael's empathy to appreciate the fascinating and unique effect of the three independent storeys circling the interior, one above the other and meeting only in the two main axes, as the result of a brilliant artistic stratagem, even he would have had a hard time justifying the way the portico connected with the rotunda or the second pediment. In his third book of 1540, Serlio silently eliminated the second pediment, established an axial continuity between the two orders of the interior, and simply dismissed the wide exedra as a later addition.[266] Perhaps after 1535, Antonio noted the many points at which the Pantheon deviated from the principle of axial correspondence (U 874A r.).[267] In the accompanying sketch he remarked that the two rows of columns in the portico correspond to Vitruvius's *dipteros*. He observed that the second and third rows each lack four columns, and that neither the two side niches nor the insertion of the central bay are in harmony with the intercolumniations of the temple front. In the accompanying ground plan he showed how all these "errori" could have been avoided with relatively simple corrections; but he had no sense of appreciation for the aesthetic effect achieved by the ancient architect precisely through these deviations from the norm. With an equally systematic perusal, he criticised the interior and proposed a more regular alternative, in which every pilaster of the upper story and every rib of the coffered dome are set axially over the members of the lower order. He even placed ascending sections of pilasters behind the colonnettes of the aediculas and tried to counter the consequent danger of overly narrow bays by adjusting the bay widths and eliminating the broader central axis.

The interior diameter of around 150 feet in the clean drawing (U 3990A) corresponds approximately to the actual building.[268] Antonio gave the portico the three continuous rows of columns of a *dipteros*, widened the central intercolumniation, eliminated the inserted portal bay and lateral niches, and added two rows of columns, leaving a square void. By widening the central bay and reducing the entrance wall, he gained enough room to continue the outer columns around the entire rotunda in the manner of a *tholos*, and even allowed for corresponding half columns on the wall. In this way he concealed the disturbing connection of the portico to the rotunda and bestowed on the exterior a splendour echoing that of the interior.

Antonio had now eliminated not just the wider bay of the longitudinal axis but also the aedicules of the ground storey. On the closed wall sections of the rotunda he continued the rhythm of the columns with applied half columns, aligning them radially with the columns and half columns of the outer ring. In this masterly achievement of systematic planning, he relied directly on Bramante's late project for the dome of St Peter's, which undoubtedly grew out of similar considerations (cf. Fig. 18) and would find an afterlife in the dome of Antonio's wooden model of 1539. His schematic succession of short, similarly shaped bays might still have won the approval of some eighteenth- and nineteenth-century architects, but they would hardly have looked with favor on the effect of the interior space.

This ideal reconstruction was not for realisation but purely theoretical, and may have been destined for engravings. On the corresponding elevation on U 1271A r. he put his signature claiming it as his invention: "OPUS ANTONII SANGALLI ARCHITECT[I] AN[NO] D[OMINI] ...." The octastyle temple front which is accompanied by a scale of measurement, extends to a width of 120 ancient feet (35.76 m.) and a height of 65 feet (19.37 m.).[269] The extension of the plinth on both sides, with no additional steps and measurements, confirms that the front is part of the reconstruction of the Pantheon.[270] Given its total width of about 240 feet (71.52 m.), it would have surpassed most of the temples and churches of Rome. With their 5-foot (1.49 m.) diameter and 40-foot (11.92 m.) height, the columns have an exact 1:8 proportion, which again corresponds to the actual building. They are furnished with Tuscan bases and capitals, an indication that Antonio was thinking of a mixture of the Doric and Tuscan orders, whose proportions had been less exactly established by Vitruvius. The double-shaft widths of the intercolumniations correspond to the systyle and the central intercolumniation has the triple-shaft width of the diastyle. The entablature, with its corner triglyphs not centred over the columns and its indication of guttae at the corner of the architrave, demonstrates Antonio's knowledge of the Doric entablature, a type he had struggled with since 1513. Yet it follows none of those in Vitruvius's temples. Antonio here obviously developed his own quite personal ideas. Both the strictness of the corrections and the rationality are in favor of a date not before 1535.

Since the exterior does not continue the Corinthian order it cannot have been been conceived as a restoration project for the Pantheon, nor can it be connected to San Giovanni or other known projects,[271] but was probably intended to be an illustration for the treatise.

And the same is true for the drawings of a Ionic peristyle temple on U 4039A r., which is represented in side view and in longitudinal section.[272] A scale of measurement is lacking, but if the height of the plinth with its seven steps on the left border is reckoned to be about 4 Roman feet high, the columns would likewise have a diameter of about 5 feet (1.49 m.) and with the plinth and entablature would reach a height of about 40 feet (11.92 m.). Despite the narrow pycnostyle intercolumniations, they are also given a proportion of 1:8 and so follow the older norms described by Vitruvius. They possess Attic bases, and the convex frieze of the entablature is the same height as the architrave. On the outer walls of the cella, arcade-like niches alternate with rectangular ones, the two rows of which rest on cornices. The two narrow sides were probably intended to have ten columns and the entrance bay to be somewhat broader. Only in the longitudinal section does the temple reveal itself to be a complex vaulted building. Above the *peripteros* rises a second, higher storey, articulated by pilasters of a similar Ionic order and crowned on the narrow sides by pediments, so that the total height is doubled. The pedestals over the columns of the porch seem to prepare for two upper rows of columns on the narrow sides. The third row of columns in the porch opens onto the barrel-vaulted atrium, which is flanked by low exedras with shell calottes and lit by lunette windows directly recalling those of the Sala Regia of 1538–39.[273] The long cella terminates in an inserted apse. The width of the apparently single-aisled room would have corresponded approximately to the distance between the third and seventh columns of the temple facade; that is, about 34 feet, with a depth of about 100 feet (10.13 × 29.80 m.). It is articulated by two orders of Ionic half-columns, the lower of which is elevated on a high base and continued into the apse. Its intercolumniations are decorated by aedicules with niches for statues and blank panels.

It is more difficult to understand Antonio's intentions for the zone above the second order, since in the drawing it is indicated only by a preliminary scoring. Although there is no indication of it, he conceivably had in mind a barrel vault with lunette windows. A reinforcement of the springing zone behind the side facades of one of the upper colonnades may have been intended. The resulting room would have been somewhat loftier than the Sala Regia, and light wells were planned for the possible installation of lunettes. In order to guarantee sufficient lighting Sangallo let the barrel vault, which rests entirely on the lateral walls, end a few meters before the apse. The rear facade is designed like the one in front. Between the *opistodomos* and the apse is the entrance to a staircase that was undoubtedly meant to lead to the upper terraces. The temple's stylistic relationship to the Sala Regia puts it in the same period of around 1538. This project cannot be associated with any known structure from antiquity, whether surviving or known from descriptions. In it Antonio combined a peristyle with an atrium, as Palladio would later do in his reconstruction of the Temple of Venus and Roma.[274] He also followed the Temple of Venus and Roma in adorning the cella with columns, aedicules, an exedra and a barrel vault. If, as it appears, he also planned to put columns over the porches and on the sides of the upper storey, the building would have required 144 columns—considerably more, in other words, than the Temple of Diana in Ephesus. The project opens partly to the sky and lacks altars, sacristies, and other references to Christianity and it is hard to imagine what function it could have served. The perfect rendering of the drawing, however, could be again interpreted as an argument that it was meant to illustrate the treatise.

STUDIES OF THE ANCIENT HOUSE

Since Alberti the reconstruction of the ancient house had been a central interest of Vitruvian studies.[275] As early as the 1480s Giuliano da Sangallo had tried to liken the villa of Poggio a Caianao to the Vitruvian house by opening the entrance wing into a transverse vestibule, as Peruzzi would later do in the Palazzo Massimo. Perhaps only in a second phase Giüliano crowned its colonnade with a triangular pediment, as Alberti had recommended.[276] Already in 1489, in his model for the palace of the king of Naples, Giuliano proposed the Vitruvian sequence of vestibule, atrium, cavaedium and peristyle; the vestibule as a triumphal porch in front of the entrance; the atrium with three barrel vaulted naves of equal width; and the cavaedium and peristyle corresponding to the Renaissance courtyard. All this went far beyond any earlier attempts to reconstruct the Vitruvian house, but even surpassed Fra Giocondo's later reconstruction of 1511, which was neither functionally nor formally convincing.[277]

Giuliano's nephew Antonio must have known these projects, and before constructing the Vitruvian atrium of Palazzo Farnese in about 1514, he had designed on U 1168A V. an ancient house with a three-aisled atrium.[278] In the large central nave of the atrium of Palazzo Farnese with its barrel vault and the smaller side aisles, however, he followed the entrance porch of the Pantheon, which is a vestibule rather than an atrium. Renouncing the vestibule he does not distinguish these two Vitruvian functions very strictly. He made the atrium as deep as the entrance wing and thus increased the number of columns from four to six, as in Fra Giocondo's reconstruction, where there are no comparable aisles.[279] In his projects for the palace of the Medici of ca. 1515 he repeated the same type and so did his brother Giovanbattista in his illustrations of Vitruvius, even after 1530.[280]

On the project U 1054A for Villa Madama (ca. 1517) Antonio went a step further in the reconstruction of the ancient house (cf. Fig. 32). The vestibule of the main front opens into a broad colonnade with a columnar arcade in the centre overlooking the Tiber valley. The vestibule continues in a transverse atrium with four columns on each side of the axis and a round cavaedium. The narrow intercolumniations of the peristyle suggest a colonnade with an entablature. (Already when building the circular courtyard of his Mantuan house Mantegna must have thought of an antique prototype.) The left wing opens into an isolated atrium which is similar to that of palazzo Farnese and which corresponds to a small courtyard in the right wing.

The atrium of Palazzo Farnese had no precise ancient prototype (cf. Fig. 30), but was well calculated for a big Italian palace and this is characteristic of Sangallo's relatively free use of Vitruvian prototypes. Not even after the Sack of Rome did Antonio and Giovanbattista regard the typology of the atrium of Palazzo Farnese as superseded.[281]

In around 1528–29, when the consequences of the Sack of Rome gave Sangallo more time to intensify his studies of Vitruvius, in his project 1074A for the Palazzo Pucci in Orvieto, he returned to the reconstruction of the Vitruvian entry sequence like the one begun in about 1517 on 1054A: The façade opens into the wide porch of the vestibule, continues in the three aisles of the atrium which are divided by rows of four columns, and ends the peristyle.

According to Sangallo's changed handwriting the project U 999A for a imperial palace cannot be dated before 1527, while the large colonnade of the vestibule with its three rows of columns and the three aisles of the atrium are still reminiscent of U 1054A.[282] Sangallo must have known that Charles V was planning a luxurious castle at the Alhambra and may have presented the plan to the emperor shortly after the occupation of Florence in 1530, perhaps recommended by the pope.[283] The palace would have been square, as the palace was then built, though twice as big, but the site next to the Alhambra would have been sufficient. In these years no other sovereign could have had similar ambitions.

Some years later Sangallo sketched on U 1188A the plan of the Vitruvian house with the temple front of the vestibule, similar to that of the Pantheon.[284] Palladio would use this idea in his villas, together with a transverse atrium with four columns and the colonnade of the peristyle.

The reconstruction of the Greek *palaestra* on U 1161A, in which he once again changed Fra Giocondo's schematic illustration (V, ch. 11), and which conformed to his current state of knowledge, must date from the same time.[285] Only later did he consider an anterior vestibule, such as Palladio was to plan from 1542 onwards for the Palazzo Thiene.[286]

In another project for the Palazzo Pucci, which is probably not much later, Sangallo reduced the transverse vestibule to the width of a serliana and omitted the columns of the atrium[287]—an arrangement Sanmicheli would soon take over in his Palazzo Canossa.[288] Although this arrangement departs once again from Vitruvius, Sangallo retained it in his designs for his house on Via Giulia of about 1535, for the patrician houses in Castro of about 1537, and for several villas.[289]

It was only in his projects for Castro that he succeeded in combining the advantages of ancient and modern houses in an organic design, well-lit and ventilated, rational and functional. In his late palace on Via Giulia, the pre-existing structure precluded such a solution.[290]

Sangallo's elevations for his own houses illustrate how he imagined the exterior of such projects. In the years after the Sack of Rome, he planned to face the ground floor of his Florentine house with rusticated stone blocks.[291] These are no longer, however, the irregular ashlar blocks of the Rucellai palace and Bramante's Palazzo dei Tribunali or the pillow-shaped blocks of the Gondi and Strozzi palaces, but instead consist of narrow layers of three-dimensional rusticated blocks of alternating width, such as we find on the papal Zecca and Giulio Romano's Palazzo Adimari-Salviati. As in those buildings, he removed the load from the lunette window above the portal by means of widely radiating voussoirs. The portal and the six windows of the ground floor follow the tapered type of Vitruvius's Doric portal, which Sangallo reconstructed here for the first time and used again for his two Roman residences.

The *piano nobile* was certainly intended to be governed by an order, such as he planned for his Roman house on Via Giulia, which rises on a similar ground floor.[292] As in the papal Zecca, the façade is dominated by the triumphal arch of the *piano nobile*, whose slender half columns correspond to the narrow windows. The motif was to be repeated on the rear wall of the courtyard. A colossal antique head and Sangallo's coat of arms and inscription were meant to show who triumphed here.[293] This triumphal claim on the facade and in the courtyard was not legitimized by any ancient palace, but from the Cancelleria onwards had become a favorite motif of secular architecture.

STUDIES OF THE ANTIQUE THEATRE

Francesco di Giorgio had already made a schematic ground plan of the Theatre of Ferento;[294] but the first exact measurement of an antique theatre—and one of the earliest comprehensive surveys of a monument of this size—is the plan and perspective elevation of the Theatre of Orange on fol. 40 r. of the Codex Barberini, which was not made until Giuliano's trip to France in the mid-1490s.[295] Like Francesco di Giorgio, Giuliano satisfied himself with schematic simplifications of the theatre, even more so than in his surveys of the Colosseum, and avoided comparison with Vitruvius's description. Fra Giocondo and Cesariano also made schematic reconstructions of the Vitruvian theatre.[296]

Long before the Sack of Rome, Antonio, too, had started to study the ancient theatre. In his designs for the Villa Madama of 1519, he was the first to attempt a reconstruction of the Greek and Latin theatre according to Vitruvius's description.[297] It was probably about 1525 when he related the ground plan of the Theatre of Ferento to the geometric construction methods of the Latin theatre as described by Vitruvius.[298] There, he showed that the orchestra and stage resembled the geometric scheme of the Latin theatre in the seventh chapter of Vitruvius's fifth book. As in Vitruvius, the circle on which the construction is based corresponds to the orchestra and is divided into twelve equal sections by the points of four inscribed equilateral triangles. Seven points establish the stairs of the cavea and three the axes of the portals of the scenae frons. Two points determine the depth of the scenae frons, and a parallel line through the centre of the circle forms the edge of the orchestra and cavea. In his design for the theatre of the Villa Madama, Antonio had already inscribed the circle of the orchestra, whereas most interpreters of Vitruvius drew it around the entire theatre and thus moved the cavea and orchestra a considerable distance from the scenae frons. In this respect, too, for a long time Antonio remained the only draughtsman who fully understood Vitruvius's intentions.

He repeated the experiment after 1531 in his survey of the Theatre of Marcellus, to which he devoted far more intensive study.[299] His external motivation was probably the renovation of the palazzo of the Savelli family, who in the Middle Ages had settled in the upper storey of the theatre.[300] Peruzzi began rebuilding its interior probably after 1522, and the palace was still under construction about

1525 when Serlio came to Rome. How close the architects were able to come to the living quarters of the Savelli even after 1530 is shown by Antonio's section, where he noted at the height of the Ionic entablature, "piano de stantie," and one storey higher than the present courtyard, "piano del cortile."[301] Antonio's first sketches of the Theatre of Marcellus once again go back to the years before the Sack of Rome. Together with numerous details of the Forum Holitorium, he sketched a cursory plan of the theatre with a semi-oval cavea and halls flanking the proscenium.[302] These were already known at the time, but the proscenium was evidently in large part destroyed. Antonio therefore reconstructed it as Fra Giocondo had done, with a colonnaded portico and its projecting center (*pulpitum*). Nor, evidently, were there any remains to guide him when—probably after the Sack—he came to the portico behind the stage, which is described by Vitruvius in the ninth chapter of his fifth book.[303]

Giovanbattista's surveys of the theatre, measured in *braccia* with the help of a compass, must also have been made before the Sack. He, too, assumed the cavea to be semi-oval.[304] When Antonio went back to these or similar surveys after the Sack, he was not content with investigating the ground plan and its geometric scheme; as he had done for the Colosseum in 1505/06, he also reconstructed its section, its entrances and their lighting, the steps of the cavea, and the construction. With Fra Giocondo (fol. 51 v.) as his starting point, Antonio now tried to reproduce the supposed semi-oval of the orchestra by means of a circle with four inscribed squares; that is, a geometrical construction such as Vitruvius had described for the Greek theatre.[305] He believed the corners and crossing points of the squares to be the centres of the four circle segments that constitute the oval.[306] Clearly, he interpreted the cavea of the Theatre of Marcellus as half a Colosseum. This is also suggested by the almost equal number of entrances, 41—exactly half of those in the Colosseum—and their corresponding corridors and stairs. Alberti (VIII, ch. 8) had already described the theatre as "half" an amphitheatre, and Antonio could thus have constructed the semi-oval with an auxiliary construction similar to that of the Colosseum.[307] Not until they had gone a step further did the brothers reach the conclusion that the cavea and the orchestra were indeed semicircular and constructed according to the scheme of the Theatre of Ferento.[308]

Serlio was undoubtedly aware of this conclusion when, soon after Peruzzi's death, he began to collect material for his treatise. He was therefore able to publish a rough copy of the reconstruction by the Sangallo draughtsmen in his third book in 1540.[309] He attributed it to his deceased teacher Peruzzi, who had carried out excavations in the theatre, and made no mention of Antonio in this context, even though in the preface of his fourth book he had commenced his list of the leading architects with Antonio and ended it with Giovanbattista: "Evi ancora Battista gia lodato muratore, ed hor lodatissimo Architetto si ne la Theorica come ne la pratica expertissimo."[310] If he bestowed such high rank on Giovanbattista, he must have known him well; indeed, it may have been owing to him that Serlio was able to see Antonio's drawings after the antique. Daniele Barbaro's Vitruvius commentary of 1556 and Palladio's fourth book likewise make no mention of Antonio's pioneering work.[311]

The Florentine Antonio del Tanghero had already measured the exterior of the Theatre of Marcellus with the greatest precision before 1520, and in all likelihood independently of Antonio.[312] As he used *palmi romani*, he could not have been part of Antonio's team. He may instead have been one of the collaborators on Raphael's corpus of surveys of ancient Rome. After 1530, Antonio corrected, enlarged, and commented on Tanghero's drawing and established that the Ionic columns were less than 9 shaft-widths high instead of 9 1/3 shaft-widths, as they would have been in the Ionic order of a theatre.[313] Here was another important building that did not follow Vitruvius's recommendations. Giovanbattista's less detailed but more exact elevation is still measured in *braccia* and therefore probably stems from the period 1525–27.[314]

With his studies of the theatre, Antonio showed how close Roman buildings could be to Vitruvian norms, despite some deviations. At the same time he created the pre-requisites for the construction of new theatres. As early as 1487–88, in the dedication of his Vitruvius edition, Sulpizio da Veroli had urged the young Cardinal Riario to restore the Theatre of Pompey, or else to construct a new theatre.[315] Soon afterwards, Giuliano da Sangallo and Giuliano da Maiano created their projects for Neapolitan theatre courtyards. Beginning in 1503, Bramante augmented the Belvedere with a giant auditorium intended for tournaments and probably also for drama, and in 1518–19 Raphael and Antonio planned the first Vitruvian theatre for the Villa Madama. Even afterwards, Antonio's real goal must have been to build an ancient theatre, especially since Bibbiena, Ariosto, Macchiavelli, and Aretino were once again writing effective plays for the stage and laying the foundation for modern spoken theatre. Even Trissino, whom Antonio surely knew, was able to achieve success with his tragedy *Sofonisba*. How single-mindedly Antonio pursued this goal is shown by his project for a wooden Vitruvian open-air theatre with *periaktoi* (triangular and movable border elements of the stage), which he proposed to erect in the spring of 1531 near the Largo Argentina for the wedding of the Cesarini.[316] In the event, the Cesarini, however, preferred Peruzzi's perspective stage. It was Palladio who towards the end of his life once again gathered the fruits of all these efforts in his Teatro Olimpico, which he adapted to the needs of his home city, Vicenza, with a protective roof and a reduced auditorium.[317]

THE VITRUVIAN ORDERS

Antonio's drawings after the antique create the impression that in the final years of his life his theoretical interests shifted from the great monuments back to the column orders, and from about 1538 onwards the sessions of the learned Accademia Vitruviana may have been a contributing factor.[318] It seems that Antonio and his "illiterate" collaborators and practitioners were excluded from this noble circle. Thus they founded their own Compagnia dei Virtuosi del Pantheon in 1543 on the themes set down in the foreword of his treatise, and among its members were his brother Giovanbattista, Labacco, Giovanni Mangone, and Jacopo Meleghino. Antonio was its first secretary, and it undoubtedly followed his line of thinking.[319] Meanwhile, in 1539 he had again taken up work on his Vitruvius commentary.[320]

Perhaps Antonio had only acquired his copies of Durantino's 1524 Vitruvius translation after the Sack of Rome,[321] and it is not obvious according to which principle he distributed the rather few comments to the two copies.[322] He had already made use of his knowledge in the copy in Parma, supplementing the incomplete illustrations of the prostyle temple and the temple in antis in the second chapter of Book III.[323] Fra Giocondo, whose illustrations were taken over by Durantino, apparently still had no clear idea of the form of these two types. He also called the portico of the Pantheon a "seudodiptero" (III, ch. 2), citing the temple "delle tre fortune ... presso ala porta collina."[324] In his other copy, Antonio corrected the reconstruction of the Tuscan temple (V, ch. 7) and the basilica "calcidica." In the copy in Parma, Antonio returned once more to the fifth chapter of Vitruvius's fourth book and commented on the proportions of the orders: "Alla jonica otto e meza hanno co[n]stituito e questo sie/ secondo fra jocu[n]do v[ero] secondo li altri viiij/ seco[n]do li altri la jonicha a essere come di sopra teste viiij/ Ma quella delli portici e chiara [?] chelle doriche sono teste 7½/ Le joniche creschono una testa e cinqu[e] sesti che sono teste 9⅓/ v[ero] la cori[n]tia li due tertij che de teste -10/ Cosi aria a stare i[n] li te[n]pli che sendo la doricha teste – 7/ e la jonicha ricreciessi una testa e ⅚ saria–8⅚/ E la corintia saria p[er]che cresci li ⅔ teste – 9/ ½/ e cosi crescie luna qua[n]to laltra i[n] proportione e sta bene."[325] In other words, he still wavered in his late years between 1:8.5 and 1:9 for the Ionic order of temples.[326] With 1:7.5, 1:9 1/3, and 1:10 the three orders of porticoes are somewhat more slender. To

FIG. 39 Palazzo Farnese brackets groundfloor (photo O. Savio, from Uginet-Fossier, 1980–94, *Le Palais Farnèse*, p. 158, fig. b)

FIG. 40 Rome, Vatican Palace, Sala Ducale, window frame (photo: Archivio Fotografico Vaticano)

come closer to Vitruvius, he increasingly relinquished the whole numbers of his earlier years, but now, as before, he strove for a systematic development of the orders. He also followed this tendency—which ultimately goes back to the spiral staircase of the Belvedere—in a sketch of 1542, where he developed the Ionic capital from the Doric, and the Corinthian from the Ionic: "Questi capitelli nascono uno dallaltro."[327] Only the ornament of the order increases; its basic forms remain the same.

For the varying heights of the Doric, Ionic, and Corinthian capitals and architraves of columns between 15 and 60 feet high, which had already occupied him before the Sack of Rome, he drew four curves on one sheet which become flatter as the height increases. He also discussed the reduction of the entasis of the columns and the tapering of the door openings with their increasing height. In this way he tried to make more understandable and relevant the optical corrections of ancient architecture, which had barely been taken into consideration by his predecessors. His commentary is unclear in some places, but it shows that in each case he proceeded in his calculations from a constant proportion of the column shaft and base, intending to enlarge only the capital and architrave by increasing their heights. It was probably as a result of these considerations that he investigated the entablatures of the most important temples in Rome and came to the conclusion that the architrave, independently of the size of the order, on average measured from two thirds to three quarters of the diameter of the columns.[328] Here, too, he had to revise his postulate of 1531 that Vitruvius's rules were corroborated by the buildings of Rome.

In 1540, Antonio had already compared the differing interpretations of a passage in the Vitruvius editions of 1487/88 and 1497 "per fare li architravi," and had shown examples with the help of fragments of Ionic-Corinthian entablatures, one of which was also drawn by Giovan Francesco.[329] At that time, he also displayed admirable humanist rigour by consulting a Vitruvian manuscript "a penna," in addition to the different printings of the *Editio Princeps* and Fra Giocondo.[330] In all, he used at least seven different copies of Vitruvius.

Finally, Antonio returned once again to the Vitruvian rule that had already occupied him on fol. 30 v. of the Prague copy of the treatise. According to this rule, the height of the lateral acroteria on an Ionic temple should correspond to the height of the central axis of the tympanum, and the central acroterion should be half as high again.[331] Antonio noted sarcastically that if this were the case, on a temple front with ten columns the acroteria would be as high as church towers. Thus he never followed blindly the differing interpretations of the Vitruvian manuscripts and printed editions, but rather, tested each of the countless recommendations

FIG. 41 Rome, Palazzo Farnese, Ionic order of the courtyard (photo: Bibliotheca-Hertziana – Max Planck Institute for Art History)

against the surviving monuments and his own reconstructions. In any case, he was not among those who paved the way for Serlio, who in 1537, in his fourth book, proportioned the orders in an ascending series of round numbers: 1:7 for the Doric, 1:8 for the Ionic, 1:9 for the Corinthian, and 1:10 for the Composite.[332] Even though Francesco di Giorgio had already considered a canon of ascending round numbers,[333] and despite the fact that since Peruzzi the canon of the four orders seems to have included the Composite, Antonio's few buildings are proof enough that he never committed himself to such rigid proportions.[334]

After leaving Bramante's workshop in about 1513, Antonio had competed for at least seven years with Bramante and concentrated on the proportion, intercolumniation and entablature of the Doric order, but had given much less attention to the Ionic. The only realized Ionic order of these years in the courtyard of Palazzo Baldassini follows the system of Bramante's Logge, though with much more slender proportions, and the heavy Ionic brackets in the ground-floor rooms of Palazzo Baldassini and Palazzo Farnese also look rather Bramantesque.[335] (Fig. 39) In around 1515, when Antonio had already penetrated more deeply into Vitruvius and articulated the courtyard and atrium of Palazzo Farnese in a more canonical manner than Bramante had done, he tried to improve on the Ionic portal of Bramante's Tempietto in the proportions, cornice, consoles, tapering and convex frieze of Johannes Gorizius' garden door.[336] After 1520 this was, however, heavily criticised by Antonio's cousin Giovan Francesco and Antonio himself called it a youthful error: "No[n] sta bene fu delle prime jo facesse non avea anchora i[n]teso vitruvio bene."[337] The proportions of 1:2.2 or 1:2.4 in the clear, the degree of tapering, the position of its volutes, and the profiles of the entablature of the Ionic portal of his project for the ambulatories of St Peter's of 1519/20, in fact, correspond more precisely to the Vitruvian canon.[338] In the double frames of the windows of the Vatican Sala Ducale, in around 1523, he then found a definitive formula for the Ionic portal.[339] (Fig. 40)

The Doric order of Palazzo Farnese and St Peter's and its continuation in an Ionic order had been decided before 1520, but it was after 1538 that Antonio had to prepare the execution of the Ionic orders of St Peter's, and he designed those of the Ionic order for the courtyard of the Palazzo Farnese and of the aedicules for the third storey of its façade as late as 1545.[340] Antonio's intensified study of the orders cannot be separated from the detailed planning of the definitive project for St Peter's from 1539–40 onwards. These were tasks that members of the newly founded Vitruvian academy, such as Philandrier, must have scrutinised with a fierce dogmatism.[341] For this reason, too, Antonio was far more careful with the geometric construction of his Ionic volutes

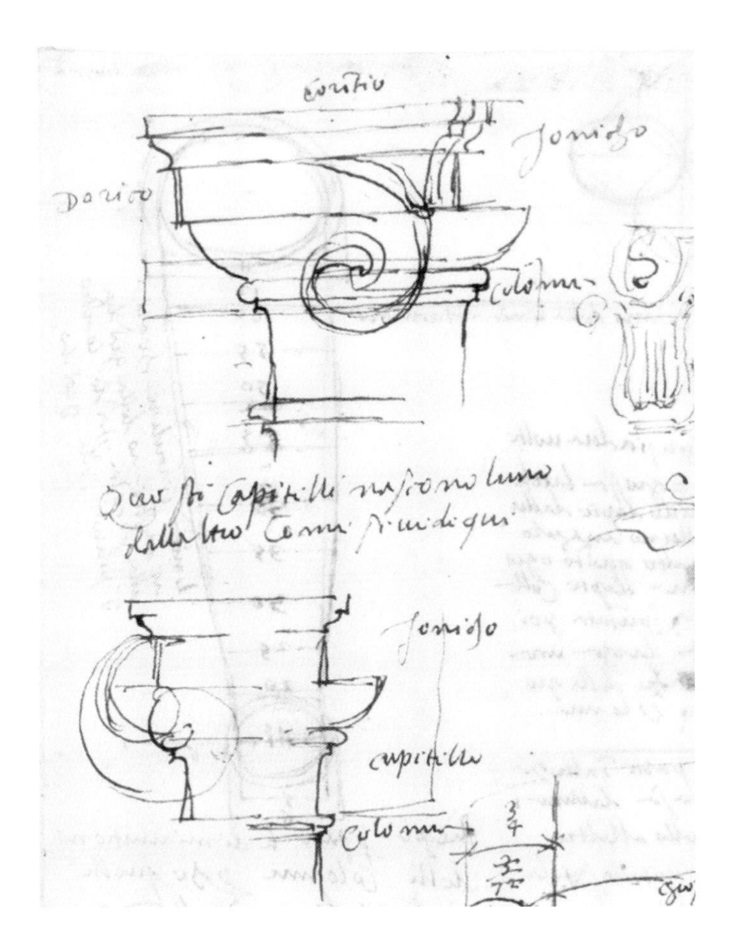

FIG. 42 ANTONIO DA SANGALLO THE YOUNGER. Studies for columns and capitals (Florence, U 826A v.), detail. (photo Gabinetto dei Disegni e delle Stampe degli Uffizi)

and bases than he had been in earlier years.[342] Only the two Ionic orders of the upper windows of the exterior and the *piano nobile* of the courtyard of Palazzo Farnese were actually constructed, and they reflect the interaction between theory and practice in Antonio's late work more clearly than any other piece of architecture. For a long time he had occupied himself with Vitruvius's partly contradictory norms for the proportioning of the orders. According to chapter three of the third book of Vitruvius, columns should increase in girth with the widening of the intercolumniation, and in the araeostyle, with its intercolumniation of more than three shaft widths, they should have a proportion of 1:8.5 regardless of the order. According to chapter five of the third book, the entasis of an Ionic column should decrease with the increasing height of the order, but its capitals and entablature should be enlarged. In addition, columns in secular porticoes should be more slender than those of a dignified temple. Finally, the proportions of an Ionic column vary in Vitruvius's conception by about three modules.

By attempting to take all of these considerations into account, Antonio added to the complication of the planning process. Even so, the two Ionic orders of the Palazzo Farnese illustrate how undogmatically he conducted himself in practice.[343] The intercolumniation between the half-columns of the middle courtyard storey, with its width of 6⅔ column shafts, is much wider than that of the araeostyle. But when Antonio gave his Ionic half-columns a proportion of about 1:9⅓, the architrave 1¼ modules, the cornice 1⅕ modules and the frieze probably 0.95 modules, he went beyond even the most slender version of the Ionic column in the different interpretations of Vitruvius (Fig. 41).[344] This was probably not only to counteract the visual foreshortening of the columns in such an elevated position and to adjust their relationship to the slender Doric order of the ground floor (cf. Fig. 31), but also because, like Alberti and Giuliano before him, he preferred more slender proportions and admired the Ionic order of the Theatre of Marcellus.

He gave the Ionic bases in the courtyard of Palazzo Farnese the normative proportion of half the width of a column shaft, but in profiling them he followed an antique prototype rather than Vitruvius;[345] and then he made light of his own scheme by allowing only a little more than the width of half a shaft for the height of the capitals (including the volutes) and that of the architrave (U 826A r.) (Fig. 42).[346] The aedicules of the third storey of the façade were further from the eye than the *piano nobile* of the courtyard, so he made their Ionic columns even slimmer, with a proportion of 1:10.23.[347] And while the diameter of the half columns of the courtyard of exactly three Roman *palmi* depended on the measuring system of the ground floor, here he could give the width of the columns the exact value of an ancient foot. Antonio also departed from Vitruvius in giving the bases, capitals, and architrave of the aedicules appreciably more than one module. In both cases, he used a convex frieze such as he had proposed for his Ionic portal, and in the courtyard he had probably intended the frieze to be lower than the architrave. Vitruvius had described the decorated frieze as being higher than the architrave and Michelangelo may have been raised in height also for this reason. The 1.7 modules of the realized frieze exceed the 1.28 modules of the architrave by a considerable margin. The Ionic order of the equally elevated south thermal window of the Sala Regia of 1538–39 has a proportion of only 1:8.5, whereas its entablature is already similar in form to that of the Ionic aedicules of the Palazzo Farnese. Even in his later work, however, Antonio could make the frieze of a giant Ionic, Corinthian, or Composite order, about as high as the architrave, or even higher; but from 1518 onwards, he kept to Vitruvius's rules when designing portals and aedicules.[348]

The doubts with which he was still beset around 1546 are revealed by his design for the fireplace of his palace in Via Giulia (U 981A).[349] There, as he had done perhaps two or three years earlier for his masterly façade windows with volutes, he once again reconstructed Vitruvius's Ionic entablature with a low convex frieze and a crowning cornice, only to condemn it with the words "Vitruvio e goffo" and give the frieze in the left variant the same height as the architrave. After careful consideration, his eye won out again. He was following not only Vitruvius but also aesthetic criteria, and as in Palazzo Farnese he could vary the proportions of the orders within one and the same building.

Tuscan and Doric orders play a much smaller role in Antonio's mature work. Apparently it was difficult for him to distinguish between the two, even though a Florentine so aware of his ancient roots must have been particularly keen on the Tuscan order. In the eighth chapter of his fourth book, Vitruvius had described the order of the *tuscanica aedes* as having torus-like bases, simple capitals without *annuli*, and little decoration. Wooden beams allowed for the broad intercolumniations of the aerostyle, which in turn required stocky proportions for the columns. This is probably also why in Vitruvius the proportions of the Tuscan and Doric aerostyle agree with each other, and why Antonio gave the Tuscan order of his pycnostyle temple project distinctly more slender proportions.[350] In determining the order, Antonio gave more weight to the simple bases he had seen at the Temple of Hercules in Cori and the mausoleum near the Ponte Nomentano than to the triglyph frieze, and so he called both—and even the Column of Trajan—"toscano."[351] Even after Antonio's death, Giovanbattista would reconstruct Vitruvius's *aedes tuscanica* with a triglyph frieze.[352]

Only in two projects for courtyards of about 1535 did Antonio return to the Doric order. He proposed to articulate the courtyard of his house in Via Giulia with a Doric order and divided its rear wall into a shorter left and a larger right half. There are two alternatives for the frieze of both halves, which recall his projects for Palazzo Baldassini and Palazzo Farnese and Bramante's prototypes.[353] In the right half a triglyph stands in the centre of the bay of both rows, while the left half proposes half a metope in the lower row and a tablet with an inscription in the upper. While the central metopes of the lower row are larger, the smaller triglyphs of the upper row allow a regular sequence of equal metopes, as in the frieze of Palazzo Fieschi. At about the same time Antonio started the palace of Luca Massimo and some years later provided the Vitruvian Doric order of its courtyard with modular triglyphs and adorned the inclined *geison* with 3 × 6 guttae.[354]

Antonio had to adapt the Doric portal of his nearby palace, the later Palazzo Sacchetti, to the proportions of the existing ground floor.[355] As in his designs of the thirties, he accomplished this by using the most minute units of measurement. His point of departure was the given overall width of the portal, 10 *piedi*, 32⅔ *minuti*. He first recalculated it as 932⅔ *minuti* and multiplied this number by two in order to avoid fractions. Finally, he rounded up the total to 1866 modules of 0.0016 m. each. Since calculations with high numbers were easy for him, he was able to use these basic measurements to calculate the frame exactly according to Vitruvius's modular system. The triple frame of the portal could not be justified by Vitruvius. Antonio had already alluded to it about 1510 in the portal of the Temple of the Dio Redicolo,[356] but he did not include it in his repertoire until 1523 with the windows of the Sala Ducale (cf. Fig. 39).[357] By continuing not only the architrave but also the frieze and moulding along the sides, he gave the aedicules a monumentality diametrically opposed to the elegance of Vitruvius's portals. In this he may also have been inspired by antique portals such as the one near Spoleto, which he had precisely surveyed before the Sack of Rome (U 1147A r) and probably even before designing the windows of the Sala Ducale.[358] There he mentioned that it was called the porta "Dorictta." Though the mouldings—"modani"—are Corinthian, the proportions of the clear opening, about 1:2.2 (8¼ × 18 p.), correspond to Vitruvius's Doric portal: "lo vano i[n] altezza sie sechondo che schrive vitruvio i[n] la doricha." Vitruvius, however, had recommended the much narrower proportion of 1:2.5 for the clear opening of the *porta dorica*; Antonio instead gave the portal of his palace the traditional proportion of 1:2. In contrast to his previous Doric portals, he now not only tapered the clear opening and the frame but also made the inner frame narrower at the top as Vitruvius had advised. Yet neither the proportions of the mighty entablature nor of its triglyphs, set slightly away from the corner, exactly follow Vitruvius's recommendations, just as the feminine caryatids are in contrast to the masculine character of the Doric. Here again Antonio united the most varied antique elements to make a new creation only partially conforming to Vitruvius, one which could hardly fail in its effect. Nowhere does one have the impression that his creative possibilities were hampered by the dictates of norms. If those possibilities occasionally seem to diminish in his last years, the cause is hardly to be found in his studies of antiquity.

IV Epilogue

Sangallo penetrated more deeply into the Vitruvian world than any other Renaissance architect. The frequent deviations from Vitruvius, however, contradict his reputation as Vitruvius's most dogmatic follower. In his palaces and his projects for St Peter's, Loreto and Castro Antonio he remained, first and foremost, a Florentine architect and a pupil of his uncles and Bramante. The typologies of his buildings are less classicising than their single parts and the details of the orders, aedicules and wall openings.

Raphael was capable of following Bramante much earlier than Sangallo; already in 1509 he had designed the temple in the *School of Athens* in his master's manner. He remained Bramante's pupil until his death and even the projects for Villa Madama are more directly inspired by Bramante than by antiquity and Vitruvius, who did not enlighten him sufficiently. Bramante taught him how to look at ancient monuments and how to combine their language and typologies with those of his own time. Without copying antiquity Raphael wanted to build papal Rome on the ruins of imperial city, and started to transform the papal apartments in the Vatican and Villa Madama into a setting for a life *all'antica*, of which Alberti had already dreamt. In the years 1513–20 Raphael was the most inventive and innovative architect in Europe.

Sangallo's projects are both less classicising, and less Bramantesque and when, from 1537 onward, the capital of Pierluigi Farnese's new duchy in Castro was projected, neither Sangallo nor his patron Paul III thought of an ancient town. While Sangallo in his last years could still return to his project of 1513/14 for the exterior of Palazzo Farnese, Raphael already went beyond Bramante in his first building and never repeated earlier schemes. He studied Vitruvius but followed not so much his rules as the ancient monuments and his own eye. He conferred on architecture more variety, beauty and splendour and pursued the creation of a language that corresponded to the radical changes in society and the mentality of his patrons. Raphael's sense of expansive space and hierarchy, his dynamism and abstractions paved the way for Vignola and for the seventeeth century.

Sangallo's buildings were more solid and functional and corresponded better to the wishes of many patrons. Not by chance, the typology of his palaces remained in use until the early twentieth century.

Peruzzi was more similar to Raphael, though only his first and his last Roman buildings were equally successful. His many drawings from antiquity show no sign of an engagement with Vitruvius comparable to that of Sangallo. Like Raphael he concentrated on exemplary ancient monuments themselves: "...cercò della bella maniera della architettura e per meglio chiaririsi qual fusse la migliore, si sottomise a ritrarre tutte le belle maniere che egli vedeva delle cose antiche maniere," as an eyewitness reported.[359] This was certainly also true, mutatis mutandis, of Sanmicheli and Jacopo Sansovino. Indeed, Peruzzi's numerous copies of Sangallo's antique drawings create the impression that he depended largely on Sangallo for the interpretation of Vitruvius's doctrines and their relationship to ancient monuments.

Sangallo's career lasted more than forty years. After the Sack of Rome he confessed that as late as 1514 he still did not fully understand Vitruvius, and he continued to correct him. On the other hand he was satisfied when his calculations proved accurate and when, as in the Theatre of Ferento and the temples of the Forum Holitorium, Vitruvius's norms were confirmed and he was able for once to shed some light on the tangle of contradictory attitudes. But he knew that Vitruvius had not introduced his rules, but had passed on the ideas of the great age of Greek architecture. These norms could not be followed to every detail and had to be adapted sensibly as the situation or task required. It was precisely in this that he differed from dogmatic Vitruvians such as Philandrier, who condemned every deviation from the canon and put Vitruvius's authority above that of the ruins.[360]

Though not as original and inventive as Bramante, Raphael, Peruzzi or Giulio, Sangallo's architecture, too, reveals a stylistic development. It leads from early works, where his formation by his uncle Antonio the Elder is still dominant, as in the castle of Capodimonte (cf. Fig. 26) and the Palazzo Inghirami Ricci in Via Giulia, to the Palazzi Baldassini and Farnese where he starts to follow Bramante, and to the vestibule and courtyard of the latter, where in 1514/15 he approaches antiquity still more directly than Bramante and reaches a higher level than in most of his later works. In 1518/19 he is inspired by Raphael and becomes his successor in 1520. In the papal Zecca he introduces the concave facade into Renaissance architecture and plays with concave and convex *casini* in his project for the villa of Cardinal Antonio del Monte in Valle Giulia.[361] In 1526, in the courtyard of the Palazzo Apostolico at Loreto, he distinguishes between the brick of the load bearing arcades and the Istrian stone of the orders, the *primum ornamentum*—an innovative experiment that he would not continue in other buildings.[362] In masterpieces like the Rocca Paolina or the restructuring of the papal ceremonial rooms in the Vatican he appears more as the unrivalled expert on all important typologies than as an innovator, and thus after his death in 1546 Michelangelo became celebrated because he opened new ways to the future.

Those who judge Sangallo primarily by his late wooden model for St Peter's do little justice to his extraordinary abilities. There he had to continue what he and Raphael had agreed upon in 1519, and his tendency to systemise led him to create an accumulation of relatively low storeys and to continue them even into the cupola and the lantern—an unmonumental articulation that he did not repeat in any of his otherwise rather parsimonious exteriors. He may have consoled himself with the thought that he had at last designed a building that would dominate its environment the way the Colosseum or Florence Cathedral did theirs. In his countless designs for St Peter's he did everything he could to give three-dimensional and corporeal articulation to the immense structure. His tendency for coherence also hindered him from distinguishing the entrance through the addition of a free-standing, colonnaded temple front. He lacked the force and authority to return to Bramante's lapidary simplicity, which he had failed to defend twenty years before against Raphael, but even then he never proposed a real temple front. Michelangelo immediately eliminated the subsidiary spaces and was the first to propose a truly classicising temple front, which we find—strangely enough—only in Sangallo's two utopian temple projects. Until his last days, however, Antonio dedicated his main forces to Palazzo Farnese, his true masterpiece.

[1] This text was written in 2003, reelaborated in 2012 and again in 2018. This may explain why the bibliography of recent publications is not complete. I am indebted to Renate Franciscono for the translation, and Deborah Howard for an ultimate revision of the text.

[2] Manetti-Saalman (1970) 53; Günther (1988) 13–26, with bibliography; Bruschi (1998); Frommel (2007, *Architecture*).

[3] Pagliara (1986, *Vitruvio*); Fiore (2002, *Trattati*).

[4] Burns (1998); Bulgarelli-Calzona-Ceriana-Fiore (2006), with bibliography.

[5] Burns (1998) 126–29; Frommel (2006, *Villa Medici a Fiesole*) 64–66. The scale of measurement, pricked with a compass, with units of 8.5 mm, corresponds exactly to a thirty-fifth of an ancient foot. If one uses a scale of 1:35, the thickness of the wall varies from 1 1/3 to 2 feet (0.397–0.596 m.). Measurements in *braccia fiorentine* (0.586 m.) would give unusually thick walls, those in *palmi romani* (0.2234 m.) unusually thin walls. The remaining measurements are also consistent with ancient feet. If the building were to be extended symmetrically over a central loggia with five arcades, it would have a width of ca. 100 feet (29.80 m); Hubert (2008) 218–21.

[6] Burns (1998) 126–29.

[7] Contardi-Lilius (1984); Frommel (1984, *Villa Madama*) 324–26; Frommel (2003, *tre progetti*) 123.

[8] Frommel (1994, *Introduction*) 1–5.

[9] Frommel (1994, *Reflections*), with bibliography; Frommel (1994, *Introduction*) 5–10.

[10] Poeschke (1990) I, 76–78, with bibliography.

[11] Poeschke (1990) I, 69–70.

[12] Günther (1988) 16–20.

[13] Borsi (1985); Günther (1988) 16–20; Frommel (1994, *Reflections*) 108.

[14] Frommel (2009, *Progetto di Sangallo*), with bibliography.

[15] Günther (1988) 26.

[16] Borsi (1985) 5; Günther (1988), 104–38; Pacciani (1998) 347–57; Nesselrath (2005 *Disegnare Roma*), Frommel S. (2014), Donetti-Faietti-Frommel (2017).

[17] Huelsen (1910); Borsi (1985) 59–112, 124, 140; Nesselrath (1989 , *Review Giuliano*); Günther (1988) 27, 112–13; Frommel (1994, *Introduction*) 17–18; Frommel S. (2008) 13–37.

[18] Like Alberti's S. Sebastiano, Brunelleschi's S. Maria degli Angeli seems to have been inspired by an ancient mausoleum. It is unlikely that the ground plan on U 4378A represents a project of Cronaca's, as has been assumed, but rather a mausoleum, as is suggested by the draughtsman's mention of travertine columns, which in Florence are quite improbable, and by G.B. Montano's print (cf. Günther [1988] 91–93). As in S. Maria degli Angeli, the interior is articulated by divided pilasters and the masonry hollowed out by niches, while the sides of the polygon are doubled on the exterior. For Giuliano's trips to Naples: del Pesco (2002), for the Taccuino Senese see Borsi (1985) 250–314.

[19] Krautheimer (1994); Frommel (2006, *Tavole*); Frommel S. (2008) 13.

[20] See below, p. 18.

[21] Borsi (1985) 250–314.; Günther (1988) 104–38.

[22] Günther (1988) 142–44.

[23] Frommel (2008, *Castel Nuovo*).

[24] Frommel (2010, *Mantegna*).

[25] Borsi (1985) 258–59; Günther (1988) 124.

[26] Frommel (2008, *Proposte*) 51.

[27] Borsi (1985) 250–314.

[28] Günther (1988) 112–13.

[29] Borsi (1985) 259–61.

[30] Borsi (1985) 297–301.

[31] Günther (1988) 66–103, 331–33, pl I–12; Pacciani (2008) 29–37.

[32] Günther (1988) 74–80; Zampa (2008), 65–75.

[33] Thus the detail on U 1594A v. agrees with that of the Taccuino; Borsi (1985) 294–97; Günther (1988) 73–89, Appendix, pls 2, 3, 6b, 7, 8a, 9.

[34] Borsi (1985) 297–99; Günther (1988) pls 1a, 5a, 12a.

[35] Günther (1988) 101–02; Pacciani (2008) 33–34.

[36] On Peruzzi see also the recent studies by Huppert (2001) and Huppert (2015).

[37] Borsi (1985) 94–95, 148–49; Günther (1988) 40–48, 148–49, fig. 8, pl. 13; Frommel (2003 *L'esordio*) 176.

[38] Frommel (2003, *L'esordio*) 178.

[39] For Peruzzi's stylistic development Frommel (2005).

[40] Günther (1988) 139–55, 333–35; I. Campbell, "Entry to U 2055A," in this volume.

[41] Frommel (2003, *Tre progetti*) 100.

[42] Satzinger (1991) 159–212.

[43] Satzinger (1991) 210–11; Frommel (2003 *Civita Castellana*).

[44] Satzinger (1991) figs 58, 70–71, 75–76, 79–80, 85, 91–92, 93, 98–100, 103–6.

[45] I. Campbell, H.C. Dittscheidt, "entry to U 1407A" in this volume; see Antonio the Elder's handwriting in Frommel (1994, *Introduction*) fig. 7 n.

[46] Günther (1982); Frommel (2002, *Lombardia*) 22–23; Frommel (2008, *Proposte*) 39–55.

[47] Günther (1982) 86–91.

[48] Bernardo probably supervised the construction of the Cancelleria where he may have collaborated with Bramante. cf. Valtieri (1983) 3–25; Frommel in Frommel-Pentricci (2009) I, 3; Günther (1988) 165–202 with bibliography; Frommel (2008, *Proposte*) 50–51.

[49] For the Codex Coner and its authorshop Ashby (1904); Buddensieg (1975); Günther (1988) 165–202.

[50] Ackerman (1954) 195, cat. 4 b.

[51] Wolff Metternich (1972) pl. 11–12; Wolff Metternich-Thoenes (1987); Frommel (2008, *Proposte*).

[52] For the late medieval origins of orthogonal representations Frommel (1994, *Reflections*) 102.

[53] A. Bruschi, "entries U 43A and 44A" in vol. II, 76–7; Frommel (2008, *Proposte*) 48.

[54] Frommel (1994, *Introduction*) 19–22; S. Eiche, "entry U 1563A," in vol. II, 254; Frommel (2008, *Proposte*) 45; Zavatta (2008) 162–65.

[55] Serlio (1540) 39–40.

[56] Borsi (1985) 197–98; Frommel (1994, *Introduction*) 19–22.

[57] See above, n. 49.

[58] Frommel (1989 Bramante); Frommel (1994, *Introduction*) 9; Frommel (2008, *Proposte*) 40–43.

[59] Günther (1988) 32; Frommel (2003, *L'esordio*) 180.

[60] See n. 58.

[61] Wurm (1984) 423, 425, 464. At about the same time Giuliano (on fol. 17 r. of the Taccuino Senese, cf. Borsi (1985) 302–11; Frommel (1994, *Introduction*) 9–19, Peruzzi (on U 1683 Orn. v.; cf. Frommel [2003, *L'esordio*] 160), and Antonio (on U 1273 A) cf. Kuntz, "Entry of U 1273 A," in this volume) studied the *Volta Dorata* of the Domus Aurea. Like Antonio also Peruzzi changed his archaic script, in particular the "ch," probably only in about 1508 and also under Bramante's influence, to a more humanistic script (Frommel [2003, *L'esordio*], 158–64).

[62] Borsi (1985) 251–52; Nesselrath in Frommel-Ray-Tafuri (1984) 406–07; Nesselrath (1993).

[63] Wurm (1984) 482; Günther (1988) 199, 341, 378, IV, figs 35, 37; see below p. 19.

[64] Frommel, in vol. II, 173–74, 258–59; Nesselrath (1992); Frommel (2009, *Palazzo Alberini*) 35–43; Frommel (2008, *Proposte*) 48.

[65] Frommel (2008 *Proposte*). See also Bramante's orthogonal sketch of the cornice for San Biagio on U 1191A r. which is inspired by the Pantheon drawn next to it and measured on Bramante's commission by the prominent stonemason Menicantonio de Chiarellis. Günther (1988) 47–48; A. Nesselrath, "Entry to U 1191A r.," in vol. II, 216; Günther (1982) 79, 102–03.

[66] Frommel (2008, *Proposte*) 48–49.

[67] Günther (1982).

[68] Nesselrath (1996).

[69] Frommel (2008 *Proposte*) 49.

[70] Frommel (2008 *Proposte*) 45.

[71] Günther (1988) 29–43; Frommel (2003 *L'esordio*) 175.; Fiore-Tafuri (1994).

[72] Frommel (2003 *L'esordio*).

[73] Giovannoni (1959) I: 396; Frommel (1994, *Introduction*] 11.

[74] Vasari-Milanesi (1906) 5: 447–49.

[75] Giovannoni (1959); Bruschi (1983) 3–23; Frommel (1994, *Introduction*), 10–26; Fiore (2002, *Roma*) 136–7.

[76] In his drawings after 1520, such as U 1039A, Antonio cites Latin passages. Before the Sack of Rome he informs Peruzzi on U 1213A r. that Vitruvius' *peristylium* is synonymous with "colonnato," and explains its relationship to the *atrium* according to Vitruvius' Book 6, chapter 3—"L VI c iiii [!]." Evidently he was not only the more profound connoisseur of Vitruvius but the better Latinist; Günther (1988) 296; G. Scaglia, "Entry to 1213A r.," in this volume. On Antonio's drawings after the antique see esp. Pagliara (1988) 184–200; Günther (1988) 243–327; C. L. Frommel, "Entry of U 1627A," in this volume.

[77] Günther (1988) 114; Frommel (1994, *Introduction*) 12 both with attribution to Antonio the Elder.

[78] Bartoli (1914–22) figs 145–54, 393–94, 401–02; Borsi (1985) 12, 78–80, 194–96, 497–502; Günther (1988) 11–18, 113–14; Frommel (1994, *Introduction*) 14.

[79] Borsi (1985) 194–6.

[80] Borsi (1985) 254–59; Günther (1988) 33, 115–6, 123–4; Frommel (1994, *Introduction*), 106, 108–9; Giuliano's ground plan is already copied in the Codex Escurialensis.

[81] Nesselrath (1986, *I libri*) 123, 129–34; Marias (1992); Nesselrath (1996); Benzi (2000); Frommel (2008, *Proposte*) 48–49.

[82] On U 1427A v. Antonio notes: "Lo mezo disegnio di termini longo b[raccia] 700 pied[i] 1400/ Le piante grande si mettino al libro secondo queste misure/ Lo Coliseo longo alto b. 85 7/24 b[raccia] 333 P[piedi] 666/ [at the edge: li templi...] La ritonda alta b. 75 longa b. 140/ [at the edge: li cerchi con questa?] la colonna storiata alta b. 66." Even before 1514 he apparently arranged his surveys of ancient monuments in separate portfolios according to types. Giovan Francesco's information on the ancient foot, which is based on a find in the Piazza of Cardinal Alborense, also appears to be from the time before 1513; see the samples of handwriting in Frommel (1994, *Introduction*), fig. 35.

[83] A. Cerutti Fusco, "Entry of U 1089A," in this volume.

[84] See above, p. 16. Giuliano added this measurement at the time when he made the much more precise surveys on fol. 68 of the Codex Barberini; Borsi (1985) 254–59; Günther (1988) 123–25.

[85] On the use of the compass, see below, p. 32; cf. Modonutti (2014).

[86] Lotz (1956).

[87] On U 480A r. from before 1520, Peruzzi shows the cross section of the exterior with measurements in *palmi* and details of the two lower orders, and from his sheer interest in ancient proportions—"sesquialtera"—goes beyond Sangallo's early measurements; Wurm (1984) 451.

[88] A. Cerutti Fusco, "Entry of U 1136A," in this volume.

[89] C.L. Frommel, "Entry of U 2043A," in this volume.

[90] C.L. Frommel, "Entry of U 2044A," in this volume.

[91] A. Cerutti Fusco, "Entry of U 1576A," in this volume.

[92] Frommel (2003 *L'esordio*) 178.

[93] Frommel S. (2008) 18–21.

[94] Borsi (1985) 423–26.

[95] Borsi (1985) 468–80; Frommel S. (2008) 18–21.

[96] Frommel (2003, *L'esordio*) 176.

[97] Borsi (1985) 191–94, 497–98; cf. Günther (1988) 98–99, figs 22, 23.

[98] Denker-Nesselrath (1990) 27–34; Frommel (2003, *Tre progetti*) 113–19.

[99] Günther (1988) 72, fig. 4.

[100] Frommel (1994, *Introduction*) 18, fig. 15.

[101] C.L. Frommel, "Entry of on U 1627A," in this volume. Cf. the later survey of the same mausoleum on Giovanbattista da Sangallo's U 1654A r. (I. Campbell, "Entry of U 1654A r.," in this volume) and on Peruzzi's U 1636A; Frommel (2003 *L'esordio*) 168.

[102] Frommel (1994, *Introduction*) 19–21; I. Campbell, "Entry U 1414A r.," in this volume.

[103] Frommel (2008, *Proposte*) 42.

[104] Frommel (2003 *L'esordio*) 181.

[105] See above, 0.

[106] End of December Bramante 1506 "cum suis socijs" was back in Rome; Frommel (1996 La chiesa di San Pietro) 48, n. 43. Antonio is probably not identical with the cabinet-maker "Magister Antonius florentinus" who in October 1506 was paid for work in Sant'Agostino; Frommel (1994, *Introduction*) 11, 19, n. 169a.

[107] S. Eiche, "Entry of U 992A verso," in vol. II, 194.

[108] Frommel (1994, *Introduction*) 22; Frommel (2008, *Proposte*) 40; H.C. Dittscheidt, "Entry of U 1413," in this volume.

[109] "In presentia mej notarij etc. personaliter constituti discreti viri sebastianus quondam marci de giano de sangallo de florentia et antonius bartolomej etiam de sangallo carpentarij in civitate lavinio prope palatium apostolicum ... recognoverant se esse veros debitores providi viri Martini de alpino romani civis de regione sancti eustachij ... jn ducatis 47 de carlenis X pro ducato ad computum monete veteris occasione et ex causa pretij venditionis certi lignaminis vel tabularum trabium et travicellorum ac diversorum lignaminum ab eodem martino habitorum emptorum et receptorum de mense martij jam proximi (?) elapsi tempore accessus et reditus sanctissimi dominj nostri pape ad urbem ex civitate bononie que lignamina dicti sebastianus et antonius debitores habuerunt pro conficiendo certo arco triumfali ad gloriam laudem et ornatum dictj sanctissimi domini nostri jn eius reditu ad urbem quos quidam 47 ducatos dictj sebastianus et antonius promiserunt solvere isto modo videlicet singolis mensibus duos ducatos auri in auro donec et quousque dicti 47 ducati fuerint integraliter ... Actum in civitate Lavinio prope palatium apostolicum jn apoteca dictorum sebastiani et antonij presentibus raffaello berti de sarto da florentia architectore johanni francisco quondam johannis de florentia et johanni jacopo ausurini (?) de radinis (?) de caravagio ferrario testibus"; Roma, AS, Coll. Not. Cap., Stephanus de Armannis, vol. 60, fol. 81r.; frammenti del documento in Jobst, Die Planungen Antonio da Sangallo des Jüngeren, 140.

[110] Sanudo (1969–70) VIII: 63–65; manuscript of Paris de Grassis, Diari, Biblioteca Apostolica Vaticana, Chigi L I 18, fol. 182 v.; Pastor (1891–1933) III: 733–34.

[111] Pastor (1891–1933) III: 739.

[112] Bruschi (1983) 3.

[113] F. Fagliari Zeni Buchicchio, "Entry of U 995A," in vol. I, 178; Frommel (2008, *Proposte*) 40.

[114] G. Scaglia, "Entries to U 1482A, 1483A," in vol. I, 243–4.

[115] Borsi (1985) 17; Frommel (1994, *Introduction*) 23–6.

[116] Frommel (1991) 180; Frommel (1994, *Introduction*) 23.

[117] Frommel (1994, *Introduction*), 13.

[118] Frommel (1994, *Introduction*) 22; S. Eiche., "Entry of U 992A r.," in vol. II.

[119] Frommel (1994, *Introduction*) 22; see H.C. Dittscheid, Entry of U 1413A in this volume; on the drawings of the Basilica Aemilia see also Zampa 2019.

[120] See above, p. 17.

[121] G. Scaglia,"Entry of U 1484A v.," in vol. I.

[122] M. Luchterhand, "Entry U 1193A," in this volume. On U 1145A, one of his two drawings for the *rocca* of Civita Castellana, Antonio uses the compass, which before 1518 is unlikely; cf. E. Bentivolglio, "Entries of U 977 and 1145A," in vol. I, 178, 198; Bruschi (2003).

[123] Frommel (2003, *Porta ionica*) 44–56; I. Campbell, "Entry of U 1168A r.," in this volume. P.N. Pagliara,"Entry of U 989A," in vol. IV.

[124] Frommel (2003, *Farnesina*) 42–3; see below, 0.

[125] Frommel (1994, *Introduction*) 24; I. Campbell, "Entry of U 1168A v.," in this volume.

[126] Frommel (2001).

[127] Frommel (2011, *Palazzo Farnese*).

[128] I. Campbell, "Entry of U 575A," in this volume. On the *vestibulum* see Frommel (1973) I 54–6.

[129] See n. 126.

[130] Frommel (1981) 134–43; Frommel (1995 *Palazzo Farnese*); Frommel (2011, *Palazzo Farnese*). On Sangallo's orders, see below, pp. 44–48.

[131] Bruschi (1992).

[132] Pliny the Elder, *Naturalis Historia*, Book 36, chapter 178.

[133] Frommel (1981) 136, where the height of Alberti's *Dorica* is incorrectly given as 14 instead of 16 modules.

[134] Denker-Nesselrath (1990) 4–17; Frommel (2002, *Lombardia*) 1–31.

[135] Frommel (2017, *Tempietto*).

[136] Frommel (1973) II 80–87; Denker-Nesselrath (1990) 22–23. According to the measurements on the rather imprecise engraving by Lafréri the upper floor was 34.5 *palmi* high, the bays were about 20 *palmi* and the columns about 2,5 *palmi* wide. The relationship of the width of the columns to the width of the bays is confirmed by the plan of the corner of the upper floor in the Cod. Icon 195 in Munich; for the detailed measurements see Fig. 24.

[137] Frommel (2017, *Tempietto*).

[138] See H.C. Dittscheidt, "Entry of U 2143A," I. Campbell, "Entry of U 1413," both in this volume.

[139] Denker-Nesselrath (1990) 17–34; Denker-Nesselrath (1996); Frommel (2003, *Tre progetti*) 116–19, 154–5, with a table of the measurements and the discrepancies in execution.

[140] Frommel (2002, *Bramante e Raffaello*).

[141] A. Bruschi, "Entry of U 43 e 44A," in vol. II, 76–77 with attribution of both drawings to A. da Sangallo the Y.; Riegel (1998) 46–50, 164–65; Niebaum (2008) 54–65; Frommel (2008, *Proposte*); Frommel (2012, *Presbytère*); Frommel (2012, *Presbiterio*).

[142] See Peruzzi's drawing U 105A; Wolff Metternich (1972), Wolff Metternich–Thoenes (1987) 132; Niebaum (2008) 63–64, Fig. 15; Frommel (2019, *Metodo progettuale*).

[143] Pagliara (1988) 181, note 12, with reference to Philandrier's criticism of this solution; Denker-Nesselrath (1990) 37–42. The measurements of the fragmentary entablature known from the drawings of the Codex Coner and of Antonio's plan U 44A allow an approximate reconstruction of the frieze.

[144] A. Bruschi, "Entry of U 257A," in vol. II, 126; see below, 00.

[145] Letarouilly (1849–86) II: pl. 195; Frommel (1973) II, 180–88; Frommel (2003, *Raffaello e Sangallo*) 263–64; Denker-Nesselrath (1990) 41–42; see Nolli's plan of 1748.

[146] After spring 1514 this cannot have been Antonio who had used such a language before 1513 in the *piano nobile* of the courtyard of the Farnese Castle at Capodimonte, on the façade of the *palazzetto* of Tommaso Inghirami and in contemporary portals and windows; Frommel (2003, *Raffaello e Sangallo*) 257–65. Next to a detail drawing for the courtyard of Palazzo Farnese which can be dated in 1513 Antonio sketches a rusticated portal with the name "fieschi," probably a 15th century portal of Palazzo Fieschi with which he was busy; Frommel (2011 *Palazzo Farnese*).

[147] Frommel (1973) III, tav. 75a.

[148] Christern-Thiersch (1969); Wolff Metternich (1972) plate 33; Wolff Metternich–Thoenes (1987) 124, 125, 200; Denker-Nesselrath (1990) 42–45. Christern's and Thiersch's doubts over whether the drawings of the Codex Coner might not be measured with the *braccio fiorentino* are not justified. The altar-house was a little larger than the old apse and its steep arcades were proportioned as about 1:2. According to the Codex Coner the triglyphs were 2 *palmi* wide and the metopes of the central bays were more than three times wider than the triglyphs. Bernardo della Volpaia seems to have measured the metope of the relatively small corner intercolumniation, which corresponds approximately to the Vitruvian norm of 1.5 modules.

[149] Frommel S. (2008) 17–18; concerning the use of the doric order by Antonio da Sangallo in general cf. Zampa (2017).

[150] Frommel S. (2008) 18–19.

[151] Frommel (1973) II, 23–29, 118, pls 10b, 12a; Pagliara (1992, *Ordini*); Frommel (2007 *colonna*) 699–700, 717; C.L. Frommel, "Entry of U 1298A," in this volume.

[152] Frommel (1981) 137–41, Fig. 24; Pagliara (1992, *Ordini*) 140; Frommel in Buranelli (2010) 327–28; Frommel (2011, *Palazzo Farnese*); C.L. Frommel, "Entry of U 1000A v.," in this volume.

[153] Frommel (1981) 136–41, Fig. 23; Frommel (2010, *Fabbrica*) 48–61, 326–35; Frommel (2011, *Palazzo Farnese*).

[154] Frommel in Buranelli (2010) 325–27; C.L. Frommel, "Entry of U 627A," in this volume.

[155] On Antonio's *Ionica*, see Pagliara (1992, *Ordini*) 143–46.

[156] Vitruvius-Fra Giocondo (1511), Vitruvius-Fra Giocondo (1513),), fol. 63v.-67r.

[157] Frommel (1981) 136–41, Fig. 24; C.L. Frommel, entry of U 1000A, in Buranelli (2010) 327–28; Frommel (2011, *Palazzo Farnese*); C.L. Frommel, "Entry of U 1000A," in this volume.

[158] Compare the three naves of equal width with rows of four freestanding columns in Giuliano da Sangallo's project for the palace of the King of Naples; Biermann (1970); Pellecchia (1992) 377–416.

[159] He owned four copies of Fra Giocondo but most of his comments were written after 1527; see Benelli (2014, *Fra Giocondo*) who analyzes the copy of the 1513 Fra Giocondo edition at the Metropolitan Museum in New York.
[160] See above, n. 152.
[161] In the 1513/14 project for the staircase the ground floor is only 36 *palmi* high; C.L. Frommel, "Entry U 1041A," in this volume.
[162] Pagliara (1992, *Ordini*) 139, 148; Günther (1988) 295.
[163] Frommel (1981) 136.
[164] Günther (1988) 298; P.N. Pagliara, "Entry U 1409A," in this volume.
[165] See the elevations of the Theatre of Marcellus in A. Cerutti Fusco, "Entries of U 932, 1966A," in this volume.
[166] The two partially different versions of the ground plan of the Cortile delle Statue are probably not based only on personal surveys but also on copies of different projects of Bramante; Frommel (2003, *Tre progetti*) 119–27, Fig. 7; Günther (1988) 165–81. The drawing of a column of the Cancelleria by Bernardo della Volpaia (Codex Coner fol. 55v., Ashby [1904], 68) directly recalls a drawing of Giovan Francesco's; S. Eiche, "Entry of 1327 U A," in this volume.
[167] Pagliara (1988) 190. The handwriting is closely comparable to that on the designs for the Palazzo Farnese; on Gianbattista's *Editio Princeps* Pagliara, "Entry of U 903A," in this volume. The handwriting is similar to that of U 1193A; Frommel (1994, *Introduction*) 13.
[168] Satzinger (1991).
[169] Frommel (1984, *Raffaello*).
[170] Frommel (1984, *Raffaello*) 19.
[171] Fontana-Morachiello (1975); Frommel (1974), 178–79; Günther (1988) 316.
[172] Valtieri (1984, *Sant'Eligio*).
[173] C.L. Frommel, "Entry of U 1898A," in this volume; Frommel (2019, *Metodo progettuale*).
[174] Frommel (2003, *Raffaello e Sangallo*); see F.E. Keller, "Entry of U 1054A," in vol. II.
[175] See F.E.Keller, "Entry of U 179A and 1518A" in vol. II.
[176] see n. 174.
[177] Frommel (2018, *Granada*).
[178] Frommel (1974) 178–79; Günther (1988) 316.
[179] Frommel (2019, *Metodo progettuale*).
[180] Pagliara (1984, *Palazzo Branconio*) 188–98.
[181] Frommel (1996, *San Pietro*) 270–74, 283–84; Frommel (2003, *Raffaello e Sangallo*) 282–5.
[182] Di Teodoro (1993); Shearman (2003).
[183] Günther (1988) p. 57; see F.-E. Keller and V. Zanchettin, "Entry of U 915A r.," in this volume.
[184] Cf. Günther (1988) pp. 61–62, whose point of departure is a close collaboration between Sangallo and Peruzzi. Therefore he dated numerous drawings after the antique by both masters, especially those of the Forum Holitorium and the Theater of Marcellus, to the time before Raphael's death. However, Sangallo's changed handwriting is enough to show that the majority of these drawings date from after 1530. On Antonio's surveys of the forum Viscogliosi (2000) and Viscogliosi (2017).
[185] Frommel (1994, *Introduction*) in vol. I, p. 26, n. 209; Viscogliosi (2000) 112–25. A date of the survey of ca. 1518 is corroborated by the sketch of Michelangelo's model for S. Lorenzo on U 790A r. (see G. Maurer, "Entry of U 790A," in this volume).
[186] See G. Maurer, "Entry of U 790A," H.C. Dittscheid, "Entry of U 1139A and 1141A," in this volume.
[187] See H.C. Dittscheid, "Entry of U 1283A," in this volume.
[188] Cf. Günther (1988) 261.
[189] Cf. Günther (1988) 261. During his last years Peruzzi collected material for a treatise and copied numerous monuments from other sources. It is no accident that he used the usual Roman *palmo* or ancient foot in neither drawing. On the copies of Peruzzi's and in Labacco's Libro from Antonio's surveys of the Forum Holitorium and Temple of Mars Ultor, see below, p. 38. Whereas Antonio had a large number of qualified collaborators and draughtsmen who also assisted him in his surveys of antiquities, Peruzzi, as his entirely autograph antique drawings show, relied largely on himself and was therefore much more poorly prepared for large surveying campaigns.
[190] Cf. Gros (2005).
[191] Viscogliosi (2000) 114–16; Günther (1988) 272, 277, 280; Dittscheidt, "Entry of U 1139A," in this volume.
[192] Günther (1988) 277–78; Viscogliosi (2000) 99–102, 125–28; Campbell, "Entries of U 1123A, 1299A," in this volume.
[193] Frommel (1981) 140, fig. 25 (U 1001A r.); Frommel (2002, *Progetto di Sangallo*).
[194] H. Burns, in Frommel-Ray-Tafuri (1984) 444 ff.
[195] Frommel (1973) vol. II, pp. 5–7; Pagliara (1984, *Palazzo Alberini*) 181.; Frommel (2009, *Palazzo Alberini*).
[196] Günther (1988) 203–41, 339–79.
[197] Günther (1988) 161.
[198] Günther (1988) 50.
[199] Fiore (2002 *Trattati*) 508–10.
[200] See below, pp. 44–45.
[201] Juren (2004) and Juren (2006). On U 903A, dating from about 1514, Antonio already refers to a Vitruvius edition of Fra Giocondo; P.N. Pagliara, "Entry of U 903A," in this volume.
[202] Viscogliosi (2000) 102–08, 162–66; G. Scaglia, "Entry of U 1113A," in vol. I, 197; C.L. Frommel, "Entry of U 896A," in this volume.
[203] Günther (1988) 193–94, 257; Jobst (1992) 21; C. Jobst, "Entry of 786 UA r.," in vol. II, 150–51.
[204] Frommel (1987) 173; M. Schich, "Entry of U 949A," in this volume.
[205] Frommel (1986) 65–66, figs 6, 13–15.
[206] H.C. Dittscheidt, "Entry of U 1716A," and I. Campbell, "Entry of U 1326A," in this volume.
[207] Günther (1988) 297–98; H.C. Dittscheidt, "Entry of U 1041A," in this volume; S. Eiche, "Entry to U 1327A," ivi, 0.
[208] In the Palazzo Balami Giovan Francesco reconstructs what is perhaps the earliest demonstrable Ionic base in Renaissance Rome; Frommel (1986) figs 13–15.
[209] Günther (1988) 256.
[210] Pagliara (1986, *Vitruvio*); Günther (1988) 256, 298; Frommel (1994, *Introduction*) 11.
[211] Frommel (1973) II, 30–38; Pagliara (1992, *Ordini*) 147–48; Antonucci (2008) 11–13; Frommel, "Entries of U 1331, 1332A," in this volume.
[212] Günther (1988) 53.
[213] On Sangallo's Corinthian order and its Composite variation, see Pagliara (1992, *Ordini*) 147–49.
[214] S. Valtieri, "Entry of U 878A," in vol. II, 175.
[215] M. Tafuri, "Entry of U 168, 304, 305, 908, 1347A," in vol. II, 110, 133–34, 181, 240; C.L. Frommel, "Entry of U 1002A," in this volume.
[216] See I. Campbell, "Entry of U 1299A," in this volume.
[217] C.L. Frommel, "Entry of U 1002A," in this volume.
[218] "Entries of U 834, 896, 1117, 1123, 1132, 1138, 1139, 1141, 1142, 1299A," in this volume.
[219] "Entries of U 1139, 1153, 1181, 1221, 1299A," in this volume.
[220] See Nesselrath (2008), and below, pp. 38–40.
[221] P.N. Pagliara, "Entry of U 1409A," in this volume.
[222] Adams-Pepper (1994) 63, Zavatta (2008).
[223] S. Eiche, "Entry of U 1336A r.," in this volume; A. Ghisetti Giavarina, "Entries of U 1117A, 1337A r."
[224] A. Ghisetti Giavarinia, "Entries of U 606A, 3974A," in this volume.

225 He may have copied Michelangelo's project for the stair of the Laurenziana, annotated in his pre-1527 handwriting, during this trip; S. Eiche, "Entry of U 816A," in vol. IV.

226 S. Valtieri, "Entry of U 1383A v.," in vol. II, 247.

227 S. Eiche, "Entries of U 887A r., U 1334A," in vol. II,176–77, 237.

228 S. Eiche, "Entries of U 887, 992, 1334A r.," in vol. II, 176–77, 194, 237.

229 S. Eiche, "Entry of U 1406A r.," in vol. II, 250–51.

230 C. Jobst, "Entry of U 172A,"in vol. II,112.

231 Frommel (1994, *Introduction*) 36–37.

232 Frommel S. (2002); Rowland (2003).

233 Frommel (2003, *Tre progetti*), 91–95; Frommel (2017, *Tempietto*).

234 Günther (1988) 225–31.

235 See below, p. 48.

236 Wurm (1965) 318–19.

237 V. Zanchettin, "Entry of U 1039A," P.N. Pagliara, "Entry of U 2056A" in this volume.

238 A. Cerutti Fusco, "Entry of U 1378A," in this volume.

239 Giovannoni (1959) I:395–97.

240 Günther (1988) 297.

241 Fiore (2001) I:21–25.

242 Vitruvius-Barbaro (1557), Vitruvius-Barbaro-Carunchio (1999).

243 See below, pp. 37–40.

244 Vitruvius-Philandrier (1544) 169–70; Günther (1988) 316; Lemerle (2000) 16 f., 42 f., 168, 190, 192.

245 Günther (1988) 62–64, 280–82, 310–16; Pagliara (1988) 190–95.

246 Günther (1988) 315; Pagliara, "Entry of U 2056A v. A," in this volume.

247 A.C. Huppert "Entry of U 1090A r., 1230A r.," P.N. Pagliara "Entry of U 1174A v." in this volume; T. Fagliari Zeni Buchicchio, "Entry of U 1074A r.," in vol. IV.

248 Günther (1988) 272–94.

249 Ivi, 257–66, 282.

250 Günther (1990).

251 Günther (1990) 256, n. 94.

252 See Günther (1988).

253 P.N. Pagliara "Entry of U 2056A" in this volume.

254 H.C. Dittscheidt, "Entries of U 1305A, 1306A," in this volume.

255 H.C. Dittscheidt, "Entry of U 1166A," in this volume.

256 Günther (1988) 194; J. Niebaum, "Entry of U 1165A," in this volume.

257 Günther (1988) 206; F.P. Fiore, "Entry of U 1096A," in vol. I.

258 Günther (1988) 209, J. Niebaum, "Entry of U 1069A," in this volume.

259 A. Cerutti Fusco, "Entry of 1233 U A v.," in this volume.

260 Günther (1988) 315–16.

261 A. Cerutti Fusco, "Entry of U 1378A," in this volume.

262 A. Nesselrath, "Entries of U 1061A r., 1157A r., 1219A r." in vol. II: 201–02, 212–13, 219–20 are still measured in *braccia*, and their dating, about 1525–27, is suggested by the "h," the upper loop of which almost disappears and thus may have contributed to the change in the "h" after 1527; Frommel (1994, *Introduction*) 37, figs 32 c, d.

263 Frommel (1994, *Introduction*) 34; A. Nesselrath, "Entry of U 69A," in vol. II, 90–91; Nesselrath (2008).

264 A. Nesselrath, "Entry of U 1219 Av," in vol. II.

265 Wurm (1984) 473. The perspective cross section of the entablature of the portal at the right edge is likewise measured in *braccia* and could go back to a drawing by Giovan Francesco or Bernardo della Volpaia; other details measured in *palmi* may be by Peruzzi himself. The detailed ground plan of the Pantheon on U 462A r., which evidently also dates from Peruzzi's late period, is also measured in *palmi*; Wurm (1984) 471. Similarly, on U 605A, Peruzzi copied Giovan Francesco's cross-section of the amphitheatre in Verona on U 1386A r. and its ground plan on the verso of the Pantheon cross-section in Ferrara, ivi: 474–75. The ground plan of the portico of Pompey on U 484A r., which is measured in *braccia fiorentine*, must also refer to a model by Antonio; Wurm (1984) 460, 469, 477.

266 Serlio, "Delle Antiquita libro terzo," in Fiore (2001) IV, 7–17.

267 U. Kleefisch Jobst and A. Nesselrath, "Entry of U 874A r.," in vol. II 171–73.

268 A. Nesselrath, "Entry of U 3990A r.," in vol. II 268–69., Benelli (2018, *Vitruvian Pantheon*) with the hypothesis to date it much earlier and to connect it with San Giovanni dei Fiorentini.

269 C.L. Frommel, "Entry of U 1271A," in this volume.

270 Benelli (2018, *Vitruvian Pantheon*) 90–93, who showed that the drawing belongs to U 3990A r.

271 For such a hypothesis cf. Benelli (2018 *Vitruvian Pantheon*) 99–102, cf. previous note.

272 C.L. Frommel, "Entry of U 4039A," in this volume.

273 Frommel (2003, *Cappella Paolina*).

274 Palladio (1570) IV, ch. 10.

275 Pellecchia (1992).

276 Frommel S. (2014) 78.

277 Burns (2017).

278 See n. 125.

279 Vitruvius-Fra Giocondo (1511) fol. 64r., Pellechia (1992) 401–2.

280 Rowland (2003) 58, 131.

281 Frommel (1973) I: 56.

282 J. Niebaum, "Entry of U 999A," in this volume.

283 Frommel (2018, *Granada*).

284 P.N. Pagliara, "Entry of U 1188A" in this volume.

285 Pagliara (1988) 195; see H.C. Dittscheit, "Entry of U 1166A," in this volume.

286 Puppi (1973) 251–54; Frommel (1990) 154.

287 P.N. Pagliara, "Entry of U 969A," in vol. IV.

288 Frommel (1995, *Sanmicheli*) 24–25.

289 Pagliara (forthcoming, *Domestic Architecture*) in vol. IV; Giess (1981) and Giess (1994).

290 Frommel (2003, *L'architettura*) 45–69.; Pagliara (forthcoming, *Domestic Architecture*) in vol. IV.

291 S. Eiche, "Entry on U 767A," in vol. IV.

292 P.N. Pagliara, "Entry on U 867A," in vol. IV.

293 P.N. Pagliara, "Entry on U 1286A," in vol. IV.

294 Günther (1988) 33; Pochat (1990) 241–77.

295 Borsi (1985) 203 f.; Günther (1988) 28.

296 Günther (1988) 303–05.

297 Frommel (1974); Di Teodoro (1994); F.-E. Keller, "Entries of U 1228A, 1267A," in vol. II.

298 Günther (1988) 307–08. A. Cerutti Fusco, "Entries of U 1131A, 1966A v.," in this volume. Both drawings are still measured in *braccia*.

299 Günther (1988) 307–09; A. Cerutti Fusco,"Entries of U 1142A, 3969A, 1225A," in this volume.

300 Günther (1988) 266; on the dating of Peruzzi's reconstruction, see Tessari (1996) 123–36; Frommel (2005) 48–49.

301 Cf. the ground plan and cross section of 1926 in Günther (1988) 264, figs 24–25; A. Cerutti Fusco, "Entry of U 1107A v.," in this volume.

302 From Peruzzi, in any case, only drawings of the "aula regia" and some details have survived; Wurm (1984) 413–16). Peruzzi measures the ground plan of the aula on U 527A r. in *palmi*, and Antonio measures it in *piedi* on U 1233A r. and U 1668A v. The description there also dates from after the Sack of Rome; A. Cerutti Fusco, "Entry of U 1142, 1668A v.," in this volume.

303 A. Cerutti Fusco, "Entry of U 1203A," in this volume.

304 Günther (1988) 257–61, 321, fig. 85; A. Cerutti Fusco, "Entry of U 1122A v.," in this volume.

305 A. Cerutti Fusco, "Entries of U 1072A, 1225A, 1240A," in this volume.

306 Günther (1988) 308. At that time, on U 844A, Sangallo believed that in the Theater of Helvia Ricina (Macerata), he had discovered a Greek theatre that was constructed with the help of squares; A. Cerutti Fusco, "Entry of U 844A," in this volume.
307 See above, p. 19.
308 A. Cerutti Fusco, "Entry of U 626A," in this volume.
309 Günther (1988) 64–65, 376–79.
310 Serlio, *Il Terzo Libro* I, fol. A ij v. Serlio probably also took over the subdivision of the systyle and diastyle from Sangallo, who had already corrected Fra Giocondo in the Prague Vitruvius; Juren 2004 and Juren 2006.
311 Günther (1988) 65.
312 Scaglia (1994) 218–45; Frommel (1994, *Introduction*) 46; C.L. Frommel Entry of U 932A," in this volume.
313 Scaglia (1991–92), Vitruvius-Durantino 1524, fol. 33r.
314 See above, n. 298.
315 Pochat (1990) 219–75; Frommel (1999).
316 Frommel (1999) 182.
317 Magagnato (1992).
318 Pagliara (1986, *Vitruvio*) 73; Pagliara (1988) 180.
319 Giovannoni (1959) 1:25; Pagliara (1986 *Vitruvio*) 73.
320 Frommel (1994, *Introduction*) 36–37, and see above, p. 98.
321 Pagliara (1988). The copy mentioned by Scaglia (1991–92), 61–63, does not come from Antonio (information kindly given to me by P.N. Pagliara); see below, 00.
322 Günther (1988) 256, 295. Pagliara (1988) 185; Juren (2004) and Juren (2006).
323 Cf. Fabio Calvo's similar but less correct ground plans of these two temple types in the Munich manuscript; Fontana-Morachiello (1975) pl 7–8.
324 I am indebted to P.N. Pagliara for showing me his valuable material.
325 Pagliara (1988) 185.
326 Pagliara (1992, *Ordini*) 143–46.
327 Pagliara (1988) 186–87; Günther (1988) 53, 256, 295, 298; P. Zampa, "Entry of U 826A v.," in vol. II, 154–56.
328 P.N. Pagliara, "Entry of U 1187A r.," in this volume.
329 Pagliara (1988) 188–87, 196–97; Pagliata, "Entry of U 1211A," in this volume.
330 Pagliara (1988) 188, n. 52.
331 Günther (1988) 299–300.
332 Fiore (2002, *Trattati*) 513.
333 Fiore (2002, *Trattati*) 507.
334 Günther (1990)155–56, 159; Lemerle (2000) 36–37. That Philandrier took over the Composite order without direct legitimization by ancient authors shows how strong an influence Serlio exercised over him.
335 Denker-Nesselrath (1990) 49–67; Frommel (2011, *Palazzo Farnese*) 35.
336 Pagliara (1992, *Ordini*) 144–45; Frommel (2003, *Porta ionica*) 49–51, 56, 84–85; P.N. Pagliara, "Entries of U 989 and 1237A" and C.L. Frommel, "Entry to U 1278A," in vol. IV.
337 P.N. Pagliara, "Entry U 989A," in vol. IV.
338 Frommel (1996, *San Pietro*) 275, 286; A. Bruschi, "Entries of U 79 and 122A," in vol. II, 97–98, 108.
339 Frommel (2003, *Porta ionica*) 56, 84–84.
340 Frommel (2010, *Fabbrica*) 59–60, 331.
341 Pagliara (1986, *Vitruvio*) 73–75; Günther (1988) 63–64; Lemerle (2000) 16–17.
342 Pagliara (1992, *Ordini*) 143–46; see also the construction of an Ionic volute for the window of the Sala Regia of 1538/39, where Antonio cites the corresponding passage of the fifth chapter of Vitruvius' third book in the original text; M. Losito "Entry of U 1078A," in vol. IV.
343 Frommel (1981) 149–55.
344 Scaglia (1991–92); Scaglia (1994).
345 Pagliara (1992, *Ordini*) 145, figs 12–14.
346 P. Zampa, "Entry of U 826A r.," in vol, 148–49.
347 See Philandrier's criticism of the two orders of the aedicules (Lemerle, "Les annotations," 68). He did not take into account that Sangallo conceived the small Composite columns of the *piano nobile* about 30 years before the decidedly more slender columns of the Ionic order in the third storey; that is, with different theoretical premises. He similarly criticised the moulding of the Doric courtyard order, which projects as far forward as in the Theatre of Marcellus; Lemerle (2000) 42.
348 Giovannoni (1959) figs 25–27, 114 f., 118, 121, 134; Frommel (2003, *Porta ionica*) 49–69.
349 Pagliara (1992, *Ordini*) 146; Günther (1988) 297, 299; Frommel (2003, *L'architettura*) 69. The Ionic doors of the *piano nobile*, which are imposingly finished in marble, do not have the same assurance of form as the windows; they are more probably by Nanni di Baccio Bigio. P.N. Pagliara, "Entry of U 981A," in vol. IV.
350 See above, p. 44.
351 Günther (1988) 193–94; J. Niebaum, "Entry of U 1165A v.," and P.N. Pagliara, "Entry of U 1204A r.," in this volume.
352 Günther (1988) 195; Günther (2001, *L'opera tuscanica*).
353 P.N. Pagliara, "Entry of U 1286A" in vol. IV.
354 C. Thoenes, "Entry of U 65A," and C.L. Frommel, "Entries of U 994, 1011A," in vol. IV.
355 Frommel (2003, *L'architettura*) 69.
356 See above, p. 123.
357 Frommel (2003, *Porta ionica*) 56–58.
358 P.N. Pagliara, "Entry of U 1147A," in this volume.
359 Cellini-Milanesi (1893) 224–25; Fiore (2002, *Trattati*) 512.
360 The rebellion of the anti-Vitruvians, which Philandrier experienced towards the end of the 1540s in Rome, was directed partly against the pedantry of learned laymen of his type and partly against the power of the *setta sangallesca*, which kept raking in important commissions: "They [the anti-Vitruvians] condemn Vitruvius's rules, which they have never read or understood, and try to prevent whatever is being read to them. If these foolhardy ignoramuses were to begin to read Vitruvius and only then to form judgments, it would count for more than any building from their imaginations.," Lemerle (2000) 42–43, 17, 161.
361 Frommel (2002, *Villa Giulia*).
362 Frommel (2018, *Loreto*) 65–70.

COMMENTARIES ON THE DRAWINGS

Note on the Organization of the Entries

The entries follow the numerical sequence employed at the Gabinetto dei Disegni e Stampe at the Uffizi, Florence. Each drawing is identified by its Uffizi number, which is followed by an indication of the subject collection it comes from. The drawings by Antonio da Sangallo the Younger and his circle, are all from the architectural collection ("Architettura") and are thus identified by the letter A. We have used the designation "U" (for Uffizi) only for the first drawing in a sequence or a drawing referred to separately.

While every effort has been made to regularize the forms of transcription used by the authors, some variations are inevitable. The designation "recto and verso" is used in the heading when we have reproduced both recto and verso, having judged that both faces of the sheet merit reproduction. In cases where only a brief text is found on the verso, scholars have been asked to transcribe the text but a reproduction of that face is not provided. In this case, a sheet is referred to as "recto" only. Numbers or other mathematical inscriptions have not been transcribed unless judged of special relevance.

The division of the sequence of drawings by subject, both for the purposes of the entries and for the format of the volumes, is a result of the vast size of this undertaking. In some instances, drawings that contain annotations related to subjects ostensibly covered in this volume have had to be reserved for another volume. References to other volumes are indicated by "vol." and the number of the volume in Roman numerals. By and large, we have tried to follow the principle that the main subject of the sheet determines its location within the corpus. Despite our best intentions this principle of order has not always been respected.

The first lines of each entry give the author, subject, and approximate date of the sheet. Next follows a summary of specifications. Dimensions (height and width) are expressed in millimeters, measured from the bottom left corner; irregularly cut sheets are described as such. References to "white paper" are assumed, since it was the standard medium used by the Sangallo workshop. Restorations to the sheet may be noted.

In the inscriptions, brackets around three dots indicate an illegible word or phrase. A slash (/) is used to mark a new line. Semicolons indicate discrete words or groups of words.

The authors are identified by their initials at the end of each entry. Authorship divided by a comma (,) indicates that the entries have been combined by the editors.

As the texts written by different authors were written at different times and have different profoundness, they and the bibliography have been updated to varying degrees for the preparation of the publication.

NA	Nicholas Adams
EB	Enzo Bentivoglio
RB	Rita Bertucci
IC	Ian Campbell
ACF	Anna Cerutti-Fusco
HCD	Hans Christoph Dittscheid
SE	Sabine Eiche
FZB	Fabiono T. Fagliari Zeni Buchicchio
CLF	Christoph Luitpold Frommel
AGG	Adriano Ghisetti Giavarina
ACH	Ann C. Huppert
CJ	Christoph Jobst
F-EK	Fritz-Eugen Keller †
BK	Bernd Kulawik
MK	Margaret Kunz
ML	Maria Losito
MLU	Manfred Luchterhandt
GMa	Golo Maurer
JN	Jens Niebaum
PNP	Pier Nicola Pagliara
SP	Simon Pepper
HR	Hannes Roser
GS	Giustina Scaglia †
MS	Maximilian Schich
VZ	Vitale Zanchettin

Antiquity and Theory

U 32A *recto and verso*

Antonio da Sangallo the Younger

Rome, St Peter's, details of a column, ca. 1535–46 (*recto*), Sketches of a composite capital, 1535–46 (*verso*).

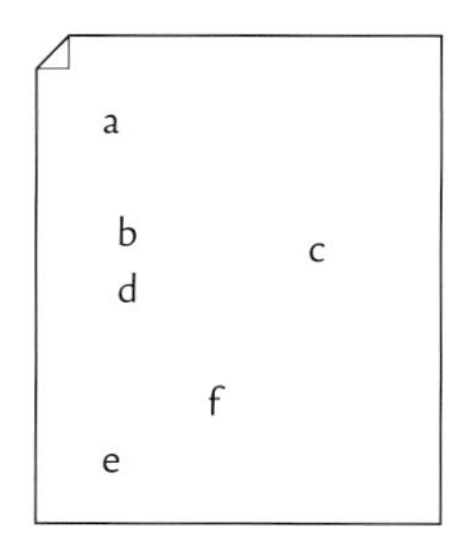

Dimensions 287 × 220 mm.
Technique Pen and brown ink.
Paper Lightweight, horizontal and vertical folds, perforated in places.

INSCRIPTION, Recto (top half) *Di Santo pietro; lo tutto alto 1 65; Tutto 1 65; Colla misura del mo/dello che l minuto si è/per due di quali di 5 per dito*; (lower half, bottom edge) *Misurato colle misure* [...]/*modello ch ogni minuto/per dito di que 10 di dito; tutto 3 95; Tutta 7 88*; (lower left) *in una te* [...] *de/delli* [...]*rmo/giallo di S.to pietr*[...]; *cinquantamilia cinquanta 71*

Verso *Di questo capitello/me stato mozzo/minuti 3/me stato mo/zzo M 3; rivedere l'agetto dell'ovolo/li membri della cimasa; la di sotto del capitello 142/la colonna da pie 1466*

The drawing on the *recto* shows details of the columns, including a sketch of the composite capital (*a*); a study of the volute (*b* and *c*); and decorations on the base of another column(?) (*d*). The latter sketch was executed by turning the sheet 90 degrees; it may have been made at a different time than the two details for the column in St Peter's and thus may be unrelated to it. On the lower half of the sheet are sketches of the shaft (*e*) and the profile of the base (*f*); these two drawings were executed by turning the sheet 180 degrees. The notes suggest that the shaft of the column, of which approximately two thirds was fluted, was to be made of *giallo antico* marble. However, as evinced by the many calculations on the sheet, Antonio seemed to have been more interested in the relationship between the measurements, so that he could study the proportions of the composite column. The elegant capital is a fine composite example as Giovan Francesco da Sangallo stated in a note on U 1804A v. (which might be a copy of U 32A r.), for which there are studies both here and on the verso; it would appear to have been used as a model for the capitals of the Ducal Palace in Urbino and by Baldassarre Peruzzi for those on the tomb of Pope Hadrian VI in S. Maria dell'Anima. In general, Antonio was not much interested in such richly decorated composite capitals, which, as Pagliara (1992, *Ordini*, p. 149) has observed, he thought more appropriate for interiors; he employed similar capitals on fluted pilasters in the Serra Chapel at S. Giacomo degli Spagnoli in Rome.

The sketches on the *verso* of a composite capital relate to those on the recto of the sheet. Here Antonio drew a good representation of the capital with a measured profile, and next to it a three-quarter view of another profile, in order to study the volutes, which are placed at 45 degrees. The latter scheme was also adopted by Giovan Francesco for U 1804A, his fair copy of the same capital in St Peter's that was sketched on the recto of this sheet, U 32A, by Antonio. However, the survey sketches made on site by Antonio were redrawn in fair copy at the drawing table by his cousin Giovan Francesco. | AGG

BIBLIOGRAPHY Ferri (1885) 130, 150–51; Bartoli (1914–22) IV: figs 351–52, pl. 210; VI: 67; CensusIDs 10014116, 10070230.

U 184A *recto and verso*

Giovanni Battista da Sangallo

Rome, Ancient basins at S. Pietro in Vincoli and at S. Marco (*recto*). Plan related to projects for Medici tombs at S. Maria Sopra Minerva (*verso*), prior to 1536.

Dimensions 199 × 268 mm.
Technique Pen and brown ink.
Paper Lightweight, fold parallel to short side, trimmed at corners, corners and upper edge reinforced.

INSCRIPTION, Recto (upper basin) *largo pie[di] 10¾*; *longo pie[di] 20*; *nel fondo pie[di] 14 [dita] 5*; *A S[an]to pietro in vincola ed e fesso*; (lower basin) *largo pie[di] 10 [dita] 10 1/2*; *longo pie[di] 20 [dita] 2*; *A S[an]to marcho*

Verso (later hand) *184A/ Sangallo Gio[vanni] Batt[ista] detto il Gobbo*

The drawings of the basins are done freehand, gone over a second time or corrected in places, and include the principal measurements. They are shown in orthographic projection with two views each: a longitudinal section and a transverse section at the left, the latter possibly added later and not to scale with its corresponding elevation. The overall proportions do not appear to have been respected, particularly in the elevations, but seem more accurate in the sketches of the transversal sections. In these, the details of the water outlet seem to have been neglected, while they are indicated on the elevations by the hatching on the lions' mouths. The basin of S. Pietro in Vincoli (at top) measures 20 *piedi* in length, 10¾ *piedi* in width (591 × 318 cm) and 4 *piedi* 14½ *dita* in height (145.10 cm) on the outside and 3¼ *piedi* in height (96.21 cm) on the inside. The basin of S. Marco (at bottom) measures 20 *piedi* 2 *dita* in length by 10 *piedi* 10½ *dita* in width (595 × 314 cm) and 4 *piedi* 12 *dita* in height (140.5 cm) on the outside and 3 *piedi* 2 *dita* in height (92.41 cm) on the inside Abandoned antique monuments were plundered from the early seventh century on, particularly such ancient basins, which were carved out of valuable types of marble and used mainly for nymphaea and baths and then were reused in early Christian buildings. In general, the basins that came to light between the fifteenth and sixteenth centuries were unearthed during digs for works of antiquity, while foundations for new buildings were being built, during inspections, or when early Christian churches were being demolished. The basin at S. Pietro in Vincoli was probably discovered in that building, which would mean that it had already been reused during the Middle Ages. The basin at S. Marco is one of two that were moved to the fifteenth-century piazza next to the Basilica of Paul II from the Terme di Caracalla in 1466. These were still in the piazza at the time of Emperor Charles V's visit in 1536. Sometime around 1536–45, Pope Paul III ordered one of these basins to be moved to Piazza Farnese. About 1580, Cardinal Alessandro Farnese, with Gregory XV's blessing, directed that the second basin also be moved to his palace. Both were reused for the extant seventeenth-century fountains.

Giovanni Battista's drawing must have been commissioned by Antonio da Sangallo the Younger around the middle of the 1530s, given that it relates closely to U 185A v., a drawing attributed to Antonio himself, and to his studies for the tombs of Popes Leo X and Clement VII (see vol. II, U 185A v.). On the recto of the same sheet, Antonio sketched ideas for mausoleum structures, which show the influence both of Michelangelo and of his own theoretical and reconstructive studies of the Etruscan tombs. Clearly Antonio intended to keep the pyramidal plan of Etruscan mausoleums with stepped levels and to adapt it according to Christian liturgical demands, which provided for the preservation of a buried body rather than ashes. Thus the apex of the structure, which has become the trunk of the pyramid, is taken up by the "antique" element consisting of the basin, with the "modern" elements of the architectural base, statues, and effigies of the recumbent pontiff nearby. Giovanni Battista's drawings for this confirm that Antonio had intended to build two tombs according to the same model. The measurements of the basins at S. Pietro in Vincoli and S. Marco are much the same; however, although formally similar, there is some difference in the size of the basin conserved in S. Salvatore in Lauro and reproduced on sheet U 185A v., which Antonio might initially have thought of using. The fair copy of a slightly modified version of Antonio's sketch in U 185A r., made by Giovanni Battista himself on sheet U 183A recto (see vol. II), gives the measurements for the basin (or basins) to be used in the monument: *20–10*, probably 20 *piedi* long by 10 *piedi* wide. These measurements agree with the dimensions of both the basins shown in U 184A r., but not with those of the basin of S. Salvatore.

On the verso of U 184A are hasty marks in ink that are not easy to decipher. The semi-octagonal shape of part of the scheme recalls the plan for the second level of the Medici tomb, sketched by Antonio at the left of U 185A r., suggesting that it may have been a study for the tomb itself. The sketch on the verso may have belonged to a planning stage in which the proportions of the second level (hypothetically corresponding to that of the seated statues of the Prophets)—proposed in Antonio's drawings on U 185A and the version in Giovanni Battista's hand on U 183A r.—have not yet reached the final proportions and dimensions of the realized project. | RB

BIBLIOGRAPHY Ferri (1885) 143, 153; Bartoli (1914–22) IV: fig. 547, pl. 328; VI: 100; Giovannoni (1959) I: 384; Heikamp (1966) 134–53; Valtieri (1986) 109–18, esp. 115 n. 13; Pagliara (1992, *Battista Sangallo*) 748–49; Kleefisch-Jobst in Frommel-Adams (2000) 117–18; CensusID 64432.

U 284A *recto and verso*

Francesco da Sangallo

Rome, plan of Baths of Diocletian, 1518.

Dimensions 662 × 815 mm; strip added at top, 77 × 315 mm.
Technique Pen and brown ink, straightedge, square, compass.
Paper Parchment, stained, one part glued and folded.
Drawing Scale Roman palmi (1 palmo = 213 mm)

INSCRIPTION, Recto (at the right) *Questa linea si e a il palmo romanescho e la canna a palmi dieci, e cioe la canna di roma colla quale ho misurata la presenta*; (below) *Questa era lentrata principale di questa terme la quale io fran[cesc]o di M[aestr]o giuliano / da sangallo feci j roma lanno 1518*

Verso *Pianta di Terme*

This ground plan of the Baths of Diocletian in Rome is dated 1518. It relates, with variations, to the incomplete study, U 1547A r., also attributed to Francesco. The present sheet highlights the contemporary interest in the large structures of these ancient baths among architects at the papal court. The ground plan is accurate and well defined, and derives from the surviving ruins, which in turn allowed for the artist's imaginative completion of the missing parts; the result reflects the early sixteenth-century taste for large, complex, covered spaces. The sequence of the spaces (*calidarium*, *tepidarium*, and *frigidarium*) was carefully studied; these are marked by the *varietas* stressed by Alberti. Solutions and inventions are suggested for the porticoed system of the courtyard gymnasia, for the articulation of the walls in relation to the architectural orders, and for the play of projections and recessions of the wall surfaces. Relationships between open and closed spaces are also defined in the rigid symmetrical layout of the central edifice.

This sheet should be compared to a series of drawings of the Baths of Diocletian by Giuliano da Sangallo (U 131A), Bramante (U 104A r.), possibly Antonio da Sangallo the Elder (U 2162A, 1546A r. and v.), Baldassarre Peruzzi (U 476A, 622A, and other studies such as U 357A, 405A, 421A, 427A, 464A, and 482A). It also should be compared with the drawings by Antonio da Sangallo the Younger (U 2134A r. and v.), and Giovanni Battista (U 2163A). The last drawing, in particular, which represents half of the plan, is identical to the present drawing. The two ground plans might derive from U 2134A r. and v., a section of a plan. Some ground plans of the Baths of Diocletian are also found among the drawings of antiquities in the Albertina, Vienna (Egger 1903, n. 13v., 14v., n. 177), the authors of which, until now anonymous, seem linked to the Tuscan ambient of the Sangallo circle. | ACF

BIBLIOGRAPHY Ferri (1885) 203; Ashby (1904) 14, n. 8; Guidi-Paribeni (1911) fig. 9; Bartoli (1914–22) IV: fig. 722, pl. 400; VI: 126; Krencker-Krüger (1929) 179–282; Giovannoni (1959) I: 99; Collobi Ragghianti (1973) 44; Collobi Ragghianti (1974) 163; Günther (1988) 199; Frommel (1989, *Bramante*); Scaglia (1995) 273; D. Donetti in Donett-Faietti-Frommel (2017) 123; CensusIDs 10084044 10007817.

U 508A *recto and verso*

Aristotile da Sangallo

Pula, Arch of the Sergi, elevation, plan, and details; Beneventum, Arch of Trajan (*recto*), Proportional scheme for a Doric portico (*verso*).

Dimensions 410 × 290 mm.
Technique Pen and brown ink, straightedge, compass, freehand.
Paper Heavy, horizontal rupture, repaired on verso.
Drawing Scale piedi antichi (recto), Scales with unknown measure unit (verso).

INSCRIPTION, Recto *L. SER GIVS / C FAED II / VIR; SALVIA POS / TVMA SERGI; L SERIVS / LF LEPIDU / S AED TR / IMILI LEG / XXIX / GN SERGIVS C F / AED II VIR QVINQ / Q* (canceled); *SALVIA PORVIMA SERG I DESVA / PECVNIA*; *piedi e l' è partito / el pie in trentadua*; *arco di bonivento*; *arco di pola i[n] schiavia*

Verso *alto questo zocholo quanto e il vano dello frontone*; *piu alto questo / una 8 tava parte*; *e a eser*[?] *alto una delle 9 / qui nel vano ma questo / disegnato è baso quanto / è la gola di sopra*; *di quelle picole che sono / nel vivo dopie*; *meza teste*; *parte tre*; *quadro*; *scompartita la cornice che chorre tuta in parte 9 e di questa*; *delle 6 / picole*; *ageto 1 delle 6 dopie*; *Nera*; *la meta del portichato in parti 14*; *parte 14*; *dopie 6*; *alto insino ad i p.*[...] *della architrave parte 14*; *Da Dapori*; *da capo 5*

In the sixteenth century, triumphal arches figured among the most frequently studied monuments of antiquity. As they combined the most important patterns of classical architecture—the order, the wall, and the arch—in constant variation, they might well have been regarded as exemplary keys to its understanding. Whereas the arches in and near Rome could be studied in the original, the more remote ones were known mainly through copies and copies of copies. Of these, the well-preserved Arch of the Sergi in Pula (Istria) is one of the most prominent examples. As Hubertus Günther has shown, the many copies can be retraced to only three versions taken from the original (Günther 1988, p. 238). The drawing on the recto of the present sheet is clearly a copy and closely related to a version by Antonio the Younger (U 1875A; Günther 1988, pp. 208/9) and anonymous renderings: U 2058A; Lille, Musée Vicar, inv. no. 772; Florence, Biblioteca Nazionale, Codex II-I-429, fol. 18 r.; "Wiener Skizzenbuch" 18 (Günther 1988, Anhang IV. 18b) and "Kassel Codex" (Günther 1988, Anhang VI. 9v.).

The larger sketch here shows the arch in its reduced outlines, drawn with a straightedge and compass but not to scale. Its plan, as well as detailed, measured renderings of the pedestal, the column's base, the entablature, and the attic are added freehand underneath and beneath. In the opening of the arch, its profile and the pattern of the coffered vault is indicated. Below is a small sketch of the much larger but structurally related Arch of Trajan in Beneventum, which might have served as a more familiar point of reference.

The many errors in the inscriptions on the frieze and on the attic show that the draftsman's understanding of Latin abbreviations and names was rather limited. The measurements refer to the *piede antico*, which is divided into 32 parts. They are largely identical to those found on Codex II-I-429, fol. 18 r. (Günther 1988, Anhang II, 40a). The mistakes in transcription and the drawing's painstaking and awkward execution make an attribution to Giovanni Battista da Sangallo (Ferri 1885, p. 13; Giovannoni 1959, I, p. 21; Vasori 1981, p. 122; Günther 1988, p. 209) improbable. A more likely author of this sheet is Aristotile da Sangallo, whose handwriting has already been identified by Vasori.

In the interesting drawing on the verso, the author described the general proportions of a Doric portico with four columns, which is shown exactly in half (Günther 1988, p. 211, no. 14). According to Vitruvius, such a portico (*diastylos*) is to be divided into 27 units (Vitruvius IV: 3, 3). the author, apparently fearful of odd numbers, preferred 28 units, or 14 for the half view. A corresponding scale can be seen at the bottom, divided into 3 respectively 6 subunits. Closely following Vitruvius's prescription, he took 14 units for the columns' height and 2 units for their lower diameter, which tapers by 1/6 at the top (Vitruvius IV: ch. 3, 4). The capital—divided into three equal sections—measures 1 unit in height and 2 1/6 units in width. In accordance with Vitruvius's unusually clear instructions, the architrave is 1 unit and the triglyphs are 1 1/2 units high. The draughtsman centered the triglyphs correctly above the columns, placing—as Vitruvius (IV: 3, 3) recommended—two between the outer and three between the inner interval, the latter being consequently wider. However, Aristotile's outer metopes are notably larger than the inner ones, for the columns are placed upon a scale of 28 instead of 27 units and avoided the odd intervals that Vitruvius's prescriptions would have required. Obviously, the intervals between the columns'outlines are taken as a basis instead of the distance from axis to axis. The much more complicated question of how to resolve the problem of the corner triglyph—discussed by Vitruvius at the beginning of chapter 3—is left unconsidered. The upper edge of the cornice is divided into 9 (4 1/2) sections, one of which indicates the height of the tympanum. Aristotile's scale is too small to render further details of Vitruvius's prescriptions for the entablature. It is perhaps for this reason that the entablature is repeated in freehand.

This sheet is a rare case of Vitruvius's text being illustrated almost word for word. It clearly shows the difficulties in harmonizing the respective intervals of the colonnade and the frieze, a problem that made the Doric order especially difficult to employ. The impeccable rendering of this complicated subject compared to Aristotile's rather limited capacities suggests that it is a copy. | GMa

BIBLIOGRAPHY Ferri (1885) 13, 117; Giovanoni (1959) I: 21; Vasori (1981) 156–58, cat. no. 122; Günther (1988) 209–11, no. 14; CensusID 10074046.

U 562A *recto and verso*

Giovanni Battista da Sangallo

Rome, Theatre of Marcellus, after 1519.

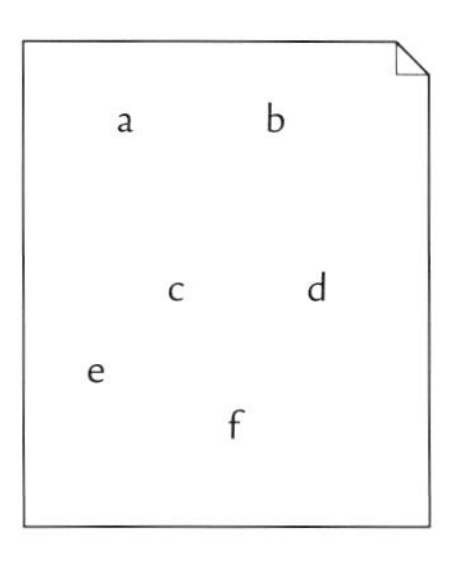

Dimensions 240 × 320 mm.
Technique Pen and sepia ink.
Paper Lightweight, restorations and additions.

INSCRIPTIONS, Recto (perspectival section) *Pane sala lata pacacio di*

Verso *Pass fu mio patre*

Sangallo has used the recto for a study of the geometrical genesis of the theater, showing the entry through the side hall (known as the *aula regia*) and along the *parodoi*, or covered entrance corridors. In Latin theaters *parodoi* were called *versurae* and served as an entrance for the spectators who occupied the places of honor. A group of sketches on the verso relates to the same theater: (*a*) Perspectival sketch of part of the ground floor ambulatory; the order of attached half-columns on the arcade at ground level is Doric. (*b*) Partial plan, indicating the vaults and a study of columns and half-columns, showing the intersection of the piers of the final rectilinear segment of the ambulatory and the piers of the stage building. (*c*) Lateral perspectival sketch of one of the aisles in the *aula regia*. (*d*) Transversal perspectival sketch of the *aula regia*; note the thermal windows in *c* and *d*. (*e*) Sketch of a base. (*f*) Partial plan of the *aula regia*. | ACF

BIBLIOGRAPHY Ferri (1885) 39, 100; Giovannoni (1958) I: 96.

U 575A *recto and verso*

ANTONIO DA SANGALLO THE YOUNGER(?) and unknown hand

Rome, Cemetery of Praetextatus, So-called Sepolcro dei Cercenii and Sepolcro dei Calventii (*recto*). Unidentified loggia (*verso*). Recto before 1512–15(?).

Dimensions 181 × 321 mm.
Technique Pen and brown ink, stylus, straightedge, compass (*recto*); red chalk, freehand (*verso*).
Paper Torn, trimmed, and patched.

INSCRIPTION, Recto [...] *i*[*n*] *vano*; *fuora di roma i miglio*; (below) *fuora di roma i miglio*

The sheet has suffered a large tear at top left, and has been cut severely on the right, losing part of the upper drawing on the recto, and part of the drawing on the verso The handwriting on the recto is similar to the early hand of Antonio the Younger (ca. 1510–13) and allows us to attribute the plans to him. They show a hexaconch-domed structure and a cruciform-vaulted structure, the remains of which still stand just north of Via Appia and west of Via Appia Pignatelli within the area of the Cemetery of Praetextatus. They were drawn frequently in the Renaissance by Peruzzi, Serlio, Ligorio, and others (Rausa 1997, 77–87). The hexaconch was named the "Sepolcro dei Calventii" by Ligorio on the basis of an inscription he records there, which, however, is uncorroborated by others (CIL VI 1422*). Nevertheless all the evidence points to its being a mausoleum dating from the late 4th to early 5th centuries AD (Spera 1999, p. 191, UT 323). Ligorio is also responsible for naming the cruciform structure the "Sepolcro dei Cercennii" again on the basis of an inscription (CIL VI 14658). It is considered contemporary with the "Sepolcro dei Calventii" (Spera 1999, p. 191, UT 322).

Antonio erred in squaring off the exteriors of the structures and in giving them both porticoes *a forcipe*, that is, with rounded ends. Later he altered the upper plan, correcting the form of the portico by making it less wide and squaring the ends. To the right, he added an extension, of which no trace now survives, but since it appears on other contemporary drawings, independent of the Sangallo circle, it can be taken to have existed. Although, no other plan shows it with stairs as here, their presence would seem reasonable to give access to the burial chamber below. His original plan had imagined two spiral stairs contained within the masonry between the portico and the hexaconch. On the verso is a freehand elevation of a suspended loggia, with a three-arched structure with cartouches above and below, suggesting an interior gallery, perhaps for a choir. The upper part of the drawing is cut off but at the centre of the cartouche there apıpears to be the lower part of an aperture or inscription panel. At the centre of the lower cartouche is a blank shield. The use of red chalk and the drawing style do not immediately suggest Antonio's hand. | IC

BIBLIOGRAPHY Ferri (1885) 174, 199; Bartoli (1914–22) III: fig. 407, pl. 234; VI: 74; Windfeld-Hansen (1969); Rausa (1997), 78, fig. 13.7 and 85, fig. 14.4; CensusID 60680.

U 606A *recto*

GIOVAN FRANCESCO DA SANGALLO

Verona, view of part of Arena, ca. 1526.

Dimensions 395 × 276 mm.
Technique Pen and brown ink, freehand.
Paper Lightweight.

The drawing is a foreshortened view of the monument, which shows both the appearance of the rusticated structure with its three orders, the lowest one partly buried in the ground, and the ruined state of the monument. The plants on the vaults of the *cavea* at the height of the second order are also evidence of its abandoned state. But, despite appearances, the view could well have been made at the drawing table with the help of sketches done on site. The circle with a cross through it in the middle of the sheet is a cross-reference to the one on U 1386A r., also by Giovan Francesco. | AGG

BIBLIOGRAPHY Ferri (1885) 225; Vasori (1981) 158–9, cat. no. 123; CensusID 10072002.

U 626A *recto and verso*

Giovanni Battista da Sangallo

Rome, Theater of Marcellus, general schematic plan, larger-scale detail of ambulatory, study of Doric columniation of latter, after 1519.

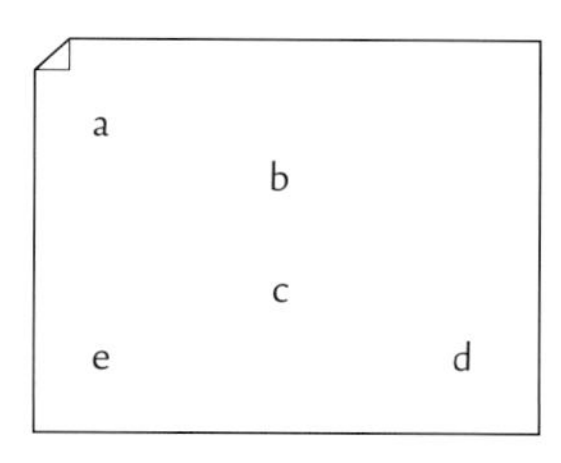

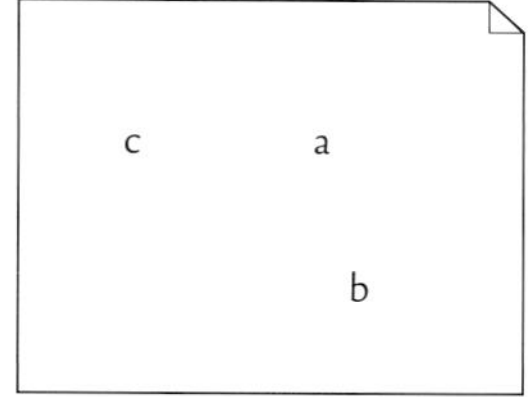

Dimensions 234 × 337 mm.
Paper Lightweight, mounted on card, fold down middle of sheet.
Technique Pen and sepia ink, freehand, stylus, compass (seven marks).
Drawing Scale Roman *piede.*

INSCRIPTION, Recto (top right) *teatro di marcello*; (center of sheet, from top to bottom) *orchestra; vano 194*; *dalla finestra del pollaro al di fuora piedi* 307; *piedi 417*; (right) *pulpito proscenio*; *vano*; (below) *piedi trecento sessanta ignoravo*; *scena*; *aula regia, sala regia*; *hospitali*; (bottom left) *al tutto della basa*; *del culiseo grande*

Verso (bottom right, turned clockwise) *dalla finestra del gallinaro al di fuora piedi 325, 325, 301, 301*; (right) *piedi*; (below) *lultima misura*

By the handwriting and drawing style, this plan can be certainly attributed to Giovanni Battista Sangallo (not to Peruzzi as by Bartoli and the Census). On the recto, there is a partial plan of the Theater of Marcellus in Rome (*b*). In the center of the sheet there is a plan of the stage with connecting guest chambers and the lateral apsidal spaces (*c*). At the top left there is a plan of a pier with a half-column, together with their relative measurements (*a*). At the bottom right is a plan of the *aula regia* with a detail of the corner solution (*d*). The plan of a freestanding column and a pier with a half- column, with relative measurements, relates to the *aula regia*. At the bottom left is there a section showing the base of an unidentifiable order above a flight of steps, with the annotation "del culiseo grande" (*e*). In Renaissance drawings, the term "culiseo" was often used to signify the Theater of Marcellus. It is quite possible that this base related to the Theater of Marcellus, and to the "Porticus in summa gradatione" of which there are drawings on sheets U 1136A r. and 1856A in particular. The absence of a tall plinth would seem to exclude any definitive attribution to the Amphitheater of Flavius; although sheet U 39A v., conserved in the Biblioteca Comunale di Torino, does contain a drawing by Juvarra of the base of one of the columns in the stalls of the Colosseum, which is similar to that depicted by Giovanni Battista on this sheet. Lastly, there are various plans of schemes for piers composed of half-columns, together with metric references relating to the measurements.

On the verso, there are various details from the same theater as on the recto: at the top right, a study, in plan, of the structural and functional layout of the ambulatory, with annular corridors, radial walls, and piers supporting the vaulting and access stairs (*a*). At the bottom right is a schematic reconstruction of the plan of the theater, including the *aule regie* (*b*). To the top left, perpendicular to the previous drawings, there is a hasty concise sketch of the first order of half-columns, which does not show the piers behind them (*c*). Giovanni Battista has made faithful drawings of the Doric order minus its base, the cornice, and the frieze with its metopes and triglyphs in the ambulatory, and provided measurements and calculations relating to the interaxes between the column shafts. | ACF

BIBLIOGRAPHY Ferri (1885) 100, 193; Bartoli (1914–22) IV: figs 529–30, pl. 319; VI: 97; Lanciani (1897) 495; Lanciani (1902–12) III: 8; Frommel (1974) 181; Günther (1988) 260, figs 19, 305, 307; Pochat (1990) 258, 271; Tessari (1995) 125, 142, 145; Jobst (1994) 441–42; CensusIDs 242279, 242341.

U 716A *recto*

Antonio da Sangallo the Younger

Profiles of entablature of the Trajan's Forum and so-called Temple of Romulus in the Roman Forum; profile of cornice of the door of the loggia of Cortile del Maresciallo to Bramante's Cordonata in the Vatican Palace, after 1538.

Dimensions 274 × 322 mm.
Technique Pen and ink.
Paper Medium, damaged at lower edge.

INSCRIPTION *In terra / questa si è in sulla piaza de Ca / valieri in roma e si e di marmo / semplice senza intagli ed e / de uno pezo architrave fregio / et cornicie e tutta dua sono / misurate a dita ma sono ri / dute qui de una medesima / grandeza per vedere la disimilitu / dine de membri quale conferentia / abbino insieme anchora / che questa sia in se molto / minore che questa a riscontro / cioe di S.to Cosmo* / (top of the sheet) *Batista Bisognia / rimisurarla / perche* (*stimo* canceled) / *ti mancha* (*ch'a* canceled) *misure / e fare li suoi intagli / misurata a dita / Questa si e la cornice / di S.to Cosimo e damiano / intagliata e suo architrave / e fregio. La cornicie si e / alta piedi 5 et Dita 15 / Lo capitello si e alto piedi 3 / et Dita 5 / La colonna si e alta cioe el suo / fuso piedi 23 Dita 12 / La colonna da pie piedi 2 Dita 14 misurata a dita questa si e la cornice fatta / sopra la porta della scala / grande di palazzo del papa / nel portichale di S.to pietro*

The drawing shows from left to right the profiles of fragment of entablature of marble facing in one of the spaces adjacent to the *murus marmoreus* of the Trajan's Forum, the profile of entablature above cipolin columns of so-called Temple of Romulus in Roman Forum, and the profile of the cornice of a door executed by Antonio that leads from loggia of Cortile del Maresciallo to Bramante's Cordonata of the Loggie. The profiles of the two antique entablatures are shown at the same height, as Antonio noted here, in order to illustrate similarities and differences. Antonio's inscription provide a clear identitification of the three pieces. The first was also drawn by Giovan Francesco (U 1326) with the annotation: "A Spoglia christo cavata di terra". The drawing was possibly taken from Giovanni Battista and copied by Antonio on this sheet. The second profile above which Antonio noted "Batista Bisognia / rimisurarla..." also features in a drawing by Giovanni Battista (U 1662A v.) in which the same measurements are given, albeit fewer of them; Antonio's explicit invitation to his brother is another illustration of his authoritarian behavior toward even his closest collaborators.

In the spring of 1538, Antonio began work on the restructuring of the southeast part of the Vatican palaces, which also included transforming the Cortile del Maresciallo. The portal leading to Bramante's Cordonata, under the portico with its four arches created using the remains of the previous portico from the time of Pope Paul II, became much less important once Pirro Ligorio's new entrance from the Cortile di S. Damaso, constructed during the reign of Pope Pius IV, had been built. | AGG

BIBLIOGRAPHY Ferri (1885) 137, 157, 183; Vasari-Milanesi (1906) V: 481, 494; Bartoli (1914–22) III: fig. 385, pl. 225, VI: 72; Sepe (1939) 43, 45; Giovannoni (1959) I: 20, 179; Lupi-Pettinau (1980) 62; Zavatta (2008) 42; Davis (2015) 135; CensusID 10071568.

U 788A *verso*

Antonio da Sangallo the Younger

Rome, Forum Romanum, Curia used as Church of S. Adriano, before 1546.

Dimensions 1096 × 474 mm.
Technique Pen and black ink.
Paper Heavy, two sheeets pasted together, reinforced on verso, and multiple folds.
Drawing Scale minuti.

INSCRIPTION, *questa si e uno architrave de una porta anticha / cavata de uno muro della chiesa di sa*[*n*]*to adriano / acca*[*n*]*to alla tribuna dove e segnato A tutta / de uno pezo / Lo he pertiro sie tre parti & l'architrave 4*; (on the entablature) *Sima*; *Listoio*[?]; *Astragalo*

The drawing shows the antique profile of a lintel from a door of the Curia that served as the Church of S. Adriano. The door is sketched into a ground plan. For the recto see vol. IV. | HCD

BIBLIOGRAPHY Ferri (1885) 134; Bartoli (1914–22) III: fig. 367; VI: 69; CensusID 10169498.

U 790A *recto and verso*

Antonio da Sangallo the Younger

Rome, reconstruction of Forum of Augustus (a); copy of design by Michelangelo for facade of San Lorenzo (b); detail of ground plan of church (c), various calculations (*recto*); Rome, ground plans of Baths of (*a*) Caracalla and (*b*) Diocletian; (*c*) bird; (*d*) schematic ground plan; (*e*) ornament; (*f*) helmet (*verso*), ca. 1518.

Dimensions 338 × 479 mm.
Technique Pen and brown ink, straightedge, compass, freehand.
Paper Center fold, trimmed, partly restored. Watermark: anchor in circle surmounted by six-pointed star.

INSCRIPTION, Recto (left half, top to bottom) (Antonio's hand) *da questa banda / qui sta lo pilastro / e no*[*n*] *dall altra*; *questo pilastro qui sta i*[*n*] *op*[*er*]*a / canalato ed e i*[*n*] *questo locho / di marmo cipollino*; *muro / pare mo/derno*; *mar/mo*; *muro*; *qui erano / colonne di mistio / non so quante se ne / cavo dua col detto / pilastro pure canelate*; *qui era / una nigia / e non e entrata / e chosi dall altra banda*; *basa bella*; *cosi stava*; *60 palmi*; (right half) (later hand, perhaps Ferri's) *foro d'Augusto; pare che questo sia per la facciata di S Lorenzo a Firenze? grde cartella dove sono*[?] *gli altri progetti per questa facciata*

Verso (Antonio's hand): *EA*; *AMA*; *SETENTRIO*; *al chontadino B. 84 / a dua manovali B. 50 / a tonio B 45 / 179*; various calculations

RECTO At the left of the sheet is Antonio's reconstruction of the Forum of Augustus. Several of his surviving drawings document various phases of his interest in the forum

(Viscogliosi 2000, pp. 112–16) where, in 1518, he had the opportunity to excavate (Lanciani 1902–12, p. 185; Bartoli 1914–22, p. 38). While the studies on U 1141A r. and 1139A r. are measured building surveys and final copies of them, on this sheet Antonio attempted to reconstruct a complex that was to a large extent buried and built over. His archaeological findings, which are remarkably accurate, are mixed with contemporary ideas of symmetrically and centrally organized rooms and surfaces. His point of departure is the large, correctly drawn exedra in the southeast. In place of the straight line that borders the Forum Iulium in the southwest, his restoration shows a slanting wall symmetrical to that on the northeast side. At the same time, by extending the southeast colonnade of the Temple of Mars Ultor to double its length—that is, by another eight columns—he created an axially symmetrical complex closed off in front by a screen of columns. The corresponding arrangement to the northwest, along with a third exedra in the southwest, is merely indicated. The idea for this scheme seems to have arisen in the course of drawing, since Antonio lined up the exedra and colonnade along a common central axis only on U 1283A. This basically consistent doubling is carried out even in the frontal colonnade of the temple, which shows that Antonio did not recognize it as such. He subsequently rejected it, because the resulting corridor, only one intercolumniation in width, would have been too narrow for a central entrance way.

Antonio himself expressly noted that the exedra precluded such an entrance (*qui era una nigia e non e entrata*). Additional details of the archeological finds—entered freehand in the finished reconstruction, which is drawn with straightedge and compass—chiefly have to do with materials and execution (inscription 2). Antonio also distinguished between ancient and modern masonry (inscription 3a).

How Antonio envisioned the elevation and original function of the area can only be surmised (Viscogliosi 2000, p. 118 f.). It was first identified as the Forum of Augustus by Pirro Ligorio and Palladio. It is indicative of how aware architects were becoming of their achievements that with the onset of the sixteenth century they increasingly found models not only among ancient monuments but in contemporary work, which they consequently studied. Michelangelo's project for the facade of San Lorenzo seemed to them especially innovative and stimulating. It was copied by Antonio but also—to name just a few—by his cousin Aristotile da Sangallo (Munich, Staatliche Graphische Sammlung, 33258), Baccio Bandinelli (attributed, Paris, Musée du Louvre, Cabinet des Dessins, 134 v.), and the circle of Etienne Dupérac (New York, The Metropolitan Museum of Art, 49.92.41 r.). The novelty of Michelangelo's project was to front the heterogeneous organism of a tiered basilica with a box-like facade independent of the interior and with the self- contained outline of a palace.

The influence of this solution on Antonio can still be traced in his model for St Peter's. There, too, the mighty three-storied zone of the facade serves to concentrate the highly differentiated building complex into a compact, palace-like block whose articulation—quite in contrast to the projects of Bramante and Raphael—is largely independent of the interior. Architectural details such as the design of the corners seem to be taken directly from Michelangelo's project, whose wholly novel solution for corners Antonio, unlike his cousin Aristotile, grasped quickly and surely (Millon 1988, no. 11). The project, probably copied from a drawing brought to Rome, differs only in the design of the attic from the final solution, which was fixed by a contract of 19 January 1518 (Millon 1988, no. 10).

(c) The detail of a ground plan at the lower right, a crossing pier with two half-executed arms, is described by Günter (1988, p. 254) as a study for Sant' Egidio in Cellere (begun in 1518). A similar ground plan on U 526A r. has been identified by Tafuri (see vol. II., from its dimensions as a study for Santa Maria di Monserrato in Rome and dated by him to the winter of 1517–18.

VERSO The great bath complexes were the principal models for the characteristic Roman manner of creating spatial structures from masses of masonry, which in constantly varying combinations of niches, exedras, and passageways were hollowed out and shaped until only a few masses remained. They also showed the many ways in which different spatial types could be joined to make a cohesive, hierarchically organized complex.

There are correspondingly numerous surveys and reconstruction drawings of these monumental complexes, which Antonio already knew from the measuring campaigns of his uncle Giuliano, Peruzzi, Bernardo della Volpaia, and perhaps also Bramante (Codex Barberini 4424, 66v.–67v.; U 104A v. Codex Coner 8, 22; Frommel 1989 [*Bramante*], p. 164 f.; Günther 1988, pp. 136 f., 252; Frommel 2003 [*L'esordio*]).

About 1518 Antonio's cousin Francesco and his brother Giovanni Battista were both studying the baths of Diocletian and Caracalla (U 284A, 1547A, 1133A). This contemporaneous sheet (see recto), which shows portions of the complexes (*a*, *b*), may be a part of the study. Antonio's cursory ground plans (*a*, *b*), undoubtedly sketched at one go, have no measurements and may have been based on another drawing rather than made on the site. In both cases, interest is focused on the central area of the complex. In the Baths of Diocletian (*b*) the peripheral areas at the right of the complex have been summarily added and parts of the surrounding wall indicated. Antonio was clearly interested in comparing the sequences of rooms along the main axes of the two complexes. The four sections of *caldarium*, *tepidarium*, *frigidarium*, and *natatio* are connected in a similar manner. In Antonio's time the function of these rooms was anything but clear (Günther 1994, pp. 14–18), but beyond such archeological and antiquarian questions as these, Antonio must have been interested in the different solutions of their spatial organization despite their structural similarity. A specific incentive for this may have been the roughly contemporary, major change in plan substantially entrusted to Antonio by Raphael (U 273A, 314A) while the Villa Madama was under construction. When a central circular court was introduced, problems developed in the arrangement of the rooms, and the bath complexes may have served as a welcome aid in solving them.

The right half of the folded sheet was used by Antonio for various calculations and small sketches which are not necessarily connected with the rest of the sheet, even though the inscription "SETENTRIO" labels it as the north side of the Baths of Diocletian. | GMa

BIBLIOGRAPHY Ferri (1885) 49, 165, 199, 209, 217; Bartoli (1914–22) III: figs 453, 454, pl 268, 269; VI: 84–5; Frey (1922–23) 221–28; Tolnai (1934) 38; Giovannoni (1958) I: 36; II: fig. 1; Tolnay (1972) 63; Tolnay (1975–80) IV: 42; Günther (1988) 254 f.; Millon (1988) no. 10; Frommel (1989, *Bramante*); Günther (1994, *Insana aedificia*); Viscogliosi (2000) 116–12, cat. no. 8; Zavatta (2008) 188; Viscogliosi (2017) 101, 106, 108, 110, fig. 5; CensusIDs 238811, 10071569.

U 815A *recto and verso*

Antonio da Sangallo the Younger

Verona, left half ground plan, elevation and details of the Arch of the Gavi, right half of facade and details of Porta Borsari, ancient pier at lower right (*recto*).

Dimensions 436 × 574 mm.
Paper Heavy; 3 folds, slightly damaged at upper edge, reinforced on back.
Technique Pen and brown ink, stylus, straightedge, compass (recto); pen and brown ink (verso).
Drawing Scale *piedi antichi.*

INSCRIPTION, Recto (left half) (below plan, later hand) *verona*; (Antonio's hand) *Diverona*; (on entablature) *qui aquesta alteza cie uno / pezo di questa cornicie non chre / do sie alsuo logo*; *questo noncie; nequesto*; *Lovano piedi 11 D[ite] 10½* (for clear width of passage); (on columns) *2 [piedi] – 6 [dite]*; *18 [piedi] 15½ [dite] lo fusco ede canalata*; *striate*; (referring to inscription below tabernacle and to place where installed on outer side of upper pier in ground plan, also marked with +) *C.GAVIO CM.F.* / *Straboni*; *queste lette/re anno asta/re dallaltra banda dietro / aquesta dove e questo con / trasegnio +*; (referring to inscription given in ground plan) *qui e laschritione / divetruvio apreso / alchapitello adua piedi – 8 [dite] / edalaltra banda da / arischontro alchonpagnio / di questo dove e una stella VIETRUVVIVS.L.L. / ARCHITECTUS / CERDO* (*CERDO* crossed out, its place marked with * in ground plan); (referring to inscription "GAVIAE.CM.F. CM" and to place installed on outer side of lower pier in ground plan, also marked with A) *queste lettere qui sotto schritte / vano dove segnato contra / segnio A*; (in ground plan, at right) *p[er] questo verso dachapo lacholona escie fora uno pie alvivo*; (far left of ground plan) *vovoli*; *foglietto*; *Dinanzi*; *p[er] fiancho*; (in cross section of column) *Dapie[di] 2–6*; *31 dite*; (near details at left of elevation) *fondo deltabernacholo*; *detabernacholi*; *questo e dimano / di vetruvio in verona / edebellissimo*; (right half; above plan, in later hand) *di Verona / 18*; *La stella e in mezo*; *colonia*; *cimase*; *membretto*; *Basamento*; *piedi 34* (for clear width of passage); (in column) *canalata*; (referring to inscriptions to be placed in aedicules framing passages) DEDICATI; *porta di basse* (*basse* crossed out) *de borsoli anticha / in verona insulpiano ciera gia / Larchitrave e spianato p[er] farne / epitafio dellultimo piano in/fuora che ne intagliato gusti*; (next to profile of architrave of passage) *archo*; (referring to detail of pier at right) *pilastro quadro / Largo piedi 3 / incircha nel chortile / delduomo diverona*

Verso (in Antonio's hand) *verona*

Together with U 1048A and U 1200A, this sheet may be one of the fruits of a tour of inspection of papal fortifications in northern Italy undertaken in 1526 by Antonio da Sangallo and the Veronese architect Michele Sanmicheli, an occasion also used by Antonio to broaden his knowledge of ancient architecture (for the tour of inspection, see Beltrami 1902). There is no evidence that Antonio stopped in Verona, but the city was not far from his route. The freehand sketch of the Porta Borsari (recto, at right) may have been made on site; however, the scored drawing of the Arch of the Gavi (recto, at left), which was constructed with straightedge and compass, and the scored ground plan of the amphitheater (verso) exhibit the characteristics of studio drawings. The representation of the Porta Borsari adheres closely to the form of the structure except for small changes and additions. In contrast, the drawing of the Arch of the Gavi differs in several respects from the presumed appearance of the structure in the sixteenth century. The architrave, frieze, and molding are described by Antonio as reconstructions ("questo noncie"). The square plinths under the column bases are free additions rather than adoptions or reconstructions. In the actual building, the column bases are placed directly on the pedestal moldings; the latter extend around the corners of the arch pylons, another detail that Antonio failed to record on the present sheet, although he did so on U 1229A r.

The wall section placed in front of the right facade of the tetrapylon, which blocks the side passage in the ground plan, is another deliberate change in the Arch of the Gavi. Antonio's drawing is thus a collage of description, reconstruction, and reinterpretation.

Since it is likely that he visited Verona, and his precise knowledge of the Arch of the Gavi is documented by a drawing on U 1229A r., the deviations from the finds must be regarded as the architect's critique of the ancient structure, whose plan he attributed to Vitruvius ("e dimano di vetruvio"; on the subject of architectural criticism, see also U 1048A, 1064A, and 1200A). The drawing of the Arch of the Gavi on U 815A is very probably the model for Giovan Francesco da Sangallo's drawing U 1382A.

The pier to the right of the drawing of the Porta Borsari stood in the cathedral during the sixteenth century and is now in the Museo Maffeiano in Verona. For the Arch of the Gavi, see also U 1229A and U 1382A. | CJ

BIBLIOGRAPHY Ferri (1885) 224–25; Giovannoni (1959) I: 21; Burns (1966) 258 nn. 33, 34; 259, fig. 11; Schweikhart (1977) 38, 41 ff.; 75, fig. 94, 83, fig. 125; Tosi (1980) 36 f., no. III.2, fig. 36; Vasori (1981) 88–90, cat. no. 65; Tosi (1983) 92–97, fig. 66; Jobst (1990); Puppi (1986) 101–07, esp. 103; Zavatta (2008) 188; Hemsoll (2014) 282, fig. 16; CensusID 10022379.

U 834A *recto and verso*

Antonio da Sangallo the Younger

Vitruvian scheme for a Latin theater (*recto*).
Sketch of a Latin theater (*verso*). After 1519.

Dimensions 128 × 143 mm.
Technique Pen and black ink, straightedge, compass (recto); pen and black ink, stylus, compass (verso).
Paper Restored in places.
Drawing Scale piedi.

INSCRIPTION, Recto (in the center) *piedi 60 diametro / dell orchestra piedi 120 longha*[?] *proscenio*; *pulpito*; *procenio*; *piedi 120 la sciena / sciena*; (at the edges of the) *schala*; (at the sides of the proscaenium) *itinera*; *ospita / lia, teatro latino*; *valva sive porta regia*; *ospitalia*; *piedi* [*cancelled 31 and other numbers*]

Verso (near the drafted sections of the steps) *Li gradi maggiori sieno / largi piedi 2½ cioe dite 40 / alti dite 22; liminori / largi dita 32 / dite 20; anchora possono sa / re cosi /* [*dita*] *32 /* [*dita*] *22;* [*dita*] *40 /* [*dita*] *20;* (in the center) *pulpito*

The drawing shows a project for a theater in which the measurement of 120 *piedi* is imposed upon the *frons scaenae*. There is also a metric calculation in *piedi* and *dita* for the levels of the seats and a scheme for the inclination of the them. All the elements of the Roman theater, as interpreted by Antonio, are placed according to a Vitruvian geometric scheme for the Latin theater. The *frons scaenae* has five columns on either side and is interrupted by the *pulpitum* (podium). It represents, therefore, an original version of an antique theater, which was proposed possibly contemporaneously or just previously, in a sketchier form, in the theater for the Villa Madama (see U 1072A v.)

The double circumference determines the position of the centers of the first two columns. One side of the triangle is not straight and for this reason has been erased; because of this error it was necessary to make another drawing. The triangle reappears, duly corrected by Giovanni Battista, on U 1378A r.

On the verso, Antonio illustrated the very deep podium, which likewise interrupts the colonnade, which here extends beyond the generating circumference of the Vitruvian- Sangallesque scheme for the theater. At the lower right is a sketch of the *cavea* with the attached levels of seats, possibly to have been built in wood; these were probably meant for dignitaries and they take over a good part of the orchestra. The levels seem to be aligned with the triangle parallel to the *frons scaenae*. The sheet includes the relative measurements of the minor levels (22 × 32) and the major levels (20 × 40), with various solutions. At the lower left, the doors that may have provided access for the actors to the orchestra and stage are drawn in perspective. | ACF

BIBLIOGRAPHY Ferri (1885) 35, 216; Giovannoni (1959) I: 23; Frommel (1974) 175, fig. 85.

U 844A *recto*

Antonio da Sangallo the Younger

Villa Potenza (Macerata), Theater of Helva Ricina, ground plan, after 1520.

Dimensions 575 × 436 mm.
Technique Pen and black ink, straightedge, compass, stylus.
Paper Folded into four; restored.
Drawing Scale *piedi* (50 *piedi* = 68.5 mm).

INSCRIPTION (top, numbered from left to right, 1 to 25); (corresponding to 13) *lo 13 archo gra*[*n*]*de*; (14–15) *archi picholi*; (16–17) *Archi gra*[*n*]*di*; (22–23) *archi picholi*; (24–25) *Archi gra*[*n*]*di*; (below ground plan, to the right) (referring to pilasters of external ambulatory) *Questo Come si passa di la bisognia rimisurarlo apu[n]to p[er]che fu preso alla grossa*; (lower left) *Teatro di ricina*; (bottom, different, later hand) *Disegni antichi di teatro di Recine a presso di macerata.*

In this sheet, Antonio superimposed one of his two versions of the Vitruvian scheme onto the ancient Greek theater, the Helva Ricina. In his first version, one side of the central square is parallel with the *frons scaenae*, following Fra Giocondo's illustration for Vitruvius (Book v); this solution was used by Antonio, for example, in U 1225A, for the Theater of Marcellus in Rome. In the second version, as illustrated here, one corner of the square marks the center of the *frons scaenae* and the opposite corner marks the apex of the semicircumference of the orchestra. In this case, Antonio specified the position of fundamental architectural elements still *in situ* following a geometric rule. Thus, the upper limits of the orchestra and the lower limits of the exedra of the *frons scaenae* are placed in relation to the *valva regia*.

This version of the scheme for the Greek theater, typical of Antonio and never again used by students of Vitruvius, allowed for more space for the proscenium and a more distant placement of the *frons scaenae*. Antonio attempted to respect the arrangement of the surviving parts of the Helva Ricina. In his interpretation, the *cavea* rests on two semicircular sectors subdivided into sevenths, which support and define the *praecintiones* (horizontal, ring-like passages between the levels of seats); and the direction of the stairs follows the corners of the inscribed squares. | ACF

BIBLIOGRAPHY Santoni (1887) 76; Inglieri (1939) 104; Giovannoni (1959) 1: 22; Frommel (1974) 181, fig. 97; Vasori (1981) 90–92, cat. no. 66; CensusID 10071974.

U 853A *recto and verso*

Antonio da Sangallo the Younger

Reconstruction of the Vitruvian stage, ca. 1535–40 (*recto*); Rome, Forum Transitorium, Basilica Julia, hypothetical reconstruction of a forum (*verso*).

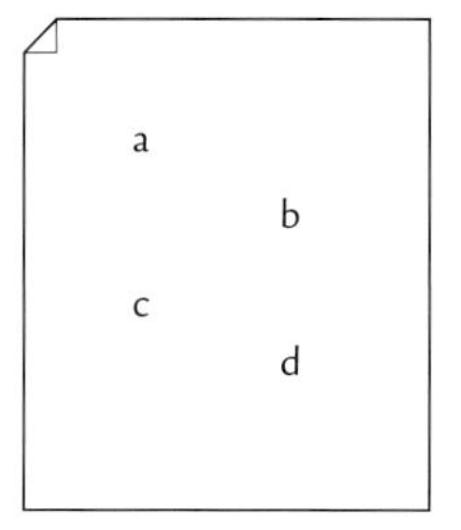

Dimensions 176 × 130 mm.
Technique Pen and brown ink.
Paper New support on left side.

INSCRIPTION, (a) *laula regia e li ospitalia si facevano i[n] sul proscenio quello che noi diciamo el parato e fingevasi una sala e da ogni canto uno ospitio overo camera donde uscivono li recita[n]ti / ed era cosa posticia p[er]che seco[n]do la materia si facieva varia adornamenti come dicie di tre sorte*; (b) *Triangolare machina quale si gira seco[n]do li efetti della comedia p[er]che i[n] ogni facia a varij li efetti cioe i[n] una laparitione delli dei nel atra un altro atto nel altra uno ato*; (c) *foro, aula regia, per ogni asciena, per ogni asciena, orchestra, teatro, machina, magine*; (d) *Del teatro, aula regia, ospitio overo hospitalia, ospitij*

Verso *per foro tra[n]sitorio*; *Basilica Juliana*; *meniana cioe abi / tatione*

U 853A, like 845A and 1094A, can be dated after 1527 on the basis of the handwriting. Antonio's reconstruction of the stage is based on the Italian translation of a passage in Vitruvius's Book v, chapter 7, although not the translation prepared by Fabio Calvo for Raphael (Fontana-Morachiello 1975, pp. 215–16). The covered stage is dominated by the central *aula regia*. The flights of steps of the auditorium lead to the projecting side wings in which the *ospitii* are located. Above the *hospitalia* are *periaktoi*, which facilitate quick scene changes and which Antonio combined with the *deus ex machina*. He was not hampered by topographical or dramatic restrictions here, as he was in the projects of 1531. However, here he interpreted Vitruvius's words "secundum autem spatia" to mean that the stage does not include the *aula regia* and the forum behind it, and that the *hospitalia* are located in the projecting side wings. These are reached by way of doors in the *aula regia*. They have windows in the front and are surmounted by the *periaktoi*.

Since Antonio sketched an Ascension of Christ in one of them, he must have intended the stage for religious performances as well. Both the text and the plan suggests that the *hospitalia* are part of the *periaktoi* and therefore to be turned and outfitted with three different facades. The central stage is constructed with a central perspective—*quello che noi diciamo el parato*—as in Peruzzi and Giovanni Battista da Sangallo. It is impossible to say what is drawn on the side scenes, or what the squiggle in the middle of the background represents. In this drawing Antonio comes close to the theater practice of his time, but not to Vitruvius, and therefore we should ask whether this really is a purely theoretical study.

On the upper half of the verso of this sheet, Antonio reconstructed an ideal, square forum with a double row of columns. His model seems to have been the Greek forum described by Vitruvius in Book v, chapter 1 (see also

Palladio's reconstruction in Palladio 1570, III,, ch. 17). Below, at the right, he attempted an imaginative reconstruction, taking the Forum Transitorium as his point of departure. The front of the temple of Minerva has eight rather than six columns. The "colonnacce" are connected to arcades, behind which are assumed to be the *tabernae* of the Basilica Julia, which of course Antonio would have known only from written sources. At the lower left he sketched the elevation of a facade bay, turning the inhabitable upper story into a *meniana*, an oriel-like balcony, as earlier drawn by Raphael about 1519 for theater sets (see U 242A and 560A). Stylistically, the elevation recalls U 750A, circa 1537, for the Osteria of Castro. | HCD, CLF

BIBLIOGRAPHY Ferri (1885) 130, 216; Frommel (1974); Frommel-Ray-Tafuri (1984) 227–28; CensusID 10081617.

U 854A *verso*

Antonio da Sangallo the Younger

Sketches for moving the Vatican(?) obelisk.

Dimensions 430 × 290 mm.
Technique Pen and light brown ink.
Paper Center fold.

INSCRIPTION *lo peso d 33 dando di tracollo / un tertio della longeza e alzare / li /dua tertij pesa Due terrij pesa d 10 fino alla / pendenzia del trigone de pittagora / e dalli in su pesa posando lo calcio pesa d 20 / a mezo camino pesa d 12 / levandoleo da imo unocapo e laltro presi pero fa d 16*

The sheet is cited by Ferri in the category "Geometry" and does not appear, neither in "obelisks" nor in "St Peter's in the Vatican." The graphs and calculations which are limited on the lower half of the recto refer to the study for the raising of an obelisk. On the left the graph with the segment diveded in three parts and the inclined lines centered on a point coinciding with a third of the length of the segment is explained by the seven lines Antonio wrote at the lower right margin of the sheet. (compare with the drawing at the bottom of the recto, vol. I, 339). The other drawing in plan and elevation at the right may refer to the wooden castle for the erection of the obelisk while the other in axonometry probably visualizes the angle of inclination of the struts of the machine. There is, however no clear indication that the sketches and calculations refer to the preparation for moving the vatican obelisk. | EB

BIBLIOGRAPHY Ferri,81; CensusID 10169553.

U 859A *recto*

Antonio da Sangallo the Younger

Rome, Forum Romanum, aedicule for the statue of Marforio, ca. 1530–40(?).

Dimensions 240 × 160 mm.
Paper Trimmed on four sides.
Technique Pen and brown ink, stylus, straightedge, compass.

INSCRIPTION *p[er] marforio*

The colossal statue of the river god Marforio was one of a number of ancient sculptures known since the Middle Ages (see Bober and Rubinstein 1986, no. 64). Until 1588, it stood in the forum near the arch of Septimius Severus. Antonio's plan was to restore the statue and place it on a socle underneath an arch. Two Doric or Tuscan pilasters support a low triangular pediment, the first version of which was considerably higher. The occasion for giving the figure this monumental setting may have been Charles V's visit to Rome in 1535, at which time the Via Sacra was rebuilt. | HCD

BIBLIOGRAPHY Ferri (1885) 192; Vasari-Milanesi (1878–85) V: 519; Bartoli (1914–22) III: fig. 406, pl. 234; VI: 75; D'Onofrio (1957), fig. 113; Madonna (1980) fig. 67; Bober and Rubinstein (1986) 99; CensusID 10012047.

U 888A *recto and verso*

Antonio da Sangallo the Younger

Ravenna, Tomb of Theodoric, details, ca. 1526.

Dimensions 429 × 420 mm.
Technique Pen and brown ink (recto); pen and two types of brown ink (verso).
Paper Medium weight, folded four times, stains, torn edges, corners restored, repairs.

INSCRIPTION, Recto (top to bottom) *Come sta la porta di sopra di dentro e di fora / e quanto larga e alta e Come sta la faccia / achanto la porta*; *Cosi*; *moza*; *alta pi-9*; *pietre 15 largo dalla / i[m]posta i[n] su*; *i[n] piano*; *Bugnie basse*; *alle i[m] poste e sopra alla / porta da basso se i[n]ginochia / Come sta i[n] disegnio*; *porta da basso larchitrave*

Verso (top right) *come i[n] poste / di volte*; *Le faccie al piano / di sopra*; (center, turned 180 degrees, in different ink) *Schizi di ravenna*; *Fora*; *Stipito della porta / di sopra dentra / e fora*; *dentro*; (lower right, turned 90 degrees) *Li manichi sono 12*; *Di pietra istriana*; *Coperchio*

After Bramante and Giuliano da Sangallo had made surveys of the Tomb of Theodoric in 1506/07 (see Frommel 1994, *Introduction*, 21), Antonio is likely to have made these studies of the Tomb of Theodoric on the spot, while exploring the monument. At the bottom of the sheet he drew a plan, with measurements, of the cruciform-shaped lower chamber. Above this is a view of the arched door at ground level, of which he drew only the upper portion, since the tomb then was buried in the ground approximately to the level of the springing of the arches. At the top right of the sheet he carefully analyzed the complicated profiles of the jamb of the interior door in the upper chamber, which had already engaged him on U 887A r. (see vol. II). Below that, he investigated the form of the exterior door on the upper level, a part of the monument that was then difficult to read, as it was largely obscured by an overhang.

On the verso of U 888A Antonio included more architectural and ornamental details of the Tomb of Theodoric, concentrating on the upper chamber and the monolithic dome. His examination must have been carried out at very close range, since he incorporated precise measurements, for example, for all of the profiles of the moldings beneath the top frieze. From the distribution of the drawings on the sheet, and from the creases, it would seem that he folded the paper into a smaller, manageable format, in order to be able to draw directly on the spot. | SE

BIBLIOGRAPHY Ferri (1885) 120; Giovannoni (1959) I: 22; De Angelis D'Ossat (1959–61) 68, 80, n. 6, fig. 5; Heidenreich-Johannes (1971) 110, 112; Zavatta (2008) 38, 40–1, 46, 51, 53, 66, 150–56, 164, 168, 172, 248; CensusIDs 10011329, 10074657.

U 894A *recto*

Antonio da Sangallo the Younger

Two plans and an elevation for reconstruction of Mausoleum at Halicarnassus, after 1527.

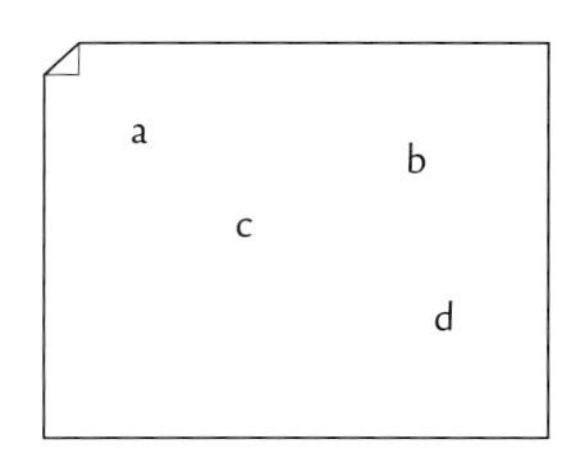

Dimensions 260 × 217 mm.
Technique Pen and brown ink.
Paper Faintly lined, watermark.
Drawing Scale Roman *piedi* (for the reconstruction).

INSCRIPTION *quadriga co'/quattro Cavalli; gradi 24; può farsi così anchora; Mausoleo alto colla piramide/piedi 140/Lo edifitio senza piramide piedi 70/La piramide colla quadriga/piedi 70 In tutto piedi 140/Cinto da 36 Colonne/giro overo circhondo/piedi 511 li fronti sono piedi 73/luna*

This study proposes solutions that had already been explored on sheets U 1039A and U 1040A r. and is a direct consequence of some of the conclusions elaborated on sheet U 1167A r., on which Sangallo established the overall measurements of the building equal to 73 *piedi* for the fronts and 511 *piedi* for the perimeter. The planimetric scheme *a* at the upper left of the present sheet is a simplified version of the articulation shown on the lower part of U 1167A r. (drawing *d*), from which the four fronts with the hexastyle pronaos that define a square deambulatory around the central body have been accurately taken. Lastly, the octagonal cella with four entrances and niches on the diagonals has been taken from the same sheet. A further alternative theory at the upper right (*b*) shows corners recessed by one and fronts with seven intercolumniations.

The central sketch *c* shows an attempt to verify the plan in the upper left corner of the elevation. The building has been drawn slightly foreshortened so as to show the depth of the pronaos, and the relationship between the external colonnade and the internal walls that support the pyramid above. On this sheet, Antonio showed greater confidence over the vertical succession of the different components than in previous drawings (U 1039A, 1040A, 1167A). As the inscription *d* says, the total height of 140 *piedi* is divided into two equal parts of 70 *piedi*, which differs from the dimensions given on U 1039A r., where a subdivision into 65 + 65 *piedi* was suggested, leaving 10 *piedi* for the quadriga. Thus, the lower part of the edifice seems to consist of the repetition of four avant-corps that are very similar to the pronaos on the Pantheon. In conformity with the ancient text, Antonio also showed the quadriga at the top of the pyramid and the four statues on the corners, which reproduce the figures shown on U 1039A r., placed according to the four cardinal points: "Ab oriente celavit Scopas / A septentrione brijaxis / A meridie timotheus / Ab occasu Leocares."

The lower part of this elevation appears to have been inspired by ancient edifices well known to Antonio, the Pantheon in particular, and he seems to have abandoned his more imaginative and uncertain hypotheses, such as the spiral top with a truncated pyramid shown in sketch on sheet U 1040A r. | VZ

BIBLIOGRAPHY Ferri (1885) 39, 97; Giovannoni (1959) I: 11, 24; Burns-Oberhuber (1984) 430; Valtieri (1986) fig. 7; Raub (2014) 180, fig. 10; Fane-Saunders (2016) 266–67; CensusID 10074661.

U 896A *recto*

Antonio da Sangallo the Younger

Rome, Forum Romanum, Curia with adjacent buildings, ca. 1522/23.

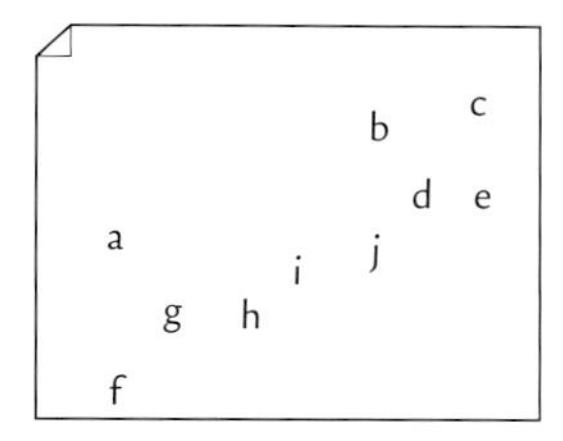

Dimensions 347 × 476 mm.
Technique Pen and brown ink, stylus, straightedge, compass.
Paper Heavy, folds, repairs on verso
Drawing Scale palmi (30 *palmi* = 31.5 mm).

INSCRIPTION, Recto (a) *Marforio*; (b, turned 90 degrees) *foro di s[an] basilio*; (b, turned 180 degrees) *questa porta saliva tre gradi duno/palmo luno avolere andare al foro/transitorio quali erano molti logori/qua[n]do si chavorno tanto vi sera caminato/sopra si che si vede che questa era una/delle entrate pri[n]cipale di questo foro/e dal piano di questa paza fino alla/cima dell archo di q[ue]sta entrata si e/palmi 31*; (c, turned 90 degrees) *Dal disopra delle cornicie/che sono alle i[m]poste di questo archone sino al piano/si e palmi 22 e p[er] e[n]trare di questo/foro i[n] quello di s[an] basilio si smonta/tre gradi duno palmo luno*; *Foro Transitorio*; (d, turned 90 degrees) *di qua ci era larchitrave solo*; *Da questa banda ci era architrave fregio chornicie*; (e) *piano del foro/transitorio*; *piano del foro/di s[an] basilio*; (f) *Marforio*; (g) *orto*; (h) *S[anta] martina ed e a[n]ti/cha qui erono i[n] torno/dentro le storie gra[n]de de/sono nel chortile di cha[m]/pidoglio quale sono/di marmo*; (h, turned 90 degrees) *Tevertini*; *Maestrali a gradi 2*; *Tevertini*; *questo e uno archo/grande aperto/va fino al tetti*; (i) *fodera di mattoni/Tufi e tevertino*; (j) *moderna*; (below this) *Le cholonne sono/modername[n]te/misse no[n] ci era/i[n] mezo niente anti/camente li pilastri/sono corinti antichi di fo/dere e fralli pilastri/e foderato di marmi/porfidi serpe[n]tini pe/zi grandi riquadrati/di piu sorte*; *S[ant]* ADRIANO; (below this) *Qui e la porta di metallo/bella*

Verso *Sa[n]to Basilio e foro di nerva e altri cose circu[m]sta[n]te*

The drawing shows the ground plans of the Church of S. Martina and that of S. Adriano, the latter housed in the ancient Curia, together with the location of the Marforio sculpture at the left, and the intersection of the Curia with the Forum of Caesar and the Forum Transitorium, also drawn in elevation, at the right. Antonio's preliminary studies for this drawing appear on U 1299A r. and 1143A r. A comparable plan of the area by Baldassarre Peruzzi appears on U 625A.

Antonio's drawing is significant for its degree of descriptive detail. He devoted much attention to the junction between the Curia and the two adjacent imperial forums. Using a cut-away section drawn in perspective, he elaborated at the right the archways connecting the Forum Transitorium with the Forum of Caesar, which he identified as the Foro di S. Basilio. He described the surviving entablature elements (*c, d*) and noted the difference in ground level between the two spaces. From the degree of wear he observed on the steps, he determined that this had been the principal entrance to the Forum Transitorium (*c*).

Antonio included a series of columns behind S. Adriano that may relate, in part, to the colonnade of the Forum of Julius Caesar. In contrast to the columns marking the passage from the Forum Transitorium, drawn with the aid of a compass, he drew these freehand and then crossed them out. The suggestion of a portico to the rear of the ancient structure may reflect his interpretation of the actual colonnade of the Forum of Caesar, which he did not otherwise include, or instead may have been a proposal for reconfiguring the rear of the church. Krautheimer considered this study to be an idealized reconstruction of S. Martina and the area surrounding it, rather than an actual survey. More recently, Viscogliosi proposed that the drawing accurately depicts the entrance wall of S. Martina and that it offers important evidence for two of the original four piers of the now-lost Arch of Marcus Aurelius.

The reference to "le storie gran[d]e" (*h*) offers a date for the drawing, as these three marble relief panels of Marcus Aurelius were moved from S. Martina to the Campidoglio in 1515. Antonio's handwriting suggests a date before 1527, but the drawing likely dates to after the death of Raphael when Antonio collaborated with Peruzzi, possibly around 1522/23, in the pontificate of Hadrian VI. Inclusion of the colossal statue known as Marforio does not help in dating the drawing, since the statue had been known from the twelfth century and remained near the Arch of Septimius Severus until 1588.

The drawing demonstrates Antonio's particular interest in the materials used in ancient buildings. This is evident in his notes concerning the "tevertini," "mattoni," and "tufi" elements of the walls of S. Martina and S. Adriano (*h, i*) and the interior marble revetment and bronze door of S. Adriano (*j*).

Notations such as "Maestrali a gradi 2" (*h*) and the abbreviations for the winds ("L," "M," and "S" surrounding the "orto" at the lower left) indicate that he surveyed the area with a compass, following the method outlined by Raphael in his Letter to Pope Leo X. | ACH

BIBLIOGRAPHY Ferri (1885) 134, 147, 165, 166, 192; Bartoli (1914–22) III: fig. 457, pl. 272; VI: 85; Krautheimer-Corbett-Frankl (1937–77) III: 84–85; Haskell-Penny (1981) 255–59, nos 56–57; Günther (1988) 254, 277–78, 280; Frommel (1994, *Introduction*) 36; Tessari (1995) 109–11; Viscogliosi (2000) 21–38, 105–08, 250–52, cat. no. 3, pl 2, 4, 5, 6; Viscogliosi (2017) 101, 104–05, fig. 2.; CensusID 237564.

U 900A *recto*

Antonio da Sangallo the Younger

Sketches of plans ancient edifices in the Horti Variani, architectural details, and land cultivated as an orchard, ca. 1525.

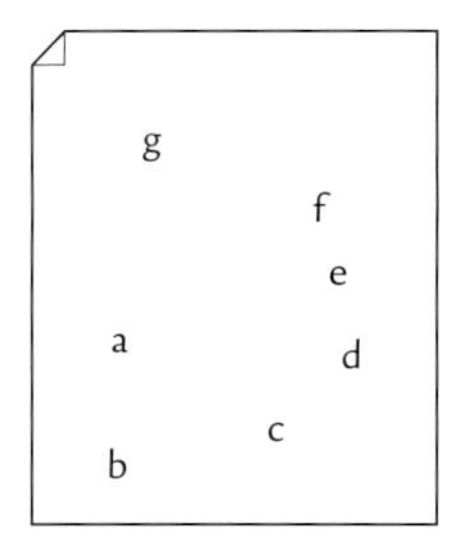

Dimensions 434 × 284 mm.
Technique Pen and ink, freehand.
Paper Lightweight, center fold, trimmed at left and top (once part of a sketchbook?).

INSCRIPTION (Numbered top right) *587*; (near fold at left center) *464* (referred to by Milanesi in Vasari-Milanesi 1878–85) (a) *queste cose sono fu[o]ra di porta maiore / p[er] la strada achanto li aquidotti i [un] miglio / fuora della porta*; (inside plan, above annotation) *strada / crociera / a schifo / schop[er]to*; (b) *posesione*; *Lo quadro e uiuo da pie / partito i[n] quattro e sei e cholli agietti dalluna / facietta allaltra sie qua[n]to / e grosa dua volte da pie ne / l uiuo la cholonna alta sanza / la cimasa qua[n]to da pie ne / l uiuo*; (c) (inside plan) *Conserua daqua apreso alle forme / fuora di porta magiore uno miglio*; various measurements; (under plan) *sono palmi e capelle 7 i[n]tere / i[n] questa facia e dua meze i[n] / sucantoni*; *Capelle 6 i[n] tere e due / meze in sucantoni*; (d) (inside plan) *tabernacholi / capelle*; (e) *grosso p[almi] 4 i[n] circa / lobelischo e fuora di porta / maiore i [uno] mezo miglio apresi li aquidottoduo tiri / di mano i[n] uno circho nauale quale dalla banda delli aquido / ti diuerso la porta di S j[ov]annj / nelle uignia di mes[ser] / di mes[ser] girolamo / milanese che ci lauo / ra rugieri scharpe / llino*; *lungi tutti edue li pezi i[n]sieme canne tre i[n] circa*; (f) *cose piantate alla vigna, 54 prungi damasceni / del reame, 8 prungi i[n] pisi, 14 grisomoli e dua datteri quali anno questo / contrasegnio * / 8 persichi*; (g) *i[n] chostantinopoli e una piaza lunga qua[n]to / nauona doue sono colonne i[n]torno a dua a dua / chome apare i[n] disegnio grose quanto quelle di santo / pietro piu presto piu grosse edanno sopra li architraui e chornicie / e fatto uno piano cholli parapetti da ogni banda / i[n] mezo ello belischo e questa piaza e i[n]anzi al palatio dello i[m] peratore / e sta i[n] una chosta come sta a roma / s [an] piero a mo[n]torio quale piaza / e palatio uede tutto chostantinopoli / chome san pietro a montorio uede roma*; (inside plan) *obelischo / palatio i[m]peri/ale*

The sketches are all of different subjects and have been executed using each of the four sides of the folded sheet. The copious annotations therefore run in the same direction of the drawings they illustrate. All the drawings, both on the recto and verso of U 900A, are attributed in their entirety to Antonio the Younger.

The recto of the sheet has been used for summary information concerning a series of ancient buildings, almost all standing in the Roman countryside, outside the city walls, near Porta Maggiore. As already correctly identified by Lanciani and by Bartoli, this was the site of the Horti Variani during the Roman Empire. Among the findings, the obelisk dedicated by Hadrian to Antinous, broken into two fragments, is immediately recognizable (*e*). Heliogabalus probably took it there as an ornament for the *spina* of his circus, having removed it from its uncertain original location on the tomb or cenotaph of Antinous.

In the mid-sixteenth century, substantial remains of the circus were still visible; this is attested to by Andrea Fulvio, Bufalini's 1551 map of Rome, and the perspectival reconstructive view by Pirro Ligorio, also 1551, in which the obelisk is shown whole and upright in the middle of the *spina*. Antonio was mainly interested in the dimensions of the piece; in fact, he wrote down the measurements of the base (approximately 4 *palmi* = 0.8963 m) and the overall height (approximately 3 *canne* = 6.702 m). The note contains other information relating to the original monument (classified as a "naval circus" and clearly regarded as suitable for the display of *naumachia*, possibly because of its proximity to the aqueduct and the reservoir); the location of the site (half a mile, that is, approximately 750 meters outside the Porta Maggiore; 1 mile = 1497.98 m); the agricultural nature of the area at the time (vineyard); who it belonged to ("Girolamo milanese"); and how it was being used ("Rugiero scarpellino" was working there).

The agricultural nature of the area seems to be directly related to the drawing on the right of the obelisk, on the other side of the page fold (*f*). This shows the layout of fruit trees, which Antonio noted had been "planted with vines," possibly the same ones that belonged to Girolamo Milanese, perhaps an allotment not too far from properties belonging or in usufruct to Sangallo.

At least three of the other subjects illustrated belonged to the area described above, which suggests that they were all sketched at the same time. The plan at the left of the obelisk is for an unidentified building, a small a mausoleum, summarily surveyed by Antonio and lacking measurements and details. The structure is composed of two circular spaces. The main one, labeled "capella," is the larger of the two, and has six radiating chapels and two rooms on an axis, at the entrance and the passage to the second room respectively. The one labeled "tabernacholo" is smaller, and has five niches along the internal perimeter. The two circular halls are preceded by a sort of pronaos on a rectangular plan, the short sides turned into semicircular niches. The external elevation was to have pilasters and niches at the sides and two freestanding columns in the central part to articulate three wide openings. This is probably the same building that appears in two drawings attributed to Sallustio Peruzzi: a measured drawing made on site (U 670A) and a fair copy (U 669A) (see Bartoli 1914–22, VI: 122, figs 690, 689), and in one of the plates in Book III of Sebastiano Serlio's treatise (1540, Book III, ch. 4, pp. 30, 31).

The identity of the buildings drawn by Antonio and by Sallustio Peruzzi is confirmed by the notes made by the latter on sheet U 669A r., which agree with those made by Antonio both in terms of the overall location of the remains and as regards the toponym "le forme" (which probably refers to the aqueduct) that appears on this sheet, U 900A r., next to the drawing at lower right (*c*). The plan of the reservoir, whose remains had already been identified by Lanciani (1897, p. 349), is a type of parallelepiped block, hollowed out on the exterior for the semicylindrical spaces of the niches that provided increased resistance against the thrust of the waters inside; this plan is quite common and is also documented by other sixteenth-century drawings (see, for example, U 1430A r., attributed to Giovanni Battista da Sangallo). Antonio took the time to painstakingly record the measurements of the structure; he also seems to have been interested in the articulation of the external surface of the walls, achieved through the regular succession of niches, and the corner solution, which again involved a connection with a niche with a quarter circle base.

The two drawings at the bottom of the left half of the sheet remain unidentified (*a*, *b*). Sketch *a* is a plan of a building that might still have been in use, since Antonio drew the type of covering used for the two main rooms. In sequence along the same axis are an atrium or *sala*, of square proportions, directly overlooking an unspecified road, and an oval *salone*, with a cross vault and a coved vault respectively. After these comes a long rectangular room, in the first part of which the longitudinal walls are articulated by seven transversal partitions followed by an uncovered space, also of square proportions. Here, Antonio seems to have been primarily interested in the orderly, balanced layout of the rooms along the entry axis leading from the *strada* outside the first *sala* to the *schoperto* at the back, which can be interpreted as a green area or a garden, and it could be related to his studies of ancient houses. Sketch *b*, with its annotation, represents the orthographic projection (*projectione*) from above the abacus of a presumably Corinthian capital at the top of a column or pier with a square base. As well as clarifying the kind of representation he had recourse to, Antonio's notes illustrate the proportions of this element, and he also made a graphic subdivision into modules of the *grossezza* (diameter or side) in plan form.

At the top left of the sheet is a representation of the only non-Roman structure, probably drawn from travel notes or from memory (see U 1218A in this volume) (*g*). This is the Imperial Palace in Constantinople, drawn in plan and accompanied by a long explanatory note. The drawing is not a faithful survey, but should be interpreted as a free re-elaboration of the Hippodrome in Constantinople and the Imperial buildings that looked onto it. Given its obvious formal analogies, as annotated by Antonio, the drawing has been related to the project for the Medici palace on Piazza Navona, drawn up by Giuliano da Sangallo, and bears witness to the fact that, even post-1516, the concept of a construction of this kind had not been abandoned altogether (Bentivoglio 1972, pp. 172–204; Tafuri 1984, *Roma instaurata*, p. 85). Around 1515 Antonio designed an alternative project for Palazzo Medici-Madama, which likewise stretched to Piazza Navona. After 1517, however, the enlargement of Palazzo Madama was no longer an issue.

On U 1218A r. Antonio analyzed details of buildings in Constantinople, using it to note down various facts relating to: the obelisk, presumably the same one that stood in the middle of the square, in front of the Imperial Palace, as here on U 900A r.; the historiated column in the same city; the basilica and convent of Hagia Sophia. The original information could have come from an unidentified traveler from Genoa in the service of the Medici, who returned to Italy in 1521. This theory would confirm a dating of after 1521 for the execution of U 900A r., close to the date of 1525 suggested by Lanciani, although without the benefit of any supporting evidence. | RB

BIBLIOGRAPHY Vasari-Milanesi (1878–85) V: 497; Ferri (1885) 37, 122, 163, 177; Giovannoni (1958) I: 22, 58; Lanciani (1902–12) III: 165; Bartoli (1914–22) III: fig. 467, pl. 282; VI: 87; Bentivoglio (1972) 196–204; Tafuri (1984, *Roma instaurata*) 85; CensusID 10034052.

U 903A *recto*

Antonio da Sangallo the Younger

Rendering of Vitruvius's passages on the fronts of systyle and diasystle Doric temples, seven reconstructions of Doric friezes with cornices, before 1520.

Dimensions 238 × 430 mm.
Technique Pen and brown ink, straightedge, compass, freehand.
Paper Trimmed on all four sides, hole at center, fold at center and in middle of right side.

INSCRIPTION (Antonio's hand) (top center) *Riprove de vetruvij*; (top left) *in xxxxiiii / Fra giochondo / la metofa viene / larga quanto le alto col chapittello / del tigrifo che chorre lo tigrifo uno modulo emezo senza lo chapitello*; (referring to top frieze) (in circle at left, diameter 17 mm) *colonna moduli 2*; *in xxxv / lo vechio*; (in circle at right, diameter 23.5 mm) *moduli 2*; (referring to second frieze from top) (in circle at left, diameter 17 mm) *moduli 2*; *in xxviii*; (at right, on first architrave from top, but referring to frieze below it) *in xxviii*; (in circle at right, diameter 18 mm) *moduli 2*; (referring to third frieze from top) (in circle at left, 15.5 mm) *moduli 2*; *in xxxv*; *in xxix* (in circle at right, diameter 19 mm) *moduli 2*; (referring to bottom frieze) (in circle at left, 15.5 mm) *moduli 2*; *in xxiii*; *in xviii* (in circle at right) *2 moduli*

On this sheet, Antonio drew some "double-checks" to graphically verify the different measurements proposed in two readings of passages from Vitruvius on the modular construction of Doric temples with fronts with four and six columns and with diastyle and systyle colonnades (*De Architectura* Book iv, ch. 3, 3; 3, 7). This explains why, on the right side of the drawing, he drew half the widths of friezes for temples with fronts of four or six columns and diastyle colonnades (the top two) and systyle colonnades (the bottom two) according to specific numbers of modules, prescribed in numerous manuscripts and in the first three printed editions of the treatise: 28 and 32 for the diastyle, 18 and 29 for the systyle. The small circles each represent two modules, which Antonio used to determine the length of the entablature in the respective drawings. On the left side, however, he adhered to the numbers given in Fra Giocondo's 1511 edition (fols 36 v. and 37 v.) amended by the latter after he had compared the excerpts on the width of systyle and diastyle intercolumniations with other passages from Vitruvius: xxviii and xxxxiiii for the diastyles and xxiii and xxxv for the systyles. The second solution from the top is the only continuous drawing that goes from left to right, because both Giocondo and the previous editions agree on 28 modules for the diastyle with four columns. The same numbers as in the 1511 edition reappear in Giocondo's 1513 edition, as well as in Durantino's (which cites Giocondo in any case), both of which Antonio possessed.

Neither the versions drawn on the left nor those on the right seem to have proved satisfactory for Antonio, because he failed to achieve square metopes one-and-a-half modules wide, as prescribed by Vitruvius, as is particularly evident in the systyle drawings at the bottom. Antonio must have been working out the articulation of the frieze in line with Vitruvius, and came up with a third solution (U 1174 v.), in which the systyle tetrastyle measures 19.5 modules and the hexastyle 29.5 modules, as in the later version published by Pilandrier that has been accepted in modern editions. | PNP

BIBLIOGRAPHY Ferri (1885) xl; Giovannoni (1959) i: 67; Günther (1988) 256; Pagliara (1988) 190.

U 911A *recto*

Antonio da Sangallo the Younger

Rome, profiles of Hadrian's Mausoleum, the base of Trajan's Column, and others, ca. 1526.

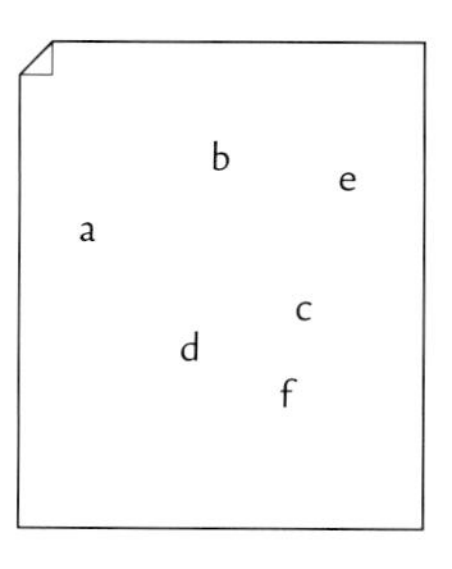

Dimensions 289 × 190 mm.
Technique Pen and brown ink.
Paper Lightweight, trimmed on three sides, traces of old glue.

INSCRIPTION (a) *Di castello s[an]to / angelo dello anticho*; (b) *lo palmo in 16*; *lo qu[...]a 20 / lo interno 10*; (e) *colonna istoriata*; (f) *Della colo / nna stori / ata / a braccia / di minuti / 60 per brazo*

The drawing shows a profile of the socle of the base of Hadrian's Mausoleum inside the fortified Renaissance walls of Castel Sant'Angelo (*a*); the base of a column on a pedestal (*b*); the profile of a pedestal (*c*); the sketch of an Attic base (*d*); the profile of a cornice (*e*); and the profile of the base of Trajan's Column (*f*). As profile (*e*) does not correspond to the moldings of Trajan's Column, it may be an attempt to reconstruct the profile of the crowning capital. Another drawing by Antonio of the same column, which is described as "historiated" because of the carved bas-reliefs on the shaft that tell the stories of Trajan's exploits, can be found on sheet U 1153A verso. | AGG

BIBLIOGRAPHY Ferri (1885) 128; CensusID 10037786.

U 913A *recto and verso*

Antonio da Sangallo the Younger

Studies of antique decorations
and architectural details.

Dimensions 323 × 238 mm.
Technique Pen and brown ink, freehand.
Paper Lightweight, folded, reinforcements on verso.

INSCRIPTION, Recto (*b–d*) *alle terme che son de fora/presso alla dogana/dove stava mess. marchi/da pistoia*

There are five drawings on the recto: (*a*) detail of a decoration with grotesques, perhaps from an antique relief; (*b*) schematic drawing of a composite capital; (*c, d*) profile of the abacus, and details, with measurements, of the profile of the echinus and abacus of the same capital; (*e*) study of a baluster (drawn with the sheet turned 90 degrees counterclockwise).

These sketches of an antique capital, perhaps from the Baths of Caracalla, can be connected with Antonio's interest in the Composite order. More difficult to identify is the work for which Antonio was designing the balustrade: he made a quick drawing of one baluster, inspired by Bramante's designs, and studied the profile of the cornice.

The verso shows a hatched drawing of the capital drawn on the recto. It is similar to that of Old St Peter's found on U 32A. Although it lacks the wealth of decorative details, it corresponds to a type that is in a certain sense canonical in ancient Roman architecture. | AGG

BIBLIOGRAPHY Ferri (1885) 161, 201; CensusIDs 10042176, 10042180.

U 915A *recto and verso*

Antonio da Sangallo the Younger

Survey of hemicycle of Naumachia of Domitian in Campus Martius, partial plan of building with two colonnaded courtyards, partial surveys in plan of buildings, probably for Villa Medici-Madama, 1519. (*a*) Position of the hemicycle of the Naumachia of Domitian in the Campus Martius with respect to the streets of the Campus Martius (via Flaminia, via Ripetta). (*b*) Survey of the plan of the hemicycle of the Naumachia of Domitian. (*c*) Detail of (*b*) in a larger scale. (*d*) Elevation of *c*. (*e*) Measurements at an unknown construction site. (*f*) Ramps and beginning of the street behind the theatre (Villa Medici-Madama theatre?). (*g*) Partial plan of a building with two colonnaded courtyards.

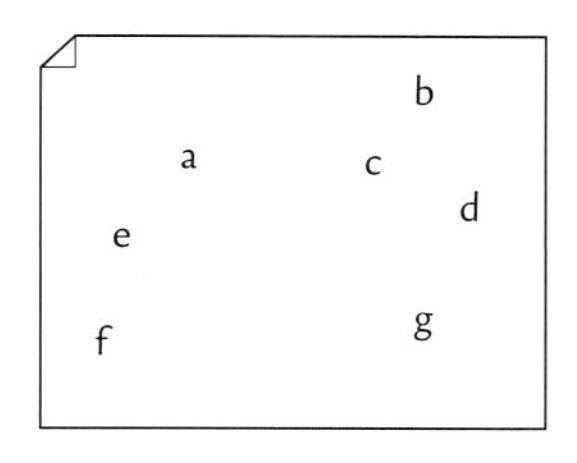

Dimensions 235 × 340 mm.
Technique Pen and brown ink, black chalk, freehand.
Paper Heavy, yellowed, stains, originally folded in half vertically, then horizontally, and again vertically.
Drawing Scale Roman *palmi*.

INSCRIPTION (Antonio's hand) (a) *quanti tabernacholi alo emicichlo e chosi/quanti ne uedirti qua[n]ti tondi/qua[n]ti quadri*/(on base line of exedra) *M 8 Concheuento*; (along the Corso) *Ma 9 strada flaminia Conche uento/Strada* (in different ink, turned 180 degrees) *Sciavona/strada noua Chon[c]he/uento*/(on diverging line) *Casa nostra po 1½*; (f) *Lastrada*

H. Günther (1988), M. Tafuri (1992), and A. Moneti (1993) misidentified the sketches *a–d* as surveys of the exedra of the Horti Aciliorum on the Pincio. Instead, the drawings refer to another exedra below the hill, which, as *a* shows, lay along the hillside on the axis of the present-day Via di S. Giacomo at the foot of the Pincio. When Antonio prepared the sheet for the surveys, noting several times "Con che uento" ("with which wind?" = "which direction of the wind rose?"), he folded it so that the verso was on the inside. When he was on site doing the survey he entered the orientations (in a different ink): for the base line of the exedra, "M 8" = maestro 8 degrees; for the line of the Corso

("Strada flaminia"), "Ma 9" = maestro 9 degrees. For Via Ripetta ("strada noua") he indicates the slightly diverging line of his own house: "Chasa nostra po 1½" = ponente 1½ degrees (for the position of the Sangallo house, see Zanchettin 2003–4). The three lines connecting the Strada Nuova and Via Flaminia could indicate the three crossroads perhaps planned and laid out by Antonio. The name Schiavonia is written upside down and in a different ink with respect to the inscription "Strada"; this could mean that it is no more than a general topographic indication, such as "on this side is the zone of the Slavs, on the other the street." To determine the position of the central axis of the exedra Antonio takes a point from the first street, the present-day Via Canova, that is 53½ *palmi* north along the "strada flaminia," and lays out the central axis at a slightly different angle. The distance corresponds to the 12-meter difference in alignment between the Via di S. Giacomo and the Via Canova, so that the axis of the exedra coincides with the former street.

The sketches *b* and *c* on the right side of the folded sheet relate to the plan of the exedra: it was 187 *palmi* wide and only 32 *palmi* deep (41.77 m by 7.15 m). It had alternating semicircular and square niches. Columns stood in front of the wall between the niches. In the elevation *d*, Antonio reconstructed the exedra as two-storied, with statues placed on top of these columns. He does not identify the "emicichlo"; his concern is with the location, the survey of the remains, and the resulting reconstruction of the building.

On Pirro Ligorio's plan of ancient Rome we see that he identified the architecture as the Naumachia of Domitian, about which Flavio Biondo had written already in 1446: "Vestigia (scil. Naumachiae Domitianae) extant certissima vineis tecta inter flamineam uiam et collem nunc Pincianum ad ipsum Sancti Sylvestri monasterium pertinentia" (Roma Instaurata, Verona 1481, lib. II, XIII). Ligorio reconstructed the imperial loggia of the *naumachia* as a two-story exedra, standing in front of the hillside of the collis hortulorum. On Falda's plan of 1676 we see, in a garden on Via Margutta, an arcade along the hillside with the inscription, "Vestigie della Naumachia di Domitiano hoggi Orto di Napoli"—possibly part of the ruins sketched by Antonio da Sangallo.

Sketch *e* is a survey of a building site, probably a little street with column in the middle (via delle Colonnette in Campo Marzio?). The same color ink and the same ductus as in the sketch *f* suggest that it, too, relates to measurements and drawings done on the site of Villa Medici-Madama, although it is not possible to say specifically which parts were being surveyed. Drawing *f* is a survey of a building similar to the beginning of the ramp and of the "strada" behind the theater of Villa Medici-Madama, a sketch done on site on the sheet that had been folded three times. This survey relates to those on U 1228A r. and v., which are then used in the planning of the villa on U 179A r. and U 1518A r. It can thus be dated about 1518–19, in any case before the large design U 314A r. of the whole layout, which is to be dated 1519 (see vol. II, pp. 137–38).

Sketch *g* is a freehand drawing in black chalk of the plan of a palace with the colonnaded courtyards, probably the first made on the right half of the sheet when it was initially folded.

The drawing drawing on the verso is the result of a survey done on site of land belonging to the hospital of S. Giacomo degli Incurabili in Rome, measured by Giovanni Battista da Sangallo. Antonio the Younger subsequently added the lines of the street, measured with the compass and indicated with wind directions. The drawing reveals the irregularities of the frontage on via Lata (today via del Corso), which follow a line broken into three segments oriented north-south (*scirocco*). The long straight side running east-west, indicated with *G 15* (*grecale* 15 degrees), coincides with the crossroad (today via Canova) joining present-day Via di Ripetta with Via Lata. Along this street are marked the position of the old hospital of S. Giacomo and that of the new wing, "spidale novo," on which construction began in 1515, following the project of Giorgio da Coltre. This wing was subsequently extended toward Via di Ripetta with an octagonal room, later transformed into the present church. S. Maria Porta Paradisi (see U 1891A r. and v. in vol. II). The long, straight side oriented "Ponente 6" corresponds to the street connecting via Lata with the zone of the port of Ripetta, before it was straightened as far as the Porta del Popolo. The presence of the small square sector jutting out from the trapezoidal shape of the main piece of land makes it possible to date the drawing after 1519, when that part of the street—thereafter called "Leonina"—was straightened and the old street was closed. The survey is therefore very likely the basis for the major unrealized projects for San Giacomo degli Incurabili of Sangallo (U 578A r., 870A r., 871A r., 872A r.) and Peruzzi (U 577A r., Wurm [1984] 252). | F-EK, VZ

BIBLIOGRAPHY Günther (1985) 277; Günther (1988) 57; Tafuri (1992) 135, n. 68; Moneti (1993); Günther (1994, *Urban planning*) 547; Zanchettin (2003–04) 241; Keller (1996) 116 n. 32; Zanchettin (2003–4); Modonutti (2014); CensusID 10034043.

U 917A *recto and verso*

Antonio da Sangallo the Younger

Villa Potenza (Macerata), plan for
Theater at Helvia Ricina, 1530ies

Dimensions 218 × 278 mm.
Technique Pen and black ink, drawn freehand.
Paper Stained, restored.
Drawing Scale Roman *piede.*

INSCRIPTION, Recto *sodo 9* [...]/ *13* [...]/ *17* [...]/ *22* [...]; *archi 5*; *teatro di recine misurato apiedi a*[*n*]*tichi* / *ma ditto piede fu fatto acaso quale sie* / *lo*[*n*]*go Dita 34 cioè D 34 li dui piedi* / [...] *tondo 36* [...]/ *Lartiglieria di civitavecchia* / *fu misurata colpiede giusto*

This on-site study is of an interesting *frons scaena*, articulated with a central exedra and large rectangular spaces decorated with small rectangular and semicircular niches, of which only the left side is visible. The stage building is set quite far from the diameter of the orchestra and this is probably the main reason why Antonio began a reconstruction of the plan of the theater on U 844A, based on Vitruvius's scheme for Greek theaters, which remained unfinished: he used the version in which the square that determines the positioning of the *scaena frons* is shown at an angle. One particularly interesting detail is the series of columns that encircle the ambulatory and run along the stage building; this is a solution that, if interpreted literally, would be unusual, not to say unique, among drawings of theatrical subjects by Antonio. A possible alternative would be to read the sign of a small circle that conventionally alludes to the diameter of the column as indicating a pier, which would then mean that this was a schematization of the piers of fornices. Sangallo may have made the drawing when working in Loreto in the early 1530s.

On the verso is a hasty sketch of a scheme for a Greek theater. No further calculations or inscriptions are given. | ACF

BIBLIOGRAPHY Alfieri (1936) 1–21; Giovannoni (1959) 1: 22; Vasori (1981) 92–3, cat. no. 67; CensusID 10042190.

U 919A *recto and verso*

Antonio da Sangallo the Younger (*recto*) and Giovan Francesco da Sangallo (*verso*)

Rome, studies after ancient profiles,
probably before 1527.

Dimensions 169 × 111 mm.
Technique Pen and brown ink, freehand.
Paper Heavy, folded, trimmed on four sides, stained, glued.
Drawing Scale braccio.

INSCRIPTION, Recto *Sa*[*n*]*lorenzo delli Spetiali*; (repeated below in a later hand)

Verso *b*[*raccio*] *1 m*[*inut*]*i 45½*

The sheet shows a section through the marble revetment in the socle zone of the Temple of Antoninus and Faustina in the Forum Romanum. The cella of the temple erected in AD 141 by Emperor Antoninus Pius in memory of his deceased wife Anna Galeria Faustina was later converted into a church, presumably in the seventh or eighth century; it is documented since 1192 under its still common name of San Lorenzo in Miranda. In 1430 Martin V presented the church to the guild of apothecaries and herb dealers, whence the designation "degli Speziali."

The Temple of Antoninus and Faustina was among the more frequently studied ancient buildings of Rome. This is attested not only by the surveys of the Sangallo circle (U 1166A r. and v., 1654A v. / 3972A r.) but by those of other architects among whom Peruzzi (U 1535A v. and U 1539A, among others) and Palladio (IV, 9). The recto shows a section through the main socle of the, whose height corresponds approximately to that of the lower third of the columns of the pronaos, and through the *plutei* of the latter. The heights indicated pertain to the larger units: 7 *braccia* for the height of the socle itself; 3½ *braccia* for that of the *plutei*, of which 1 *braccio* 16 *minuti* is for the profile of its Attic base. Evidently Antonio was less precise here, for a comparison with other drawings (U 1535A v., 1166A v., 1654A v. / 3972A r.) shows that plate and apotheosis, which are excluded in this sketch, should however be included in the calculation of the base height. The number "48" at the upper edge of the attic can only refer to *minuti*, but this measurement cannot be corroborated by any comparable drawing (not even in Peruzzi's very precise survey U 1535A v.). The height written above the cornice of the attic should probably be read as "18–14" and understood as *braccia*; it evidently refers to the height of the wall up to the attic of the pronaos order (see U 1166A v., where this measurement is given as 35¾ feet, or about 18.3 *braccia*).

On the verso are sections through the base and cornice of the socle are to be found. The given heights indicate the use of an ancient foot of 32 *minuti*, as is evident from a comparison with other drawings (in particular U 1166A v. and U 1654A v./U 3972A r., measured in ancient *digiti*, and U 1535A v. by Peruzzi, measured in Roman *palmi*). Next to the individual measurements a summation of 1 *braccio* 45½ *minuti* is given as a check (this *minuto*, as on the recto, corresponds to 1/60 of a *braccio*, an invented measurement not infrequently used at the beginning of the Cinquecento, and one that closely approximated the *minuto* of 1/32 of a foot). The use of a *minuto* measuring 1/32 of a foot on the verso makes it probable that this drawing at least, or its model, was among the surveys made in the circle of the so-called Master C, whom Günther has identified as Riniero Neruccio da Pisa. The model, according to Günther, would then have been made in 1515 or the following years.

Based on the characteristic writing of the numbers (especially the 3), the verso can tentatively be attributed to Giovan Francesco da Sangallo, while the recto, as the inscription shows, is probably by Antonio the Younger himself. Because the unit of measurement is the *braccio*, which according to Frommel is no longer encountered after the Sack of Rome, the drawing was probably made before 1527. | JN

BIBLIOGRAPHY Ferri (1885) 142, 193; CensusIDs 10043279, 10043880.

U 930A *recto and verso*

Circle of Antonio da Sangallo the Younger (Antonio Labacco?)

Rome, Theater of Marcellus and Arch of Septimius Severus, measured details, after 1520.

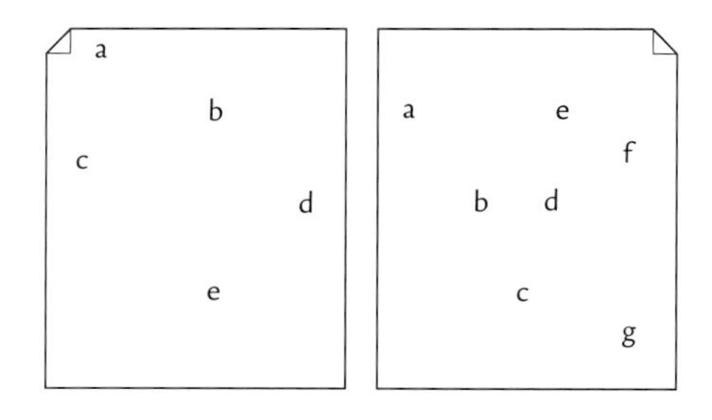

Dimensions 439 × 291 mm.
Technique Pen and black ink, straightedge, compass.
Paper Creased, stained, and restored.
Drawing Scale braccia.

Inscriptions, Recto: (left) *quadri sette egli altri quadri 15*

Verso (Top left) *Delarcho dinanzi piccolo*; (center) *Delarcho dilatio*[...(?)]; *settimio*; *membretto, delarcho didentro*; (bottom right) *architrave che gira intorno alarcho magiore*

The drawing in the lower half of the recto (*e*) is a schematic study of a section of intermediate superimposed orders enclosing three barrel vaults; these may have belonged to the ambulatory of the Theater of Marcellus, which was in a partly buried state and therefore not wholly visible, or they may have been arches belonging to a portico clearly inspired by the Theatre of Marcellus. The three column shafts are, however, incomplete: the base of the Doric order is missing, whereas only the pedestal and the base of the Ionic order above it can be seen, the shafts only partly drawn. No measurements are provided and the purpose of the study seems simply to focus on the articulation of the vaults, the Doric order, the frieze with its triglyphs, and the other architectonic members. During the Renaissance, interest in the Theater of Marcellus chiefly revolved around the architectonic orders: from Giovanni Monsignori, also known as Fra Giocondo (U 7997A) to Antonio the Elder (U 1602A), Giuliano da Sangallo (see Cod. Senese Falb. pl. 34), Antonio the Younger, Peruzzi, Bastiano da Sangallo (U 1742A v. and 1743A), Giovanni Francesco da Sangallo (U 1705A), and Pietro Rosselli (U 932A and U 1579A).

A propos the elevation of the double Doric and Ionic order of the ambulatory, it is worth comparing this drawing with the more precise drawing by Antonio Tanghero and Antonio the Younger on U 1296A r. Drawings of elevations of a wholly Doric arcade and of a Doric and Ionic arcade are held in the graphic collection at the Albertina Museum (Egger 1903, nos 165 r. and 166 r.).

The other drawings on the recto are as follows: (b) a sketched plan of the Arch of Septimius Severus with some metric notes; (d) (turned 180 degrees) axonometric elevation of a pillar, showing thearchitectonic order with pedestal, and and the attic; (c) two sections of the coffers of the vaults; (a) impost moulding of side arch. On the verso are: a measured profile of the cymatium of the pedestal and base of the column of the Arch of Septimius Severus (*a*); a measured profile, with an axonometric sketch of the archivolt of a barrel vault, the impost cornice, base and cornice of the pier (*b*); a perspectival sketch and survey of the Corinthian column with its base and some of the entablature (*c*); profiles and an axonometric sketch of some of the cornice details (*d*); a sketch of a composite capital (*e*); a sketched plan of the Arch of Septimius Severus (*f*); and a measured profile with an axonometric sketch of the cornice of the archivolt (*g*). | ACF

BIBLIOGRAPHY Ferri (1885) 126, 193; Egger (1903) nos 165r. and 166 r.; Lanciani (1902–12) III: 8; Bartoli (1914–22) III: figs 431–32; pl 250–51; VI: 80; Brilliant (1967) 258; CensusIDs 10043888, 10044995.

U 932A *recto and verso*

Antonio del Tanghero and Antonio da Sangallo the Younger

Rome, elevations of Theater of Marcellus and of details of both orders, ca. 1518–22 and after 1527.

Dimensions 432 × 565 mm.
Technique Pen and brown ink; straightedge, stylus, compass, details freehand (verso).
Paper Mediumweight, folded, restorations on verso, refiled.

INSCRIPTION, Recto (Antonio del Tanghero's hand): *I fra una la[l]ttra palmi 3 once 3 / nona fronta*; (Antonio's late hand) *In sul picolo sta cosi / El palmo in once 12 loncia minuti 5 / ridotta tutta minuti 60 per palmo / quanto el monto dove e segniato A / pende el disotto del gociolatoro*

Verso (Antonio's late hand) *In sul grande / Secondo Vitruvio / aria a essere nove / teste uno tertio cioe 2006 1/3 / e la 1920 che dia circha 9 teste / mancho 15 a teste 8 minuti 200 (modern hand) Pietro Rosselli; Teatro di Marcello*

The handwriting of the Florentine Antonio di Filippo del Tanghero is known from a letter he wrote to Michelangelo, dated 1518. At that time he was working on the altar of San Silvestro in Capite in Rome under the supervision of his older countryman Pietro Rosselli (1474?–ca. 1564). Michelangelo had provided a design for the altar, and Antonio del Tanghero sent Michelangelo a plan of the church drawn to scale. The altar was finished in 1522, and so we can assume that Tanghero was in Rome at least during the period 1518–22. Antonio's notations (in his post-1527 hand) of "rossello" on U 1150A and U 1335A suggest that he believed Pietro Rosselli was the author of the two drawings. Since Tanghero worked for Rosselli, he probably measured the church under Rosselli's guidance. It is possible that only a fragment has survived. Unlike Giuliano da Sangallo, Cronaca, the author of the Codex Strozzi, and Antonio the Younger, Tanghero used *palmi romani* and *once*, in other words, a Roman unit of measurement. However, he followed the orthogonal method for measuring used above all by Cronaca (1457–1508), who may have been Rosselli's and perhaps even Tanghero's teacher. The units of measurement and Antonio's inscriptions lead us to believe that we are dealing with original surveys, and since Antonio still refers to them in his detailed calculations of the Vitruvian orders, we can assume that even by 1530 their precision had not been surpassed. Rosselli could have left them with Antonio in the years following the Sack of Rome, a period when Antonio had considerable time to devote to the Vitruvian orders (Frommel 1994, *Introduction*, pp. 36–39, 46). It is possible that also Giovanni Battista da Sangallo's related drawing U 1966A—which is, however, measured in *braccia*—was made in connection with Antonio's studies of Vitruvius. He used Tanghero's measurements from U 932A and discovered that the proportions of the Ionic columns are slimmer, 1:9.5, than those recommended by Vitruvius. | CLF

BIBLIOGRAPHY Bartoli (1914–22) II: figs 335–36; pl 195–96; VI: 62; Giovannoni (1959) I: 20, 24; Günther (1988) 230–31; Scaglia (1994) 224–25; CensusIDs 10054804, 10071358.

U 949A *recto*

Antonio da Sangallo the Younger

Rome, survey of area north of Church of S. Luigi de' Francesi showing houses, Church of S. Andrea de Fordivoliis, and northwestern exedra of Thermae Neronianae- Alexandrinae.

Dimensions 420 × 578 mm.
Technique Pen and brown ink, straightedge, pin, compass(?).
Paper Heavy, textured, fold at center, tears at left and right edges, stains, large inkblots, traces of glue(?) on borders of verso. Watermark: encircled anchor and six-pointed star.
Drawing Scale Scale of pinholes (12 units corresponding with 5 *palmi romani* each = 88 mm (scale ca. 1:150).

INSCRIPTION, Recto (signatures) (bottom left) *949*; (top right, Ferri) *635*; (far left, in pen) *134*; (far left) *strada*; *piazetta*; *strada*; (left) *Case di bene in bene*; *67*; *Andito Comune Cop[er]to*; *ii*; (top center) *largo buono Cannae 13 / longa Cannae 25*; *Le Case chi sono sulla strada di S maria f[...] vengono fino a questo muro*; *Casetta di bene [in] / bene*; *2[6]*; *Chiesa di Spadri / [...] labro di S. Luigi*; *Casetta di S. Luig*; (center) *fondame[n]to anticho*; *33*; *45*; *fondamento anticho*; *60*; *palmi [150]*; *52*; *[comune]*; *scho[perto]*; *muro anticho*; *8½*; *Di bene [in] bene*; (depth of exedra) *56*; (width of exedra) *100*; *muro moderno*; *[15½]*; *muro antico*; *51*; (bottom center) *150½*; *orto*; *55*; *fratta*; *30*; *orto*; (right) *11¼*; *30*; *vi cullo di mastro do[...]cho*; *50*; *28*; *Casa di S Luigi logata / auno Sartorio*; *22½*; *Casa di Sta maria ritonda alogata amastro pietro fallegniame*; *25*; *palmi 65*; *34*; *14⅓*; *12*; *7⅔*; *60*; *28½*; *schoperto*; *44*; *40½*; *Casa di mastro giovanni da macjerata*; *79*; (far right) *28*; *21*; *34*; *25*; *42*; *56*; *34*

Verso (far right) *Datario cioe Messer guglielmo / in che forte le terme alexandrine / parti di esse*

The present survey is aligned orthogonally to the points of the compass. As the inscriptions are tilted in all four directions, the plan has no articulated top (a triangular inkblot lies on the northern half). Superimposed on a modern map, the area shown here corresponds to the northern half of the block of S. Luigi de' Francesi and the southern wing of the next block to the north. The modern Via di San Giovanna d' Arco bisects the courtyard directly behind the exedra. The southern half of the block of S. Luigi de' Francesi is shown on U 868A (vol. II).

Bartoli dated the present sheet between 31 August 1522 and 10 September 1523, when Willem van Enckenvoort, probably identical with the "datario cioe messer guglielmo" mentioned on the verso, was *datario* of Hadrian VI, but not yet cardinal. Frommel suggested that the purpose of the survey was to settle a dispute about Enckevoort's property to the north of the depicted area.

A very similar survey, U 996A, apparently by the same hand, also includes an inscription referring to a datario on the verso and is dated 1518. Comparison of that drawing with U 949A r. (together with U 868A) suggests that the present sheet is a preliminary survey of the building project for S. Luigi de' Francesi of 1518. If this is the case, the inscription on the verso may have been added later.

The present sheet sheds light on Roman church history. Observed in raking light, the drawing shows a series of four spaces to the north of the common courtyard (below the triangular inkblot). Three of them are annotated with the word "cassetta," or house. The second one, which is almost completely obscured by the inkblot, contains the inscription "Chiesa di Spadri / [...] labro di S. Luigi." The entrance to this church is visible in the southwestern corner. Close to the right edge of the inkblot is an altar at the eastern wall, formed by a small square with an inscribed cross. It seems very likely that the church represents S. Andrea de Fordivoliis, a small chapel belonging to S. Luigi, which was inaccessible from the street. Huelsen proposed that the building became used for secular purposes in the beginning of the sixteenth century, since it is not mentioned in the church catalogues of 1492 and after. If the identification is correct, U 949A not only proves the existence of S. Andrea about 1520, it also provides the only exact topographical record, including its interior size of 24 by 40 *palmi*.

As the above inscriptions indicate, the houses to the left of the inkblots, marked with the notation "bene in bene," belonged to the Benimbene family (as suggested by Bartoli). The buildings along the north wall were owned by the fraternity of S. Luigi. The western entrance, as well as the courtyard and its eastern loggia, were of common use.

Two properties north and south of the eastern house of S. Luigi were rented by a tailor. The northern one belonged to a "maestro berardo" or "domenicho," and the southern one to the Chapter(?) of S. Maria Rotonda, rented by Pietro Fallegniame. The properties in the southeastern corner belonged to Giovanni da Macerata. The inscription along the northern wall at the top of the sheet most likely refers to S. Maria Cella Farfae, the church preceding S. Luigi.

From an archaeological point of view, this study is very important. Modern reconstructions of the Thermae Neronianae-Alexandrinae, shown on U 949A, are primarily based on drawings by Palladio and on evidence collected by Ghini in a survey of the still extant other northern exedra of these ancient baths. The present drawing differs from that by Palladio and improves on the findings of Ghini. Ancient walls and foundations are clearly marked in the inscription. The western and northern walls of the common courtyard base are built on ancient foundations, and the eastern and southerm walls are entirely ancient. A modern wall closes the exedra on the south side. The columns shown in the exedra need not have been intact, but presumably the draftsman saw enough to reconstruct six columns in the south entrance of the exedra, as well as a wall system with a smaller order and four rectangular aedicules on both sides of the northern entrance. As this wall system is very similar to those in the Baths of Caracalla, which Antonio and his circle drew in U 1656A and U 1545A, it might well be extrapolated from there. Spiral staircases are shown on both sides of the exedra, the eastern one in part by pinholes in the design.

On what Palladio probably used to base his reconstruction—the record shown on R.I.B.A. XIV 4v.— the exedra differs from that shown in U 949A. Instead it seems more similar to the northeastern exedra on U 3931A, another rather crude reconstruction of the Thermae Neronianae-Alexandrinae made after 1518 by an unknown hand.

In U 3931A, the northwestern exedra is not articulated. In addition, we must suspect that Palladio's record is also based on the eastern exedra. Thus the present sheet seems to be the only existing survey of the northwestern exedra of the Thermae Neronianae-Alexandrinae before it was partly torn down to be incorporated in succeeding buildings, as seen in the survey of Clement IX dated 1667 (ASR Coll. Disegni e Mappe I, Cart. 86°, n.ord. 513). | MS

BIBLIOGRAPHY Vasari-Milanesi (1906) V, fig. 481; Bartoli (1914–22) III: fig. 491, pl. 300; VI: 92; Lanciani (1893–1901) pl. 15; Ghini (1998) 130–33 ff.; Buchowiecki-Kuhn (1967–97) II: 308–13; Huelsen (1927) 183 f., 326 f.; Frommel (1987) 173; Frommel (1973) II: 166 f.; CensusID 10070169.

U 992A *recto*

Antonio da Sangallo the Younger

Rome, Zecca Antica at SS. Cosma e Damiano, ca. 1508–10.

Dimensions 226 × 330 mm.
Technique Pen and grayish-brown ink, incised lines, compass, straightedge, pin.
Paper Medium weight, trimmed, creased, stains, repaired at lower left edge.

INSCRIPTION *tevertino; tufo; tevertino; tutto tevertino da qui i*[*n*] *giu; la zecha anticha / a san chosimo e damiano*

In this elevation of the left part of a facade, Antonio seemed most interested in the building materials used and in the courses of the stones. The shading of the rectangular aperture (niche?) at lower left gives a sense of plasticity to the otherwise flat orthographic representation. While most of the drawing was prepared with the use of a compass and a straightedge guided by incised lines, some of the stones were drawn freehand, as were the three steps in front of the door.

There is a series of arbitrary pinholes, unrelated to the drawing, in the wall between the top and bottom apertures immediately to the left of the door, suggesting that at some point, either before or after it was drawn, U 992A r. served as an underlying pad for another sheet. Günther referred to another drawing in a private collection in Rome that has a representation of the same portal.

Frommel dated the drawing to 1507–08 on the basis of Sangallo's handwriting. Ferri identified the subject as the "Palazzo della Zecca vecchia Banco di S. Spirito," which is impossible also in view of the date when Antonio made the drawing, since the name "Zecca vecchia" was applied to the Banco di S. Spirito building only after the mint was transferred to another location in 1541. | SE

BIBLIOGRAPHY Vasari-Milanesi (1878–85) V: 489; Ferri (1885) 185; Giovannoni (1959) I: 22; Günther (1988) 343; Frommel (1994, *Introduction*) 12–13, fig. 7h; CensusID 10010325.

U 1037A *recto and verso*

Antonio da Sangallo the Younger

Reconstructions of the Mausoleum at Halicarnassus and Porsenna's Tomb, between 1526–27 and 1531.

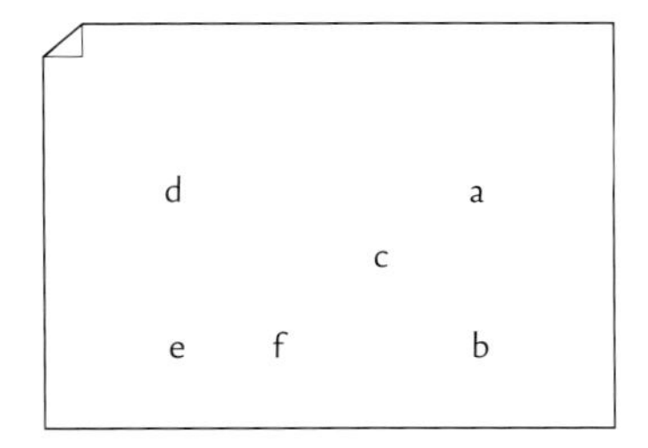

Dimensions 289 × 426 mm.
Technique Pen and brown ink.
Paper Lightweight, trimmed on four sides, reinforced on left side, various holes, possibly caused by acid ink.
Drawing Scale Roman *piedi.*

INSCRIPTION, Recto (in 19th-century hand, Ferri?) *Mausoleo in alicarnasso / Tucta lacirconferentia / sia p*[*iedi*] CCCCXL / *Le 36 Colonne / sono grosse p*[*iedi*] *3 luna / lo intercolumnio p. 8¾ / excetto quelli di / mezo p*[*iedi*] *10 luno pro de li fronti p*[*iedi*] *63 / circhonda p*[*iedi*] *440 / alto cubiti 25 sono p*[*iedi*] *37½ / La colonna alla* [...] *testa e mezo p*[*iedi*] *22½ lacornice p. 4½ / lofrontespizio p*[*iedi*] *10½ / in tucto p*[*iedi*] *37½ / Lapyramide alta p*[*iedi*] *102½ in tutto p*[*iedi*] *140 alta dove* [...] *dice che gira / p*[*iedi*] 4XI [...] CCCCXL

Verso (Antonio's hand) *Prosenna Rex hetruriae sepulcrum eam sit ut externorum / regum vanitas r*[*sic*]*quoque ab italis superaretur sed cum excedat / omnia fabulositas* [*utemur* canceled] *ipsius M. Varronis in exposi/tione eius verbis sepultus est inquit sub urbe / Clusio in quo loco monumentum reliquit lapide quadrato / singula latera pedum lata tricenum alta quinquagenum / in quo basi quadrata intus labyrinthusm inextrichabilem Quo / si quis improperet sine glomere lini exitum invenire / nequeat. / Supra id quadratum pyramides stant quinque Quattuor / in angulis et in medio una in imo latae pedum septua/genum quinum altae centum quinquagenum ita fastigatae / ut in summo orbis aeneus et pegasus unus omnibus sit / impositus ex quo pendeant excepta cathenis tintinnabula / quae vento agitata longe sonitus referant ut dodonae olim / factum. / Supra quem orbem quattuor pyramides insuper singulae / extant altae pedum centenum sup* [*sic*] */ supra quas uno solo quinque pyramides quarum altitudinem / Varronem puduit adiicere fabulae Hetruscae tradunt eandem / fuisse quam operis adeo vesana dementia quesisse gloriam / impendio nulli pro futuro praeterea fatigasse regni vires / ut tamen laus maior artificis esset*

On the right side of this sheet, Antonio drew a reconstruction of the Mausoleum at Halicarnassus on a cruciform plan, based on the hypotheses put forward on sheets U 894A, 1039A, 1040A, and 1167A. The drawing was probably the last to be made during his study of the monument, and must have been executed before he decided to draw the fair copy of the reconstruction of the edifice with a stylus and straightedge on a rectangular plan, on sheets U 1127A r. and 1128A r. On the left he sketched a plan for the reconstruction of Porsenna's tomb in Chiusi (*d*, *e*).

The reconstruction of the Mausoleum at Halicarnassus is confidently set out, with two sketches in the center of the right side of the sheet (*a* and *b*), in which the elevation appears to be exactly aligned with the projection of the plan. The sure lines in the freehand part of the drawing show that by this time, Antonio had a clear idea of the overall measurements of the edifice after partially rectifying the conclusions he had elaborated on U 894A recto. He did not consult his previous transcriptions of Pliny's text, but went over the ancient text again, rectifying the measurement of 411 *piedi* given for the perimeter of the edifice in U 1039A recto, which does, in fact, appear to have been correctly fixed at 440 *piedi* as in the ancient text. The result is an edifice 110 *piedi* wide, with four *avant-corps* measuring 63 *piedi* each with two bays measuring 23½ *piedi* set back from the corners on each side, verified in addition (*c*). The measurement of the columns is fixed at 3 *piedi*, the intercolumniations measure 8¾ *piedi* with the exception of the central one, which is 10 *piedi*. Although he kept the height of the building at 140 *piedi*, Antonio distributed the heights in a different manner than in the previous versions, bringing the height of the lower part as far as the top of the tympanum down from 70 *piedi* to 37½ *piedi*, and envisioning a stepped top pyramid of 102½ *piedi*. In so doing, he would have had a much taller pyramid in mind, keeping to the 24 steps shown on sheet U 894A r. This meant that he had to employ Doric columns, to which he seems to allude in this schematic drawing, 21 or 22½ *piedi* high, that is, measuring seven modules, which is why he had to dispense with the Corinthian columns shown on sheet U 1039A r.

On the verso Antonio jotted down a passage from Pliny the Elder, taken from Varro, on Porsenna's sepulcher at Chiusi (*Naturalis Historiae, XXXVI*, 36, ch. 13, 91–92). On the recto's left, he sketched a plan for its reconstruction. On the right he drew Halicarnassus's mausoleum, which Pliny discussed in chapter 4 of the same volume (*XXXVI*), basing his drawing on a careful reading of the text and on a study of the monuments it described. A lengthy note on the ruins at Cizico on another sheet, U 1218A r., is further evidence of Antonio's interest in architecture cited by Pliny.

The passage transcribed by Antonio on Porsenna's tomb contains an alteration of the name of the Etruscan king, Prosenna, which would appear to be a printing error in the Venetian edition of 1519. Another detail, "petasus" transformed into Pegasus, which is misleading for Antonio's reconstruction, occurs throughout this edition and in most of Pliny's incunabula and publications available to the architect during the early sixteenth century (the correct lection "petasus" is printed in N. Perotti's edition, Rome, 1474, fol. 384v., and in Froben's, Basel, 1530, p. 641). Several abbreviations found in Antonio's transcription are in line with those of the 1519 edition, but there are many others besides, which do not appear within the main fifteenth- and sixteenth-century editions of Pliny. It would seem that, while transcribing the passage from the 1519 edition, the architect has added abbreviations of his own, and there are several errors, variations in the use of capital letters, and a division of the text into paragraphs. The note probably dates from the period between 1527 and 1530, given the occurrence of two different sorts of "h," employed by Antonio before and after these years, respectively (Frommel 1994, *Introduction*, p. 36). There are two drawings by Antonio on U 979A r., datable to April 1526 at the earliest, in which the reconstruction of the sepulcher is less clear, supporting the hypothesis that U 1037A is posterior to that date. Even though it is drawn freehand, the proportions of the elevation on U 1037A r. do not correspond to the annotated measurements, and are closer than U 1038A to the fair copy U 1209A in incorporating Pliny's measurements by interpolation and are evidence of a mature reconstruction of the sepulcher. Attempts to determine the date are furthered by Baldassarre Peruzzi's reconstruction of Porsenna's tomb, U 634A v., and by Giovan Francesco da Sangallo, who in U 1385A, as his cousin does in U 1037A, annotated both drawings of the sepulcher (recto) and of Halicarnassus's mausoleum (verso). These reconstructions, in fact, provide diagrams that correspond with Antonio's more mature scheme as well as diverging elaborations and, given that it would have been difficult for either Peruzzi or Giovan Francesco to enter into any exchange of ideas with Antonio after their departure from Rome in 1527, any mutual discussion of the subject must have taken place after April 1526 and no later than the first few months of 1527.

Antonio drew two plans of the sepulcher on the lower part of the sheet (*e*, *f*), one at the level of the labyrinth inside the first basement, and one that depicts the whole of the upper part, composed of four podiums on a square plan, which are superimposed and rotated by 45 degrees to each other. There are four conical "pyramids" on the corners of each of the three lower podiums, while a thirteenth "pyramid" is positioned at the center of the top pedestal. Sidetracked by the corruption of the word "petasus," which was the name for a certain type of vault, into Pegasus, Antonio topped each "pyramid" with a winged horse instead of the roof covering and the shelf onto which the top spires should have been placed. In order to support these, he had to add a square plan podium to each level, thus doing away with the fifth "pyramid" that Pliny spoke about at the center of the first level. In the elevation, a few slanting lines next to the fourth pedestal appear to show that this, which also agrees with the plan, was added as a *pentimento*, correcting a larger upper "pyramid" positioned, as in U 1038A r., on the same plan as the four spires of the third order. The annotated measurements that refer to the partial and overall measurements of the sepulcher, which is 600 *piedi* high (circa 180 m), are those cited by Pliny, apart from the height of the "pyramids" of the third order, extrapolated from the heights of the first two. The proportions of the freehand drawing do not, however, correspond to the annotated measurements, the spires are all approximately the same height and the sepulcher is noticeably more slender than in Antonio's reconstructions of U 1038A and U 1209A. In the latter, drawn in a fair copy in 1531, the doubts on the top spire have been overcome and the proportions of the drawing now respect the measurements. | VZ, PNP

BIBLIOGRAPHY Giovannoni (1959) I: 11, 24; Vasori (1979) 130; Vasori (1981) 95–6, cat. no. 69; Borsi (1986) fig. 4; Günther (1988) 256; Raub (2014) 192–93, 197–98, fig. 18; Fane-Saunders (2016) 262–63, 273, 280; CensusIDs 252453, 10081635.

U 1038A *recto*

Antonio da Sangallo the Younger

Chiusi, elevation of Porsenna's Tomb, before 1531.

Dimensions 293 × 170 mm.
Technique Pen and brown ink, freehand.
Paper Mediumweight, trimmed, glued.

INSCRIPTION (in 19th-century hand, Ferri?) *731*; 771A

On this sheet, Antonio sketched Porsenna's sepulcher, described by Varro and cited by Pliny, in perspective from below, showing some of the pyramids on the rear facade and thereby offering an insight into the depth of the volumes, of the lower podium in particular, which is delimited by planes receding by 45 degrees with respect to the frontal plane. The sketch, similarly to U 1037A of the same subject, shares the profiled frames of the vertical faces of the plinths, the arrangement of the three groups of spires and traces of *pentimenti* with regard to the position of the top cusp. In U 1037A, it appears that Sangallo corrected a large spire, with a base on the same plane as the four corner ones, by introducing a podium that is as high as they are, and on which he has positioned a smaller top pinnacle. In U 1038A, however, at the height of the tops of the third group of corner cones, there are traces of the upper edge of a fourth podium or of the molded base belonging to the central spire that has been scratched out in order to place a 300-*piedi*-high cusp, which he has placed lower down, on the third podium. In the fair copy U 1209A, Antonio adopted a solution that he found more satisfactory, reducing the height of the third group of pinnacles and the adjacent podium on which he placed the thirteenth spire by a third with respect to the ones beneath. All the measurements given in *Naturalis Historia* appear in the right-hand margin of the sketch, to which Antonio has added the total height of 300 *piedi*. The height of the third row of spires, about which Pliny says nothing, is not given, but Antonio sets it at 66⅔ *piedi* in U 1037A and U 1209A, which is ⅔ the height of the spires in the second row. Here, on the other hand, the spires in the second row appear taller than the ones beneath. U 1038A would therefore appear to be a preparatory drawing for the definitive version on U 1209A, possibly even earlier than U 1037A. | PNP

BIBLIOGRAPHY Ferri (1885) 97; Giovannoni (1959) I: 24; Vasori (1979) 132; Vasori (1981) 96, cat. no. 70; Günther (1988) 256, n. 88; Fane-Saunders (2016) 273; CensusID 252462.

U 1039A *recto and verso*

Antonio da Sangallo the Younger

Transcription from Pliny the Elder's (Gaius Plinius Secundus) *Naturalis Historia* and preliminary information pertaining to the reconstruction of the Mausoleum at Halicarnassus; reconstruction of the Temple of Diana at Ephesus (*recto*), Reconstructions of the Mausoleum at Halicarnassus based on Pliny the Elder's *Naturalis Historia* (*verso*).

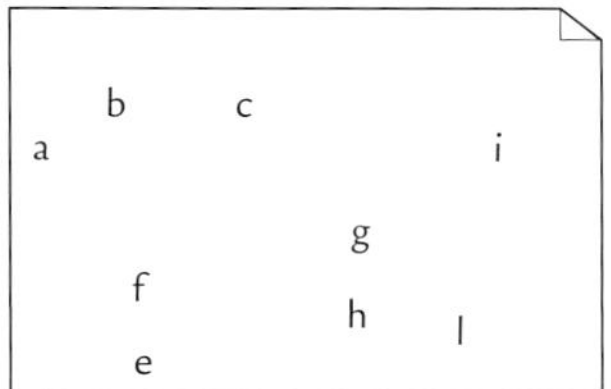

Dimensions 423 × 287 mm.
Paper Lightweight, watermark of a shield emblazoned with a goose and a star, conservation lining, top margin partly reinforced, pin holes under ink blots.
Technique Pen and brown ink.
Drawing Scale Measurements in Roman *piedi*.

INSCRIPTION, Recto (Pliny *Naturalis Historia*, Book 36, Chapter 4, with occasional discrepancies) *Mausoleum hoc est sepulc(h)rum ab uxore Artemisia / factum Mausolo Cariae regulo qui obiit olympiadis(?) / centesimo anno secundo* (instead of 107). *Opus id ut esset inter / septem miracula ij maxime artificis fecere* (instead of fecere artifici) / *patet ab austro & septentrione sexagenos ternos / pedes, Brevius afrontibus toto Circumitu pedes / quadringentos xi* (instead of: CCCCXXXX) *attollitur in altitudinem 25 cubitis* / (to the side*: sono piedi 37½ Corintia*) / *Cingitur Columnis XXXVI* (omitted: pteron vocavere circumitum) / *Ab oriente celavit Scopas / A septentrione brijaxis / A meridie timotheus / Ab occasu Leocares / Priusque quam peragerent Regina Artemisia ope mariti / memoriae id op(er)a exteri Juserit objit. Non tamen / recesserunt nisi absoluto, iam id gloriae ipsorum / artique* *monumentum* (instead of: monimentum) *Judicantes hodieque certant manus/ accessit ex quintus artifex. Namque supra pteron pyramis/ altitudinem inferiorem aequat xxiiij gradibus/ In metae cacumen se contrahens In summo est quadriga/ marmorea quam fecit pythis Haec/ adiecta* CXL *pedum altitudine totum opus includit/* (bottom of the left-hand side) *Voldire che supra alla prima alteza sopra altero muro/ anco di qua. La prima* (cancelled:"*che fa la soma di 75 piedi*") / *et le sta fori la metà alto* (cancelled: "*quanto*") *lo resto che in tutto/ fa la somma di piedi 140 (… …) 65 piedi 102* ½; (on the right-hand side) *plinio Capitulo 4 dellibro 36/ Diano (…) longo 425 piedi largo 220/ columne 127* (corrected below with: *questo* vol dire *128) alti piedi 60 et 36 intagliati/ di columne sendo joniche sono* (cancelled: "*nove teste*") *teste 8½ che sono/ alte piedi 60 rimangono grossi piedi* (cancelled: "*6⅓*") *7 4/3 / sendo Columne 128*; (lower right-hand side) *La columna e grossa p. 7 4/3 / lo intercolumnio sia p/ lo lato sia per columna 23/ piedi* (cancelled: "*153⅓*") *174 1/7 / per 22 intercolumnij sendo piedi 12⅓* (cancelled: "che") *fanno/ la soma di piedi 271⅓ /* insieme le *Colonne colli/* inter*columnij fanno/ la somma di piedi 424⅔/ avanza uno tertio (…)/ delle Columne di canto anno a farsi/ più grosse 1/50 (sic.)/12 columne occupano/ piedi 80 per fino a 220/* (cancellato: "*resti*") *tocha pro intercolumnio/ piedi 12⅓ per inter/columnij fa piedi 123⅓/* (cancelled: "*e 80 le colonne fa 220*") */ lo intercolumnio di mezo/ resta piedi 16 (⅔?) insie/me tutti fanno la soma/ di piedi 220/ Le 18 circondatei sono le inta/gliate da ogni banda/ che sono 36/ (…) n-12 in testa in li lati 23*

Verso on the left-hand side of the sheet, written vertically: *que*(sto *gira) 390 per intercolumnij (resta)* (cancelled: "*88*") *p(er) colonne 12 36/ primo/ tertio/ questo giraria piedi 343½/ piedi 63/ questo se notano Colonne 14/ p(er) lo (-) gira p. 14 Colonne p. 72 p. 13 intercolumnij/ pronao.* Left-hand side of the sheet, written horizontally: *questo sian colonne 36/ e la piramide quatro/ Doricho (…) sta 7½/ Doricho/ Colonne 6 in fronte/ Colonne 14 in li lati.* On the right-hand side of the sheet, from top to bottom: *nel riverso della medaglia/ sta Come dalli frontespitij e sta/ Colle quattro statue p(er) sulli anguli/ e nelli gradi sono scolpiti anima/li quadrupedi che caminano l'uno/ dietro all' altro e in cima alli 24/ gradi sta la quadriga/ Questa saria molto/ Bella e grande nelle/ piramidi volessere in sul muro segniato */ e di vera in proportione/ di due quadri alla cima/ del suo piano di (…)*

The recto of the sheet documents the first steps taken by Antonio the Younger in his reconstruction of the mausoleum based on Pliny the Elder's *Natural History.* He begins by transcribing a passage from the 4th chapter of the 36th book. Sangallo's transcription contains some slight differences from the modern philological editions of the ancient text as well as an error in the measurement of the perimeter of the building, which he gives as being equivalent to 411 piedi whereas there is a general consensus that this should be 440. Although this measurement was put right by Sangallo in the more advanced stages of the reconstruction (cf. U 1037A r. and U 1039A r.), it did impinge on the first graphic reconstructions of the edifice. Furthermore, Sangallo failed to heed the words: *patet ab austro & septentrione sexagenos ternos / pedes, Brevius afrontibus,* which clearly specify the rectangular shape of the building, with two shorter fronts and two longer ones.

It is extremely likely that Sangallo consulted a printed transcription of the Latin text such as the one printed by Giovanni and Bernardino Rossi in Venice in 1507, as some of the punctuation would seem to confirm. None of the references suggest that he might have made use of Vulgar translations of the text, such as that published by Cristoforo Landino in Venice in 1534.

Even in its earliest stages, the transcription, which takes up almost the entire left half of the sheet, is supplemented with comments, as evidenced by the conversion of units of measurement in the right-hand margin of the text referring to the height of the columns of *25 cubitis,* in which Sangallo correctly notes: *sono piedi 37½ Corintia.*

The first thing Sangallo verified was the vertical progression of the edifice, continuing to use measurements in ancient *piedi.* Given the overall height and that of the columns, as indicated by Pliny (equal to 140 *piedi* and *37½ piedi* respectively) Sangallo subdivided the edifice into three levels, one on top of the other: the lowest part 65 *piedi* high (columns 37½ piedi and pediment 37½), the pyramid above 65 *piedi* high and the *quadriga* at the very top 10 *piedi.* These measurements are often found in later reconstructions.

On the right half of the sheet, Sangallo made a note of the source of the quotation: *plinio Capitulo 4 dellibro 36,* corresponding to the description of the mausoleum at Halicarnassus. Lower down, on the same side of the sheet, he drew up a description together with an attempt at a reconstruction of the Temple of Diana at Ephesus. The edifice *longo 425 pedi e largo 220* with 128 columns, 36 of which were *intagliate,* gives an incorrect width that does not tally with the accepted 225 *piedi* that appears in modern editions of Pliny. It should also be noted that the reference to the Ionic order of the Temple does not come from Pliny's text, and it is therefore extremely likely that at the same time Sangallo was also drawing on Vitruvius' treatise (III, 2.7; X, 2.11–12), from which Pliny had derived information on the temple at Ephesus.

Here again, Sangallo corrected the number of 127 columns given by Pliny to 128, in order to complete the symmetry of the edifice. This correction seems to agree—and may also be contemporaneous—with that inserted in a postil to Vitruvius' edition, now conserved in the library in Parma. In that 1542 edition of Vitruvius by Durantino, which had belonged to Antonio the Younger, there is an autograph postil which describes an edifice enclosed by a double peristyle with 126 columns, and a central column bearing an image of the goddess (Pagliara 1988, p. 185). In the hastily sketched plan on the right side of the sheet, the rectangular edifice is shown surrounded by a double colonnade with 22 axes on the longer side and 11 interaxes on the short side. 18 columns are circumscribed with a hasty sign on each of the two fronts; there were 36 columns overall, carved in accordance with the ancient description.

Sangallo used the bottom part of the sheet to give further consideration to the reconstruction, with a calculation of the proportions of the columns: given that the height of the Ionic column was 60 *piedi* and that the diameter to height ratio was defined as being equivalent to 8½, Sangallo deduced that the diameter had to be the equivalent of 7 *piedi* and 4/3. Finally he calculated respectively: the length of the edifice, equal to 424 *piedi* and 2/3 and its width, equal to 220 *piedi*, justifying the jettisoning of the 1/3 of a *piede* between the length envisaged by Pliny and that arrived at through his own calculation thus: *le Columne di canto anno a farsi / più grosse.*

The collection of solutions on the verso illustrates Sangallo's first attempts to devise an edifice that was congruent with the indications given in Pliny the Elder's (Gaius Plinius Secundus) *Natural History*. The sheet contains almost all the possibilities envisaged in Sangallo's reconstruction, based on the scant information provided by the ancient text. The study starts off with several variations on a rectangular plan (*a, b, c*) to which another two analogous solutions (*g, h*) were added, possibly at a later date. The vertical inscriptions belong to the first three examples. The first (*b*) proposes an edifice articulated around a square central cella with three external bays on each side, enclosed by a colonnade with 9 interaxes on the long sides and 5 on the short ones. This scheme was briefly verified in solutions *a* and *c*. Later on, Sangallo had to turn the sheet 90° in order to draw the later solutions on a square plan that were to influence most of the later reconstructions. In scheme *d*, he had to come to grips with the possibility of having to create corner recesses in order to produce four equal fronts with an empty central bay in each front. Schemes *e-f* represent extremely brief syntheses of a perfectly measured plan of an edifice with columns of 3 *piedi*, intercolumniations of 8 and 3/4 *piedi* and a central intercolumniation of 10 piedi, making a total of 110 *piedi* on each front. The total perimeter in this case would have measured 440 *piedi* as indicated by Pliny, which is at odds with the 411 *piedi* erroneously specified in Sangallo's transcription on the recto of this sheet. Both measurements recur in the successive reconstructions, and it therefore seems probable that, even at this early stage, Sangallo had again consulted the text, rectifying the information erroneously transcribed on U 1039A r. From scheme *e* onwards he continued to work on the possibility of articulating the edifice with four equal sides and corner recesses, and again in *f* which he then verified more thoroughly in sketches *i–l*. Plan *e* amplifies the concept of an edifice having four equal fronts with 5 bays and 6 columns and corner recesses on two interaxes for a total of 36 columns. Elevation *f* represents a first check of this solution, recognizable through the two bays seen on the right of the pediment. Here we find the reference to the *Doricho* order: columns three *piedi* in diameter and 22 ½ high, an entablature measuring 4½ *piedi* and the supporting socle for the 10½ *piedi* pyramid, making a total of 37½ *piedi* which correspond to Pliny's 25 *Cubitis*. His next attempt (*i–l*) probably constitutes the first drawing to appear as a complete elevation. In this case too, the main constraint seems to consist of the entire 36 columns, although this would appear to be a simplified solution compared with schemes (*e–f*), given that the corners recede by one bay only. All these examples demonstrate that Sangallo had rejected any notion of creating fronts with equal intercolumniations and columns on the median axis, which had proved acceptable for the most up to date reconstructions of ancient edifices (Jeppesen 1981-).

Here, for the first time, we are presented with the idea of an octagonal cella and a complex system of stairs, located within the avant-corps so as not to interfere with the load-bearing function of the walls of the cella, which supported the pyramid above. There is a swift but effective sketched elevation of the edifice with the four corner statues described by Pliny. Sangallo appears to have drawn on a medal for his reconstruction, which the inscription "*...nel riverso della medaglia sta Come dalli frontespitij...*" refers to. The circle of Raphael and Giulio Romano frequently relied on numismatic sources for their reconstructions of ancient monuments, and the images featured on ancient coins provided them with material for the reconstruction of Augustus' and Hadrian's mausoleums in Constantine's Adlocutio in the Vatican. (Burns 1984).

Although this was one of Sangallo's first attempts to draw the edifice in its entirety, it is clear that this has been achieved through a swift analysis of possible solutions. By drawing on what little information was to be gleaned from Pliny's ancient text, combined with some elementary calculations, he succeeded in producing a perspectival elevation that accentuates the simple structure of the square edifice, with four avant-corps crowned by an equal number of pediments. He also managed to determine the tripartition of the edifice in elevation (37½ + 37½ + 65 *piedi*) described on the recto of the sheet, analogous to the one shown in drawing U 1040A, which should be regarded as the immediate next stage in the reconstruction. | VZ

BIBLIOGRAPHY Ferri (1885) 97; Giovannoni (1959) I: 11, 24; Burns (1984) 448–49; Pagliara (1988) 185; Borst (1994); U 1039A r/v; Raub (2014) 171, 173–74, 178, 181, figs 3–4; Fane-Saunders (2016) 260–61, 270; CensusIDs 10077170, 10074721.

U 1040A *recto*

ANTONIO DA SANGALLO THE YOUNGER

Hypothetical graphic reconstructions of the mausoleum at Halicarnassus.

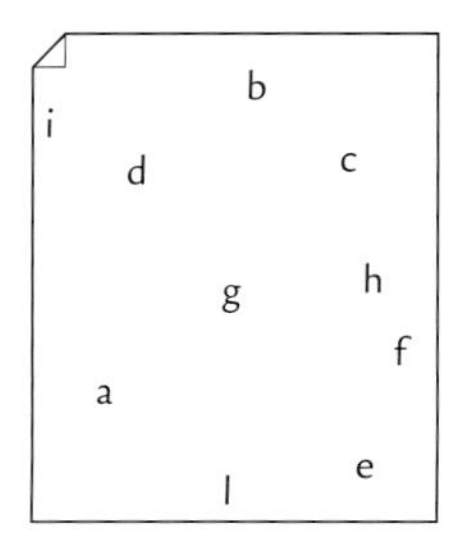

Dimensions 215 × 85 mm.
Paper Lightweight, glued onto thicker paper, good condition, small ink holes on the plan in the top half of the sheet.
Technique Pen and brown ink.
Drawing Scale No drawing scale, reconstruction measurements given in Roman *piedi*

INSCRIPTIONS (right side) *gira 411 piedi*, numbers and sums

This group of sketches should be considered as the immediate successors to the earliest designs, which appear on U 1039A v., and they demonstrate the way in which Sangallo at this stage, following Pliny's indications, pursued several solutions contemporaneously. The reconstruction evolves through three square-based designs (*a-b-c*) and one rectangular-based one (*e*). The possibilities of creating avant-corps with three (a), five (*b*) and seven intercolumniations (*c*) have been explored. The smallest scheme *a* has been rejected out of hand because the dimensions are too small. Two solutions are left open, the first involving corner recesses with two bays (*b*) and the second involving recesses with one bay only (*c*). The design with five interaxes (*b*) is of an edifice with a square central cella, with entrances on all four sides accessed through thick perimeter walls. Scheme *c* is a design for an avant-corps with seven interaxes and single bay corner recesses involving a total of 36 columns altogether. Elevation *d* provides an intermediate solution between schemes *b* and *c*, in which Sangallo was exploring the idea of an articulation of fronts with seven intercolumniations and corner recesses with two bays, which would have brought the total number of columns to 40, contrary to Pliny's final count of 36. The heights of the edifice first explored in scheme (*l*) have also been verified and then related to sketch *d*. Here, Sangallo seems to be considering the option of creating a pediment that is as high as the columns (37 ½ *piedi*), along the lines of the subdivision indicated on sheet U 1039A r. and v.

This is where the concept of superimposing a truncated pyramidal block originates, and it is represented here by two vague oblique lines which Sangallo appears to be using in order to call attention to the excessive height of this component set between the pediments and the topmost pyramid.

The variables left open by Sangallo at this point in the reconstruction can be deduced from the changes made to the solutions involving five (b) and seven intercolumniations (c). He then concentrated on the number of intercolumniations required for the central body of the building and the back wings. The resulting fronts measure 63 *piedi*, with intercolumniations of approximately 12 and a half *piedi*. The dimensions of the total perimeter of the edifice *d* have been worked out in column *i*, assuming interaxes of approximately 12 *piedi*, giving a total of 448 *piedi*, which therefore exceeds the indication "*gira 411 piedi*." This confirms that this must have been one of Antonio's earliest designs, still based on the erroneous measurement of 411 *piedi* transcribed onto U 1039A r.

Antonio's uncertainty over whether to opt for a square plan or a rectangular one is confirmed by scheme *e*, which puts forward designs previously drawn up on sheet UA 1039A v. This solution involves four fronts articulated by 5 intercolumniations on the short side and 13 (later reduced to 12) on the long side, making up the desired total of 36 columns. This solution is not unlike the fair copies on sheets UA1127 and UA1128.

The two designs involving spiraliform crowning parts (g-h), which may be an allusion to the processional function of the funerary pyramid, are evidence of a point at which the architect's attention seems to have shifted away from the metric reconstruction of the edifice. This spiral *g*, articulated by arches, is evidently an allusion to the picture of the Tower of Babel, absolutely analogous with the one that appears in the background of the drawing of the Balbi Crypt by Giuliano da Sangallo (Vatican Apostolic Library, Cod. Barb. Lat. 4424 fol. 4 verso). In the drawing, designs deriving from what was clearly a source familiar to Antonio resurface; this might well have been in Raphael's *bottega* after the death of Giuliano da Sangallo (Pagliara 1984, p. 417). | VZ

BIBLIOGRAPHY Ferri (1885) 97; Giovannoni (1959) I: 11, 24; Pagliara (1984, *Cripta Balbi*) 417; Raub (2014) 174, 178, 181; CensusID 10074675.

U 1042A *recto*

Antonio da Sangallo the Younger

Studies relating to the Mausoleum at Halicarnassus; inscription discovered at Perugia; Vitruvius on acroteria, ca. 1540.

Dimensions 550 × 440 mm.
Technique Pen and brown ink, stylus, straightedge, pin.
Paper Medium weight, folded once, edges torn, reinforced on verso.
Drawing Scale Unidentified, along upper right edge

INSCRIPTION (upper half) (left, turned 90 degrees) *·P· AEMILIO·P·F·VOPISCO / SEVIRO EX TESTAMENTO ~~HS~~ CIƆ CIƆ CI / Questo sie le Caratero del sextertio ~~HS~~ / Questo sie el caratero del mille CIƆ / Questo è lo Carattero del 500 CI / p[er]che lo mezo mille* (*questo sie i[n]* canceled) */ questo si era i[n] perugia i[n] una spo[n]da de uno pozo / jo lo fatta murare nel portone del corritoro della rocha /* [...] *acio no[n] vadia a mala via; sestertij 2500 / Bisognia chiarire se / dicie mille overo milione / questo carattero; ~~HS~~ / Sextertio*; (turned back) *è necesario chel pri / mo grado stia a scarpa / fino che a dato*[?] *una volta / tonda e poi sieno a pi / ombo tutti a volere / chella piramida Comi[n] / ci quadra*; (top right) *Fuvi il qui[n]to artefice i[n]pero che / appareggio la parte i[n]feriore / & Collalteza della superiore / pirramide ristri[n] gnie[n]dosi Cu[m] xxiiij / gradi i[n] pu[n]ta di meta nella sum[m] ita / sua era una quadriga di marmo / cioe Carro Con quattro cavagli la quale / fece pitis questa arro / tovi fece che tutta lop[er] a / fussi alta CXL piedi*; (below this) *Cerchare la medaglia a questi / medagliai di mausolo come qui sotto / a quelli di medici / Domitio Cechini / Antonino Feriapani / Mariano guardaroba / Lore[n]zetto / Antonietto delle medaglie / Andrea fratello di rinieri / Rafaello orefice / Biagio di bono ragugeo / i[n] anchona*; (below this) *Jo o visto la medaglia stare Così / Colla pirramide sola Con sette / gradi oltre alla basa Co[n] queste / statue i[n] sulli Cantoni & nelli gradi / animali che paiono muletti e i[n] cima / la sua driga & auricha & li genti / montano a uso di scala*; (lower half of sheet, turned 90 degrees) *La colonna è grossa piedi 3 Dita 11 Minuti 11 / La colonna e basa alta piedi 27 Dita 11½ minuti 43 / la basa piedi* (*uno* canceled) *i D 13 minuti 45 / La colonna sola cioe lo fuso alto p[iedi] 25 D 13 minuti 77 / Capitello architrave triglifi Cornice p[iedi] 9 D 12 minuti 36 / capitello alto piedi 1 D 15 minuti 23 / Larchitrave alto piedi 1 D 15 minuti 23 / Li triglifi sono alti piedi 2 D 14 minuti 74 / La cornice sie alta piedi 2 D 14 minuti 74; Lo primo grado della faccia gra[n]de mo[n] ta 1¼ del grado / lo grado della faccia picola mota 1¾ del grado / Laltra faccia gra[n]do mo[n]ta 1¼ del grado / Laltra faccia pichola mo[n]ta 1¾ del grado / quale al tutto*; (to right of this) *Cerchare di*; (*La regolla* canceled) */ La regola che mette Vitruvio delli agroterij chel dice / che quelli delli angoli sieno alti qua[n] to è lo ti[n]pano / i[n] mezo e quello del mezo sia la ottava parte più alto / Questa regola parte excettione p[er]che no[n] può ess[er] e / generale bisognia darli* (*darli* rewritten in margin) *termjni & p[er] qua[n]to si trova / i[n] roma si vede essere fatta i[n] sul tetrastilo cioe di / quattro Colonne e Così torna Come li antichi e di / gratia p[er] che* (*sel si s* canceled) *si sa che el tetrastilo cio e di quatro / Colon[n]e sia lo tinpano de una alteza tale quale / si li tocha quale sie la nona parte de la cornice piana* (*piana* written above line) *nel cimatio / da stremo a stremo di detta longeza dello cimatio / Quelli che sono di sei Colonne anno più alto lo tinpano / Quelli di otto Colonne lo anno più alto / Queli di dieci più e quelli di dodici più / di sorte se savesse a fare qua[n]to è alto lo ti[n]pano di questi / gra[n]di parerieno Campanili p[er] ta[n]to Iudico se li abia / a dare termine e pigliare lalteza del ti[n]pano a tutti / Come se fussino di quatro Colon[n]e i[n] fro[n] te e Così / tornerà bene a fare la regola generale a tutti / i[n] pro portione Colle loro Colonne a ciascuno*

At the upper left of this sheet, Antonio copied an inscription that he discovered in a well in Perugia, and which—in order to preserve it—he had set into the doorway of the corridor of the fortress. The architect was particularly interested in the inscribed symbols denoting 1,000 and 500.

The sketches of the Mausoleum at Halicarnassus on the sheet are among several that attempt to reconstruct this monument. Antonio's main source was Pliny's *Natural History*, Book XXXVI, ch. 4, 30–32, as a part of his written description, lifted word for word, attests (from *Fuvi il quinto artefice* ... to ... *alta* CXL *piedi*). Antonio claimed to have seen a representation of the mausoleum on a medal, and he made a note to search for such a medal among various medalists, listing their names.

In a long text on the lower half of the sheet, Antonio analyzed Vitruvius on *acroteria* (Book III, ch. 5), concluding that Vitruvius's general rule needed to be adapted to the different sizes of the portico. | SE

BIBLIOGRAPHY Vasari-Milanesi (1878–85) V: 496; Ferri (1885) 97; Giovannoni (1959) I: 23; Camerieri-Palombaro (1988) 144, fig. 32; Günther (1988) 294 n. 171, 297, n. 206, 299 n. 221; Zavatta (2008) 44, 214; Raub (2014) 171, 178, 185, 187, 191, fig. 15, 16; Fane-Saunders (2016) 268–71; CensusID 10075100.

U 1043A *recto*

Aristotile da Sangallo and Antonio da Sangallo the Younger

Perugia, elevation of Porta Marzia; elevation of bastion on northeast face of Rocca Paolina, ca. 1540.

Dimensions 290 × 438 mm.
Technique Pen and brown ink, straightedge.
Paper Lightweight, folds.

INSCRIPTION, Recto (Antonio's hand) *Voglio si vega tutto larcho anticho / e tutte due li pilastri grandi si vegino / e lo muro novo non lo stia come sta el tocho / di penna*; (below this, Aristotile's hand) *Dangholone del dentro sopra larcho di / marzo e il fino a langlolone e da fare / di gismondo sono p[almi] 17 e bisogno / fare giunctione / langlio e altre*; *la chortina di gismondo e piatta sopra angholone / perfino al piano dale sogie dele finestre da destra anzi di dritto*; (right, center) *belguardo verso S[an]to Arcolano*; (top right, in Antonio's hand) *qui non posso terminare se non so dove lalteza / delle 17 palmi se afronta colli regoli del / baluardo col malanno che dio vi dia / segniateli come stanno in opera le loro / alteze come si afrontano luna collaltra / accio le possano terminare non qui sono segniate / ci oscura dapresso e non si vide dove safrontano uno / collaltra ne per lo scritto mancho si puo cn prudenza*[?] / *togliere uno poco piu contra / Lopitaffio voglio stia come e qui segniato sopra colonia vibia*; (at left) COLONIA VIBIA; (lower right, in later hand) *Rocha di perugia*

Verso (Antonio's hand) *A maestro Aristotile ala / rocha in perugia*

This sheet contains two formal studies: an elevation of the Arco di Marzo, the monumental Etruscan gateway to be incorporated into the Rocca Paolina (later called Porta Marzia), and the elevation of the bastion toward the church of S. Arcolano. The verso bears Antonio's inscription "A mastro Aristotile ala rocha di perugia," revealing that the architect, probably coming from Rome or Florence, was working with Aristotile on the site at Perugia. Both have written extensively on the recto, which shows Antonio's characteristic messy script and Aristotile's hand, sloping to the right rather distinctively.

Giovannoni (1959, I, p. 16) concluded that Antonio the Younger ruled his team with an iron hand, calling it "if it was a military system." The annotations on the present sheet were also discussed extensively by Bacile di Castiglione (1903, p. 360). | NA/SP

BIBLIOGRAPHY Ferri (1885) 111; Bacile di Castiglione (1903) 359–60, fig. 10; Giovannoni (1959) I: 16; Grohmann (1981 *Perugia*), fig. 84; Vasori (1981) 179–81, cat. no. 136; Ghisetti Giavarina (1990) 57, n. 1; Zavatta (2008) 59, 88; CensusID 233032.

U 1044A *recto and verso*

Antonio da Sangallo the Younger and Giovanni Battista da Sangallo

Rome, details of a tomb outside Porta S. Pancrazio; sketches of measuring rods (recto). Fragment of a poem (verso), before 1546.

Dimensions 276 × 183 mm.
Technique Pen and brown ink, freehand.
Paper Partly yellowed, patched, edges trimmed, one vertical fold

INSCRIPTION, Recto (top left) (unknown hand) *che l rosso abbia legna parte del cottimo / Lo breuiario nouo*; (center left) (Antonio's hand) *Volta i[n] botte de una sepoltura / fuora della porta S[an]to branchaltio a ma[n] ritta appresso alla seco[n] da strada / mattoni bianchi* (canceled) / *che va alle fornacie a ma[n] ritta i[n] una vignia de uno vaccinaro*; *matoni rossi*; (right) *forma del passo i[n] pres[en]tia / ma no[n] pe[r] mesura propria*

Verso (Giovanni Battista's hand) *Tuo volsi essere senpremai / sol pensando a te piacere / ne mai ebbi altro volere / Ma invano in te sperai / Tuo volsi essere se[m]pre mai / Alla m*[...]

On the recto, Antonio drew a few details of the tomb outside the Porta S. Pancrazio, as his text tells us. The squares in the center of the sheet look like compartments of a stucco vault. The sketch below could be the archivolt, that is, the molding where the vault meets an end wall. The patterns of hexagons and triangles, however, are composed of red and white bricks, which would be unusual for a vault, although not out of place for a floor or external elevation if the tomb was a second-century AD tomb when polychromatic brickwork was fashionable.

The two other drawings on the sheet depict measuring rods. The text at top left is by an unknown hand and does not relate to the drawings, nor do Giovanni Battista's lines on the verso. | IC

BIBLIOGRAPHY Ferri (1885) 179, 192; Bartoli (1914–22) fig. 443, pl. 261; VI: 82; CensusID 10071991.

U 1046A *recto*

Antonio da Sangallo the Younger

Rome, Janus Quadrifrons; (a) reconstructed elevation of left half of a façade; (b) ground plan of a pylon; (c) groin vault of tetrapylon; (d) base molding of a pylon pedestal; (e) portico of a temple(?), 1526–33(?).

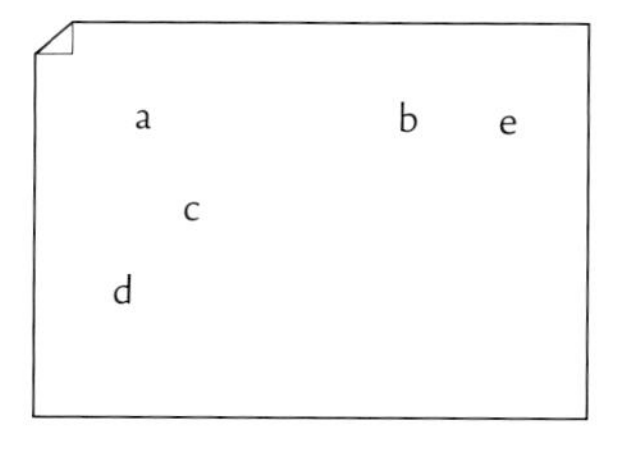

Dimensions 218 × 280 mm.
Technique Pen and brown ink, drawn freehand.
Paper Lightweight.
Drawing Scale Roman *palmi*(?).

INSCRIPTION (a) *inbasamento dellarcho / quadro* (b) *IMP CAESA / DITICO / DIABENICO / SPQR / M.F.PP*; (c) *sotto larcho sta cosi*; (d) *Loarcoquadro / sono pilastri / quattro cosi*; numerous measurements, including (a) various measurements (for molding); (b) (measurements diverging from this) *3–10*; (for width and apex of the wall niches) *7–4*; (d) *3–12* (for width of wall niches); *18–4* (for length of edge of a pylon); *22–12* (for clear width of passages between pylons).

The condition in the early sixteenth century of the late-antique tetrapylon, Janus Quadrifrons, near S. Giorgio in Velabro is shown by Heemskerck (see Huelsen-Egger 1913–16, I: 17, fol. 29r., Bartsch 2019, cat. 46). Antonio's freehand sketch combines depictions of the finds with reconstructions. The base molding of the pedestal (*d*) and the groin vault (*c*) are in accordance with the finds, but in the elevation drawing *a*, the medieval brick tower over the arch, shown by Heemskerck, is replaced by an attic zone and a low triangular gable spanning the whole width and crowned by figures (see the similar gable construction over the Arco di Augusto in Fano, on U 1220A r.). This is an invention of Antonio, as is the inscription on the attic story ("IMP CAESA …"), which makes it clear that he interpreted the tetrapylon as an imperial triumphal arch. The columns framing the wall niches of the two superimposed stories (*a, b*) are also added by Antonio, but they are consistent with modern reconstructions of the antique monument. The different measurements given for the clear width of the wall niches in the ground plan of the pylon (*b*) and the elevation (*a*) indicate that in this drawing Antonio was compiling measurements from various sources. For the Janus Quadrifrons, see also U 1064A. | CJ

BIBLIOGRAPHY Ferri (1885) 121, 168; Bartoli (1914–22) III: fig. 416, pl. 238; VI: 77; Giovannoni (1959) I: 24; CensusID 10072006.

U 1057A *recto and verso*

Giovanni Battista da Sangallo

Rome, Forum Romanum, Basilica Aemilia, Doric capital and entablature, ca. 1520.

Dimensions 412 × 268 mm.
Technique Pen and brown ink.
Paper Folded in eight parts.
Drawing Scale *minuti* (not indicated).

INSCRIPTION, Recto (Antonio's hand) *Batista*; (Giovanni Battista's hand) *questa e di mia mano no ne penso che sia buona / io nono sonone di mia mano siche noscho*[?] *quali / voi dite hano mi dato nomeno richordo ameno di nostra mano*; (later hand) *513*

Verso *Porta i*[*n*] *mano di maestro / ant*[*onio*] *da sangallo*; various calculations

This sketch by Giovanni Battista da Sangallo shows a Doric capital in profile and a Doric entablature in perspective from the Basilica Aemilia. It is carelessly drawn and has been left incomplete: the details of the egg-and-dart molding beneath the bracketed cornice are missing. The measurements differ slightly from those on U 1413A v. by Antonio.

Giovanni Battista's inscription was perhaps intended as a satirical verse aimed at Antonio, who seems to have given his brother an unwelcome task in asking him to draw the entablature; this may provide support for Vasari's description of the tense relationship between the siblings. | HCD

BIBLIOGRAPHY Bartoli (1914–22) IV: fig. 533, pl. 322; VI: 98; Giovannoni (1959) I: 96; Frommel (1973) III: pl. 189d; CensusID 10028355.

U 1064A *recto and verso*

Antonio da Sangallo the Younger

Rome, Janus Quadrifrons, two ground plans of pylons, steps of amphitheater in Tuscolo, a window(?) (*recto*); Loreto, window of a papal palace(?), part of a gable (*verso*). 1526–33.

Dimensions 213 × 269 mm.
Technique Pen and brown ink, red chalk, freehand.
Paper Center fold, repairs on verso.
Drawing Scale *dita.*

INSCRIPTION, Recto (Antonio's hand) (near upper pylon) *larcho stacosi cioe i / suoi pilastri*; *in suquesto angolo / li architravi si tagliono / in nicchie*; *morte p*[*er*] *none indebolire / langolo*; (lower sketch of pylon) *P*[*er*] *lacorrettione dello / archo stana / meglio cosi*; (in red chalk) *gradi del coliseo di / tuscholano del diazo / mata*; various measurements; (another hand) *questo e uno di gradi delculiseo di tuscolano / e di quello dello diazomata secondo vitruuio*; *misurato a dite*

Verso (19th-century hand) *finestra del* […] *pal. apt. / in Loreto*

Antonio depicted the ground plan of a pylon from the late-antique Roman Janus Quadrifrons in two freehand sketches (see also U 1046A). The drawing on the recto, at upper left, largely accords with the finds ("larcho stacosi …").

The columns between the wall niches, however, are additions, though they are also found in modern reconstructions of the building. Antonio justified the use of a blind niche at the corner of the pylon for structural reasons. The drawing below it is designated as a "correttione" and can be classified as one of Antonio's critical drawings of ancient triumphal arches (see also U 815A r. and 1200A r., as well as his critique of the facade of S. Francesco in Rimini on U 1048A r.). The term "correttione" also appears in his critique of the Pantheon on U 306A. The inner corner of the pylon is beveled to create—if the procedure is extended to all four pylons—an octagonal space in the center of the tetrapylon, which is erected over the square ground plan. At the same time, the pedestal zones beneath the columns are set back from the corners of the building and the wall niches are placed closer together. What Antonio designated the "coliseo di tuscholano" in the inscription for the drawing at the right is in reality an amphitheater. The measurements of the stepped tiers are compared with those in Vitruvius (Book V, ch. 7). The profile of a window frame or door jamb in the upper right corner cannot be clearly identified. It is possibly related to the drawing on the verso, which may be a design for the new form of the botteghe of the papal palace in Loreto. Antonio completed a model for the papal palace in 1526, but the windows were not executed until 1533. This sheet can thus be dated between 1526 and 1533. | CJ

BIBLIOGRAPHY Ferri (1885) 79, 86 (under "Loreto"); Giovannoni (1959) I: 20–21; Vasori (1981) 96–7, cat. no. 71; Jobst (1990); CensusID 10016646.

U 1065A *recto*

Antonio da Sangallo the Younger

Terracina, Temple of Apollo

Dimensions 230 × 143 mm.
Technique Pen and brown ink
Paper Restored at top edge.

INSCRIPTION, Recto (later hand) *798*; *Schizzi dellamarcha e campagnia di roma*; (later hand) *83*; *dalla striscia* i[n] *su a* [losses] / *vie basse nelfregio* / *sei uno bello fogliame* / *quale altro sei mo*[*n*]*to i*[*n*] / *mezo di lunet*; *fascia*

Verso (later hand, twice) *1065*

Vasori identified this sheet as representing details of the engaged Ionic columns and podium of the Temple of Apollo at Terracina. During the thirteenth century, the temple was incorporated into the Cathedral of S. Cesareo. Vasori associated the drawing with those by Peruzzi of the same structure (U 400A, 401A, 421A, 422A). The details shown here are of the northwest corner, which is still visible today and was probably the only portion visible in the sixteenth century (see U 1210A v.).

The lower portion of a fluted Ionic column with the base drawn in profile (Vasori identified the base as "ionico-microasiatica") is repeated at the upper left corner of the sheet. This same detail is drawn again at the center, but here Antonio included the profile of the podium. He also noted the undecorated fascia, indicated by the isolated word "fascia," as well as the approximate height of the wave motif that separates the marble facing and drafted masonry of the exterior temple wall. This detail, the column base and exterior temple wall, including the first and second course of drafted masonry, is shown in profile at the right. | MK

BIBLIOGRAPHY Vasori (1981) 97–8, cat. no. 72; CensusID 10016567.

U 1066A *recto and verso*

Antonio da Sangallo the Younger

Cassino, theater and amphitheater (*recto*),
Aquino, elevation of left half of arch;
plan of entire arch (*verso*), ca. 1531.

Dimensions 212 × 142 mm.
Paper Lightweight, edges reinforced.
Technique Pen and brown ink, freehand.

INSCRIPTION, Recto top right, numbering, black pencil, nineteenth-century hand, *84* (cancelled), 799; *I*[*n*] *cima de gradi de uno* / *teatro amo*[*n*]*te Casini apie del* / *mo*[*n*]*te ci e la nfiteatro apresso*; *mo*[*n*]*te*; *mo*[*n*]*te*

Verso *Archo de aquino* / *doue nascie una* / *aqua fuora* / *della terra*

The sketch at the top of the recto is an elevation of the *frons scaena* of the Roman theater at Cassino and the one immediately below is a schematic overall plan of the theater. The theater as a whole can be traced back to about 40 BC, shortly after *Casinum* was refounded as a colony. An inscription records a restoration by a notable local citizen, Ummidia Quadratilla, whose tomb is still located nearby. She is known from one of Pliny the Younger's letters to have died around AD 107. This is consistent with the appearance of the *scaena*, built largely of brick with some marble ornaments (Coarelli 1982, pp. 222–23). The broken pediments at either end recorded by Antonio the Younger are similar to those of the Markets of Trajan.

The bottom sketch is a schematic plan of the amphitheater of Cassino, built entirely through the munificence of Ummidia Quadratilla, and hence datable to the late first century AD. The overall dimensions of the amphitheater are 85 by 69 meters and the outer wall rose to 18 meters. It had six entry passages. The plan errs in adding a seventh in the northwest (top right) quarter, an area where the amphitheater is built into a hillside (Coarelli 1982, p. 220; Golvin 1988, I, p. 114, no. 82).

Giovannoni (1959, I, pp. 20–21) associated the sheet with a sketchbook he proposes Antonio the Younger used on his travels. He believed that U 1119A of the Arch of Trajan at Ancona and U 1220A of the Arch of Augustus at Fano formed part of the same sketchbook. Antonio had opportunities to visit the remains of Roman *Casinum* while working on the project for the mausoleum of Piero de' Medici at the abbey of Montecassino around 1531 (see vol. II, U 172A r.).

The top study on the verso is a perspectival elevation of the left half of an arch that stands south of the town of Aquino on the Via Latina toward Cassino, while the lower sketch shows a plan of the entire structure. The arch, now in very poor condition, measures 6.10 meters wide by 1.70 meters deep and is entirely constructed in travertine *opus quadratum*. No documents have survived to confirm its purpose or date, but it is probably connected with the founding of Aquinum as a colony in 41 BC (De Maria 1988, p. 231, no. 4). The lower part of the arch is buried, as shown in the top sketch. The small inner columns supporting the archivolt had Ionic capitals, while the outer corner columns had Corinthian, rather than Ionic, as depicted here. Giuliano da Sangallo instead showed them as Composite in the *Taccuino Senese* (Siena, Biblioteca Comunale, Ms S.IV.8, fol. 25v.; Falb 1902, pl. XXVI). A watercourse still runs through the arch, as the inscription indicates. | JC

BIBLIOGRAPHY Giovannoni (1959) I: 20–21; Vasori (1981) 98–101, cat. nos 73, 74; De Maria (1988) 231; CensusIDs 10016130, 49437.

U 1067A *recto and verso*

Antonio da Sangallo the Younger

Tivoli, Sanctuary of Hercules Victor
("Villa di Vopisco"), 1539.

Dimensions 296 × 440 mm.
Technique Pen and brown ink.
Paper Medium weight, vertical center fold, lower right edge reinforced on verso.

INSCRIPTION, Recto (inside rooms) *a schifo*; *i[n] botte*; *Botte*; (outside, at right) *triangoloare* (referring to pediment); *colonne e me[m]bretti*; *op[er]a reticulata*; *piano del/ giardino*; *piaggi che va p[er]fino nel fondo del fiume/ e i[n] questa piaggia sie edifichato u[n] lato/ dello edefitio*

Verso *A charrara qua[n]do cavono gra[n] saxi l'alzono colle/ zeppe e poi vi mettono sotto palle de ferro da cannoni/ i[n] cambio di curri e cosi la fanno andare fino alla/ ripa poi la fanno tonbolare a basso*; *Ricordo di cose di tigoli e maxime/ di porta scura Villa di Nerone/ altri dicono di Vopisco sechretario/ d'adriano secondo statio in la sua/ selva*

The Sanctuary of Hercules Victor, which dates from the first century BC, was securely identified as such only in the nineteenth century. In the sixteenth century, by which time a church and convent had been constructed on the ancient site, it was believed to have been originally a villa of Maecenas, subsequently owned by Augustus. Among the several other names associated with the site, Antonio seemed to have preferred Porta Scura and Villa di Vopisco.

Antonio was on the site when he drew this perspectival section of the northern part of the Sanctuary. It is the only section he drew that shows more than a single story. He appears to have been interested primarily in the vaulting systems and in the levels of the site. The diagonal line demonstrates the steep slope of the hill towards the River Aniene.

Giuliani and Vasori pointed out that Antonio's note "a schifo" in the outermost vault at left is an error, since those vaults were *a padiglione*, that is to say, coved or cloistered. Other drawings recording Antonio's studies of the Sanctuary of Hercules Victor are U 1156A r., U 1159A r., U 1176A r., U 1208A r., and U 1351A r.

The fact that Antonio described the mode of transport of blocks of marble out of the quarries of Carrara on the verso of a sheet that has a drawing of the Sanctuary of Hercules is baffling, unless he intended to add a relevant drawing, but then never did. In any case, the inscription about Carrara is not on the verso of the blank half of the sheet, but on the verso of the half with the Tivoli drawing. | SE

BIBLIOGRAPHY Vasari-Milanesi (1878–85) V: 494; Ferri (1885) 21, 220; Giovannoni (1959) I: 22; Giuliani (1970) 166, figs 181, 188; Zorzi (1957); Vasori (1981) 101, cat. no. 75; CensusID 10016174.

U 1068A *recto and verso*

ANTONIO DA SANGALLO THE YOUNGER

Rome, S. Bartolomeo in Isola, sketches of antiquities (*recto*); notes on columns and capitals (*verso*); after 1523.

Dimensions 272 × 221 mm.
Technique Pen and brown ink, freehand.
Paper Mediumweight, tear, reinforced.

INSCRIPTION, Recto *Ricordo come a Santo Bartolomeo in isola sie in sulla / piaza uno coperchi di marmo di una sepoltura di uno pezo / e in la chiesa sie uno bello pilo di porfido che in fa/cie ale zampe di lioni*; (on tomb) *porfito*; *in la chiesa a riscontro cie due tripodi intriangula / uno a tre ucelli grifoni e in mezo uno albero; laltro sie tri*[...]*fi e in uno / lato uno corvo*; *in casa Julio matei sie una basa intagliata / conpagnia ala mia che in casa e de in dua / pezi lo pezo magiore si scerve per scalino per intra/re in una stanza laltro pezo ellintranto*; (on portal) *tondo*; *quadro*

Verso *Lo vivo della colonna di pie 5½ / Lo capitello e alto p. 7⅓ / La colonna ala chapa p. 5 Ditta 9¼*; *Lo capitello se alto ditta 88 alto / La cimasa avendo essere la settima parti / aria essere —— minuti* [...] *12⁴⁄₇ / e si trova esere in questo capitello dita 11⅔ / Le foglie grande arrivano a essere la terza*(?) */ parte de l*[...]*e dalle cimase in giu quali sie*; (later hand, upside down) *106*

In the interior of S. Bartolomeo in Isola, Antonio drew this antique object, its hypothetical groove, and an architectural profile. The piece was drawn also by Baldassarre Peruzzi in U 550A v. (Wurm 1984, pl. 436). On the right, the inscription "uno bello pilo di porfido che in fa/cie ale zampe di lioni" refers to the sketches of the front and side of an urn containing the relics of the church's saints. The urn was donated by Otto III, and now serves as the base of the church's main altar. The lion's paws, which may have not been original, are missing. The two tripods below with griffins and a raven (eagle?) could not be identified.

Two inscriptions in the lower part of the sheet here are important for dating the drawing. The first, "casa Julio matei" refers to Giulio Mattei, who was likely related to the Mattei in Trastevere and whose house was located across the bridge. The only documentation on Giulio regards his engagement in 1498 to Caterina Maffei (Burckardus, R.I.S., II, 380, n. 4). The second relevant annotation refers to Antonio's house in S. Rocco and dates to after 1523; his other house located in Via Giulia dates to after 1541. | EB

BIBLIOGRAPHY Bartoli (1914–22) III: fig. 373, pl. 219; VI: 70; CensusID 233109.

U 1069A *recto and verso*

ANTONIO DA SANGALLO THE YOUNGER

Tivoli, mostly sketches for the so-called Temple of Vesta, before 1535. Recto: (left half) (*c*) ground plan; (*d*) section through the order of the peristasis; (*e*) section through the stylobate and column base; (*f*) section through the entablature; (right half) (*a*) half the ground plan of an unknown rotunda with a stilted apse, two rectangular niches, and pairs of columns; (*b*) sketch of a volute. Verso (left half) (*a*) portal; (*b*) section through the lintel; (*c*) detail of *b*; (*d*) inner window frame; (*e*) section through the inner window lintel; (*f*) outer window frame; (*g*) section through the outer window lintel; (*h*) detail of the lower strip of the outer window frame; (right half) (*i*) section of an unknown ancient stylobate; (*j*) section of an unknown ancient door lintel.

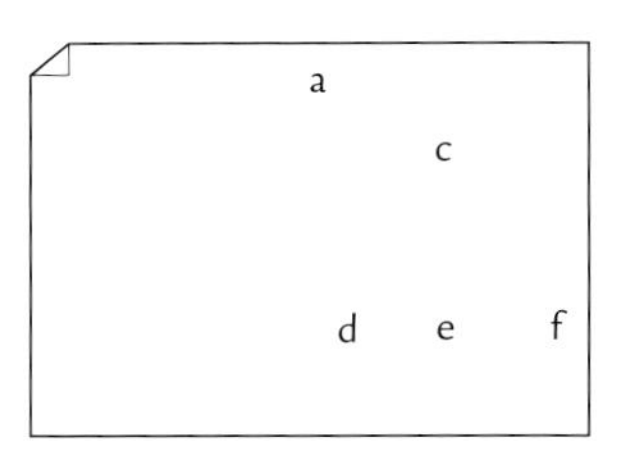

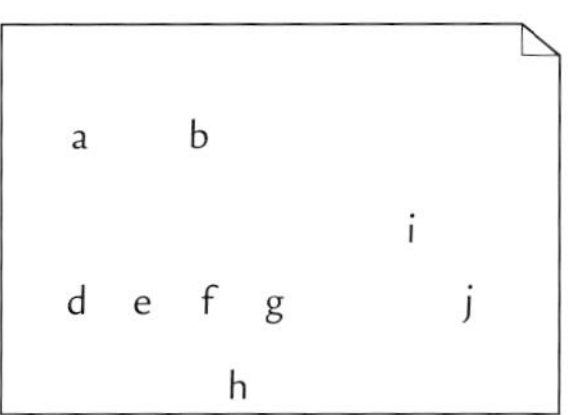

Dimensions 286 × 426 mm.
Technique Pen and brown ink, compass, freehand.
Paper Lightweight, center fold, partly glued, trimmed on four sides, reinforced on left edge, stains.
Drawing Scale Approx. 1:95.6 (*recto* c).

INSCRIPTION, Recto (below c Antonio's hand) *Questo sie lo te*[*m*]*pio di tigoli dicto dauitruuio peripteros auto da rinieri / quale e misurato a piedi antichi e minuti delli quali minuti ne / ua 32 p.*[*er*] *ciaschuno piede auto adi 6 dottobre 1535*; (below, on entablature of f) *Cornicie sopra le colonne*

Verso (Antonio's hand) (in *a*) *la porta*; (next to b) *Cornicie della porta / e sua architravatura*; (in d) *finestra di de*[*n*] *tro del tempio*; (above e) *Cornicie della finestra / di dentro*; (in f) *finestra di fuora*; (above g) *Cornicie della fin/estra di fuora*; (above i) *sotto la sofitta del porticho / overo lacunario*; (next to j) *Modano de una porta / i*[*n*] *Casa dello stipido*

Günther has argued convincingly that the sheet originally constituted a page in a sketchbook in half-recute format. This is supported not only by the fold, which divides the sheet almost exactly in half, but also by the fact that the drawings of the circular temple in Tivoli on the recto and verso are restricted to one of these halves and terminate at the center fold (see especially the section of a window frame *g* on the verso). The obviously unconnected sketches on the other half of the sheet have not yet been identified.

On the recto Antonio himself explained what lay behind the drawings of the so- called Temple of Vesta. "Rinieri," from whom he states to have received the material on which these sketches are based, undoubtedly refers to Riniero Neruccio da Pisa. His note that the delivery of this material occurred on the 6th of October 1535 gives the terminus post quem for our sketch. Probably this took place in Loreto, where Antonio was at times present at the building site of the sanctuary of the Santa Casa from time to time between 1530 and 1539, Riniero beeing his collaborator and, from 1539 on, the architect of the Santa Casa under Sangallo's supervision. The measurements are given in ancient feet of 32 *minuti* each. Günther has hinted at a drawing by the so-called Italian X (Gabinetto Nazionale delle Stampe, Rome, vol. 2510, fol. 36 v.) which contains precisely measured surveys of the window frames, pedestals, and column bases. Numerous analogies among the measurements reveal a close relationship between the two surveys. However, contrary to Günther, the numbers do not correspond precisely, even though the differences are frequently minimal. Moreover, differences occur in the rendering of the profiles, e.g. in the placement of the great cyma on the bottom plate of the base of the stylobate (here Antonio, or Riniero, is nearer to the archaeological remains), in the connection between the cyma and the stylobate itself (where the "Italian X" comes closer to the actual construction), or in the rendering of the profiles between the lower ogee molding and the quarter-round on the pedestal molding (where Riniero once again more accurately reproduced what is found on the building). So it seems reasonable to conclude that during one and the same survey campaign, Riniero and the "Italian X," or his informant, prepared mutually independent drawings, at least of the details.

The ground plan of the *peristasis*, which was already in ruins during the Renaissance, incorrectly shows sixteen columns, while the temple actually was equipped with eighteen (this is how Giuliano da Sangallo and the Codex Coner, for example, had already reconstructed it). In view of the fact that Bramante's Tempietto also has a *peristasis* with sixteen columns, Riniero may to some extent have seen his work of reconstruction through the glasses of Bramante, who was widely regarded as the "reviver" of the ancient art of building. In his own survey of the temple (U 1216A), made just almost four years later, Antonio corrected Riniero's errors. | JN

BIBLIOGRAPHY Ferri (1885) 220; Vasori (1981) 101–3, 103, cat. nos 76, 77; Günther (1988) 206–09, 237; Frommel (2003, *porta ionica*) 47f; CensusIDs 10016578, 10016592.

U 1071A *recto and verso*

Antonio da Sangallo the Younger

Ancona, Arch of Trajan, ca. 1532–35.

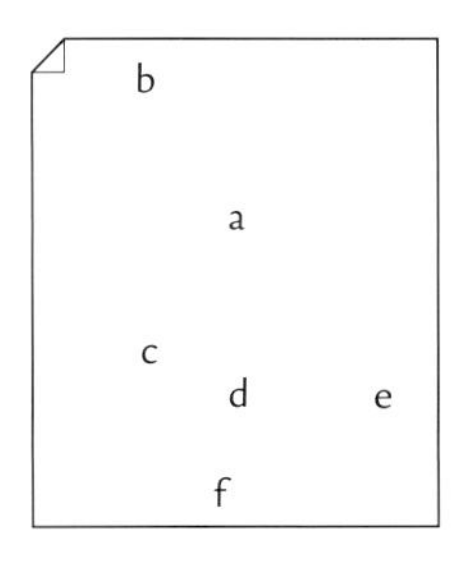

Dimensions 217 × 140 mm.
Technique Pen and brown ink, freehand.
Paper Torn at lower right edge, trimmed.
Drawing Scale Roman *palmi.*

INSCRIPTION, Recto (on a, turned 90°) *diminuolo piano*; (key letter) *A*; (on d) *mare*; (on *e*) *i*[*n*] *basame*[*n*]*to / sotto li zoch*[*oli*]; *mare*; (key letter) *A* (on f) *li dadi sotto le base delle Colonne*

Verso *lo palmo i*[*n*] *parti 12*; *Archo i*[*n*] *sulporto dancho / na*; *lo vano O 13–12*; *diverso larcho*; *Diverso lato* [...]; *Archo danchona*

The date for the sheet is most likely between 1532 and 1535, when Antonio was working in Loreto and on fortifications in Ancona (see vol. I, U 978A and U 1020A), although there he was involved with a villa project in about 1540 (see Frommel- Adams 2000, U 721A), and thus must have visited earlier than the 1530s (see Frommel- Adams 1994, U 1446A).

The principal study *a* depicts the left half of the seaward elevation of the Arch of Trajan at Ancona. It includes little detail, which is supplied by the remaining sketches here and on the verso. The inscriptions on the arch itself are represented by repeated short vertical strokes. The comment "diminuolo piano" seems to refer to the lack of pronounced entasis on the engaged columns. Antonio appears to have speculated (wrongly) that a bust sat on the lower of the two small cornices between the columns of the pier. Another thumbnail sketch of a bust *c* appears in the margin at left.

At the very top of the sheet is a profile *b* across the middle of the attic. The key letter *A* (*e*) refers to the *A* at the bottom left of *a*, indicating that it is the continuation of the latter, showing the basement on which the whole arch stands. Drawing *d* shows an irregular vertical line meeting a horizontal wavy line at the bottom, representing the distance between the podium and the sea ("mare") lapping at the bottom plinth. Finally, *f* shows the unusual moulded plinths between the bases of the columns and the supporting pedestals.

The verso shows three details of the Arch of Trajan at Ancona related to the studies on the recto. The uppermost sketch is a plan of one of the piers. The annotation *lo vano O 13–12* would seem to refer to the width of the opening of the arch between the piers, but it is difficult to make sense of: *O* cannot be an abbreviation for *oncie* as Vasori speculated, nor can it be a mistake for *p* for *palmi*, since it was divided into twelve parts, as the annotation above the sketch makes clear. Below this at the right is a sketched elevation of one of the capitals and shafts of one of the Corinthian columns of the arch. Why the base should be excluded is a mystery. The sketch at left center is a horizontal section through the shaft of one of the outer three-quarter columns and the immediately adjacent parts of the pier.

The Arch at Ancona was erected on the harbor breakwater, which had been restored by Trajan. The inscription dates the arch to AD 115, that is, almost exactly contemporary with Trajan's arch at Benevento, which it resembles in its broad outlines: a single arch with four engaged Corinthian columns on a podium to each front, supporting an entablature and attic, which break forward over the central bay and angle columns.

However, the Ancona arch differs in that it had more slender proportions, its podium breaks forward under each column, and it bore no figurative reliefs. The front of each pier between the columns was divided into three fields by pairs of corniced panels. *Rostra* occupied the upper two fields. The arch is made of marble and measures 9.75 meters wide by 13.80 meters high. It stands on a travertine podium, 10.80 by 5.30 meters and 5.35 meters high, with front and rear access stairs, but these are thought to be late-fifteenth-century in date.

It is thought that, originally, the ground level was higher and the arch stood on a lower, octagonal base with sloping sides through which ran a road on a slight incline (De Maria 1988, p. 227 f.). | JC

BIBLIOGRAPHY Vasori (1981) 104–05, cat. nos 78, 79; CensusIDs 10016191, 10016630.

U 1072A *recto and verso*

Antonio da Sangallo the Younger

Studies of ancient theaters, after 1527.

Dimensions 285 × 214 mm.
Technique Pen and brown ink, compass, straightedge.
Paper Thin, horizontal fold.
Drawing Scale *piedi* (120 *piedi* = 74 mm).

INSCRIPTION, Recto (lower part of the sheet) *ciello; vaso; ciello; vaso*

Verso (top to bottom) *cuneo; orchestra; pulpito; proscenio; proscenio; itinera; hospitalia; aula regia, hospitalia*

In the upper, central area of the recto, Antonio traced a schematic section of the plan he had drawn on the verso (also visible on the recto). He represented exactly the height of the *summa cavea* to the left and introduced some changes. By contrast with the solution for the colonnade with architrave on two superimposed levels, which is laid out on the corresponding section on the verso to the left, he proposed an aedicule on the first level and a system of arches and pilasters with attached half-columns, inspired perhaps, at least in part, by the proposed reconstruction of the *porticus* in the *summa cavea* of the Flavian Amphitheater, studied in U 1136A r. Furthermore, at the left, there appears a more accurate delineation of the rings of seats. The diameter of the orchestra is subdivided into five parts, beginning at the left with two sections of 30 *piedi* and three of 20 *piedi*. The levels of the seats are extended on the hypotenuse of a right triangle, which has a base of 32 *piedi* and a height of 20 *piedi*. The upper of the two lines might indicate the position of a *precinctio*.

On the verso is a ground plan developed from the Vitruvian scheme for the Latin theater *ad triangulum*. Antonio, in his original reinterpretations of ancient theaters, generated circumferences that coincide with the external limit of the orchestra. The diameter of the orchestra measures 120 *piedi* and the erasure at 96 indicates a *pentimento*. The placement of the steps is marked by the peaks of the triangles inscribed in the generating circle and the *cuneo* (wedge) of the first *praecinctio* as specified by the arcs of the circle contained within the edges. The presence of the *preacinctiones* makes the organization of the passages in the *cavea* more complex, with the stairs in alternate position. The inscriptions "cuneo," "orchestra," "pulpito," "proscenio," "itinera," "hospitalia," and "aula regia" specify the principal parts and the placement of the constituent elements of the theater. The section cuts the levels of the *cavea* and notes at the left, without great conviction, a *porticus* in *media gradatione*, articulated in two superimposed orders supported by a high base that functions as a pedestal. The open gallery in this way would have created a diaphragm through which the spectators could enjoy the play while being shielded from the sun. At the same time this would have helped the acoustics of the building. Beyond the prescriptions of Vitruvius, the description of Alberti in *On the Art of Building* (Book VIII, ch. 7) once again seems to be among the sources for Antonio ("Et praesertim theatrum ... omnino esse a sole aversum atque obtectum oportet ... et in supremo ambitu porticus et tecta, quibus vox diffusa contineatur fiatque sonorior"). In the lower part of the sheet is a theater in the *aovata* form, with an orchestra and half-oval *cavea,* and the Vitruvian scheme *ad quadratum* for the Greek theater.

With such a scheme, it is difficult to place the wedges of seats (the *cunei*) and the rising ramps that are situated according to a complex system consisting of horizontally projecting the placement of the corners. Moreover, Antonio seems to be searching for a form of *cavea* that narrows at the extremities according to the indications suggested by Alberti in Book VIII, ch. 7: "Nam ex his (spectaculis) id quidem cuius forma senescenti lunae simili est, theatrum nuncupatur." In this passage, he proposes a geometric form similar to the waning moon; in another, he describes the geometry of the theater as similar to a marshalling of an army in fighting trim ("Spectacula ferme omnia structam cornibus ad bellum aciem imitatur"). This is a more complex polycentric figure than that for the construction of an oval plan studied by Antonio in the upper part of U 1240A v. In fact, the limits of the orchestra are determined by three arcs of a circle with centers respectively in the points corresponding to the letters *A, B, C* in U 1240A v. The curve, which sets the boundaries of the *cavea,* is obtained by means of a central arc that has its center at the point corresponding to *C* in U 1240A v. and in two arcs of a circle with a center at the intersection between the straight line passing through the diameter of the generating circumference and the circumference itself. Antonio determined the placement of the stairs by projecting in a horizontal direction, parallel to the *scaena,* the points that mark the corners of the squares inscribed in the generating circles, in the half-oval of the external limit of the orchestra. | ACF

BIBLIOGRAPHY Ferri (1885) 19, 35, 216; Cerutti Fusco (1986) 462, 690.

U 1088A *recto*

Antonio da Sangallo the Younger

Studies of temples and a Doric portal according to Vitruvius, 1530–40.

Dimensions 191 × 195 mm.
Technique Pen and ink, freehand.
Paper Lightweight, trimmed on four sides, with traces of glue on verso.

INSCRIPTION, Recto (Antonio's hand) *Li[bro]* IIII / *De interiori cellarum / et pronai distribuitione*; (inside plan at left) *paries*; *valve*; *pronai*; *pronai*; *paries*; *pteromatos*; (under plan) *pteromatos*; *pronai*; *pteromatos*; (lower left) *cioe alia/ pteromatos eneciesario / sia lointercolunio laterale / overo lastrada o piaza / inanzi altempie*; (center, on surround) *corona* (19th-century hand, Ferri?) *822*

Verso *1088*; *686* (canceled)

There are five drawings on the sheet, from left to right: the plan of a temple; a barely started sketch; the corner part of a surround for a portal; a piece of molding broken down into six parts; and a measured scheme of a plan for a temple. In the plan at the left, Antonio adhered faithfully to Vitruvius's passage (Book IV, ch. 4, 1) concerning the proportions of the cella and the pronaos of temples: the longest side has been divided into 8 parts of which he took 4 to obtain a width equal to half the length; he has then attributed 5 parts to the length of the cella, leaving three for that of the pronaos. The two columns between the *antae* that provide a very wide central intercolumniation are followed by two rows of internal columns, as prescribed by Vitruvius for widths of over 40 *palmi,* and Antonio continued to abide by the treatise by closing the spaces between the *antae* and the columns with low walls. In the drawing in the middle of the sheet, the wide internal fascia and the lack of volutes are characteristic of the type of Doric portal such as that in Palazzo Farnese, but the small section at the bottom does not appear to have derived from the relevant passage in *De Architectura* (Book IV, ch. 6, 2). On the right is a swift sketch of a plan for a scheme for a temple, possibly peripteral, with a length-to- width ratio of 11:5 and a cella 3 parts wide.

Apart from the Doric portals that Antonio often created and designed with different permutations in his own architecture, the Vitruvian subjects of this sheet conform less than some of his others to the usage of the time. This sheet is evidence, however, of the attention with which Antonio studied all the books in the treatise, particularly during the 1530s and 1540s, in an attempt to fully master the Vitruvian rules. | PNP

BIBLIOGRAPHY Ferri (1985) 217; Giovannoni (1959) I: 23.

U 1089A *recto and verso*

Antonio da Sangallo The Younger

Rome, plan for Flavian Amphitheater (recto and verso); plan for Baths of Diocletian (verso).

Dimensions 288 × 413 mm.
Technique Pen and brown ink (recto), black ink (verso), straightedge, compass, stylus.
Paper Lightweight, mounted on heavier paper, stains, damaged, restored at center.
Drawing Scale *braccia.*

INSCRIPTION, Recto (from top right, turning sheet clockwise) *murato B[raccia] 87–25; dali entro al rigo B 33–35; dali rientro dentro B 81; dali entro al rigo B 33–35; mura[...]to B.87–25; el tutto B 323;* (lower right, across from outside to inside) *murato B.87–9; dal i rigo al i rientro B 73–44* (numbers canceled, possibly substituted with *75–44*); *dal i rientro al i rigo dentro B 74–25* (numbers canceled, possibly substituted with *11–25*); *dal i rigo al i rigo dentro B 93–10; dal i rientro al i entro B 120* (canceled) *116; dal i rigo al rigo di fu[o]ra B 267–28;* (perpendicular to preceding inscriptions along diameter) *dal i rigo al punto B, dal punto al punto B 120;* (center, from left to right) *dal i rigo al i rigo B; dal i rigo al punto B 45;* (slightly below) *da punto a punto B 81*

This drawing shows the geometric scheme for the graphic reconstruction of the Colosseum, a theme particularly dear to Antonio the Younger, and one to which he dedicated a series of interesting studies. In this one, his primary interest was to trace the polycentric figure, establishing four points that define a rhombus. He fixed the length of the lines of the two corresponding circumferences on the elongation of the fixed sides, the not-visible circumferences running together to form the polycentric curve. The geometric system was studied instead on the verso. On the recto, Antonio inserted the pillars of the barrel vaults of the colonnade and showed the substructures in the zone of the change of the line. He then inserted on the exterior of the *cavea* a sketch of the profile of the levels of seats that rise from a high base into the arena. He also inserted a *praecinctio* (horizontal passage) and proposed a solution that allows good sight lines and comfortable seating. A hint of the geometric scheme of the polycentric figure is found in U 854A at the bottom left with Antonio's notation: "Cosi e fatto lo Culiseo di Roma."

On the verso is a sketch of the external perimeter of the enclosure of the Baths of Diocletian. It is one of a series of drawings dedicated to the baths, a typological theme that particularly engaged Bramante and his followers. As mentioned above, at the right of the sheet is the scheme of the geometric construction of the polycentric figure used for the graphic reconstruction of the oval of the Flavian Amphitheater. As such, it belongs to a group of geometric exercises especially important for Antonio's projection of the reconstruction of the Colosseum. See also the entry for U 830A r. and v. | ACF

BIBLIOGRAPHY Ferri (1885) 7, 79, 81; Giovannoni (1959) 1: 23; Vasori (1981) 105–06, cat. no. 80.

U 1090A *recto* / **U 1230A** *verso*
U 1090A *verso* / **U 1230A** *recto*

Antonio da Sangallo the Younger

Rome, temples of Forum Holitorium (S. Nicola in Carcere), after 1527.

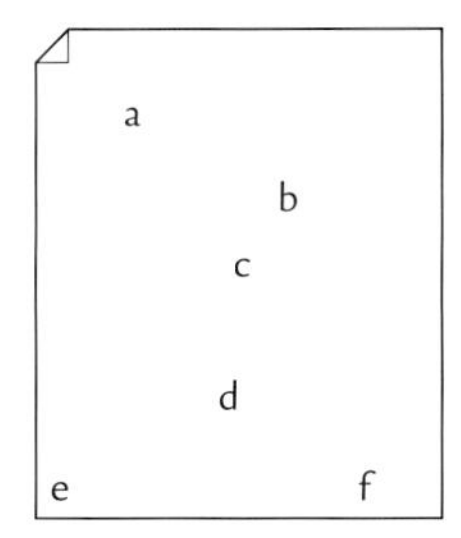

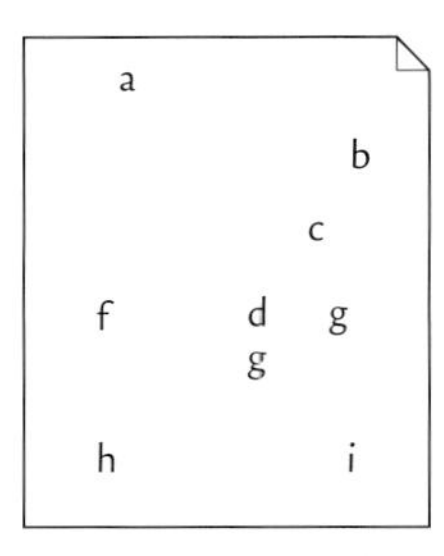

Dimensions 445 × 297 mm.
Technique Pen and brown ink.
Paper Lightweight, restored.
Drawing Scale *piedi* and *dita.*

INSCRIPTION, Recto (b) *La cornicie doricha di giove statori;* (g) *questo era doricho e aveva / lo i[n]tercolumnio delli angoli / piu stretto ta[n]to chel tigriffo / veniva i[n] sul ca[n]to e le metope / si erano equale e le colonne / no[n] avevano base*

Verso (a) *Jove Statori;* (b) *la porta non arriva allo architrave / a dito-38; p[er] la ca[n]tina p. 47 D 8; p[er] lo piano di sopra p. 46 D 8;* (c) (turned 180 degrees) *alta p 24½;* (d) *architrave; piedi 6; colonna 31-D 8;* (e) *porta doricha;* (f) *S[an]to nichola; Le Carcere; Le Colonne sono alte piedi 32 D 14;* (g) *onori e virtute; Larga piedi 13–14;* (h) *S[an]to nicola di ermodi* (canceled); *Honori & virtute / i[n] le Carcere Cori[n]tio;* (i) *onori e virtute / La porta lo suo va / no e larga piedi 13 D 14 / alta lo vano / piedi 24 D 8 / cornicie della porta / piedi 5 D 8*

The middle of the three republican temples of the Forum Holitorium had been converted into the church of S. Nicola in Carcere by the eleventh century. Like Giovanni Battista da Sangallo and Baldassarre Peruzzi, Antonio the Younger devoted considerable attention to the area's ancient remains. On this sheet, at one time divided and now rejoined, he focused primarily on the Doric temple at the south end of the group.

At the upper left (*a*), Antonio made a preliminary

schematic study of its intercolumniation and frieze, which he developed more fully at the center of the sheet (*c*). Between these two studies is a sectional view of the Doric trabeation (*b*); at the bottom of the sheet is a plan reconstruction of all three temples (*d*). The additional drawings on the sheet are a pediment study (*e*) and a measured plan detail (*f*). The sketches and notes correspond closely with Antonio's drawings on U 1174A and seem to be preliminary studies for those reconstructions. The wording of his note concerning the placement of the triglyph at the corner of the Doric temple is very close to that on U 1174A r., where he explicitly related this treatment of the corner to the text of Vitruvius. Antonio also indicated a wider intercolumniation at the center front of the Doric temple. As Pagliara has noted, Antonio's measurement for the central column spacing differs from those given by both Peruzzi and Giovanni Battista, which may indicate that Antonio's drawing represents a theoretical reconstruction of the Doric temple based on Vitruvius rather than a true survey drawing. The triglyphs and metopes of the frieze do not appear in other Renaissance drawings of the temple, and it is possible that Antonio reconstructed these as well on the basis of the Vitruvian text. His identification of the Doric temple here as that of "giove statori" (*b*) is another indication of his reliance on Vitruvius. The Temple of Jupiter Stator in the nearby Portico of Metellus is one of three peripteral temples named by the ancient author in his third book, and on this and other sheets, Antonio identified the three temples at the Forum Holitorium with those specified by Vitruvius. Bartoli grouped this drawing in a "series B," which he dated not earlier than 1519. Antonio's handwriting suggests a date after 1527.

On the verso Antonio used red chalk for the initial drawings, which he then retraced in ink, providing additional information and measurements. Here, as on the other side of the sheets, he equated the Doric temple with Temple of Jupitor Stator and identified the adjacent temples with "ermodi" and "onore e virtute" (*a, g, h, i*), all of which Vitruvius named in his discussion of peripteral temples in Book III. Whereas both the central and northern temple of the group in fact had Ionic capitals, in drawings *c* and *i*, Sangallo drew a Corinthian capital for the north temple. The drawings here closely correspond with his other studies of the temples on U 1174A and U 1270A v. | ACH

BIBLIOGRAPHY Ferri (1885) 148, 195, 199; Bartoli (1914–22) III: fig. 417, pl. 239, fig. 418, pl. 211; VI: 77–8; Crozzoli Aite (1981) 34–38, nos 17, 18; Campbell (1984) I: 229–30, 236–38, 243, II: fig. 18, 40; Campbell-Nesselrath (2006) 27–29; Günther (1988) 262, figs 115; 282–83, figs 47; 312–16, 282, 313–16; Pagliara (1988) 190–95, fig. 16; Frommel (1994, *Introduction*) 36; Huppert (2001) 141–44; Engel (2014) 113–14, fig. 9; Huppert (2015) 80–83; CensusIDs 10012456, 10013627.

U 1093A *recto*

Antonio Labacco and the Circle of Antonio da Sangallo the Younger

Rome, plan of enclosure of Baths of Caracalla.

Dimensions 195 × 285 mm.
Technique Pen and brown ink, red pencil.
Paper Trimmed, restored border.
Drawing Scale *canne.*

INSCRIPTION (red pencil, later hand) *terme*, measurements

To the right on this sheet is a plan of the northwest angle of the peripheral areas of the Baths of Caracalla. To the left is a sketch of a plan without measurements of several rooms in the exedra and a more detailed plan with measurements of the same spaces. These include the small octagonal room with niches on four sides that are set at an oblique angle to the entrance, the circular stairs ingeniously imbedded in the thickness of the walls, the small square room, and the small rectangular room with apses. This is a preparatory drawing related to U 1206A by Antonio the Younger, U 1514A r. and v. by Labacco, and U 1546A and U 4117A by Giovanni Battista da Sangallo. | ACF

BIBLIOGRAPHY Ferri (1885) 202; Lanciani (1897) 524; Jordan-Huelsen (1878–1907) I, 3: 192; Bartoli (1914–22) V: fig. 609, pl. 351; VI: 110; Valori (1985) 136; CensusID 10081509.

U 1095A *recto and verso*

Antonio da Sangallo the Younger

Narni, view of the Bridge of Augustus, partial section through one of the piers (*recto*); Rome, measurements of the window grille of Palazzo Baldassini (*verso*), ca. 1514–15

Dimensions 147 × 293 mm.
Paper White, trimmed at right edge, folded twice; restoration along three edges, stains from tape.
Technique Pen and brown ink, incised lines, pin pricks from compass.
Drawing scale: Roman *palmi* (verso)

INSCRIPTION, Verso *lo vano dove vanno le / ferate dalla soglia / al di sotto del gociolatoio / sie palmj 10¾ e piu / questo x----x / larghe cholli stipiti 8.*

The Bridge of Augustus at Narni crosses the river Nera. Although the view is precisely drawn with a compass and incised lines, it lacks measurements. Vasori notes the similarity to Peruzzi's drawing (U 478A) of the same bridge, of which only one of the four arches was still intact by the sixteenth century. Abandoning his original intention of drawing a detailed reconstruction, Antonio sketched a parapet on top of the bridge, along which a boar pursues a snail. The snail in turn pursues a stick figure, which has just turned around and shot an arrow.

Unlike Peruzzi, Antonio indicates some structural details, such as the blocks used for centering and the construction of piers, which are normally below the water line.

The drawing on the recto can be dated with the help of the inscriptions on the verso, referring to the iron grilles for the ground floor window of Palazzo Baldassini. These grilles were crafted at the earliest a year or two after the beginning of construction (ca. 1513), and therefore the view of the Roman bridge must have been drawn about 1514–15. Such a date is confirmed by the handwriting, which is comparable to that on U 1002A, a drawing for the stair of Palazzo Farnese. During those years Antonio used the same abbreviation for *palmo* as for the Latin "per" (see U 2002A) and "pro" (as on the present drawing, or on U 1228A, done about 1519, for the theater of Villa Madama).

Also, his method of rendering the bridge semi-perspectivally suggests a date in his early maturity. He drew the five piers, the parapet, the intrados, and indicates the hillside and river with delicate lines and without straightedge, but uses a compass for the archivolts of the four arches, the second of which is considerably wider. He was mainly interested in the design of the piers, with the jutting ashlar in the two top and two bottom rows reminiscent of wooden beams, and in the plain archivolts (which have a returned end short of the impost on two of the arches) and the intrados. The latter are reinforced through four ribs, square in section. The dentilled plan at upper right relates to the impost molding of the first arch on the left. The erect bug, the snail, and the boar, which are marching in single file leftward on the parapet, are a rare instance of Antonio's humor. | MK, CLF

BIBLIOGRAPHY Ferri (1885) 114; Giovannoni (1959) I: 21; Vasori (1981) 106–07, cat. no. 81; CensusID 0075148.

U 1099A *recto*

Antonio Labacco

Ancona, Arch of Trajan, ca. 1532–5

Dimensions 264 × 158 mm
Technique pen and brown ink, freehand.
Paper white paper; left edge cut.
Drawing Scale Roman *palmi*

INSCRIPTION, top centre, old numbering, black pencil, *833*; bottom left, ink *Lo rituro*[?]

A measured profile of the lower parts of the Arch of Trajan at Ancona, running from the base of the engaged columns down to the lowest plinth of the basement. Its dimensions correspond closely with those of drawing *d* on U 1119A v. and may be a worked-up version combining that drawing with drawing *b* on the same sheet. Labacco accompanied Antonio to Ancona to inspect fortifications (Frommel 1994, *Introduction*, 39), in which case the date of execution would be similar (ca. 1532–5). | IC

BIBLIOGRAPHY Ferri (1885) 12, 115; CensusID 10074639.

U 1107A *recto and verso*

Antonio da Sangallo the Younger

Rome, study of ground plan of Theater of Marcellus (*recto*). Ground plan and section of barrel vault, sketch of ceiling (*verso*). After 1519–20.

Dimensions 426 × 572 mm.
Technique Pen and brown ink, straightedge, compass, red pencil.
Paper Folded into four parts.

INSCRIPTION, Recto (top left, another hand) *teatri antichi*; (Antonio's hand) *Teatro de Savilli*; (in plan) *cimasa* [...]; various other inscriptions Verso (at the section) piano del chortile, pano di stantie, andito, architrave, (at the ground plan) di termini, *archi di S.pietro*[...]

The recto shows a Vitruvian scheme for the genesis of the plan of the Latin theater applied to the Theater of Marcellus. In the center of the drawing is a semicircular *cavea* and on the right half, a rectilinear form of the colonnade. The survey includes twenty-one arches, labeled beginning at the center of the *cavea*. The area closest to the orchestra appears undefined, because of the impossibility of carrying out metric verifications, except in the area of the ramp of stairs at the center of the *cavea*.

On the verso, Antonio drew a small-scale section of the two main floors with mesasurements. To the right, in red pencil, he sketched hastily various buildings labeled as St Peter's and Baths of Diocletian. | ACF

BIBLIOGRAPHY Ferri (1885) 193, 203; Lanciani (1902–12) III: 8; Jordan-Huelsen (1878–1907) I, 3: 518; Bartoli (1914–22) IV: figs 435, 436, pl 254, 255; VI: 80; Metternich (1972) Fig. 34; Frommel (1974) 180–81, fig. 92; Cerutti Fusco (1987) 302, 306, fig. 3; CensusIDs 242381, 10071450.

U 1112A *recto*

Giovanni Battista da Sangallo and Antonio da Sangallo the Younger

Rome, Forum Holitorium (S. Nicola in Carcere), details of the Ionic and Doric temples, probably early 1520s or later.

Dimensions 288 × 108 mm.
Technique Pen and brown ink.
Paper Fold marks, reinforced on verso.
Drawing Scale *piedi* and *dita*.

INSCRIPTION, Recto (Antonio's hand) *aca[n]to s[an]to nichola i[n] carcere; la colonna capitello e basa e alto pie 31–13; la[rch]itrave tutto e largo / dita 24½*

Verso (Antonio's hand) *Doricho aca[n]to s[an]to nichola / i[n] carcere Jovi statoris*

Giovanni Battista drew these sketches of the Forum Holitorium temples freehand. The column with its entablature section and the adjacent portal sketch at the top of the sheet are of the Ionic temple adjacent to the Theater of Marcellus, while the profiles on the lower part of the sheet are from the portal of the Doric temple at the south end of the group. Antonio and Giovanni Battista made sketches of the same elements on U 1090 and 1230A r. and v., 1174A r. and v., and 1270A v., with measurements that closely correspond to those given by Giovanni Battista. Giovan Francesco da Sangallo and Baldassarre Peruzzi drew comparable details of the Doric portal on U 1375A r. and 477A, but with measurements in *braccia* rather than *piedi*. For a discussion of Antonio's identification of the Doric temple as the Temple of Jupiter Stator, see U 1090A, 1230A, and 1174A.

This drawing should be dated no earlier than Antonio's and Giovanni Battista's studies of the early 1520s. Frommel has observed that Giovanni Battista began using *piedi* after about 1525 and his writing on this sheet corresponds with that of U 1657A v., which Frommel dates to after 1534. Antonio's handwriting suggests that he added his note after 1527. | ACH

BIBLIOGRAPHY Ferri (1885) 195; Bartoli (1914–22) IV: fig. 509, pl. 308; VI: 95; Crozzoli Aite (1981) 42, no. 34; Frommel (1994, *Introduction*) 45; CensusID 10018205.

U 1115A *recto*

Antonio da Sangallo the Younger and Francesco di Bartolomeo da Sangallo (?)

Survey of an ancient(?) volute, before 1528.

Dimensions 234 × 217 mm.
Technique Pen and brown ink.
Paper Lightweight, left edge restored
Drawing Scale Florentine *braccia*.

INSCRIPTION (Francesco's hand?) *inel mezzo da pie* (canceled); (Antonio's hand, before 1528) *dal chapo*

The timid strokes and the numerical values suggest that this detailed measurement of a volute was made by the same hand as U 310, 311, 980, and 1082A, and that Antonio made minimal additions. With its length of 2¼ *braccia*, or 1.26 meters, the volute is of considerable size, and the irregular measurements in *braccia fiorentine* point to an ancient piece. From these measurements it appears to be the same volute that Antonio drew again more exactly on U 1405A about 1519, probably from the present sketch (Frommel 1984 *San Pietro*, 291). There the lower end is shown as a fragment and the tapering of the three channels is rendered more precisely. In any case, U 1115A is one more piece of evidence for the close collaboration between Antonio and this rarely seen hand, perhaps that of his younger brother Francesco di Bartolomeo da Sangallo. The methodical representation in side view, perspective view, and profile, both at the top and in the middle, is also characteristic of Antonio, who corrected the draftsman only in what he called top and bottom and added two measurements together. The two sketches at the lower edge are hardly recognizable. | CLF

BIBLIOGRAPHY Ferri (1885) XVII, 92 (as Antonio Labacco); CensusID 10169518.

U 1117A *recto and verso*

Antonio da Sangallo the Younger

Verona, details of an arch of the exterior of Arena (*recto*), superimposed arches of Arena (*verso*); ca. 1526.

Dimensions 205 × 255 mm.
Technique Pen and brown ink.
Paper Lightweight, trimmed, mounted on another sheet.
Drawing Scale *piedi*.

INSCRIPTION, Recto (top left) *capitello*; (right, near center) *Lo penultimo* (*L'ultimo* canceled) *grado si è in piano / col di sotto dello architrave secondo*; (above this, turned 180 degrees) *sono archi 72*; *Di fora*; *in fondo* (repeated and canceled) / *al secondo / piano / pie 14*; *Drento*

Verso *cornicie / frecio / architrave*; *cornicie / fregio / architrave*; *Di dent[r]o*; *le porte sono alte / [come] quelle de fianchi*; *Dent[r] o allandito / in bracha [braccia] / dentro*

The recto of the sheet shows one of the impost capitals of the arch—of which the profile is also shown above the cornice, with the sheet turned 90 degrees—the subdivision of the blocks, and a sketch of the architrave and pilasters surrounding it. At the bottom is a plan showing the piers that served to support the arch and the piers at the back that defined the width of the deambulatory gallery on the ground floor. The measurement of the width of the arch shown here, 13 *piedi*, corresponds to the measurement noted on Giovanni Battista's perspectival drawing (U 3974A r.). The annotation in the middle of the right side states that the level of the penultimate tier of the *cavea* corresponds to that of the underside of the architrave of the second order on the facade. At the bottom are sketches showing the elevation of a pier surmounted by an entablature and a plan that Antonio may have been using to study the arrangement of columns in proximity to a series of walls. At the top, turning the sheet upside down, is a plan of two piers supporting the arches of the second order. The sketch shows that the section of the piers on this level is smaller, with the obvious result that the arch openings are larger than those on the level below. With the sheet turned another 90 degrees, Antonio drew the section of one of the piers and noted its dimensions.

The central part of the verso of the sheet shows three superimposed arches belonging to the surviving part of the outer ring of the Arena. There is only a sketchy drawing of the bottom arch, presumably because it was still partly buried during the first half of the sixteenth century. We can see that the arch of the second order sits on top of the lower entablature, above a course of stone blocks, whereas that of the third order, which is less tall, opens out onto three courses of blocks placed on top of the entablature, giving the appearance of a window. The proportional ratios of the heights of the courses of the third order up to the impost of the arch and the entablature of the second order are provided. The height of the course that acts as a base for the piers is fixed at 1; Antonio noted that the architrave, the frieze, and the cornice below this and the other courses, were of double height, whereas the course under the impost cornice of the arch was even higher (given as 3). One of the openings providing access to the tiers on the second level (visible in the background in Giovan Francesco's perspectival drawing on sheet U 606A r.) is shown as an example of a second order arch, with the note "Di dentro," because, as specified in the note lower down, these openings ("le porte") are of the same height as the arches on the facade: beneath this note a measured section appears to relate to an access corridor leading to the tiers or to a deambulatory gallery.

The small sketch at bottom right is also interesting, and is amplified by a note on the recto of the same sheet to the effect that the foot of the penultimate tier of the *cavea* is at the same level as the bottom of the architrave of the second order. | AGG

BIBLIOGRAPHY Giovannoni (1959) I: 20–21; Vasori (1981) 107–10, cat. nos 82, 83; Zavatta (2008) 188; CensusIDs 10072096, 10072115.

U 1119A *recto and verso*

ANTONIO DA SANGALLO THE YOUNGER

Ancona, Arch of Trajan, ca. 1532–35.

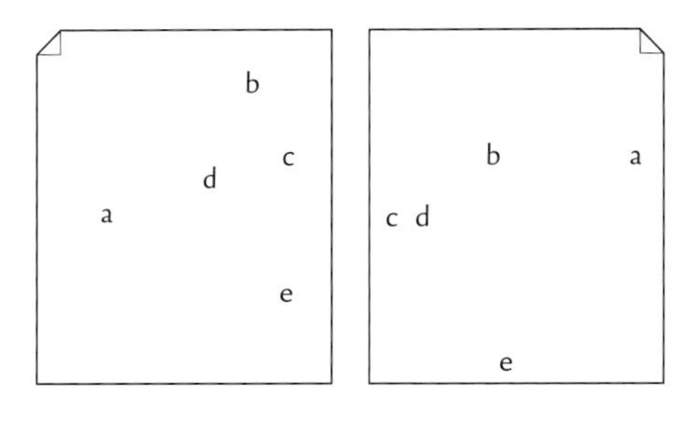

Dimensions 233 × 154 mm.
Technique Pen and brown ink, freehand.
Paper Reinforced at upper left edge.
Drawing Scale Roman *palmi.*

INSCRIPTION, Recto (c) *i[n] cima*; (e) *Dentro de / llo archo liscio / no[n] corre se non e / lo menbretto et / collarino*

Verso (d) *4 facie*; (e) *aqua*

All the drawings on the recto. are details of the Arch of Trajan at Ancona. Their sketched nature suggests that the sheet is probably a companion to U 1071A r. and v., the slight difference in size is due to the trimming of the latter, in which case the dating would be the same. Giovannoni (1959, I, pp. 20–21) posited that this sheet formed part of a sketchbook Antonio the Younger used on his travels. He believed that the book also included U 1066A, dated here to about 1531, which accords well with the presumed dates of the present drawings.

Drawing *a* is a side elevation, complete except for the lower part of the basement; *b* is an abandoned sketch, probably intended to be the profile of the entablature of the arch, *c*, drawn immediately below. Between *c* and *a* is a profile of the attic cornice, *d*, as the annotation confirms. Drawing *e* shows the inner face of one of the piers, which the annotation explains was smooth apart from the astragal and fillet running just below the impost.

All the drawings on the verso are details of the Arch of Trajan, continuing the series on the recto. Drawing *a* is the profile of the lower apophyge of a column shaft, obviously abandoned in favor of *b*, which has the same detail at the top and continues through the composite base of the column, its two plinths and pedestal, to the top of the basement. What appears to be a copy of the profile of the base molding of the pedestal immediately to its right is probably the set-back base molding in the intercolumniation between the pedestals. The projection of the cornice of the pedestal strays over into the field of drawing *c*, which is an elevation and profile of the archivolt of the arch and profile of the impost and the astragal and fillet molding just below it. Drawing *d* repeats the last detail at the same scale for no obvious reason. Drawing *e* is a profile of the basement, stretching from the base molding of the pedestal down to the lowest plinth at sea level, indicated by the reference to *aqua* (water). | IC

BIBLIOGRAPHY Giovannoni (1959) 1: 21; Vasori (1981) 110, cat. nos 84, 85; CensusIDs 10072125, 10072138.

U 1120A *recto and verso*

Antonio da Sangallo the Younger

Rome, Quirinal, Temple of Serapis;
Circus Maximus, before 1546.

Dimensions 268 × 200 mm.
Technique Pen and brown ink.
Paper Center fold, tears, repairs.
Drawing Scale *stadii* (verso).

INSCRIPTION, Recto si trova alpalazo di f[...]; *piano; architrave de lo [e]lifizio di mecenate / si trova cosi i[n] [...] dello edifizio* (*uno sasse* [...] canceled) *al presente / i[n] santo apostolo i[n] palatio de cholona / e stava cosi; questo e i[n] pie / come uno lato; tutto questo e i[n] pie*

Verso *circo massimo / era longo tre stadii / largo uno stadio / che sono piedi quadri— 1.171.875 / e pare che privio voglia che sia / quattro iucheri e nove* [...] *fronte / p[er]che 4 iucheri sono 115.200 /* [...] *dire che questa parte / chede edifichata ochapa 4 iugieri*

On the recto is a study of the right part of the still-extant gable wall of the monument, which Antonio the Younger, partly following the interpretation of his uncle Giuliano, cautiously referred to here as a neutral "edifitio di mecenate" rather than a palace. The gable wall terminates in a corner pilaster. The indication of an altar within an apse is evidence that the structure was recognized as a sacred building and not a palace. The related study is a perspective view of an entablature. Below it is the *drawing* of a entablature zone and a pediment with a scrollwork frieze and a figure. The brilliant small sketch in the lower edge looks like a reconstruction of a part of the Temple of Maecenas.

The verso gives the measurements of the Circus Maximus, possibly part of the survey of ancient Rome initiated by Raphael. | HCD

BIBLIOGRAPHY Ferri (1885) 156; Vasori (1981) 110, cat. no. 84; CensusIDs 10072388, 10081737.

U 1121A *recto*

Antonio da Sangallo the Younger

Study in plan and elevation of a
Corinthian capital, ca. 1530.

Dimensions 237 × 175 mm.
Technique Pen and ink, straightedge, compass, stylus, freehand.
Paper Trimmed at bottom edge, tears, reinforced, mounted on another sheet.

INSCRIPTION (19th-century hand, Ferri?) *854*; *212*; (Antonio's hand, in same ink as drawing) *L iiij*; *sechondo vitruvio vole sieno / alti quanto elacholonna dapie collagietto / della campana e la cimasa sia la settima / parte e la cimasa sia largha da angolo ad angholo / per la linia in quarto buono*[?] *overo diagonia / due tanti e poi sia schavato in dentro / la cimasa una nona parte della sua faccia. / non fa mentione della facietta delli corni / pare voglia che ditti corni siano / puntati*; (at right) *sono puntuti li chorni*[?] */ a chasa pierantonio mattei in tresteveri ne sta uno cholli*[?] *Corni puntati / in la strada abozate e quelli disanto stefanello ritondi aponte / santa maria*; (in plan) *vivo da chapo / vivo da pie / collarino da pie*

Antonio drew three drawings in an attempt to interpret Vitruvius's directions (*De Architectura*, Book IV, ch. 1, 11–12) regarding the *symmetriae* and the decoration of Corinthian capitals, and the proportions of the abacus in particular, on an already partly damaged sheet of paper. The notes, in fact, follow the irregular line of the left margin; at the top, the plan, broken off on the diagonal, seems to have been added after the tear to the right corner of the sheet, given the fact that the lines appear to be unbroken. At the left of the geometrical construction of an abacus with pointed ends, partly drawn freehand, Antonio referred to the ratio 1:9 prescribed by Vitruvius between the rise of the hollow curve of the abacus and the side of the square in which it is inscribed, which, in the plan below, he rightly divided into nine parts. Below that is a half plan of the capital, together with its graphic construction, still at the level of the abacus but with projections of sections of the column at the upper and lower shafts as well as at the *collarino da pié*, and an elevation of the capital itself, closely correlated with the plan as in Serlio's *L'Architettura* (Fiore 2001, Book IV, fol. LXVIII r.). The face of the abacus has been divided into nine parts so as to achieve the rise.

Vitruvius indicated that the total height of the capital should be equal to the diameter of the column at the lower shaft, and the vertical subdivision of the two orders of leaves, the *caulcoles* and the thickness of the abacus, the length of the diagonal of the abacus being equal to twice the height. Antonio endeavored to follow him precisely and took the overall diameter of the *collarino da pié* as being that of the lower shaft, which he showed on his plan. The Latin treatise, however, did not indicate the center point from which the curvilinear sides of the abacus should be drawn. Neither Fra Giocondo (1511), nor Cesariano (1521) showed how they managed to draw the curve in their illustrations. Antonio first placed his compass on the intersection between two arcs of circles that he drew, taking the edges of the side of the abacus as his center, with a radius equal to the length of the latter. This is a procedure similar to that of Serlio, who constructed an equilateral triangle with its base on the side of the abacus and then took the angle opposite as being the center of curvature. Antonio, however, seemed not to have been satisfied with this solution, having followed the same procedure when constructing the section of the abacus above the elevation, because he crossed it out with strokes of his pen. Then, starting at the intersection between the curve thus obtained and the side of the abacus, he found a closer center, from which he drew another minor curved arc that enlarges the concavity. A speedy solution that agreed with Vitruvius's text was later proposed by Jean Gouion in the edition of *De Architectura* published by Jean Martin (Paris, 1547), which involved duplicating the square, constructing a square taking the side of the abacus as its diagonal (*Vitruve, De l'Architecture, Livre* IV, trans. and commentary by P. Gros, Paris 1992, pp. 80–81).

The detail of the *chorni* is the only one on this page that Antonio compared with ancient examples, recalling the capitals at *Santo Stefanello ritondo*, that is, the round temple of the Forum Boarium, in which the proportions of the abacus are in fact similar to Vitruvian ones, with corners that really are *puntuti*, like many from the Hellenistic era and like one that Antonio had seen at one of the Mattei houses in Trastevere, probably the one in Piazza Piscinula. Although he was familiar with these ancient examples and noted that Vitruvius's lack of comment suggested that the latter had an abacus with acute angles in mind—"non fa mentione della facietta delli corni / pare voglia che ditti corni siano / puntati"—Antonio cut the points off what he described as the *chorni* of the abacus, thus achieving a less graceful and elegant shape than other graphic interpretations of the same subject published in his day. *Chorni* that have been blunted in the same way also appear, however, in U 1385A by Giovan Francesco da Sangallo, again in a drawing in which the plan and section of the Corinthian capital are accompanied by a paraphrase of the text of *De Architectura*, using the same vocabulary as Antonio, which would attest to the existence of a connection between the Vitruvian studies of the two cousins. | PNP

BIBLIOGRAPHY Ferri (1885) 17; Giovannoni (1959) I: 23, 27.

U 1122A *recto and verso*

ANTONIO DA SANGALLO THE YOUNGER AND GIOVANNI BATTISTA DA SANGALLO

Rome, plans and section of the Theater of Marcellus, after 1519–20.

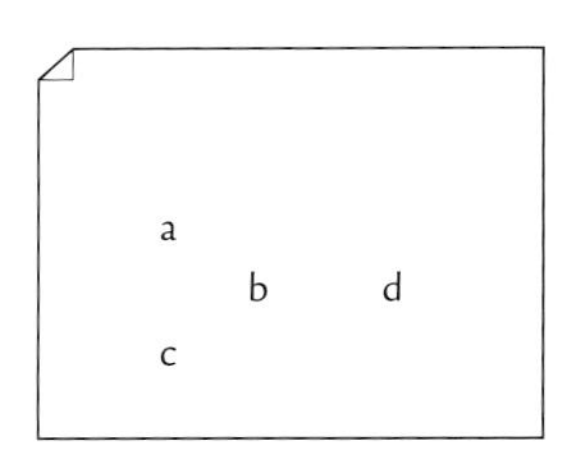

Dimensions 463 × 587 mm.
Technique Pen and brown ink, straightedge, stylus.
Paper Center fold.
Drawing Scale Roman *piedi.*

INSCRIPTION, Recto (upper left) [turned 90°] *teatro delli / signori Savelli / Quarto*; (a) *a scontro al / XII arco; andito di sopra; volta che/piglia due / vani e uno / muro*; (b) *piano; imposta; colonna; volta in testa / le due branche*; (c) *mezo; andito di sopra; questi non ci / sono; da tutto il pilastro che / 36 a 35 fino allamezo della / finestra dell andito pie[di]; piedi; piedi; della facia del porticho / fino alvivo delli mem / bretti di fuore sia piedi 31; dalluna loggia allaltra sie piedi 301. tutto sie piedi 442; dal vivo delli secondi / pilastri dalluno allal / tro lasando landito / e li pilastri di fora / sie piedi 405 e 8½ / Landito e pilastro sie / piedi – 19 6 / laltro sie 19 6 / Tutto sie 444 4½*; [cancelled] *Dall uno de pilastri / secondi allaltro / sie piedi colli pilastri/ sie 325/ lapiaza colli due/ portici sia/ 465–4; la vorrebbe essergni quella/ inposta di volta che qui/ sotto; la quale* [unreadable] *i[n]posta*; various measurements

Verso (left half) *greco; libeccio* (repeatedly); (right half) *cornice; zocolo; pilastro; pie 34*; various measurements

On the left half of this sheet's rectp are three sketches of the Theater of Marcellus. At the top (*a*) is a study of the passages and ascending ramps; the sketch below (*b*) [turned 180°] shows a detail of the vaults, with some measurements noted. The plan below (*c*) is an attempt of a graphic reconstruction of the plan of the theater in the *a ovato* version. This hypothesis is supported by Antonio's Vitruvian geometric scheme for the Greek theater, elaborated, for example, in U 1072A r.; the geometric construction, however, does not appear overtly in U 1122A.

The constituent elements of the Theater of Marcellus are all present in this sheet and bear witness to Antonio's deep understanding of the typology of the antique theater. The scenic structure, however, appears unresolved, especially in the *paradoi* (*itnera*) and *columnatio* of the *frons scaenae*, which appears just faintly sketched in the row of four columns. At right is a schematically drawn *porticus post scaenam* with a row of pilasters, inserted in strict relation to the apsed *aula regia*.

On the right half of the recto (*d*) is a representation of the section of the *cavea* and the colonnade, with a few measurements. Many uncertainties remain concerning the crowning of the attic zone, the functionality of the intersecting ramps of stairs, and the complicated construction system of the vaults. These difficulties derive above all from the impossibility of surveying the entire ancient structure and of reconstructing it from the spotty mosaic of remaining fragments.

On the right half of the verso is another unfinished sketch of the same section, which has some differences and additional measurements. The study of the ramps appears more precise and a series of indications underline the position of the levels of seats. At the upper right are two measured profiles of a base and a cornice. On the left half is an unfinished sketch of a plan that seems to suggest a horseshoe form for the theater. | ACF

BIBLIOGRAPHY Ferri (1885) 193; Lanciani (1902–12) III: 8; Jordan-Hülsen (1907) I, 3: 518; Bartoli (1914–22) III: figs 433–34, pls: 252–53; VI: 80; Giovannoni (1959) I: 20 n.; CensusIDs 242533, 243008.

U 1123A *recto*

Antonio da Sangallo the Younger

Rome, Forum Transitorium, ca. 1520.

Dimensions 498 × 342 mm.
Technique Pen and grayish black ink, scored, straightedge, compass.
Paper Two sheets glued together, tears, lower right corner missing, restored.
Drawing Scale Roman *palmi* and Florentine *braccia.*

INSCRIPTION *foro di S basilio*; *questi i[n]tercolunni sono/ i[n]equali cosi come segniato/ riprovati*; *queste anchora/ sono canalure fine/ i[n]fondo grose palmi 6⅔/ canali 24*; *palmi 30/ canna di palmi*; *B[raccia] 12*; *B 4 partito i[n] sesanta/ p[er] bracio/ canna di bracia*; *palmi 426*; *questo sta bene riprovato*; *canali 24/ grosa B 1 minuti 45/ grosa B 1 mi 45/ canalte fini i[n] fondo*

This sheet is a continuation of U 1139A on the same scale depicting the Forum of Augustus, here called the "Foro di S. Basilio." The fact that the Forum Transitorium is measured in Roman *palmi* and the Forum of Augustus in Florentine *braccia* suggests that the work of measuring the dimensions of the imperial forums was given to different assistants.

Antonio's plan of the site records the congestion around the Temple of Minerva, including the exedra of the Forum of Augustus and the *porticus absidata*; the exedras placed back to back and the sketched apse of the Temple of Minerva are recognized as characteristic aspects of Roman forum architecture. Next to the six-columned pronaos of the Temple of Minerva, Antonio noted with singular precision the unorthodox deviations of the bay widths, which must have irritated him. On the interior, he reconstructed a triple-aisled arrangement with six columns per aisle, probably a freehand invention. | HCD

BIBLIOGRAPHY Ferri (1885) 165; Lanciani (1883, *Aula del Senato*) 24; Bartoli (1914–22) III: fig. 463, pl. 278; VI: 86; Nash (1961–62) II: 235, fig. 982; Günther (1981) no. 80; Günther (1988) 257, 271, 277, 279, nos 103, 150, ill. VII 35; Viscogliosi (2000) 125–28, cat. no. 10; Viscogliosi (2017) 101, 106, 111, figs 9–10; CensusID 239053.

U 1124A *recto and verso*

Antonio da Sangallo the Younger

Rome, Septizodium; reconstruction of the plan of the Mausoleum at Halicarnassus, ca. 1540.

Dimensions 289 × 429 mm.
Technique Pen and two shades of brown ink, stylus, straightedge, compass, pin.
Paper Medium weight, reinforced on verso.
Drawing Scale Roman *piedi* (1 *piede* = 3 mm) on verso.

INSCRIPTION, Recto (at left, turned 90 degrees) *Setto[n] Sola*; *p[er] setti[n]solea / ma sono tre ordini*; (at right, written in opposite direction) *Mausoleo*; *no[n] riesce Così*; *moduli 37*; *questo mezo / sie moduli / 98½ quali / sono piedi / 163–51/70* (canceled) / *elgiarebbo ae*(?) / *sserio p[ie]di 205 1/2*; *Lo moduio sie uno / piedi 36/37 di pie 1 36/37 / se fusi dui piedi no[n] / basta afare 411 piedi / ma[n]cho piedi 14*; (bottom right) *Colonne 36 Con quella / dentro al portico*

Verso *piedi uno* (calculations)

On the left half of this sheet, Antonio drew a perspectival view of part of a structure that he had labeled Settinsola, that is, the Septizodium, the ruins of which remained standing until 1588–89. As depicted, the construction has two unarticulated lower stories, with an upper story composed of a colonnade surmounted on the left by a stepped pyramid reminiscent of the Mausoleum at Halicarnassus, and on the right by a spire recalling the Tomb of Porsenna. It seems that Antonio was indulging in a fantasy reconstruction, combining unrelated ancient monuments about which he happened to be thinking at the time.

The partial plan immediately above the Septizodium relates to the plan of the Mausoleum at Halicarnassus, more of which is drawn on the right half of the sheet. For the more complete study, Antonio carefully used a stylus, a straightedge and a compass, as can be clearly seen in the areas of the plan that were not drawn over in pen and ink. It is, however, an unsatisfactory ("non riesce Così") effort to translate Pliny's verbal description (see U 1042A) into visual terms; the many cancellations and calculations are proof of Antonio's frustration in his attempt to reconstruct the ancient monument.

On the verso are calculations in Antonio's hand. | SE

BIBLIOGRAPHY Ferri (1885) 97, 174, 191; Bartoli (1914–22) III: fig. 441, pl. 259; VI: 82; Raub (2014) 181, fig. 11; Fane-Saunders (2016) 264–65; CensusID 10072399.

U 1126A *recto*

Giovanni Battista da Sangallo

Rome, section of the Flavian Amphitheater.

Dimensions 199 × 140 mm.
Technique Pen and brown ink.
Paper Stains.

INSCRIPTION *Coliseo*; *fa sol la fa*; (later hand) *Gobbo*

This is an incomplete and schematic section of the Flavian Amphitheater, in which a hypothesized arrangement of the rows of seats below the portico in *summa cavea* is represented; the vaulting system of the so-called *velarium* remains unresolved. Giovanni Battista interpreted the *velarium* as if it were supported by poles placed on the consoles of the attic and by cables attached on the inside rather than the outside of the structure, where they were in fact fixed. The drawing should be related to U 1136A r. and 1555A v. by Antonio the Younger and with 1126A by Giovanni Battista, as well as with a drawing in the Albertina (Egger 1903, no. 23v.). | ACF

BIBLIOGRAPHY Ferri (1885) 123; Egger (1903) no. 23v.; Bartoli (1914–22) IV: fig. 493, pl. 301; VI: 93; CensusID 10012682.

U 1127A *recto*

Antonio da Sangallo the Younger

Plan for a reconstruction of the Mausoleum at Halicarnassus, ca. 1540.

Dimensions 440 × 315 mm.
Paper Watermark featuring a shield with a star above and keys.
Technique Pen and Brown ink, prepared with stylus.
Drawing Scale Roman *piedi* (11,3 mm = 40 *piedi*).

INSCRIPTION (top from left) calculation of the total perimeter / *parte orientale scolpì Scopa*. (Center, from left to right) *settentrionale scolpì Briase / questo viene 412 incircuito / p[iedi] 9 D[ita] 2⅔ / piedi 30 / Prova p(er) trovare lo disegnio / delmausolio ma non riferi[to] / alle misure torna piedi / 412* eliaessere *411 / cioè* elorecinto / *questo veniria intorno piedi 423 Dita 8 / meridionale scolpì Thimotheo.* (Lower part of the sheet) *piedi 9 D[ita] 2⅔ / piedi* (cancelled: "*30*") *28 D[ita] 14 / piedi 53 D[ita] 12 / parte occidentale scolpì Liocaro / Corintio.* (In the margin of the sheet, in later handwriting) *128*

Like sheet U 1128A r., this drawing is an attempt to reconstruct the shape of the Mausoleum at Halicarnassus, which deviates slightly from Pliny the Elder's description and ties in with various schemes based on rectangular plans shown on sheet U 1039A verso. Sangallo drew on the ancient text only to mention the perimeter of the edifice which, as the inscription in the middle of the page states, measures 412 *piedi* rather than the 411 indicated by Pliny. The drawing differs deliberately from the ancient model and from the reconstructions in the sketches on sheets U 1040A, U 894A and

U 1037A. Nevertheless, this design also seems to have been influenced by data furnished by earlier reconstructions, such as the width of 73 piedi of the side avant-corps, which possibly derives from notes on sheet U 894A. The octagonal shape of the cella, adapted for the longitudinal crossing, takes up a similar space to that explored in the left scheme of drawing U 894A recto. The total number of 56 columns appears to be the result of a loose interpretation of the ancient text, which actually prescribed 36 columns. Two different designs for the intercolumniations are shown on the sheet, on the top and left sides they measure 7 *piedi*, but are reduced to 6 ½ on the top and right sides and the central axis widened to 9 *piedi*. Despite these variations, Sangallo had to begin his drawing with a subdivision in stylus that envisaged entirely homogenous intercolumniations. This serves to confirm the function of measurements in Sangallo's project, given that he continued to work on new designs even after he had produced a fair copy. The edifice as a whole has a central crossing axis, which divides the cella, articulated on the exterior by pilasters with alternating niches, into two parts. This method was frequently adopted in ancient architecture, as demonstrated by the alternating square and apsided niches. | VZ

BIBLIOGRAPHY Ferri (1885) 97; Giovannoni (1959) I: 11, 24; Raub (2014) 181, 190–91, fig. 12; Fane-Saunders (2016) 265–66; CensusID 10074770.

U 1128A *recto*

Antonio da Sangallo The Younger

Plan for a reconstruction of the Mausoleum at Halicarnassus, ca. 1540.

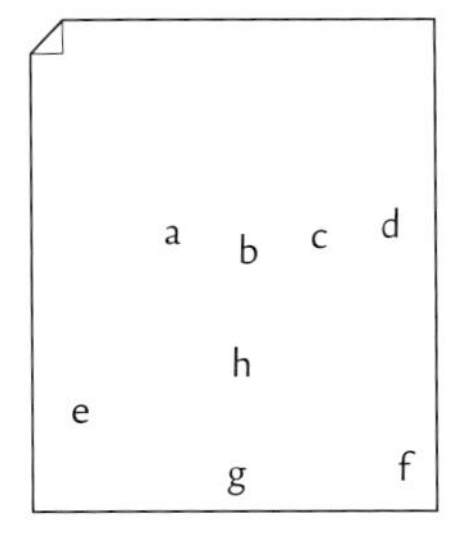

Dimensions 430 × 317 mm.
Paper Watermark featuring a shield with a star above and keys, excellent condition.
Technique Stylus construction; pen and brown ink.
Drawing Scale 11.3 mm = 50 modules.

INSCRIPTION (*a*) *questa piramide e necesario sia longa / in cima perche laquadriga di quattro Cavagli / e la carrozza sie più longa che larga*; (*b*) *piedi 25 / piedi 10 / Longo p(er) laquadri (…) e carrozza incima della piramide*; (*c*) *questo viene così egiraria piedi 400 & Dita 14 / facendo lo intercolumnio dellotastilo Comequello / de mezo delli fronti viene apunto 4ii*; (*d*) *questo così non viene piedi 73 come lui adavenire / viene piedi 67 Dita 15 / Allargando quello tercolumnio di mezo viene apunto 411*; (*e*) *L' intercolumnij demezo / lottastilo bisognia farlo / moduli ii come que / lli delli fronti* (…) *piedi* (cancellato: *piedi*) *10 D*(ita)*2; 50/79; Lipilastri bisognia siano piedi i d 18/79*; (*f*) *Lo modulo sie Dita 14 62/79 / La colonna e grossa moduli / 4 che sono piedi 3 D*(ita) *11 & 11/79 / Lo intercolunnio picolo sia moduli 6 che sono piedi – 5 D(ita)8 & 56/79 / moduli 6 che sono / piedi – 5 D*(ita) *8 & 56/79 / Lo intercolunnio per avanti sia moduli 11 sono piedi 10 D*(ita) *2 & 50/79*; (bottom center) *moduli X; tutto moduli L*. In the margin of the sheet, in later handwriting: *129*.

This drawing is a design similar to the one on sheet U 1127A r., to which it also relates in terms of the size of the sheet, the stylus preparation and the almost identical drawing scale. Despite these analogies, however, the edifice on this sheet should be regarded as a more realistic proposal, with four avant-corps and a double colonnade on all four fronts. The rectangular cella, devoid of architectural articulations to the walls, is connected to the two shorter fronts and surrounded by large walls 14 *piedi* thick. On the outside, the cella is articulated by alternating quadrangular and rectangular niches separated by narrow pilasters. The drawing shows a pentimento near one of the entrances (*h*). The cancelled solution had envisaged freestanding columns by the entrance, which means that the cella would have been open right along the two shorter sides.

It is impossible to state with any certainty which of the two sheets shows the most advanced design, although the more simplified transcription of the measurements would suggest that the version on sheet U 1128A is later than the one on U 1127A r., but unlike the drawing on U1127A r., the central intercolumniation of the hexastyle front is wider than the side intercolumniations. Here again, Sangallo deviated from the measurements prescribed by Pliny, using the need to place the quadriga on the top to justify his solution (inscription *e*, *d*). He does not, therefore, appear to be paying attention to Pliny's indication, which describes an edifice with two shorter fronts. As in the very first solutions on a square plan, Sangallo has again kept to the idea of making the corners of the edifice recede, thus rendering the colonnaded avant-corps visually independent of the volume of the cella. | VZ

BIBLIOGRAPHY Ferri (1885) 97; Giovannoni (1959) I: 11, 24; Raub (2014) 181, 185, 190–91, fig. 13; Fane-Saunders (2016) 265; CensusID 10074822.

U 1131A *recto*

Antonio da Sangallo the Younger

Ferento, Roman theater, measured ground plan, ca. 1536.

Dimensions 406 × 288 mm.
Technique Pen and black ink, stylus, straight-edge, compass.
Measurements: Roman *piedi* (60 *piedi* = 82 mm).

Inscription (to the right) *archi 27; non torna lo vano 144; in quadro; passi 28*; measurements.

This is an attempt at a graphic restitution of the ground plan of the theater at Ferento. It is part of a series of five drawings by Antonio the Younger dedicated to the same subject (U 1131A, 1132A, 1300A and 1301A r/v). Furthermore, the plan of the theater is related to, but in many ways different from, the drawings of Baldassarre Peruzzi (U 364A v., 387A, and 491A) as well as the drawing by Giovanbattista (U 1966A v.) The number of the arches was easily discovered *in situ* and with reference to this, Antonio hypothesizes the geometric matrix of the corridor and of the auditorium. It is clear that the scena is the part of the theater best conserved and most stimulating for Antonio, who attempts as faithful as possible a restitution. This plan, accurately surveyed, with measurements carried over in an ordered way, is the result of profound study, as is the drawing U 1300A, carried out, as one can gather from some marginal notes on the drawing, with the help of collaborators, among them probably Giovanbattista, author of another graphic restitution in U 1966A v.

There are many contradictory and difficult points which remain in an undetermined state in the drawing, such as the entire system of interconnection between the scenic structure and cavea, which in Latin theaters is typically resolved in a different way from the Greek theaters: this was a difficult knot to unravel because of the scarcity of information on site and because of the difficulty of interpretation of the descriptions provided by Vitruvius and Leon Battista Alberti, which were presented without illustrations. The relation of the drawing to Alberti's *De Re Aedificatoria* reveals that the theater is in the shape of a horseshoe, clearly visible thanks to the imprint left by the stylus and the barely-sketched cavea, placed inside the orchestra facing the doors of the hospitalia. This solution is studied on the left half of the ground plan of the Theater of Ferento by Antonio the Younger in U 1132A and also in a theoretical study, visible in U 1240A r./v. (in the lower part of the drawing), which concerns the Vitruvian scheme for the Greek theater interpreted in two alternative versions. | ACF

Bibliography Ferri (1885) 193; Galli (1911) 215–17; Giovannoni (1959) I: 22–23; Vasori (1981) 111–12, cat. no. 86; CensusID 10077047.

U 1132A *recto*

Antonio da Sangallo The Younger

Ferento, ground plan of Roman theater.

Dimensions 297 × 434 mm.
Technique Pen and brown ink, straightedge, stylus, compass.
Paper Center fold, restored.
Drawing Scale Florentine *braccia*.

Inscription (top left) *guarda le porte che altezza anno e che larghezza quando hai trovato lo cientro gira lo filo altondo nelo dove lo puoi girare perché dubito che non sia tondo cosi abia dello aovato. avresti poi bene fatti dauna banda e risolvimi tutti questi dubij e guarda a non mela fare virare indietro e trovato* [...] *che tu hai lo cientro gira conuno filo dove puoi per vedere se va altondo e se aovato*; (left, inside parascenia) *Questa parte non va al punto diritta qui sopra secondo vitruvio ci ha da essere li gradi fino a diritto della sciena e da questo muro inanzi sono tagliati per di questa entrata sicche guarda setucivedi misure segnate di questi tramezzi che sono pareggiati ivero setucivedi segniale di volta*; (further down) *itinera ospitalia*; (at margin) *Questi pilastri che sono* [...] *in sino questo muro grosso*; (center, lower edge) *tutta la faci larga b 110 porta regia*; (top right) *vedi se il primo regolone quale e sopra alti archi da questa banda fa fronte con quello recolone della facciata e colle cornicie della sciena si piglia tutte le misure se possibile e massimo della pianta e massimo dove vedi puntato e dove schrito e soprattutto tira quello filo dritto da luna allaltro delultimi pilastri e vedi quanto el passa fuora dalla sciena overo discosto e gosi quanto lo cientro si discosta dal ditto filo*; (below, turned perpendicular) *Tira qui uno filo che vada parallelo col muro grosso discosto tanto da un capo quanto dallaltro e fa che tochi lo tondo come e seguitato e segnia quanto andra discosto dal muro grosso*; (right, inside parascenia) *Vedi se potesi vedere questi archi se bene li dovesse fare cavare mena teco due o tre uomini con gravine e pale da potere scoprire*; (at margin) *Questo muro in sul tuo disegno sta gosi braccia 2 me lo desti palmi 9½ guarda come li sta e se sta cosi fuora di squadra e quanto sta fuora di squadra*; (along fold) *dal cientro al circolo sie bracia 53*; (along diameter of orchestra) *e qui tira lo filo ancora e trova bene questo cientro e vedi questo si schosta dal filo diritto tira qui uno filo diritto P su questo filo and angolo retto b 166*; (in vertices of triangles) *scala*

This is one of the most significant early sixteenth-century drawings of a restoration of an ancient theater completed with the help of the Vitruvian scheme for the Latin theater.

In this study, Antonio the Younger presented the typology of the Roman theater in a substantial way, although it is incomplete and not without errors. The restitution offered by Antonio for the *cavea* and for other parts of the theater of Ferento, however, does not correspond with that which the most recent excavations have brought to light, as noted by Vasori. The fortunate circumstance of the conservation of an adequate part of the scenic structure allowed Antonio to reconstruct it graphically, with few reworkings. The version at the right, in fact, varies with that at the left in several important details concerning the parascenia and the connection of the *cornua* of the *cavea* to the scenic structure. Indeed, at the left, the connection is a horseshoe and the proposed opening that ought to correspond to the *parados* is quite broad and just next to the *frons scaenae*, while at the right, the scenic structure is connected to the *cavea* by means of a section of rectilinear wall interrupted by a narrower door. These doors allow for communication between the proscenium and the parascenia but do not seem to have the value of *paradoi*, since the inscription "itinera" seems rather to indicate the *valvae hospitales*. As for the parascenia, in his annotation Antonio expressed doubts about the inclined position of the walls, which do not seem to agree with Vitruvius's description of this feature: this is confirmation of Antonio's practice of consulting Vitrivium, also evident in his studies of ancient theaters and theaters *all'antica*, where he consistently employed the Vitruvian scheme for the Latin theater. He also expressed doubts concerning the dividing walls at the left, which are indicated by hatching, possibly to denote, correctly, the different period of construction.

The Vitruvian scheme also allowed Antonio the place the seven access ramps, denoted by the inscription "scala"; the alignment, with a slight disparity of the *frons scaenae*; the royal door, the *itinera*; and the limit of the *post scaenium*. Antonio suspected, however, that the form of the orchestra and the *cavea* was *aovata* rather than round, and in order to clarify this uncertainty, he noted at the left margin of the sheet all of the verifications and surveying methods that had to be applied, presumably by his brother Giovanni Battista with assistants. A similar uncertainty is shown by Antonio in U 1300A v. for the theater at Ferento, in the drawings of the Theater of Marcellus, and in the theoretical studies and projects for theaters *all'antica*, including those for the Villa Madama.

Regarding the *cavea*, the proposal for substructures and pilasters placed concentrically supporting the levels of seats has been shown to be mistaken in the light of the excavations of 1911, as Vasori has observed. The solution of the sustaining pilasters is different from that conjectured in drawing U 1131A, in which the division is set along the radius of the *cavea*. | ACF

BIBLIOGRAPHY Ferri (1885) 193; Galli (1911) 215–17; Giovannoni (1959) I: 12, 22; Frommel (1974) 181–82, fig. 98; Vasori (1981) 112–14, cat. no. 87; CensusID 10075588.

U 1133A *recto*

Giovanni Battista da Sangallo

Rome, ground plan of Baths of Caracalla.

Dimensions 396 × 273 mm.
Technique Pen and brown ink, straightedge, stylus, compass.
Paper Fold, stains, traces of glue.
Drawing Scale Florentine *braccia*.

INSCRIPTION (Antonio's hand) *terme antoniane in braccia fiorentine*; *aria* (repeated several times)

This measured and scaled plan is identical to U 476A r. by Baldassarre Peruzzi (the plan that serves as the basis for Serlio 1540, III, p. 88), with the exception of small omissions or changes in the graphic reconstruction of certain parts. For example, here, in the enclosure of the baths, there are no columns on the left side of the apsed space at the top, nor on the wall at the end of the two small rectangular rooms to the side, columns that do appear in the Peruzzi drawing. The same omission is to be noted in the central body, on the side of the portico facing the apse, where the solution is different from Peruzzi's, and once again on the left side of the apsed space at the bottom right, where instead of the four columns in Peruzzi's version, only two are indicated. The measurements correspond exactly. Details of the enclosure of these same baths are studied in the drawings U 1093A by Labacco and U 1381A, 1656A, and 4117A by Giovanni Battista da Sangallo, and U 1227A and U 1369A by Antonio the Younger. The drawing under consideration seems to be the final version based on U 1381A r. by Giovanni Battista. There are many studies and plans of the Baths of Caracalla; see, for example, the drawings of Bastiano, known as Aristotile (U 1827A v.). | ACF

BIBLIOGRAPHY Ferri (1885) 202; Lanciani (1897) 542; Lanciani (1902–12) II: 183; Bartoli (1914–22) IV: fig. 524, pl. 314; VI: 97; Valori (1985) 134; CensusID 10072264.

U 1134A *recto and verso*

PIETRO ROSSELLI

Rome, ground plans of temples (*recto*); Theater of Marcellus(?); general schematic sections (*verso*), after 1519–20.

Dimensions 214 × 291 mm.
Technique Pen and sepia ink, freehand.
Paper Paper, mounted on card, signs of restoration to the recto.
Drawing Scale Roman *piedi.*

INSCRIPTION, Recto *p[er] lo Culiseo / p[er] uno verso el uino 628 e 2/3 / p[er] l altro 523. Bisognia / diminuirsi le proporzioni / overo lo modulo; p[er] le plastine p[er] un verso 240 / p[er] l altro 160*; several plans and volumetric sketches, numerous calculations and sums

Verso *dua quadri e mezo; ionicho; Doricho*, calculations

At the top right of the recto there is a volumetric sketch of a pier with an Ionic order. At the center left there is a rather hastily sketched concise plan, which presumably relates to the side of a proscenium pulpit, showing the apsidal spaces taken up by the aula regia, which Bartoli ascribes to the Neptunium. There is a plan of a temple at the bottom right, drawn extremely schematically, which Bartoli ascribes to the Ionic temple at the Forum Olitorium, later the site of S. Nicola in Carcere. At the top left of the sheet, there is a detail of the temple study in plan form. In the same position, at the bottom of the sheet, there is an oval (polycentric) plan, attributable to the Savelli Theatre. The inscription "Savilli," next to the scheme, presumably denotes the Theater of Marcellus.

On the verso first a rectangle with additional subdivisions was drawn, corresponding to the sequence of orders along the outside wall of the theater: "dua quadri e mezo [corintio] […]; ionicho; doricho" can be read., in which later on were inserted two hastily drawn sketches of a longitudinal and a transversal section of a *cavea* and the relative ambulatory. The flights of steps have been rather vaguely illustrated, and the tiers are barely distinguishable. There are also various additions and calculations. | ACF

BIBLIOGRAPHY Ferri (1885) 123, 193, 199; Egger (1903) no. 23v.; Bartoli (1914–22) III: figs 423, 424, pl. 244; VI: 63, 79; Tessari (1995) 127, 146; CensusIDs 242954, 243000.

U 1135A *recto*

ANTONIO DA SANGALLO THE YOUNGER

Rome, Flavian Amphitheater, section of the attic zone, before 1527.

Dimensions 291 × 213 mm.
Technique Pen and brown ink.
Paper Lightweight, mounted on cardboard.

INSCRIPTION *I[n]tenne / di travi; Coliseo aveva 80 archi e ogni aveva / tre i[n]tenne e ciascuna i[n]tenna aveva uno / paro di traglie di modo erono 240 para / di traglie a tirare el cielo qual era di panno rosa/to ordinariamente e alcuna volta di panno / de oro; travi; Colle me[n]sole e tra/vi come qui sta/va i[n] le teste cioe / travi […] p[er]cio / fa una testa / p[er]che no[n] ci sono / li pilastrelli e ci so/no ditte me[n]sole; Questi sono qui li / pilastrelli che sono / nel di de[n]tro della faccia / del culiseo che sono i[n] / su tre me[n]solee sopra del/le quali posava archi / dove si faceva sopra / lo solaro p[e]r stare in suso / attirare le traglie / del cielo e questo si era / nelli fianchi soli pilastrel/li […] p[er] ciascuno fia[n]/cho nelle teste stava / colle me[n]sole e travi / come qui aca[n]to; tetto; scala i[n]aria; volta acroseria; Colonne*

The drawing shows a profile of the attic zone with a detail of the system of cables of the so-called *velarium*, or, more precisely, the velum and the beams placed on large consoles. In addition, the sheet includes an axonometric sketch of the small internal pilasters supported on three consoles and the archivolt that rises above, as well as a sketch of the *porticus in summa cavea*, with an indication of the column, the rings of seats and the cross-vault that supports a stair. As for the sketch near the bottom of the sheet showing the roof on the inside of the Colosseum, a more detailed drawing of this area is found on U 1136A. | ACF

BIBLIOGRAPHY Ferri (1885) 123; Bartoli (1914–22) IV: fig. 372, pl. 219; VI: 70; CensusID 10072411.

U 1136A *recto*

ANTONIO DA SANGALLO THE YOUNGER

Rome, Flavian Amphitheater, perspective section of restitution, before 1527.

Dimensions 233 × 135 mm.
Technique Pen and black ink.
Paper Folded at the center and pasted.

This is a sketch of a perspective section of the *summa cavea* of the Flavian Amphitheater. It is an attempt at the restitution of the portico, a portion of which is sketched in the drawing at the bottom of U 1135A. To the right, there is a reference to a drawing which was subsequently cut away. Below is an axonometric sketch of the volume of the Colosseum. An interesting solution concerns the arched colonnade at the top of the *summa cavea*, a solution which Antonio the Younger proposes again, modified in a system of half-columns attached to pilasters linked by arches, for the project of a theater *all'antica*, U 1072A r. In the graphic restitution U 1555A v. Antonio the Younger imagines instead a system of arches sustained by vaults rather than by columns as considered in the drawing. Yet another system was proposed by Giovanni Battista in U 1887A. | ACF

BIBLIOGRAPHY Ferri (1885) 123; Bartoli (1914–22) IV: fig. 371, pl. 228; VI: 70; CensusID 10072423.

U 1137A *recto*

Pietro Rosselli and Antonio da Sangallo the Younger

Rome, Flavian Amphitheater.

Dimensions 263 × 156 mm.
Technique Pen and brown ink.
Drawing Scale Roman *palmi.*

INSCRIPTION *Colonna prima / del Culiseo di roma / sta cosi*; *palmi romani; tutto*

This is a survey with measurements in *palmi* of the Tuscan half-column at the first level of the Colosseum with base and capital. | ACF

BIBLIOGRAPHY Ferri (1885) 123; Bartoli (1914–22) IV: fig. 398, pl. 231; VI: 74; CensusID 10072452.

U 1138A *recto and verso*

Antonio da Sangallo the Younger

Rome, Piazza Giudea, so-called Porticus Pompeii, ca. 1520(?).

Dimensions 440 × 290 mm.
Technique Pen and black ink.
Paper Folded.
Drawing Scale Roman *palmi* and *minuti.*

INSCRIPTION, Recto (lower half) (left) *finestra*; *questo piano / della saglia e a mezo l archo / della faria; strada maestra*; *mezo*; (turned 180 degrees) *dal mezo* [...] *al chanto no / si vede 7 archi chomputando / quello del mezo fino a macielli / cioe ne poteva e*[*ss*]*ere un altro*; Upper half: (left) *tevertino*; *mezo*; (right) *questo / al sechondo pilastro* / [...] *della cholonna / che* [...]; *questi sono / i archi di so/pra; Tevertino*; *Dala porta di mezo fino / al mezo del pilastro qua in cha*[*sa*] / *lo notaro B*[*raccia*] *93 cio*[*e*] *deli scharpe/llini notaro*

Verso *Cachabario*; *Cantina del / notaro 15*; *serata di legnio*; *pilastro*; *Cantina / del chande/lottaro*; *da questa banda sie dal mezo / fino al pilastro sotto la chasa del notaro / delli scharpellini sono B*[*raccia*] *90, cioe a lo / pri*[*n*]*cipio del pilastro quale p*[*a*]*ia gro/sso chelli alto e p*[*er*] *questo pare la fine / di detto* [*e*]*difitio ed e mezo i*[*n*] *cantina / del notaro e mezo i*[*n*] *cantina de/1 chandelottar*; *Diciesi porticho di ponpeio / vulgarmente Cachabario e chi dicie / Casa di mario apreso a piazza giudea / santo salvatore e i*[*n*] *detto* [*e*]*difitio*; *S Sal/vatoris*; *qui si vede archi 7 i*[*n*] *opera / co*[*m*]*putando quello del mezo / cioe no poteva essere uno altro / fino alli macielli al chantone*

This sheet includes several sketches—probably made *in situ*—of the Porticus Pompeii, which during the Renaissance was thought on the basis of ancient descriptions to be part of the Theater of Pompeius. The recto has two ground plans and elevations, as well as a perspective view of a pier. On the verso, Antonio tried to reconstruct the ground plan, his interest being primarily in the corner pier.

Antonio's sketches were used by Peruzzi for the overall reconstruction of the ground plan on U 484A, which was published in Serlio's third book on architecture (Serlio 1540, fol. LVII). | HCD

BIBLIOGRAPHY Ferri (1885) 163, 191; Huelsen (1910) 9; Giovannoni (1912) I: 202; Bartoli (1914–22) III: figs 425–26, pl 245, 246; VI: 79; Günther (1981) 376–82, figs 17–18, 22; Günther (1988) 257, 267, 377, n. 102, figs VII: 31, 32; CensusID 10072515.

U 1139A *recto*

Antonio da Sangallo The Younger

Rome, Forum of Augustus, ca. 1520.

Dimensions 380 × 550 mm.
Technique Pen and dark brown ink, scored, straightedge, compass.
Paper Center fold, tears.
Drawing Scale Florentine *braccia* and Roman *palmi* (section adjacent to Forum Transitorium).

INSCRIPTION (top left) *Foro transitorio; questo e misurato a palmi/ 20* [...]; (on exedra) *questo e stato levato*; (center, left) *questo e misurato a bracia fiorentine/ e pero nella attachatura doue/ se attachano i[n]sieme ci sono le misure/* [...] *de palmi e delle bracia*; (below) *B 19–6 al fondo deli chanali/ della colonna a lo regolo/ sie B 18–56½/ da mezo a mezo*; (center, right) *lo bracio partito i[n] 60*; *pincnostilo lo i[n]tercholunnio/ sie uno diamitro e mezo della/ colonna e quello di mezo e dua diamitri*; (lower right) *questo e misurato a palmi/ romaneschi*; measurements: diameter of columns, *B 3–2*; pilasters, same size; thickness of wall of cella, *B 2–1½*; intercolumniation, *B 4–32* (last bay); other bays, *B 4–22½*; width of cella, *B 38–40*.

This is a clean drawing of U 1141A r. and is continued on U 1123A. In a second phase, the drawing was corrected. The exedra oriented toward the Forum Transitorium was initially a quarter circle; it was later changed to a flatter curve. The Temple of Mars Ultor is partly reconstructed. Its square cella opens through a door into the pronaos; but where U 1141A shows an apse, 1139A lacks a solution. The interior arrangement is ignored. On the other hand, the colonnade surrounding the temple on three sides has been completed with eight columns in front and on each flank. This allowed Antonio to classify the temple as a *pyknostylos* in the Vitruvian sense. The three sketched-in sides of a square corresponding to six-and-a-half of the front columns probably belong to the medieval Church of S. Basilio. The open back of the church indicates that the drawing was left unfinished. | HCD

BIBLIOGRAPHY Borsari (1884) 5, 11, pl. 1; Ferri (1885) 166; Bartoli (1914–22) III: fig. 462, pl. 277; VI: 63, 86; Günther (1981) no. 80; Günther (1988) 257, 261, 272, 277, 280, ns. 103, 111, 150, fig. VII: 37., Viscogliosi (2000) 114–16, cat. no. 7; Raub (2014) 190; Viscogliosi (2017) 101, 106, 108, 110, figs 7–9; CensusID 238779.

U 1140A *recto and verso*

ANTONIO DA SANGALLO THE YOUNGER

Rome, Largo Argentina, Temple "A" (S. Nicola ai Cesarini); Forum Transitorium, Temple of Minerva; Forum Romanum, Temple of Vespasian (*recto*). Forum Romanum, Temple of Vespasian, Temple of Saturn (*verso*). After 1527.

Dimensions 294 × 437 mm.
Technique Pen and brown ink.
Paper Lightweight, center fold.
Drawing Scale *palmi* and *minuti*.

INSCRIPTION, Recto (left half) *Tempio deto al cardinale/ Ceserino fatto di tufo cop[er]to/ di stucho refatto come chiesetta/ che si domanda Sto apresso al ditto ce ne e uno/ tondo similme[n]te/ fatto di tufo e stucho; di foro tra[n]sitorio/ dal cornicione primo i[n] su; di foro tra[n]sitorio/ larga piedi 12–12; Cornicie di sopra/ del foro tra[n]sitorio/ cioe l'ultima*; (right half) *Capitolio; dalla facciata alla faccia di canpitolio p[almi] 94–6; Capitolio e qui l'opera doricha; facia dina[n]zi/ ne e i[n] pie solo queste/ tre colonne di questo/ edifitio qual e i[n] fra l'archo/ di luti settimio e Campitolio/ l'archo e qui; questo e tratto dal libro delli epitaffij/ questo pocho e i[n] o/pera*

Verso (left half) *qui e vachuo; queste parole solo; cimasa del capitello/ cori[n]tio; La basa e alta 2–6/ La colonna solo alta 9–10/ Lo Capitello alto 5–8; 1 uno ha le misure/ dell cornicione/ 1 Logetto delle base/ 3 Lo regolo sotto la base*; (right half) *Tempio dello i[n]ce[n]dio presso a Ca[m]pidoglio/ fatto di spoglie no[n] troppo bona cosa/ fatto di cattiva maniera; e mal co[m]posto cosi*

On the upper left half of the recto of this sheet, is a partial ground plan of the so-called Temple "A"—one of the four republican temples on Largo Argentina—which had housed the Church of S. Nicola ai Cesarini since the Middle Ages. Antonio correctly assumed that the front had six columns. The remaining sketches on the left half relate to the Temple of Minerva. They show a pilaster, the lower and upper profile of the Attic story of the forum wall, and the profile of the temple door. The right half of the recto shows more than half the ground plan of the Temple of Vespasian, which Antonio completed as a *peripteros* with 6 by 8 columns *sine postico*; the sole surviving three columns of one corner are drawn again at the lower right. The sketch at the right, next to the ground plan, is an attempt to complete the frontispiece of the temple with its inscription (CIL, vol. 6, 938); Antonio specifically identified the only surviving part, "STITVER" (cf. Codex Rootstein Hopkins fol. 16 *recto*, in this volume).

The verso shows the ruins of the Temples of Vespasian and Saturn, two nearby monuments. The left half of the sheet includes the entablature, the cyma of a capital, and the profile of the base of a column from the Temple of Vespasian. The Temple of Saturn on the right half is criticized by Antonio for its use of spoils, as "di cattiva maniera." He drew the shortened shaft of a column together with an entablature and inscription, and beside it, at the right, a partial ground plan with a six-columned pronaos. | HCD

BIBLIOGRAPHY Ferri (1885) 166, 198–99; Lanciani (1883, *Portici*) 12, pls. A, B; Lanciani (1902–12) III: 123; Bartoli (1914–22) III: figs 474–75; VI: 89; Giovannoni (1959) I: 25, 436; Günther (1988) 313, no. 269; CensusID 10072798, 10072698.

U 1141A *recto and verso*

Antonio da Sangallo The Younger

Rome, Forum of Augustus, Forum Transitorium (*recto*). Forum of Trajan (*verso*).

Dimensions 487 × 345 mm.
Technique Pen and brown ink.
Paper Center fold.
Drawing Scale Florentine *braccia* and *minuti.*

INSCRIPTION, Recto (left half) *S[an] basilio*; *stantia; moderno*; *camino*; *foro transitorio*; (right half) *questo va almezo*; *questo porta bungnie / vivo alfondo / aregoli*; *ne fondi / deli chanali*; *50 camino*[?]; *S[an] basilio*; *50 camino*

Verso *foro traiano*

The two parts of the drawing on the recto correspond to the two folded halves of the sheet, which must be read at right angles to each other. The sketch includes the exterior wall of the Forum of Augustus and the Temple of Mars Ultor, which is augmented by flanking columns and an apse and is referred to as S. Basilio, the monastic church into which it was transformed in the Middle Ages. This cursory drawing, with its numerous measurements, was probably made *in situ*. The three columns adjoining the pilasters of the exterior wall, the only ones standing at the time and still standing today, are drawn in detail; Antonio initially assumed that they were equidistant, then corrected himself.

Related to the Forum Transitorium are the two freestanding columns of the exterior wall, the so-called *colonnacce*, which are mistakenly shown as larger than the half *porticus* of the Temple of Minerva opposite.

On the verso is a sketch of what lies across from the Forum Augustus, that is, the Forum of Trajan, which, as conceived in the drawing, symmetrically encloses the Column of Trajan with six exedras. | HCD

BIBLIOGRAPHY Ferri (1885) 165, 167; Borsari (1884) 11; Bartoli (1914–22) III: figs 460–61; VI: 85–6.; Günther (1981) no. 80; Günther (1988) 257, 261, 272, 277, 279–80, ns. 103, 111, 150; VII: 36, 43; Viscogliosi (2000) 111–12, 112–14, cat. nos 5, 6; Viscogliosi (2017) 101, 105–06, 108, 110–11, figs 4–6; CensusIDs 238549, 238535.

U 1142A *recto and verso*

Antonio da Sangallo the Younger

Rome, Theater of Marcellus (*recto*); Temple of Forum Holitorium (*verso*); 1519 or later.

Dimensions 433 × 283 mm.
Technique Pen and brown ink (recto); pen and black ink (verso).
Paper Center fold, restored.
Drawing Scale Florentine *braccia.*

INSCRIPTION, Recto (upper half) (top right) *difitio della chiesa di S Nichola / come stava antichamente / saria sopra alle navette pichole / in questo difitio doricho*; (below, left to right) *travertini perini*; *peperini*; (next to profiles) *architrave sopra / alla cholonna*; *questo architrave / e quello che fa di quadraffondati / dalle cholonne al muro e / di travertino*; (slightly above these) *lo muro fatto li architravi* [...] / *tutto peperino* [...] *fregio*; (right, next to half-plan of royal hall) *Savelli*; (below apse) *qui sta cosi*; (lower half) (next to plan of temple) *carciere di tulio / ostilio dite tuliano*; (below Ionic capital, different ink) *Sine postico / Lo primo che verso / li Savelli achanto sto nichola*; (next to Corinthian capital) *di peperigno foderati di tufo*; *peperigno*; *travertini sopra le colonne*; various other inscriptions relating to materials

Verso (upper half) *varie piante*; (turned 180 degrees, in the plan) *porticho / porticho /S nichola / in charciere / stava cosi antichamen / te secome lo si vede / per le antichita sono / nelle mura della chiesa / moderna che si vede / precise che stava chosi*; (in the center of the sheet) *pelle* [= covering] *delle colonne / canalate murate nela faciata / dinanzi della chiesa di santo nicola / quale sono di peperini e sono/ ioniche foderate di stucco*; *pilastro canalato*; (vertical) *La diverso chiesa in la nave grande/di santo nichola*; (lower half, in the plan) *porta della chiesa*; (vertical) *s. nichola ioniche; Dove la fine del muro / anticho da ogni banda*; *qui non si vede/morse* [= clamps] *del muro della / porta*; (lower margin) *Pilastro fino al piano /di terra fura di tera 4 dita/canali 7 e da canali da dua/bande*; (right margin) *Doricho achanto S nichola*

On the recto, near the center fold, the solution with the oval form of the *cavea* for the Theater of Marcellus with uncovered *paradoi* in the Greek manner is typical of Antonio's typological research into ancient theater. The reconstruction of the royal hall is interesting. It is differentiated in its two sides, with the roofing with cross-beams at the center and the connection of the walls and the *porticus post scaenam*. The placement of the *columnatio* of the *frons scaenae* seems to have been in doubt, as revealed in the alternative versions at left and right: at the center, the *columnatio* is interrupted, corresponding to the *pulpitum* that projects into the proscenium, as in other drawings of theaters by Antonio (notably U 314A for Villa Madama). The orchestra appears excessively reduced and the two structures, the *cavea* and the *scaena*, appear close together in a paratactical way, in the Greek manner. An important detail is the *porticus in summa gradatione* sketched with a *columnatio* on the external curve of the *cavea*. Above this plan of the Theater of Marcellus are two profiles of architraves and an axonometric sketch of the detail of the colonnade of the pronaos and of the *perestasi* of a temple, perhaps from the Forum Holitorium. To the right of the plan, half of the royal hall is shown, cut at the level of the windows, rather than at the pavement.

On the lower half of the sheet is a measured plan of a detail of a temple of the Forum Holitorium at S. Nicola in Carcere, with a study of the relationship between colonnade and walls through the passage of pilaster strips that corresponds to the columns, a detail not found in the royal hall of the Theater of Marcellus, where there are half-columns attached to the walls. On the inside of the plan, a schematic Ionic capital is sketched. Perpendicular to this is the outline of a Corinthian capital. Finally, there is a trabeation indicating the different stone: travertine for the architrave and the frieze, and peperino for the cornice.

On the two halves of the verso, turned 180 against each other, there is a series of sketches in plan and elevation of the three temples, two Doric and one Ionic, adjacent to the church of S. Nicola. | ACF

BIBLIOGRAPHY Ferri (1885) 132, 143, 193, 195; Bartoli (1914–22) IV: figs 421–22; pl 247–48; VI: 78; Frommel (1974) 181, fig. 95; Günther (1988) 254, 316; Engel (2015) 110, 114, fig. 5; CensusIDs 10014174, 10014799.

U 1143A *recto and verso*

ANTONIO DA SANGALLO THE YOUNGER

Rome, Forum Romanum, curia with adjacent buildings (*recto*). fragment of *fasti* of priests of Tempio Propugnatore; sketches of unidentified ground plan and profile (*verso*); ca. 1520(?).

Dimensions 292 × 435 mm.
Technique Pen and brown and black ink.
Paper Heavy, folded twice, grid.

INSCRIPTION, Recto (left half) *Sta Martina*; (right half) *fodera / tufi e tevertini*; *facia ornata*; *foro o piaza / di S basilio / dalle imposte delli archi di foro / transitorio* [...]; *foro transitorio / piano / piano della pi/azza di S basilio*

Verso *qu[e]sto era i[n] terra i[n] sa[n]ta martina / acanto a marforio dov[e] erano / le storie d a[n]tonino pio che sono / i[n] capitolio*; various antique inscriptions

The recto is a preliminary drawing for U 896A, showing the location of the Marforio, the ground plans of S. Martina and the Church of S. Adriano in the curia, and, at the upper right, the exterior wall of the Forum Transitorium. The verso reproduces the fragment of the *fasti* (CIL VI. 2004–09). | HCD

BIBLIOGRAPHY Lanciani (1883, *Aula del Senato*) 14, 16; Ferri (1885) 134, 147, 166, 192; Bartoli (1914–22) III: figs 455–56; pl 270–71 VI: 84–85; Giovannoni (1959) I: 21; Günther (1981) no. 80; Günther (1988) 254, 265, 278, 280, ns. 68, 120, 144, 150; Viscogliosi (2000) 102–04, 108–09, cat. nos 2, 4; Viscogliosi (2017) 101, 103, 104; CensusIDs 237441, 238500.

U 1144A *recto*

ANTONIO DA SANGALLO THE YOUNGER

Rome, Campus Martius, studies of Temple of Hadrian, after 1527.

Dimensions 262 × 200 mm.
Technique Pen and black ink.
Paper Lightweight.

INSCRIPTION *Plastine*; *Le Colonne pu[n]teggiate / manchano*; *[e]difizio delle plastine / plastine*; *questa uolta / da questa banda / e qui e secondo questa / ma[n]cha una Colonna da / questa banda li verso sa[n]to apostolo*; *38* (canceled, possibly by Antonio)

The right half of the sheet shows a partial ground plan of the Temple of Hadrian, which Antonio had begun to reconstruct. Besides the eleven columns standing at the time, as they do today, four more can be identified by their dots as hypothetical additions, making a total of fifteen columns on either flank of the reconstructed building. The fourth column from each end is aligned with a corner pilaster. In the cella, the long wall is surprisingly thick, while each of the short walls has been replaced by two parallel walls enclosing narrow rooms. One of these rooms contains flights of stairs running in opposite directions. The freestanding columns of the interior are not extant and are probably also hypothetical. Their placement along the wall is established by the pilasters.

Antonio's conception of the pronaos is visible only in part. At one end he lengthened the wall of the cella by adding a parallel colonnade of three columns on axis with the corner pilaster. The number of columns on the front is not specified, but we can conclude from the drawing that there are eight. We thus have a temple with 8 by 15 columns; that is, a peristasis. The latter was known to Vitruvius only in connection with a *pseudodipteros*, which, as is made clear by the distance between the colonnade and the cella wall known from the ruins, is not what Antonio's drawing shows. On the other hand, the ruins leave no doubt that the temple had a colonnade with more than eleven columns. Accordingly, Antonio's conception can be defined as a compromise between what was extant and Vitruvian theory.

The top left of the sheet shows a cross section through the colonnade at the height of the Corinthian capitals, along with its entablature and the longitudinal vault above it. The connection of a second vault suggests that the cross section is made at the height of the pronaos, though exactly how high is not clear. The beginning of the longitudinal vault of the cella above the cornice of the interior order is also sketched in. In the lower left corner of the sheet, we see a perspective cross-section through an unrelated denticulated cornice. | HCD

BIBLIOGRAPHY Ferri (1885) 165, 195; Bartoli (1914–22) III: fig. 358, pl. 213; VI: 68; CensusID 249724.

U 1147A *recto*

Antonio da Sangallo the Younger

Spoleto, reconstruction in elevation
of portal of S. Salvatore.

Dimensions 276 × 200 mm.
Technique Pen and ink, straightedge, compass, stylus, pin.
Paper Heavy, trimmed on four sides, traces of glue, one edge reinforced on verso.
Drawing Scale Roman *palmi* (3 *palmi* = 35 mm.; ratio 1:20).

INSCRIPTION (19th-century hand, Ferri) *879*; (Antonio's hand) *palmi 8¼ larga*; *in Sangorzo fuora di Spuletj / in verso fulignio uno tiro / di balestro anno difitio qualera ra*[*sic*] *antichamente doricho / e per questo la chiamava porta doricha / Doricha ma li modani sono cori/nti elovano in alteza si e sechon/do che schrive vitruvio in la doricha*; (along metric scale on vertical axis) *palmi*; *alta palmi 18*; *moduli 12 alta*; (on base) *Larga dapie / palmi 8¼*; *larga moduli 5½ / da pie*

The Church of S. Salvatore near Spoleto, built between the fourth and fifth centuries reusing older materials for a largely Doric interior, then modified several times (Pietrangeli 1939; Ward-Perkins 1949; Salmi 1951), attracted the attention of the late-fifteenth-century Renaissance architects. Francesco di Giorgio Martini reproduced the facade and the central apse (see U 321A r. and his *Trattato I*, p. 287, pl. 93; Serlio 1537, fol. LII), and included an illustration of the central portal among examples of the Corinthian; it was presumably also surveyed by Michele Sanmicheli, who replicated it several times in his architectural works. It was also drawn by Palladio along with some other details of the interior (London, R.I.B.A. IX: fol. 17 r.; Zorzi 1956, p. 63, fig. 82). Antonio's is the oldest drawing of the portal to have been conserved, and the annotation "in San Gorzi fucra di Spuleti" is similar to Palladio's "questa porta si e sotto di Spoieti a una giesa dita di S. Giorzo." The relics of S. Concordio are preserved in the church, perhaps called "S. Gorzio" in the vernacular; Salmi (1951, p. 69) proposed, without justification, a "S. Senzio?"

Antonio first drew a scale version of the door with the caption "Doric," topographical directions, and measurements. He then checked his proportions against those prescribed by Vitruvius for the doors of Doric temples and added the second part of the caption (using a slightly different ink); the drawing thus documents his recognition and selection processes of the components of the orders from ancient architecture.

Antonio could still see that the nave had originally been delimited by columns with Doric capitals supporting an entablature with a Doric frieze and a cornice with brackets, and he therefore considered the entire edifice to be Doric. The portal should also have been so, as confirmed by its proportions, which he thought corresponded to Vitruvian ones, but the profiles and the richness of the carvings in particular persuaded him that it was Corinthian. Sanmicheli opted for ambiguity, including the portal with a simplified version of its carvings in the Doric construction of Porta Palio, but employing a richly decorated version in the Corinthian construction of the Pellegrini chapel. | PNP

BIBLIOGRAPHY Ferri (1885) 214; Giovannoni (1959) I: 22, 249; Salmi (1951) 65; Pagliara (1995) 144; CensusID 10074790.

U 1150A *recto*

Antonio del Tanghero and Antonio da Sangallo the Younger

Rome, Ionic entablature of church of S. Sebastiano della Valle, ca. 1518 and after 1527.

Dimensions 566 × 438 mm.
Technique Pen and brown ink, stylus, straightedge, details freehand.
Paper Mediumweight, watermark (ladder), center fold, restaured, edges reinforced, stains.

INSCRIPTION, Recto (Antonio del Tanghero's hand) *Da un moddello al attro cioe dove e rosone*; (Antonio's late hand) *a San Bastiano della / Valle sopra le colonne / del portichale in la facia / dinanzi in propria forma / levata el Rossello*

Verso (Antonio's later hand) *cornice di piu sorte antiche*

Bartoli, Giovannoni, and Scaglia incorrectly identified the subject as a detail of S. Sebastiano in Vallepiatta in Siena, where there is no comparable entablature. The drawing obviously represents an antique fragment that had been reused in the portico of S. Sebastiano della Valle, the church that preceded Sant'Andrea della Valle. | CLF

BIBLIOGRAPHY Ferri (1885) 154; Bartoli (1914–22) fig. 339, pl. 199; VI: 62; Giovannoni (1959) I: 102; Hibbard (1961); Scaglia (1994) 225–26; CensusID 10079150.

U 1152A *recto and verso*

Antonio da Sangallo the Younger

Rome, two ancient triumphal arches; sketch for decoration of a wall (recto). A molding and a console (verso). Before 1527.

Dimensions 340 × 463 mm.
Technique Pen and brown ink (recto); graphite, pen and brown ink (verso).
Paper Heavy, center fold.

INSCRIPTION, Recto (left half) *sala longa B[raccia] 38¾ / larga B[raccia] 22 1/1; chamera longha B[raccia] 22 1/1 / p[er] chiachuna parte; la chamera di sopra p[er] lunghe/zza B[raccia] 30 larga B[raccia] 22 1/1*; (right half) *Porte di metallo*; *archo di / chamiglia/no*; *i[n]giano achanto la minerva / doue la chonpagnia della / nuntiata* (these 3 lines canceled)

The left half of the recto shows the ground plan and elevation of a niched wall for an unspecified secular building. The right half contains sketchy ground plans of two ancient triumphal arches, the lower one located on the Campus Martius next to S. Maria sopra Minerva. The drawings of a console and molding in elevation on the verso are for a modern building. | HCD

BIBLIOGRAPHY Ferri (1885) 125, 164; Bartoli (1914–22) III: fig. 451; pl. 266; VI: 84; CensusID 57962.

U 1153A *recto and verso*

Antonio da Sangallo the Younger

Rome, Trajan's Column, pedestal, base, capital, and other details (*recto*); Trajan's Column, with measurements and annotations (*verso*), 1518–20.

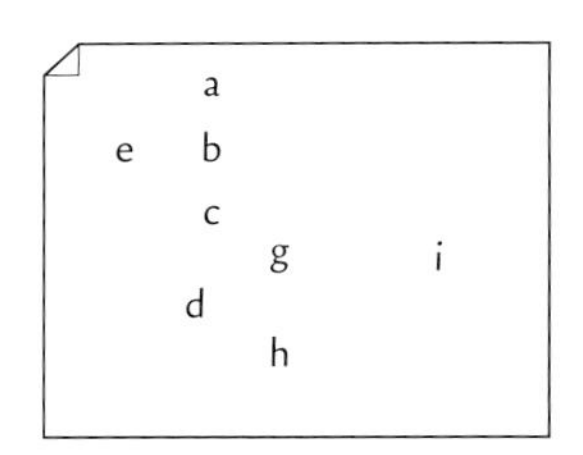

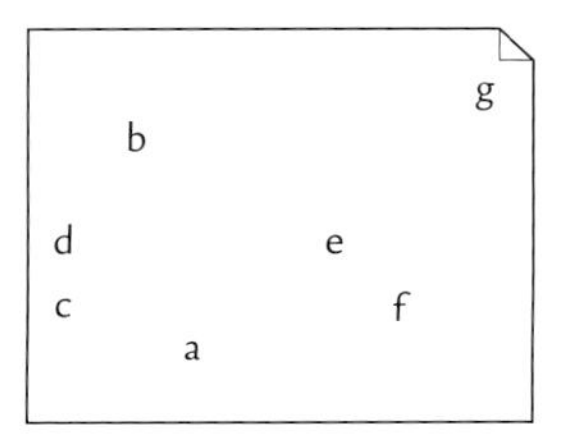

Dimensions 345 × 484 mm.
Technique Pen and several inks, straightedge, stylus, freehand.
Paper Heavy, trimmed, center fold, reinforced at right edge and along fold.
Drawing Scale Florentine *braccia* and *minuti*.

INSCRIPTION, Recto (19th-century hand, Ferri) (top right) *885*; (Antonio's hand) (top left) *volte 11 dala schala tonda*; (below, next to [e]) *chanali 20*; (top right, partly overlapping base of previously drawn column) *senatus populus que romanus / imp caesari divi nervae f. nervae. / traiano aug germ dacico pontif / maximo* (*masim* canceled in space between lines) *trib pot XVIII imp VI* (*con* canceled) *cos VI pp. / ad declarandum quantae altitudinis / monset locus tantum* (outline of a hole) *ibus site giestus* [*sic*]; (top right corner) *colonne storiate*; (half way up, center, to left of plan [g]) *porta in cima*[?]; (above plan) *facia dinanzi*; (right margin, written in redder ink) *l antoniana alta piedi 176 / schaloni 206 spirachuli 56 / lalbertino e pomponio leto / piedi 128 alta la traiana / schaloni 185 spirachuli 45*; (bottom center, to right of pedestal) 6[?] *schaloni quadri daldiso / tto delle chornici in su equatro / tondi insino al chor[ona]mento / alti 20* [*minuti*]; (in same ink as that used for quotations from Albertini and Pomponio Leto) *in tuto 10*

Verso:: Left half: (Antonio's hand) (lower left, with sheet turned 180 degrees) *b 6 24 al rilevo*; *al vivo* / 6[?] *28*; *23 al di sopra delli intagli / li intagli 5* (*23* and *5* corrected in dark ink of kind used on recto); *dita 35¾* (height of cove above pedestal, in reddish ink like that used for additions on recto); (on pedestal, written vertically) *Lo zocholo alto 9–28 insino a dove / posano li piedi le aquile*; (next to base of pedestal; turned 180 degrees) *foglie frapate di basso rilievo / chiociola in tertio* (next to *taurus* with carved cable motif); (next to plan *c*, written vertically) *da questa in su* (correction to "*i*" in reddish ink) *c°* [*cento*?] *57 schalonj*; (in same plan) *busa donde si entra* (upside down); (next to plan) *porta di sopra*; (beneath plan) *di chiesa dove / lo epitafio*; (higher up next to plan, *d*) *li schaloni sono / alti 20 / larghi 36*; numerous sums. Right half: (Antonio's hand) (under capital [*e*]) *chonvento*; (top of column, bottom edge of cove above pedestal, turned 180 degrees) *qui ariva / li piedi 128*; (to right of column at top) *la cholonna della lumacha*[?] / *da chapo grossa 1.32 / da pie 1.48 / La schala da pie 1.17 da chapo 1.13 lo guscio da pie1–1 / da chapo 49½*; (below) *C 57 li schaloni tondi*; (to right of column, vertically) *la cholonna alta cholla base / chapitello b.*[*raccia*] *50–57*; (at join between second and third drum, in reddish ink) *chonvento*; *la cholonna grossa da pie b. 6–22* (the second 2 corrects a *4*); (between first and second drum) *chonvento*; (on bottom edge of *taurus* of base) *chonvento*; (next to horizontal joins of blocks making up pedestal) *chonvento / chonvento / chonvento*; (top right, vertically) *Lo dado b. 9–28 / La cholona b. 50 57 / lo dado sopra / lo chapitello b. 4 50½*[?] / (sum =) *b. 66 / 132 piedi*; (in bottom right corner, vertically, in reddish ink, written later given line between this and the sum in blacker ink) *lo inbasamento 9–28 / la colonna basa / capitello 50–57 / Dal capitello insu 5–35 / tuto b. 66.00*

On this sheet, Antonio brought together nine drawings of important components of Trajan's Column, which he analyzed on the verso in a drawing of the entire column, together with other details.

In the middle of the left half of the recto is a succession of different measurements set out in vertical order: from the top, an elevation of the abacus of the capital with the beginning of the pedestal of the statue surmounting it *a*; an elevation of the upper shaft of the column with the width of the nucleus and the outer casing and the width of the stairwell *b*; an unfinished sketch similar to the previous one *c*; a measured synthesis of the lower shaft, with the widths of the nucleus, the stair and the outer casing, together with base and pedestal *d*; at the upper left, a schematic plan of the top shaft of the column with flutes *e*; at the upper right, a partial elevation of the block of the capital with fluted upper shaft *f*; below, a small square unmeasured schematic plan (of the podium?) *g*; at the bottom, an axonometric view of a step of the spiral staircase *h*. On the right half of the sheet, on a larger scale, Antonio drew part of the elevation facing the Basilica Ulpia from the upper shaft of the column to the top half of the podium, synthetically but assiduously showing the main sculptures: eagle, festoon, and figure holding up the epigraph *i*.

The preparation with straightedge and stylus of this latter elevation means that the drawing couldn't have been made on the spot and raises the question whether any of the others were, although the fact that they have been annotated freehand on a sheet folded in two (in a notebook?) and turned over several times in order to make full use of the empty spaces suggests otherwise. There is also a correction inserted as the text of the epigraph was being written, which suggests that the copy was made *in situ*. Later on, at home, Antonio would have completed his findings with calculations and information taken from books by Pomponio Leto and Albertini. The measurements of the drawing in Florentine *braccia* (*d*) and others on the verso that agree with those noted by Baldassarre Peruzzi on U 484A v. (Bartoli 1914–22, fig. 324) on the same subject have led to a supposition that the two sheets belonged to a group of surveys jointly undertaken by the two architects. Some mistakes in the text of the epigraph (C.I.L., 6, 1, 960), which Antonio annotated down in cursive script on U 1153A r., and which Peruzzi set out carefully in capital letters in the drawing of the pedestal, confirm the relationship between the two sheets. Common to both, in fact, is the "XVIII" in the fourth line instead of "XVII" and the omission of the dash above the number and the partial integration of a *lacuna* in the fifth line. Most importantly, Peruzzi has repeated Antonio's erroneously broken-up phrase "site gestus" (this should read "sit egestus"), so as not to interfere with the baseline of an already extant drawing by partially covering it up with writing.

For his part, Peruzzi erased with a slip of Antonio's, the extra "i" in *egiestus*, and in a couple of other places, where Antonio did not transcribe breaks or conjunctions between words correctly. Elsewhere, however, he incorporated mistakes of his own and then crossed them out twice. We must conclude that whichever of them first reproduced the inscriptions in capital letters must have based them on the text in U 1153 r., and checked it on their own. Various graphic peculiarities also prove that the two sheets are connected: in Antonio's drawing *i* the almost vertical and barely unfolded wing of the eagle is more faithful to the original than his figure of the same subject on the verso, a detail to which Peruzzi comes closer. In the margin of drawing *i*, Antonio noted measurements and quantitative information taken from Albertini and Pomponio Leto about the Aurelian Column, so that he could compare these with measurements he took himself from Trajan's Column.

On the verso hhere are six drawings of details and one of the whole of Trajan's Column by Antonio the Younger on U 1153A v. On the left half are: (*a*), a more detailed elevation, upside down, of the pedestal than the one on the recto, showing the base and upper shaft of the column with all the carved motifs clearly defined; some thicker pen lines in black ink amplifying and correcting the drawing, calculations, and measurements in sepia ink; *b*, *a* cable motif carved on the *taurus* at the base of the pedestal; *c* and *d*, plans of two levels of the pedestal of the column showing the stair, with straight flights at the beginning and then spiral. On the right half are: *e*, the fluted upper shaft of the column with its capital; *f*, an elevation of the column from the podium to the pedestal of the statue at the top, divided into sections by the joins, *chonventi*, numbered from the bottom upward, each with its own height. The sum of the heights of the sections equals the total height. At the bottom and top, in a vertical section, Antonio also set out the widths of the corona, the stairwell, and the cylindrical nucleus; and at the top right, is *g*, a sketch of a plan of a half-column(?) with a projecting pedestal, which has no obvious relationship to the subject of the sheet. As on the recto, almost all the measurements match those given by Peruzzi on U 484A v., which confirms the relationship between the two sheets of Uffizi drawings.

The collection of drawings on the recto and verso demonstrate the diverse interest with which Antonio examined the column, focusing on the order, the tapering, and the ornamental details, and analyzing the stair and the superimposed blocks of the pedestal and the shaft, making notes of the dimensions in order to study them from a construction point of view. It thus comprises the most exhaustive graphic documentary record of Trajan's Column of the time. Antonio measured the thickness of the cylindrical nucleus of the column, the corona, and the width of the stairwell precisely, both at the lower level and at the upper shaft, where all these measurements diminish along with the tapering.

The Florentine *braccio* used in this survey is subdivided into *minuti*, equal to 1/60 of a *braccio*, as can be seen in a calculation running perpendicular to the drawing of the entire column, in which the total, 39 *braccia* and 717½ *minuti*, is converted into 50 *braccia* and 57 *minuti*. What is particularly striking is the care with which Antonio measured the heights of each of the drums to within ½ a *minuto* (.48 cm). Of twenty or so measurements, only a couple differ by 1 centimeter from the measurements taken during restoration work of the 1980s, the rest are off by only a few millimeters (Martines 2001). Antonio must have taken the measurements from the bottom upwards, since his dimensions and the numbers assigned by him to each drum are given in this order, as they follow on upward from each other inside the stairwell. | PNP

BIBLIOGRAPHY Ferri (1885) 156; Bartoli (1914–22) V: figs 458–59, pl 273–74; VI: 85; Günther (1988) 257, 377; CensusIDs 10073128, 10073082.

U 1154A *recto and verso*

Pietro Rosselli and Antonio da Sangallo the Younger

Rome, Campo Marzio, Piazza Capranica, and Temple of Matidia, after 1527

Dimensions 421 × 566 mm.
Technique Pen and brown ink, wash, straightedge, compass (recto); graphite (verso).
Paper Center fold, trimmed, left edge restored.
Drawing Scale Roman *palmi* and *minuti*.

INSCRIPTION, Recto (left half) (Antonio's hand) *Lo capitello sie alto tutto palmi 7 minuti 21 / che sono minuti 441 / La cimase sie minuti 51 che viene* adesse / *partito lo tutto i[n] parti 8⅔ p[er]* che / *fa 442; la quarta [parte] sie 92½; aessere; lacolonna 38½ / Lo i[n]tercolunnio* [...] due *ggroseza / e uno quarto* [...] / *che sono 867 sono p[almi] 14–27* / [...]; *Alto teste 9⅙ p.[er] soli* [...] *senza lo / capitulare quale sie la settima parte della / colonna dappie ch' e di teste 9 – iii 3/7*; (Rosselli's hand) *In piazza chapranicha; Eustili 2¼ / 3 2¼* (right half) (Antonio's hand) [...] *che la colonna sie palmi 6–30 sono minuti 390 / Lo i[n]tercolunnio essere palmi 14–13⅓ che sono 853⅓ / soma tutto 1252⅓ / di queste* se ne *a fare 13 parte e una di dette parte / fa una quarta parte della colonna & nove parte allo / i[n]tercolunnio se nelo Eustilo a essere lo i[n]tercolunnio due grosseze di colonna e una quarta parte / La detta tredecima parte sie 96⅓ e 13 vie 96⅓ fa / 1252⅓ di modo che la colonna aria a essere 385⅓ / che sono p[almi] 6 minuti 25⅓ / Lo i[n] tercolunnio sie 867 che sono palmi 14–27*; (Rosselli's hand) *In piazza chapranicha*

The recto shows one of the Corinthian capitals of the temple in two plans and an elevation, along with a ground plan of two column bays of differing width. Reference to Vitruvius's *eustylos* is made only in Antonio's inscription and the related sketch at the lower left edge of the sheet. The graphite sketches on the verso are by Antonio, who made use of Rosselli's separate bits of information to reconstruct a *peripteros* with 6 by 11 columns; the measurements are added up at the left. This sheet is the model for U 1305A. | HCD

BIBLIOGRAPHY Lanciani (1883, *Basilica*) 12; Ferri (1885) 131, 199; Lanciani (1897) 505; Bartoli (1914–22) III: figs 481–82, pl 294–95; VI: 90; Giovannoni (1959) I: 102; Günther (1988) 230, no. 107; Huth (2014) 162; CensusIDs 10072229, 10072221.

U 1156A *recto and verso*

Antonio da Sangallo the Younger

Tivoli, Plan of Sanctuary of Hercules Victor ("Villa di Vopisco"), 1539.

Dimensions 276 × 437 mm.
Technique Pen and three shades of brown ink.
Paper Medium weight, vertical center fold, stains, repaired on verso.

INSCRIPTION, Recto (on left side, turned 180 degrees) *una sta[n]tia / fino alla fine*; *ruinati*; *andito*; *Ruinati*; *Botte*; (next three words turned 180 degrees) *archo*; *archo*; *archo*; (turned 180 degrees) *qui i[n] giu la strada pendeva circha / al quarto li archi e la volta / lo demostra*; (turned 180 degrees) *spiracolo*; (turned 90 degrees) *spiraglio*; (turned 90 degrees) *botte*; *spiraglio* (canceled); *botte* (canceled); *Botte; B*

Verso (on the right half of the sheet) *Parte della pia[n]ta de porta scura / subteranea dove sopra la villa / de vopisco*

According to Vasori, on this sheet Antonio drew a plan of the substructures along two sides of Via Tecta, but without the northern end of the site, which is drawn on U 1159A. Together with U 1159A, which continues the drawing to the right, this sheet shows Antonio's partial survey sketches of the foundations of the Heracles temple, built by the Romans and once thought to be part of Villa di Vopisco. The two drawings, U 1156A and U 1159A, were never, however, part of a single sheet. Sangallo's plans are of great importance because he was the only architect ever to have made a record of this part of the complex.

Other drawings recording Antonio's studies of the Sanctuary of Hercules Victor are U 1067A r., 1176A r., 1208A r., and 1351A r. | SE

BIBLIOGRAPHY Vasari-Milanesi (1878–85) V: 494; Ferri (1885) 220; Giovannoni (1959) I: 22; Giuliani (1970) 167, 181–85; Vasori (1981) 116–17, cat. no. 89; CensusIDs 10022112, 10082060.

U 1159A *recto and verso*

Antonio da Sangallo the Younger

Tivoli, Plan of Sanctuary of Hercules Victor ("Villa di Vopisco"), 1539.

Dimensions 282 × 230 mm.
Technique Pen and two shades of brown ink, freehand.
Paper Medium weight, folds, stains.

INSCRIPTION, Recto (in plan) *schala; botte*; (turned 180 degrees) *spira/culo*; (turned 180 degrees) *Botte*; (turned 90 degrees) *masicio*; *tutte le volte / che sono segniate / stella vano alte / p[er]fino al pie / di quelle di so/pra*; measurements, with orientation of walls done by compass readings of the winds *G[reco]*; *M[aestro]*

Verso *Questa sio una parte della / pianta de l difitio de porta / scura dove sopra era edi/ficato la villa di vopisco.*

Antonio the Younger drew this plan freehand, recording the northern subterranean area of the Sanctuary complex. U 1159A r. is the continuation to the right of the plan that he drew on U 1156A r.; both are sketches of the Roman Temple of Hercules at Tivoli, once thought to belong to the Vopisco villa. Antonio also included notes about the height of the vaults. Antonio's other studies of the Sanctuary of Hercules Victor are U 1067A r., 1176A r., 1208A r., and 1351A r. On the verso is only a note. | SE

BIBLIOGRAPHY Vasari-Milanesi (1878–85) V: 494; Ferri (1885) 220; Giovannoni (1959) I: 22; Giuliani (1970) 167, 181–85; Vasori (1981) 117, cat. no. 90; CensusID 10022106.

U 1161A *recto and verso*

Antonio da Sangallo the Younger

Plan of a gymnasium, according to Vitruvius (*recto*); five plans of parts of Greek houses, the *palestra* and the *domus magna*, as described by Vitruvius (*verso*), after 1527.

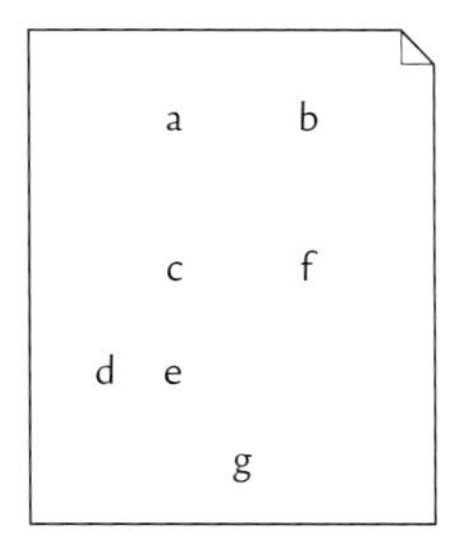

Dimensions 293 × 236 mm.
Technique Pen and brown ink, straightedge, grid, pin, freehand.
Paper Lightweight, trimmed on three sides, stains, holes made by acid ink, reinforced.
Drawing Scale Roman *piedi*, *passi*, and *stadia.*

INSCRIPTION, Recto (Antonio's hand) (top center) *edifitio della palestra greco / quadrato di circuito di due stadij*; (top left, key to plan) *A peristili tre*[?] *overo / tre portici dove sono / le exedra / B exedre / C Duplici portici conversi ameridie / D ephoebeum colresto*[?] *de bagni*; (top right, continuation of key) *E sixtus per hyberna tempora*; (on section) *margine*; *lo portico largo p. 36*; (in thickness of wall) *pariete*; (center of top margin of plan) *Portico duplo que spectat a setentrione*; (below) *E*; (left edge) *uno stadio sono piede 625*; *250 passi 125*; *sinistra stadiata*; (right edge) *destra stadiata*; (bottom left) *p. 34½* (*4* correcting a *3*) (measurement of 3 interaxes of colonnade); *11½* (correcting *11¼*) (referring to interaxis of colonnade); (inside plan, left margin) *margine*; *planitie*; *margine*; (in upper wing, from left) *scoperto*; *frigidarium*; *elaotesium H*; *calida la/vatio*; *laconico*; *concamerata/ sudatio due / quadric*; *propugneum*; *Ephoebeum / exedra amplissima D*; *10½* (width); *7* (length); *corticeo*[?]; *conisterium*; *frigida lavation*; *scoperto*; (in left wing) B (repeated in each room); *exedre tutte*; (in two top porticoes) *C*; (in side porticoes and at bottom) *A*; (in right and lower wing) *B* (repeated in each room); (in courtyard, on steps) *gradi spectaculorum*; (below): *hipetra / silve*; (in center) *portica dupla que spectant admeridiana regione* (canceled); *sotto*; *quarta quae ad meridianas regiones est conversa dupplex*; *le colonne di dentro girano dua stadij / sisto allo scoperto per li belli tempi*; (outside plan, below) *porticus exeuntibus*; (bottom right, in red pencil, 19th-century hand) *Vitruvio*

Verso (Antonio's hand): (plan *a*) (in external portico) *sixto coperto per li mali tenpin*; (left room) *Exedre alte/uno quatro et/mezo collese/die in torno*; (right room) *Exedre quadra/ te alte uno qua/tro et mezo colle / sedie in torno*; (in internal colonnade) *peristilio*; (below plan) *sixto sub divo scoperto / per li belli tenpi*; (plan *b*) (above plan) *Ephoebeum grande / cioe Exedra grande*; (below plan) *Ephoeboeum in medium hoc autem est / exedra amplissima cum sedibus quae / tertia parte longior sit quam lata*; (in plan *c*) *Li* VI *cap°* VI */ Triclinio*; (left of plan) *li oeci corintii / edegitij sono / come li triclinij*; (above plan *d*) *Triclinio*; (above plan *f*) *almo dogreco*; (in plan) *Libro sextus Cap°* VI */*; *oeci quadrati / ipsi autem sint ita longi / et lati uti duo triclinia / cuncircuitionibus inter / se spectantia possint esse / collocate / alto uno quatro e mezo*; (in plan *g*) *oeco greco quadratos tam / ampla magnitudine / uti fa/ciliter in eis triclinijs quatuor stratis*[?] */ ministrationum ludorumque*

Vitruvius dedicated a chapter of *De Architectura* (Book V, ch. 11, 1–4) to a description of the *palestra*, or gymnasium, which Antonio on the recto of U 1161A interpreted rather differently to the illustrations published at the time, as well as from the later reconstruction by his brother Giovanni Battista. The measurement of three interaxes of the outer portico, noted by Antonio on the plan, allows for a calculation of the length of the longest side.

Excluding the colonnade on the north side, this measures 625 *piedi*, equal, therefore, to a *stadio*, as the reference passage from the treatise in the margin states. Antonio adhered to Vitruvius's text regarding the reconstruction of the width of the portico, which he also drew in sections, and which he used to gauge the measurements of the capital and the overall colonnade, attributing a width compatible with an architraved covering to the intercolumniation. Working out his plan on squared paper, he attributed the measurement of the width of the portico to the sides of the small square exedras, placed on the east, west, and south sides, in which Fra Giocondo had depicted *viridaria*. They do not derive from the Vitruvian text, and the octagonal rooms that Antonio placed on the southeast and southwest corners of the *palestra* would appear to have been inspired by ancient baths. On the northern side of the peristyle, turned south toward the interior of the *palestra*, Antonio followed the treatise, as did Fra Giocondo, placing the *ephebeum* on axis and spaces for *balnea* to the left and right. However, unlike Fra Giocondo, who merely supplied a brief sketch of this, Antonio created a large space, following the ratio of 2:3 suggested by Vitruvius, and he showed the seats and the walls with their niches.

Rather than being interested in the gymnasium complex as a whole, which was generally not of great topical interest during the sixteenth century, Antonio appears to have been more interested in the parts at the sides of the *ephebeum* from a practical point of view. Therefore, the *laconicum* and *frigidarium* are represented here, as well as rooms for the various types of *lavatio* and other connecting rooms, that he often included in projects for *stufette* for palaces and houses, although in this drawing they assume more defined shapes and have been incorporated into a more complex building.

Antonio used the verso of U 1161A to detail parts of the plan of the *palestra* that he drew on the recto, and then moved on from Vitruvius's Book V in *De Architectura* to Book VI in the bottom half of the sheet, drawing some of the rooms found in the *domus* and in Greek houses.

Plan *a*, on the subject of *exedrae*, is a graphic interpretation of information gleaned from Vitruvius in Book V, ch. 11, 2, on the presence of seats in these rooms, integrated with a passage in Book VI, ch. 2, 8, concerning *exedrae* in the *domus*. From this passage, he learned that these rooms could have been on a square plan, in which case their height would have been equal to one and a half times the side of the square. He therefore drew one part of the *palestra* with two square exedras contained between a segment of the external portico and part of the internal peristyle. In plan *b*, which refers to a passage (Book V, ch. 11, 2) on the *ephebeum*, Antonio repeats that this involves a large exedra and illustrates the ratio of 1:1.5 between the two sides of the rectangular plan. Regarding *triclinia* and *oeci*, Antonio's main point of reference was the passage in Book VI, ch. 3, 8, which he specified as Book VI, ch. 6, possibly based on the chapter divisions in Cesariano's translation, or Durantino's, which he owned. He learned from the treatise that *triclinia* should be twice as long as they were wide, but nothing suggests that they were *sale*[?] with columns on three sides as shown in plan *c*. His interpretation is perhaps due to the fact that in the same paragraph and in the following one, Vitruvius cited the various types of *oeci*, all with columns, sometimes placed next to the *triclinia*, with the result that Antonio noted next to the plan: "li oeci corintii edegitij sono come li triclinij." The reconstruction is perhaps also due to a confusion between the two meanings of the word "triclinim": a dining couch and a dining room. In plan *f*, in fact, Antonio came up with a square *oecus* with columns along all four sides, consisting of two *triclinia* of the kind he drew on the left, misunderstanding Vitruvius (Book VI, ch. 3, 10), who prescribed a width ample enough to be able to take two *triclinia*, meaning two pieces of furniture, for the *oeci ciziceni*. Plan *d* shows a *triclinium* longer than it is wide, and plan *e* shows a square *oecus* surrounded, through the same misunderstanding as above, by four *triclinia* of the same sort as plan *c*. In plan *g*, at the bottom of the sheet, a large rectangular Greek *oecus* has been created by putting together four rectangular *triclinia*, again of the same sort as in plan *c*. | PNP

BIBLIOGRAPHY Ferri (1885) 218; Giovannoni (1959) I: 23; Pagliara (1972) 26, 28; Frommel (1973) I: 78; Fontana-Morachiello (1975) 41; Vasori (1981) 117–18, cat. no. 91; Pagliara (1988) 186, 195; Pellecchia (1993) 332; Fane-Saunders (2016) 262.

U 1162A *recto and verso*

Antonio da Sangallo the Younger

Campello sul Clitunno (Spoleto),
Temple of Clitunno, before 1527.

Dimensions 220 × 290 mm.
Technique Pen and brown ink.
Paper Medium weight, folded twice, stains, trimmed, edges reinforced on verso.

INSCRIPTION, Recto (left) *del Zocholone*; *del zocholone*; (right, top to bottom) *strada alta quale cho*[*n*] *mano / sariva al chornicione*; *questo difitio e i*[*n*] *fra spuleti / e ttrievi i*[*n*] *sulla strada che va / a trievi apresso dove nascie / lo fiume chlitondo / quale mette plinio p*[*er*] *chosa / mirabile di belleza chiare / za daqua*; (on plan) *botte*; *scala*; *qui e uno pocho di piazeta piu alta che l fiume / qualche Canne .5. / La cholonna grossa p*[*almi*] *1⅞*; (on plan) *sotto lo porticho*; *fiumane*; *la chornice e della / medesima sorte / chella grande cho me / desimi i*[*n*]*tagli e i*[*n*] *sulle / cholonne li risalti nonanno / niente sopra lo fronte spitio e i*[*n*] */ sul vivo del muro e chosi la chornicie / del fronte spitio e questo e allo altare grande*

Verso (left) *Le cholonnette sono / a fogli dedera / Li pilastri sono chanalati*; (right, turned 180 degrees) *sotto larchitrave /* (in portico) *i*[*n*] *botte*; *Li pilastri diminuischano chome / la cholonna sono chorinti li chapitelli / La chornicie alagola quella che chorre i*[*n*] *pia / chome quella del frontespitio*

This sheet depicts plans and details of the Temple of Clitunno, an early Christian church built of antique spoils. Its date—which is linked to that of S. Salvatore in nearby Spoleto—has been much disputed in the past, though now it is generally agreed that the Temple was constructed in the fifth century (see Salmi 1951, p. 44; Russo 1992, pp. 84–89; Jäggi 1998, pp. 149–94 proposes seventh century).

At the left of the recto Antonio drew the profiles of the base and cornice of the basement level of the temple (see elevation on verso). At the upper right is a plan, with measurements, of the main level of the edifice, including the external stairs. Salmi (1951, pp. 41, 54 n. 65) observed that Antonio's drawing is considerably more accurate than that of Francesco di Giorgio, of decades years earlier (U 321A). In the lower part of the sheet, Antonio included a hastily drawn plan of the T-shaped space below the portico, which is entered through the door at basement level (see verso). To the right of that is an elevation of the apse of the main space.

On the verso at left is a perspectival view of the main entablature of the Temple of Clitunno, with indications of the ornaments, below which Antonio drew an elevation of the facade of one of the sides of the temple. The two plans of the column/pilaster/wall details to the right and left of the entablature view refer to the porticoes of the side and main facades. At the bottom is a close-up of the leaf motif decorating the columns. The right half of the sheet shows a view of the principal face of the temple, above which is a detail of the decorated intrados of the main portico architrave. Antonio drew the pilasters with their fluting, the columns with their leaf motif and the spirals, with a close-up of the spiral pattern beneath the right column. | SE

BIBLIOGRAPHY Ferri (1885) 214; Salmi (1951) 41, 54 n. 65; Benelli (2014, *Tempio*) 177; Jäggi (1998) tav. 165, 166, CensusIDs 10074832, 10076376.

U 1163A *recto*

Giovan Francesco da Sangallo

Rome, ancient cornices conserved at
the Sangallo house, ca. 1514–20.

Dimensions 388 × 204 mm.
Technique Pen and ink, compass (curve of the Doric *cyma*), freehand.
Paper Lightweight, reinforced at edges.

INSCRIPTION (Giovan Francesco's hand) *in chasa*; (below this, Antonio's hand) *mia / ando afirenze*; (in Doric cornice, Antonio's hand) *in casa mia*; (Giovan Francesco's hand) *in chasa*; *Le gutte e none*[?] *mezo tonde*

This sheet contains several meticulously measured drawings of two ancient cornices, made by Giovan Francesco on site at the Sangallo family house in Rome, perhaps near the Tomb of Augustus, where they were conserved at that time. The house passed into his cousin Antonio's hands either when Giovan Francesco left Rome to return definitively to Florence in 1527, or on his death in 1530. Antonio added his notes on the ownership of the pieces and recorded the removal of the Corinthian cornice to Florence. At the top, Giovan Francesco drew a measured and defined elevation/section of a Corinthian cornice with modillions, including all its carved details, and on the right he drew a pair of modillions in elevation, indicating their distance from each other in order to achieve an integral frontal reconstruction of the whole.

At the bottom of the sheet, a Doric cornice in isometric section is surrounded by details of various parts of the entablature to which it had belonged: on the left, a hasty sketch in elevation of the frieze with triglyphs and *guttae*; in the left corner, a drawing of the *fulmina* that articulate the soffit of the cornice; in the right corner, an annotated detail of one of the *guttae*.

On another sheet, U 1329A, Giovan Francesco drew only the drip molding, claiming to have drawn everything that still survived, which leads one to consider that the Doric *cyma* at least, and perhaps some of the other details, were partly hypothetical reconstructions.

The present sheet is a testament to the thorough and meticulous manner in which Giovan Francesco surveyed ancient pieces of architecture, but it should be noted that U 1329A was later corrected, albeit only very slightly, to take account of the more precise measurements for the Doric cornice provided on U 1163A, and that Antonio the Younger corrected the lower side of the drip molding in section, his cousin having represented it horizontally in both U 1163A and U 1329A, rather than hanging as it actually was. It was, in any case, fundamental to the consolidation of Giovan Francesco's position within the circle of Antonio the Younger, with whom he shared the residence in Rome near S. Rocco. | PNP

BIBLIOGRAPHY Ferri (1885) 32, 45; Giovannoni (1959) 1: 320; Buddensieg (1975) 104–05, 108; Frommel (1994, *Introduction*) 42; CensusID 10026897.

U 1165A *recto and verso*

Antonio da Sangallo the Younger

Cori, the so-called Temple of Hercules and the Temple of Castor and Pollux; Rome, the Temple of Hadrian, after 1527.

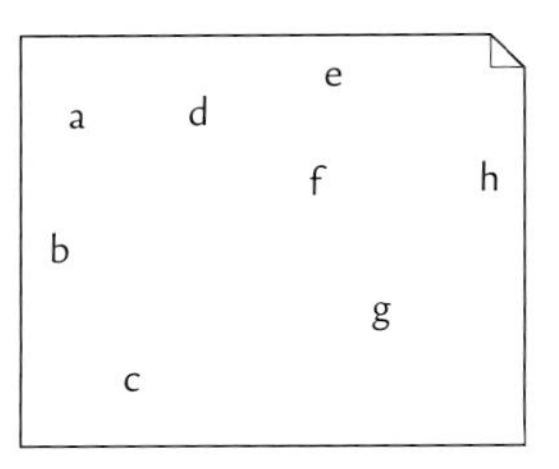

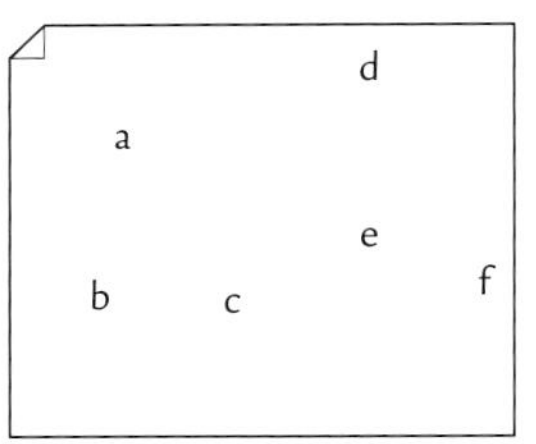

Dimensions 291 × 437 mm.
Technique Pen and ink.
Paper [?]
Drawing Scale Roman *palmi* (recto).

INSCRIPTION, Recto (b) *porta del te*[*m*]*pio toscano i*[*n*] *Cori / di Canpagnia di roma*; (c) *modano della me*[*n*]*sola*; (d) *M·MANLIVS M·F·L TVRPILIVS·LA·DVOM / VIRES DE SE NATVS SENTENTIA AEDEM / FACIENDAM COERAVERV*[*N*]*T EISDE*[*MQVE PROBAVERE*]; *larga p*[*al*]*mi 10.1*; *palmi 22*; (e) *questo portico era / de ogni testa ed e cori*[*n*]*tio*; (f) *dentro*; (g) *Le plastine quale aueua / el porticho dinanzi e dirieto / simile*; *Colonne 10*; *Colonne 15*; *gradi piedi 22*; (h) *Basa di queste colonne*; *Le plastine*

Verso (a) *Lo fiancho del te*[*m*]*pio toschano*; *La cornicie no*[*n*] *risalta qua*[*n*]*do ariva alpilastro / p*[*er*]*che li pilastri diminuiscono qua*[*n*]*to lacolonna*; within the elevation: *plutei*; (b) *te*[*m*]*pio di Castore e polluce / Cori*[*n*]*tio li suoi capitelli / sono alti palmi 4 e le / Colonne sono grosse da pie / p*[*almi*] *4 le colonne i*[*n*] *faccia / sono piu larghe che quelle / de fianchi e questo sie / i*[*n*] *la terra di Cori presso / a velletri di roma nel suo / fregio sono queste lettere / TENPLV*[*M*] *CASTORIS E POLVCI*; *a palmi romaneschi*; (c) *facciata del te*[*m*]*pio toscano / di Cori*; (e) *Te*[*m*]*pio toschano a cori*; (f) *Bug*[*n*]*e lassate / p*[*er*] *li traui*; *questo elcapitello / del pilastro*; *Della Colonna*; *Colonna e Capitello 27–10*; *di fuora*

This sheet shows survey drawings of three temples: the so-called Temple of Hercules (recto, *a–d*; verso, *a*, *c–g*) and the Temple of Castor and Pollux (verso, *b*), both in Cori; and the Temple of Hadrian in Rome (recto, *e–h*). These Cori drawings are the oldest ones to be known of these two temples. The Temple of Hercules was particularly interesting for Antonio because it showed an order similar to the Greek Doric, which he identified as the Tuscan order. On the recto, he drew a scrupulously measured partial survey of the doorframe (*d*), which is ionic, however, as well as the profiles of the architraved lintel (*b*), the corona of the cornice (*a*), and a section of the consoles (*c*). In the right half of the verso, there is a ground plan of the temple with measurements (*e*), and a detail of the tympanum (*d*), as well as a measured view of the order (*f*), The survey was carried out in Roman *palmi*. On the left half of the sheet, Antonio drew his reconstruction of the front and side views of the temple.

All that remains of this temple are the pronaos (however roofless), which is a tretrastyle and three intercolumniations deep, and the entrance wall of the cella including the beginning of the side walls. Other contemporary drawings do not exist. It is therefore not possible to state with certainty to what extent Antonio reproduced the actual situation, and to what extent he may have reconstructed missing parts. The fluting of the pilasters along the wall of the cella is, however, contrary to the archeological findings. Moreover the 9⅓ *palmi* height of the podium given is too high (Brandizzi Vittucci 1968, p. 88). The acroteria and the statues to either side of the stairs are likely to be Antonio's additions.

The ground plan of the Temple of Castor and Pollux on the verso (*b*) seems rather dubious. Antonio drew a rectangular cella decorated with pilasters, that has 8 by 5 intercolumniation and a tetrastyle portico, that is two intercolumniations deep. Today all that is left are two fluted Corinthian columns. The excavated ground plan, however, reveals a much smaller, transversally oblong and tripartite cella (Brandizzi Vittucci 1968, p. 58, fig. 78); consequently the portal cannot have been the simple one shown here. It is likely that this plan is to a large extent a rather free reconstruction of Antonio, who, by adding the two portico axes to the ground plan, was trying to achieve the ideal proportion of 2:1 (10:5 intercolumniation).

The drawings of the Temple of Hadrian, all concentrated in the right half of the recto, show a partial elevation of the right flank (*e*), a half section through the cella and side portico (*f*), and a partial ground plan *g*, as well as the profile of one of the column bases (*h*). It seems that within the Sangallo circle, the small order of columns, which carries the reinforcing arches of the barrel vault within the cella, was envisioned as standing on a continuous pedestal set against a smooth wall (see Giovanni Battista da Sangallo, U 1661A v., as well as the Codex Hopkins Rootstein); but compare to this, for instance, the later reconstructions by Palladio (half-columns flanking semicircular niches in the wall) or by Sallustio Peruzzi (U 662A v., where half-columns are set against both the interior and exterior of the side walls of the cella). The reconstructions made by the Sangallo circle also diverge from the abovementioned later attempts with respect to the entrance walls of the cella. Antonio the Younger and his circle referred to the structure on several of their drawings as *le Plastine* (see U 1180A, 1187, 1661). | JN

BIBLIOGRAPHY Ferri (1885) 31; Günther (1988) 194; Bartoli (1914–22) V: figgs 478–79, pl 291–92; VI: 90; Vasori (1981) 118–21, cat. nos 92–93; Brandizzi Vittucci (1968) 58–66, 77–96; Delbrück (1907–12) II: 23–36; LTUR III (1996) 7 f.; CensusIDs 10020791, 10020795.

U 1166A *recto and verso*

Antonio da Sangallo The Younger

Rome, Forum Romanum, Temple of Antoninus and Faustina; Forum Boarium, Temple of Protumnus (*recto*). Temple of Antoninus and Faustina (*verso*). After 1527.

Dimensions 294 × 428 mm.
Technique Pen and light brown ink.
Paper Lightweight, center fold.
Drawing Scale Roman *piedi* and *dita.*

INSCRIPTION, Recto (left half) *444/p[er] fiancho*; (right half) *Sta maria egiptiacha/si doma[n]da og[g]i questo/tenpio qual e i[n] roma/apresso ponte Santa maria/ricoperto tutto di stucho*; *I[n] botte sopra/questo porticho*; *Capitello dell/canto sta cosi;* *Le bugnie sono 25 luna/Lo vano della porta e alta piedi 22½/ larga piedi 10½/secondo vietruvio sia alto p. 22 D 13/e larcho piedi 9 D 2*

Verso (left half) *antonino e faustina*; *piedi*; *di fuori*; (right half) DIVO ANTONINO/DIVA FAUSTINA/*I[n] la faciata di qua*

On the left half of the verso of this sheet, the ground plan of the Temple of Antoninus and Faustina corrects the measurements and proportions of Giovanni Battista's U 3972A; whereas the length remains the same, 85 *piedi*, the width is given here as 55 *piedi* 5 *dite*. The diameter of the columns is 4 *piedi* 15 *dite*, the middle intercolumniation measures 13¼, and the remaining intercolumniations are 12½ *piedi*. Thus Antonio's corrections of Giovanni Battista's measurements include even the diameter of the columns. On the right half of the verso, the partial elevation of the front shows a sculpture on the parapet of the staircase. The partial elevation of the lateral view on the left half of the recto includes staffage figures in the pronaos behind gates placed between the columns. Next to this is a partial elevation of an entablature showing a section of the decorative frieze with a winged griffin between vases and acanthus vines, the distinguishing feature of this temple.

The sketches of the Temple of Portunus on the right half of the recto are for an extensive reconstruction; they include a ground plan, a side elevation, and a partial elevation of the front. A corner of the pronaos has been enlarged in the ground plan; Antonio's interest lies in the Ionic corner volute and its diagonal placement. The side elevation freely—and incorrectly—reconstructs a podium and the returned pedestals of its engaged columns; this is probably an attempt to interpret Vitruvius's concept of "scamilli impares." | HCD

BIBLIOGRAPHY Ferri (1885) 144, 193, 195; Lanciani (1902–12) II: 194; Fiechter (1906) 222; Bartoli (1914–22) III: figs 476, 477, pl 289, 290; VI: 89–90; Benelli (2018, *Sostegno e adornamento*) 47; CensusIDs 64044, 10073077.

U 1167A *recto*

Antonio da Sangallo the Younger

Two designs for a planimetric reconstruction of the Mausoleum at Halicarnassus, based on a description by Pliny the Elder (Gaius Plinius Secundus), after 1527.

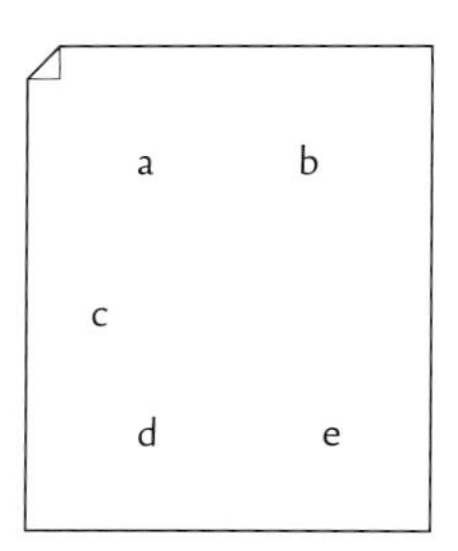

Dimensions 204 × 177 mm.
Paper faintly ruled, watermark with lamb and flag, excellent condition.
Technique Pen and brown ink.
Drawing Scale and Dimensions Roman *piedi.*

INSCRIPTION (*b*) *Lo modulo sii 30 dita e ¾ / cioè uno piede e dita 14¾ /* (cancelled: *lacolona grosso / piedi 4 lo intercolunio / piedi 13¾*) */ la colona grossa p*[*iedi*] *3 dita 13½ / Cioè due moduli / Lo intercolunio largo moduli / tre cioè piedi 5 D*[*ita*] *12¼ / exciette quello di mezo / è moduli 4 cioè piedi 7 d*[*ita*] *11 / In tutto la fronte sia piedi 73 / dalle bande colli angulari / sono Colonne 12 sono moduli / 24 sono piedi 92 dita quattro / Li intercolumnij sono 11 che sono / moduli 33 sono piedi 189 D*[*ita*] *4¼ / tutto gira piedi 524 D*[*ita*] *9 no ne affronta / perché a agirare 411 e acingerlo ncolone 3 Le Colone* (*e*) *La Colona moduli due / Lo intercholunnio moduli quattro / Lo modulo sia piedi 2 D*[*ita*] *4½ / La fronte sono Colonne sei sono / piedi 27 dita 12 – p. 27* (*12* cancelled and then corrected to *6*) */ Lintercolunnij sono 5 quali in tu / tto sono moduli 20 quali so / no piedi 45 e dita 10 – p. 45 10 /* (somma) *73 / Le rivolte sono due colonne e due / intercolumnj sono in tutto moduli / 12 in tutto piedi 27 Dita 6 / Le fronti sono 4 che sono piedi 292 / le rivolte sono 8 insieme – 219 / piedi 511 / dove dicie che gira piedi / 411 bisogna dicho 511 questo sie*

The sheet contains two possible solutions for the reconstruction of the mausoleum at Halicarnassus, which follow on from the earlier designs on U 1039A *verso* and U 1040A *recto.* Sangallo drew the solution on the top half of the sheet first (*a-c*), which he later rejected, and went on to develop a second version on a square base in the bottom half (*d, e*).

The fixed point for Sangallo was the 36 columns indicated by Pliny, however the measurement for the fronts has been extended to 73, despite the fact that the transcription on U 1039A *recto* specifies a length of 63 *piedi.*

In the rectangular solution (*a, b*), Sangallo had a rectangular edifice in mind, with fronts of 7 and 11 interaxes articulated by a module of 30 and ¾ *dita.* He then assigned a diameter of two modules to the columns, a width of three modules to the intercolumniations and a width of four modules to the central intercolumniations on the shorter sides. Lastly he worked out the measurement for the side of the edifice as being 189 *piedi* 4 and ¼ *dita* which, added to the measurement of the shorter sides, gives a total of 524 *piedi* and 9 *dita,* which is absolutely at odds with the 411 *piedi* taken from Pliny's text on U 1039A *recto.* It was for this reason that he rejected this solution and passed on to the next.

The second square designs *d, e* with corner recesses amplifies the ideas set out on U 1040A r., adapting them to the measurement of 73 *piedi* for the four hexastyle avant-corps. Having established one module as equaling 2 *piedi* and 4½ *dita,* Sangallo added together the measurements of the columns on each front, equivalent to 27 *piedi* and 6 *dita,* and those of the five intercolumniations, which add up to 45 *piedi* and 10 *dita,* making a total of 73 *piedi* for each avant-corps. He then calculated the measurements of the corner recesses, or "*rivolte,*" which prove to be 27 *piedi* and 6 *dita.* Lastly, he added together the four fronts and the 8 corner recesses, which gave him a total perimeter of 511 *piedi,* which was still 100 *piedi* longer than in Pliny's description. Notwithstanding the fact that this result was much the same as the first, Sangallo did not reject this second version, noting: *dove dicie che gira piedi / 411 bisogna dicho 511 questo sie.*

Although the purpose of both designs was to define the overall measurements of the edifice and its fronts, Sangallo has also used them to start delineating two different solutions for the central octagonal cella. In the first sketch *a*, access to the cella is gained via two colonnaded atria, in a solution that he took up again in U 1127A r. In the second example *d* the cella is articulated by niches on the diagonals and the avant-corps, inside which the staircases can be seen: these are detached from the central block in a solution that was taken up again on U 894A r. Sangallo had no antique source material regarding the articulation of the internal space of the cella, and thus he suggested solutions that frequently appear in his project. Octagonal plans have also been brought into play for the small temples on the Isola Bisentina U 962A r., for the church of Santa Maria Porta Paradisi U 870A r., for Santa Maria di Loreto 786A r., in a project for San Giacomo a Scossacavalli U 305A r., San Giacomo degli Incurabili U 782A r. and for the chapel in the monastery at Montecassino U 172A r. Furthermore, although the first design would appear to have been crossed out, it was not rejected out of hand, and both the planimetries illustrated on the sheet reappear in various later solutions. | VZ

BIBLIOGRAPHY Ferri (1885) 97; Giovannoni (1959) I: 11, 24; Raub (2014) 178, 199, fig. 9; Fane-Saunders (2016) 262, 266; CensusID 10075084.

U 1168A *recto and verso*

Antonio da Sangallo the Younger

Rome, Tomb of Annia Regilla (*recto*); Rome, antique house near Aventine; so-called Tomb of the Bracciolini (*verso*), before 1527.

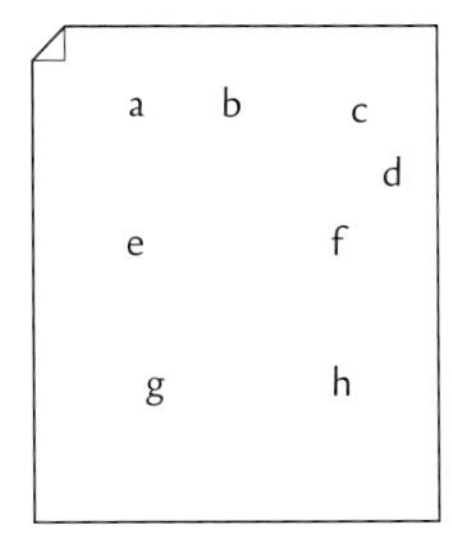

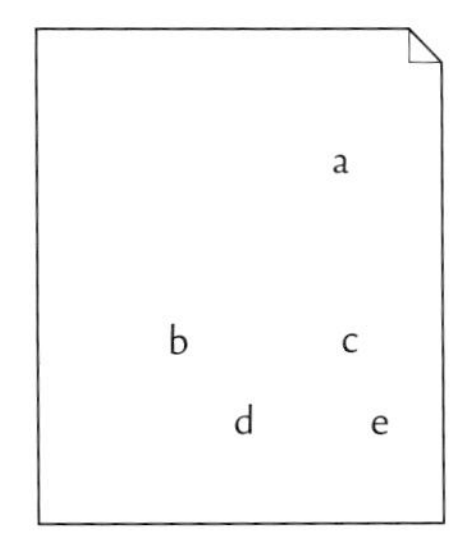

Dimensions 275 × 210 mm.
Technique Pen and brown ink.
Paper Partly yellowed; central vertical and horizontal folds.

INSCRIPTION, Recto top right, black pencil, nineteenth-century hand, old numbering, 901; (*b*) *pietra* [twice]; *matoni* [three times]; (*g*) *pianta di sopra*; *questo edificio e di matonj / bene lavorato i*[*n*] *sul fiume daqua / dacia i*[*n*]*fra la strada di santo bastiano / ela strada di porta latina achanto a / una gualchiere di pannj e dalla facia / di retro sono tre finestre simile e nelle / facie laterale sono una p*[*er*] *facia chome / a pare*; (h) *pianta di sotto*

Verso bottom left, black pencil, nineteenth-century hand, numbering, 1168; (*a*) *schala a gradi*; (turned 90 degrees) *mo*[*n*]*te alto fino / al primo piano*; *questa schala mo*[*n*]*ta / neli due prime branche / al primo e le altre / dua che sono piu chorte / montano al sechondo pi / ano*; *strada va s*[*an*]*ta stasia / p*[*er*] *lo piano A pie del mo*[*n*]*te / aventino*; *Questo edifitio si / pasato schola grecha alle / radicie ove chomi*[*n*]*cia mo*[*n*]*te / aventino*; (bottom half) (left edge) *Schala p*[*er*] *andare / a chauallo*; (*b*) *colarino / staua meglio / questo*; (*c*) *cornicione* [twice]; *fregio* [twice]; *architrave* [twice]; *A*; *mura / di roma / dalla bancha / di fiume*; *banda / di fuora / delle mura*; (*d*) *di roma / nelle mura infra / lo populo el fiume / doricho*; *mura di roma* [twice]; *A*; (*e*) *mattoni*; *pietra* [twice]; *piano* [twice]; *vano*; (*f*) *stipito piano*

The subject of all the drawings on the recto is the second-century Tomb of Annia Regilla in Valle Caffarella, between Via Appia Pignatelli and Via Appia Nuova. Drawing *a* is a sketch of the entablature of the window of the west elevation. Drawings *b* and *c* show the entablature of the doorway. Drawing *d* is a section through the doorway architrave and the molding surrounding the consoles supporting the cornice. Drawing *e* is a perspective reconstruction of the east elevation. Drawing *f* is an elevational reconstruction of the cella entrance wall. Drawing *g* is a plan of the cella, and *h* is a plan of the podium and reconstructed front steps.

The Tomb of Annia Regilla was much admired in the Renaissance for the detailing of its polychrome brickwork and for the recessed columns of the east elevation (a possible source for Michelangelo's Biblioteca Laurenziana). The sketches do not have the character of survey drawings (no measurements) and seem to be a record of details and attempts at reconstruction, which err in omitting a pronaos or portico in front of the cella.

The verso shows a plan of what appear to be the remains of an antique house and *horrea* (*a*) and studies of the so-called Sacello dei Bracciolini. Drawings *b* and *c* are perspective reconstructions; *d* is a plan; *e* is an elevation of the architrave of the doorway; and *f* is a section through the same architrave.

The house has a plan similar to many at Ostia, with rooms opening onto a central courtyard and stairs at the back, leading to the upper floors as Antonio indicated here. Clearly the remains stood to a considerable height, which raises the question why this sheet, another by Antonio (U 1201A r.), and one by Peruzzi (U 397A r.) are our only records of the house. A possible explanation is that, as with so many details of the temples at S. Nicola in Carcere, only the Sangallos and Peruzzi seem to have been interested enough to record them while they were exposed, during some building or excavation works. The unshaded part of the plan at the front of the house appears to be conjectural reconstruction, since it differs from both U 1201A r. and 397A r. Behind the house, Antonio included a range of chambers, probably belonging to a *horreum*, on which see U 1201A r.

The Sacello dei Bracciolini was an unusual T-plan tomb, incorporated into the Aurelian walls, between the Tiber and the Porta del Popolo. It attracted attention in the Renaissance, one imagines, mainly due to of its use of the Doric order. Other drawings of it by Sallustio Peruzzi and anonymous hands are preserved in the Albertina in Vienna and the Hermitage in St Petersburg.

For the dating of the sheet, see U 1223A, which is of similar size and includes the drawings of the Tomb of Annia Regilla in a similar style. | IC

BIBLIOGRAPHY Ferri (1885) 174, 199; Lanciani (1891) 140–41; Lanciani (1893–1901) no. 34; Bartoli (1914–22) III: fig. 469, pl. 283; VI: 88; Kammerer-Grothaus (1974) 187–88, no. 110.2; Wurm (1984) pl. 22; Frommel (2003, *porta ionica*) 44; Campbell (2004), I: 163–65, fig. 44 (ii) and 305; CensusIDs 60670, 60672.

U 1171A *recto and verso*

Antonio da Sangallo the Younger

Terracina, Temple of Jupiter Anxur (*recto*); Cassino, amphitheater and Tomb of Ummidia Quadratilla (*verso*), after 1527

Dimensions 214 × 150 mm.
Technique Pen and brown ink.
Paper Medium weight, trimmed, creases, reinforced at upper edge, hole at lower right, reinforced on verso.

INSCRIPTION, Recto *i[n] Sul mo[n]te sopra al passo di terra cina / quale vede el mare quasi da ttre banda e sopra / sta al saxo tagliato e al porto i[n] mo[n]te altissimo; p[er] adiquame[n] to e i[n] cima / era lo palazo abita[n]to / elevato qua[n]to uno omo / sopra questo el p[ri]mo piano / è piu alto i[n] cima al mo[n] te / era la forteza i[n] su uno / piano quale è piu alto / chel piano della bitatione / piu di 40 piedi; ripe; ripe; ambulatorio; ripe*

Verso *p[er] tirare lo cielo; porta a bugnie; piedi 25; a presso al palazo di ragona / e i[n] el palazo ne una simile sopra a una / antichaglia overo sepoltura di pietra / tutto dentro e fora*

Giovannoni observed that this sheet originally formed part of a "taccuino di viaggio," of which several other sheets have also survived. Antonio's view and plan of the Temple of Jupiter Anxur are thoroughly discussed by Vasori, who points out that in the view Antonio accurately recorded the lowest level, but inaccurately interpreted the upper level as living quarters. In the plan, the architect correctly drew the layout of the spaces, though he was mistaken in representing the enclosure as a rectangle, for it was slightly rhomboid. These divergences can be explained by the fact that the site was largely buried until the excavations carried out by Borsari in the nineteenth century.

At the top of this sheet, Antonio drew one of the five rusticated entrances into the amphitheater of Cassino and a mechanical device for raising and lowering the awning. Below this is a plan of the Tomb of Ummidia Quadratilla, located to the west of the amphitheater. In the tenth century, the mausoleum was transformed into a church, whereby a facade was added, and the corresponding arm of the Greek cross plan was extended to become the entrance into the church. This is what Antonio recorded. The profile to the left may relate to the base of the ancient sepulchre. The drawing is extensively discussed by Vasori. | SE

BIBLIOGRAPHY Ferri (1885) 217, 219; Giovannoni (1959) I: 20–21; Vasori (1981) 122–24, cat. no. 94–95; CensusIDs 10075109, 10021860.

U 1172A *recto*

Bernardo della Volpaia and Antonio da Sangallo the Younger

Survey of the obelisks of Mausoleum of Augustus and Circus Maximus.

Dimensions 333 × 393 mm.
Technique Stylus, pen and brown ink.
Paper Fold, trimmed on right side, restored.
Drawing Scale piedi antichi.

INSCRIPTION (Antonio's hand) *Pantano, santo rocho, capo di bove, questo sie b[raccia] 26 minuti 24 senza la punta / che sono piedi 52 m[inut]i 9 1/7 / lo bracci partito i[n] 60 / lo bracio sie mancho di dua piedi / 4/7 duna sesantesimo cioe parti lo bracio / i[n] 420 e due piedi sono 424*

The half-perspectival method of representation and the original, badly faded measurements point to the author of the Codex Coner. The sheet must therefore have been made before the presumed death of Bernardo della Volpaia in 1521 (Günther 1988, p. 170). In his pre-1527 hand, Antonio converts the measurements into *piedi antichi* and comments that the *braccio fiorentino* (.586 m) is 4/7th of a 60th smaller than two ancient feet. Thus 424/20 *braccia* equal two ancient feet (Günther 1988, p. 227). When Antonio put his drawings in order, he located, in his post-1527 hand, one of the obelisks in the neighborhood of San Rocco and the other in the Circus Maximus.

On the left side of the sheet there is a quick sketch of the relationship between an element with profiles, that refer to a "Tuscanic" order and a curve, probably allusive to a wall with an arch. The lower left corner beneath, is a baseline in a ratio of 1:2 to a vertical line. | CLF

BIBLIOGRAPHY Ferri (1885) 176–77, 219; Bartoli (1914–22) III: fig. 412, pl. 236; VI: 76; Günther (1988) 227, 257, 377; CensusID 10071277.

U 1174A *recto and verso*

Antonio da Sangallo the Younger

Overall plan of the temples at Forum Holitorium and various details in elevation; Attic Ionic base, after 1527 (*recto*), Temples of Forum Holitorium and modular articulation of Doric and Ionic colonnades (*verso*).

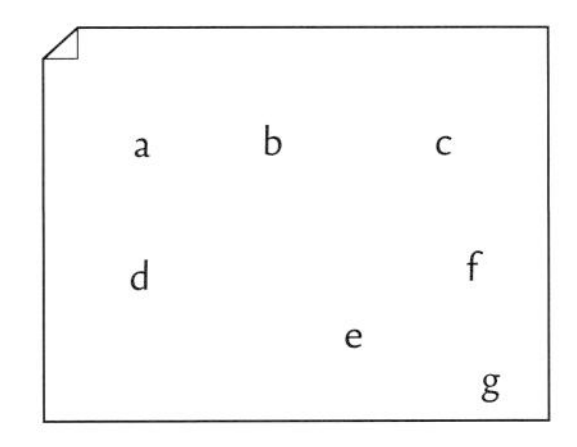

Dimensions 285 × 443 mm.
Paper Lightweight, right side partly trimmed, the rest fully trimmed, central vertical fold possibly made earlier than the drawings, reinforcements to left edge and in two places on bottom edge.
Technique Pen and brown ink, freehand.
Drawing Scale Roman *piedi*, *dita*, and modules.

INSCRIPTIONS, Recto: (Old marks, top center in brown ink, 17th–18th-century hand) *492*; (top right) (black 19th-century pencil) *907*; (Antonio's hand) (from top left, next to drawing (*a*), *iove statori*; (vertically) *piedi 13–10*; (below entablature of Ionic entablature) *sant nichola*; (under same drawing) *Linbasamenti di questi / edifitij erono in piano / cio[e] li piani loro perche que/llo di statori no navea base el capitello di santo / nicola e piu alto che quello / di Jove statori piedi 13 dita 10*; (above *b*) *la colonna si parte / in parte 16 qui e la base / nel piano da basso si e/ moduli 22 cioe 3/16 / per banda*; (top right corner) *porticho del teatro*; (top of right margin) *qui viene al de/ntro del muro a diretro / della colonna / come sta*; (below *d*) *Questo aveva li trigrifi in sul canto e lle metofe / equale. ma lli intercolunnij di sulcantone erono / più stretti che lli altri Dita 8 così dalli ii lati / come per faccia quale è uno de dua inconvenienti / che dice Vitruvi che fa quando si mette li tigrifi / in sulli canti che necesario o che si facia ditto / intercolunnio più stretto o lametofa Delcanto / piullonga chellaltre*; (under drawing *e*) *Jove statori, nello stesso, all'altezza dei capitelli, lacunari*; (in section *f*) *le carcere*; (below vertically) *basa capitello colonna 31–15*; (center *g*), *Sto nichola*

Verso (Antonio's hand) (from left, upper margin, turned 90 degrees) *30 Dita / perfino allo / architrave / della colonna*; (on entablature of door, at bottom) *carciere / Porta delle carciere*; (center top, in line with cornice of door of Doric temple to the right, and entablature of colonnade to the left) *e questo piano / afronta el capitello*; (beneath door frame, turned 90 degrees, referring to width, not height, of aperture) *dicie batista 13–12*; (beneath, at center, with reference to north temple) *La colonna capitello / basa del difitio corinto di / Sto nichola e alta p. 31 Dita 13 / La porta e alta pp. 25–4 / Larga 13–12 e vani*; (next to it, in right margin, referring to drawing above) *5–14 / queste de cantone / da mezo a mez [o] / L altre sono 6–6 / quella del mezo / più largo*; (below) *Lo capitello di Sto/ nicola e piu alto / che questo piedi 13*; (bottom center, referring to partial elevation of Doric temple below) *Libro quarto Capitolo tertio*; (beneath elevation) *si tetrastilo sara sia / moduli 19½ / si exastilo sara sia / moduli 29½ / si ottastilo sara sia moduli 49½*; (next to it, to right, above Ionic temple) *libro tertio / Capitolo secundo*; (beneath same elevation) *si tetrastilo sara sia / moduli / [x]ii½ / si exastilo sara sia moduli / xviij / si ottastilo sara sia moduli / xxiiij.s.*; (next to it, in right margin) *5–14 / queste de cantone / da mezo a mez[o] / L altre sono 6–6 / quella del mezo / più largo*; (below) *Lo capitello di Sto / nicola e piu alto / che questo piedi 13*

On U 1174A r. and v., Antonio grouped together various notes on the three temples at the Forum Holitorium in plan, section, and elevation form, together with a reconstruction of an Ionic base according to Vitruvius. The sheet can be dated post-1527 because of the shape of the "*ch*" in the handwriting. Antonio was not merely interested in the topography of the site and the reconstruction in plan and elevation of the architecture as a whole, which was one of major focuses of study toward the end of the second decade of the sixteenth century for anyone interested in reconstructing the various types of ancient temple. He drew on the Latin text in an attempt to reintegrate the shapes, but he appears to have primarily been interpreting various passages from Vitruvius, some of which have been expressly annotated on the verso, in order to verify the ruins against the latter's text.

The drawings on the recto are as follows: (*a*) the distance between the Doric temple of the Forum Olitorium (to Spes), which Antonio mistakenly identifies as the Doric peripteral temple of Jupiter Stator cited by Vitruvius (Book III, ch. 2, 5), with the Ionic temple in the middle and a comparison of their heights; (*b*) proportions of an Attic Ionic base (*De Architectura*, Book III, ch. 5, 2–3); (*c*) a reconstruction of the three temples in the plan; (*d*) the front of the upper part of the Doric temple; (*e*) a section showing the portal of the latter; (*f* and *g*) sections as above of the north temple (to Janus)—which Antonio considered to be Corinthian but which is actually Ionic, as he himself noted on U 2056 v.—and of the middle, Ionic temple (to Juno Sospita). In drawing *b* he drew the proportions of the various parts of the Ionic base in height from the plinth upward, according to the text (Book III, ch. 5, 2), and has applied the Vitruvian rule concerning the projection of the base itself as related to the thickness of the column, "Proiectura erit spirae pars octava et sextae decuma pars crasitudinis columnae" (Book III, ch. 5, 3), put briefly, 3/16 of the diameter, which makes the rule easier to apply. In drawing *d*, he observed how the narrower breadth of the corner intercolumniation ("li intercolunnij di sulcantone erono / più stretti che lli altri") corresponded to one of the expedients described by Vitruvius (Book IV, ch. 3, 2) for solving the problem of Doric friezes on corners; the same drawing shows the modulation of the front of the Doric temple, a theme taken up again with reference to all three temples on the verso. Lastly, in drawings *e*, *f*, and *g* the focus is on the upper edges of the portals, for which in the Doric, Vitruvius (IV, ch. 6, 1) prescribed an alignment with the tops of the capitals of the colonnade. In Antonio's reconstruction of the south temple (*e*), on the other hand, the casing of the portal comes up higher, corresponding to the cornice of the colonnade. In the north temple, the top edge of the casing remains 30 *dita* (approximately 56 cm) below the bottom edge of the cornice; in the middle, only the Ionic temple is its top aligned with that of the capitals. There is a suggestion of vaulting over the cella in all three drawings, a solution that is unlikely to have been evoked by any visible remains of the temples but one that Antonio and his brother Giovanni Battista both employed, the latter proposing it for the north temple (Campbell 2005, p. 31, and also p. 23 for the Adrianeum).

On the verso, in the left part of the sheet, Antonio drew a detail of the corner of the door of the north (Ionic) temple, with exhaustive information about much of the portal, giving the principal measurements and drawing the carved ornamentation in the door frame, in the arabesque frieze, and in the lower cornice with dentils and egg-and-dart. The note at the top regarding the distance of 30 *dita* between the upper edge of the cornice of the portal and the *architrave della colonna* reveals that here, as on the recto, Antonio was at pains to check whether Vitruvius's indications about the modular composition of temple portals coincided with the practice of the ancients. He confirms it in the right half of the drawing at center top, where he compares a section of the capital and upper corner of the architrave of the Doric temple with the upper cornice of its portal and establishes a correspondence, showing the cornice with the same height as the architrave of the colonnade. The sum of the partial measurements that he notes on the same cornice seems, however, to contradict the drawing, since the result is a height of 16 *dita* against the 20 *dita* of the architrave. The note at the center of the sheet also regards the relationship between the portal and colonnade: the height of the colonnade, base and capital included, "del difitio corinto di / Sto nichola" (north temple, Ionic), 31 *piedi* and 13 *dita*, is juxtaposed to the height of the door aperture, 25 *piedi* and 14 *dita*. If we add to this the height from the aperture to the top of the cornice (obtained from the large detail drawn at left), which is 6 *piedi*, we have a total height of 31 *piedi* and 14 *dita* for the portal, only one *dito* less than the height of the colonnade. The result, summarized in drawing *f* on the recto, is the only one in the three temples of the Forum Holitorium corresponding to Vitruvius's prescriptions for portals. The Corinthian capitals drawn by Antonio and Giovanni Battista da Sangallo in their reconstructions of the north temple do not, however, correspond to the actual architecture, which is Ionic, as Antonio himself writes on U 2056A v. and as appears already in Labacco's reconstruction. It is difficult to explain how the two Sangallos arrived at the idea of a Corinthian temple, but Antonio's interpretation is nevertheless a significant example of how the architect tended to reconcile the antique with Vitruvius, at least when the condition of the ruins made hypothetic solutions possible.

The second theme explored on the verso is the Vitruvian modulation of the intercolumniation of different kinds of temples, which Antonio dealt with also on the measured plans of the three temples in drawing *c* on the recto. At the upper right, a section-elevation of the capital and the full entablature of the Doric south temple, with triglyph in the corner, is accompanied by the measurements 5 *piedi* and 14 *dita* of the corner fields, 6–6 of the intermediate ones, and 9–9 of the central one. This is therefore connected, together with the note beneath it, to the elevation *d* on the recto. At the bottom of the sheet Antonio represented the modular division of the colonnade of a Doric temple (at left) and of an Ionic temple (at right), referring to the relevant passages in *De Architectura*. From the number of modules proposed we recognize a systyle intercolumniation (Book IV, ch. 3, 7) in the Doric temple and a eustyle intercolumniation (Book III, ch. 3, 7) in the Ionic temple. The number of parts that Antonio gives to the front of the tetrastyle Doric temple—"XVIIII S"—and to the hexastyle—"XXVIIII S"—are still considered correct, but did not appear in the printed editions of *De Architectura* before G. Philandrier's *Annotationes* to Vitruvius, published in 1544. This solution (repeated several times also by Giovanni Battista) may have been reached by the two Sangallos independently in the course of the 1530s, while thinking about the modules of the Doric frieze, as Philandrier was to do later. Using the same method, Antonio obtained and added the 49½ modules for the octastyle temple, for which Vitruvius had not given any indications. The division of the Ionic eustyle temple front in XII S parts is one less than the lection still accepted today, which is also found in the edition of Fra Giocondo. The numbers for the hexastyle—XVIII—and the octastyle—XXIIII S—are correct. | PNP

BIBLIOGRAPHY Ferri (1885) 195; Huelsen (1906) 171, 174; Bartoli (1914–22) III: figs 472–73, pl 265–66; VI: 88–9; Crozzoli Aite (1981) 37–38; Campbell (1984) 230, 236 ff., 243; Günther (1988) 262, 281–82, 312–13, 316; Pagliara (1988) 191–94, 198; Campbell (2005) 54 f.; Campbell-Nesselrath (2006); Engel (2014) 107–08, 113–14, fig. 4; CensusID 10015263, 10015666.

U 1175A *recto*

Antonio da Sangallo the Younger

Rome, Campus Martius, Temple of Hadrian, after 1527.

Dimensions 292 × 430 mm.
Technique Pen and brown ink.
Paper Lightweight, center fold.
Drawing Scale Roman *palmi.*

INSCRIPTION, Recto (left half) *fodera di marmo*; *peperigni*; *fodera di marmo*; (right half) *vedesi che i[n]tagli sono quelle / della gola dell architrave*; *i[n] botte p[er] / [...]*; *sotto terra / i[n] botte p[er] questo verso*; *19*; *4*; *sopra terra / 26 / arco [...] largo / p[almi] 26 apalmi / sottoterra*; *arco ne / volte*; *alti 6 palmi sta [...] p[er] testa*; *apunto delle / bande*; *festono largo / legato [...]*

The sheet brings together four sketches showing portions of the Temple of Hadrian. On the left half of the sheet, at the top, is the profile of the foot of a column with its plinth and Attic base, the latter characterized by an additional round swelling above the upper *torus.* At the right angles to this is a cross section through the vaulted cellar and the long wall of the cella with the peristasis in front of it. This drawing is probably a correction of the corresponding sketch on U 1144A r. The large exterior Corinthian order carries a longitudinal vault over the peristasis. The smaller freestanding interior Corinthian order carries a much wider vault spanning the entire width of the cella. Antonio conscientiously noted the different materials of the cella wall: the peperine core and the marble covering of the interior and exterior.

Antonio assumed in his ground plan that the pronaos is in *antis.* He was also interested in the various shapes of the barrel vaults in the cellar and the cella, as well as the longitudinal vault that, he assumed, covered the pronaos. The inclusion of the partially preserved vaulting of the cellar gave him, in contrast to U 1144A r., a more precise figure for the width of the temple, half of which he assumed to have had 4 by 15 columns—that is, 8 by 15 in total. The position of the smaller interior order is uncertain and is thus clearly a hypothetical reconstruction. Its entablature shows some peculiarities: the architrave is not divided into fascias but rather is adorned with festoons; the frieze, like the entablature of the exterior order, is pulvinated. On the other hand, the dentils and mutules are omitted.

Chronologically, this sheet probably follows U 1144A and 1661V., which is a preliminary typological study by Giovanni Battista. | HCD

BIBLIOGRAPHY Ferri (1885) 199; Bartoli (1914–22) III: fig. 464, pl. 279; VI: 86; CensusID 10073080.

U 1176A *recto*

Antonio da Sangallo the Younger

Tivoli, Plan of Sanctuary of Hercules Victor ("Villa di Vopisco"), 1539.

Dimensions 291 × 423 mm.
Technique Pen and two shades of brown ink, incised lines, straightedge.
Paper Lightweight, horizontal and vertical center folds, creased, stained.
Drawing Scale Three scales. The one at left is incised only; that at center bottom, which was too large, is canceled; that at right is the definitive one: 100 *piedi* = 52 mm. Measurements on the plan are given in *palmi* and *piedi.*

INSCRIPTION, Recto *Valle della strada / romana*; *edifitio*; *piedi 487 / palmi 649⅓*; *piedi 71 / palmi 94⅔*; *Giardino*; *piedi 182 / palmi 242⅔*; *Giardino; piedi 22 / palmi 29⅓*; *p[iedi] 84 / p[almi] 112*; *p[iedi] 32 / p[almi] 42⅔*; *p[iedi] 22 / p[almi] 29 1/3; edifitio pri[n]cipale*; *piedi 138 / palmi 184*; *edifitio*; *Longo tutto piedi 644 / quali sono palmi 858⅔*; *Di verso la terra*; *Giardino*; *piedi 194 / palmi 258⅔*; *piedi 182 / palmi 242⅔*; *p[iedi] 91 d[igiti] 8 / palmi 122*; *edifitio*; *piedi 71 / palmi 94⅔*; *Valle del fiume*; *piedi 487 / palmi 649⅓*

Verso *Boza della villa di vopisco / sopra a porta oscura*

In this drawing, a schematic plan of the Sanctuary at the level of the terrace, Antonio the Younger made a clean copy of his detailed study U 1208A. Since only half of the site was accessible, he reconstructed the project symmetrically, which does not, however, correspond to the real situation.

Antonio's other studies of the Sanctuary of Hercules Victor are U 1067A r., 1156A r., 1159A r., 1208A r., and 1351A r. | SE

BIBLIOGRAPHY Ferri (1885) 220; Giovannoni (1959) I: 22; Giuliani (1970) 166, fig. 177; Zorzi (1957); Vasori (1981) 124–25, cat. no. 96; CensusID 10022019.

U 1177A *recto*

Giovanni Battista da Sangallo

Rome, Nymphaum of the Orti Linciniani.

Dimensions 277 × 396 mm.
Technique Pen and brown ink.
Paper Mediumweight, restored at edges.

INSCRIPTION (later hand) *503* [cancelled] *504*

The sketch shows part of the circular room of the Orti Linciniani, the so-called Temple of Minerva Medica. It is an approximate drawing that records some characteristics of the structure: the system of the vault with its segments, the system of archivolts of the drum, and the room with niches. | ACF

BIBLIOGRAPHY Ferri (1885) 217; Bartoli (1914–22) IV, fig. 492, pl. 301; VI: 93; CensusID 10072209.

U 1178A *recto*

Antonio da Sangallo The Younger

Rome, Torre delle Milizie, plan of portion of ancient building, after 1527, about 1540?.

Dimensions 286 × 424 mm.
Technique Pen and brown ink, freehand.
Paper Trimmed on three sides, center fold, restored at edges.

INSCRIPTION (in Antonio's hand) *Diquesto e difitio se cavato in Casa / messer gieronimo Cuccino e se tro/vato molti framenti in ruina / dove e quello e emiciclo a pie delle / militie e setrovato questi Capitelli / Cioe A. B. C. D. e la Colo/nna E e molti altri framenti / di pilastri gialli pianj / Una storia de uno sacrifitio / grande lo ferne quanto* [...] */ Dua tondi per mettere una testa / Come quelli di ravenna dellarcho / della porta aurea / in ditta storia ne tinpano del tempio / di Judei cie Iove in mezzo di dua / donne asedere a pie di sua sca/la qui la e nel basso dello* (word canceled) */ timpano daogni banda sia una / Biga / in sulmezo delfronte spitio in su un / dado sia una quadriga / in sulli angoli una biga che corre in su / in fralla biga e quadriga dua statue ritte*; *in sullo cantone laterale u / architrave una aquila al/quanto larchitrave collali*; (later hand) *291*; *911*

The importance of this archaeological note is its representation of a lost building not documented in later archaeological maps. The building could be part of the Market of Trajan complex. The Coccini family is a well-known and important family in Rione Monti, as testified in later documents. Girolamo, son of Mariano Coccini and described as "procur. fisc." in the tombstone (formerly in S. Lorenzo in Damaso), was still alive in 1544 (J. Burckardi, *Liber notarum, R.I.S,* II, p. 53 n. 1). In another drawing by Antonio, U 1211A, as remarked by himself is a cornice "cavata nel 1540 in lorto dello emiciclo delle milizie del quale vi e' larchitrave in casa col fregio de grifoni" (cf. also Giovannoni 1959, I, p. 94). | EB

BIBLIOGRAPHY Ferri (1885) 34, 213; Viscogliosi (2000) 137–38, cat. no. 15; CensusID 239351.

U 1179A *recto*

Antonio da Sangallo The Younger

Rome, tomb probably unearthed during building of Bastione Ardeatina, after 1527, about 1540.

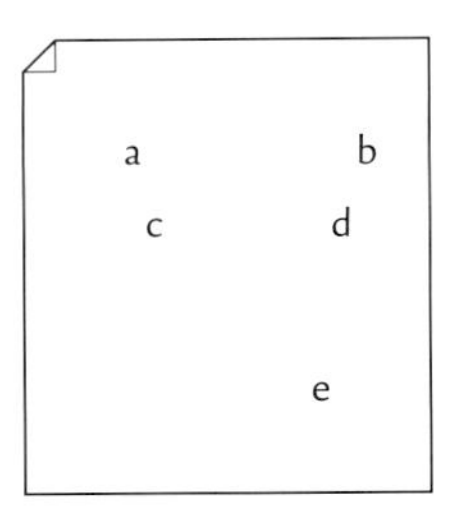

Dimensions 360 × 281 mm.
Technique Pen and brown ink.
Paper Partly yellowed, folded, patched.
Drawing Scale Roman *palmi.*

INSCRIPTION top right, black pencil, nineteenth-century hand, old numbering, *912* (*a*) *Tevertino* [three times]; lega; (*b*) *qua*[*n*]*to sia largo li / me*[*n*]*soli / Qua*[*n*]*to sia dalluna / allaltra me*[*n*]*sola / Qua*[*n*]*to sieno larghi / li di*[*n*]*telli / qua*[*n*] *to sia da luno allaltro / selbasto*[*n*]*cino si gira / sopra alle me*[*n*] *soli*; (*c*) *palmi 10 / ne lo regolo di teuertino*; (*d*) *i*[*n*] *tertio*; (*e*) a calculation of the height of the tomb by adding together the heights of each part, the sum of which is given *sono dita 228–7/10*; (bottom left) *le porte di roma i*[*n*]*comi*[*n*]*cia*[*n*]*do / al fiume ci era una porta ca*[*n*]*to / al fiume ditta* [...] */ seco*[*n*] *da porta quella che ogi s*[*an*]*to pagolo / canto la meta quadra di caio Cestio / chel uulgo dice la meta romulo / Tertia porta si e i*[*n*]*crusa nel bastione / della*[*n*]*toniana al fianco diuerso la porta di / sa*[*n*]*to pagolo quale ueniua dalla apia / e metteua a sa*[*n*]*to sau* (i.e. Saba) */ La quarta porta ditta apia s ie i*[*n*]*crusa nell / altro baluardo quale metteva a santa / balbina e dipoi a santa prisca i*[*n*] *ave*[*n*]*tino / quale viene i*[*n*] *mezo al ditto baluardo / e viene alinia adirittura Colla via / apia di Capo di bove ditta porta apia / e se afro*[*n*]*tava i*[*n*]*sieme / collaltra cioe colla / tertia nel circha a / sa*[*n*]*to balbina / La qui*[*n*]*ta porta si e la porta sa*[*n*]*to se/bastiano ditta Capena quale no*[*n*] *viene /*

diritta colla apia p[e]rde al fiumicello / della travicella piglia una storta i[n]verso / porta latina

All the drawings show parts of a tomb thought to have been found by Antonio the Younger while he was building the Bastione Ardeatina. The form of the base molding precludes the possibility that it is the tomb still surviving in Via Lucio Fabio Cilone, just north west of the bastion. Clearly the tomb was very grand both in size and ornament, and, had it been exposed before the construction of the bastion, it would surely have attracted the attention of others. The fact that only a segment of the plan is recorded suggests, perhaps, that only a fraction of the whole was excavated. Drawing *a* is upside down and shows a section from the basement to the cornice of the tomb; *b* is a section and projection of the cornice and cap; *c* is a diagram of a segment of the tomb, allowing one to estimate its full size; *d* is a sketch of part of the door frame; and *e* is a sketch section showing the heights of the various members illustrating the adjacent calculation. The drawings appear to be survey drawings made on site. The text accompanying drawing *b*, of the cornice, largely consists of questions about dimensions that still needed to be taken. Most of the details here are repeated *in pulito* on U 1287A r.

The text at the bottom of the sheet is the beginning of a list of the gates of ancient Rome, and is unrelated to the drawings. It is interesting in that it makes reference to the gates between the Porta S. Paolo and the Porta Ardeatina, which Antonio mistook for the Porta Appia and said was enclosed within the bastion (hence allowing us to date the text to at least after the construction of the latter). He identified the Porta Appia as the Porta Capena, a common mistake among Renaissance topographers (see also the locations given by Giovanni Battista on U 1636A r. and 1638A r.). | IC

BIBLIOGRAPHY Ferri (1885) 157, 189; Bartoli (1914–22) III: fig. 440, pl. 258; VI: 81–82; Eisner (1986) no. R6; Huth (2014) 151, fig. 1; CensusID 10072552.

U 1180A *recto*

Antonio da Sangallo The Younger

Rome, Campus Martius, Temple of Hadrian, after 1527.

Dimensions 225 × 163 mm.
Technique Pen and black ink.
Paper Lightweight, reinforced on verso.
Drawing Scale Roman *piedi*, *dita*, and *minuti*.

INSCRIPTION *Lo architrave delle plastine sie alto / piedi 3½ quali sono — D[itta] 56 / Lo gocciolatoio sie* (*p. 1 Dita 9 mi 1* canceled) *D 25 M 1*; (dripstone) *D 25–1*; (architrave) *p. 3½ alto apunto / cioe D 56*

The sketches show two views of the entablature of the peristasis. Below is a cross section through the architrave characteristically showing two fascia on the outside but three fascia within (see Cozza 1982, figs 6, 9, 53). On the upper half of the sheet, in perspective, is part of a cornice with a projecting, beam-like console and above it a coffer with a rosette. The underside of the portion of cornice beyond the console has a channel concluded with a fillet (see Cozza 1982, fig. 21). This study was probably made together with U 1144A and U 1175A. | HCD

BIBLIOGRAPHY Ferri (1885) 195; Bartoli (1914–22) III: fig. 357, pl. 213; VI: 68; Günther (1988) 230, no. 104; CensusID 249698.

U 1181A *recto and verso*

Bernardo della Volpaia (recto), Giovanni Battista da Sangallo (verso) and Antonio da Sangallo The Younger

Rome, Forum Romanum, Temple of Castor and Pollux, ca. 1513–15.

Dimensions 322 × 299 mm.
Technique Pen and light brown ink (Bernardo), pen and dark brown ink (Antonio), scored.
Paper Heavy.
Drawing Scale Florentine *braccia* and *minuti*.

INSCRIPTION, Recto (Antonio's hand) *le tre colonne*; *bernardo*; *Da meza cholonna a meza / cholonna sie B*[*raccia*] *6 e 27 e* dieci / *me*[*n*]*sole 3 i*[*n*]*teri e dua meze / e dentelli 11 i*[*n*] *teri e dua mezi*

Verso (Antonio's hand) *batista*; *Tre cholonne / Queste o prese 10 la cholonna / grosa da pie b 2 mi 31½ / la basa ad agietto 29 / Da cholonna a cholonna b 3–55½*; *cholonna; da cholonna a cholonna*; *da chapo b 2 minuti 10 la diminutione / e partita in 14 da pie e 12 da chapo b 2–31½ / I*[*n*]*fondo la cholonna e chrosa b 2–31½ / la basa adogietto 29 che metagola b 3–30;* [...]

The recto shows a perspective cross section through the entablature of the Corinthian "tre colonne" on the Forum Romanum, drawn by Bernardo della Volpaia, author of the Codex Coner (Buddensieg 1975), whose first name was recorded on the frieze by Antonio. The latter corrected the details of Bernardo's drawing, evidently after reexamining the monument himself. In the spaces between the dentils he drew, in perspective, the small, flat pieces overlooked by Bernardo. In a profile sketch, he also made it clear that the consoles of the cornice start from such pieces and that their independent character is emphasized in this manner. Antonio further insisted on an axial correspondence between the individual ornaments, a correspondence that he was apparently the first to discover or hypothesize. The lower inscription tells us that his point of departure was the axial measurement of the columns (6 *braccia* 27 *minuti*). At the same time, he presented a hypothetical reconstruction of the cornice, which, then as now, was preserved only above the three middle columns (see Lisbon, National Museum, inv. no. 1713; Buddensieg 1975, fig. 4). This brought him to the conclusion that there is a correspondence between the axes of the columns, consoles, and dentils of the molding, 3 + 2/2 consoles and 11 + 2/2 dentils corresponding to one intercolumniation; that is, there are 2 + 2/2 dentils to one console "bay." This unity and its subdivision is what interested him, as is demonstrated by the sketch in the lower right corner, an orthogonal view of two 38-*minuti*-wide consoles, the space between which is given as 58¾ *minuti*. Unlike the perspective view, the frontal orthogonal view allows a graphic, precisely measured reconstruction of the axial correspondences. Three dentils (two and two half), each 21½-*minuti* wide with 10¾-*minuti* spaces, correspond to the axial measurement of 96¾ *minuti*. Dentils and spaces are thus in a ratio of 2:1. This axial division did not interest Bernardo; in his perspective view, one console axis corresponds to three and two half dentils, that is, each console has one dentil more (information from Christoph Jobst). Despite this obvious error, Antonio copied Bernardo's measurements into his perspective drawing.

But where did Antonio get his detailed measurements? Did he, or his assistants, use a scaffold to measure the molding? Buddensieg (1975, p. 94) assumed that Bernardo made an "analysis of the entablature based on one measurement," which Antonio then corrected. The various columns of addition on the recto and verso and the two different measurements in Antonio's sketch make it clear, however, that he began with only one exact measurement, the axial measurement of the columns (387 *minuti*), which could easily be determined from the ground. All the other subdivisions were derived by mathematical trial and error, not by taking further measurements. Antonio initially gave the width of the dentils as 22 *minuti* and that of the spaces as 11 *minuti*. As if to conceal this experiment, he crossed out his orthogonal sketch after it had served its purpose. Its existence demonstrates the inadequacy of perspective representation as a means of showing ratios. The sheet provides a welcome illustration of the value of orthogonal drawing, such as Raphael advocated in his letter to Leo X.

In this conflicting form—with Bernardo's partly erroneous notations and Antonio's corrections—the Uffizi sheet was included in Bernardo's Codex Coner, where the number of dentils per console "bay" is given as three and two half but where the small flat pieces added by Antonio also appear (see Ashby 1904, no. 85). Yet surprisingly, the measurements ascertained by Antonio are not included in the Codex Coner. We may conclude from this that he corrected Bernardo's drawing in two stages: his additions to the perspective view must have been made before the Codex Coner; the rest, his calculations and orthogonal sketch, must have been made afterward. Bernardo probably manipulated the length of the console bay so that he could show on the underside of the cornice the coffer with its rosette, which would have inevitably been overlapped, given the closeness of the consoles (information from Christoph Jobst).

The verso shows a sketch in perspective of a cross section through the same entablature, with measurements different from those of the recto. We can assume, however, that the artist was not Giovanni Battista da Sangallo (Bartoli 1914–22; and Buddensieg 1975), who is referred to here by name, but Antonio himself; the cursory style, as in the drawing of the consoles, is exactly like that on the recto, and the details in the spaces between the dentils, about which Antonio complained on the recto, are here taken into account from the start. At any rate, the inscriptions are in his hand. The measurements differing from those on the recto, however, are by Giovanni Battista; he was probably sent to the actual site with the drawing and returned with his data, although they could no longer be used by Volpaia for the Codex Coner. | HCD

BIBLIOGRAPHY Ferri (1885) 127, 197; Egger (1906) I: 88; Jordan-Huelsen (1878–1907) I, 3: 666; Bartoli (1914–22) III: figs 380–81, pl. 223; VI: 63, 71; Buddensieg (1975) 90–94, figs 1, 3; Günther (1988) 165, 200, 252, 257, no. 102, fig. V5; CensusIDs 10006809, 10006907.

U 1182A *recto*

Antonio da Sangallo The Younger

Rome, Monte Cavallo, Ionic base, after 1527.

Dimensions 205 × 203 mm.
Technique Pen and brown ink, stylus, pin.
Paper Glue stains on four edges on verso.
Watermark: fleur-de-lis within a circle.
Drawing Scale Florentine *braccia*.

INSCRIPTION, Recto *191*; (later hand) *915*; *Questa basa sie appie della Croce di mo[n]te Cavallo / sotto uno portichale bene i[n] tagliata*; *Abraccia Fiorentini e minuti 60 p.[er] braccio*; *minuti 72*

Verso (later hand, in blue pencil) *1182*

This is a measured drawing of an Ionic base as described by Vitruvius (*De Architectura*, Book III, ch. 5). The inscription indicates that it was at the foot of a cross on Monte Cavallo, located under a portico, and considered to be well carved. Antonio sketched the decorative motifs of each section of the base and measured each molding, as indicated by the numerical notations along the left and right edges.

Günther compared this sketch to U 1850A, attributed to Labacco, and to folio 19 of the Cassel Codex. | MK

BIBLIOGRAPHY Ferri (1885) 128; Bartoli (1914–22) IV: fig. 353, pl. 211; VI: 67; Günther (1988) 372; CensusID 206968.

U 1183A *recto*

Antonio da Sangallo The Younger

Civitavecchia, Trajan Baths, caldarium, after 1527.

Dimensions 186 × 174 mm.
Technique Pen and brown ink.
Paper Mediumweitght, white.

INSCRIPTION *bagni di civita vechia cioe / el corpo pri[n]cipale quale a i[n] / torno ale mole altri corpi / e abitatione*

This sheet portrays the caldarium at the Trajan Baths, still visible near Civitavecchia. Antonio wanted to know first-hand how the vaults were designed, and he drew two elevations of the interior that make the vaulted covering of this antique Roman structure more understandable. | FZB

BIBLIOGRAPHY Ferri (1885) 28; Giovannoni (1959) I: 20–21; Vasori (1981) 125, cat. no. 97; CensusID 10074949.

U 1184A *recto*

Antonio da Sangallo The Younger

Frascati, Ionic base, after 1527?.

Dimensions 215 × 268 mm.
Technique Pen and brown ink, red chalk.
Paper Restored.
Drawing Scale Roman *piedi.*

INSCRIPTION *Infrascati* [repeated by other hand]; *questa basa e partita i[n] parte 4 dal regolo i[n] su / e uno sie lo bastono e letre parte sie partito i[n] / dua e uno scotia coli suoi piani e tre basto[n] / cini sie la meta*; *Bisognia partire / dalabaso i parte* (*38* canceled) *22 / e* (*32* canceled) *16 e luine della / colonna e* (canceled) *8 sie / alta in baso*; *piedi 3*

As the inscription "Infrascati" indicates, this is a measured drawing of a base found at Frascati. Like U 1182A, the profile corresponds to Vitruvius's description of an Ionic base (*De Architectura*, Book III, ch. 5). Vasori associated this sheet with drawings by Peruzzi (U 416A r.) and Dosio (U 2011A v.), which presumably record the same base. Similarities to Dosio's sheet prompted Vasori to identify the subject as a base from the Villa of Lucullus. Additional remains of this villa were found in 1854 under the small Villa Pentini.

Antonio reinforced the profile of the base with red chalk, and remeasured and corrected notations, as indicated in the second inscription in the lower right corner. Each section of the base has been measured and noted on the profile at the left. At the base of the column, the diameter is noted as 3 *piedi*. It is unclear if the unit of measure is *piedi antichi* or *piedi romani* as on Dosio's sheet. | MK

BIBLIOGRAPHY Ferri (1885) 79; Vasori (1981) 126, cat. no. 98; CensusID 10021813.

U 1186A *recto*

Antonio da Sangallo The Younger

Palestrina, details of an antique building, after 1527.

Dimensions 286 × 407 mm.
Technique Pen and brown ink, stylus.
Paper Heavy, folded, trimmed, restored along top edge.

INSCRIPTION (sketch at top left) (not Antonio's hand) *misure dello edifitio di palestrina*; *unovoli*; *fusaiole*; *unovoli*; *fogliette / fregiate*[?]; *fogliette liscie*; (sketch at lower left) *fusaiole*; *Vnovolo*; *fusaiola*; *alta Dita 55–3*; *archetti*; *archetto*; *lumaca i[n]tertio*; *fogliette nel piano*; *sopra li Capitelli*; *li bastonccinj*; (sketch at top right) *Colonne da capo*; *Capitello questo sie / alto D 90 minuti / Vno*; (sketch at lower right) *Capitello questo / sie alto D 90*; *La cimasa sie la / settima parte del / Capitello & la otta / va parto dil tutto*

The present drawing is extensively discussed by Vasori, who suggested that the architectural fragments may represent elements of the Sanctuary of Fortuna Primigenia. She further proposed that the perspectival view of the upper part of the corner of a wall supporting a soffit panel (upper left of sheet) may refer to one of the extant upper porticoes of the Sanctuary. Vasori also hypothesized that in addition to these details, Antonio is likely to have drawn plans and views (now lost?) of the entire Sanctuary.

What has not been noticed until now is that in the upper left quarter of the sheet there are three sets of sums inscribed with a stylus only. The numbers correspond to measurements written on the drawing, and look as though they are by the same hand. | SE

BIBLIOGRAPHY Ferri (1885) 108; Vasori (1981) 126–28, cat. no. 99; CensusID 10075002.

U 1187A *recto and verso*

Antonio da Sangallo the Younger and Giovan Battista da Sangallo

Comparative studies of the proportional relationships between diameters of columns and heights of -architecture in ancient buildings in Rome, 1527–30(?).

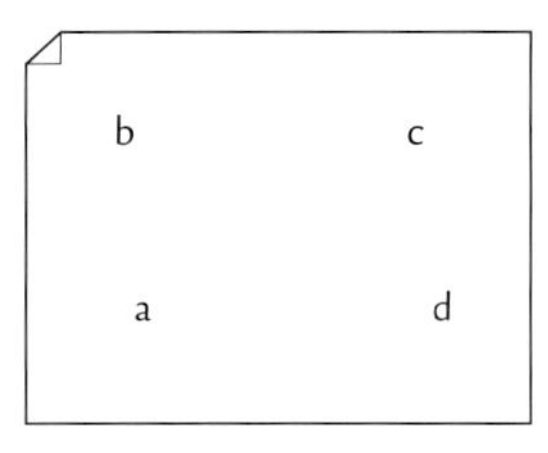

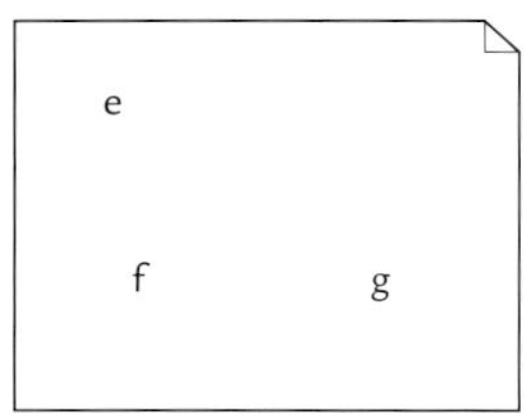

Dimensions 292 × 436 mm.
Technique Pen, with two different brown inks.
Paper Thin, trimmed on all four edges, slightly creased, one vertical fold.
Drawing Scale Roman *piedi, dita, braccia,* and *minuti.*

INSCRIPTION, Recto old reference numbers, black pencil, 19th-century hand: top right corner, *210*; bottom right corner, *920*. On the right half, turned 90°, to the left, on a), Giovan Battista's hand, on the section of an architrave, *72 dita*; below, on the bottom of a column shaft, *Monte cavallo / pie 6 dita 10*; below, Antonio il Giovane's hand, *monte Cavallo a piedi la colonna / grossa D 106 / La architrave D 72 / Quale sie vel circha li due tertij*; to the right, on b), Giovan Battista's hand, on the section of an architrave, *pie 3* — [*dita*] *9*; on the bottom of the column shaft, *Le tre colonne*; below, Antonio's hand, *a pie di la colonna sie D 78 / Larchitrave sie D 57 / quale sie circha li ¾ della colonna.* Antonio again on the sheet upside down: *per 12 piedi ad 15 in* (crossed out, illegible) *14*, on the margin *mezo / A* (?) *15 ad 20 in 13 / A 20 a 25 in 12½ / la colonna alta da 25 a piedi 30 in 12 / Larchitrave viene li 5/6 7/12 / partendo li 30 piedi in 7 teste viene / grossa la colonna piedi 4 e 2/7 e facendo / de pie quatordeci minuti* (?) *viene 60/ et partendo 30 pie in 12 e quello fa / larchitrave viene piedi 2½ quali / sono 35/14 de 35/14 sono li 7½ di / di 60/14*; numerous calculations. On the right half of the sheet, column of text to the left, Antonio's hand: *Ledifitio di monte Cavallo la co/lonna Dita 106 / Larchitrave alta Dita 72 / velcircha li ⅔ / Santo basilio la colonna xxxx* (crossed out, illegible)*/ fatto a bracci a moduli 60 per braccio / si e lacolonna moduli 181 / larchitrave moduli 121½ / vel circha li ⅔ /Antonino e faustina la co / lonna grossa dita 79 / larchitrave alta D 56 / vel circha li 2/3 / Spoglia χpo la colonna / moduli 147½ 147⅓ / larchitrave 111¾ / Vel circha li 3/4 / Lo porticho di foro transitorio la colonna / Dita 78 / Larchitrave dita 60 / Vel circha li ¾ / Le tre Colonne di Campo / grosse Dita 78 / Larchitrave alto Dita 57 / vel circha li ¾ / Le tre Colonne sotto campi/doglio / grosse Dita 76 / Larchitrave alto Dita 50½ / Vel circha li ⅔ / Le Colonne delle plastine / del tempio della minerva D* [*sic*] */ le Colonne grosse D* [*sic*] */ l architrave alta / Velcircha* [*sic*] */ Antonino e faustina / A piedi la colonna grossa D 79 / L architrave alte / vel circha D* [*sic*]*; / Questa si è vel circha li ⅔*; still on the right half of the sheet, Giovan Battista's hand, left, on the section of an architrave, *Antonino e Faustina*; *pie 3*—(dita) *8* (altezza dell'architrave); on the base, *pie 4*—(dita) *15*; below the same base, Antonio's hand, *a piedi la colonna grossa D 79 / larchitrave D 56 / quale si e vel circha li ⅔*; right on d) Giovan Battista's hand, on the section of the architrave, *pie 3*—(dita) *2½* (height of the architrave); on the bottom of the column shaft, *4¾ pie / sotto canpidoglio quelle 3 colonne*; below, Antonio's hand, *A pie di la colonna grossa D 76 / architrave alta D 50½ / viene vel circha li ⅔*

Verso (Left half, with sheet turned 90 degrees) (Giovanni Battista's hand) (on cornice *g*) *3–12* [height]; (on base *h*) *el tempio di foro transitorio 4–14* [diameter of column]; (Antonio's hand) *Lo architrave si e vel circha / alli ¾ della cololonna*; (under base) *A piedi et dita lo vivo della Colonna si e piedi 4 dito 14 – cioe D 78 / Lo suo architrave si e piedi 3 D 12 cioe D 60 / quale sie circha li ¾*; (Giovanni Battista's hand) (right, on cornice *i*) *braccia 2½* [Antonio's hand] *Batista la data in due modi*; [height of the cornice]; (on base) *braccia 3–1 "A"*; (below) *san basilio*; (Antonio's hand) (to right of cornice) "A" *Li quattro quinti della colonna*; under the base: *questa Credo sia errata / Colonne misurate a braccia /* ea *minuti di 60 per bracio lo vivo / delle colonne sie minuti 181 cioe – 181 / Lo suo architrave si e minuti 145 / quale sie li 4/5 / et sendo la colonna 181 / et larchitrave 121½ viene vel circha li ⅔*; (Giovanni Battista's hand?) (below) *questa credo stia bene.* (Right half) (Giovanni Battista's hand) (on cornice) *bracia*; *spoglia cristi*; (Antonio's hand) (on cornice) *vel circha li ¾ della / colonna mancho 3 minuti*; (under base) *A braccia partito in moduli 60 / grossa la colonna moduli 147½ / lo architravo alto moduli 111¾ / quale sie velcirca alli ¾ della colonna mancho 3 minuti*

The sheet, recto and verso, is a good example of both how much care Antonio and Giovan Battista took to check the findings of their investigations on ancient buildings, which they had surveyed and analysed, against the information supplied by Vitruvius on the heights of ionic architraves (*De Architectura*, III, 5, 8), and of how the two brothers shared the tasks. Firstly, on a sheet folded in half, which thus made a four-page notebook, Giovan Battista has assembled, from his own surveys or copies, a composite summary of drawings of architraves and column bases with the beginning of their shafts, belonging to seven buildings in the Corinthian style, mostly measured in *piedi* and *dita*, except for one in *braccia* and *moduli*. On the recto are bases and architraves of: (*a*) Monte cavallo (Temple of Serapis); (*b*) "Tre colonne" (Temple of Castor and Pollux); (*c*) Temple of Antonino and Faustina; (*d*) the three columns under the Campidoglio (Temple of Vespasiano). Antonio has then converted almost all the measurements into *dita* (1 *piede* = 16 *dita*) to make the calculations easier by using the only the smallest unit of measure. He has then calculated the ratios of the heights of the architraves and diameters of the columns and has set out the results in a list, in which the ⅔ ratio occurs slightly more than than ¾. Antonio knew well that Vitruvius had stipulated that the height of the architrave should be half the diameter of the column at the bottom, only for columns from 12 to 15 feet high, while for taller ones he had related the height of the architrave to the height of the shaft. Antonio has transcribed the relevant passage of *De Architectura* (III, 5, 8) on the sheet, but has tried to unite the two methods reported in the treatise, making the height of the architraves of columns 12 to 15 feet high a fraction, 1/14, of the height of the column, assuming a column 7 diameters high and thus translating the half diameter proposed by Vitruvius.

On the verso, Giovan Battista has drawn the profiles of cornices and bases, including the bottoms of the shafts, of three buildings in Rome: (*e*) the Temple of Minerva, Forum Transitorium; (*f*) the Temple of Mars Ultor, San Basilio; (*g*) "Spoglia Christi" (Forum of Nerva). Antonio has then added his own comments and calculations, noting the results in the list on the recto. | PNP

BIBLIOGRAPHY Ferri (1885) 128, 157,65,166,17; Bartoli (1914–22) III: figs 465, 466, pls: 280, 282; VI: 87; Günther (1988) 230, 301–02; Pagliara (1988) 195, note; Viscogliosi (2000) 139–40, cat. nos 16, 17; CensusIDs 239360, 239401.

U 1188A *recto*

Antonio da Sangallo The Younger

Plan of Greek house according to Vitruvius., after 1527.

Dimensions 219 × 163 mm.
Technique Pen and ink, freehand.
Paper Lightweight, trimmed, one corner and center reinforced.

INSCRIPTION (Upper right) (modern hand, in black pencil) *421*; (upper left) *106*; (Antonio's hand, from right of plan) *A vestibolo / B peristilio portico / rodiaco / C portico / D triclini ziciceni*[*sic*] */ pinacothece / F Bliotece*[*sic*] / *G* (blank) / *H gimnasio / exedre / H oeci quadrati grandi*[?] / *L Bagni*; (plan marked with letters) (at left) *H / F / G*; (at top) *K / C*; (in porticoes) *C / B / B / B /*; (at right) *L / H / I / F*; (at bottom) *D / A* [in entrance], *A* [in front projecting portico], *E*; (to right of portico) (*settentrio* canceled) / *meridie*

In the larger plan at the center of the drawing, the courtyard surrounded on all sides by peristyles reveals that Antonio the Younger is representing the *andronitis*, that part of the Greek house reserved for men (*De Architectura*, Book VI, ch. 7, 3–4). This is confirmed by the disposition of the rooms, which nearly always follows Vitruvius' description for the men's quarters: at the bottom of the plan, *A* marks the vestibule, referring to both the entrance and the preceding portico. In the same front wing Antonio locates the Cyzicene dining halls and the picture galleries, both on the side of the peristyle facing north.

Following the text of Vitruvius's Latin treatise, the left wing behind the peristyle facing east contains the library, and across from it is an exedra. At the top of the plan, and entered from the south, is a large square *oecus*, which projects at the rear into a second courtyard. (For a similar *oecus*, see the one Antonio draws on U 1161A v.). The Rhodian peristyle that Vitruvius locates only on the side facing south, and therefore in front of the *oecus*, is here found instead on the other three sides. This may be due to an error in marking the plan with the key letters rather than a misunderstanding of Vitruvius's text. The baths are Antonio's addition; Vitruvius refers to them only in the chapter on the *domus* (Book VI, ch. 5, 1). To right and left of the larger house, Antonio draws two plans that are fundamentally identical in their layout. In the one on the right, the space to the left of the entrance is clearly a stable. This feature, together with the peristyle around three sides of the court, corresponds to Vitruvius's description of the *gynaekonitis* (Book VI, ch. 7, 1–2). The peristyle around three sides of the courtyard appears also in the house on the left, although it is drawn more sketchily. Most likely this house was a *domuncula* for guests (Book VI, ch. 7, 4). Courtyards or gardens lie behind the two smaller houses, filling in the vast perimeter of the rectangular site.

Antonio's reconstruction of the Greek house differs from the corresponding illustrations of both Fra Giocondo and Cesariano. Fra Giocondo (fol. 01.66v.) only draws a *gynaekonitis*, omitting the *andronitis* for lack of space on the page of his edition of Vitruvius's treatise; Cesariano (fol. CIIIr) places the *gynaekonitis* and *andronitis* on a longitudinal axis, the former entered from the south, the latter from the north. Antonio the Younger's plan, less strictly tied to a practical purpose than was his reconstruction of the *domus*, could have been one of the drawings he made beginning in the 1530s, in which he systematically studied the various books of the treatise, perhaps in preparation for an illustrated translation. | PNP

BIBLIOGRAPHY Ferri (1885) 39, Giovannoni (1959) I: 20, 21, 23; Pagliara (1972) 26; Frommel (1973) I: 55; Fontana in Fontana-Morachiello (1975) 24; Pagliara (1988) 186; Pellecchia (1993) 333; Günther (2001, *Palazzo di Mecenate*) 231; Benelli (2018, *Sostegno e adornamento*) 44–5.

U 1189A *recto and verso*

Antonio da Sangallo The Younger

Studies of Ionic capitals according to Vitruvius, after 1527.

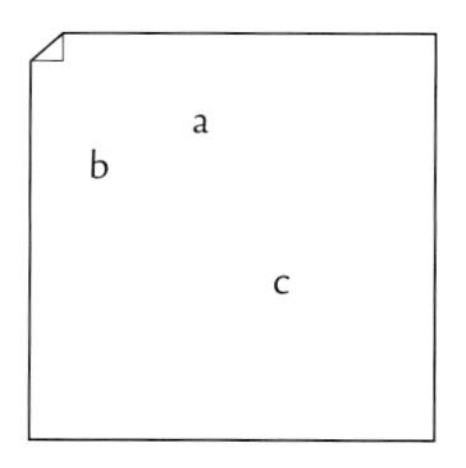

Dimensions 183 × 175 mm.
Paper Thin, trimmed on four sides, eight paper reinforcements on verso.
Technique Pen and brown ink, freehand.
Drawing Scale Measurements in modules.

INSCRIPTION (top right) (in black 19th-century pencil) *922*; Antonio's hand) (at top edge) *Tertio*; top between drawings (b) and (a) *parti in 40*; (below) *de unochio*; below bottom edge of plan (a) *abaco*; to its right *Colonna da pie/nelvivo*; below plan *agiunto una diciottesima/ diventa diciannove/ le volute se anno a rimettere in dentro*; vertically, to left of elevation (b) *di nove parte e ½/ ne pende in su stragulo/ 3⅙ / e cosi resta e capitello/ la terza parte della colonna 6⅓*; on drawing (c) *canali/ cimatio*; below it *cavato lo cimatio/ e canali e lo resto si e al cimatio*; to right of this elevation, under compass incision *1a*[?] *dellochio*; below *baltei anno/ avere fuora/ dello abaco de/ agietto quanto dua ochij*; (at bottom) calculations relative to the proportions shown above

Verso (16th-century hand, in pen and brown ink) *Al molto onorando mesere Antonio da Sangalo Architeto de la Santita/ De nostro Signore in roma/ dare lo diporto uncharlino.* The breaks that appear vertically along each of the four lines demonstrate that the address was written after the papers had already been bound with string. Beside it, Ferri annotated in black pencil: *Aristotile ad Antonio/ il Giovane.* Below left, Ferri has written another note in black pencil that has largely disappeared: *di Gaye N 861*[?]/ [...] *quale* [...]

Antonio has made several sketches of Ionic capitals on this sheet: above, a plan at the level of the abacus (*a*); on the left a scheme of the front elevation (*b*); below center an elevation with greater definition of different parts at the two extremities (*c*). The drawings have been annotated on the verso of a packet of papers addressed to Antonio during his term as master of the works at St Peter's, and therefore certainly after 1520. The "*ch*" with the loopless "belly" of the "*h*" in "*ochio*" means that the writing can be dated post-1527 (Frommel 1994, *Introduction*, p. 36), while the cross turned 45 degrees for the construction of the volute, alluded to here, can be found among Antonio's papers relating to a drawing for Villa Madama (U 718A r., before 1520), then in U 1218A r., and finally in a project for an Ionic capital for the loggia in the courtyard of Palazzo Farnese (U 983A r.). Antonio used the same procedure to delineate the volute in the latter in around 1539–40, and this was later published by Francesco Salviati (Günther 1988, p. 223, and Losito 1993, *La ricostruzione*, pp. 149–50).

The three drawings, with their relative notes, would seem to be a first attempt at a graphic interpretation of various points made by Vitruvius in his guidelines for Ionic capitals (*De Architectura*, Book III, ch. 5, 5–7), made by Antonio during his systematic study of the treatise, not as part of any ongoing project, and set out methodically, as specified in Book III. Antonio starts at the top, with a drawing *a*, in which the side of the abacus is equal to the diameter of the shaft of the column at its bottom plus 1/18 (*De Architectura*, Book III, ch. 5, 5), and after having also expressed this length in 40 submodules, he attributes 35 of these units to the length of the dosseret. The difference between the two measurements is thus reduced to ⅛ of the side rather than ⅙ (2 × 1½ modules out of 18) envisaged by Vitruvius, and therefore the projection of the abacus diminishes in relation to the dosseret. In elevation *b*, Antonio replicates an abacus with a length of 40 submodules and on the left he calculates the height of the capital as 9½ modules, which is the sum of the 8 modules of the volute plus the 1½ of the abacus (*De Architectura*, Book III, ch. 5, 6). In elevation *c*, on the left, the heights of the parts of the capital corresponding to the volute are given: 3 for the lower part of the volute up to its "eye" (1 for the "eye"), 4 for the height of the channel (and 1½ for the abacus) (*De Architectura*, Book III, ch. 5, 6–7), giving a total of 9½ modules. Here Antonio has inexplicably placed the vertical line of the column shaft on the inner side of the volute and caused the center of the "eye" to recede further from the edge of the abacus than prescribed in *De Architectura*, possibly because he was less interested in this than in other points raised by Vitruvius in this part of his treatise. In the right corner, the projection of the "*cimasa*-echinus" beyond the abacus is shown, equal to one "eye," as is that of the baltea, equal to two "eyes," indicated by one and two compass arcs denoting the width of the diameter of the "eye" (*De Architectura*, Book III, ch. 5, 7).

Antonio would have been able to draw on the Latin text with pictures by Fra Giocondo (1511, fols 29v.–30r. and 1513, fols 51r. and v.) and Durantino's translation as a basis for his interpretation of these passages from the treatise. He also added significant emphasis, however, to the ratio of 1:3 between the central body of the capital and the module of the column, the outline of the dosseret in plan A, a different take on the construction of the volute and the details of the projections of the echinus and baltea, which he obtained by following the treatise, which he kept to faithfully on the whole, to the letter. The slight deviation from *De Architectura* regarding the overhang of the abacus may be due to a desire to simplify and rationalize the calculations on Antonio's part, rather than to his predilection for following ancient methods, and negligible dissimilarities with Hermogenes's directions for this detail, taken from Vitruvius, can also be noted.

Ferri had attributed the address on the verso to the hand of Aristotile da Sangallo. The note bears some similarities with the handwriting of Antonio's cousin (see U 1043A r. and 1070A r.) regarding the ductus and the extremely elongated pen strokes, but these are insufficient in terms of a positive identification, in addition to which the writing used for the address is more careful and formal. | PNP

BIBLIOGRAPHY Ferri (1885) 17; Giovannoni (1959) I: 23, 67.

U 1190A *recto*

Antonio Labacco

Rome, Forum Romanum, Basilica Aemilia, ca. 1527–46.

Dimensions 219 × 259 mm.
Technique Pen and gray ink, scored with straightedge.
Paper Heavy, vertical fold.
Drawing Scale Florentine *briaccia* and *minuti.*

INSCRIPTION, Recto (Antonio's hand) *del labacho misurata braccia fiorentina / in foro bovaro cioe lo difitio* ascontro *al fiancho / di Sto adriano i*[*n*] *sul ca*[*n*]*tone pro proprio*

Verso *schizi di cornizi*

The survey on the recto deals entirely with the parts of the column order of the basilica. From left to right, there is a capital in profile, an entablature in perspective, and the upper part of a column and entablature in elevation for an imagined corner arrangement with corner triglyphs. The name "Forum Boarium" follows the current belief of the building's site among the circle of the Sangallo since Giuliano da Sangallo; Antonio the Younger was Labacco's master. The weak drawing compiles the surveys of others and is theoretical in character. It departs from the measurements of the Sangallo circle by making the frieze too low: on U 1716A it measures 82 *minuti*, on U 1057A, 85 *minuti*; here it is only 60 *minuti*. The drawing is probably connected with the preparation of Labacco's *Libro appartenente all'Architettura* (Rome, 1552), where the basilica is reconstructed as a rectangular building. | HCD

BIBLIOGRAPHY Lanciani (1883, *Aula del Senato*) 30; Ferri (1885) 166; Bartoli (1914–22) IV: fig. 606, pl. 350; VI: 109; Buddensieg (1975) 95; CensusID 239698.

U 1192A *recto and verso*

Antonio da Sangallo the Younger

Rome, Ionic capitals from S. Giovanni in Laterano, Rome; figures, one seated, one kneeling (*recto*); plant of the ionic portico of S. Giovanni in Laterano (*verso*), 1540–45

Dimensions 275 × 250 mm.
Technique Pen and black ink.
Paper Reinforced in five locations.

INSCRIPTION, Recto *Capitello de langolo Jonicho; santo Janni sotto l'andito di Santo Santorum uno capitello ionicho quadro in su n uno pilastro quadro di granito groso p[er] uno verso palmi 2 p.[er] laltro palmi 3 e non e piu in roma e sta chosi*

Verso *Capitello Jonicho*

On the recto of the sheet, Antonio represents three ionic capitals from pilasters most probably belonging to the portico of S. Giovanni in Laterano, under the chapel of the Sancta Santorum, now belonging to the Padri Passionisti. The portico was built in the 9th century and its ionic pilasters, designed by Antonio, according to the documentation, belonged to the vestibule or *macrona* which Pope Zaccaria and Pope Hadrian I had beautified, Leo III had rebuilt and Gregory IV had restored (see *Libr. Pont.* II, 76, 81).

The pilasters of the granite portico, faced with a line of columns, are rectangular and their dimensions (2 × 3 *palmi*) correspond exactly with those shown by Antonio. On site, three lines of pilasters are still visible, probably belonging to a large room, a vestibule or possibly a portico.

Two ionic columns (originally probably three) in Cipollino marble, which Antonio seems to have designed in plan in U 1192A v. are aligned with the three pilasters. The two marble shafts are of different sizes; the smaller is 3.6 meters high, the other is 3.8 meters high. Their bases have different profiles and heights. The height of the western base is 0.31 meters; the width 0.60 meters. The height of the eastern base is only 0.22 meters. The intercolumniation is approximately two meters. The capitals of the columns are surmounted by a dado prior to the architrave and they have the same character as the three capitals of the pilaster drawn by Antonio, which is no longer on site. The abacus is quadrilateral in form with the ionic cyma on the four attached edges; below is the diagonal canal of the volute (the only feature to distinguish these capitals from those of the pilaster so precisely drawn by Antonio). | MLU

BIBLIOGRAPHY Ferri (1885) 141; Bartoli (1914–22) fig. 389, pl. 227; VI: 73; CensusID 10073156.

U 1193A *recto*

Antonio Labacco and Antonio da Sangallo the Younger

Rome, Sketches of the aula of S. Giovanni in Laterano, 1512.

Dimensions 220 × 329 mm.
Technique Pen and black ink, red chalk. *Paper* Folded in eighths, repairs on the fold.
Drawing Scale Roman *canne* and *palmi*.

INSCRIPTION, Recto (top left quarter) (red chalk) *chane cinqe p/almj sete / chane ventj 3 p.[almi] ii*; (top right quarter) (red chalk) *channe v p.[almi] iiiiiii /* (pen and black ink) *sala di santo ianni / Larga channe v p.[almi] vii / Lunga channe xxiii p.[almi] ii /* (red chalk) *channe xx 3 p.[almi] ii*; (bottom left quarter) (red chalk) *channe / viii p.[almi] ii / channe xxx 3 p.[almi] iiiiii /* (black ink) *nave grande di Santo ianni / Lunga channe xxxiii p.[almi] vi / Larga channe viii p.[almi] ii*; (bottom right quarter) (red chalk) *channe / oto p[almi ...]*; *channe trenta 3 p.[almi] iiiiii*; (later hand, pencil) *926*; *40*

Verso (red chalk) *ixi 1/1*; (later hand, pencil) *Abaco* [twice]; (later hand, blue pencil) *1193*

The sheet contains two measured drawings each of the large Leonine aula in the Lateran Palace and the nave of S. Giovanni. The drawings of the aula are sketched only as rectangles, with five apses on one side. Some dimensions are indicated in red chalk: length, 23 *canne*, 2 *palmi*; width, 5 *canne*, 7 *palmi*; width of the first and third apses, 3 *canne*; width of the first section of wall, 10.5 *palmi*; depth of the third apse, 2½ *canne*. In the left drawing, the lower apse is 2 *canne* deeper [not "deeper" but "has a depth of 2 *canne*"]. Except for the depth of the apses, the measurements agree roughly with those given by Fontana in about 1585/86 in his "archive plan" for the same hall (Luchterhandt 1999).

The sketch at the lower left gives the measurements of the nave of S. Giovanni: width, 8 *canne*, 2 *palmi*; length, 33 *canne*, 6 *palmi*. The lower right corner presumably shows the 3-*canne*-long papal *quadratura*. It was evidently intended at first to be installed to the right of the main altar, as in the Sistine Chapel. The sketch at right basically repeats the information on the left, this time with the *quadratura* in the upper left corner. The draftsman's scrawled measurements were repeated legibly in ink by another hand in all the red chalk sketches.

Presumably Labacco made the survey sketches at the site for Paris de Grassis, the papal master of ceremonies. The sheet was folded twice, and a rough drawing was scribbled on each quadrant. In March 1512, Julius II had appointed a commission of cardinals and architects to plan installations for the council in the nave of the Lateran Basilica. In the course of the planning, De Grassis succeeded in becoming head of the commission and sought to collect information about older councils. Eventually, word came back to Julius II that it would be desirable to follow the example of the Council of Constance and arrange for a supplementary *secretum conciliabulum* in the Leonine aula of the palace, where higher level political deliberations could be held.

In the Lateran Basilica the room of the council was arranged in front of the tomb of Martin V as an enclosed chamber surrounded by a stone wall 4.50 meters in height. In the palace hall the papal consultation room [better:

room of the papal council] was shifted toward the north, in front of the doors of Pilate, because of the reliquaries of Christ in the central axis. The aula was used only once for a consultation, in May 1513, but from that time on it was called the "Aula del Concilio." | MLU

BIBLIOGRAPHY Ferri (1885) 141; Minnich-Pfeiffer (1981) 147–72; Frommel (1994, *Introduction*) 12, Luchterhandt (1999) 109–22.

U 1195A *recto*

Antonio da Sangallo The Younger

Rome, Porta del Popolo, cornice.

Dimensions 170 × 152 mm.
Technique Pen and brown ink, freehand.
Paper Heavy.

INSCRIPTION, *sopra la porta / del populo*

The cornice represented here, drawn by a number of Renaissance architects (Giuliano da Sangallo, Baldassarre Peruzzi, Codex Coner), belongs to the original decoration of the Porta Flaminia. The old gate was expanded and modified as part of Pius IV's architectural renovation between 1561 and 1563. | EB

BIBLIOGRAPHY Ferri (1885) 189; Bentivoglio (1987); CensusID 237965.

U 1197A *recto*

Antonio da Sangallo The Younger

Rome, Campo Martius, Baths of Nero-Alexander, before 1527.

Dimensions 186 × 210 mm.
Technique Pen and light and dark brown ink, stylus, compass.
Paper Heavy, trimmed.
Drawing Scale Florentine *braccia.*

INSCRIPTION *una torre*; *bronzo*; *i[n] chasa mes[ser] marcho dei sbizeri / di quadretti di selcie e di marmo / a uso di musaicho quale erano le terme / alessandrine da santo stato*; (on mosaic) selcie; *marmo a uso / di musaicho*

The drawing shows two patterns for the white marble floor with black intersections of the Baths of Nero Alexander. Inscribed in the circles of the pattern at the left are black stripes running in three directions; the circles are 1 *braccio* in diameter. In the pattern at the right, the perimeter of each circle is overlapped by six other circles; the overlapping areas are distinguished by black stones.

For the topographical situation of the baths, see also U 949A r. | HCD

BIBLIOGRAPHY Ferri (1885) 161, 201; Bartoli (1914–22) III: fig. 409, pl. 235; VI: 75; CensusID 10072896.

U 1200A *recto*

Antonio da Sangallo The Younger

Rimini, bridge over the Marecchia, parapet, Arch of Augustus, after 1527.

Dimensions 222 × 289 mm.
Technique Pen and brown ink, freehand.
Paper Lightweight, yellowed, upper edge restored on verso.
Drawing Scale *piedi antichi, dita*? (1 *piede* = 2.96 mm; 1 *dito* = 185 mm).

INSCRIPTION (left half) (over bridge) *ponte di riminj*; *parapetto tondo disopra*; *p[ie]di 2*; (on parapet) *epitaffio*; *archj cinque / larcho circa piedi / 32 luno*; *parapetto – 2 [piedi] – 4 [piedi]*; *cornicie tozo*; (to indicate level of street on bridge) *terra*; *modelletto*; (right half) (for arch) *dalla stella ingiu / cie in pie dalla stella / in su cie cierto p[a]rete / dentro cierte lettere / rusticate grande epi/cole parono ricolte / duna ruina e mura/te poi acaso* (*stella* refers to corresponding sign at levels of socle and gable); (left of elevation) *corintio*; *Largo circa piedi 30 / circa 30* (canceled; refers to clear width of roadway); *e molto largo e basso / dalla stella in su credo sie / uno quadro tutto penso sia uno quatro Lo mezo*; *in rimini lagola delcornicione sie / in la cornicie che sta in piano come in quello / del frontespizio*

The drawings on the sheet all done freehand. The sketches for the Augustinian bridge over the Marecchia, in which the clear width of the arches is given as 32 *piedi antichi* (ca. 8.7–8.8 m), are, by and large, in line with the finds (Gazzola 1963, II, p. 73 f., no. 83). However, in the elevation drawing of the Arch of Augustus, which was erected in 27 BC over the restored Via Flaminia as a city gate (see Mansuelli 1941, pp. 78 ff.), the description of the finds is mixed with reconstruction and critical assessment of the structure. The clear width of the opening— "*circa piedi 30*"—is very close to the actual measurements (8.84 m, according to Mansuelli). But the attic story above the low triangular gable is a reconstruction, and both Antonio's remark about the cramped proportions of the passage and the change in the socles beneath the engaged columns and the piers of the wall (unlike the finds, the engaged columns are given their own pedestals) may be regarded as deliberate corrections of the architectural finding (see also U 815A, 1048A, and 1064A).

Antonio may have visited Rimini during one of his trips to Ancona and Loreto. | CJ

BIBLIOGRAPHY Ferri (1885) 121; Giovannoni (1959) I: 20, 21, 156; Pasini (1974); Vasori (1981) 128–30, cat. no. 100; Zavatta (2008) 38–40, 47, 115, 118, 134, 216–17, 232, 249; CensusID 10076301.

U 1201A *recto*

Antonio da Sangallo The Younger

Rome, remains of antique house and *horrea* between S. Maria in Cosmedin and Aventine, before 1527.

Dimensions 315 × 224 mm.
Technique Pen and brown ink, freehand.
Paper Partly yellowed, folded, trimmed.
Drawing Scale Roman *palmi.*

INSCRIPTION top right, brown ink sixteenth-century hand, old numbering, *296*; black pencil; nineteenth-century hand, old numbering, *934*(; upper sketch, turned 90°) *schala a bastoni / monta palmi 2½ per channa*; *A* (various measurements); *A*; *monte di tufo*; (lower sketch) *questa e una Casa anticha / dala scuola grecha in sulla / strada*; *queste muri erano / sopra la volta / sotto era tutto uno / Corpo*; *aria* [twice]; *coridoio*; *qui non si puo / avere lume*; various measurements

The key letter "A" indicates that the two plans are related, the upper being the continuation of the series of chambers on the lower. The subject is the same as that on U 1168A v., where, although the house is drawn in a more finished manner than here, it lacks measurements and some of the present plan's details. This is especially clear at the front of the house, which, on 1168A v., appears to be reconstructed conjecturally, while here Antonio drew a vault and referred to it in the text. He also made clear the substantial scale of the building behind the house. He was specifically interested in the ramp to the upper stories and gave detailed dimensions. On 1168A v., he speculated that it was for the use of horses. Similar ramps occur in *horrea* at Trajan's harbor at Ostia, but are likely to have been designed to help men carrying burdens rather than horses (Rickman 1971, 17–24, 128–30). Certainly, those in the Trajanic-Hadrianic (early 2nd century AD) *horrea* known as the "Piccolo Mercato" cannot have been used by horses, since they are preceded by five or six steps. The vaulted portico running along the front of the chambers, implied by the criss-crossed lines (absent on U 1168A v.), is a feature of the largest *horrea* at Trajan's harbor at Ostia, which has Aurelianic brick stamps (mid- to late 3r.d century AD), and also had ramps.

Antonio's plan also bears a resemblance to the remains of the long brick portico and chambers, which were excavated at the foot of the Aventine in 1891 and which appear on Lanciani's Forma Urbis (1893–1901, pl. 34). The structure was almost certainly one of the many *horrea* located between the Tiber and the Aventine. | IC

BIBLIOGRAPHY Ferri (1885) 133, 162, 163; Bartoli (1914–22) III: fig. 375, pl. 220; VI: 70–1; CensusID 60671.

U 1202A *recto*

Antonio Labacco

Rome, Trajan's Column, three profiles of cornices.

Dimensions 302 × 220 mm.
Technique Pen and brown ink.
Paper Fold.

INSCRIPTION (Antonio's hand) *Colonna storiata*

The drawing is generally referred to by Ferri in the category "cornicioni" (Ferri 1885, p. 32). The note "colonna storiata" next to the profile with hints of the decorative apparatus points towards the crowning frame of the "pedestal" of the Trajan's Column. The cornice is measured in detail in the extension of each member and in their projections. The drawing reproduces exactly the profile drawn by Giuliano da Sangallo in the Latin Barberinian Vatican Code 4424, in the scale of reduction of 1:3 (fol. 18 of the old numbering). The other profiles are without measurements and identification. | EB

BIBLIOGRAPHY Ferri (1885) 32; Bartoli (1914–22) IV: fig. 613; pl. 352; VI: 110; CensusID 10081578.

U 1203A *recto and verso*

Antonio da Sangallo The Younger

Rome, Theater of Pompey, after 1527.

Dimensions 257 × 403 mm.
Technique Pen and brown ink.
Paper Fold, restored.

INSCRIPTION, Recto (left half, from top) *post sciena portichus/ costitue[n]da[e] uti cu[m] i[m]bres/ repe[n]tini ludos i[n]terpellaveri[n]t/ habet populo quo se recipiat/ ex teatro curagia que laxame[n]tu[m]/ habea[n]t ad comparan[n] dum uti su[n]t/ poritcus po[m]peiane cioe lo teatro di ca[m] po di fiori; Teatro; orchestra; pulpitto; proscienio; sciena; porticho dopo la sciena; lu[n]go uno stadio; Libro v capitolo viiij/ Trallibus porticus ex u/ traq[ue] parte ut sciene/ supra stadiu[m]* (right half) *e come i[n] attene il phano dellibero patri cio e di bacho; e come sono li portici eumenmici i[n] attene*; calculations

Verso (upper part of the sheet) *e come i[n] attivi* [...] *quelli che soljono del teatro trovano/ sinistri lo Odeun quale* [cancelled: *Atrium*] *Odeun pericles colle/ colonne di saxo lo disposi*; (middle of the sheet) *ma chi ara buono architetto circha al teatro fara li/ portici e le ambulatione dopie che abbia le colonne di fuora/ doriche colli sua epistilij*

This plan of the Theater of Pompey reveals uncertainties about the form of the *cavea* and the orchestra, which appear in a solution showing an oval form superimposed upon a semicircular form: both of these possibilities were thoroughly investigated by Antonio. The scheme attempts to clarify the description of Vitruvius, as is made clear by the annotation in which Book v, ch. 9 is cited. The *frons scaenae* is rectilinear and exceptionally wide, the proscenium is quite elongated and the *pulpitum* extremely extended toward the orchestra. The *scaena* and *cavea* are connected, since the *columnatio* turns along the proscenium and is joined to the supporting structures of the auditorium. A *porticus post scaenam* completes the theater, which thus decisively assumes the form of a horseshoe described by Alberti, and which is present, for example, in U 1122A v. and 1131A r. | ACF

BIBLIOGRAPHY Ferri (1885) 191; Giovannoni (1959) I: 22; Frommel (1974) 182, fig. 96; CensusID 10075032.

U 1204A *recto and verso*

Giovanni Battista da Sangallo and Antonio da Sangallo the Younger

Rome, bases and pedestals of Trajan's Column and Antonine Column (*recto*). Fragment of a plan for unidentified house; note on Trajan's Column and Antonine Column (*verso*).

Dimensions 290 × 208 mm.
Technique Pen and brown ink, freehand (recto); straightedge, stylus, pin, freehand (verso).
Paper Trimmed on four sides, reinforced.
Drawing Scale Roman *palmi* and *dita* (for Trajan's Column); *piedi* and *dita* (for Antonine Column).

INSCRIPTION, Recto (19th-century hand, Ferri?) (top right) *937*; (lower left corner) *Gobbo*; (Antonio's hand) (top right) *in la piazza de bufali* (canceled); *traiana*; (Giovanni Battista's hand) measurements on drawing at top; *La colonna di colonna lopalmo e partito indita 12*; (Antonio's hand, referring to central drawing) *a piedi misurata*; (on torus) *Antonina*; (on cove) *Misurata per batista*; (Giovanni Battista's hand) (also on cove) *piedi*; *i non o di questa altre misure/ la troiana almacello decorbi* (canceled); (Antonio's hand) (right margin, center) *La meza colonna/ sie grossa 105 e la/ base e alta 97½/ 17½/ e mancho che/ lla meta dita 7½*; (on base, bottom right) numerous measurements in *dita*; (on plinth) *palmi 22 Dita 10 sono/ in tutto dita 274*; (on right) *34*[+]/ *176* [=]/ *210*; (to right of cove) multiplication and a sum with the result in *dita, 274*; (written over column of numbers visible in middle of note) *Bisogna avertire bene alla Campana della colo/nna perche cie quella fodera della storia che ingrosa la colonna/ perche co*[...] *la colonna grossa Dita 212 e la base sie/ alta Dita 97 perche sella Colonna fuse solo grossa dua alteze di/ base come arebbe ad essere*[?] *saria Dita 195*[?] *ela base/ aria dagetto Dita 39½ in tutto fa Dita 274 che tolto*[...]/ *la basa nel regolo e lagettosaria laquarta parte de lovivo della/ colonna e colli agetti saria 7 circum circha*; (on base at bottom left) measurements in *dita*

Verso (Antonio's hand, referring to recto) *parte del/ Lin basamenti delle due colonne storiate/ cio della antoniana in sulla piaza debufoli/ Et della traiana a santa maria delloreto/ presso alli macelli delli Corvi/ Quale sono opera toscana*

First, on the top half of the recto, Giovanni Battista made drawings of the measured elevations of the base with the top of the pedestal of Trajan's Column, and, below that, of the Antonine Column, later annotated by Antonio, who corrected his brother's apparently mistaken identifications. A note by Giovanni Battista on the "colonna di colonna" (Antonine) states that the *palmo* is divided into 12 *dita*, which agrees with the scale of the top drawing, which, however, is actually of Trajan's Column, where, for example, the height of the plinth is given as both 3 *palmi* and as 36 *dita* and that of the *torus* as both 3 *palmi* and 1½ *dita* and as 37½ *dita*. The survey of the Antonine Column, on the other hand, is measured in *piedi* divided into 16 *dita*, since the height of the plinth of 1¼ *piedi* is equivalent to 20 (16 + ¼ *dita* 16) *dita*, 1 *piedi* and 2 *dita* = 18 *dita*. Later on, a partial elevation of the base of the Antonine Column was added on the left of what little space remained at the bottom of the sheet, and on the right, an elevation of the base of Trajan's Column. Both had measurements exclusively in *dita*, some of which had been noted by Antonio, who was probably responsible for these two hasty sketches, based on the surveys by his brother directly above, selecting the lines and the measurements and converting the latter into *dita* to facilitate the process of verifying the proportions in which he was interested.

The notes on the recto and the verso and the workings out in his hand show, in fact, that Antonio's main objective was to select columns that he judged to be Tuscan and to check the ratio between the heights of the bases and the diameters of the shafts at the bottom as proposed by Vitruvius for this sort of column, with the added complication of having to subtract the thickness of the reliefs on historiated shafts, which were regarded as being add-ons to the "real thing."

The sheet shows the manner in which the two brothers divided up the tasks inherent in the study of ancient architecture in this instance—in this instance, Giovanni Battista was responsible for surveying and taking measurements on site, or possibly copying a survey done by somebody else in one case, which would explain the utilization of two different units of measurement; Antonio then used them for his drawings of the monuments themselves, in order to put Vitruvius's theories to the test.

On the verso Giovanni Battista had drawn a plan of a house from which is left only one half remains. The front of the house is approximately 32.5 *palmi* wide (over 7 m), and the facade wall has a thickness of 2 *palmi*; like the side walls, it was broken off by the cutting up of the sheet, which it abuts, forming angles that are out of true. The room on the right has an opening for a *bottega* and a staircase in the corner, but no internal doors leading to the rest of the house, unlike the room on the left (bottom of sheet), which has no openings onto the street or to the side but has a door in the back wall; this door obstructs a wide recess delineated in the back wall at the center of the opposite side. The presumably narrow dimensions of the entire plan justify the use of such a small ratio of reduction, which is unusual in a planimetric scheme. The continuous side walls make it clear that this fragment could have hardly belonged to a palace of any great size and, in any case, the few geometrical features described do not serve to trace it back to known projects for palaces or houses in which Antonio the Younger was involved. It was probably part of a minor, not easily identifiable, project. | PNP

BIBLIOGRAPHY Ferri (1885) 156; Vasari–Milanesi (1878–85) V: 493; Lanciani (1902–12) II: 123; Bartoli (1914–22) III: fig. 379, pl. 222; VI: 71; Giovannoni (1959) I: 20; Günther (1988) 194; CensusIDs 10073056, 10073502.

U 1206A *recto and verso*

ANTONIO DA SANGALLO THE YOUNGER

Rome, Baths of Caracalla, measured survey of the passage from the frigidarium to adjacent palaestra with detail of a pedestal; survey plan of the natatio and adjacent room to the east, 1545–46.

Dimensions 279 × 212 / 273 × 209 mm.
Technique Pen and brown ink.
Paper White, cut down on four sides.
Drawing Scale Roman *palmi.*

INSCRIPTION, Recto (upper left) *144*; (upper right, later hand) *939*; *Lo tutto largo palmi 109*; *Bagnio piu basso della / Sala palmi 5½*; *palmi 77*; *Collone grosse*; *Sala grande della / antoniane*; *I[n] li i[n]tercolumnij segnati B/ furo[no] trovati li dui erculi di/ Casa farnese lobello siera dove/ sie lo B: cholli due pu[n]ti et / volta va[no] lafaccia i[n]verso la Sala / gra[n] de*; *i[n] el piede della Colonna / e scritto le i[n]frascritte paro / le et numeri* NIIII DIADVMENI; *p. 4½ mi.ti 2 cioe diti 54 mi.ti 2*; *p[almi] 5½ cioe dita 61*; *palmi 5½*; *La colonna alto p[almi] 39⅔*. Verso *Questo sie magiore assai / piu dello arisco[n]tro*; *lo cortile aveva quattro colonne grosse et era scop[er]to*; *Bagno scop[er]to*; *porta*; *Li canali che sono i[n] lafaccia / difuora dove e segnato A / erata[n]to qua[n]to sporgevano / fuori li corni di capitelli et / erano foderati porfidi et / serpentini detti canali*; (later hand, blue pencil) *1206*.

Antonio the Younger has recorded one of the two tripartite passages marking the east/west axis of the central cross vaulted frigidarium of the Baths of Caracalla. These passages gave on to the adjacent vaulted room inscribed "bagnio più basso..." which in turn led to the adjoining palaestrae. Antonio designated the frigidarium with the inscription "la sala grandi della antoniane," yet it is not possible to determine with certainty which of the two identical passages he has represented, that to the east or the west. Yegül believes this drawing records, "the extreme intercolumnation of the colonnade that divides the frigidarium from its extension to the west." Bartoli mistakenly identifies this as the passage to the south leading from the frigidarium to the tepidarium. This southern passage is also tripartite, but with a different plan and flanking spaces. Moreno maintains that it is one of the north wall openings flanking the passage to the natatio.

Antonio's notations regarding the width of the room, 109 *palmi* (24.3m.), conclusively demonstrate that he is documenting either the east or west wall of the frigidarium, for the width of this room is equal to the larger dimension of the adjacent spaces to the east and west. According to the reconstruction drawings published by Iwanoff and Huelsen (pl. J), the width of the frigidarium and the larger dimension of these flanking rooms are measured between 23.65m. and 24.10m.

This drawing is most interesting because it is the only known document indicating precisely how and where the two freestanding colossal Farnese Hercules statues were displayed in the central hall of the Baths. Several other statues are believed to have come from this room, but how and where they were situated is not known.

Antonio has created a key that serves for the verso drawing as well. The letter "A" indicates the "colonne grosse" at the base of each cross-vault of the frigidarium. The letter "B" specifies the symmetrical arrangement of the two Farnese Hercules statues which were found between the columns flanking the central passage. The so-called Latin-Hercules now in Caserta, was located where the letter "B" is noted. Its pendant, the "Lo bello" figure signed by Glykon and now in Naples, was found where "B" is written. Antonio also indicates that both figures faced the frigidarium: "volta va[no] lafaccia i[n]verso la Sala gra[n]de." Thus, this drawing conclusively demonstrates where the two colossal statues were found and how they were originally displayed. Some authors have argued that the colossal figures were commissioned for the site (Marvin). Both statues were set up in an analogous manner at the Palazzo Farnese shortly after their recovery.

The notations for the Hercules figures enable the drawing to be dated to sometime between August 1545 and Antonio's death in September 1546. The *postquem* is established by an entry dated September 1st, 1545 from the diary of Angello Massarelli, the papal secretary for the Council of Trent, which mentions that the Farnese Hercules, the Farnese Bull and a third unidentifiable statue—due to a lacuna in the text—had been found during the previous August.

On the lower half of the sheet, Antonio has penned a measured sketch of a pedestal which bore the inscription "NIIII DIADVMENI." He notes that the pedestal was topped by a column which stood 39⅔ *palmi* high (approx. 8.8 meters). These are perhaps the pedestals supporting the large columns indicated by the letter "A." The notations are from Antonio's hand contrary to suggestions made by Moreno (p. 389).

The verso is an unmeasured plan of the natatio (not the frigidarium as suggested by Bartoli), the large open-air swimming pool, indicated by the inscription "Bagno scop[er]to," and the smaller changing room to the east. The colonnade separating the natatio from the adjacent space has not been drawn. The letter "A," corresponding to the recto, designates the large columns, eight of which stood in the natatio. Antonio also notes that behind the columns were fluted pilasters which projected beyond the "corni di capitelli" and were faced with porphyry and serpentine. The relationship of these parts is noted where he sketched the plan of the capitals at the north flank of the natatio. The colored marbles may have been used for use at New St Peter's under Pope Paul III. Excavations began at the Baths in 1545, initially in search of colored marbles to be used for New St Peter's. By the end of the century, the Baths were stripped of all incrustation; in 1597 only eleven *scudi* worth of marble was retrieved.

The south wall of the natatio is articulated by two large round niches which housed large fountains and flank the central square niche passage leading to the frigidarium. The north wall is articulated by colossal columns that divide the wall into three bays which are further articulated by smaller columns flanking square niches. According to reconstructions of the Baths these niches were located above a high socle zone and held large-scale statues. See the entries for U 1133 and U 1227. | MK

BIBLIOGRAPHY Ferri (1885) 202; Vasari – Milanesi (1878–85) V: 494; Lanciani (1897) 542; Lanciani (1902–12) II, 183; Jordan-Huelsen (1878–1907) 192, 196; Bartoli (1914–22) III: figs 359–60, pl: 214; VI: 68; Yegül (1992) 154, 444 n. 55; Günther (1988) 255 n. 81; CensusID 10072317.

U 1207A *recto and verso*

Antonio da Sangallo The Younger

Perugia, Porta Marzia and Tempio Sant'Angelo (*recto*); Perugia, Porta Sant'Angelo (Arco di Augusto) (*verso*), 1540.

Dimensions 295 × 408 mm.
Technique Pen and brown ink, red chalk (*recto*), pen and brown ink (*verso*).
Paper Medium weight, folded twice, creased, e dges restored.

INSCRIPTION, Recto *piatti stanno Cosi / sono circha piedi 4 / luno; fralluno pi[l]asto e lalto sono / pilastretti 2; li tondi / sono gra[n] / di piatti ri[n]pochiati; Questo portone sie i[n] sulle / mura vechie di perusia / perche dipoi a cresciuto uno / gra[n] pezo fino alla porto / S[an]to agniolo si dice el por / tone di s[an]to agniolo & / Le lettere che sono i[n] lo archo / sono le i[n] frascritte /* AUGUSTA / PERUSIA; AVGVSTA PERVSIA / *porta an / ticha dice si* [...] *da portone di S[an]to / agniolo / porta Circha / piedi 15 larga / alto dua quadri / e mezo / piedi 15; una torre / p[er] banda gro/sse Circha 30 / piedi; questo archo / e ma[n]cho che / quadro e sta / sopra laltro archo / dove A questo segnio; Questa porta al sup[er]bo p[er]che / e alta e gra[n]de*

Verso *agio[n]ta / Cavalie / ro / porta S[an]to ant[oni]o; Porta bornia / di perugia / p[i]edi 12; questi archi servo / no p[er] i[n] cavellature / altetto; questo sie apresso / alla porta S[an]to angni / olo a ma[n] retta p[er] / andare fuora della / terra; Le fiure anno parapetti / di gelosie fino a mezo* (*petto* canceled) */ el bellico e sono tre fiure / e dua Cavalli cioe uno p[er] ba[n] / da & dove e la me[n]sola de / llo archo era uno animale / ma e ta[n]* *to Consumato che no[n] si / Conoscie p[er] essere de preta tener / e tutto e malfatto di modani / & fiure ma solo se ne pigli / la i[n] ve[n]zione p[er] quello chelli / perche e variata dalli altri archi / triu[n]fali; S[an]to argniolo di perugia / sie Cosi uno te[m]pio che a / 16 Colonne tondo Colli / Capitelli Cori[n]tij di spoglie / perche nelle Colonne nelli / Capitelli ne base sono si / mili luno allaltro solo se / ne pigli la forma overo / i[n]ve[n]zione altro di bono / no[n] cie se no[n] qualche Capitello / Cori[n]tio di boni e qualche fuso / di Colonna / Lo Corpo di mezo e circha 30 piedi / la nave picola i[n]torno e circha 15 / piedi*

The left half of recto shows a perspectival elevation of a part of the Arco di Augusto, the best-preserved city gate of the Etruscan walls of Perugia. Antonio included studies of the architectural and decorative details, accompanied by his notes.

The upper part of the arch—a smaller arch framed by pilasters—is drawn as a separate detail on the lower part of the sheet because Antonio had run out of space at the top of the paper. The drawing has been carefully analyzed, also with regard to the present state of the monument, by Vasori (1979, 1981). Borsi dated the drawing to 1541–42. (For the red chalk drawing of fortifications, see vol. I, U 1207A)

On the right half of the verso, Antonio drew an elevation of the upper part of the Porta Marzia (known as Porta Bornia in the Middle Ages) in Perugia. This city gate was incorporated by the architect into one of the bastions of the Rocca Paolina (see left half of sheet), which was built on the site of the Baglioni houses adjacent to the gate. In a lengthy inscription to the right of the drawing, Antonio described the decorative details of the gate, commenting on their degraded condition, due to which he was taking note only of the "invenzione," since it was different from that of other triumphal arches. The drawing is fully discussed by Vasori (1979, 1981).

Below the Porta Marzia, Antonio drew the plan and a section of the left half of the so-called Tempio di Sant'Angelo, which is believed to have been built in the fifth century with a dedication to S. Michele Arcangelo. In a note to the right, Antonio referred to the sixteen columns of the interior, which are antique spoils, all with different capitals, shafts, and bases. The section shows how the inner ring of columns had to be strengthened eventually with buttresses in the vault of the ambulatory. (Subsequently, presumably after Antonio's visit, the exterior of the church also had to be reinforced with buttresses, to counteract the thrust from those in the ambulatory.)

Borsi dated the sheet to 1541–42. The drawing of the fortifications is discussed in vol. I. | SE

BIBLIOGRAPHY Vasari-Milanesi (1878–85) V: 495; Ferri (1885) 110; Giovannoni (1959) I: 20–22; II: figs 40–41; Vasori (1979) 136–39; Vasori (1981) 131–3, cat. nos 101, 102; Borsi (1986) 452; Camerieri-Palombaro (1988) 130, fig. 8; Frommel-Adams (1994) 200; CensusIDs 10075868, 233030.

U 1208A *recto and verso*

Antonio da Sangallo The Younger

Tivoli, Sanctuary of Hercules Victor ("Villa di Vopisco"), 1539, (*recto*); Tivoli, details of architectural ornament and two sculptures, ca. 1539, (*verso*).

Dimensions 438 × 293 mm.
Technique Pen and brown ink.
Paper Medium weight, stained, repaired on verso along one long side.

INSCRIPTION, Recto (on plan at top right) *A*; *B*; *C*; (outside plan) *ripa altissima verso lo fiume*; *tutti sono archi*; (next to *A*) *i[n] questa volto sotto e i[n] botte di sopra al piano del giardino / di sopra al capo sono a schifo comme quelle delle logoge* [loggie?] *e di palazo*; *B so i[n] volte a botte dal uno tramezo / all altro*; *C la logia di de[n]tro sia i[n] botte dal muro / a pilastri e li archi sono sotto la i[n]posta / e sono mezo colonne de op[era] retigulata*; *giardino*; (left side) *Via che va al po[n]ticello e a po[n]te lucano verso roma*; *Terazo scop[er] to*; *qui e edifitio p[er] largeza di piu di sei canne largo*; *questa loggia aveva i[n]anzi / uno terrazo scoperto*; *i[n] alto al piano che sopra / al giardino era una logia / di colonne di cime[n]to e calci/na e lavorate di stucho che / ci e ne uno anchora i[n] pie col capitello e basa jonicha e alta circha piedi 24 gro/ssa circha 3 piedi bella*; (under plan) *monte*; *mo[n]te*; *qua e uno gra[n] paese dove si vede vestigie di gran difitio / i[n]chognito*; *mo[n] te che va salendo i[n] verso / la terra*; *i[n] questo muro no[n] ce nisuna porta*; *Ambulatorio*; *giardino*; *Habitatione del pri[n] cipe*; *giardino*; *Jardino e fino a questo piano e uno piano di / sta[n]tie e i[n] su questo piano / sono l'altro piano ta[n] to se alza quanto e uno piano di sta[n]tie / e le volte i[n] aria e dalli i[n] su e ruinato / e cosa divina avederla e mirabile / e ci puo venire tutta laqa di tigole / e dicano villa neroniana*; (turned 90 degrees) *vista i[n] verso Roma / e ruinatissima* [...] / *mirabilissima*; (column of writing below plan) *questo piano sie al piano di sopra / dello edifitio e a questo piano / si era l abitation p[er]che tutto quello / che de i[n] pie adesso s[er]ve quasi o i[n] ma/giore parte p[er] adiquame[n]to e qua / si vede vestigie o ruine che poteva essere uno gra[n] difitio e* (*p[e]rfino* canceled) *alla / terra che cie canne piu di 200 va / sempre mo[n] ta[n]do la colonna joni/cha nominata nel disegnio quale / e di cime[n]to cioe di pietre pichole di scaglia /* (*e co* canceled) *di trevertino e calce e al capitello jonicho / e basa otigurge*[?] *di vertino e coperta la colonna / di stucho sola lei e da questo piano i[n] su / altro no[n] cie e da questo difitio i[n] giu e una / Isola continouata p[er]fino al piano con una / pendeza dolcie p[er] i spatio de uno miglio / o piu che poteva essere una bella possesione / p[er] questo edifitio p[er]che al prexente e bella /*

cop[er]ta di ulivi e altri pomerij e vite e dalla / Banda di verso mo[n]ticelli e palo[m]bara sia el / fosso del fiume e dall altra el fosso della strada / romana e dalla da ditta strada / a cierti colli e piage amene piene de / ulivi e altri alberi fruttiferi i[n] una parte / e i[n] la medesa facia vede tigoli vechio cioe Villa adriana e pilestrina e selva dell aglio / e tutto el mo[n]te di tuscolano fino al mare

Verso *uno fr[egi]o co[n] dua tori che una / vittoria p[er] toro chella amaza / e due grifoni che sono trameza/ti da candellieri come vede / e vanno seguita[n]do duo tori e uno / candelliere e dua grifoni come / si vede; questa motofa / sie al piano del tigriffo come se de/vessi a i[n]tagliare con uno / smusso i[n] torno*; (to right of *guttae*, continuing down, partly invading space of an earlier note, which Antonio separated with a wavy line) *questo corre i[n] sununa piaza / nell alto della terra / i[n] una facciata d'una casa e sono le gutte* (*duna* canceled) *fino a mezo e tiglifo / volte sottosopra e ve ne dua / pezi*; (left of above passage) *li canali de tigriffi no[n] ne sfondano / fino i[n] su* (*il* canceled) *regolo dell architrave / e p[or]ta i[n] piano lo tiglifo col regolo / dell architrave*; (right of telamon) *dua di queste / di pietra rossa / della guglia / e sono alte circha / piedi 10 luna / e sono belle egitie / bisognia disegnia/rle bene / e fra queste dua cariatide cie una diana che cami/na e de vestita e non a / testa*; (right of seated figure) *Cie uno ercole che siede i[n] sununo / scoglio e posa una mana i[n] sunu[n]o / otro e premelo ce solo el culo elle / dua coscie e uno pezo del corpo fino / al bellicho e lo scoglio dove siede /* (*e la mana* canceled) *e de su p[er] la strada pu/blicha; la mana che preme lotro / collotro i[n]sieme sie i[n] vesco/vado el braccio la mes[ser] / giovanni gaddi e de / nel numero delle cose belle; i[n] chiesa sono dua triangoli bellissimi / piene di belle cose quali regano una sepul/ tura; Tutte le soprascritte cose le o schizate p[er] rico/rdo poi che sono tornato a roma p[er] tornarci / a disegniarle o mandarci*; (right, at bottom, 19th-century hand) *Ricordi di Villa di Mecenate* (*di Mecenate* written above *Adriana*) *in Tivoli*

In the freehand plan on the recto, drawn on site, Antonio made copious notes concerning the general layout, the location and the view, and the fragments of architectural details that he was still able to see in the ruins. He showed particular interest in the vaulting systems, which he studied again in another visual document, U 1067A r. Where possible, he also recorded the kind of materials (cement, etc.) used. U 1208A r. must have been drawn on his first visit ever to the Sanctuary, because he peppered his notes with expressions of excitement (*cosa divina* and *mirabilissima*). U 1208A r. served as the basis for the clean copy in U 1176A r. Antonio's other studies of the Sanctuary of Hercules Victor are U 1156A r., 1159A r., and 1351A r.

Antonio made quick drawings and notes on the verso of the sheet upon returning to Rome from Tivoli, as a reminder of what he wanted to draw for when he would go back to Tivoli or alternatively send someone there in his place. His eye seems to have been caught by unusual details. Vasori observed that the frieze with Victories, bulls, and griffons can be related iconographically to two friezes in the Forum of Trajan. She identified the telamon in red granite as one that was probably excavated at Villa Adriana and which is now exhibited in the Vatican Museums. | SE

BIBLIOGRAPHY Vasari-Milanesi (1878–85) V: 494; Ferri (1885) 220; Giovannoni (1959) I: 22; Giuliani (1970) 166, fig. 176; Zorzi (1957); Vasori (1981) 133–37, cat. nos 103, 104; Huppert (2001) 105–06; CensusIDs 10022021, 63921.

U 1209A *recto*

Giovanni Battista da Sangallo (?) and Antonio da Sangallo the Younger

Chiusi, reconstruction in plan and elevation of Mausoleum of Porsenna, 1531.

Dimensions 426 × 262 mm.
Paper Trimmed on four sides, creases near lower left corner, stains along bottom edge, traces of glue on edges of *verso*.
Technique Pen, straightedge, compass, brown ink over preparatory drawing with stylus and pin, freehand, stylus.
Drawing Scale *piedi antichi*; beneath bottom base of elevation a scale in *piedi*, divided into 10 *piedi*, marked in groups of 50; 300 *piedi* = 131 mm.

INSCRIPTION (Antonio's hand) (lower right) *Di Porsena secondo / Plinio per le parole di M. / varrone*; (beneath elevation) *fata nel* MDXXXI

Antonio the Younger dated the drawing, as he did in other instances where laborious studies finally led to satisfying results (U 991A r.), but it may have been his brother Giovanni Battista who, following Antonio's indications, meticulously drew a clean copy of the plan and elevation, finishing the latter with light shading. Antonio reconstructed the tomb, trying to follow Varro's description in Pliny (*Naturalis Historia*, XXXVI, ch. 13, pp. 91–92). He was misled, however, by the fact that in almost all fifteenth- and early sixteenth-century printed editions available to him, the term petasus, which in Pliny indicates a type of vault, was wrongly translated as Pegasus. Thus Antonio crowned the "pyramids" at the first level with the mythological winged horse in place of the cover and level surface on which the guglios of the upper level should have rested. In order to support the latter, he had to install a square podium, which led to the elimination of the fifth "pyramid" at the center. In accordance with the text, the monument is composed of three orders of four "pyramids" each and a final "pyramid" at the center of the upper group. By giving the guglios a conical form, which facilitated the composition, Antonio is referring back to the sepulchre known as "degli Orazi e dei Curiazi" at Albano (U 1414A v.), and by rotating each of the superimposed prismatic bases by 45 degrees with respect to the one below, he is reworking the top of a belltower of the Templars in Piacenza (U 979A r.). The reconstruction is faithful to the text of *Naturalis Historia* for the width (300 *piedi*) and height (50 *piedi*) of the first podium and for the heights of the first and second order of "pyramids," 150 and 100 *piedi*, respectively. After assuring that the height of the second order is equal to 2/3 the height of the first, Antonio extrapolates an identical reduction for the heights of the "pyramids" of the third order, about which Pliny is silent, giving them a height of ⅔ of 100 *piedi*, that is, 66⅔ *piedi*. The top guglio is 233⅓ *piedi* high, and by adding the height of its pedestal (66⅔ *piedi*), aligned with the guglios of the third order, the total height is the 300 *piedi* given by Pliny.

For the plan, and in particular for determining the width at all levels, Antonio uses a geometrical matrix based on the square. Composing two concentric squares rotated 45 degrees with respect to one another was usual in medieval project designs, and Antonio himself uses this scheme several times when planning fortifications (see U 758A r., 973A r., 1344A v. in vol. I). As in the plans of schema d in U 979A r., he had composed two squares of equal size, with the corners of each protruding from the sides of the other. But here, Antonio inscribes the rotated squares of decreasing size in the square one size larger. He divides each square into 16 minor squares and inscribes the circular bases of the guglios in the four corners. With this geometric construction, the diameter of the pyramid of one order is equal to $\frac{1}{2}\sqrt{2} = .707$ diameters of the order below. The difference with respect to the reduction of ⅔ (= .666) is minimal, and by application of this geometrical method, the architect, working upward through the orders, manages to reduce also the diameters of the bases of the cones in almost the same proportion as he reduces their height. He tends to keep to the ratio of 1:2 of width to height in each order, which derives from Pliny's description of the pyramids of the first order, 75 *piedi* wide at the base and 150 *piedi* high. In the same way Antonio extrapolates the numerical indications from the text and applies them to all but the lowest pedestals, which do not feature in Pliny's description and to which he gives the same height as the adjacent "pyramids." Thus Antonio's coherent synthesis is based on a careful reading of the Latin text, an extrapolation of measurements given by Pliny, an examination of one antique and one medieval example, and the use of a geometrical matrix, all in ways that can also illuminate methods and objectives of other interpretations of the antique by Antonio. This reconstruction provides the architect with ideas when designing classicizing projects for suitable themes; for instance, on U 185A r., a project for the 1535 funerary monument for Clement VII in the choir of S. Maria sopra Minerva, Antonio roughly sketched the plan of the Mausoleum of Porsenna in the right margin; the forms are partially reworked also in another project for the tombs of Clement VII and Leo X (Frommel 2003, *Disegni sconosciuti*, pp. 346–350).

The projects for the top of the belltower of St Peter's (U 81A r., 82A r., 86A r., 261A r., 262A r.) are even more liberal interpretations of the scheme of the ancient Etruscan sepulchre. | PNP

BIBLIOGRAPHY Ferri (1885) 97; Giovannoni (1959) I: 24; Vasori (1979) 139; Vasori (1981) 137–38, cat. no. 105; Günther (1988) 256; Raub (2014) 196; Fane-Saunders (2016) 273–74; CensusID 252465.

U 1210A *recto and verso*

Antonio da Sangallo the Younger

Terracina, view of so-called Pisco Montano (*recto*); Terracina, plan of substructions of so-called Minor Temple next to Temple of Jupiter Anxur; plan of external perimeter of part of so-called Temple of Apollo (*verso*), after 1530.

Dimensions 195 × 145 mm.
Technique Pen and brown ink, freehand.
Paper Lightweight.

INSCRIPTION, Recto *Questo si è uno sasso ta/gliato per antonino pio/ e nel taglio si è lassato que/sti epitaffi con questi nu/meri e sono larghi quello/ da basso p. 2 D 4 e li altri/ parono piedi 2 e dal di/sopra dello ultimo per fino/ al di sopra del penultimo/ si sono palmi 40 di que/sti qui da pie segniati; mare*

Verso *stufa; conserva; pilo; caldara; Le stantie segniate A B C D/ sono foderate di stucco belle/ a bugnie e finte di prete mischie; in terracina/ in el di fuori della/ chiesa Cattedrale è questo/ edificio lavorato molto bene/ quanto nessuno che resta arro/ ma dichono ed è lo tempio/ de apolline*; (a sinistra) *passi 7*; (in basso) *passi 14 andanti/ le colonne sono grosse circha piedi 3½ l'una*

The drawing on the recto, made with swift but effective strokes, is of the Pisco Montano, showing the cut in the face of the cliff made during the Trajan era, complete with the tablets enclosing the incised marks giving the various heights in Roman *piedi*, the Porta Napoletana on the edge of the shoreline, and, to the left, the opening of a grotto from which access could be gained to a tower above via a ladder and through an underground passage. A parapet can be seen at the top of the cliff cutting and, higher still and barely sketched, are what are probably the medieval fortifications. In his annotation, Antonio cited the *palmo* that he used to measure the distance between the two lowest tablets, as indicated on the drawing; the sheet must, however, have been cut down because, below, there is no sign of the measurement to which he refers.

On the upper part of the verso, the plan of the substructions of the Minor Temple is incomplete: three rooms and two tanks are missing. Furthermore, in the building's present state, the rooms marked "B" and "pilo" are no longer to be seen and the five rooms at the bottom are open at the front. The reference in the annotation to the stuccowork painted to resemble a flat, rusticated polychrome marble paramento is interesting. The lower part of the sheet shows the so-called Temple of Apollo, over which the Cathedral of Terracina was constructed, with projecting half-columns on the northwest corner. These were never incorporated into the various transformations undergone by the church and are still visible, with narrower intercolumniations on the long side of the cella (on the left) and wider ones on the short side (below). The "passi andanti," meaning that Antonio actually measured by paces gone by himself, give the impression of being slightly over 60 centimeters and, therefore, the measurements would appear to be close to the actual ones. | AGG

BIBLIOGRAPHY Ferri (1885) 218, 219; Lugli (1926) pl. V, fig. 1; Giovannoni (1959) 1: 20n, 21; Vasori (1981) 138–40, cat. nos 106, 107; CensusID 10075568.

U 1211A *recto and verso*

Antonio Labacco and Antonio da Sangallo the Younger

Rome, isometric section and section of cornice belonging to entablature with griffin frieze from Trajan's Forum, after 1540.

Dimensions 285 × 215 mm.
Technique Labacco's drawing, top left: pen, straightedge, black ink, over stylus, details of decoration drawn freehand. Below, by Antonio: pen and sepia ink.
Paper Four corners trimmed, reinforced at bottom edge.

INSCRIPTION, Recto (19th-century hand, Ferri?) *Gobbo* [Giovanni Battista da Sangallo]; (top left, Labacco's hand, same ink as drawing) *Misurata chon el bracio partito in 60*; (Antonio's hand) *Cornice dell'architrave e fregio de / grifoni di casa mia*; *cornice cavata nel 1540 / in l orto dello emiciclo dele melitie / del quale si e l'archi/trave in casa col fregio de gri/foni*; *ridotta a moduli di / cinque per ogni dito overo / 80*[?] *per ogni piede*; (top right) *Quando vitruvio dice che / la gola sia la ottava / parte coronarum / intende che coronarum fre/so e cornicie sia / una ottava parte di/tta gola e lo resto 7 / Cosi torna questa / perche l fregio si è quanto / lo architrave per essere inta/gliato*

Verso (Antonio's hand) *per fare li architravi / quelli della seconda stampa dice che l dentello col suo / cimatio sia tanto alto quant e dello epistilio media factigia / chredo voglia dire meza fascigia cioe quanto meze / tutte le fascie che Cosi afrontano li antichi*; (in margin) *cioe meze tute e tre le fascie senza lo cimatio / Di poi dice che la corona sia quanto la media fascia dello / epistilio cioe quanto la fascia di mezo e così afrontano / li antichi e maximo questo che de bello / Quelli della prima stampa dice el dentello col cimatio quanto / meza fastigia e lacorona quanto la fascia di mezo / simile dice quello a penna / Questo bisognia chiarire se dicessi fascigia aria avesse quanto meze le fasce Se dice fastigia direbbe quanto meza lalteza dello epistilio / ma li antichi afrontano quanto meze le fasce e la corona / quanto la fascia di mezo*

Buddensieg recognized Labacco's hand in the isometric section of the cornice of the east hemicycle in the Trajan's Forum, a sketch previously attributed by Bartoli with reservations to Giovanni Battista da Sangallo. This precise drawing by Labacco, one of Antonio the Younger's collaborators, passed, like several others, into Sangallo's collection. In his notes, Antonio dated the discovery of the piece drawn here to 1540 and connected it with the fragment of the cornice and griffin frieze that he already owned. He also sketched a section on the recto with a couple of enlarged details measured in modules, so as to facilitate the verification of the proportions by a minimal unit of measurement. Furthermore, he covered the sheet with notes and calculations, taking the opportunity to interpret various passages from Vitruvius's De Architectura on the Ionic entablature. On the recto, Antonio transcribed a passage concerning the cymae above the top cornice (*De Architetectura* III, ch. 5, 12), using the Trajanic entablature to determine whether he read the text correctly, despite his conviction that the cyma should be one-eighth of the sum of the frieze and cornice, which actually is a misinterpretation. In the correct version, the cyma should be one-eighth higher than the cornice. On the verso, under a heading beneath the title "on making architraves," Antonio discussed two readings of a passage concerning the height of dentils in the Ionic entablature that he came across in different editions of De Architectura (Book III, ch. 5, 11): one came from Sulpicio da Veroli's first edition and from a manuscript, which he attributed to the "second printing," although it is actually from the third edition published in Venice in 1497. In the first edition, we are told that the dentil had to be made "... tam altus quam epistilii media fastigia" and in the second "... quam epistylii media factigia," "Factigia" is presumably a printing error; Antonio, however, substituted it with "fascigia," and used this term to denote the fascia bands of the epistyle in their entirety without the cymatium and concluded that a height equal to half the sum of the heights of the fascia should be ascribed to the dentil. Given that a study of ancient monuments serves to confirm this interpretation, he tended to prefer it, rejecting the idea of a dentil as tall as the intermediate fascia of the architrave, which is in fact the correct interpretation, as clarified in an amendment by Fra Giocondo, in which "fascia" is substituted for "fastigia" (1511, fol. 30 v., and 1513, fol. 54 v.), as proposed also in the translation published by Durantino (1524, fol. 30 v.), editions that Antonio owned and had consulted (see U 903A r., 920A r.). This is followed, however, by a correct reading for the corona to be constructed at the height of the architrave's intermediate fascia, which is confirmed through the studying of ancient monuments. Antonio's notes on this page allow us to add to the list of versions of Vitruvius's treatise known to have been consulted by him and demonstrate that, although he reached wrong conclusions, he studied the Latin text in a thourough manner, acknowledging several different versions, and based what he assumed was correct primarily on the examination of numerous examples of ancient architecture. | PNP

BIBLIOGRAPHY Ferri (1885) 160; Milanesi in Vasari-Milanesi (1906) V: 493; Lanciani (1902–12) II: 123; Bartoli (1914–22) III: fig. 384, pl. 224; VI: 72; Giovannoni (1959) I: 17, 67, 84; Buddensieg (1975) 95, no. 18; Viscogliosi (2000) 136–37, cat. no. 14; Günther (1988) 248, 255, 295, 297–98; Pagliara (1988) 188, 196; CensusID 239317.

U 1213A *recto and verso*

Antonio da Sangallo the Younger

Comments on Vitruvius' VI book; circular ground plan, before 1527 (*recto*); studies of a sarcophagus; aedicule-like frame of a vertical rectangular opening (*verso*).

Dimensions 102 × 213 mm.
Technique Pen and brown ink.
Paper Heavy, yellowed, folded, reinforced at edge.

INSCRIPTION *Li[ber] VI Ca[pitolo] iiii. Vol chello inpluvio del chortile e non dello atrio / non sia ne mancho a una quarta parte ne piu / che una tertia parte dello largeza dello atrio / La longeza in proportione allo atrio*; *L[iber] VI Ca[pitolo] iiii. Peristilio e tanto quanto dice colunnato / perche dicie che quanto sara in traverso lo peri/stilio la tertia parte di ditta longeza / sia introrsus cioe lo colonato sia indentro / dischosto dalla parete*; (at left edge) [...] *Ant.o da Sangallo* (at right edge, later hand) *Baldassare*

The chapter number indicates that Antonio's notes on the recto were paraphrased from Cesariano's edition of Vitruvius (1521): "De la longitudine de li atri e de le loro ale e tablini. Capo quarto" [page LXXXXVIII v.], which corresponds to the modern division (Book VI, ch. 3, 6–7) on the *impluvium* of the *tablinum* and the peristyle. The circular plan is Antonio's own sketch, and does not rely on Cesariano's volume. Antonio's use of Cesariano's edition is noteworthy again in U 1409A v., 1444A r., 1447A r. and v., 1458A r. and v., 1461A r., and 1492A r. The name "Baldassare" has been written at the right edge of the sheet rather recently.

On the verso, sketches at the upper far left and right show two variants of the front of a sarcophagus in an antique style, loosely connected by a roughly indicated mask in the center between volutes. At the left, the casket tapers toward the bottom to form a single convex shape, while the variation at the right begins as concave and then swells outward to describe a convex base. The corner of the casket at the left shows an upright figure of a sphinx, whose legs are lost in the abundant leafy decoration toward the base, whereas at the right, a degree of clarity is achieved by the greater separation of figural and ornamental elements. The now-reclining sphinx has been moved to the front as a supporting element, while the corner is entirely given over to the leafy decoration.

At the bottom of the sheet, thumbnail sketches of the sarcophagus develop the solution worked out in the variant at the right as seen from its narrow end. The cover of the sarcophagus, which is flat and concave at one end and a steep half barrel at the other, is further elaborated in these small insights. Between these two drawings is a sketch of a vertical rectangular opening flanked by two slender columns or pilasters and crowned by a triangular gable. While there is no obvious connection between this and the other representations, such a relationship is likely.

The Florentine point of departure for the form of this sarcophagus and its manner of decoration is Desiderio da Settignano's monument for Carlo Marsuppini in S. Croce from about 1453–54. Verrocchio's monument for Giovanni and Piero de' Medici in San Lorenzo (ca. 1472) is an early example of a sarcophagus richly decorated in the antique manner without a reclining figure of the deceased on top. Sphinxes on the corners may be found, for example, on the sarcophagus of Francesco Tornabuoni (ca. 1480) in S. Maria sopra Minerva in Rome, which may be by Mino da Fiesole or his workshop. Sphinxes placed under the front of the sarcophagus, in a more delicate form, can be seen on the tomb of Cardinal Pietro Riario in SS. Apostoli in Rome (ca. 1474) by Andrea Bregno and Mino da Fiesole, as well as on the two monuments for cardinals by Andrea Sansovino in the choir of S. Maria del Popolo (ca. 1505–10).

Although the four studies shown here reflect an equal interest in the long and narrow sides of the sarcophagus, a freestanding solution was not necessarily intended. The additional drawing of the aedicule suggests instead an arrangement similar to that of Michelangelo's ducal tombs in the New Sacristy of S. Lorenzo in Florence (1520–34) or the Cappella del Monte in S. Pietro in Montorio in Rome (1550–52). | GS

BIBLIOGRAPHY Ferri (1885) 97; Giovannoni (1959) I: 23; Benelli (2018, *Sostegno e adornamento*) 46.

U 1214A *recto*

Antonio da Sangallo the Younger

Rome, two antique Ionic capitals from the Sangallo house in Via Giulia, after 1527.

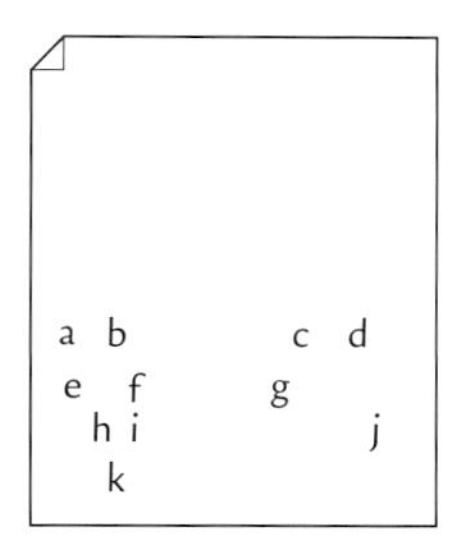

Dimensions 359 × 288 mm.
Technique Pen and brown ink, freehand.
Paper Medium weight, partly trimmed on right side, completely trimmed on the other sides, folded in four, reinforced with paper on the verso, small reinforcement at lower edge, traces of glue on edges of verso.
Drawing Scale *dita*.

INSCRIPTION, Recto (upper right corner) (black pencil, 19th-century hand) *170*[?] and *949*; (Antonio's hand) (beneath *b*) *mezo / ovolo, sono ovoli 5*; (beneath *c*) *quatro bacelli / tre ovoli interi / due mezi*; to the right: *quatro rose*[?] / *lo fiancho*; (beneath *e*) *anno lo pianetto / di dentro e de fori / el pianetto di fora / in lo interno fa li bacelli* [referring to plan *f*]; (beneath *h*) *ulivella*; (beneath this) *in l canale fogliamj / nel cimatio fogletta*; (between *i* and *j*) *questi due capitelli sono in casa mia*; (at the top) a calculation

VERSO (ink, 16th-century hand, Antonio the Younger?) *capitelli ionici*; (at bottom, in black chalk Ferri) *La casa di Antonio da sangallo è il palazzo dei Sacchetti a piè di via Giulia*

The two capitals of unknown provenance were part of Antonio the Younger's collection of architectural sculpture. Antonio carefully analyzed the richness of ornaments in eleven drawings that depict the entire capitals as well as their details: *a*, partial section of the abacus, the channel of the volute and the echinus of the capital shown in drawing *b*; *b*, partial elevation of an Ionic capital; *c*, view of another Ionic capital with rosettes adorning the neck; *d*, section of the capital shown in drawing *c*; *e*, molding of capital shown in drawing *b*; *f*, plan from below of capital shown in drawing *b*; *g*, an ovolo(?) of an echinus; *h*, *i*, *j* are ornamental details; *k*, sections as in drawings *a* and *d*. With the sheet turned 180 degrees, he drew the view of the abacus and volute of the left portion of an Ionic capital, probably a first incomplete sketch for captial *b*. | PNP

BIBLIOGRAPHY Ferri (1885) 131; Bartoli (1914–22) III: fig. 354, pl. 209; VI: 67, CensusID 10072558.

U 1216A *recto and verso*

Antonio da Sangallo the Younger

Tivoli, so-called Temple of Vesta, 1539. Recto: (a) Door. (b) Ground plan. (c) Section through the peristasis. (d) Capital. (e, f) Section through the lintel of the door. (g, h) Profile sections. (i) Section through the profile of the podium and the column bases. (k) Outer window frame. (l) Inner window frame. (m) Sketch of abbreviated columns and entablature with inscription.

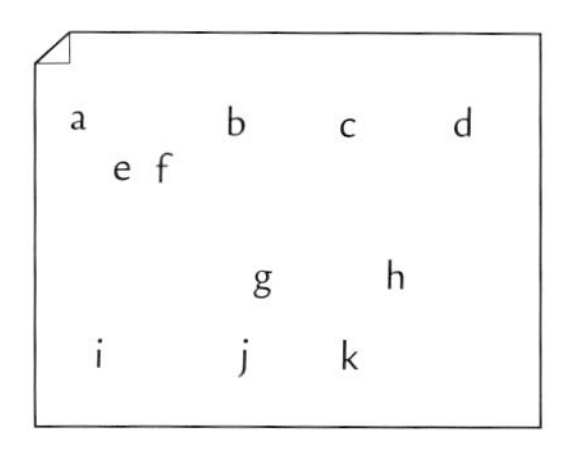

Dimensions 437 × 578 mm.
Technique Pen and brown ink, freehand.
Paper Heavy, folded twice vertically and horizontally, cut on all sides, edges partly torn and pasted, one fold reinforced.
Drawing Scale *Piedi antichi*.

INSCRIPTION, Recto (lower right corner, turned 90 degrees, other hand) *del tempio di tigoli di mia mano levato questo / dì 5 di settembre 1539 essendovi papa paolo terzio*; (below m) *In di sotto dello architrave*; (inscription in *m*) CELLIO·L·F·; (by l) *finestra di de*[*n*]*tro*; (by k) *finestra di fora*; (above e) *lo fregio e de*[*n*]*tro allogiato / dello architrave*; (by a) *la portta sie diritta*; (between a and b) *Lo capitello e alto p*[*iedi*] *2 dita 7 1/2*; (below b) *canali 20 p.*[*er*] *colonna*; (next to f) [...] *li sopra della / Cornicie fino al / di sotto* [...]

Verso *Del te[m]pio to[n]do di tigoli / di mia mano levato a dì / 5 di settembre 1539 [es]sendo sua s.ta a tigoli papa pa / golo*

On the 5th of September 1539, about four years after receiving Riniero Neruccio da Pisa's survey of the round temple of Tivoli, a copy of which has survived (U 1069A), Antonio made a new survey when he was in Tivoli together with Paul III, as stated on this sheet.

The folds in the paper were probably produced in the course of the drawing. This time the unit of measurements is the ancient foot with 16 *digiti*. The heights vary only slightly from those of Riniero and are within the usual range to be expected when different measurements are made. Of greater significance is Antonio's correction of Riniero's erroneous count of sixteen columns in the *peristasis*. He drew in nine columns on one side of the portal axis to produce a symmetrical total of eighteen columns. Perhaps Antonio had become suspicous of the correctness of Riniero's version because, with a sixteen-column *peristasis*, Riniero's measurements for the intercolumniations and diameters of the columns would have resulted in a circumference too small for the diameter. | JN

BIBLIOGRAPHY Ferri (1885) 220; Giovannoni (1959) I: 22; Vasori (1981) 140–42, cat. no. 108; CensusID 10077247, 10082081.

U 1218A *recto*

Antonio da Sangallo The Younger

Notes on various antiquities and sketches for volutes, 1519–20(?), with additions after 1521.

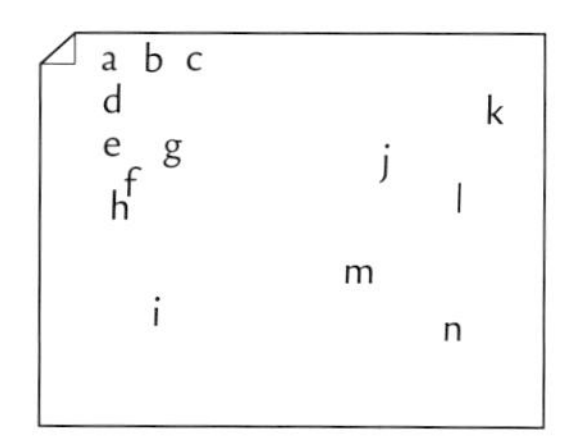

Dimensions 430 × 568 mm.
Technique Pen, straightedge, and compass over stylus; straightedge and compass holes for *j–m*; impression of a scheme between *l* and *n* that cannot be seen in the photograph, freehand sketch of a squared scheme and compass-drawn circle to the left of *n*.
Paper Vertical center fold with three pairs of small holes close to it, top, center, and bottom (marks left by stitches in a notebook?) trimmed, creased; torn at right edge, reinforced.

INSCRIPTION (Antonio's hand) (left of center fold) *Uno delli sette miracholi e in cizicho / lo quale monta gradi el vul* [*ul* interlinea] *go dicie / non si potere contare quando sono / più e quando mancho di poi saliti / li gradi cie infinita grandissima / di colonne grande fralle quale / in su dua ci e una archa la quale / chilla vole ruinare satacha le / mane alarcha nelmezo ci e / uno obelischo grande / autore uno gienovese quale sta / con zanobi de medici nel 1521 / torno di quelle parte li gradi sta / no Come li sopra disegnati luno / che legalaltro ogni preta / e alta dua gradi come stanno / Le bianche le negre* [refers to drawings *c, d, e*]. *Lo belischo / di Costantinopoli fu quello celle*[?] */ traglie si tochavano quandoera / preso aritto e non potendo ri/zallo una dona dise auno / servo che bagnassi le corde / e cosi finire per lo rachorcia/re le chorde e chosi e schol / pito nella basa apresso / alli dad*[...] [?] *stano una cinta / intorno di bataglie e lo / belischo e intagliato di le/tere egittie Lacholon*[*a*]*/ storiata in chostantinop/oli e intagliata del testa/mento vechio enovo/ sta sofia e una cupola/in pie grande dove*[?] *era uno difitio grande di portici e abitatio/ne de frati tutte*[?] *che / magiore di dua terme e da pontte*[?] */ 189*; (at left, under drawing *h*) *denti alli gradi del tempio / dAntonino e faustina / alti uno palmo / largi* [*sic*, without value]

When the plan on what is now the verso was drawn, the page was spread out and used lengthways. It was then folded in half when Antonio used the right side of what is now the recto to enlarge one of the schemes, a series of concentric squares (*k*) used to determine where to place the compass point when constructing a volute, and when he made several sketches of volutes (*j, l, m, n*). In fact, none of the volutes cross the folded line. Furthermore, the compass holes that came with the drawing of a volute on the left side of the page has left clear marks on the right-hand part, which had been folded under the left-hand part. On the left side, Antonio outlined this volute (*i*) and sketched an Ionic capital using a "cathetus" to try and determine the position of the "eye" as specified by Vitruvius (*g*). Then, he used the empty spaces to sketch examples of flights of dovetailed steps (*a–f, h*) and also wrote a lengthy note on the ruins of Cyzicus and on architecture in Constantinople, to the left of the fold.

The inscribed note is from after 1521, the year in which Sangallo accounts that an unidentified Genoese traveler returned from the East telling him about Cyzicus, and it must be prior to 1527 because the architect uses a shape of "ch" which was altered from that year onward (Frommel 1994, *Introduction*). Numerous unfinished curving lines in some of the volutes suggest that Antonio may have been experimenting, attempting to find the fastest and simplest geometric system to determine where the compass points should be fixed within the eye so as to describe the arcs of the circle that make up the volute. There are schemes made up of squares rotated by 45 degrees and circles (*i, n*) as well as one with many concentric squares (*k*), which is similar to that shown on U 718A v., a sheet of drawings for St Peter's and Villa Madama. The drafts on U 1218A r. may be roughly contemporaneous with the spirals drawn in 1519 on the recto and verso of that sheet (Losito 1993, *La ricostruzione*, pp. 133–75), where the marks in the middle of each square suggest that Antonio must have fixed each center using Euclid's theorem and reduced the radius of each quadrant by the half of the diameter of the eye and that, therefore, he had not yet discovered a quicker method. Assuming that this was the case, he would have gone on to add the other drawings to the recto a couple of years later. In his lengthy note, Antonio refers to one of the Seven Wonders of the Ancient World as being a building of Cyzicus with tall steps and numerous columns, identifiable as the Temple of Zeus described by Pliny the Elder (*Naturalis Historia*, XXXVI, xxii, 98–99), which he was particularly interested in because of one of its elements of construction, the dovetailing device that ensured the integrity of the blocks of the steps, which he draws on the basis of the description by the Genoese traveler (*a–e*). Sangallo adds that he recalls dovetailing being used to much the same effect at the Temple of Antoninus and Faustina in Rome (*f–h*). The references to the various monuments in Constantinople presumably derive from the same source: an obelisk, possibly that of Theodosius, although the description of the reliefs of battles on the plinth would appear to suggest the podium of the historiated column (of Arcadius?), referred to immediately thereafter, and finally the church of Santa Sofia. | PNP

BIBLIOGRAPHY Ferri (1885) 37; Huelsen (1910) 81; Bartoli (1914–22) III: 201, pl. 341; VI: 64; Günther (1988) 294, 296; Chatzidakis (2017) 158, fig. 345; CensusID 10072710.

U 1220A *recto*

Antonio da Sangallo the Younger

Fano, Arch of Augustus, ca. 1532.

Dimensions 212 × 148 mm.
Technique Pen and brown ink, freehand.
Paper Trimmed.

INSCRIPTION (top left), black pencil; nineteenth-century hand, old numbering, 82; top right, black pencil; nineteenth-century hand, old numbering, *354*; Antonio's hand, brown ink, *Sopra meze Colonne / Canalate*; *Arco i[n] Fano*

This sketch shows just over half of the Arch of Augustus at Fano, which formed the western gate of the ancient city and dates from AD 9–10. The lower stage consists of two plain travertine facades, pierced by a large central arch, with two smaller pedestrian arches at either side, under an entablature, which carries an inscription to the divine Augustus. The gate was originally flanked by towers; remains of the northern one are still standing today. The attic, an arcade of seven arches separated by fluted Corinthian pilasters, was destroyed in 1463 during Federigo da Montefeltro's attack on Fano. Its form is known from later drawings and a relief, which, however, depend on a drawing executed before its destruction (Nesselrath 1984–86, III, pp. 102–04). The attic entablature carried an inscription rededicating the arch to the divine Constantine, probably following its restoration by L. Turcius Secundus Asterius, a native of the region, who was Urban Praefect at Rome in AD 339 (De Maria 1988, p. 242 f.).

Antonio may have seen the extant lower part, since he was given responsibility for repairing the dilapidated fortifications of Fano in 1532 (Giovannoni 1959, I, p. 75), and the sheet is one of the series that Giovannoni (1959, I, p. 21) believed was part of a travel sketchbook, other sheets of which we have dated to a similar period (see U 1066A r. and v.). However, the sketch does not have the character of a record drawing, as it lacks measurements and inaccurately shows the smaller pedestrian arch with impost moldings. The reconstruction of the upper part differs from all others in omitting arches between the half-columns, which the annotation tells us were fluted. The presence of a pediment indicates that Antonio studied Giuliano da Sangallo's drawing in the Barberini Codex (Biblioteca Apostolica Vaticana, Barb. lat. 4424, fol. 61v.), in which a pediment is also present, although Antonio avoided the many other fanciful aspects of Giuliano's reconstruction. | IC

BIBLIOGRAPHY Huelsen (1910) I: 61, fig. 65; Giovannoni (1959) I: 20n, 21; Vasori (1981) 142–43, cat. no. 109; Brands (1988) 510–11, fig. 15; Raub (2014) 176, fig. 6; CensusID 10074764.

U 1221A *recto and verso*

Antonio da Sangallo the Younger

Rome, Forum Transitorium, ca. 1520.

Dimensions 215 × 254 mm.
Technique Pen and black ink.
Paper Lightweight, center fold.

INSCRIPTION, Recto *antiche/i[n] istorie; frachasso; chosi fino*
Verso *a foro traiano dalla cholonna/al pilastro fa chosi alle mensole*

On the recto at the left is a partial view in perspective of the "colonnacce," part of the exterior wall of the Forum Transitorium, and below it, two solutions for the corner of a door jamb. At the right is a ground plan of the entablature of the Temple of Minerva at the point where it is joined to the pronaos by a projection. On the verso, left, is a plan of half of the Forum Transitorium, which Antonio called the "Foro di Traiano." The Temple of Minerva with its pronaos juts out from the lower, concave, short side of the forum. The attachment of the pronaos is drawn at the right in three perspective views, the two at the top showing details of the entablature, the one at the bottom a column and a pilaster at the height of the capital. The sheet is a preparatory study for U 1123A. | HCD

BIBLIOGRAPHY Ferri (1885) 126, 161, 163, 167; Bartoli (1914–22) III: fig. 364–65, pl. 216; VI: 69; Günther (1988) 280, no. 150; Viscogliosi (2000) 129–31, 131–34, cat. nos 11, 12; Viscogliosi (2017) 112, 113, fig. 11; CensusID 239170.

U 1223A *recto and verso*

ANTONIO DA SANGALLO THE YOUNGER

Rome, details of S. Marco, study for New St Peter's, study for the niche with the bust of Hadrian in Castel Sant'Angelo (*verso*); near Rome, details of the Tomb of Annia Regilla and the so-called Grotto of Egeria, (*recto*), ca. 1544.

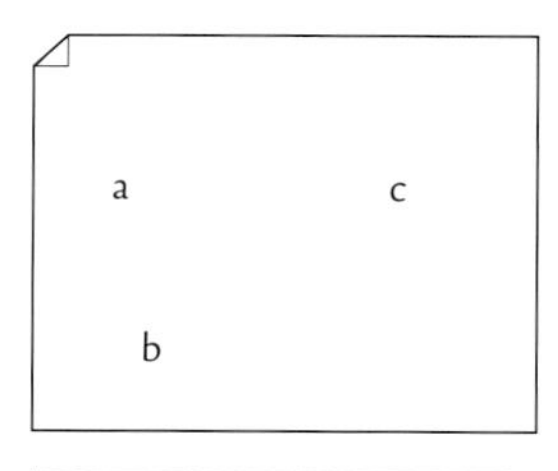

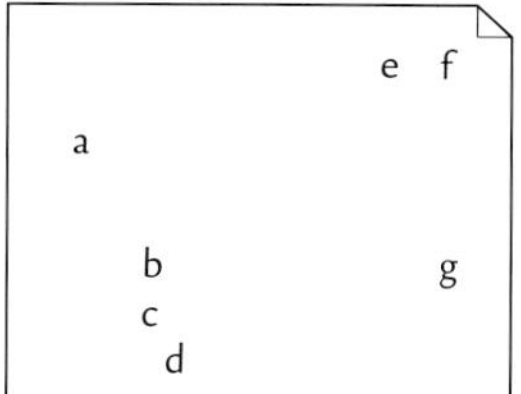

Dimensions 278 × 219 mm.
Technique Pen and brown ink, freehand, stylus, compass.
Paper Partly yellowed, central vertical fold, trimmed, repaired.

INSCRIPTION, Recto *(a) alla vignia/di Mes[er] Ja[m]petro/Caferello fuora/di porta latina; (b) Finestre di questo te[m]pio; aquedotto suteraneo; (c) i[n] la vignia di Mes[ser]/Ja[m]pietro Caferello*

Verso *a pie della porta di S[an]to marcho i[n] chiesa/e torna molto bella; M[armo]; S[erpentino]* [*twice*]; *(a) Porfido; (c) sacristia; portichо; canpanile; (e) 4; 1; 2 1/2; (g) nichia sopra la porta*

On the left half of the recto is a plan of the exterior of the Tomb of Annia Regilla *a*, and a sketch of one of its windows *b*, although the lack of detail prevents us from establishing exactly which one. The sketches probably belong to the same group of studies as those of the tomb on U 1168A, a sheet of similar size and paper. The plan at the right *c* shows the so-called Grotto of Egeria, a nymphaeum built into a bank in the Valle Caffarella, close to the tomb and probably also part of the Triopion of Herodes Atticus, and hence from the 2nd century AD. The inner part still exists with its barrel vault of brick, but the front is reduced to the foundation courses. Antonio's reconstruction, with the outer part also vaulted, cannot be confirmed from the existing evidence, although the thoroughness of his investigations can be confirmed by the inclusion of the underground aqueduct feeding the nymphaeum.

On the verso is a series of apparently unrelated monuments. The first drawing on the left *a* is a plan of part of a cosmatesque pavement, executed with stylus and compass, which the text above seems to put by a door in S. Marco, presumably in Rome, where the pavement was repaired some time between 1503 and 1523, while Domenico Grimani was titular cardinal (Krautheimer-Corbett-Frankl 1937–77, ch. II, p. 219). The pavement consists of fragments of white marble, red porphyry, and green prophry (*serpentino*), arranged in patterns of interlocking circles with squares and triangles in the interstices. This pattern is common in the work of the "Paulus group," the earliest known group of the marble workers known generically as the "Cosmati." The sons of Paulus signed the now lost ciborium of S. Marco in 1154. Fragments of the cosmatesque floor include, for example, the pattern of the panel in front of the relics of Pope St Mark. The incised circles of the plan extend further down the sheet but only one other small area is inked in *c*, forming a slightly different pattern, of unspecified materials. This pattern cannot be seen today at S. Marco, but it does occur at S. Maria in Cosmedin. On top of the incised circles Antonio has added two other drawings. One, *b*, in slightly darker ink than the other drawings on the page, shows crossing piers and adjacent piers above and to the left which are a reminder of Sangallo's projects for New St Peter's of around 1518 (but such a date is excluded here by the handwriting, see Frommel 2019, *metodo progettuale*). The two freehand circles to the left of the pier may represent domes. On the left opens either an apse or the doorway to an octagonal sacristy drawn as alternatives, but might also belong with drawing *d* at the bottom of the sheet, the vaguest of plans, which the text tells us represents a campanile and a portico. Bartoli believed these too belong to S. Marco, but the Romanesque campanile is nowhere near the portico, and we have no evidence that Antonio was involved in any scheme to alter the church, although the drawing of the pavement, a subject rare in Antonio's oeuvre, demonstrates he had some interest in S. Marco.

The right half of the verso contains a proposal for one of the niches in the Cortile dell'Angelo in the Castel Sant'Angelo (*g*). It bears no apparent relation to the circular ones actually executed by Raffaelle da Montelupo, but Gaudioso shows the evolution of the design. He proposes Raffaele as the author of the present drawing and of U 846A, but the writing and drawing styles both seem closer to Antonio's. It is more likely a case of Antonio helping Raffaele with the design of the aedicule. The present design, with the end of the pediment and entablature projecting forward, links it to the aedicule over the door of the Tomb of Annia Regilla, details of which are drawn on the recto, although the bracket supporting the colonnette is reminiscent of the aedicules on the facade of the *frigidarium* of the Baths of Diocletian. Drawing *f* may be a study of this bracket, while drawing *e* is probably best explained with reference to U 846A, where we see the conventional pedimented aedicule in the process of transformation as the round-headed niche bursts out and becomes independent. Payments to Raffaele for work on the niches date from July 1544 to August 1546, and hence these drawings can probably be dated to about 1544, although other items on the sheet, like the cosmatesque pavement, may be earlier. | IC

BIBLIOGRAPHY Ferri (1885) 147, 162, 174, 199; Bartoli (1914–22 III: figs 403–04, pl. 233; VI: 74–5; Kammerer-Grothaus (1974) 149 ff.; Gaudioso (1976) 39 ff.; Glass (1980) 145, pattern 20; Campbell (2004), I: 344; CensusIDs 60669, 10072907.

U 1225A *recto*

Antonio da Sangallo the Younger

Rome, Theater of Marcellus, ca. 1519–20.

Dimensions 264 × 424 mm.
Technique Pen, straight-edge, compass, stylus and black ink.
Drawing Scale Roman *piedi*.

INSCRIPTION (top left, turned outwards) *quella di de*[*n*] *tro elabona questa e fatta dapoi no*[*n*] *bisognia chominciarsi conquesta ma conque*/ *lla di de*[*n*]*tro si*; (lower right, crossed out) *questa linia a* [...] *mezza*/ *i*[*n*]*mezo qui*; (below) *archi*

The drawing is an attempt at the graphic restitution of the ground plan of the Theater of Marcellus in aovata form with the geometric matrix of the Vitruvian scheme for the Greek theater, as interpreted by Antonio the Younger. For this reason, it should be compared to U 1107A r for the study of an alternative version, correctly rendered, and obtained by employing the Vitruvian scheme for the Latin theater, with semicircular orchestra and *cavea*. The present drawing is only partially completed but uses technical tools for precision such as straight-edge, compass, and stylus. Cavea and orchestra have an oval form obtained through a polycentric figure, worked out by Antonio the Younger in other theoretical studies, while the frons scenae is tangent to the generating circumference.

With this interpretation of the Vitruvian scheme of the Greek theater, Antonio the Younger obtained a greater expansion of the auditorium in comparison to the Latin scheme, making use of the available depth and, at the same time, placing the frons scenae at a greater distance from the orchestra. A knowledge of these possible alternatives of geometric proportions is also evident in the studies for the theater at Villa Madama U 1267A (a preliminary study with respect to drawing U 314A) by Antonio the Younger, where the Vitruvian schemes are applied, even if with some uncertainties. This consideration suggests a date for the drawings related to the Theater of Marcellus around the 1520s, contemporary with or just after the project for Villa Madama. In the drawing, the three points of projection are marked by a small circle (that at the bottom is partially covered by the stamp of the Sopraintendenza). Furthermore, Antonio the Younger has constructed with the stylus the rays for the placement of the pilasters of the external colonnade and the cunei of the cavea. Beginning from the right, the rays converge at the center corresponding to the intersection of the side of the square which marks the frons scenae and the generating circumference. From pilaster 14 to 27, the ray has its center in the external point of the circumference below, from pilaster 28 to 39 they converge at the center symmetrical to the first and marked with a small circle. An interesting detail is the sketch of a ground plan at the bottom right where Antonio the Younger tries to resolve the joining of the royal hall with the columnatio of the frons scaenae. | ACF

BIBLIOGRAPHY Ferri (1885) 216; Bartoli (1914–22) VI: 97; IV: Pl. CCCXVIII, fig. 528; Frommel (1974) 181, fig. 94; Cerutti Fusco (1987) 303, fig. 4, 306; CensusID 10072241.

U 1226A *recto*

Antonio da Sangallo the Younger

Study for the geometric construction of capital and shaft of Ionic column from Theater of Marcellus, after 1527.

Dimensions 570 × 424 mm.
Paper Center fold.
Technique Pen and ink and compass.
Drawing Scale *Moduli.*

INSCRIPTION *La linia del cavetto ouero/piombo del centro sie reste/re sotto A et non sotto B* – (word canceled: *Cimatio*?) *Abbacho – Canali* –; (to the right, turned 90 degrees) *moduli 6. – Capitello la tertia parte della/grosseza della colonna dappie* –; (along right edge of sheet) *Lo cimatio sia/lo resto che rimane/va del tutto levato lo abba/cho e li canali/Lo getto suo sara uno mo/duli ouero ochio fuori/dello abbacho/Li baltei ouero pulvini/sia fuori del cimatio/quanto dua moduli/ouero occhij* –; (at center of sheet) *Cimatio – parte della colonna – 15* [*ochija* canceled]; – *grosseza Della Colonna da capo quale sendo piedi 15/re moduli 15 – grosseza della Colonna da pie nel vivo quale/sia moduli 18 la meza parte*; [*fare sia in* cancelled] *moduli 9 – nella campana fare 20 moduli 20* –; (lower right edge of sheet) *A piedi 15 la colonna/et repartita in parte 6/el da pie el da capo se fa 5/*[*lo dagapo* for *da capo*? canceled]/*che vi e* [*ochij mo*/canceled] *ochij*/[*duli* canceled] *18 da pie fa ochij* [*br* canceled]/*13 lo dagapo nelvivo*

This drawing relates to others by Antonio with studies of the Ionic capital (U 983A, 1600A). U 1226A represents half of a front elevation and half of a side elevation.

Antonio cuts the column shaft at the top and bottom and draws the sections juxtaposed in order to reveal the significant difference due to entasis between the diameter at the base—represented perspectivally to show that it is a column and not a pilaster—and the diameter below the capital. | AGG

BIBLIOGRAPHY Giovannoni (1959) I: 23, 67; Günther (1988) 223, nn. 47 and 49.

U 1227A *recto*

Antonio da Sangallo the Younger

Rome, Baths of Caracalla, calidarium, 1545–46.

Dimensions 111 × 186 mm.
Technique Pen and brown ink.
Paper lightweight.

INSCRIPTION *Laconico/Efebep* [canceled]/*sudatorio*; *dellantoniana li tondi sono/pozi che scaldano lastantia*

This is a sketch of the plan of the calidarium of the Antonine Baths, showing the pools that produced the steam. For the dating of this drawing, see also U 1206A r. and v., which, as noted by Bartoli, should be dated to the years 1545–46 due to the reference to the Farnese Hercules. | ACF

BIBLIOGRAPHY Ferri (1885) 202; Lanciani (1902–12) II: 183; Bartoli (1914–22) III: fig. 361, pl. 215; VI: 64; CensusID 10072728.

U 1229A *recto and verso*

Antonio da Sangallo the Younger

Verona, socle zones of the Arch of the Gavi, of an unknown building and of Porta Borsari; two sketches of a drawbridge in Verona (*recto*); an ornamental hanging with bay leaves (?) (*verso*), 1526(?).

Dimensions 283 × 217 mm.
Technique Pen and brown ink, freehand.
Paper Heavy, trimmed at lower edge, reinforced on verso.

INSCRIPTION, Recto (bottom left, Arch of the Gavi) *loinbasamento delarcho di/vetruvio verona* [...] *sta* [...]; (bottom right, Porta Borsari) *Loinbasamento/della porta di bo/rsoli inverona/sta cosi*; *Borsoli*; (top right, drawbridges) *ponte – ponte – contrapointe*; *modo di pontelevatoro/averona chesono due/ponti uno dentro laltro di/fora quali si serrano/tutte due alchontrario/luno dellaltro luno cascha/ingiu cioe quello didentro/equando questo di dentro vie/ne abasso quello di fora siriza/cosi quando quello dentro salza/quello di fora se abaso*; (19th-century hand, lower edge) *Arco dei Gavi* distrutta/nel 1805; *Arco de Borsari in Verona*

Verso *schizi di verona*; various sums

This sheet was probably made during Antonio the Younger and Sanmicheli's 1526 tour of inspection of papal fortifications in Northern Italy (see also U 815A, 1048A, and 1200A). The freehand drawings scattered loosely over the page are characteristic of sketches made on a journey (see also U 1048A and U 1200A). The minute description of the drawbridge (possibly the one installed in front of the Castelvecchio in its former state) also seems to indicate that Antonio visited Verona. But there are differences from the finds in the structures represented here. In the drawing of the Arch of the Gavi, the base of the engaged column at the left is placed directly on the top molding of the pedestal, as it is in the erected structure. Beneath the right engaged column, however, a square plinth has been introduced by Sangallo between the column base and the upper molding of the pedestal, as in the elevation of the arch on U 815A recto. In his sketch of the Porta Borsari ("Borsoli"), Antonio also drew a high pedestal beneath the passage pier and its fluted engaged column, another difference from the erected structure and from his drawing of the Porta Borsari on U 815A. All these changes must be understood (as on U 815A, 1048A, 1064A, and 1200A) as deliberate corrections of the ancient buildings. See also the entries for U 815A and U 1382A.

The ornamental hanging, probably an antique necklet, on the verso is not identified. | CJ

BIBLIOGRAPHY Ferri (1885) 225 (under "Arco de' Leoni"); Giovannoni (1959) I: 20n, 21; Burns (1965–66) 258 n. 33; Schweikhart (1977) 38, 75, fig. 96; Tosi (1980) 37, no. III.3; Vasori (1981) 144–45, cat. no. III; Tosi (1983) 95, fig. 67; Puppi (1986) 103, fig. 3; CensusID 10075389.

U 1231A *recto*

Antonio da Sangallo the Younger

Rome, details of the Arch of Titus, after 1527.

Dimensions 283 × 285 mm.
Technique Pen and brown ink, freehand.
Paper Partly yellowed, left and bottom edges trimmed.
Drawing Scale Florentine *braccia*.

INSCRIPTION (top right), brown ink, old numbering, sixteenth-century hand, *23*; black pencil; nineteenth-century hand, old numbering, *964*; lower left, brown ink, Antonio's hand, *Dillarcho di tito uespasiano / misurato a braccia fiorentine / e minuti di 60 per braccio*; various measurements and calculations

Both drawings are sections. The first, spanning the length of the sheet, includes the full height of the podium, the column plinth and base, and the lowest part of the shaft. It is measured. The other, drawn at 90 degrees to the first, shows the top of the cornice of the podium, the plinth and column base, and the lowest part of the shaft. It is unmeasured and was clearly abandoned in favor of the first, perhaps because Antonio realized he could not include the podium in the space available. The presence of so many measurements and the freehand nature of the drawing suggest that this could be an on-the-spot survey drawing.

The Arch of Titus, standing at the highest part of the Via Sacra, was in a very fragmentary state at the start of the sixteenth century, lacking the greater parts of both piers. It attracted the interest of Raphael and his circle, who attempted to reconstruct it on paper, as did Antonio the Younger (see U 1255A). | IC

BIBLIOGRAPHY Ferri (1885) 126; Bartoli (1914–22) III: fig. 374; pl. 273; VI: 70; Pfanner (1983) 6; Frommel-Ray-Tafuri (1984) 440; CensusID 60673.

U 1232A *recto*

Antonio da Sangallo the Younger

Rome, proposal for the base of the obelisk in Piazza del Popolo; schematic reconstruction of the plan for the Mausoleum in Halicarnassus, after 1527.

Dimensions 163 × 276 mm.
Technique Pen and brown ink, freehand.
Paper Restored.
Drawing Scale Roman *palmi.*

INSCRIPTION (top right, black pencil; nineteenth-century hand, old numbering), *965*;(below the base, Antonio's hand, brown ink) *per lobelisco nella piazza del popolo come nel S. Rocco/ 110*; right of the plan *medaglia de/ mausoleo/ Colonne 36*; calculations

The top design shows a proposal for the base of the obelisk that was to be placed in the Piazza del Popolo in Rome under the supervision of Raphael and Antonio the Younger, as part of the urban development instigated by Leo X (Tafuri 1984 *Obelisco*, pp. 229–30; Günther 1985, pp. 249–51.) The caption specifies that the obelisk to be relocated is the one found in July 1519, during work on Via Ripetta; together with another obelisk, it flanked the entrance door to Augusto's Mausoleum (Lanciani 1902, I, p. 192; Tafuri 1984 *Obelisco*, p. 229.) In the same year, Raphael proposed placing it in Piazza S. Pietro (Marino Sanudo, *Diari*, ed. Fulin, Stefani, Barozzi et. Al. 1879–1902, XXVI, pp. 470–71.) It was probably shortly thereafter that the decision was made to put it in the new Piazza del Popolo, where the bivium formed by Via Lata and Via Ripetta converges; the drawing, however, due to Antonio's handwriting, cannot be dated before 1527.

Four elephants, placed on the diagonals of the square plan, stand on the three steps. The elephants support a platform on which eight sphinxes hold an inscribed cube; four turtles are squeezed in between the cube and the obelisk. The use of an ancient monolith to give distinction to a new piazza was typical of the cultural trends under Leo X; the use of sculpture enhances the visual effect of the obelisk with regard to its function as a vanishing and/or urban focal point. The elephant-obelisk association recalls a well-known engraving in Francesco Colonna's *Hypnerotomachia Poliphili* (1499;) it also brings to mind the pairs of elephants in the interior of the Malatesta temple in Rimini that were designed by Antonio in U 1048A (D'Onofrio 1976, p. 208; Tafuri 1984, *Obelisco*, p. 230.) Leo X's affection for Annone, the elephant given to him by King Manuel of Portugal, should also be noted. From an iconographical point of view, the *virtus* and the *sapientia* of the elephant join the *prudentia* of the turtle (Hypnerotomachia,) while the sphinxes asking riddles demonstrate the interest for Egyptian things in that period – the telamones in the Raphaelesque "Stanza dell'Incendio" are another example. The grouping probably alludes to the wise rule, virtue, and culture of the Medici pope. The amusing combination of figurative elements and architectural abstraction may be a result of collaboration between Raphael and Antonio, consultants to the "masters of the streets" during Leo X's renovation of Rome (Tafuri 1984 *Obelisco*, p. 230; D'Onofrio 1976, pp. 202–04, 206.) The proposal was never carried out; it was not until 1585 that Sixtus V decided to put the obelisk in the piazza facing the apse of S. Maria Maggiore (D'Onofrio 1967, pp. 156–57.)

The sketch below it is an attempt to reconstruct the plan of the Mausoleum at Halicarnassus, with 36 columns, according to Pliny's description (73 × 132 1/2 *palmi*.) It is not known to which medal Antonio is referring. Two sixteenth-century medals showing reconstructions of the mausoleum are discussed by Greenhalgh (1972) but neither appears related to the present plan. The calculations in the margin refer to the monument's perimeter. The presence on the same page of the design for the Popolo obelisk and the plan of the ancient monument is probably due to the thematic affinity inherent in the stepped base proposed for the obelisk. | IC

BIBLIOGRAPHY Ferri (1885) 176; Lanciani (1902) I: 192; D'Onofrio (1967) 155 ff.; Frommel (1973) I: 19; D'Onofrio (1976) 202–18; Bruschi (1983) 9; Tafuri (1984, *Obelisco*), 229–30; Günther (1985), 249–51; Zavatta (2008) 204; Raub (2014) 171, 173, fig. 1; Fane-Saunders (2016) 262; CensusID 10073044.

U 1233A *recto and verso*

Antonio da Sangallo the Younger

Rome, Theater of Marcellus, Obelisk of Mausoleum of Augustus (*recto*); Doric Temple at San Nicola in Carcere, Ponte S. Angelo, Detail from Marcus Aurelius reliefs in the Palazzo dei Conservatori, so-called Arch of Drusus, (*verso*), after 1527.

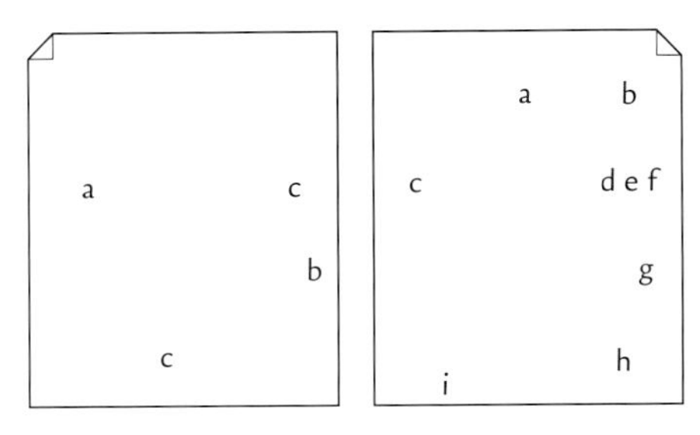

Dimensions 295 × 219 mm.
Technique Pen and brown ink, freehand.
Paper medium weight, pachted on right side.
Drawing Scale Roman *piede*.

INSCRIPTION, Recto (top right, black pencil; nineteenth century hand, old numbering) *966*; brown ink, Antonio's hand, top left, calculations; bottom left, *A piedi e dite*; all over, measurements; *(a)* and *(b) Savelli*; *Porticho de Savelli dove sta el lucchese manischalco*; *questa faciata e fro[n]tispitio*; *Le Colonne sono / alte con* base & / *Capitello piedi 26 1/2; (d) obelischo / da s[an]to / rocho*; measurements

Verso (bottom left, black pencil, nineteenth-century hand, current numbering), *1233*; brown ink, Antonio's hand, (top right) *18, 9*; *Li modani* [numbers?] *uolte ta[n]to che no[n] ue[n] gono i[n] disegnio* [?]; *(c) di Jove Statoris*; *(g) archo picholo / di ponte santo / agniolo*; *(h) nelle storie / di Campidoglio*; measurements on *(b)*, *(g)* and *(i)*; black chalk, later hand *dell'Arco di Druso*

Most of the drawings here have more finished parallels by Giovanni Battista da Sangallo on U 1270A r where their relationship is discussed.

The text at the top of the recto identifies its drawings apart from *(d)* as parts of the Theatre of Marcellus. It is not clear if the 'Manischalco' from Lucca referred to as living there is an individual with that surname (still common), or to his trade as a blacksmith. Drawing *a* is a half plan of a part of one of the *aulae* of the Theater of Marcellus. The notation gives the height of the columns as 26½ *piedi*, including the capitals, which is 2 *piedi* lower than Giovanni Battistas's measurements on U 1657A v. The section, *b*, cuts through the *aula* with the exterior to the height of the entablature on the left and the interior to the springing of the vault on the right – the reverse of the more detailed parallel drawing on U 1270A r. The profile *c*, of an Attic base, is drawn to a larger scale. ithas similar but not identical measurements to that on *b*. From its position it would appear to belong to the internal column of the *aula*. The small sketch, *d*, on the bottom shows the obelisk of the Mausoleum of Augustus which was discovered near San Rocco in 1519.

The note at the top right appears to refer to some moldings (*modani*) of the vaults of the Doric temple at S. Nicola in Carcere, which are not drawn in the two sections, *a* and *b*, of the upper parts of the temple, the latter appearing to show the pronaos. The measured section, *c*, shows a detail of the entablature of the peristyle, paralleled on U 1270A r. Antonio's identification of it as belonging to the Temple of Jove Stator is discussed on U 1090A v+1230A r).

The three profiles of Attic bases, *d*, *e* and *f*, are unidentified. Below them is a perspectival sketch, *g*, of one of the small side arches of the Ponte S. Angelo, the Hadrianic *Pons Aelius*. The parallel on U 1270A r shows the parapet above the arch. At lower right is a perspectival sketch, *h*, of a tetrastyle prostyle temple. It is a reconstruction of the Temple of Capitoline Jove depicted in one of the reliefs from a triumphal arch of Marcus Aurelius, housed in the Palazzo de' Conservatori on the Campidoglio. Giovanni Battista also tried reconstructing the same subject on U 1270A r and U 1657A v, but in both cases makes the temple pseudoperipteral rather than prostyle. At lower left is a plan, *i*, of one of the piers of the so-called Arch of Drusus spanning the Appian Way just inside the Porta S. Sebastiano. The sketch is paralleled on U 1270A r, where the plan is complete and accompanied by an elevation. | IC

BIBLIOGRAPHY Ferri (1885) 163; Huelsen (1906) pp. 172–3; Bartoli (1914–22) III: fig. 419, pl. 215; VI: 78; Righetti (1833–36) I: 168; Crozzoli Aite (1981) 37, no. 19; Campbell (1984), I: 146; II, fig. 5.15; Günther (1988) 254, n. 65–67, 266; CensusIDs 242505, 10012251.

U 1240A *recto and verso*

Antonio da Sangallo the Younger

Schemes and studies of the ancient theater, after 1519.

Dimensions 278 × 206 mm.
Technique Pen, stylus, compass and straight-edge, brown ink.
Paper Restored.

INSCRIPTION, Recto (lower right) *A-B-C-: centri*; (inside the plan) [...]/*pulpito*

Verso (top and bottom) *A B C centri*

The drawing shows two studies of Vitruvian schemes for the plan of ancient Latin and Greek theaters. In the first, above, the scheme is correctly interpreted by Antonio the Younger, who, following the suggestions of Fra Giocondo, translates the Vitruvian description of the generating geometric system of the Latin theater (Vitruvius, *Ten Books on Architecture*, V.4). Antonio's drawing differs in the reconstructions of Fra Giocondo and Cesariano not only for the placement of the generating circumference tangent to the extremity of the orchestra, but also in the half oval-oval form of orchestra and cavea. Antonio's reading was based on the authority of Alberti (as well as Vitruvius) who in several passages (for example,"amphitheatrum vero duobus constat theatris, iunctis gradationum cornibus unter se ambitu perpetuo. In hocque differunt, quod est quidem theatrum velut pars amphitheatri dimidia ..." Alberti, *On the Art of Building*, Book VIII) emphasizes that the theater consists of half an amphitheater. Antonio the Younger therefore constructs an orchestra on the Vitruvian scheme ad triangulum and traces at the right the furthest cunei of the cavea and some pilasters of the barrel-vaults of the external corridor up to the joining of the porticus post scaenam, as well as the rayed sections of the underpinning of the seats.

In such a typological study of the hypothetical theater, the joining of the scenic structure to the cavea is not clearly resolved, even though there is an attempt to join the two bodies of the structure organically. The alignment of the scena would coincide with the side of the triangle that has its vertex at the center of the oval of the orchestra. The version aovata must be related to that of the drawing on the upper half of the verso. In the drawing of the lower half, Antonio the Younger gives a geometric interpretation for the passage in Alberti relative to the horseshoe form of some theaters ("The theater takes the lineament of its area from the hoofprint of a horse," Alberti, *On the Art of Building*, Book VIII). A horseshoe form, elaborated by means of the Vitruvian sheme for the Latin theater, is barely sketched on the right side of the graphic restitution of the Theater at Ferento U 1131A by Antonio the Younger, then placed in comparison with another in drawing U 1132A. A different version is represented in the solution at the bottom of drawing U 1240A v. In the second study on the lower part of 1240A r, Antonio the Younger constructs a theater all'antica, using the Vitruvian scheme for the Greek theater ad quadratum, which allows him to configure an orchestra decidely more spacious than that obtained by the Vitruvian scheme ad triangulum. The basic scheme derives from that presented by Fra Giocondo to illustrate the relevant passage from Vitruvius: the derivation is also taken from the drawing U 1463A r., where a note records the geometry of Fra Giocondo. With respect to Fra Giocondo's scheme, however, the form of the theater here is certainly a horseshoe and the geometric construction is more complicated: in fact, the orchestra and the proscenium are inserted into a space which is drawn from a polycentric figure obtained by means of three arcs of a circle and three points of projection: A.B.C., indicated in the drawing by a small circle. This solution is differentiated from that proposed at the bottom of the verso in the choice of three centers aligned on the diameter of the orchestra.

On the verso, Antonio the Younger studies two other solutions which are presented as alternatives to those on the recto. In the first, above, he proposes a form of theater laid out with the help of the scheme of the Greek theater ad quadratum. Up above is the version of the half-oval orchestra. The polycentric figure presents three centers A B C, emphasized by Antonio, and turns out to be compsed of three connected curves, of which the highest one has its center at point C, vertex of the equilateral triangle which has as its base the side of the square AB and is tangent to the generating circumference, and those at the sides have as their centers A and B respectively, and as rays, the segments lying on the lines CA and CB, individualized by the centers A and B and by the intersections of the lines CA and CB with the highest arc of the circle. It is, therefore, an alternative version of the form of the theater as half of an amphitheater according to the description of Vitruvius. The interpretation of the form of the theater as half of an amphitheater is Alberti's *On the Art of Building*, Book VIII:"Quae vero duobus theatris iunctis frontibus concludebatur, caveam nuncubant; quod ipsum opus amphitheatrum dicitur." This hypothesis is proposed by Antonio the Younger on other occasions for the graphic reconstructions of ancient Roman theaters; for example, the Theater of Marcellus (U 1225A r. and 1122A v., in which there is a sketch at the bottom of a plan with alternative solutions for the cavea as half-circle and aovata); the Theater of Cassino (U 1066A r.) and the Theater at Ferento (U 1301A v.). The drawing at the bottom is a different interpretation of a theater as half of an amphitheater, but in an opposing sense to the preceding one, that is, with a development of the frons scaenae along half of the smaller diameter of the oval. This variation would also be compatible in part with the passage in *On the Art of Building* which describes the form of the theater as a horseshoe. The polycentric figure in this case has the three centers of the arcs of the circle inside the orchestra. This tighter form of theater is proposed in the sketch to the lower left of U 387A by Baldassarre Peruzzi. | ACF

BIBLIOGRAPHY Giovannoni (1959) I: 23.

U 1243A *recto*

Antonio da Sangallo the Younger or Antonio Labacco

Partial plan and view of an unidentified circular(?) structure, before 1515(?).

Dimensions 164 × 201 mm.
Technique Pen and three types of brown ink, stylus, compass, straightedge, pin.
Paper Medium weight to heavy, fold marks, trimmed, stains.

INSCRIPTION (left segment) *botte* (*bassa* canceled); *piano*; (*botte* canceled); (central passage) *botte alta trebuna*; (right segment) (illeg. word canceled) *piano*; (*botte* canceled); (illeg. word, *piano* canceled); (*botte, bassa* canceled)

On this sheet is a partial plan of a circular(?) building with three rings of aisles or ambulatories. The outer wall has applied pilasters on the exterior and large semicircular niches flanked by half-columns on the interior. The inner wall is reduced to a series of piers with applied pilasters and half-columns. The entrance passage has a domed vault at center and two freestanding columns at the far end. A series of incised lines guided Antonio in drawing the outer and inner walls, and the outermost ambulatory. The innermost ambulatory, on the other hand, does not have any corresponding incised lines. The view at the right seems to be from the center of the passageway looking down the middle ambulatory, curving out of sight.

From the many architectural terms that Antonio wrote on the plan and then modified or canceled, one can infer that he was drawing an imaginary architecture, perhaps as an exercise. This conclusion is further supported by the absence of measurements, and the many changes that were made to the form and position of some of the architectural elements. The fact that there are at least three different kinds of ink used in this drawing could mean that Antonio worked on it over a long period of time.

The fragment of a plan on the verso reveals that the sheet was considerably trimmed along the upper edge. | SE

BIBLIOGRAPHY Ferri (1885) 39.

U 1249A *recto and verso*

Antonio da Sangallo the Younger

Reconstruction of the human body according to the Vitruvian canon (*recto*), Ancient measurements with notes on metrology taken from Vitruvius (*verso*), post 1532.

Dimensions 284/285 × 211/214 mm.
Technique Pen and brown ink, freehand.
Paper White, thin, trimmed edges except for the left one; right edge stained, 3 small paer reinforcements on the verso.

INSCRIPTION, Recto (Antonio's hand: close to the left edge, left of the man seen side-on) *petto*; (right, above drawing of 'Homo ad circulum') *cubito / amezo peto*

Verso (Antonio's hand, close to the top edge, above a line divided into 24 equal parts, representing the cubit) *ditto / palmo D*[*ita*] *4 / piede D 16 / cubito D 24*; (top left) *si puo intendere per 18 e per 9 / si puo intendere per 18*; (next to these two lines, at right) *siemialtera*[*sic*] *si e · 9 · e per uno e mezzo / sesquialtera si e 18 e per uno e mezo*; (top right) *Numero perfetto anticho se* [*?*] *X· / secondo le dita di tutte due / le mani el numero / Di poi sono venuti al palmo e al piede / e alcubito come qui apare / e ancora a platone piaque el numero X*; (below) *Di poi anno detto el sei essere perfetto perche anno tre partitione in se e molta ragione / perche el sestantes si e uno lo triente si e Duo* [...] *lo semis si e tre / lo Bessem si e · 4 · cioe li dua tertij quintarium s e cinque lo perfetto si e sex / e agiunto sex sopra sex fa lo axe quale e xij li greci diceno—axe / agiunto la sexta parte al sei fa—vii / agiunto la tertia parte di sei alsei fa—viij / agiunto la meza parte al sei fa—viiij / agiunto li due tertij alsei quali · 4 fa—x / agiunto giunto* [*sic*] *cinque al se*[*sic*] *fa—xi / due simplici numeri cioe se*[*i*] *agiunto alsei fa—xij*

On the sheet, Antonio seeks to interpret some passages from Vitruvius (*De Architectura*, III, 1–3) on the proportional canon of the human body, and the principal units of measurement derived from the body. On the left half of the recto are two drawings of a man seen from the side, rarely so depicted among the innumerable Renaissance reconstructions of Vitruvian man, and probably inspired by an illustration by Dürer on human proportions, who schematizes the proportions similarly. (*A. Dureri clarissimi pictoris et geometrae de Symmetriae partium in rectis formis humanorum corporum in latino conversi*, Nuremberg, 1532, fol[...]). A parallel drawing by Giovanni Battista is found in his annotated copy of the 1486 *De architectura* (Inc. Corsiniano, f. 28v.). To the right are two smaller sketches of the more familiar 'Homo ad circulum ed ad quadratum' and, above, a geometric diagram showing the width of a man with open arms as four cubits, equal to his height, although for some reason Antonio divides the cubit into 23 rather than 24 *dita*, making the total 92 rather than 96.

For the human canon, besides the overall proportions, Vitruvius had proposed detailed information on smaller parts of the body, expressed sometimes in decimal terms and other times as duodecimal, which Antonio tries to apply in the two larger figures, to superimpose and integrate Vitruvius' differing prescriptions into a homogenous system. The first figure is more finished and includes some details of musculature, while the second is more schematic and a little slenderer. In the former, the architect starts from the Vitruvian ratio of 1: 10 between the height of the head from the chin to the forehead, and the total height of the man. He then divides the first measure, below the right side of the leg, in 12 units and, again to the right of the figure, expresses the total height of the man as 12 × 10 = 120 of these small units, which to the left of the drawing is then grouped into four larger units each comprising 30 of the small units (the second from the bottom is 27 to allow for the three assigned to the foot), based on the passage of *De Architectura* which proposes a total height of four cubits. Vitruvius had given two cubits to the upper part of the human body: one from the top of the chest to the top of the head, and the other that of the entire chest, without, however, specifying exactly how far it extended below. For the upper part of the body Sangallo used the text's indications, but for the lower part he completed it by adding two more cubits, one to the height of the leg below the knee but excluding the foot, and the other from the knee to the penis. To reach a total of four cubits he adds the three *dita*, which has allowed for the thickness of the foot. All the measurements are expressed in the small unit (*moduli*), which is also used in the upper part of the drawing for the proportions given by Vitrivius for the head.

To the left of the second figure, Sangallo, instead expresses the measurements in *dita*, 1/24 of a cubit according to the diagram on the verso. He then divides each *dito* into five small *moduli*, which he uses to indicate the measurements in whole numbers closer to the drawing. Here the lower half of the man is longer than the former, while the curved lines on the left show that the architect is still trying to divide the height of the man into four equal parts, with the expedient already seen of giving a whole cubit to the part of the leg below the knee, and then subtracting the three *dita* assigned to the height of the foot from the part above the knee.

The figures, however (from the bottom: D[ita]3; 23; D20 (23 i 3 digiti del piede); D7+12; D8+5+12+2) reveal that Sangallo fails to make every quarter equal to a cubit. Dissatisfied, especially in the upper part, he corrects some measurements in *dita*, which therefore, do not always match those in *moduli*: D20 in the upper part of the leg, he amends to 19, corresponding to 95 *moduli* below; at the height of the upper part of the chest, measured in *dita*, he puts an 8 and a 9, and only the 40 *moduli* would lead one to prefer the first measurement with which it agrees: finally, at the height of the neck, one sees a 5 and a 6 above, the first confirmed by the 25 *moduli* below. Hence, there remains some doubt on the total, which would seem to be 92 *dita*, assuming four cubits of 23 *dita* instead of 24, as in the upper right of the diagram.

The ithyphallic figure below with arms and legs akimbo in the 'homo ad circulum' and with legs together in the 'homo ad quadratum,' suggest that Antonio had in mind the illustration in Cesariano's translation, especially that of f. LIr, rather than the woodcuts of Fra Giocondo's edition.

The diagram at the top of the verso illustrates the sexagesimal and quadragesimal relationships between the four measurements given for the human figure in Vitruvius's *De Architectura*, Book VI, ch. 1, 5: *dito*, *palmo*, *piede*, and cubit. After this, there are paraphrases of various passages from this and the following paragraphs of the treatise, with minimal comment. Apart from the addition of a *semialtera*, there appears to be nothing to indicate whether Antonio was working from Fra Giocondo's edition of Vitruvius or from translations by either Fabio Calvo or Cesariano. The sheet proves that Antonio was interested in ancient metrology, a subject that needed to be fully understood by anybody really wishing to comprehend *De Architectura* and survey the ancient monuments in conformity with the original dimensions. To this end, in Rome, during the second decade of that century, Fra Giocondo, Fabio Calvo, and Angelo Colocci all dedicated careful studies to this subject. | PNP

BIBLIOGRAPHY Ferri (1885) XL; Giovannoni (1959) I: 23.

U 1253A *recto and verso*

Antonio da Sangallo the Younger

Rome, entablature of the Quirinal temple, before 1546.

Dimensions 163 × 219 mm.
Technique Pen and light and dark brown ink, red chalk, freehand.
Paper Partly yellowed, trimmed and patched, folded (twice).
Drawing Scale Florentine *braccio.*

INSCRIPTION, Recto Top right, black pencil; nineteenth-century hand, old numbering, 957; (Antonio's hand, darker brown ink) *Lo pilastro sie sexa[n]tesimi di br / coie 206 / Lo architrave sie minutij 154 / che sono li ¾ del pilastro*; *pilastro B[raccia] 3 minuti 26*; (lighter brown ink) *minuti 154 sono / B[raccia] 2 minuti 34 / pilastro e largo B[raccia] 3 minuti / 26*; other measurements

Verso Bottom left, blue ink, nineteenth-century hand, *1253*; three fragmentary drawings in brown ink, one plan in red chalk.

The recto shows a section and projection of a fragment of the entablature of the enormous temple on the Quirinal, the largest in ancient Rome, with a total area of 135 by 98 meters, identified by by Hülsen as Caracalla's temple of Serapis. The fragment still in the gardens of the Palazzo Colonna is the largest surviving block of marble in Rome, weighing 100 tons and measuring over 34 cubic meters.

The different shades of ink suggest the drawing was executed in two stages. The earlier is represented by the lighter ink. At some later date, the darker ink was used to add the second modillion, measurements, and various comments. The drawing was copied by Bartolomeo Baronino (see U 4003A). Antonio's unusual use of "sexantesimi" instead of "minuti" also occurs on U 1652A r.

The left half of the crude plans on the verso includes three drawings: one in dark brown ink, the other two in lighter ink. The first drawing at the upper left may be either a profile of a hemispherical vault, or, a plan showing a pier and part of an apse. To its right is a perspectival sketch of a pointed vault. At the lower left is a faint sketch, which could be another pier if the first drawing above is a plan. Otherwise, it resembles a profile of a ramped wall. The probability that the first and third drawings are indeed plans is strengthened by the crudely-drawn plan and the plan drawn in red chalk on the right half of the verso, with figures in an unstated unit of measurement, maybe of the same building. The apse at the top and the angled corners appears to echo the two inks and may represent the same building, which appears to be modern in its planning rather than antique. This is assumption is also supported by the small sketch of a part of a vault with lunette cap. | IC

BIBLIOGRAPHY Ferri (1885) 222; Lanciani (1897) 428; Bartoli (1914–22), III, fig. 370; VI, 69; Giovannoni (1959) I: 229, 334; CensusID 1073033.

U 1255A *recto and verso*

Antonio da Sangallo the Younger

Rome, details of Arch of Titus, before 1527.

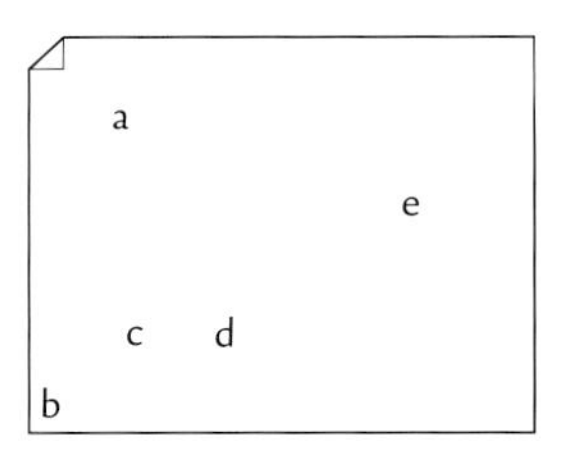

Dimensions 194 × 270 mm.
Technique Pen and brown ink, freehand.
Paper Partly yellowed, central vertical fold, torn and patched.
Drawing Scale Florentine *braccia.*

INSCRIPTION (top right, brown ink, old numbering, sixteenth-century hand) *64*; (black pencil; nineteenth-century hand, old numbering), *969*; (Antonio's early hand, brown ink) *basa che corre i[n] testa della/rcho*; *Tito vespasiano*; measurements

On this sheet, all the drawings are of details of the Arch of Titus. On the left half of the sheet, in the upper part, *a*, is a profile of the podium coping, column plinth, base and lowest part of the shaft. In the lower part of the left half, from left to right, are: *b*, a part plan of the corner of a pier; *c*, plan of one of the piers, an elevation, partly in perspective, of details of the architrave and cornice of one of the aedicules on the piers and of the cartouche above; and *d*, a profile of the aedicule cornice. On the right half of the sheetis a plan, *e* reconstructing a pier.

The reconstruction of the pier agrees with those made by members of the circle of Raphael, such as Master C of 1519, whose reconstructions survive at the Albertina and at Chatsworth. The meaning of the inscription near the top drawing is unclear, as is the presence of the dimension giving the conjectural width of the pier (or at least between the columns). It will be noted that the measurements of the base and plinth are not entirely in line with those on U 1231A, suggesting that one or the other is copied from another source. Given that far more dimensions appear on U 1231A, it is likely that the present drawing is the copy. | IC

BIBLIOGRAPHY Ferri (1885) 126; Bartoli (1914–22) III: fig. 366, pl. 217; VI: 69; Pfanner (1983) 6; Frommel-Ray-Tafuri (1984) 440; CensusID 60674.

U 1270A *recto and verso*

GIOVANNI BATTISTA DA SANGALLO?

Rome, Mausoleum of Augustus, details of the Theater of Marcellus, the so-called Arch of Drusus, the Doric Temple at S. Nicola in Carcere, Ponte S. Angelo, details from Marcus Aurelius reliefs in the Palazzo de'Conservatori (*recto*); near Rome, on the Via Prenestina, the tombs known as Le Capellette and Tor de'Schiavi; in Rome, the Theater of Marcellus and the north temple at S. Nicola in Carcere, (*verso*), before 1548.

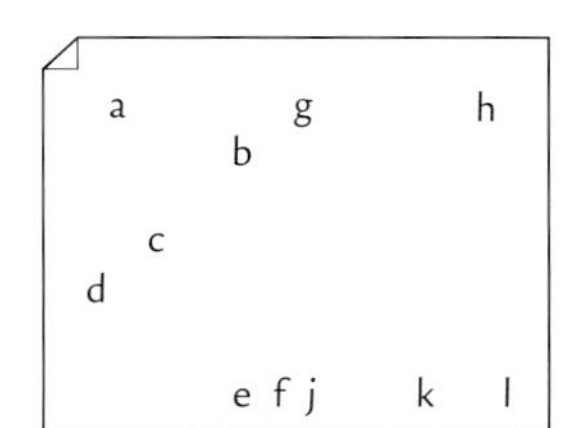

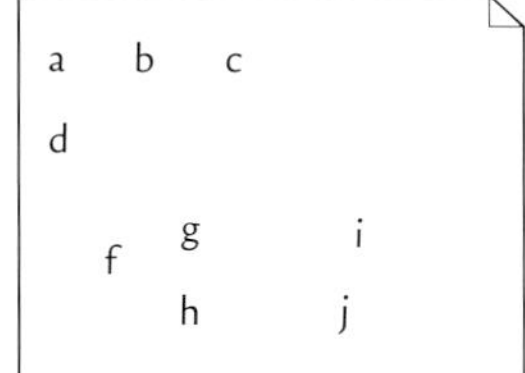

Dimensions 428 × 572 mm.
Technique Pen and brown ink, stylus, straightedge, compass, freehand.
Paper Partly yellowed, central vertical fold.
Drawing Scale Roman *Piedi*.

INSCRIPTION, Recto (top right, black pencil; nineteenth-century hand, old numbering) *1004*; (brown ink, Giovanni Battista's hand?) (b) *Ebelisco a sancto Rocco i roma al mausoleo dagosto*; (c) *dalla terra alla cima del capitello sie 27/ cioe 27*; *Savelli*; *Apreso a savelli*; (d) *Savelli*; (g) *Cornice doricho di quel tempio presso S[an]to nichola*; (h) *archo picholo di ponte S[an]to angnolo*; (i) *aquidotto dentro alla porta s[an] to bastiano*; *Laqua correva qui a questo piano*; (g) *Savelli*

Verso (bottom left, blue pencil, numbering) *1270*; (brown ink) (a) *fuor di porta magiore come a quest altro*; (c) *fuor di porta maiore 2 milglia*; (d) *suo Rilievo*; (f) *porta delle carcere*; (i) *Savelli*; *pulpito latino*; *pulpito greco*; *scena greca*; *sciena latina*

The sheet seems to be mainly the work of Giovanni Battista, with an odd note by Antonio. Its central vertical fold suggests it may have formed a fascicle perhaps of a sketchbook of antiquities. Many of the drawings are paralleled elsewhere, especially on U 1233A r. and v., leading Bartoli to believe that the drawings on U 1270A depend on that sheet, but this is unlikely since in some cases those on U 1270A are more detailed. Here, the Mausoleum of Augustus is represented by a reconstruction in the plan *a*, and by an elevation of one of its two obelisks at *b*. On U 1233A r., only the obelisk is drawn in a sketchier form. Also, among the drawings of the Theater of Marcellus, the reconstructed plan (interesting for including different positions for the *pulpitum* and *scaena*, according to Greek and Roman theory, as expounded by Vitruvius) and the section verso *h* and *i* are not found on other sheets. On the recto, the plan and section of one of the aulae that flanked the *scaena* (recto *c* and *d*) both include more information than their counterparts on U 1233A r. (The two Attic bases, recto *e* and *f*, belong to the aula, as is demonstrated by the measurements on the identical base on U 1233A r.). The pattern is repeated in recto *h*, showing part of the Ponte Sant'Angelo, first built by Hadrian to link his mausoleum to the Campus Martius: on U 1233A v., only the arch of the bridge appears, without the parapet of the causeway. Crowds thronging the bridge during the holy year of 1450 caused the collapse of some of the parapet. It was immediately restored, very likely under Alberti's supervision. Perhaps the part shown here, at one of the ends of the bridge, was still largely original. Yet again, recto *i* and *k*, an elevation and plan of the so-called Arch of Drusus, incorporated into the Aqua Antoniniana, are represented on U 1233A v. by the plan of a single pier. The real identity of the arch is not known, but it must have provided a monumental entrance to the city, and was probably flanked by side arches, before it was utilized to carry the Aqua Antoniniana over the Via Appia. This aqueduct was a branch of the Aqua Marcia, built by Caracalla between AD 211 and 216 to supply water for his baths. The final strict parallel between U 1233A and U 1270A is recto *g*, the section through the entablature of the Doric temple incorporated into S. Nicola in Carcere.

There is, however, a looser connection between recto *l* and another drawing on U 1233A v., both of which attempt reconstructions of the temple seen in the background of the second-century relief depicting a triumph. It is one of three reliefs, all now in the Palazzo de' Conservatori, which are believed to have belonged to an arch in honor of Marcus Aurelius. However, whereas on U 1233A v. Antonio reconstructs the temple as prostyle, that is, the cella wall is plain masonry with pilasters only at the corners, here he makes it pseudoperipteral, articulating the cella with seven engaged columns or pilasters. This is more similar to a third reconstruction of the same temple found on U 1657A v., which is pseudoperipteral, but with only four columns or pilasters along the cella. The strange arrangement of the pronaos on U 1657A v., with steps up to the side intercolumniations, as well as the front, an attempt to make sense of an ambiguity on the relief itself, is not shared with recto *l*, which in this respect resembles more closely the drawing on U 1233A v., filling in the side intercolumniations with low fences. U 1657A v. also provides a parallel for recto *j*. Both are studies of the Temple of Capitoline Jove, as represented on another of the group of reliefs just discussed, which shows a sacrifice. The main points of difference are the omission on recto *j* of the nails on the central doors and the flanking of the steps by the extensions of the podium, while on U 1657A v. they run across the whole front. Since the lower part of the temple on the relief is obscured by the figures in the foreground, either interpretation is valid.

On the verso, the group of plans and elevations reconstructing the tombs known as Le Capellette (verso *a* and *d*) and Tor de' Schiavi (verso *b* and *c*) match a group on U 1654A r. and U 3972A v., where the tombs and the problem of which drawings came first are discussed. The fact that the groups here are upside down in relation to the other drawings on the sheet, suggests they were added later, using some free space. There remain now to be discussed verso *e*, *f* and *g*. The elevation *f* shows the cella doorway of the northern temple at S. Nicola in Carcere, while *g* is a profile and projection of the doorway's entablature. Slightly above and to the right of *g*, is *e*, which appears to be the outline of a Corinthian capital. In two other drawings (U 1174A r. and U 1090A r.), Antonio reconstructed the temple with Corinthian capitals, suggesting that its Ionic capitals were not readily accessible at the time of his surveys, although one must have been visible long enough for Peruzzi to note the fact on his U 478A v. and U 631A r.

The fact that virtually all the drawings on U 1270A have counterparts elsewhere and yet cannot be dismissed as merely a collection of copies helps to throw light on the process by which Antonio and Giovanni Battista da Sangallo shared information and ideas in their attempts to understand antique architecture. | IC

BIBILIOGRAPHY: Ferri (1885) 122, 124, 176, 188, 195, 199; Bartoli (1914–22 III: figs 437, 438, pl 256, 257; VI: 81; Crozzolli Aite (1981) 32, no. 22; Luschi (1984) 30–31; Campbell (1984) I: 145–46, 243; II: 5, fig. 14; La Rocca (1986); Campbell (2004) II: 472; Zavatta (2008) 219; CensusIDs 60677, 60678.

U 1271A *recto*

Antonio da Sangallo the Younger

Project for a temple-like building, ca. 1540.

Dmensions 200 × 458 mm.
Technique Pen and ink, straightedge.
Paper lightweight, white, traces of glue.

INSCRIPTION *piedi* LX, OPUS ANTONII SANGALLI ARCHITECT[*I*] AN[NO] *D*[OMINI] [...]; scale of measurement in ancient feet

In his inscription, Antonio states that this elevation of a Tuscan Doric building is his own invention. Its closeness to the Ionic building on U 4039A dates it to about 1540. The building rises on a socle about 15 feet (4.47 m) high. In front of the central temple facade, he placed a flight of stairs with twenty-one meters high steps. The octastyle temple facade extends to a width of 120 feet (35.76 m) and is 65 feet (19.37 m) high. With their 5-foot (1.49 m) diameter and 40-foot (11.92 m) height, the columns are exactly 1:8 in proportion. They are furnished with Tuscan bases and capitals and lack fluting, an indication that Antonio was thinking of the Tuscan order, whose proportions had been less exactly established by Vitruvius, rather than those of the Doric order. The double-shaft widths of the intercolumnations correspond to the systyle, whereas the center intercolumniation exceeds even the triple-shaft width of the diastyle. The extension of the socle on both sides with no additional steps can be reconstructed in two different ways.

While the orthogonal elevation of the facade could suggest that it has been intended as the front of a closed oblong structure with a total width of about 240 feet (71.52 m) and to have been articulated by pilasters of the same order, neither in antiquity nor in the Renaissance has such a type been found, and it hardly would correspond to Antonio's ideal conceptions. In fact, it corresponds a centralized, round building, to the plan of the idealized Pantheon on U 3990A r., as Francesco Benelli has shown (Benelli 2018, *Vitruvian Pantheon*). | CLF

BIBLIOGRAPHY Giovannoni (1959) I: 24; Benelli (2018, *Vitruvian Pantheon*).

U 1273A *recto and verso*

Antonio da Sangallo the Younger

Rome, Domus Aurea, details of Volta Dorata (*recto*); details of Volta Gialla (*verso*), ca. 1508/09.

Dimensions 330 × 470 mm.
Technique Pen and brown ink.
Paper Center fold (repaired on verso), losses at corner and edges. Watermark: letter "T" inscribed within circle.
Drawing Scale Florentine *braccia.*

INSCRIPTION, Recto *altondo damezo*; *achanto e dallato/ fanno pettorale/ lamedisima chornicia*; *i*[*n*]*torno alemandorli*; *alquadro deltondo*; *alton do/ de lchanto*

Verso [deleted inscription on verso]

The drawing records the decoration of the Volta Dorata (recto) and the Volta Gialla (verso) of the Domus Aurea. The sheet has been folded to form two separate drawings and was flipped from top to bottom as each drawing was made. The handwriting suggests a dating around 1508.

The left half of the recto has been divided into eight rows, with measured sections indicating the spacing of the individual members of vault decoration. Bartoli interpreted this as wall decoration but it seems more likely to be a record of a vault, analogous to the right half of the sheet. The individual members follow what appear initially to be somewhat regular divisions, though in fact they vary considerably. When the total length of each row is calculated the sum exceeds the 50½ *braccia* indicated at the bottom (when the drawing is flipped). The decorative moldings of the central tondo of the vault have been drawn as indicated by the inscription.

The right half of the recto records one-quarter of the vault articulation with additional detailed sketches of the cornice and individual moldings of the vault. Extensive calculations are scattered at the bottom of the sheet.

The verso records the grotesques that decorate the Volta Gialla. Citing such drawings, Dacos has argued that the Volta Gialla was widely studied by sixteenth- century artists and thus very influential on the development of architectural decoration.

Giovannoni cited this sheet as an example of Antonio's rapid sketches made without the use of underdrawing. He also suggested that this sheet was one of a larger group of drawings for the wooden ceilings and associated it with Antonio's origins as a woodworker. | MK

BIBLIOGRAPHY Ferri (1885) 103, 213; Bartoli (1914–22) figs 345, 346, pl 205, 206; VI: 65–66; Giovannoni (1959) I: 12, 68; Egger (1906) II: fol. 75 v; Dacos (1969) 38 n. 2; CensusID 10072736, 10072757.

U 1283A *recto and verso*

Antonio da Sangallo the Younger

Rome, Forum of Augustus, Temple of Mars Ultor, projects for a palace (*recto*); Plan of a house (*verso*), before 1527.

Dimensions 469 × 330 mm.
Technique Pen and dark brown ink, straightedge, stylus, compass.
Paper Center fold.
Drawing Scale Florentine *braccia.*

INSCRIPTION, Recto *p*[*er*] *quatro some/ di legnie b. 40/ p*[*er*] *lasagnie chacio/ frutte e insalata b. 6*; *questo*; *qui*

Verso *La puma 3³/₅ / la luaga 17³/₅*

Antonio the Younger used the ruins of the Temple of Mars Ultor to make a fanciful reconstruction not of a temple but of a palace that incorporates a counterpart of the temple by mirroring it at the cross axis of the exedra. The cella with its freestanding interior order becomes the cortile. The numerous staircases allow us to assume that at least two stories were planned, here represented in ground plans of details. The reconstruction recalls Giuliano da Sangallo's reconstruction of the Temple of Serapis on the Quirinal as the palace of Maecenas; like the latter, it is a theoretical experiment. Bartoli, in contrast, considered it to be an actual building project. The unrelated inscription is an example of Antonio's early script; it was probably written at a time when the sheet had lost its usefulness.

On the verso is a small sketch of an unidentified house. | HCD

BIBLIOGRAPHY Ferri (1885) 133, 165; Bartoli (1914–22) III: fig. 452, pl. 267; VI: 84; Viscogliosi (2000) 122–25, cat. no. 9; Viscogliosi (2017) 101, 106, 108–09, figs 3, 8, 9; CensusID 238815.

U 1287A *recto*

Antonio da Sangallo the Younger and Collaborator

Rome, tomb near Bastione Ardeatina, ca. 1540.

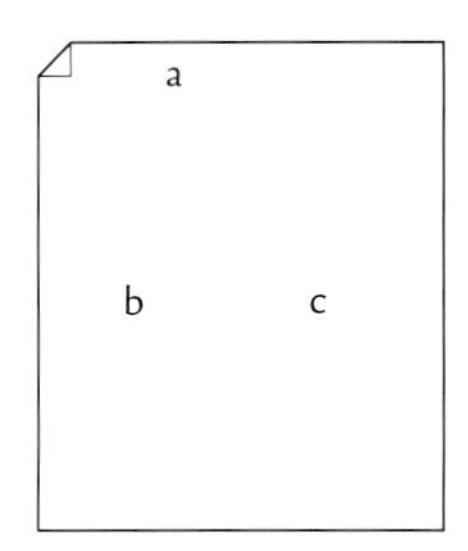

Dimensions 425 × 280 mm.
Technique Pen and brown ink, pencil, stylus, straightedge, compass.
Paper Partly yellowed.
Drawing Scale Roman *piedi, dita,* and *minuti.*

INSCRIPTION (top right, black pencil; nineteenth-century hand, old numbering) *1021*; (brown ink; Antonio's hand) (a) *questo sie lacircu*[*m*]*fere*[*n*]*tia del tondo della sepultura i*[*n*] *sullo / Regolone di tevertino sotto lo i*[*m*]*basame*[*n*]*to segniato A/quale sia diamitro piedi 68*; *i*[*n*] *Dita 60 aquiste Minuti 23*; (drawing b) *Marmo* (three times); *Tevertino* (four times); *A* (refers to drawing a) *Lo piede Dita 16 / lo dito Minuti 5 / che sono lo piede*; *Mi 80*; (bottom left) *Misurate aminuti di 5 p.*[*er*] *dito overo 80 p.*[*er*] *ciascuno piede*; (bottom left) *piedi 3/ Questa ditta sono minuti 5 nelli modani che riesce sie 5 tanti*; (scale at bottom left, many measurements of which the most important is) *Lo tutto p*[*iedi*] *14 D*[*ita*] *4M*[*inuti*] *31* (upper half, left); to (drawingc, bottom right), *piedi Uno Minuti l*[*n*] *o questo regolone*

All three drawings are clean versions of Antonio the Younger's studies on U 1179A r., drawn by another hand but with notes by himself. Drawing *a* is a segment of the circumference; *b*, an orthogonal section through the podium; and *c*, detailed orthogonal sections of the cornice and base molding. The monument is discussed in the entry on U 1179A r., on which the dating of the present sheet depends. | IC

BIBLIOGRAPHY Ferri (1885) 12; Bartoli (1914–22) III: fig. 480, pl. 293; VI: 90; Huth (2015) 153, 159, 161, fig. 2; CensusID 60679.

U 1296A *recto and verso*

Antonio Tanghero and Antonio da Sangallo the Younger

Rome, Theater of Marcellus, elevation of exterior and details of the two orders, ca. 1518 and after 1527.

Dimensions 418 × 560 mm.
Technique Pen, stylus, compass, straight-edge, black ink.
Paper Folded in half.
Drawing Scale Roman *piedi* and *dita.*

INSCRIPTION, Recto (Sangallo's hand) *Credo cuesto dica once 16*

On the recto of the drawing to the right is an elevation with inscribed measurements of the external corridors of the Theater of Marcellus. As more precisely on U 932A r., the corridors here are represented entirely with the use of straightedge, compass, and stylus. The Doric order is drawn without a base. In the central arch of the view at ground level, travertine ashlars are sketched following the line of the arch when in reality they are to be placed behind the half-column at the impost. The same mistake is found in Serlio's *Libro della Antichità* (Book III, f. 17), where, however, in order to obviate the widening of the metopes, an additional metope is inserted. For many reasons, there seems to be a common source of reference, represented possibly by U 930A r. A preparotory drawing for 1296A r., in which the arches have more massive ashlars, is on 1966A r. On the upper level, two masks placed on the head of the arches record those actually visible at the time. The metopes appear decidedly broadened in order to attain a uniform rhythm of the triglyphs placed on the axes of the columns: three per span. Particular attention is paid to the Ionic order, at the left of the sheet: the capital appears with two volutes slightly different to the left and right, according to the method of comparison generally employed by Antonio the Younger in his drawings. Above the capital is a detailed profile of the architrave of the frieze and the cornice. The drawing in question should be considered in relation to a series of drawings of the same subject: beginning with the drawing from the Codex Escurialense (Egger 1906, p. 132, f. 54). from the workshop of Ghirlandaio, continuing with the drawings of Giuliano da Sangallo (Hülsen, p. 9, f. 4 r), Antonio the Elder (U 1602A), and onto Peruzzi, who dedicates a remarkable series of studies to the Theater of Marcellus (U 84A, 412A, 414A, 415A, 416A, 417A, 431A, 434A, 435A, 459A).

On the verso, there is a cyma of a plinth and the attic base of a column. | ACF

BIBLIOGRAPHY Ferri (1885) 17, 32, 39; Bartoli II: figs 337–38, pl 197–98; VI: 62; Scaglia (1994) 227; CensusID 10079186, 10079214.

U 1299A *recto*

Antonio da Sangallo the Younger

Rome, Forums of Augustus, Caesar and Nerva, Curia Julia and S. Martina, ca. 1520.

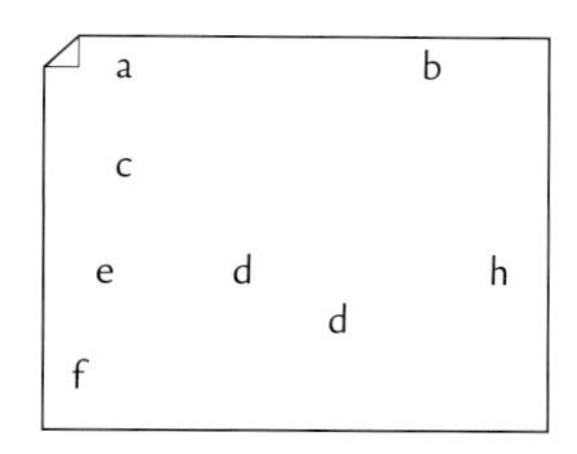

Dimensions 281 × 383 mm.
Technique Pen and gray and brown ink, freehand.
Paper Lightweight, central vertical fold, trimmed.
Drawing Scale Roman *palmi.*

INSCRIPTION (top left) *quanto dall achanto della chiesa alle cholonne* (added later by same hand) *p[almi] 9 1/2 lo di sopra dello archo e al di* (corrected from *'sotto'*) *sopra del architrave lo di sopra dello archo e al di sopra del architrave;/ a che alteza va la chornicie delle cholonne;/ Le sue misure; se qui e volto e chome qua[n]te groso/ lo muro di pe/perigni; se dall altra banda della tribuna* (cancelled)/ *se dall altra banda della trebuna/ nell archo come di qua fornire/ lo epitafio*; (drawing a) *se qui e volto e chome; qua[n]te groso/ lo muro di pe/perigni* (added later by same hand) *4½; qua[n] to largo questo/ archo*; (drawing b) *entrata dei fori*; (drawing c) *chome sta questa cholona/ e qua[n]to mura a p[er] banda/ e dove guardi*; (drawing d) *Dove batte questo diritto/ e se queste facie dei contraforti/ sono a filo;/ o se stanno chosi*; (drawing g, upside down) *(right half) Foro transi/torio;/ archa di noe*; most drawings measured; some calculations on right half

The sheet contains sketches and notes made on site of parts of the Forums of Augustus, of Caesar and of Nerva, the Curia or Senate House, mostly drawn without reference to each other making comprehension very difficult.

Most of the notes are queries to be answered, in two cases with the answers added after. Drawing *a* is a plan showing the northwest angle of the Forum of Nerva and the southern perimeter wall of the Forum of Caesar. Drawing *b* is an elevational sketch, probably of the *Arcus Nervae.* Drawing *c* shows in plan the external outline of the structure in the garden behind S. Martina where the Marforio statue was located. The reference to the column in the accompanying note connects it with drawing *e*, a plan and part elevation of the column which stood behind the Marforio. Drawing *e* is a plan showing the southeast angle of the Forum of Augustus with the south exedra and the line of the peristyle on the south side of the Temple of Mars Ultor, which extends to the northern side of the Curia, where Antonio explores whether its corner buttresses ran parallel to the walls or at an angle to them. Drawing *f* is a plan of the northwest corner of the Curia. Drawing *g* is a plan showing Porticus Absidata behind the Temple of Minerva at the east end of the Forum of Nerva, with the adjacent parts of perimeter wall as far as the *Colonnacce.* Drawing *h* is a plan of a half column and the pier to which it is attached, while *i* is a plan of a column shaft. | IC

BIBLIOGRAPHY Ferri (1885) 166; Bartoli (1914–22) III: fig. 348, pl. 207; VI: 66; Giovannoni (1959) I: 21; Günther (1988) 271, 278, nos 144, 280, 150, fig. VII 34; Viscogliosi (2000) 99–102, cat. no. 1; Zavatta (2008) 101, 103–06, 108, 109, 111–12, fig. 1; CensusID 237320.

U 1300A *recto*

Antonio da Sangallo the Younger

Ferento, plan of the *scaena* for the theater, ca. 1534.

Dimensions 240 × 406 mm.
Technique Pen and black ink.
Paper Mediumweight, white, glued.
Drawing Scale Roman *piedi* and *dita.*

INSCRIPTION (between *frons scaenae* and last *cuneo*) *sono dita 332*; (right, inside room/space) *p[iedi]17 d[ita]12 sono d[ita 204]*; *apri da basso overo/ dinanzi dalle porte D 65; questi due pilastri non ci sono/ come A B*; (lower right, outside plan) *p[iedi] 18 d[ita] 2 sono d[ita] 296*; (center lower edge) *passi 120 colla corda piedi 100*

This is an accurate, measured survey of half of the plan of the scenic structure of the Theater at Ferento and as such it should be related to U 1301A r. and v. by Antonio the Younger and U 1966A r. and v. by Giovanni Battista da Sangallo. The remains of the *scaena* are conserved in quite integral and complex form and their survey permits an understanding of the articulation of the walls of the architectonic *scaena* of a Roman theater.

At the center, the scenic structure forms an interpenetration with a plan composed of straight and curved lines that opens by a very deep royal door inserted in the rectilinear, central piece. To the right, the articulation of the walls is complicated by a play of projections and foreparts alternating with receding niches that frame the *valva hospitales* that, though narrower than the *regia*, is aligned with it. Even further to the right, the wall is articulated again and then closes upon itself at the side, leaving open another passage that leads perpendicularly into the preceding passages. This is the most interesting section, because it shows how the scenic structure is tightly joined to the *cavea* by means of the *versurae procurrentes.* Sangallo misunderstood the vast space at the end of the *scaena*, a kind of *parascaenia*, closed at the right by a long wall; excavations carried out at the beginning of the 20th century and documented by Galli have shown that this was a zone with a portico, which was then substituted with a wall in *opus reticulatum* constructed in a later period (see Vasori 1981, pp. 145–46). A notation, probably not in Antonio's hand, related to the two long sections of wall marked *A* and *B*, indicates their presence by conjecture. Antonio referred to the joining of the scenic structure, pilasters of the external corridor and the farthest *cuneo*, and sought to delineate the resulting triangular space. The excessive angling does not create an elegant result.

The Theater of Ferento was also surveyed by Peruzzi who, in U 387A and U 491A, drew, among other things, the *frons scaenae* as a ruin and as a graphic reconstruction; in the rather confused and synthetic campaign survey U 364A r. and v., Peruzzi organized the access stairs on the level below the proscenium and at the *episcenio* of the theater differently than Antonio, even with respect to U 1301A v. Also by Peruzzi, in the *Taccuino Senese* (Sienese sketchbook), we find the drawing on folio 85 v., where two picturesque perspective sketches appear at the top and in the center, showing the ruins of the *frons scaenae* from both sides of the *valva regia*; at the bottom of this folio, he attempted a graphic reconstruction of the front face of the proscenium. In the drawing on folio 95 v., Peruzzi represented, at the top, a reconstruction of the plan of the *frons scaenae* of the Theater of Ferento, with an interesting proposal of a semicircular *pulpitum* supported by small columns; at the center, there is a sketch of the ruins of the front face of the *post-scaenium* emerging from the ground and, at the bottom, the external corridor almost completely buried. The same version presented by Peruzzi appears again in Serlio, who did not follow Peruzzi's proposal of the two colonnettes flanking the *valva regia*, sketched in the left half of the sheet. Serlio furthermore did not seem to understand the turn of the corners of the *versurae* since he left a broad passage for the *paradoi* (*itinera*) rather than closing off the *scaena* perpendicularly to the final *cuneo*. Theaters with a *scaena* articulated with projections and niches were being surveyed at the same time as the one of Ferento: one recalls the Theater at Spello surveyed by Peruzzi (U 634A v.), which shows a penetration at the center of the *scaena*, and that of Helvia Ricina, surveyed by Sangallo in U 844A and U 917A. | ACF

BIBLIOGRAPHY Serlio (1619) Book III, fols 73 ff.; Ferri (1885) 41; Galli (1911) 213–26, fig. 6; Giovannoni (1959) I: 22; Vasori (1981) 145–46, cat. no. 112; Zavatta (2008) 125; Cerutti-Fusco (1987) 307–11, figs 7–11; CensusID 10075459.

U 1301A *recto and verso*

Antonio da Sangallo the Younger

Ferento, theater, after 1534.

Dimensions 295 × 432 mm.
Technique Pen and light brown ink.
Paper Restored at center.
Drawing Scale Roman *piedi* and *dita*.

INSCRIPTION, Recto *Lultimo grado sie* [word cancelled] / *al di sopra del primo re / golone; mezo*

Verso (Left half) *li archi sono 27*; (right half) *Larcho piedi 163 D 14 / Longo piedi 190 D 6*

On the recto at the bottom of the sheet, Antonio the Younger has drawn a reconstruction of the *frons scaenae*, with doors with flat arches and relieving arches and niches, inserted into the forward projection, alternating large rectangular with small semicircular forms. The *valva regia*, in the reconstruction, is ornamented by an order, which seems to agree with the solution provided by Peruzzi at the left of U 363A r. This suggests that indications of an architectural order were evident on site, according to Peruzzi, who, with notable sculptural vigor and pictorial sensitivity, sketched the ruins of the *frons scaenae* with a wider opening of the *valva regia* and the sketch of an architectural order. Above this, to the left, is a profile of a cornice. Perpendicular to the drawing of the *frons scaenae* is a sketch of the view of part of an arch of the corridor with the membretto and ashlar blocks. At the right of the sheet is a graphic reconstruction of the front face of the proscenium with construction details.

On the right half of the verso is an approximate sketch of the right half of the scenic structure. On the lower left half is a sketch of the *cavea* in *aovata* form, a recurring proposal in the drawings of theaters by Antonio. In this case, he was perplexed and proposed it, presumably to his brother, in the drawing of the *scaena* in U 1132A r. in a note at the upper left margin of the sheet. At the top are three small sketches of Vitruvian schemes of plans for the Greek and Latin theaters. One is *ad quadratum*, and for this reason related to the Greek theater applied to a half-oval *cavea* such as that proposed for Ferento on the same sheet. Antonio drew a similar proposal at the top of U 1240A v. and in a clearer way on U 1225A for the geometric layout of the pilasters of the external corridor of the Theater of Marcellus. | ACF

BIBLIOGRAPHY Ferri (1885) 41, 216; Galli (1911) 213–33; Giovannoni (1959) I: 22; Vasori (1981) 146–49, cat. nos 113–14; Cerutti Fusco (1987) 307–11; CensusIDs 10075684, 10075695.

U 1305A *recto*

Pietro Rosselli(?) and Antonio da Sangallo the Younger

Rome, Campo Martius, Piazza Capranica, Temple of Matidia and Marciana.

Dimensions 438 × 290 mm.
Technique Pen and ink, straightedge, compass.
Paper mediumweight, white.
Drawing Scale Roman *palmi*(?).

INSCRIPTION (Antonio's hand) *Eustilo*; *Diastilo*

The ground plan, probably drawn by Pietro Rosselli, was annotated by Antonio the Younger. It is a clean drawing after U 1154A v. | HCD

BIBLIOGRAPHY Ferri (1885) 199; Bartoli (1914–22) III: fig. 483, pl. 296; VI: 90–1; Giovannoni (1959) I: 43, 50, 52; CensusID 10072307.

U 1306A *recto*

Pietro Rosselli(?) and Antonio da Sangallo the Younger

Rome, Campus Martius, Temple of Hadrian, ca. 1520(?).

Dimensions 435 × 280 mm.
Technique Pen and brown ink, straightedge, compass.
Paper mediumweight
Drawing Scale Roman *palmi* and *dita*.

INSCRIPTION (Antonio's hand) *L'entrato* [...] *da questa banda / dite ante*; (possibly Rosselli's hand) *a questo amphi prostilo sie argiunto uno / filo di colonne intorno di colonne 42 / & di exastilo e fatto ottastilo*; *Questo mezo sie amphiprostilo*

Bartoli identified this sheet as an incomplete drawing by Pietro Rosselli, to which Antonio added comments. Rosselli's point of departure for this design is a Vitruvian six- columned amphiprostylos, which would have been completed as an octastylos. This may be the drawing that introduced *antae* as lateral terminations, at least on one side, into reconstructions of the Hadrianeum, which are also approached here from a theoretical point of view. This sheet is thus probably a contemporaneous alternative to Giovanni Battista's U 1661A. | HCD

BIBLIOGRAPHY Ferri (1885) 217; Bartoli (1914–22) III: fig. 484, pl. 296; VI: 91; Giovannoni (1959) I: 22; CensusID 10072934.

U 1318A *recto and verso*

Antonio da Sangallo the Younger

Study for a peripteros (*recto*); Rome, Forum Holitorium, Ionic peripteros(?), mathematical calculations (*verso*), before 1546.

Dimensions 275 × 238 mm.
Technique Pen and brown ink (recto); pen and brown ink, scored (verso).
Paper Folded twice, cut to form oval at lower right, pasted down.
Drawing Scale Florentine *braccia* and *minuti*.

INSCRIPTION, Recto [...]*ichi boetij*(?); (later hand) *Aritmetricha*

Verso (Left half) *l architrave cioe circa grosso minuti 630*; (right half) *la cholonna e alta / bracia 12' quello si vede*; *e quanto e grossa la cholonna / e quanto e la basa nella regola / e quanto e dall una e l altra basa / e quanto e alta la cholonna cho*[*n*] */ capitello e basa*; *se questo e canalato / dale bande*; *se i*[*n*] *questa banda sono li gradi*

The recto contains the sketch of a peripteros with 6 by 12 columns that has probably been influenced by Vitruvius's 6- by 11-column peripteros. This connection is suggested by the verso, where, besides illustrations of Pythagoras's theorem, there are sketches of an Ionic column in elevation, ground plans of columns, and fluted *antae*. The measurements (diameter of the columns, one *braccio* and 56 *minuti*; intercolumniation, two *braccia* and 46 *minuti*) permit us to identify the monument with some certainty. It must be the central of the three temples on the Forum Holitorium, into which the Church of S. Nicola in Carcere was later built. | HCD

BIBLIOGRAPHY Ferri (1885) 39, 217; Giovannoni (1959) I: 13, 20.

U 1319A *recto*

Giovanni Battista da Sangallo and Antonio da Sangallo the Younger

Rome(?), design for windows of Sala Ducale in Vatican, ca. 1523.

Dimensions 404 × 277 mm.
Technique Pen and ink, straightedge.
Paper Heavy, tears in center reinforced on verso.
Drawing Scale Roman *palmi*.

INSCRIPTION, Recto (Top) *larga da capo palmi 5 10/16*; (below this) *alta palmi 15 canne*; (below this) *larga palmi 6 lo vano*; (lower edge) *finestra che va i[n] palazzo del papa*; (right edge) *Alta lo tuto palmi 18*; (above this) *un quarto di palmo meno el gocciolatoio ella gola*; scale of measurement in *palmi romani* at lower edge

Verso (in Giovanni da Sangallo's late hand) *finestra di palazo del papa alle Sale de Concistori*

The design, the first in Giovanni Battista's hand that can be dated with some certainty, was subsequently executed in a similar form by Antonio the Younger. After having tried in 1514 to reconstruct Vitruvius's *porta Ionica* in the garden portal of Gorizius (U 989A, 1278A) and to come even closer to this goal in his design for the exterior of St Peter's (U 122A) in about 1519, Antonio began to take on a different direction at the beginning of the 1520s. He was no longer content with a fascia frame but now extended the frieze and the molding to frame the sides of the wall opening with a tripartite entablature. That he was thinking of a tripartite entablature is shown most clearly by the great volute portals of the Sala Regia from about 1538–40, where the convex frieze also continues on the sides (Frommel 2003, *Porta ionica*, p. 66). Antonio could not find confirmation for this in Vitruvius or Alberti. His visual preference for a stronger, more light-catching frame than the one described by Vitruvius could, however, find support in the structural logic requiring the completion of an architrave by a frieze and cornice. Giovanni Battista may have accepted Antonio's criticism, and perhaps Giovan Francesco's as well, when he decided, according to his inscription, to somewhat reduce the size of the dripstone and throat. | CLF

BIBLIOGRAPHY Ferri (1885) 184; Giovannoni (1959) I: 67; Frommel (1994, *Introduction*) 45; Frommel (2003, *porta ionica*) 56, 58, 84.

U 1325A *recto*

Giovan Francesco da Sangallo

Rome, detail of Arch of Septimius Severus, before 1530.

Dimensions 108 × 200 mm.
Technique Pen and brown ink, pencil, stylus, compass (*recto*); pencil, pinholes in corners.
Paper Partly yellowed, trimmed.

INSCRIPTION *Architrave dello archo didrento da chanpidoglio*; *foglie frapate* (twice); *fu serola*; various measurements

The drawing is an orthogonal section through the archivolt of one of the arches of the passage connecting the side arches to the central one. The inscription "foglie frapate" refers to the leaf ornaments carved on the two Lesbian cymas. The notation "fu serola" is more puzzling, but, from its position, probably describes in some way the adjacent bead- and-reel astragal. This sheet forms part of the group attributed by Buddensieg to Giovan Francesco. Brilliant (1967, p. 259), writing about a drawing of the same detail on U 930A r., suggests that the arch was so buried at this period, that it would have been easy to measure the archivolt from ground level. On the verso are two parallel, thick pencil lines across one corner. One assumes they made some sense before the sheet was cut down, but little more can be said of them now. | IC

BIBLIOGRAPHY Ferri (1885) 171; Bartoli (1914–22) IV: fig. 573, pl. 340; VI: 104; Buddensieg (1975) 108; CensusID 47338.

U 1327A *recto and verso*

Giovan Francesco da Sangallo

Rome, Santa Prassede, column and entablature (*recto*); Profile of a cornice (*verso*), ca. 1518.

Dimensions 335 × 231 mm (without strip).
Technique Pen and two shades of brown ink, black chalk, incised lines, compass, straightedge, pin.
Paper Medium weight, trimmed along right and lower sides; right side reinforced; top edge patched on verso; creased.

INSCRIPTION, Recto (Upper left, inside flutes) *chanali di cholone*; *chanali di cholone*; *chanali di cholone*; (center of flutes) *fatta*; (right of column) *Questi sono mi* (rest of word cut off) / *dordini di cholone* (writing to right cut off?) / *antique / tuschanicha / doricha / ionicha / chorinta / Antiqua latina* (writing to right cut off?) / *siracusana* (writing to right cut off?) / *frisia* (end of a word, beginning of which was on line above and cut off?; (along side of column) *questa cholona sie alta b[raccia] 6e[?] minuti* (canceled number) *3*; (left of column, Antonio's hand) *Colonna di / santa pro/sedia*; (bottom center of sheet) *la cholona e otto teste pigliando la testa / ne regolo da pie / la diminuzione della cholona p[iedi] 41 / da pie i[n] parte 37 e da chapo remetta / 33 che vene adiminuire 4 pie[di]*

The flutes at the upper left of the recto were first drawn in black chalk and then gone over in pen and ink. Three sets of differently profiled flutes are disposed around the inside of a circle, which has been incised with a compass. The profiles move from shallow to deep in a counterclockwise direction. The fifteen measurements in the column record the varying thicknesses of the shaft along its height.

The drawing was carefully prepared. All horizontal lines for the entablature were first incised and then gone over with pen and ink. There is some trace of black chalk in the curves. The underside of the cornice is represented partly in section, showing one rosette of the coffers. Antonio added the name of the chuÒrch, S. Prassede, where the column is found, as well as some measurements at the top and to the right and left at the bottom of the column shaft. These digits are clearly done by a different hand (and with different ink) from the rest of the drawing of the entablature and column. Toward the bottom of the shaft, between the two measurements "39¾," are myriad pinholes, disposed horizontally, which are unrelated to this drawing.

The drawing on the verso is turned 90 degrees with respect to the drawing on the recto. There may be some traces of black chalk beneath the pen and ink lines, but they are almost indiscernible. Some of the lines were drawn freehand. It is difficult to say if the draftsman intended to fill in the various moldings. It may simply have been an exercise in drawing the profile of a cornice. The profile is not of the same cornice as that of the entablature shown on the recto.

The date suggested is based on a comparison with the writing samples published by Frommel. Günther (1988, p. 296 n. 199) proposed a date around 1513–15. | SE

BIBLIOGRAPHY Ferri (1885) 153; Günther (1988) 125–27 n. 144, 152 n. 78, 296 n. 199, 298 n. 213; Frommel (1994, *Introduction*) 41, fig. 35e; CensusIDs 62118, 10072197.

U 1329A *recto*

Giovan Francesco da Sangallo and Antonio da Sangallo the Younger

Rome, two antique cornices, one of which was conserved at Sangallo house, Via Giulia, 1514–20.

Dimensions 328 × 235 mm.
Technique Straightedge, pen and ink, freehand.
Paper Medium weight, tattered, trimmed, restored with paper reinforcements to parts of the edges on verso.

INSCRIPTION (top right) (17th- to 18th-century hand in ink) *139*; (top right) (Giovan Francesco's hand) *Questa cornicie si trovo drieto/a mariano in stalla preso a San/marcho in roma*; (below) (on dripstone of Doric cornice) *il gociolatoio pende innazi tanto che bate/in sul piano delo tavolato degliarcheti cho me/sivede in disengnjo*; (below) (Antonio's hand) *questo a stare apiombo ello di sotto/pende in giu*; (below, small section to its right) *Cosi*; (near bottom edge) (Giovan Francesco's hand) *Questa chornicie dorica nose ne vede/se none tanto quanto e in disegnio/ed e in chasa nostra a San rocho in roma*

On the bottom half of the sheet, Giovan Francesco has made a fair, isometric copy of a Doric cornice that he had drawn freehand in situ on U 1163A, but he has not included either the Doric cyma or the drawings of details likely to have belonged to the same entablature. In a note, he states that he has drawn everything that was still visible of the cornice and he may, therefore, have left the Doric cyma out of U 1329A because of its doubtful inclusion, despite the fact that he had given its measurements on U 1163A. Furthermore, he must have measured the ancient fragment meticulously again, given that it was conserved in the communal Sangallo family house in Rome and therefore readily available, since some of the dimensions, particularly those of the minor parts of the framework differ, albeit fractionally, from those on the previous survey. For example, the molding on the top edge has gone from 3½ to 3⅓ and the fillet above it from 1¾ to 2.

Giovan Francesco has also added a note to this drawing, in which the front of the dripstone is detached from the vertical and inclines downward and outward, drawing attention to this detail, and he has sketched a dotted vertical line to show that the top fillet is flush with the lower corner of the dripstone. He has made no reference, however, to the fact that the lower fascia of this dripstone "pende in giù," as his cousin Antonio points out, together with a small illustrative section.

The Corinthian column with modillions in the top half of the sheet is quite similar but not identical to the one drawn at the top of U 1163A, and, unlike the Doric cornice in the bottom half of U 1329A r., there is no question of this being a fair isometric copy by Giovan Francesco of the survey made freehand on site. Giovan Francesco does not replicate the information given on U 1163A to the effect that the fragment is at the Sangallo house, as he does for the latter cornice, but he does specify its provenance, unlike on the other sheet. The dimensions of the corresponding parts of the framework differ considerably in the two drawings and the variations in ratio between each of them excludes the hypothesis that this could simply be the result of a change in units of measurement. Moreover, there is a fillet above the cyma reversa at the bottom of U 1163A, whereas on U 1329A there is a fillet and a rod, and there is a fillet beneath the ovolo in the former and a rod in the latter. Finally, where there are dentils in the under- cornice on U 1163A, there is a fascia in U 1329A, and U 1163A has a cyma reversa on the top edge whereas U 1329A has a cyma recta.

According to a doubtful identification suggested by Bartoli, the top cornice might have belonged to the Villa Publica, below the Mausoleum of Augustus. | PNP

BIBLIOGRAPHY Ferri (1885) 159; Bartoli (1914–22)) IV: fig. 553, pl. 330; VI: 101; Lanciani (1902–12) II: 13; III: 128; Giovannoni (1959) I: 68 [attributed to Antonio the Younger], 94 [with a mistaken identification]; Buddensieg (1975) 104, 108; Günther (1988) 296–97; Frommel (1994, *Introduction*) 40; CensusID 10026918.

U 1335A *recto*

Pietro Rosselli and Antonio da Sangallo the Younger

Rome, Temple of Serapis on the Quirinal, ca. 1520(?).

Dimensions 428 × 291 mm.
Technique Pen and brown ink, straightedge.
Paper White, center fold.
Drawing Scale Roman *palmi, piedi, dita,* and *minuti.*

INSCRIPTION (top right, Antonio's hand) *la gola sie l ottava parte Coronarum*[?]/ *cioe lottaua parte dell architrave*/ *fregio cornicie* [...] *p*[*er*]*che*/ *sono insieme p. 19¼ sono d*[*ita*] *154 in tutto*/ *la cornice sie 9 cioe d*[*ita*] *173¼*; (Rosselli's hand) *1 pallmo esse i*[*n*] *se soparttitto in otto parte, ogni oncia in se soppartita 8 minuti*; *Lagetto de tutto p. 6 d 1 m 5*; *I*[*l*] *vivo de pillasttro*/ *da pie p. 8 d 7 m 3*; (Antonio's hand) *Lo pilastro d*[*ita*] *71 e ottavi 21 mi*[*nu*]*to 3*/ *Larchitrave sie d*[*ita*] *52 mi*[*nu*] *ti 6*/ *li ¾ efusto ⅔ elli ¾*/ *secondo questo*; (Antonio's hand) *questa architrave sie*/ *li tre quarti del pilastro*/ *p*[*er*]*che lo pilastro sta* circha/ *piedi 6¾*; *a che fa* [...] *io proprio.*

Rosselli's drawing brings together the base of the extant pilaster of the temple and the entablature in an orthogonal profile view. It was used by Sangallo as the basis for the consideration of their proportions. | HCD

BIBLIOGRAPHY Ferri (1885) 12, 207; Bartoli (1914–22) II: fig. 333, pl. 193; VI: 61; Scaglia (1994) 227–9; CensusID 10079957.

U 1336A *recto and verso*

Antonio da Sangallo the Younger

Verona, surveys of the Arena: (a) sketch of the elevation of the lower part with the four remaining arches of the outer ring; (b) schematic plan with indications for the construction of the elipse; (c) section along the minor axis; (d) (with the sheet turned 180 degrees) perspective and profile of the final tiers of the cavea; (e) plan of two piers in the second order on the façade; (f) profile of a pilaster capital of the second order (recto); Verona(?), windows or niches (*verso*), 1526.

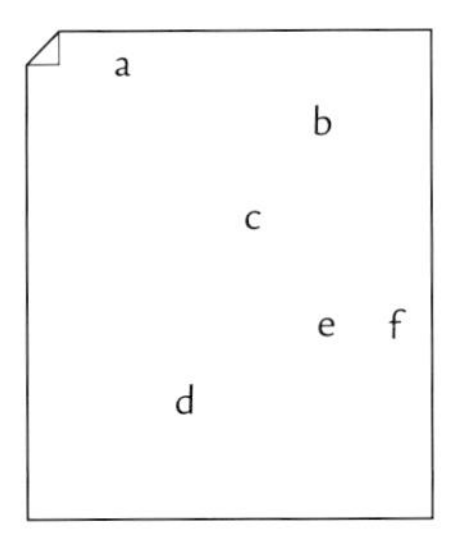

Dimensions 164 × 223 mm (with restorations).
Paper Lightweight, crease marks, restored along bottom and right sides, patch, stains.
Technique Pen and brown ink.
Drawing Scale Roman *piedi* and *dita.*

INSCRIPTION, Recto (a) *Laregeza* [for "larghezza"]; (c) *per laregieza 203 piedi*; *lo tutto longo pie 465 D 10*/ *lo tuto largo* [piedi] *369 D 06*/ *li archi sono 72*; (d) [sheet turned 180 degrees, right] *ultimo*/ *gradi*; (e) *al sechondo* [crossed out]/ *piano*/ *di fondo*/ *di fora*

The measured drawings *a* and *c*, together with other surveys by Antonio were probably used by Giovan Francesco da Sangallo when he sat at his drawing table, reconstructing the section of the Arena on U 1386A r. With regard to the tiers, Antonio observes that the last one was slightly wider and lacked the recesses that make up the stair proper, thus functioning only as seating (*d*). Back at his drawing table, Antonio must have become aware of the difference between the measurement of the interaxis of these piers and that noted on sheet U 1117A r. and therefore, in both cases, he seems to have been unsure whether or not these were arches belonging to the second order (*e*). According to Burns [(1966) p. 255, no. 29], sheets U 1336A and U 1337A are halves of the same sheet of paper.

The drawing on the verso represents an elevation, drawn freehand, of one and a half round-arched niches or windows surrounded by triangular-pedimented aedicules. Though drawn summarily, the rendering of the capitals on the left aedicule suggests that they could be either Corinthian or Composite. While it has not yet been possible to identify the windows or niches, the fact that the recto of the sheet has drawings relating to the amphitheater of Verona might indicate that the verso, too, is of Veronese architecture. | AGG, SE

BIBLIOGRAPHY Ferri (1885) 41, 224; Giovannoni (1959) I: 20n, 21; Vasori (1981) 149–50, cat. no. 115; Zavatta (2008); CensusID (recto) 10075994.

U 1337A *recto*

Antonio da Sangallo the Younger

Verona, drawings and surveys of the Arena: (a) perspective of one of the exits seen from the cavea (b) section of the cavea, the exit systems and the tiers; (c) profile of the cornices of the first and second orders and profile of a pilaster capital with a perspective of the abacus, 1526.

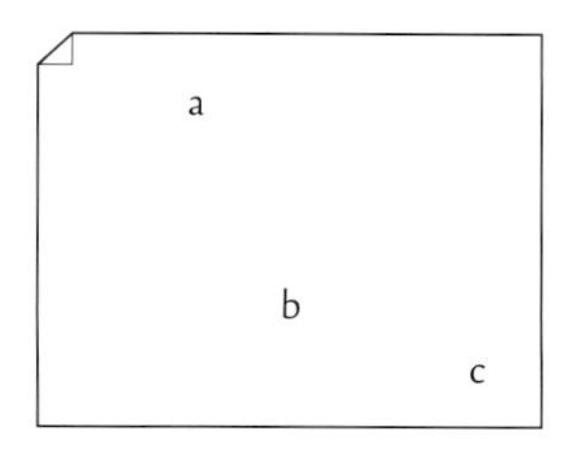

Dimensions 160 × 222 mm.
Paper Light, edges damaged and restored.
Technique Pen and brown ink.

INSCRIPTION, Recto (*a*) *uscita*; (*b*) (left) *da ogni uscita di sopra / si parte una schala / e viene in basso dalle / teste sopra lentrate / e poi da ogni testa 3 per banda / e che ne ve*[*n*]*gono sopra quelle / di sotto e in ne fianchi ne vie / ne una in mezo infra 2 / dua uscite quale dua uscite / sono più propinqua / che allaltre l'una alla / ltra*; *a questo piano / sono uscite 8 per banda / in tutto 16*; (top right) *a questo piano sono in ogni testa / una uscita e poi da ogni banda / 7 che in tutto sono 16 uscite*; *6 schaloni*; *schaloni*; *a questo piano / sono da ogni banda / otto uscite in tutto 16*; (turning the sheet 90 degrees) *pertiche* (crossed out); (*c*) *cornicie prima / e seconda*; (with the sheet turned back to its original position) *alle*[...] (but the margin has been cut)

Verso (In another hand) *Di verona*

These are hasty drawings which, like others by Antonio, appear to have been made on site and were subsequently used by his cousin Giovan Francesco for his own drawings at his drawing table (see U 1386A r. and v.). | AGG

BIBLIOGRAPHY Ferri (1885) 224; Vasori (1981) 150, cat. no. 116; Zavatta (2008) 188; CensusID 10076151.

U 1338A *recto and verso*

Antonio Labacco and Antonio da Sangallo the Younger

Rome, details of the Arch of Septimius Severus (*recto*); fragmentary studies (*verso*), after 1527.

Dimensions 216 × 296 mm.
Technique Pen and brown ink, pinholes in corners.
Paper Heavy, folded once, repaired.
Drawing Scale Roman *palmi.*

INSCRIPTION, Recto (Antonio's hand) *archo di* (*domitiano* canceled) / *lutio septimio*

Verso (Bottom left, blue pencil, nineteenth-century hand, numbering) 1338; (Antonio the Younger's hand, brown ink) *Loncia se / partita i*[*n*] *5*; *Lalteza del capitello p*[*almi*] *4 o*[*ncie*] *5 / Lalargeza del pilastro p*[*almi*] *3 o*[*ncie*] *11.2 / qua*[*n*]*to e dalluno corno / allaltro p*[*almi*] *5 o*[*ncie*] *5 / se Uie ta*[*n*]*to dalluno corno / allaltro del capitello tondo / del quadro p*[*almi*] *5 o*[*ncie*] *4*

The drawings are in Labacco's hand, but Antonio the Younger added the identification on the recto, which has three studies of a capital of the Arch of Septimius Severus. That on the left is a carefully detailed, measured elevation, while the other two are rather schematic sections, the one on the lower right appearing to cut through the center of the capital, if one interprets the top convex member as the flower at the center of the abacus. The upper right section appears to have been taken off-center. The question is whether Labacco has drawn the capital of a pilaster or of a column of the arch. The text on the verso speaks of the width of the "pilastro," but we are also given the distance across the top of both the column and pilaster capitals ("tondo" and "quadro"), and so the drawings could refer to either. However, the lower section through the capital measures the overhang—that is, the projection of the flower forward from the base of the capital—as one *palmo* and a quarter, which would correspond more or less with the column capitals.

On the verso, entirely in Antonio's hand, appear two sketches. That on the right illustrates the space between the back of a column capital and a pilaster capital on the arch, which Antonio discusses in the accompanying note. The sketch on the left seems to show two volutes connected by a straight line, which may be an abandoned elevation of part of the whole of a capital. | IC

BIBLIOGRAPHY Ferri (1885) 126; Bartoli (1914–22) IV: fig. 607, pl. 350; VI: 109; Brilliant (1967) 259; CensusIDs 60610, 10082367.

U 1351A *recto*

Antonio da Sangallo the Younger

Tivoli, Sanctuary of Hercules Victor
("Villa di Vopisco"), 1539.

Dimensions 437 × 582 mm.
Technique Pen and two types of brown ink.
Paper Medium weight, folded, tears along edges, repaired on verso along edges and center.

INSCRIPTION, Recto (top right, another hand) *Villa di Vopisco quale sop[r]a porta scura porta anticha/di Tigoli overo porta Romana*; (top left elevation, Antonio's hand) *Contra forte della faccia dove v[er]so/el fiume; piano delle/meze Colonne; piano dell/a[n]ta di sotto* (canceled); *Contraforte; piano da basso; Bugia; pia[n] o[?] verso/el fiume; piano piu/basso* (canceled); *piano piu basso*; *·L·OCTAVIVS·L·F·CAM·VITVLVS·IIII·VIR·I·D·ITER*; (plan below this) *infondo de sop[r]a.4.p.; alta a bote al/pia[no] del disop[r]a/.p. 17.8; archo; volta alta/al pia[no] delj/voltj desop[r]a*; (under sketch of arcade at right) *colonne 24 dite/grossa*; (across center of sheet) *archj.19..p. 176 sino ala stela*; (lower half of sheet) *Tutti li archj sono 24; archj 18. p. 175; palazo; ma[n]ca* (canceled) *ala volta dj gotia; la nona* (canceled) *stantia/Duodecima; nona* (canceled) *undecima; questo e largo.p. 6.i.; 11 la nona stantia p. 16. d. 6/12 la decima.p. 17.d.ii; ascifo p[er] 4/faccie*

Verso *Tigoli porta scura/& te[m]pio tondo della/sibilla; Villa di vopischo quale è sopra/lo difitio di porta scura porta/anticha di tigoli porta romana*

The Sanctuary of Hercules Victor, which dates from the first century BC, was securely identified as such only in the nineteenth century. In the sixteenth century, by which time a church and convent had been constructed on the ancient site, it was believed to have been originally a villa of Maecenas, subsequently owned by Augustus. Among the several other names associated with the site, Antonio seems to have preferred Porta Scura and Villa di Volpisco.

On this sheet, Antonio studied the remains of the ancient architecture in the northern area of the site. His drawings, notwithstanding the haste with which they were made, and the occasional "misreading" or "reconstruction," are still invaluable for modern students of the monument. At the upper left of the sheet, Antonio drew a view of the elevation of the substructure, with its superimposed arches and buttresses, on the hill above the River Aniene. Along the left side of the sheet is a part of the plan of northern perimeter of the sanctuary, with its gallery originally twenty-four bays in length. At the upper right, Antonio drew an elevation and section of half of one of the arcades around the ancient piazzale, clearly indicating the *opus incertum*. Below that is a schematic outline of the temple with its double niches, which was thought at that time to have been the main villa building (Antonio labeled it "palazo"). At the lower right is a view of one of the upper bays of the arcade facing the river, with a note regarding its vault.

The inscription on the verso suggests that U 1351A had served the architect as a kind of folder to contain the other "Porta Scura" drawings and those of the round temple at Tivoli (U 1069A?). This sheds some light on how the drawings were stored in the Sangallo workshop, where—given the huge numbers of sheets relating to different projects that were produced and kept—a "filing" system was essential (see also the entry for U 763A). | SE

BIBLIOGRAPHY Ferri (1885) 220; Giovannoni (1959) I: 22; Giuliani (1970) 168, fig. 180, 188; Vasori (1981) 151–53, cat. no. 117; Nesselrath (1993) 34, 150–51; CensusID 10022114.

U 1357A *recto*

Antonio Labacco and Antonio da Sangallo the Younger

Ancona, Arch of Trajan, 1532–34.

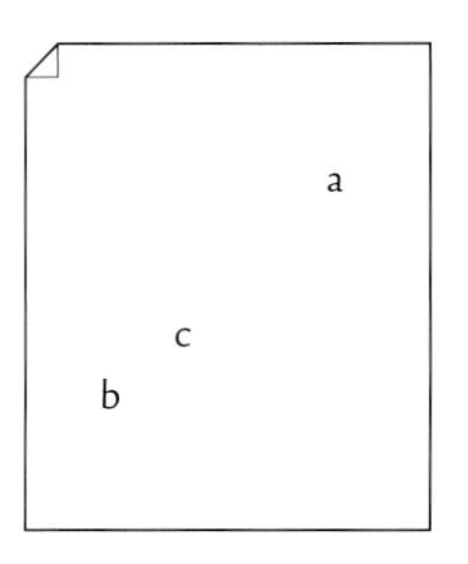

Dimensions 336 × 200 mm
Technique Pen and brown ink, straightedge and freehand.
Paper White, central horizontal fold, trimmed.
Drawing Scale *palmi* and *oncie.*

INSCRIPTION, Bottom centre, Antonio the Younger's hand) *Archo danchona*; (lower left, Antonio the Younger's hand) *Lo palmo è oncie 8/Loncia è minuti 8;* centre (drawing a, from top, written horizontally, Labacco's hand) *lalteza del friso .p. 2; lalteza del archi/travo. p.2 e mezo/de u[na] o.; El quadro/della cimasa delo/Capitelo, p, 4.o./4; el sporto/. p.1 oncie 3 dela ci(ma)sa; Imfra le colone/sporto della colona/.p. 2 e mezo e u[na].o.; La groseza da/pie.p. 3.o.)1 e 1; La colonna da/piede in ver (so) lar/co sporsj.p. 2/ma[n]co u[na].o./e mezo; el resto dela/basa [cancellation] u[no].p..o./5; el zocolo della basa u[no].p/alto; la cimasa del zocolo/.o. 5. min[u]ti.7; Imfra/el mezo dellj zoculj.p./.5. minutj.6; in saldo (?)/o.5./.e. i (?); el zocolo.p. 4. e mezo e una.o.(ncia); la basa d. zocolo alta/u[no]. p. e mezo e mi[n]utj/5;* (from top to bottom written vertically, Labacco's hand) *la grosseza/de la cornise/.p. 3 et sporto/alt[a] tanto; dal archo/in fino archi/travo.p. 2/e mezo; lalteza.p/3 e mezo.o.) una; la grosseza/del archo.p. 9./e mezo e tre parti/di una .o.; la cimasa del pilastro col bastone* (?)*.p. 7/* [...?] *i. o.; alta .p. 3.o. 2; la longeza della collonna.p. 23; da una cima della cor/niseta ala cima de lal/tra.p. 10. ma[n]co u[na]).o. e m/ezo); lalteza del pilastro de dentro in fine et baston /della cimasa .p. 26. ma[n]ca duj.o.* (written obliquely:) *El vano del archo .p. 14 e.mezo El pilastro de dentro col li cornisi (?) delle collone/ .p. 17.e u[na] .o.*

There are three drawings on the sheet. The largest, *a*, occupies most of it and shows the right half and central arch of one of the fronts of the Arch of Trajan at Ancona, excluding the attic and the basement on which the arch stands. It is a measured orthogonal elevation and is schematic, ignoring the details of the capitals and fluting of the columns. The second drawing, at lower left, *b*, is a freehand profile of the basement on which the whole arch stands. To the right of *b*, is a freehand sketch, *c*, a part-plan of a pier showing two of the three-quarter columns.

The drawing was classified in the "Categoria Ornato" by Ferri and attributed to "Ignoti architetti del secolo XVI". It is not cited by Giovannoni, while Vasori (1981) records it without offering any attribution. Here it is suggested that the measured drawing is by Labacco, while the plan and the profile are in Sangallo's hand, as are all the extensive notes. U 1099A r., which is attributed to Labacco, has a profile of the pedestal and basement of the arch which includes the base moulding of the latter, which is not unlike *b* here. U 1071A r. has a half elevation of the arch but includes the attic and the basement, while U 1071A v. includes a plan of a whole pier. It is not clear if they are related to this sheet. See the other sheets for the argument concerning the dating. | EB, IC

BIBILIOGRAPHY: Ferri (1885) 7; Vasori (1981) 34–5, cat. no. 18; CensusID 10071605.

U 1366A *recto*

Antonio da Sangallo The Younger

Schematic plan of the reconstruction of a Roman bath.

Dimensions 182 × 230 mm.
Technique Pen and two types of brown ink.
Paper Lightweight, trimmed, creased, ink stains.

INSCRIPTION, Recto (top left, two rows of three rooms) *propi[n]gare; frigidario*; (*efebeo* canceled) / *leoteseo*; *laconi/cho*; *Cocamera/te suidario*; *Calda / lavationo*; (central room and those to right of it) *Efebeu[m]*; *Coricieo*; *Coniste/rio*; *frigida / lavationo*; (above rooms at right) *apoditerio*; *apoditerio*; (two rows of rooms below) *Coricieo*; *Conisterio*; *propignie*; *frigida / lavationo*; (right edge of sheet) *Conisterio lo spogliatoro / quale si chiama apoditerio*; *Leotesio cioè untuario / frigidario*

Verso (beginning of inscription cut away) *informatione A nos.tra S.ta delli Conti di me ant[oni]o da Sangallo / sampa (?sanissa?)*; (19th-century hand, pencil, below inscription) *Questa è scrittura di Bast[ian]o da Sangallo / Ant[oni]o il Vecchio*

In this hastily drawn plan, Antonio the Younger seemed to be trying out different ways of arranging the various spaces found in a Roman bath and *palestra*, as described in Vitruvius's *De Architectura*, Book V. A circle faintly traced in the space inscribed "laconi/cho" suggests that this room was to have had a domed ceiling. Vasori suggested that U 1366A r. may be related to baths that Sangallo could have seen in Campania. | SE

BIBLIOGRAPHY Ferri (1885) 11; Vasori (1981) 153, cat. no. 118.

U 1369A *recto and verso*

Antonio da Sangallo The Younger

Rome, Porta Maggiore, Claudian aqueduct (*recto*); Baths of Caracalla (*verso*), after 1527?.

Dimensions 216 × 255 mm.
Technique Pen and brown ink.
Paper Restored, corners reinforced.

INSCRIPTION, Recto *Epitaffio*; *Epitaffio*; *Epitaffio*

On the recto is a beautiful perspective sketch of part of the Claudian aqueduct at Porta Maggiore. The rustication and sense of the typical construction material of the Claudian period is made very evident. Note that the Corinthian order is coupled with the rustication, a Roman practice that Antonio the Younger never employed in his architecture, but that evidently interested him for the sense of solidity and strength of the wall. Despite its roughness, it contains the most elegant architectural order. At the lower edge of the sheet is an unidentified plan.

On the verso is a part of the plan of the enclosure of the Baths of Caracalla, without measurements. | ACF

BIBLIOGRAPHY Ferri (1885) 189, 204; Jordan-Huelsen (1878–1907) I, 3: 365; Bartoli (1914–22) III: figs 362–63, pl. 215; VI: 69; CensusIDs 10072596, 10072771.

U 1372A *recto*

Giovan Francesco da Sangallo and Antonio da Sangallo the Younger

Rome, Doric temple podium and portico of Forum Holitorium (S. Nicola in Carcere), ca. 1519.

Dimensions 254 × 225 mm.
Technique Pen and brown ink.
Paper Medium weight, restored.
Drawing Scale *braccia* and *minuti.*

INSCRIPTION (right center) (Antonio's hand) *Tempio doricho acanto S[an]to nichola / S[an]to nichola i[n] carcere*; (within column) (Giovan Francesco's hand) *b 7 minuti 38*; (between columns) (Giovan Francesco's hand) *b 3 ii / da mezo a mezo*

This is a freehand sketch showing the outer two columns of the Doric temple of the Forum Holitorium and the edge of the temple's podium. The elements are only roughly sketched so as to provide the intercolumniation measurement and a column height (no capital is even indicated). Buddensieg recognized the handwriting concerning the measurements as that of Giovan Francesco, revising the earlier attribution of the sheet solely to Antonio the Younger (Ferri 1885; Bartoli 1914–22). The drawing is significant in that it shows the podium of the temple and gives dimensions for the top three steps.

The podium also appears on a drawing by Giovanni Battista, U 1883A v., a more complete and detailed view of the temple front with extensive measurements, also in *braccia.*

On the basis of the type, format, and watermark of the paper, Bartoli grouped this sheet with U 1172A, which he dated not earlier than 1519. Giovan Francesco's handwriting suggests a date of about 1520. Antonio may have added his note later, as the handwriting suggests the period after 1527, probably after his cousin's death 1530. | ACH

BIBLIOGRAPHY Ferri (1885) 195, 199; Bartoli (1914–22) III: fig. 413, pl. 236; VI: 76; Buddensieg (1975) 108; Crozzoli Aite (1981) 26–27, 34, no. 16; Campbell (1984) I: 235, II: fig. 36; Frommel (1994, *Introduction*) 36, 40; CensusID 10012196.

U 1373A *recto and verso*

Giovan Francesco da Sangallo

Rome, S. Nicola in Carcere, ca. 1524–25.

Dimensions 434 × 290 mm.
Technique Pen and two types of brown ink, straightedge.
Paper Medium weight, folds and creases, ink stains, repaired.

INSCRIPTION, Recto (inside plan) *le charciere cioe qella / rimurata achanto a santo / nichola i[n] charciere / lo fatto a chaso nono / preso misure*; (beneath plan) *Questo none buono*

Verso (upper left) *di marforio*; (plan at right, along left wall, turned 90 degrees) *b[raccia] 24½ quanto e dalluno / pilastro allaltro*; (inside plan, turned 90 degrees in other direction) *S[an]to nichola / fattole A S[an]to nichola*; (inside same plan, at upper right) *b[raccia] 8–50 / dal pilastro al m / uro e basi vede*; (in plan at lower right, turned 90 degrees) *Questo fecila / a santo nichola*; *Qello del fieno / achanto a S[an] to nichola*

On the bottom half of this sheet, Giovan Francesco attempted to reconstruct the plan of the Ionic temple that stands to the right of S. Nicola in Carcere, the left side of which is incorporated in the right side of S. Nicola. The plan, for which he did not take any measurements, was dismissed by him as unsatisfactory, "none buono." Above the plan and to the right is a partial plan of an unidentified structure with colonnades and an apse. On the left side of the upper half of the sheet are three bands of ornament, the first and last a kind of double guilloche and the one in the middle a simple guilloche, which is flanked by two other summarily drawn ornamental bands. Ferri identified the partial plan drawn at the right on the upper half of the sheet as of the pronaos of the Pantheon.

On the verso, according to the inscription on the plan at lower right on the sheet, Giovan Francesco here attempted to reconstruct the plan of Doric temple to the left of S. Nicola in Carcere, the right side of which is incorporated in the side of the church. He specified that he drew these plans using measurements, something he specifically stated he did not do for the plans on the recto.

In the upper left quarter of the sheet, Giovan Francesco drew a perspectival view of part of an Ionic capital and below that, three details, very finely executed, of the same capital. The inscription "di Marforio" suggests that this capital was found near the statue of Marforio, which at that time was still in the Roman forum, near the Arch of Septimius Severus. Marforio was moved to the Capitoline Hill around 1587 and now reclines in a fountain in the courtyard of the Palazzo Nuovo of the Capitoline Museum. | SE

BIBLIOGRAPHY Ferri (1885) 148; Bartoli (1914–22) VI: 94; Crozzoli Aite (1981) 41, no. 30; Günther (1988) 281 n. 153; Frommel (1994, *Introduction*) 40–41, fig. 35; Eiche, Nesselrath in Frommel-Adams (2000) 246; CensusIDs 10008907, 10016111.

U 1374A *recto*

Giovan Francesco da Sangallo

Partial plan and details of the Doric temple at the Forum Holitorium, ca. 1519–20.

Dimensions 233 × 209 mm.
Paper Lightweight, torn on left side, holes in top right corner, trimmed on three sides, reinforcements to left side, top right corner, and entire right margin.
Technique Pen and brown ink, pencil, freehand.
Drawing Scale Measurements in unspecified units (*minuti*?) in section of jamb.

INSCRIPTION (top) (Giovan Francesco's hand) *batente dello stipito*; (top left) (*Di Santo* [*sic*] canceled); (below) *achanto a San nichola / in charciere*; (on plan) *lo piano della porta posa in sulo piano delle cholonne*; (on right *anta*) *qui didrento chore larchitrave*; (top right) *stipito*; (in door opening) *chosi / porta*; *sotto, soglia di marmo / a lo batente chome gli stipiti / La soglia*

Giovan Francesco has made a hasty drawing of a partial plan of the Doric temple at the Forum Holitorium (at the bottom), to which he has added some details of the door in section, elevation, and axonometric projection at the top of the sheet, paying particular attention to the marble of the threshold and the fact that the leaves of the door folded across all four sides of the opening and that there was a continuous cornice which ran along the internal fascia of the temple *anta*. The drawing can be dated to around 1525, when the Sangallos were particularly interested in the temples at the Forum Holitorium and the Theatre of Marcellus, which corresponds also to some characteristics of Giovan Francesco's writing, such as the "*h*" minus the dash that completes the vertical stroke. | PNP

BIBLIOGRAPHY Ferri (1885) 186; Jordan-Huelsen (1878–1907) I, 3: 511; Huelsen (1906) 173; Bartoli (1914–22) IV: fig. 507, pl. 308; VI: 95; Burns (1965–66) 254; Buddensieg (1975) 108; Crozzoli Aite (1981) 42; CensusID 10012212.

U 1375A *verso*

Giovanni Battista Da Sangallo

Rome, Plan of the Ionic Temple Forum Holitorium (*verso*).

Dimensions 267 × 203 mm.
Technique Pen and brown ink, black chalk (*recto*); black chalk (*verso*).
Paper Lightweight, reinforced at right edge and lower left corner.
Drawing Scale Florentine *braccia*.

INSCRIPTION (lower left) (later hand) *Sangallo il / Gobbo*; (lower right) (later hand) *Gobbo / di / Sangallo*

On the verso is a chalk sketch of the peripteral pseudodistyle Ionic temple of the Forum Holitorium, although the architect has drawn it as a 6 by 10 rather than a 6 by 11 column temple. The corner of a second dipteral temple was partly sketched in the lower right corner.

Bartoli attributed the recto of this drawing to Giovanni Battista and noted that the words "saria bassa" were added by Antonio the Younger. Giovannoni attributed the sheet to Antonio and placed it among his designs for the Palazzo Parisani in Tolentino, which he began after 1529 when Ascanio Parisani was made bishop of Rimini. This misidentification can perhaps be attributed to a misprint of the drawing number, for the drawing identified by Giovannoni as U 1375A r. is not the same drawing published here, but U 988A r. | MK

BIBLIOGRAPHY Ferri (1885) 148, 198; Bartoli (1914–22) IV: fig. 508, pl. 308; VI: 95; Giovannoni (1959) I: 284–85; II: fig. 292; Günther (1988) 297; CensusID 10037557.

U 1376A *recto*

Giovanni Battista Da Sangallo

Rome, details of the Doric Temple of Forum Holitorium.

Dimensions 257 × 216 mm.
Technique Pen and brown ink, red chalk.
Paper Wrinkled, stains, repair at center, reinforced at corners and three edges.
Drawing Scale Florentine *braccia*.

INSCRIPTION *la porta no*[*n*] *diminuisce*; *peperrigni*; *peperigni*; *la porta di marmo tutto / loresto travertini*; *3 alto quanto uno uno*; *questa era esere perche / safrontano le teste degliarchi / travi apunto sopra*; *A Santo nichola i*[*n*] *charciere da* [...]*tro*; *chapitegli di queste edifizio*; *di stucho*

On the upper portion of the sheet, sketched in red chalk, is a detail of the portico elevation of the Doric temple of the Forum Holitorium. At the left is a molding profile. The center of the sheet, drawn in ink, is a measured plan of the porch and portal of S. Nicola in Carcere. Notations indicate that the portal is made of peperino and the remaining parts are of travertine. Superimposed over this, in chalk, is a plan of what appear to be columns and perhaps the cella wall; however, these details are unclear.

At the bottom of the sheet is a measured profile of the Doric capital from the smallest of the three temples of the Forum Holitorium located to the south of S. Nicola, which was partly incorporated into the later church fabric. An additional notation "di stucho" suggests that the decorations are of stucco and may refer to the capitals as noted in the adjacent inscription. Günther has noted that the decoration of these three temples was done in stucco.

Bartoli attributed this drawing to Giovanni Battista and Günther included it among the drawings that were to be used to record the Forum Holitorium. Günther also noted that drawings U 1376A and U 1377A correspond to drawings done by Peruzzi (U 477A r.) and Giovanni Battista (U 1658A v.). | MK

BIBLIOGRAPHY Bartoli (1914–22) IV: fig. 498, pl. 302; VI: 95; Ferri (1885) 190, 195; Jordan-Huelsen (1878–1907) I, 3: 511; Huelsen (1906) 17; Günther (1988) 257 n. 101, 377; CensusID 10016416.

U 1377A *recto and verso*

Giovanni Battista Da Sangallo

Rome, plan of the Doric temple of Forum Holitorium, Temple of the Vestal Virgins.

Dimensions 284 × 442 mm.
Technique Pen and brown ink.
Paper Darkened, wrinkled, folded at center, trimmed on three sides, losses at right edge, lower right corner, and left edge, repaired on verso.
Drawing Scale Florentine *braccia.*

INSCRIPTION, Recto (right half) *damezo amezo delle cholone*; *dachapo*; *p[er]che no/si puo misurare dapiu*; *A chanto a Santo nichola i[n]charcere* [...]; *colli stipiti*; *Lacholonna e grosa / bracia uno minuti / 41.2*; *da mezo amezo delle cholone / dapiu*; (left half) *Sfondati del tempio della vergine vestale / edevano 2 i[n]sieme*; *chosi vano al piu* [...]; *Sa[n]to Stefano roto[n]to alponte / S[anto] maria alias tempio de / la vergine vestale*; *al piano delle cholon[n]e e piu baso / che la porta Bi 10*; *modanatura della chornj* [...] / *che gira drento*

Verso *el didrentro / B. 2.7*; *didentro posono lavolta / sullarchitrave / chome qui i[n] disegnio*; *Architrave groso elsuo letto / dove posa sulle cholon[n]e B i.3 / B.i.3*; *Dapiu 80 / Dapiu / 80*

This sheet was folded in half and turned 180 degrees, top to bottom, to make the sketches on either side. The right half of the recto bears a plan of the Doric temple to the south of S. Nicola in Carcere. The architect has noted the intercolumnations in Florentine *braccie* (the calculations for the full width of the temple are noted at the lower right edge). The width of the central portal, including the door jambs, is noted as 5 *braccia*, 23 *minuti*. Losses along the edge of the sheet prevent us from knowing Giovanni Battista's calculations for the length of the temple.

The left half of the sheet records details of the coffering, architrave, and portal of the Temple of Vesta. At one edge, when the sheet is folded, is a measured profile of the coffering. Next to it, the coffers are drawn in plan. The central rosette was 37 by 41 *braccia*, and additional decorative details are noted: the ovolo was decorated with an egg-and-dart motif while the scotia was covered with a guilloche pattern. At the top of the sheet the coffers are drawn in perspective with the incomplete inscription, "chosi vano al piu [...]." The origin of these details is identified by the inscription "Sfondati del tempio della vergine vestale / edevano 2 i[n] sieme"9, which, according to Bertoli, was added by Antonio the Younger.

At the center is a schematic sketch of the central portal, the height of which was 9 *braccia* and 18 *minuti*. To the right, notations indicate it is the door of the Temple of Vestal Virgins. Above, on the right, there is a measured profile of the doorframe and below is the profile of the architrave moldings found on the interior.

The verso also has been treated as two independent sheets. The left half shows a measured elevation of the upper portion of an unidentified Doric temple. The profile of this frontispiece corresponds exactly to Serlio's woodcut of the Doric temple of the Forum Holitorium, yet the measurements are somewhat different. Unlike the Doric temple of the Forum Holitorium, the interior vault springs from an impost block. The right half of the sheet bears a sketched plan of unidentified structures. | MK

BIBLIOGRAPHY Ferri (1885) 148, 154, 163, 195, 198; Bartoli (1914–22) IV: figs 499, 500, pl 303, 304; VI 93–4; Günther (1988) 257, 377; Jordan-Huelsen (1878–1907) I, 3: 511; Huelsen (1906) 174, figs 1–2; CensusIDs 10016517, 10017078.

U 1378A *recto and verso*

Giovan Franceso Da Sangallo

Vitruvian geometric sheme of the Latin theater (*recto*), about 1525; Perspectival section of a Vitruvian basilica with details of roof structure (*verso*), before 1527(?).

Dimensions 196 × 280 mm.
Technique Pen and ink, freehand.
Paper Restored and stained.
Drawing Scale Roman p*iedi.*

INSCRIPTION, Recto (on the outside of the major circumference) *schala*; (at the top) *itinera*; *hospitalia; valva sive porta regia; teatro latino*; (on the inside) *piedi 160.0 diametro dellorchestra; orchestra; proscenio; pulpito; piedi 120; scena; scena*; (to the left, on the stairs; from the top to the bottom) *li gradi maggiori sieno lunghi piedi 2½ cioe dita 40 alti dita 22; li minori sieno lungi dita 32 alti dita 20; anchora possono stare chosi*

Verso (top drawing) *chaprioli*; *trasti chantere; muro; questa sta bene; Basiglicha*; (bottom drawing) *sta bene*

This is a geometric study, formulated on the Vitruvian sheme, of a project for a theater all'antica. There are precise indications for the measurements of the stairs with alternatives, for the measurements of the diameter of the orchestra (ca. 160 *piedi*) and of the frons scenae (120 *piedi*). The drawing should be related to U 834A r. and v. from which it seems to derive since the stairs with their respective measurements are identical. It is, however, a more elaborate and precise version. An interesting element, already projected by Antonio the Younger in U 834A r. and v., is the depth and breadth of the pulpitum with respect to the proscenium. This solution seems to suggest a deep understanding of *De Architectura* in which Alberti emphasizes the difference of the role of the pulpitum and the orchestra in the Greek and Latin theaters: "Greek theaters differed from Latin one in the size of their stage: they required a smaller one, becayse the chorus and theatrical dancers performed in the central area, whereas we preferred a larger stage, because there all our action took place." (Book VIII, ch. 7, p. 149 a).

The colonnade of the frons scenae is interrupted along the entire length of the pulpitum, probably in order to leave room for a stage-set according to the modern usage. If this were a preparatory study of a project for a theater *all'antica* for Villa Madama, as analogies related to the measurements suggest (notably different from those of U 845A by Antonio the Younger for the *apparato* of the Cesarini wedding, which has a frons scaenae measuring 60 *piedi*) its nearest analogy would be U 1267A in which the pulpitum is rather elongated in contrast to the proposal worked out in U 314A. There, the columnatio also doesn't surpass the space reserved for the orchestra and the proscaenium. The double circumference, which in U 834A r. seemed to specify the intercolumniation of the columnatio of the frons scenae, does not seem to have a precise function in this drawing.

On the verso, the drawing at the top of this sheet is almost identical to drawing *m* on U 2056A r. by Antonio the Younger and the one at the bottom to *i*, also on U 2056A r. In the bottom drawing, a secondary and casual line like the horizontal one across the central space of the basilica also coincide; in the first the hatching on the lower face of the cornice and the beams, the position of the terms that Vitruvius used to designate the components of the structure, the numbers of the measurements, their position and writing style, all correspond, right down to the note of approval. On this sheet, the notes, undoubtedly in the hand of Giovan Francesco, are characterized by their Tuscan phonetics, by the "ch" rather than the hard "c" that he tended to use more often than his cousin. It is difficult to establish whether, and indeed if, one of the two architects was copying the other's drawings. Drawing *i* on U 2056A r. is more complete in parts—in the ground line, for example—but the corresponding drawing on U 1378A is rather more precise regarding the joins between the beams of the side porticoes and the columns or piers. The diagonal volutes of the capitals are more clearly delineated in the top drawing of this sheet. In conclusion, it would appear that the two cousins may have been working on their interpretations of the passage from *De Architectura* on the basilica (Vitruvius Book V, ch. 1, 4–10) simultaneously and in collaboration and that after some discussion they made the joint decision not to cover the central space of an edifice of this kind with a vault, which Giovanni Battista da Sangallo also accepted as the solution that "sta bene." | ACF, PNP

BIBLIOGRAPHY Ferri (1885) 216 (recto only); Burns (1965–66) 254; Buddensieg (1975) 108; Günther (1988) 297 n. 201.

U 1381A *recto and verso*

GIOVANNI BATTISTA DA SANGALLO

Rome, studies of Baths of Caracalla, ca. 1525.

Dimensions 436 × 584 mm.
Technique Pen and brown ink.
Paper Stains, restored.
Drawing Scale Florentine *braccia*.

INSCRIPTION, Recto (inside room) *sale in una brancha / braccia 7 e 4*; (inside room) *scala*; *scoperto*; *architrave*; (in circular space) *il diametro b 63; finestre; porta*; (other hand) *saliva 5 braccia p[er] branca / questa scala*; measurements

Verso (right margin) *pilastri 14 / senza quelli / di centro*; (top left) *fato questo questo sedile si domanda scapo*; (top center) *sette stanze / doppie*; (bottom left) *fa la sollafami*; (lower right, later hand, pencil) *Terme di Caracalla / e Diocleziano* [...] *fianc* [...] / *tutto questo e nello cortile sie* ... [...] *capo*

On the recto is a sketch of the central body of the Antoninian Baths of Caracalla. The drawing should be related to U 1133A by Giovanni Battista, which represents the final version in a fair copy, including the enclosure. This sketch corresponds in its layout and measurements to U 476A r. by

Baldassare Peruzzi (Bartoli 1914–22, II, pl. CLXXX), proving the fact that drawings had broad circulation among architects interested in antiquity. The enclosure alone is the single subject of the drawing U 1093A, attributed to Labacco, while the enclosure and an elevation of the *frigidarium* are the subjects of U 1656A by Giovanni Battista.

On the verso in the right half of the sheet is a survey of the enclosure of the Baths of Caracalla with enlarged details, including two frontal and upside sketches of columns with Corinthian capitals. At the center of the sheet, Giovanni Battista drew a simple outline of the central portion of the Baths. To the left of the sheet is a sketch of the lower elevation of the *frigidarium*, with the giant order that frames two superimposed orders; this sketch connects with U 1656A by Giovanni Battista and U 1545A v. by Labacco. To the right of this elevation appear some decorative elements of the *frigidarium*. | ACF

BIBLIOGRAPHY Ferri (1885) 202; Lanciani (1902–12) II: 183; Jordan-Huelsen (1878–1907) I, 3: 192; Bartoli (1914–22) IV: fig. 521, pl. 312; VI: 96; CensusID 10072900.

U 1382A *recto*

GIOVANFRANCESO DA SANGALLO

Verona, Arch of the Gavi, ground plan and elevation, after 1526(?).

Dimensions 282 × 223 mm.
Technique Pen and brown ink, freehand, scoring (cross section of column shaft at lower left).
Paper Lightweight, corners reinforced on verso, paper strips attached to verso at left and right edges.
Drawing Scale *Piedi antichi* (see U 815A).

INSCRIPTION, Recto (for Arch of the Gavi – on entablature) *qui aquesta alteza cie uno / pezo da questa chornicie / non chredo sia alsuo / Luogo*; *Questo non cie – nequesto*; (below archivolt in elevation) *Questo archo e dimano / di vetruvio ede bellissimo / in verona*; *DIVETRUVVIO IN·VERONA*; (clear width of passage) *Lovano piedi 11 D[ite] 10½*; *piedi 18–18 [piedi] 15½ [dite]*; (on columns) *lofuso ede chanalata*; *18 piedi 15½ [dite]*; *striate*; (inscription below tabernacle and between the columns) *GAVIO·C·F· / STRABONI*; (referring to this inscription) *queste lettere / anno astare / dalatra banda / dirietro aque/ste dove / e questo cho/ntrasegnio / +*; (referring to inscription given in ground plan) *Qui elaschrizione divetruvio / apreso allo chapitello adua / piedi cioe pie 2 D[ite]9 / edalatra banda darischontro / alchonpagno diquesto dove sie una stella*; (in ground plan) *L·VITRUVIUS·L·L·CERDO· ARCHIT (CANCELLED) C R / ARCHITECTVS CERDO*; (referring to inscription "*GAVIAE.CM.F.*" in ground plan) *equeste lettere quisotto schritto anno / doue eseguito lo chontro asegno / A* (*A* encircled; (in ground plan, at right) *p[er] questo/ verso lach/olonna da cha/po escie fuora/ uno pie alui/uo*; (for cross section of column, lower left) *Dinanzi*; *p[er] fiancho*; (inside column) *Lamezacholonna / achanali.ii.interi / e dua mezi piedi 2.D[ite] 6–31 dite*; (for studies of details on left half of sheet) *fondo deltabernacho/lo* (with measurements); *detabernacholi* (with measurements)

According to Burns (1965–66, p. 258 n. 34), Antonio's drawing U 815A very probably served as a model for the present sheet. The artist here took over the unclear arrangement, the measurements, and the inscriptions from that model. The encircled *A* in the inscription refers to the place where inscription at lower edge, "GAVIAE·MC·F," was installed and to the place where it appears in the ground plan. By adding the conjunction "e," Giovan Francesco combined the two sentences succeeding each other on Antonio's sheet U 815A into a single sentence. Burns's theory is also supported by the corruption of various words (e.g., "ARCIHITECTVS" instead of "ARCHITECTVS"), which may have resulted from the copy. The present sheet is one of a series of drawings, long attributed to Giovanni Battista da Sangallo, depicting North Italian monuments. Burns (1965–66, p. 254f. n. 28) was the first to question the attribution, and Buddensieg (1975, p. 118) recognized in them, and in U 1382A as well, the hand of Giovan Francesco da Sangallo. For the Arch of the Gavi, see also U 815A and U 1229A. | CJ

BIBLIOGRAPHY Ferri (1885) 225 (under "Arco dei Leoni," as Giovanbattista); Giovannoni (1959) I: 21, 77; Burns (1965–66) 254 n. 28; 258 ns. 33 and 34; 261, fig. 12; Buddensieg (1975) 118 (table, as Giovanfrancesco); Schweikhart (1977) 38, 75, fig. 94; Tosi (1980) 37f., cat. III. 4, fig. 36; Vasori (1981) 160–62, cat. 125 (as Giovanbattista); Tosi (1983) 92–97, fig. 68; Hemsoll (2014) 282, fig. 17; CensusID 10029389.

U 1383A *recto*

GIOVAN FRANCESCO DA SANGALLO

Verona, Porta dei Leoni, ca. 1520–30.

Dimensions 418 × 285 mm.
Technique Pen and brown ink.
Paper Mediumweight, folded, creases, trimmed, right side repaired, small patch on recto.
Drawing Scale *Piedi.*

INSCRIPTION *none sta bene*; *a chavanate*; *none schornicito / se none e risalti*; *architrave dove sono / le lettere*; (on column) *achalanate tutte*; *piana*; *piana*; *piana*; *TI FLAVIUS F NORICUS IIII VIR I D*; *schornjciata*; *schorniciata / a punto e risalti*; *porta della chontrada de lionj / i[n] verona anticha ed erano / 2 porte cioe 2 archi / lo pilastro veniva i[n] mezo la strada / quello cha 2 meze cholonne*; *mezo*; *lo fuso della cholon[n]a è alto p[iedi] 12–2 / lo chapitello è alto chol cimazo p[iedi] 1.11½*; *basa sua*; *vano p[iedi] 10*

In this sheet, Giovan Francesco began drawing the elevation of the three levels of the internal (town) facade of the Porta dei Leoni on the left side. However, realizing that he had not rendered the intermediate level accurately, he crossed it out and redrew it correctly. He then finished the elevation by drawing the main ground level arch at the right, below the newly drawn intermediate level. Included are various details of the architectural elements of the Porta dei Leoni.

Vasori, in her entry on U 1383A r., pointed out the draftsman's various inaccuracies with respect to the real structure. While Ferri and Vasori attributed the sheet to Giovanni Battista Sangallo, Frommel (Frommel 1994, *Introduction*, p. 42) —who also dated the drawing to 1526—gives it to Giovan Francesco. | SE

BIBLIOGRAPHY Ferri (1885) 225; Giovannoni (1959) I: 21; Burns (1965–66) 254 n. 28; Vasori (1981) 162–63, cat. no. 126; Frommel (1994, *Introduction*) 42; CensusID 10030902.

U 1384A *recto*

Giovan Francesco da Sangallo

Survey of an ancient cornice with measurements (profile and horizontal projection of the carvings on

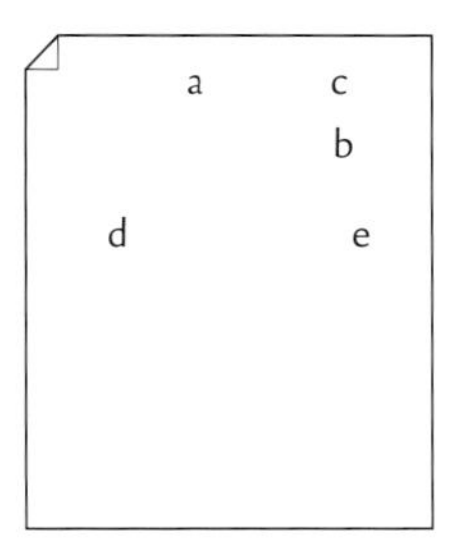

the cornice soffit and on the brackets), ca. 1520–27.

Dimensions 254 × 179 mm.
Technique Pen on white paper, dark sepia ink.
Paper Worn sheet with badly trimmed edges, a triangular fragment is missing from the bottom left-hand corner, which has been restored.
Drawing Scale Roman *piedi* and *minuti*.

INSCRIPTION, Recto (top, sheet rotated anticlockwise by 90 degrees): (a) *la mandorla doue e larosa / sia piu sfondata chome / uedi*; with the sheet the same way round, lower down: (b) *Questo la sima saria / lottaua parte de tu / tto architraue fregio e cornice cioe / 7 li me*[...] (membri?) *e lagho / la i* [una] *chesono 8*: The note apparently ends with the calculation on the right, which reads as follows: (c) *1½* [+] 2 [+] *1?* [+] *7* [+] *2½* [+] *9?* [+] *8* [+] *1½* [=] *33½*, the result corrected, evidently adding the 6 minutes of the ovolo beneath the dentil, obviously, in: *39 1/2*; the sum continues: *39½* [+] *39½* [+] *39½* [=] *118½*. About half the way up, on the left-hand side: (d) *Sulla piaza / della minerua*; on the right-hand side, referring to the detail drawn on the immediate left: (e) *lo dentello chauato uedi / come ua a smuso*

Verso (blue pencil, repeated twice) *1384*

Drawing U 1384A r. was originally thought to be the work of Giovanni Battista da Sangallo, but Buddensieg later attributed it convincingly to Giovan Francesco (Buddensieg 1975, p. 108) and modern critics have accepted it as such (Frommel 1994, *Introduction*, p. 42). There are two different calligraphies, probably that of Giovan Francesco in the letters in notes *a*, *d* and *e* and that of Antonio the Younger in note *b* and calculation *c*. The sheet contains drawings of the profile and horizontal projection of a Corinthian entablature as seen from below. One of the notes identifies it as having been discovered in Piazza della Minerva, and with the same identification it is reproduced in drawing U 549A by Baldassarre Peruzzi (Bartoli 1914–22, II, fig. 277; VI, p. 51). Both versions appear to be on-site surveys, drawn freehand and are probably unconnected (the measurements on Peruzzi's sheet, in Roman *palmi* divided into *once* and *grani*, are at a slight variance). The orthographic projections of the profile and the view from below are not shown in relation to each other, and the individual components appear to have been drawn using different proportions. This particular sort of representation seems to reflect the interests of both artists in Corinthian architecture, about which Vitruvius was both less clear and less forthcoming in his Treatise than he was about Ionic and Doric architecture. In Book IV in particular, he suggests referring to Doric and Ionic proportions and carvings for a cornice, given that the Corinthian style was devoid of truly characteristic shapes (L. IV, ch. 2). The only part of the entablature to feature in Giovan Francesco's drawing (as in Peruzzi's) is the cornice, probably because no parts of the underlying frieze or architrave had survived. The initial survey measurements of the members appear to have been crossed out in the area of the cymatium, the cyma reversa beneath it and the overhang of the brackets in the horizontal projection, presumably because the measurements are deemed to be correct, are shown on other parts of the drawing (projection of the brackets) or they are given as parts of a whole that includes others (cymatium and cyma reversa). In order to reconstruct the correct height of the cymatium, in particular, Antonio the Younger takes the completed survey and he calculates the total height of the entablature, ascribing identical measurements to the frieze (without cymatium) and the architrave in proportion to the cornice. He thus succeeds in working out the height of the cyma as a proportional measurement relative to the height of the entire entablature. This process can be deduced by the addition and the nearby note *c* and *d* and would appear to be motivated as much by a desire to fully understand the ancient "object" as by the possibility of borrowing shapes and proportions from it for contemporary projects. The proportions that Vitruvius suggests for the height of the Corinthian entablature are around one and two thirds module (the module being the diameter of the column shaft at the base) this amount being divided unequally between the architrave, the frieze and the cornice. Antonio's empirical procedure seems to relate more directly to the Corinthian entablatures that were visible at the time, with a total height usually of about two and a third modules (Temple of Mars Ultor, Temple of Apollo 'in Circo'). The sheet is also interesting because of its treatment of the moulded elements of the soffit. Handsome elongated rectangular carved lacunars are inserted between the brackets, which overhang considerably, the wider volute placed on the inside of the "S" shaped profile, and they are decorated with fine acanthus leaves with raised central stalks. The geometric patterns of the perimeter and an inscribed rhombus are repeated on squared lacunars, with realistic rosaces and rosettes in the intervening spaces, in the centre and at each of the four corners. The decorative theme adopted for the lacunars is quite unusual among surviving Corinthian examples. The survey was probably carried out both because of the rarity value of the object in question and because of the obvious references to Vitruvian precepts, particularly the mixture of Doric and Ionic elements, in this sort of entablature. The identification of the fragment is somewhat uncertain. A great many ancient finds were made in the area between the Pantheon and the Church of S. Maria sopra Minerva where Roman buildings had stood since the reign of Emperor Augustus. A. Gatti has established without doubt that the Septa Julia stood in this area, and it seems fairly likely that the fragment of entablature may have belonged to the *Porticus Argonautarum* at the furthest end, near the Pantheon (A. Gatti, *I Saepta Julia nel Campo Marzio*, in "L'Urbe," bundle 9, 1937, pp. 8–23). Gatti's theory is borne out by the "Hadrianesque" appearance of the cornice and the restoration of the portico walls that are still visible along the eastern side of the temple. As regards the exact designation of the cornice, it should be noted that the measurements given on the Sangallo drawing—that were elaborated by Antonio the Younger—relate to a complete entablature only slightly over two *braccia* high (2 b., 2 d. 4 2/3 m), equivalent to approximately 1.30 m Assuming it was equal to two and a third modules, it would have had to be supported by columns ca. 0.58 m in diameter (approximately 2 ancient *piedi*), that were ca. 5.80 m high including bases and capitals. The unusual angular shape of the fragment suggests a piece of façade that protruded from the normal alignment of the elevation or a porticated enclosure like that of Nerva's Forum, in which the columns are detached from the walls and the entablature follows suit as regards the articulation of the overhangs, typical of the triumphal arch style. Frommel's dating of U 1384A r. (Frommel 1994, *Introduction*, p. 42), to shortly after 1520, a time when Giovan Francesco and his cousin Antonio were studying antiquities and working closely together again, is perfectly acceptable. The characteristics of Antonio's calligraphy are consistent with the suggested time frame. | RB

BIBLIOGRAPHY Ferri (1885) 159; Bartoli (1914–22) IV: fig. 541, pl. 326; VI: 99 Giovannoni (1959) I: 66; Buddensieg (1975) 108; Frommel (1994, *Introduction*) 42; CensusID 10029248.

U 1385A *recto and verso*

Giovan Francesco da Sangallo

Studies of Bramante's conclave hall, reconstructions ancient monuments such as the Mausoleum of

a b c
g j
c d
h
k
f e

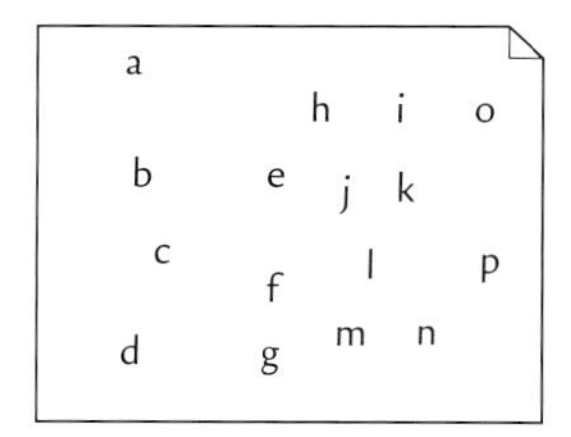

Halicarnassus, chimneypieces, machines, before 1530.

Dimensions 290 × 440 mm.
Technique Pen and brown ink, all freehand.
Paper Lightweight, central vertical fold, reinforced on recto.

INSCRIPTION, Recto (a) and (b); *choncravo*; (c) and (d) *Sepultura/ un miglio fuori/ di porta salara/ si vede una boza*; (e) *sepultura*; (f) [(upside down), *Lo fiore da essere largo/ una quarta parte più/ chella cimasa cioe/ se lla chimasa e qua[n]o/ lo fiore sara 5 chosi/ vole dire lo vetruvjo/ vecchio; Lo chapitello sie chavato duno pezo disaso alo quanto/ e grosa lacholon[n] a dapie nello regolino overo chanpana/ Laquale chanpana sie partita i[n]part 16 c die ditte 16 partte/ lacholon[n]e sara 14 nello vivo dapei e nello vivo da chapo sie parte/12 e choli agetti dello cholarino sara 14 cioe quanto velusu/ da pie e ditto saso fia largo disopra daangollo a angolo 2 volte/ quanto e la cholona da pie [cioe] 32 moduli cioe i[n] sulla linea/ diagona e chosi le fronte [avranno?] l[a r]agione loro* [...]

Verso (a) *Mausoleo*; (four lines encircled) *di prinio/ nelultimo allibre 36 prla di piramide/ e alabirinti e obelischi; e sfigne e pictura e schultura/ e chose grande; rota a cavallo/ abracia*; (c) (all three lines encircled) *L.M.D.M.L.V./ quando si trova questo epitaffio dicie/ Lamoltitudine denemici lanno uciso*; (p) *rota a chavallo/ a bracio*

This sheet was formerly attributed to Giovanni Battista da Sangallo by Ferri. The *ante quem* dating is provided by the Medici papal coat of arms drawn on two of the five studies for chimneypieces. The fold and the disposition of the drawings suggest the sheet was used as a four-page fascicle for a notebook. The heterogenous nature of the subject matter suggests that the sketches, all freehand, were made at different times.

On the recto at the top left *a* is part of the plan of the conclave hall designed for Julius II by Bramante as seen on U 287A r., while *b* shows a perspectival elevational detail of a bay and vaulting of the hall (Fernández 2009, pp. 32–38). Drawing *c*, a diagram of an octagon within a square with crossed diagonals, appears to be a schematic plan of the structure shown in the perspectival elevation, *d*, with a square basement, on steps, supporting an octagonal drum and cupola, which the accompanying inscription identifies as a tomb a mile out of the Porta Salaria to the north of Rome. Lanciani (1902–12, I, 170) draws attention to a description of a tomb in the vicinity, described by Albertini (1515, f. 63v.) as a temple. The perspectival elevation below, *e*, also said to be a sepulchre, may be a similar tomb or more likely an alternative reconstruction of *d*, differing only in the basement having pediments to each of its faces, and the cap being a facetted cone rather than a cupola. Pirro Ligorio drew a tomb on the Via Salaria with a square basement set on two steps, which he records as already very ruinous (Naples, Biblioteca Nazionale, MS XIII.B.10, fol. 163v., datable to the early 1560s). He appears to reconstruct the superstructure as a truncated pyramid, but Rausa (1997, 139–40, no. 33) thinks it more likely was a cylindrical drum or an aedicule. Drawing *f* combines a plan and an elevation of a Corinthian capital which the inscription says was excavated as a single piece but doesn't indicate where. Drawing *g* is a schematic plan of the top of the campanile of S. Maria in Tempio in Piacenza, copied from Giovanni Battista da Sangallo's parallel plan on U 979A r., where the campanile is discussed. The plan is closely related to reconstructions of the Etruscan tomb of Lars Porsenna, described by Varro and Pliny, drawn by Antonio the Younger and Giovanni Battista da Sangallo several times, including on U 979A, 1037A, 1038A, 1124A and 1209A, all of which Pagliara dates between 1526 and 1531. The part plan *h* below appears to be of Porsenna's tomb as are the reconstructed elevations *i*, *j*, and *k*, the first of which is very similar to a reconstruction by Antonio the Younger on U 1037A r.

On the verso, the part plan *a*, accompanied by an elevation *b* below, is identified as the Mausoleum of Halicarnassus as described by Pliny. The plan is close to two reconstructions drawn by Antonio the Younger on U 894A r. and U 1039A r. The seven steps of the pyramid on the elevation are similar to those shown on Antonio's reconstruction on U 1042A r., which he claims may be based on a medal.

The apparent inscription drawn at *c* is spurious, as demonstrated by its expansion in the accompanying inscription, which is copied from Landino's translation of Pliny, *Naturalis Historia*, XXIX: "hinc illa infelicis monumenti inscriptio: turba se medicorum perisse." The second 'M' of the 'inscription' should be an 'N'.

Drawings *d*–*g* and *j*–*l* are all sketches of chimneypieces or their details, none of which has been identified. Drawing *d* has a parallel on U 1439A r., by Antonio the Younger, both with Medici coats of arms, and can also be compared to one with an inscription to Pope Hadrian VI on the upper right of U 717A.

Drawing *h* shows the upper part of an octagonal tower, topped by a pavilion, more likely to belong to a castle than to a church. To the right is *i*, a detail of a Serlian arcade supported by a system of twin columns and pillars. Drawing *m* is a study of intersecting circles which has been crossed out, while *n* shows an octagon within a square, possibly related to *c* on the recto. The last two drawings, *o* and *p* are of machines, *o* being a crane paralleled on U 1439A v., the same sheet as the fireplace *d*, while *p* appears to be part of the machinery of a mill powered by a horse. No exact parallel drawing has been found but U 1471A v. (vol. I) is similar. | EB, IC

BIBLIOGRAPHY Vasori (1981) 163–64, cat. no. 127; Ferri (1885) 15, 89, 97, 174, 222; Günther (1988) 256, n. 88; Rausa (1997) 139–40, Fernández (2009) 36, fig. 1.4; Fane-Saunders (2016) 273; CensusID 252479.

U 1386A *recto and verso*

Giovan Francesco da Sangallo

Verona, section of the Arena and details of construction techniques (*recto*); Verona, Arena: sections of the façade, views of an arcade on the first level and of the cavea, Arch of Jupiter Ammone: details of the impost capital and of the shaft of a half-column with spiral fluting (*verso*), 1526.

Dimensions 289/95 × 441/45 mm.
Paper Thin, sides repaired, vertical center fold.
Technique Pen and brown ink.

INSCRIPTION, Recto (top left) *in piano cho*[n] *l'ultimo schalino / da sedere si è lo di sotto dello / architrave*; *parapetto*; (bottom) *questo sta male / segniato a dire / 15 perché a esere / al pie tanto chome / a questo segnio / che sara 18*; *nelle*[n]*trate dalle tese fra questi pilastri*; (top centre) *Questi zocholi erano intorno a ogni tramezo lo suo / e dove fornischano li gradi* (crossed out) *li 41 gradi e / e in fra l'uno zocholo e l'a*[l]*tro lo regolo dello inbasamento / faceva u*[n] *grado stretto che bastava a sedere che facieva / lo qualantaduesimo grado*; (lower down) *parapetto*; *chosi a stare*; (back to top) *qui si posava lo inbasamento / del zocholo*; (right) *in su piani delle schale ci era cierti chanali / SS / e chosi era sulle schale*; *Tutti li gradi stanno chosi chon questa chresta / in sulli chorrenti perche laqua non potesi penetrare*; *lo schavato si è uno dito / anchora pendano inna*[n]*zi / uno dito*; (further down) *li quala*[n]*tuno gradi sono a dita / 36 l'uno sono largi piedi 97 D 6 lo tutto*; *gli schalini delle / schalette sono inchastrati chosi*; (lower down) *parapetto*; *nota chome ogni grado / da sedere fa 2 schalini da salire / chome vedi in disegnio*; *li schalini delle schale / sono largi uno pie / alti dita 12*; (turning the sheet 90 degrees) *li qualantuno grado / tutti insieme sono alti / in tutto piedi 56 D 6 / perché sono alti l'uno piedi 1 D 6*

Verso (top) *qui chredo seguitasi lo quarto* [i.e. a fourth order]; *prima e sichonda* [an indication that the first two cornices have the same profile] *chiave*; *piano terreno*; (with the sheet turned 90 degrees to the right) *questo 3 ordine è alto dal di sopra dello sichondo cornicione / infino allo suo quale si è lo terzo quanto è alto lo sichondo ordine / dal primo chornicione cioè dal di sopra infino al diso*[tto] *del architrave*; (with the sheet turned the right way up) *us*[c]*ita*; *per salire si fa de l'uno dua / chome To dato a vedere / qui nello schizo*; (with the sheet turned 90 degrees to the left) *uno pezo d'un archo*

On the recto, at the centre, a circle superimposed with a cross corresponds to the symbol on U 606A r.—and as Burns has observed (1965–66, p. 255, n. 29), also on sheet U 1393A—which are all the work of Giovan Francesco. It seems simply to serve as an indication that these drawings all concern the same subject, the Verona Arena. The section on this sheet, drawn on a drawing table, seems to be a reconstruction of sketches of surveys by Antonio, of which probably more existed than have been preserved. By and large, the measurements agree with those on sheets U 1336A and U 1337A by Antonio. With the intention of giving as much information as possible in a single drawing, Giovan Francesco superimposes on the cavea tiers and walkways, the elevation of four of the lower arches of the surviving part of the outer ring, disregarding the fact that they were buried in the ground. There are detailed drawings of the tiers and the seats, focusing on constructive and functional details. Some of the details are concerned with canalization for the discharge of waters and with protecting the tiers from water, achieved by raising the horizontal surface slightly (which Giovan Francesco aptly refers to as the *chresta*) at the junctions of the blocks of stone. There is a drawing of part of the socle at the top left, showing the pedestals of the top inner order of the upper perimeter of the cavea. Some of the notes suggest that Giovan Francesco was addressing his remarks to an interlocutor (*chome vedi*), possibly his cousin Antonio, or perhaps Baldassarre Peruzzi, author of a drawing (U 605A r.) very similar to this, so similar in fact that it could be a copy with just a few variations; Peruzzi's sheet provides a few extra details that suggest that he might have used Giovan Francesco's drawing as a basis, and added information from another source to it. Baldassare's drawing also shows an elevation of the section on the façade, providing a view of the outer arches and their depth.

The verso shows on the left half three more detailed studies of the mouldings and the stone courses on the façade of the Arena than Giovanni Battista's drawing on U 3974A ("A"). On the right half, there are copies of details that also feature on sheets U 1117A, 1336A, 1337A. An arch on the façade with its plan, one of the exits seen from the cavea and, with the sheet turned upside down, disregarding the annotation, the cavea with the tiers, the seats and the socle of the crowning order. In the note, written as if addressing an interlocutor, Giovan Francesco points out that each row of stone seats corresponds to two of the steps.

By the 16th century, all that was left of the Arch of Jupiter Ammon were a few fragments. The drawing on the lower left corner (turned 90 degrees) shows the impost capital of the arch enlarged and embellished with decorative features, part of the half-column is drawn in section to render a better idea of the spiral fluting. According to U 605A v., Peruzzi drew the section of the façade using the same measurements as Giovan Francesco, but his response to whether or not there had been a fourth order was that there appeared to be no good reason to assume one might have existed. | AGG

BIBLIOGRAPHY Ferri (1885) 225; Giovannoni (1959) I: 21, 77; Burns (1965–66) 255, n. 29; Buddensieg (1975) 108; Vasori (1981) 165–67, cat. no. 128, 129; Franzoni (1980) 64–65; CensusIDs 10027350, 10027382.

U 1387A *verso*

Giovanni Battista da Sangallo

Rome, Forum of Trajan, details of column of Trajan, ca. 1521–27(?).

Dimensions 339 × 240 mm.
Technique Pen and brown ink.
Paper Heavy, fold, patches.

INSCRIPTION *la cholonna storiata sia 24 chanali e 24 uovoli / ogni uovolo fra lasua chanale ogni lancetta fra / losuo spigolo delchanale e ogni chanale a 2 fusaiuole / chome i*[*n*] *disegno*; *Questo sta bene*; *24 chanali / 24 uovoli*

Just below the inscription is a detailed sketch of a portion of the capital illustrating the text above it. A complete plan of the capital is to the right and another more schematic division of the parts is drawn again below. Giovanni Battista has not represented any of the relief carving, only the flutes that emerge above the continuous scroll indicated by three sinuous lines that wind around the shaft. An astragal is decorated with bead-and-reel, two beads per flute. The echinus is decorated with egg-and-dart and as the inscription on the plan to the right indicates, the twenty-four flutes correspond to the twenty-four eggs.

The inscription "sta bene" suggests this was done for Antonio the Younger and indicates his approval. Frequently, drawings such as this would be done while Antonio was occupied with a project at a nearby site. In this case, this sheet may have been executed during his tenure at S. Maria di Loreto (ca. 1521–27). In 1536 preliminary clearing around the column was begun, and it was only in 1545 that the column was liberated from surrounding encumbrances and the base uncovered, thus perhaps explaining why only the capital is represented here. | MK

BIBLIOGRAPHY Ferri (1885) 131, 187; Bartoli (1914–22) IV: fig. 538, pl. 325; VI: 99; CensusID 10026248.

U 1388A *recto*

Giovan Francesco da Sangallo

Notes on rules for Corinthian cornices, for bases and 2 profiles of ancient cornices, circa 1520–26.

Dimensions 195 × 250 mm.
Paper White, worn.
Technique Pen and brown ink, freehand.

INSCRIPTION (all in the hand of Giovan Francesco da Sangallo: to the right of the cornice profile, vertically), *partesi in parte 7 come vedi e la gola si parte in 2 / e una delle due si e lo piano disopra. Lo restante / si parte in parte 12, lo primo piano si e 3; lo sechondo / si e 4, lo terzo si e 5; ese voi fare chon 2 piani / leva lo primo etutieni lordine medesimo. / Larchitrave aesere alto quanta la groseza della / cholonna dachapo. Larchitrave avera dagetto quanto lo regolo della champana dapie e de sechondo / gli antichi*; (in the drawing at bottom left) *tanto quanto è l'angolo tanto sta bene perlagetto di base*; *A*; *A*; (at bottom right on the top cornice) *sopra porta piciana di roma*; (on the bottom one) *chavosi asanto rocho*

This sheet is mainly concerned with the proportions of the Ionic cornice and of its components, which Giovan Francesco deals with more comprehensively on U 2056A v. On U 1388A, however, he uses the drawings and the accompanying text to explain, following *De architectura* (III, 5, 9–10) to the letter, how the heights of the fasciae and the cymatium should be proportioned. Oddly, he applies Vitruvius' indication for the width of the lower fascia, equal to the diameter of the top of the column, to the overall height of the cornice. Lastly, he adds the height of the *regolo* above the cymatium, equal to half of the cymatium itself, for which Vitruvius supplied no indications (cf. U 2056A v.), and he concludes by stating that this is the manner in which ancient examples should be followed. The sheet is therefore an excellent example of how Giovan Francesco worked from the text of the ancient treatise, interpreting many of the indications to the letter, some arbitrarily or even incorrectly, and integrating and verifying the text through comparisons with antique architecture. The drawing at the bottom left seems to be an attempt to graphically fix the projection of a base and at the bottom right, sections of a cornice at Porta Pinciana and another unearthed at S. Rocco are illustrated. | PNP

BIBLIOGRAPHY Ferri (1885) 157, 189; Bartoli (1914–22) IV: fig. 542, pl. 326; VI: 99; Giovannoni (1959) I: 67; Buddensieg (1975) 108; Günther (1988) 296, 298; CensusID 10026548.

U 1393A *recto*

Giovan Francesco da Sangallo

Verona, amphitheater, 1526.
Dimensions 289 × 369 mm. (with restorations)
Technique Pen and brown ink.
Paper Lightweight, left side torn and restored, upper right corner rubbed, stains, patches on *verso*, corners reinforced.
Drawing Scale *canne* (5 *canne* = 35 mm).

INSCRIPTION (top right) *Tutte sono piedi e dita*; (between stairs) *questa pasa*; *questa*; (top center of arena) *porta*; (center arena) *daluna stella alatra aesere pie 184*; *piedi.279. dita 8. / dalle stelle ultime*; *pasa / pasa*; (bottom left, beginning of inscription torn away) *rto sta bene*

The drawing is thoroughly described by Vasori, who believes that it was drawn with firsthand knowledge of the building. She also followed Ferri's and Giovanonni's attribution to Giovanni Battista da Sangallo. In 1966, Burns had suggested that U 1393A r.—which he discussed in relation to Peruzzi's plan of the amphitheater on the verso of the sheet in the Biblioteca Comunale, Ferrara—was based on a source shared with Peruzzi's drawing, and therefore not drawn directly from the monument. Burns observed that U 1393A r. was more informative and more accurate than the Peruzzi drawing.

Moreover, he pointed out that the author is not Giovanni Battista, but another Sangallo collaborator whose hand can be seen in numerous Uffizi drawings, and who has since been identified as Giovan Francesco da Sangallo. | SE

BIBLIOGRAPHY Ferri (1885) 225; Giovannoni (1959) I: 21; Burns (1965–66) 254 n. 28, 255–56; Vasori (1981) 168, cat. no. 130; Günther (1988) 257 n. 97; Frommel-Adams (1994) 42; CensusID 10027431.

U 1394A *recto and verso*

Giovan Francesco da Sangallo

Ravenna, Tomb of Theodoric, partial elevation of exterior and half of plan combining upper and lower levels (*recto*); Roman theater at Verona (*verso*), 1526.

Dimensions 414 × 292 mm.
Technique Pen and brown ink.
Paper Lightweight, folded several times, wrinkled, stains, trimmed, edges torn and repaired.

INSCRIPTION, Recto (clockwise from lower center) *pianta di sotto / per di fuora*; *pianta di sopra ottusa e donda / di dentro*; *pianta di sotto / questa i*[*n*] *chrocie / di dentro*; *piedi.30. lo tutto dello djametro*

Verso (Lower half) (left side center) *profilo monte monte*; (inside the theater) *orchestra pulpito scena*; (to the right) *questo portico era al piano dell'acqua poco più alto*; (to left of porticus post scaenam) *ponte*; (at center) *fiume in dir.*; (lower left) *nel fregio dolivo*...[?] *Nel fregio erano nelle fuora della scena sopra una porta del teatro* (Top half, turned 180 degrees) *reticulata*; (to side of profile of Corinthian capital) *chapitello*; (to right) *imposte*; (below profile) *lordine chore chosi, quadri sfondati, altra sfondatura e per uno grande chosi una sfondatura*

This drawing is a freehand copy of U 1406A by Antonio the Younger. The inscriptions are in the same locations on the sheet, but the measurements expressed in Roman numerals on U 1406A have here been translated into Arabic numerals. Ferri, Giovannoni, and Heidenreich-Johannes associated U 1394A r. with Giovanni Battista da Sangallo, whereas Frommel has attributed it to Giovan Francesco.

The two freehand drawings on the verso (only on the left half of the sheet) of the plan, profile of the steps, and partial front of the scaena are highly interesting for the artist's capacity for recreating and comprehending the structure and function of the theater at Verona, based on the Vitruvian model, with a few variations. The colonnade of the frons scaenae corresponds to the diameter of the orchestra. The portico at the top (of which the columns are drawn) traces the semi-oval form of the theater. The cavea and orchestra follow the same curved line, inside which the pulpitum advances for about one third. The rear of the stage building marks the back of the theater, giving it the characteristic horseshoe shape described by Leon Battista Alberti. The theater is linked to the river by way of a Vitruvian porticus post scaenam, which contains the access stairs. Two bridges lead to the rectangular spaces with double colonnades placed symmetrically to the right and left of the theater. A hasty sketch of a section of the steps up the slope shows the sounding vessels within, according to the recommendations of Vitruvius.

The drawings at the top, turned 180 degrees, show an elevation of the rear of the scaena. The wall is articulated with a colonnade in front of pillars with lintels and is closed with opus reticulatum, which also appears in the profile of the plan drawn above.

The verso shows, all on the left side of the sheet, freehand sketches of a plan, profile of the steps and partial front of the scene. These two drawings are very interesting for the graphic restitution and the understanding of the structural and functional organism of the theater of Verona, reconstructed on the Vitruvian model, with some variations. The *columnatio* of the *frons scaenae* is identified with the diameter line of the orchestra. The *porticus in summa gradatione* (on which the columns are marked) traces the semi-oval shape of the theater. Inside the same line runs the area of the *cavea* and the *orchestra*, within which the pulpit advances by about a third. Then follows the *frons scaena* whose back wall delimits the building, giving it the characteristic horseshoe shape, theorized by Leon Battista Alberti. The theater itself is related to the river through a *porticus post scaenam* of Vitruvian reminiscence, inside which are arranged the access stairs, while two bridges constitute the access to the rectangular porticoed rooms. Two rooms symmetrically arranged, with double porticoes flank on the right and left the theater building. A brief sketch of the section of the steps, lying on the slope, shows the inserted resonating vases, according to the instructions of Vitruvius.

On the upper side, turned 180 degrees, the sheet shows a study of the elevation of the back of the *frons scaenae*: the wall is articulated plastically by columns that frame large pilasters connected to each other with flat bands, buffered with opus reticulatum. The profile of the structure also appears in the ground plan. | SE, ACF

BIBLIOGRAPHY Ferri (1885) 121, 216; Giovannoni (1959) I: 22; Burns (1965–66) 254–55; Heidenreich-Johannes (1971) 110; Buddensieg (1975) 108; Vasori (1981) 168–72, cat. no. 131; Frommel (1994, *Introduction*) 42; Zavatta (2008) 38–9, 41, 66, 144, 147, 164, 172–76, 181, 183, 187, 195, 249; CensusIDs 66984, 10027166.

U 1402A *recto and verso*

Giovanni Battista da Sangallo

Rome, Forum Transitorium, elevation of the "recinto," intercolumnation of the pronaos of Doric temple (*recto*); measured details of Temple of Antoninus and Faustina (*verso*).

Dimensions 143 × 218 mm.
Technique Pen and brown ink.
Paper Extensive losses at upper edge.

INSCRIPTION, Recto and Verso Various measurements

According to Bartoli, the upper half of the recto of this sheet is an elevation of the enclosing wall of the Forum Transitorium. Bartoli identified the drawing along the lower edge as a diagram of the intercolumnation of the Doric temple of the Forum Transitorium. However, this sketch may be a measured diagram of the enclosing wall.

Giovanni Battista penned a schematic profile of the fluted Doric order with the triglyph and metope frieze above. Günther suggested that this is one of several drawings that reconstruct the Doric frieze originally decorated with stucco. Although the unit of measure is not indicated, the intercolumnations measure 100 units, whereas the central intercolumnation is 150 units. Each metope measures 30 units and each triglyph 20 units. The measurement of the intercolumnation to the far left has been changed from 100 to 90 units, whereas the members of the frieze remain the same. The diameter of the columns is 40 units.

The left half of the verso shows a detail of what may be stucco decoration and at the left edge is a plan that may represent the height of the decorative motif. The right half of the sheet shows the profile of the Doric architrave, including a plumb line. A second architrave has been drawn directly below, in reverse. Both sketches perhaps should be associated with the recto drawing. Bartoli suggested that these sketches are measured drawings of details of the Temple of Antoninus and Faustina. Barely visible in the upper right corner is a fragment of what might have been a sketch of a Corinthian capital. | MK

BIBLIOGRAPHY Ferri (1885) 31, 39; Bartoli (1914–22) IV: figs 514, 515, pl. 309; VI: 95–6; Giovannoni (1959) I: 21; Günther (1988) 313; Viscogliosi (2000) 205–6, cat. 59; Viscogliosi (2017) 112; CensusIDs 241696, 10072546.

U 1404A *recto*

Antonio Labacco for Antonio da Sangallo the Younger

Rome, Doric temple of Forum Holitorium.

Dimensions 153 × 235 mm.
Technique Pen and brown ink.
Paper Stains, corners reinforced, trimmed.

On this sheet, Labacco sketched the corner of the Doric temple of the Forum Holitorium. To the right is a detail of the portal. The study might be a preliminary sketch for U 3965A. | MK

BIBLIOGRAPHY Ferri (1885) 39; Bartoli (1914–22) IV: fig. 605, pl. 350; VI: 109; Crozzoli Aite (1981) 43; CensusID 10015527.

U 1407A *recto*

Unidentified Sixteenth-Century Hand, Possibly Pietro Rosselli

Rome, Campo Marzio, Temple of Hadrian, ca. 1520.

Dimensions 336 × 279 mm.
Technique Pen and brown ink, scored, straightedge.
Paper Heavy, cut out and glued, left side missing.
Drawing Scale *Piedi* and *minuti*.

INSCRIPTION [...] *O DA SANGALLO / ARCHITET; Questo difi/zio e alla pi/aza de preti*

As the inscription at the lower left indicates, the drawing was ascribed to either Antonio da Sangallo the Elder or Antonio the Younger at one point.

The sheet brings together a detailed elevation of the main entablature of the exterior order (upper left) of the

Hadrianeum, a related cross section and ground plan of the console geison (lower left), and a reconstruction of half the front without a gable (lower left). No comparable exact clean drawing by Antonio the Younger is known.

Moreover, the script is by another hand. The different forms of the architraves of the interior (3 fasciae) and exterior (2 fasciae) are taken into account. Measurements are given for the column axis, 17 *piedi* 15 *minuti*, the height of the capital, 7 *piedi* 26 *minuti*, and the height of the base, 3 *piedi* 37 *minuti*. | HCD

BIBLIOGRAPHY Ferri (1885) 196; Jordan-Huelsen (1878–1907) I, 3: 609; Bartoli (1914–22) I: fig. 155, pl. 87; VI: 32; Cozza (1982) 18–19, fig. 20; CensusID 249474.

U 1409A *recto*

Antonio da Sangallo the Younger

Comparisons of various indications by Vitruvius on proportions of columns, before 1525–26.

Dimensions 413 × 288 mm.
Paper Medium weight, poor condition, trimmed, many repairs to right margin, reinforcements to part of bottom edge, integral reinforcements to other sides.
Technique Fine pen and brown ink, freehand over preparation with straightedge and stylus.

INSCRIPTION (top right, under shaft of a column) (Antonio's hand) *qui*; (below) *alli capitelli/ Dorici/ Ionici/ Corinti/ allintercolunnij/ allaltezza delle colonne/ alli architrave e corona; alla base/ allalteza e agietto*; (from left, to left of first Doric column) *per li templi moduli 14*; (to right of latter) *per li teatri moduli 15*; (on next column) *e pigliare nel vivo 8½ lo fuso solo per li teatri*; (on Ionic column) *e pigliare nel vivo lo fuso solo per li teatri*; (to left of fifth column) *A pigliare nello regolino 8½/ col capitello e basa per li templi*; (to right of same column) *moduli 15 per li teatri*; (middle of bottom margin) *Liiij*

Sheet U 1409 r. has been dedicated entirely to the study of *De Architectura*. On the verso (see entry in vol. I), there are references to Book X on machines, Book VIII on *il coronate*, Book V with a sketch of a basilica, and to the terms "pronao" and "pteromatos," taken from Book III. The main subject of the recto is a comparison of the differing proportions of the various types of columns as prescribed by Vitruvius, first for temples and then for theatres. Antonio has aligned the bottom ends of the column shafts along a horizontal line, underneath which he has added Attic bases to the four Ionic columns in the center, making a graphic representation of the proportions of the columns with their respective capitals. In addition to this group, there is a reduced drawing at the top left showing the top and bottom ends of a column, at the top right there are two column shafts, in the bottom right margin there is a pedestal with an Attic base, and below that a proportional scheme of a Doric capital. The sheet is testament to Antonio's assiduous comparison of the indications given for the proportions of columns, which vary according to context, in order to determine clearly defined rules which he can then put into practice. | PNP

BIBLIOGRAPHY Ferri (1885) 29; Giovannoni (1959) I: 23; Günther (1988) 187, 298.

U 1410A *recto*

Unidentifiend Sixteenth-Century Hand, Possibly Pietro Rosselli, and Antonio da Sangallo the Younger

Unknown monument, entablature, first quarter of sixteenth century(?).

Dimensions 107 × 408 mm.
Technique Pen and brown ink, wash.
Paper Heavy.
Drawing Scale *palmi* and *minuti*.

INSCRIPTION (Antonio's hand?) *Queste dista[n]tie non sono uguali sono come qui si vede*

This precise drawing seems to have been made by the same hand as that of U 1407A r. If its inscription is in fact by Antonio the Younger, it would indicate that the sheet was part of his collection of drawings. The ground plan of a console geison seen from below belongs to a Corinthian entablature. The consoles are decorated with acanthus leaves. | HCD

BIBLIOGRAPHY Ferri (1885) 32; Bartoli (1914–22) I: fig. 156, pl. 87; VI: 32; CensusID 10012636.

U 1413A *recto and verso*

Antonio da Sangallo the Younger

Rome, Forum Romanum, Basilica Aemilia, profile of a base, capital of a pilaster, architrave and frieze (*recto*); Basilica Aemilia, views of an entablature (*verso*), ca. 1508(?).

Dimensions 332 × 236 mm.
Technique Pencil, pen and brown ink, straightedge, compass (recto); pencil, pen and gray-black ink (verso).
Paper Heavy.
Drawing Scale *Minuti.*

INSCRIPTION, Recto *125 collagetto*; *pilastro – 80*; *pilastro a chanali / la meza cholonna a 13 chanali*; *92 alto / 80 la* [...]; *fregio e arcitrave sta cosi*; *al piatto sta cosi modanato*;
Verso *quadro sfondato*; *cornicione di foro in bouarum*; *lacolonna a grossa 80 minuti da chapo; minuto*; *lacitraue 59⅓*; *fregio 95*; *cornicione 88*

The capital and base on the recto are probably copied from a drawing in Codex Barberini (Huelsen 1910, fol. 71 v.), as the measurements are similar. The model in the Codex Barberini, where the capital is incompletely drawn, may explain why Antonio drew the egg-and-dart molding of the capital with too many eggs. In contrast to the perspective view of the capital, the architrave and triglyph-and-metope frieze of the entablature are shown in orthogonal top view. Antonio possibly saw the original fragments, which at that time were might have already been in the Palazzo Giraud (see Frommel 1973, II, p. 207 n. 1).

Such minute measurements (for instance, of the height of the lower fasciae, 19⅓ *minuti*) are unparalleled elsewhere, while the relief decoration of the metopes, patera, and bucranium is only sketchily indicated.

The verso shows an axonometric view of the entablature seen from below, extending from the abacus of the capital of an engaged column to the sima. The choice of motif seems to have been inspired by a direct comparison with a drawing in the Codex Coner (Ashby 1904, fol. 61 r.). But how different these drawings are! In contrast to Bernardo della Volpaia, the presumed draftsman of the Codex Coner, Antonio achieved a decided spatial effect, showing every detail up to the taenia. He furthermore preferred not to use a simple sectional plane as a starting point for his axonometrical view; instead, he allowed a metope to project, so that Bernardo's strict schematic character is masked. While Bernardo's entablature is carried by a pilaster, Antonio put an engaged column and next to it, toward the cross section, even added the rectangular concluding wall ending in a convex molding. Antonio's confident sketch has the effect of putting us before the actual ruin. If the ruin had in fact already been torn down by Antonio's day, his artistic achievement is even more impressive. His strong feeling for haptic and spatial values is best revealed by his drawings for the Palazzo Farnese. For the datation see Frommel (1994, *Introduction*, p. 22). | HCD

BIBLIOGRAPHY Ferri (1885) 166; Huelsen (1884) 326, 329, 331, 333, 335, 339, 341–45; Huelsen (1910) 76, pl. R; Bartoli (1914–22) III: figs 391, 392, pl. 278; VI: 73. Frommel (1994, *Introduction*) 22; Benelli (2014, *Tempio*) 178; Hemsoll (2014) 287, fig. 25; CensusIDs 239630, 239653.

U 1414A *recto and verso*

Antonio da Sangallo the Younger

Ostia, the so-called Temple of Portunus (*recto*); Ostia, so-called Temple of Portunus; Albano, so-called Tomb of Horatii; Via Appia Antica, tomb near S. Sebastiano (*verso*).

Dimensions 335 × 227 mm.
Technique Pen and brown ink, brown wash, stylus and compass, freehand.
Paper Tear at left edge.
Drawing Scale Roman *palmi* (?) *(recto)*, Florentine *braccia (verso)*.

INSCRIPTION, Recto *di drento*; *queste la pianta di sotto di questo tenpio*; *tanto alto quanto largo / al di drento*; *queste quella di sopra*; (lighter ink, another hand) *a porto dostja*

Verso (bottom left, blue pencil, nineteenth-century hand, numbering, 1414; Antonio's hand, dark brown ink, top left) *pianta di sotto / deltenpio da porto / dostia*; (top right) *3 quadri*; *una sepultura fuora / della porta a S. Sa*[*nto*] *bastiano / .12. miglia*; *channe .3 larga / alta ancora .3. cioe queste quadro sanza la pirramide*; *3*; (on lower plan) *Vna sepultura a santo bastiano*; *b*[*raccia*] *20i*[*n*] *tutto*

The drawing on the recto shows a section, two plans, and a detail of the so-called Temple of Portunus, datable by its brickwork to the third century AD. Its function is uncertain but it resembles late antique imperial mausolea. In later antiquity, it was converted to a church dedicated to St Peter and St Paul.

The perspectival section at the top shows a circular domed cella, the wall punctuated by niches, alternately semicircular and rectangular in plan, which is confirmed by the extant part of the cella that contains two such niches, but it is likely that most of Antonio's drawing is a reconstruction, since the only measurement he gave is the height of the podium. The internal decoration of the dome and the external balustrade suggest knowledge of Giuliano da Sangallo's reconstruction (Barb. lat. 4424, fol. 37; Huelsen 1910, I, p. 54), but Antonio added, freehand and in a darker ink, an exterior peristyle, possibly in response to a plan by Baldassare Peruzzi (U 538A; Vasori 1981, p. 66, no. 48), which provides more measurements. Though it is likely that any columns had been removed as spolia long before, the imprints of their bases on the podium testify to the presence of the peristyle. What is unlikely is that the peristyle was an arcade rather than a trabeated colonnade but the detail at the bottom left, an elevation of arches springing from a capital, seems to support this possibility.

The lower half of the sheet has a plan of the superstructure of the monument to the same scale as the perspective, agreeing in all respects, while within it is drawn, to a smaller scale, the plan of the basement, more accurate in its details than its counterpart by Peruzzi (see above). For a dating to about 1506–07 see Frommel (1994, *Introduction*, pp. 16–17), and Frommel (in this vol., p. 20).

On the verso, the two freehand sketches in dark brown ink, at the upper part of the sheet, were probably added at the same time as the peristyle to the plan on the recto. The annotation on the plan at the top left indicates that it is the lower part of the so-called Temple of Portunus at Porto, but it differs greatly from that on the recto. The grid lines do contain four larger squares, which resemble the four square piers shown on Baldassare Peruzzi's plan (see above) but these do not correspond with reality.

The perspectival view at the top right is a reconstruction of the so-called Tomb of the Horatii at Albano. The abence of measurements suggests that it is copied from another drawing. Like most contemporary reconstructions, Antonio's wrongly shows the cones untruncated.

The annotation on the lower drawing of similar style and technique to the plans on the recto, states it to be a plan of a tomb near S. Sebastiano, that is, on the via Appia Antica. The exterior with an entrance and fifteen niches alternately semicircular and rectangular, and the annular corridor match a plan by Giuliano da Sangallo with identical location (Barb. lat. 4424, fol. 39; Huelsen 1910, p. 56), suggesting that Antonio was copying. The subject is probably the Tomb of Priscilla, though it has thirteen exterior niches, all concave (see Campbell 2004, II, p. 574). This possibility is strengthened by the fact that Antonio deviated from his uncle's plan and correctly made the tomb chamber similar to a Greek cross rather than Giuliano's circular interior with niches.

The fragmentary drawing at the lower right may be part of another circular plan. | IC

BIBLIOGRAPHY Ferri (1885) 105; Giovannoni (1959) I: 22; Vasori (1981) 153–55, cat. nos 119, 120; Campbell (2004), II: 568, 722; CensusIDs 100076743, 10077227.

U 1427A *recto and verso*

Giovan Francesco da Sangallo and Antonio da Sangallo the Younger

Notes on units of the ancient foot (*recto*); Notes on measures of ancient buildings (*verso*), before 1520.

Dimensions 136/136 × 334 mm.
Paper White, with an extensive reinforcement to verso on the right.
Technique Notes in pen and ink; the measurements are given on the lines incised with straightedge and stylus.

INSCRIPTION, Recto (Old marks, 19th century black pencil) *27*; (in the hand of Giovan Francesco da Sangallo, top line between two measurement markers) *piede anticho chavato da tre piedi antichi in roma. Uno in chasa chapo di fero, latro in chasa* (last word crossed out); / *in sulla piaza dalborensi cioe delchardinale in unno muro duno barbiere latro in tresteveri adese ealle chanale* / *di tregui in roma*; / below: *palmo anticho era chosi* (between two measurement markers); / *dito* (between two measurement markers); bottom: *mezo chupito anticho era chosi e riprovato asai volte in roma*; *questo* (between two measurement markers) / *sie mezo*

Verso In the hand of Antonio da Sangallo the Younger, top left: *Lomezo di segnio di termine longo b*[raccia] *700 piedi 1400* / *le piante grande si mettino allibro se Condo queste misure* / *Lo Coliseo longo alto b*[raccia] *85 7/24 b*[raccia] *333 p.* [iedi] *666* / *Laritonda alta b*[raccia] *75 longa b*[raccia] *140* / *La colonnastoriata alta p*[?] *b*[raccia] *66*; there is a later note in the left margin of this list *li templi con queste* / *li archi con* / *questa*

During the early 16th century, a thorough understanding of the exact values of the ancient units of linear measurement would have been crucial to anybody involved in two fields of study, in particular. Whoever had to carry out surveys of ancient architecture would have been well advised to measure them using the units of measurement with which they had originally been planned and constructed in order to finally have measurements in round numbers. Students of Vitruvius's Treatise would have needed to be familiar with the measurement of the *piede* and other units in order to comprehend and apply the numerous passages in which indications of size are given. Ancient metrology was thoroughly researched by serious scholars of *De Architectura*, such as Fra Giocondo, Fabio Calvo and Angelo Colocci, in Rome. Fra Giocondo, a friar from Verona, was well-acquainted with the second of the three epigraphs of the ancient *piede* that Giovan Francesco da Sangallo has mentioned on this sheet, inscribed on the front wall of a barber's house in the *Foro dei Giudei.* Fra Giocondo had brought it to Colocci's attention (A. Lattès, *A proposito dell'opera incompiuta "De ponderibus et mensuris" di Angelo Colocci*, in "Atti del Convegno di studi su Angelo Colocci," Iesi 1972, p. 107). Fra Giocondo had also long known about the third source cited by Sangallo, which was the well-known funerary altar of the architect Cossutius, which came from Trastevere, and was already then part of the antiquary Angelo Colocci's collection at his gardens near the Acquedotto dell'Acqua Vergine, *Il chanale di trevi* (V. Fanelli, ed., Federico Ubaldini, *Vita di mons. Angelo Colocci*, Città del Vaticano 1969, p. 45, note 53 and Günther 1988, p. 228).

Based on the three examples cited, on the recto of the sheet Giovan Francesco gives the length of a *piede*, 296.5 mm, from which, following *De Architectura* (III,1,8) he works out the length of the ancient *palmo*, equal to 1/4 *piede*, and therefore 74 mm long, and that of the *dito*, equal to 1/16 *piede* and therefore 18mm long. He ends with a half cubit, 222mm long, which he claims to have come across more than once in Rome. The drawing is datable to before 1520 because of the horizontal dash across the downstroke of the '*h*' (Frommel 1994, *Introduction*, pp. 40–41).

On the verso, on the same theme as Giovan Francesco's notes on ancient units of measurement on the recto, Antonio the Younger has written down the overall measurements of some of the most important ancient monume4a nts in Rome in *braccia* and *piedi*: The Baths of Diocletian, *Termini*, the Colosseum and the Pantheon. The main and marginal notes indicate where to place the major surveys of various types of ancient architecture within a planned book ("si mettino al libro"). Evidently Antonio had the measurements only in *braccia* but now wanted to have them also in ancient feet. He simply divides simply the *braccia* in two, though it is slightly less than two feet. Antonio is likely to have written the note in or after 1527 because the shape of the '*h*' is one that he had started to use in that year (Frommel 1994, *Introduction*, p. 36), and he must have been in possession of the sheet on which his cousin, who had left Rome in 1527, had made notes on units of measurement some years previously. On page 227, Günther (1988) cites the verso, which he attributes to Antonio, although he is referring to the subject on the recto, and on page 229 he cites U 1427 without, however, specifying whether he is referring to the recto or the verso, and attributes it, as Ferri did, to Giovanni Battista da Sangallo. | PNP

BIBLIOGRAPHY Ferri (1885) 33, 161; Buddensieg (1976) 108; Günther (1988) 227, 299; CensusID (verso) 10076536.

U 1428A *recto*

Pietro Rosselli and Antonio da Sangallo the Younger

Rome, Forum of Augustus, Temple of Mars Ultor, ca. 1520(?).

Dimensions 388 × 236 mm.
Technique Pencil, pen and brown ink, straightedge.
Paper Center fold, reinforced at edges.
Drawing Scale *palmi* and *minuti.*

INSCRIPTION, Recto (Rosselli's hand) *Lachittrave d edifittio di satto basilljo overo* li Savelli; parmo sco*partito que 12 d*[*ita*] *ogni d*[*ita*]*a 5 minutti*; *I*[*n*] *tutto de chapitello p*[*almi*] *9*; (Antonio's hand) *questo di Sto basilio / larchitrave sie le due terzi / della Colonna da pie*; *Dieci dapie & 9 da capo / Dodici dapie 11 dacapo*; *Lo pilastro dappie p*[*almi*] *7 d*[*ita*] *10 minuti / quali sono d 94 mi*[*nu*]*ti 4 / Larchitravio sie* [*cancelled*] *d 62 mi*[*nu*]*ti 3 li due teatij s*

The sheet shows a schematic elevation of the architrave and the upper part of a Corinthian column from the Temple of Mars Ultor. The leafs of the capital are just indicated. Antonio the Younger, who added a note after 1527, was interested in the proportional relationship between the heights of the capital and the architrave. | HCD

BIBLIOGRAPHY Ferri (1885) 165; Bartoli (1914–22) III: fig. 332, pl. 193; VI: 61; Günther (1988) 230, no. 107; CensusID 10079346.

U 1430A *recto*

Giovanni Battista da Sangallo

Fragments of plans for ancient edifices.

Dimensions 258 × 232 mm.
Paper Lightweight white paper, yellowed and worn, all four corners reinforced.
Technique Pen and sepia ink, drawn freehand.

INSCRIPTION, Recto Top left, in ink, the number *37*; above the top plan, with the sheet turned 180 degrees *la longeza palmi 100 40 / can*[*ne*] *14*; vertically, reading parallel to the left side of the sheet *la groseza del muro 10 p.*[*almi*]; below, vertically reading parallel to the right side of the sheet *palmi 86*; beside the left margin of the sheet, reading parallel to the top side of the sheet *Channe 21*; various measurements

Verso In the middle of the sheet and in the margin, bottom left of the reinforcement the number *1430*

On the sheet are three plans of unidentified ancient structures. The drawing at the top is probably a plan of a water cistern. It has been hastily drawn and is not geometrically accurate with no particular attention having been paid to the correct proportions of the components. The cistern is rectangular, and has been divided into ten internal chambers, arranged in two parallel rows. The outside wall is articulated in a succession of niches, six along the longer side and four on the shorter one, to contain the water pressure. Inside, the author of the drawing shows the openings that will enable water to flow from one chamber to another, and there is a small square element in each space, which may be a pier. This interpretation does not, however, agree with the indicated barrel vault in the first chamber on the top right. The central pillar would, in fact, be more suited to a cross vault or for a pavilion vault, centred over it. | RB

BIBLIOGRAPHY Ferri (1885) 143, 153; Bartoli (1914–22) IV: fig. 516, pl. 310; VI: 96; CensusID 10083807.

U 1453A *recto*

ANTONIO DA SANGALLO THE YOUNGER

Calculations and construction of a circular structure.

Dimensions 525 × 350 min
Paper Lightweight, center fold.
Technique Pen and brown ink, compass and straightedge.
Drawing Scale Probably Roman palmo.

INSCRIPTION (left side) *moduli, minuti / Questo circulo sie in diametri moduli 126 | / Lo modulo sie minuti 2 | 7 / che* [...] *sono ditto diametro minuti* [cancelled *882*] *| 882 / La circonferentia sie moduli 393 | 2751 / quali sono minuti – | 2751 / Lo settimo del diametro sie minuti – | 0126 / E tre diametri sie minuti 2646 / Questo aria a esso minuti 126 et minuti 105 /* [below, sum] *2751 / di sorte chelli mancho di 3 diametri / e uno settimo minuti 21 / Di modo che la circunferentia sie tutta / minuti 2751 et tre diametri sono 2646 / per andare a 2751 ci vole 105 e sol fussi / Come si dice 3 diamnetri et 1/7 aria a essere / 126 di modo che ... Tre diametri / et 105* [below: *882*] *di diametro / O vogliamo dire 21 settimo di diametrio / et 105* [below: *126*] *di settimo di diametro / Lo mezo diametro sie minuti 441 / La meza circunferentia sie 1375½ /* [below calculations]; *questo sia un archo(?) /* [...] *questo ariscontro / minutti quattri* (?) */ 4630½; che questo sie* [...] *archo che questo / a riscontro mi minuti 4630½ / quadri*; (right side) *Lo diametro sie moduli 63 lo modulo / sie minuti 14 – cioe 14 / Li 63 moduli sono minuti – 882 / Lo settimo del diametro sie minuti – 126 / La circunferentia sia partita in 22 et / ciascuna parte sie moduli – 9 / che in tutto moduli – 198 / quali sono minuti 277½ / per tre diametri sarieno – 2646 / per uno settimo del diametro 126 /* [sum] *2772; Ora per que bisogna pigliare / Meza la circonferentia quale 1386 / et multiplicare colle meta del diame/ tro quale sie minuti 441 /* [calculations]

The sheet shows the part of a large circle drawn with a compass and two small rectangles, accompanied by extensive inscriptions and calculations, which discuss two different modules, that used for the circumference being 7 *minuti* of some unspecified unit. Assuming it to be the *palmo romano*, the *minuto* would be 3.724mm, making the module about 2.6 cm and the total circumference 10.218m The diameter instead is based on a module of 14 *minuti* or about 5.2 cm These probably correspond to the depth and width/ half-length of bricks, which may be represented by the two rectangles at the lower left. According to the calculations, the circumference comprised 393 of the bricks set vertically on edge making it about 10.22m in total while the diameter measured 63 of the half-bricks, which is about 3.28m wide. The reference to an arch in the inscriptions suggests that the sheet is concerned with the construction of a cupola without centering, similar to that drawn and discussed by Antonio the Younger on U 900A v.: "volta tonda di [mattoni] mezane quale si voltano senza armadure a firenze" (vol. II). | EB, IC

BIBLIOGRAPHY Ferri (1885) 81.

U 1465A *recto and verso*

ANTONIO DA SANGALLO THE YOUNGER

Geometrical plan, or scheme for decoration of a twelve-sided vault (*recto*); Geometric construction of a theater (*verso*), before 1527.

Dimensions 295 × 275 mm.
Technique Pen and black ink, stylus, straightedge, pin.
Paper Heavy, folds.

INSCRIPTION, Verso *prospettiva*; *Prospettiva*

Antonio the Younger employed drawing tools for a series of geometrical sheets such as U 1463A r. and v. (see vol. I), which he annotated "Giometria di fra Jochundo." The dodecagon, a polygon of twelve angles, on the latter sheet is different than the present one, which was drawn with a straightedge, excepting the freehand drawings of eleven of the twelve triangles outside the perimeter. The intended purpose of the drawing is unknown, as it doesn't seem to be a mere construction of a dodecagon, nor the plan of a chapel or church. The absence of an oculus furthermore sets the drawing apart from the category of a vault.

On the verso, a geometrical sketch, datable prior to 1527, was made in order to calculate the form of ancient theaters. It may have been used for the theater at the Villa Madama, Rome. See also U 1267A. | GS, FZB

BIBLIOGRAPHY Ferri (1885) 81.

U 1489A *recto and verso*

Antonio da Sangallo the Younger

Studies of oval constructions.

Dimensions 292 × 188 mm.
Technique Pen and black ink, freehand.
Paper White, laid down on secondary support.

INSCRIPTION, Recto *tre mandorle/ l'una i*[*n*] *altre/ le a*[*l*]*tre capovolte*

On the recto and verso are studies of polycentrics for drawing an oval of different widths. Antonio studies the variations of the oval according to the position of the circumferences and their reciprocal dimensions and positions. The purpose of these geometrical exercises probably was to facilitate the rendering of hemicycles (in the periboli of the Baths, such as those of Diocletian in U 1089A v.), amphitheaters (for example, U 1089A r.) and theaters (U 1225A), according to the interpretation already proposed by Alberti, of the theater as half of an amphitheater. These kinds of studies can be related to the rendering of antique monuments and to other geometric exercises, as in U 1089A v. or U 1240A v.

At the center of the verso is an oval with the measurements of the two diameters—the major (324 [*piedi*]) and the minor (270 *piedi*)—of the arena of the Flavian Amphitheater. | ACF

BIBLIOGRAPHY Ferri (1885) 81.

U 1544A *recto*

Antonio Labacco

Rome, plan of Baths of Caracalla, before 1518(?).

Dimensions 215 × 213 mm.
Technique Pen and brown wash, straightedge, compass, black ink.
Paper Heavy, yellowed.
Drawing Scale *Canne.*

INSCRIPTION *cortile/ aperto; aperto; botte; tutto cortile c*[*anne*] *24*; measurements; (lower edge) (unknown hands) *Terme di Caracalla; o antoniane*

This drawing by Labacco should be associated with the series related to the Baths of Caracalla: U 1093A, 1545A r. and v., 1546A by Labacco; U 1133A, 1206A, 1381A, 1656A by Giovanni Battista and U 1227A, 1368A v. by Antonio the Younger. It is a graphic reconstruction developed from the information of the survey, gathered on U 1545A r., also by Labacco. It deviates in many ways from the reconstruction of Giovanni Battista (U 1133A) and is nearly identical to the one worked out by Baldassarre Peruzzi (U 476A r.); the most apparent differences with the latter are found in the system by which the arcade of the large gymnasium is resolved and in the form of the *tepidarium* and *frigidarium*, with connected spaces. | ACF

BIBLIOGRAPHY Ferri (1885) 202; Bartoli (1914–22) IV: fig. 610, pl. 351; VI: 110; CensusID 10081401.

U 1545A *recto and verso*

Antonio Labacco

Rome, plan of the Baths of Caracalla, before 1518(?).

Dimensions 291 × 257 mm.
Technique Pen and brown wash, straightedge, compass.
Paper Restored.
Drawing Scale *Canne* (1 *canna* = 45 mm).

INSCRIPTION, Recto measurements; (lower edge) (unknown hand) *Terme di Caracalla?/ Labaco*

On the recto is a reconstruction of the plan of about two-thirds of the central body of the Baths of Caracalla. Some measurements are inscribed for reference whilst some areas are left undetermined. The drawing is closely connected with U 1544A and with those in the series related to the Baths of Caracalla.

On the verso are sketches of the plan and elevation of the *frigidarium* with two attempts at the reconstruction of the front views, which are particularly important for the system of the giant order framing the smaller order; the principal order has a double trabeation projecting over the capital with the effect of emphasizing the verticality of the already slender pilasters and which constitutes on its own the trabeation of the secondary order. At the lower right is a detail of the giant order, possibly composite. | ACF

BIBLIOGRAPHY Ferri (1885) 202; Bartoli (1914–22) IV: fig. 611, pl. 351; VI: 110; Valori (1985) 134. CensusID 10081406.

U 1547A *recto and verso*

Francesco da Sangallo

Rome, plan of Baths of Diocletian, before 1518.

Dimensions 377 × 367 mm.
Technique Pen and ink, watercolor.
Paper Parchment, mounted on cardboard, large section cut out.
Drawing Scale Probably Roman *palmi*.

The drawing on the recto is an unfinished version of the plan of the Baths of Diocletian. In many ways, it varies from the one presented by Francesco in U 284A of 1518. In particular, the *calidarium*, *tepidarium*, and *frigidarium* of the central body are different: the *exedrae* of the *calidarium* have four rather than two columns serving as a screen on the front face and there is a different solution for the rectangular niches. The forms of the *tepidarium* and *frigidarium* are notably different as well; the courtyards with porticos of the *gymnasia* here have sustaining pilasters rather than columns, as in the finished and more accurate version of U 284A, while small variations are found in the spaces of the enclosure. In substance, the drawing seems to precede the definitive one dated 1518 by Francesco.

On the verso is a faint sketch of an unknown, centrally planned building, possibly a mausoleum. | ACF

BIBLIOGRAPHY Ferri (1885) 203; Bartoli (1914–22) IV: fig. 721, pl. 399; VI: 126; CensusID 10074092.

U 1553A *recto and verso*

Antonio da Sangallo the Younger

Composite capital from the arch of Septimius Severus, 1536.

Dimensions 214 × 292 mm.
Technique Pen and black ink.
Paper Trimmed at edges, folded, darkened at edge where earlier attached to backing sheet.

INSCRIPTION, Recto *del pilastro*; (bottom right, later hand in pencil) *Abaco*; (verso, blue pencil later hand) *1053*

This is a pilaster capital corresponding to the capital of the column of the arch of Septimius Severus shown on drawing HdZ 4151, fol. 59 r. (Berlin, Kunstbibliothek). The capital of the pilaster of the arch of Septimius Severus visible on site corresponds in its proportions to the one drawn by Antonio (height 102 cm; 1st crown height 38 cm; 2nd crown height 53 cm; kalathos height 80 cm; full height including the volutes 150 cm; diagonal abacus 139 cm; base 86 cm).

Antonio marks several quotes on the drawing, and he seems particularly interested in the leaf proportions. This drawing includes several views of details (both front views and axonometric or perspective projections). A superposed sketch of a volute can also be seen.

The typology of this capital is of a sort that is notable in the Flavian period, and continues through the second century, notable in Hadrian's Villa and remains common throughout the third century notably at the baths of Caracalla.

On the verso is a front view of the capital combined with a proportional scale. | ML

BIBLIOGRAPHY Brillant (1967) 77–78; von Heilmeyer (1970) 139–40; Zavatta (2008) 162–69; CensusID 10081408, 10081500.

U 1555A *recto and verso*

Antonio da Sangallo the Younger

Rome, reconstruction of plan of Flavian Amphitheater, ca. 1505(?).

Dimensions 187 × 227 mm.
Technique Pen and brown ink, straightedge, compass.
Paper Parchment, stains.
Drawing Scale *Braccia*.

INSCRIPTION, Recto *LUNGO b[raccia] 333 IL TUTTO; LARGO B[raccia] 278 IL TUTTO; Il tutto p[er] longeza e partito in parte scritte*

Verso *16/spazi*[?] *sta p[er] lato; 5 finestre; 4 finestre. V. 3F. V. 4F. V. 3F. V./V4/sono lameta*

On the recto is an accurate reconstruction of the plan of the Flavian Amphitheater, taken at the level of the arena. It relates to Antonio's drawings U 1089A (a preparatory plan with a formulation of the polycentric figure for the construction of the oval of the arena), 1126A (a section), 1135A (a profile of the attic zone with the system of the *velarium*), 1136A r. (a perspective section of the *porticus* in *summa cavea*), 1883A r. (a perspective section of the *porticus* in *summa gradatione*), and above all, to Giovanni Battista's 3969A v. This last drawing is different from the present sheet especially in the form of the ramps and of the sustaining sections of the *cavea*.

A plan of the Colosseum is found in the Codex Escurialensis (Egger 1906, p. 160, fig. 70). It is also interesting to compare the plates of Giuliano da Sangallo (Codex Barberini

4424, fol. 12v.; and *Taccuino senese*, fol. 7). Although Antonio seems to have referred to his uncle's drawings as a point of departure for this study, he achieved a step forward with regard to the rounding-out of the form of the arena, which was then corrected by Giuliano himself (Codex Barberini 4424, fol. 68 r.), and also in resolving the system of the ramps. Equally important are the well-known drawings by Peruzzi on U 480A r. (Bartoli 1914–22, II, fig. 286) which are not very detailed and, in particular, with the plates of Serlio (1540, Book II, fols LXIII–LXV) which present some similarities to and differences from those of Antonio. Notably, the plan at the right by Serlio is similar to the present reconstruction, while there are differences in the system of the ramps and in the length and form of the sustaining sections of the *cavea*. Although this is not the place to discuss in detail the drawings concerned with the architectural orders of the Colosseum, it is worth mentioning, for example, U 1887A r., showing the Tuscan half-column laid against the pilaster of the first order of the exterior arcade. Notable is Antonio's rather neutral solution, common to all of the aforementioned graphic reconstructions of the Colosseum, applied to the problem of the entrances onto the axes which coincide with the major and minor diameter of the arena. The entrances are emphasized only by a greater width of the span of the front face and by the continuity of the system of pilasters which penetrates as far as the arena. There is no sign here of the little portico (probably added after the Flavian period and already documented at the time of Alexander Severus), the traces of which are visible in the northern entrance, the only entrance preserved.

On the verso is a graphic reconstruction of the perspective section of the Flavian Amphitheater. It differs from those proposed by Antonio the Younger himself in U 1136A and by Giovanni Battista da Sangallo in U 1883A r., the first showing the portico with arches on giant columns that rise to the height of approximately two stories, and the second, a portico with a double order of columns with architraves. There are doors or windows with architraves with aedicules and triangular pediments inserted into the spans of the first order. Here, Antonio imagined a double order of piers and arches with attached pilasters and, below, rectangular windows decorated with very simple ornamentation. The drawing relates to that by an anonymous Italian B(?) in the Albertina (Egger 1903, no. 23 v.) which shows a simple section and seems to reflect the section found in Serlio (1619, Book III, fol. 80). | ACF

BIBLIOGRAPHY Ferri (1885) 123; Huelsen (1910) fol. 68; Bartoli (1914–22) III: figs 395, 396, pl. 230; VI: 74; Cozzo (1971); Valori (1985) 68; Frommel (1994, *Introduction*) 15; CensusIDs 10072970, 10072987.

U 1565A *recto*

Antonio Labacco

Ancona, Arch of Trajan, ca. 1532–35.

Dimensions 150 × 180 mm.
Technique Pen and two shades of brown ink.
Paper Lightweight.
Drawing Scale Roman *palmi*.

INSCRIPTION *aqua*; (another hand) *p[almo] 4 12 p.[er] testa / Batte la mare*

Both of Labacco's drawings correspond to some extent with two of Antonio the Younger's drawings of the Arch of Trajan at Ancona, suggesting some degree of reliance and collaboration.

The schematic sketch at the top shows the sea's relationship to the lowest plinth of the arch. The annotation and the dimension are identical to those on U 1119A v., where the same detail forms part of a larger drawing. The lower drawing is a plan of one of the arch's piers at the level of the column shafts. The annotation "Batte la mare" suggests that the pier is located to the left of the arch as seen from the sea, keeping in mind that the annotation is in a different handwriting and may have been added a little later. The outline appears to have been emphasized at the same time with the same darker ink. The dimension *p[almi] 3–2* is given on U 1119A v. as the diameter of the shaft and the same dimension appears on Sangallo's plan of the pier in U 1071A v. (uppermost sketch). Three other dimensions correspond on the two drawings. | IC

BIBLIOGRAPHY Ferri (1885) 6; Vasori (1981) 188–89, cat. no. 142; CensusID 10082538.

U 1576A *recto and verso*

Antonio da Sangallo the Younger (?)

Rome, archivolts of Flavian Amphitheater, ca. 1504–06(?).

Dimensions 335 × 235 mm.
Technique Pen and brown ink.
Paper Stains, restored.

INSCRIPTION, Recto *al prjmo pjano / di stuchi*

Verso *Culiseo dentro / al secondo piano e chosi istano tutti e dua i / primi archi e sechondi e cosi quei dua di sopra / el resto an[n]o larchitrave solo e gli archi e membretti / et tutti i membretti sono chome questi di sotto*

On the recto, Antonio the Younger drew a perspective sketch of the vault with stucco decoration on the ground level of the Colosseum. He understood very clearly the contrast between the powerful, bare pilasters of the barrel vaults and the ornament of the stucco ceiling, which is represented as graceful and rich in floral motifs. At the lower right some measurements are noted.

The verso shows the interior arcade of the second order without decoration. | ACF

BIBLIOGRAPHY Ferri (1885) 123, 163; Bartoli (1914–22) III: figs 393, 394, pl. 229; VI: 73–74; CensusIDs 10072968, 10072961.

U 1578A *recto*

Pietro Rosselli and Antonio da Sangallo The Younger

Rome, Piazza di Pietra, Temple of Hadrian.

Dimensions 288 × 422 mm.
Technique Pen and brown ink, straightedge.
Paper *Lightweight, center fold, trimmed on all sides, patches.*
Drawing Scale Roman *palmi.*

INSCRIPTION, Recto (left half) *Il palmio qui(?) se repartjtto 12 oncie ogni ocia in mjnutti 5 / Larchjttrave dedifittjo della piaza de prettj* (*sic* for *pietra*); *Lalteza de*[*l*] *chapitello* [...] *p. 7½* (right half) *s ellavesse infratta due li ogetti o ¼ o ⅛ / saria grossa la colonna palmi 7 oncie 5 minuti 4 / e secondo la ... La sua alteza venire palmi 7 oncie 3 minuti 3 / bisognia vedere quanti canali ci sono / canali 24 sodi 24 / La colonna gira oncie 244 minuti 4/ viene avere di di diametro oncie 777 minuti / che sono p(almi) 6 oncie 5 minuti 7 / e per rispetto delli 4 minuti se puo dire palmi 6 oncie 6 /* (vertically) *La colonna a ric / ressere palmi 7 oncie 3 minuti 3*

Verso numbers

The two measured drawings show details of the Hadrianeum. The drawing on the left, *a*, shows a part of the entablature supported by the colonnade of the peristyle with both the external (left) and internal (right) profiles of the architrave drawn, the pulvinated frieze and the lowest mouldings of the cornice. A drawing of the full entablature is found on U 1407A r. Drawing *b* is a detail of the fluted shaft and Attic base of one of the columns. | IC

BIBLIOGRAPHY Ferri (1885) 196; Bartoli (1914–22) IV: fig. 334, pl. 194; VI: 61; Scaglia (1994) 231; CensusID 10081311.

U 1579A *recto*

Antonio del Tanghero and Antonio da Sangallo

Rome, Theater of Marcellus, Doric entablature, capital and cornice, ca. 1518 and after 1527.

Dimensions 430 × 576 mm.
Technique Pen and brown ink.
Paper Folded at the center.
Drawing Scale *Palmi* and *dita.*

INSCRIPTION (on the left half) *La chimasa dell archo de membretto/ de primo ordine de Savelli. I fra una lattra. palmi 3 once 3*; (on the right half) *basa de seconda ordine;* (in Sangallo's handwriting) *dei Savelli*

This is a relatively accurate survey drawing which represents measured profiles of the Doric order, of the capital of the entablature and of the of the impost of the arcades (left half of the sheet). On the right half is the profile of the Attic base of the ionic order with measurement, and the profile (turned 180 degrees), without measurements, of the cornice of the Doric entablature, which is then reworked in greater detail at the left of the sheet. The present drawing should be considered along with drawings U 932A, 1296, 1335 and 1428A by Antonio del Tanghero. This drawing is an early recognition of the correctness of the architectural orders on the Theater of Marcellus with respect to the Vitruvian canon, which Serlio writes about in Book III, f. 71. | ACF

BIBLIOGRAPHY Ferri (1885) 193; Bartoli (1914–22) IV: fig. 334, pl. 194; VI: 62; Scaglia (1994) 231; CensusID 10079381.

U 1627A *recto and verso*

Antonio da Sangallo the Younger

Ground plan of Heroon of Romulus (*recto*); head of Caesar and view of Colosseum (*verso*), ca. 1506–07.

Dimensions 225 × 289 mm.
Technique Pen and ink, wash.
Paper Trimmed at bottom edge, tear reinforced on verso.

INSCRIPTION, Recto *pianta dj sotto; pianta dj sopra*

Neither ground plan contains measurements, unlike most of the building surveys by Antonio the Younger himself. He must therefore have copied them from another plan. The hastily drawn strokes also suggest that it might not be a clean copy of one of his own surveys. Antonio could have copied the two plans from the same model followed by Giuliano's son Francesco on fol. 43 verso of the Codex Barberini (Borsi 1985, *Giuliano*, p. 214 f.). His other surveys from these years lack both the portico and its staircase, as well as the plan of the ground floor and the articulation of the exterior wall (Günther 1988, p. 334, pl. 17a). The Leonardesque head of Caesar on the verso is further evidence of Antonio's unusual ability and practice in drawing figures. The view of the Colosseum was probably made at about the same time as the studies on U 2043A. The handwriting seems somewhat more mature than that of the parchment sheets in the presumptive Taccuino (U 2043–2047A) and could be from about 1506/07. | CLF

BIBLIOGRAPHY Ferri (1885) 35, 39, 199, 209, 217; Bartoli (1914–22) III: figs 401–02; pl. 232; VI: 74; Günther (1988) 114; Frommel (1994, *Introduction*); CensusIDs 60618, 10073040.

U 1630A *recto and verso*

Giovan Francesco da Sangallo (?)

Florence, ground plan for S. Miniato al Monte, before 1530.

Dimensions 220 × 280 mm.
Technique Pen and dark brown ink.
Paper Lightweight, fold, corners reinforced on verso, probably trimmed on four sides.

INSCRIPTION, Recto *champanile*; *chapela*; *Sanminiato*

On the recto of this sheet is a hasty sketch—though with measurements—of the ground plan of the three-aisled basilica of S. Minato al Monte, including the southeast boundary of the forecourt created by the monastery buildings. Less attention has been paid to the front two-thirds of the church, the lay area. While the entrance wall with its three doors is depicted in its entirety (with overly narrow lateral doors), the walls of the side aisles in the north and south are only roughly marked. The two buttresses corresponding to the western pair of compound piers have been omitted. The southern aisle is shown as somewhat narrower than the one to the north, leading to problems in the depiction of the crypt (see below). The position of the quattrocento ciborium altar in the center aisle, in front of the steps to the presbytery, or crypt, is indicated with a rectangle. The Chapel of the Cardinal of Portugal is mistakenly attached to the northern aisle at the level of the fifth, instead of the fourth, intercolumniation from the west. The characteristics of the chapel (the scale of which is too small in the ground plan)—a square block with four attached, narrower "cross arms," the southern arm serving as the entrance arcade—are only vaguely realized. What is shown is an incomplete Greek cross with very short arms, pierced on the south by a wall with a narrow opening that can be interpreted as a door. This conception of the room becomes more comprehensible if one assumes that the chapel is being viewed from outside the church. When he depicted the eastern third of the church, the draftsman decided to take the crypt into account: a seven-aisled hall on an east-west axis, with five bays, whose three center aisles have been extended to form an apsidial conclusion at the west.

The arrangement of the stairs is not precise. The stairs to the presbytery (in the side aisles) are merely indicated with narrow strips. It should be noted that the three middle flights of stairs are separated by clearly drawn sections of wall instead of the reinforcing arches present today. This may be the result of a reinforcement removed in later attempts to preserve the monument. In the area of the crypt, the draftsman made an effort to draw the supports precisely, including the foundations of the columns of the presbytery above that disturb the regularity of the hall. When he drew the south aisles of the crypt, their width, which was less than those on the north, led him to add, in a somewhat improvised manner, the third row of columns from the south. Initially he may perhaps have drawn in one aisle too few.

The verso includes a detail of the S. Minato ground plan: the short wall, pierced by a door, between the two building blocks depicted on the recto.

The ground plan was probably intended purely for study purposes; it has no known connection with a specific project, such as a restoration of the complex. Other ground plans also have the character of studies, for example those on U 1160A (S. Pietro in Vincoli, Rome, vol. II) and 1383A v. (S. Antonio, Padua, vol. II). The handwriting on the latter sheet is similar to the one on U 1630A (especially the "ch" and the "p"), which argues for ascribing this plan to Giovan Francesco da Sangallo. | HR

BIBLIOGRAPHY Ferri (1885) 72.

U 1631A *recto and verso*

Giovanni Battista da Sangallo

Tivoli, Temple of Vesta, sketches of elevations, perspectival plans and sections of details (*recto*); sketch of theater stage, general sketch of plan (*verso*), probably after 1519–20(?).

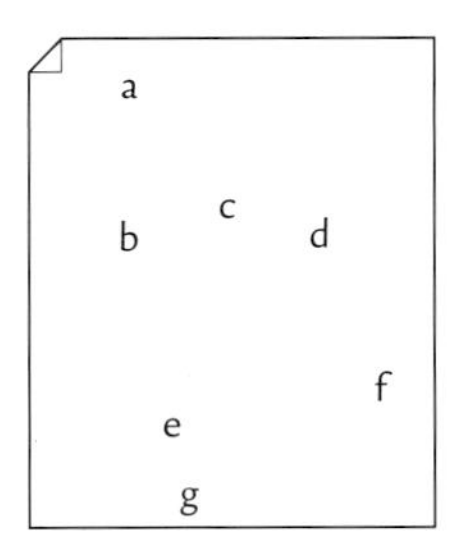

Dimensions 407 × 275 mm.
Technique Pen and brown ink, freehand.
Paper Heavy, folds, trimmed on four sides, at times irregularly, edges reinforced.

INSCRIPTION, Recto (a) *cholonne 20.*; (b) *Laporta dapiedi.* / *quanto la si discosta*; (c) *a lafinestra*; (d) *basa senza zoch[ol]o.*; (e) *palmi 33 tutto eldidrento deltenpio*; *a laporta.*; *alalte[zza]* / *della*[?]; (f) *chanali vinti.*; *lagroseza deltenpio landito.*; *disporto ¼–½ dipalmo* / *labasa*; *el fusto dela chol[onna]*; *drento p. ¼*; *de fuora p ½*

Verso (center) *la scena*; (bottom) *lavorato a grottesche*

This sheet belongs in the series of drawings by the Sangallo circle after the famous circular temple located above the falls of the Aniene in Tivoli. Unlike the other drawings by the Sangallo circle (U 1069A, 1216A), this one is measured in Roman *palmi*. At the upper left is a partial ground plan of the circular temple with the cella and five columns in the lower quarter (*a*). Below the plan are studies of the window with its characteristic form, wider at the bottom than at the top, and its location above the pavement of the peristasis (*b*), of the door and the window cornice (*c*), as well as a perspectival view from the peristasis toward one of the columns, next to which is a measured plan of the column and a profile of its base (*d*). Below, turned 90 degrees, is a section through the peristasis in the vicinity of the cella door (*e*), as well as a measured partial plan, seen from a low bird's-eye view. The ground plan of a column has been drawn, almost orthogonally, in the outer cylinder, barely sketched at the lower right (*f*). Finally, at the bottom of the sheet is the profile of the jamb and the cornice of the temple's door.

What is remarkable about this drawing is that the temple's peristasis, which was already in ruined condition in the sixteenth century, has been reconstructed with twenty columns. It is unlike Antonio the Younger's other 1539 drawings of the temple, showing eighteen columns, the correct number (U 1216A), which had been preceded by studies he made four years earlier, based on drawings by Riniero da Pisa, mistakenly showing sixteen columns (U 1069A). The only parallel in the early sixteenth century is to be found in a ground plan in the Fossombrone sketchbook (fol. 6 v.), where, however, an amazing erroneous correction alters the number of columns from eighteen to twenty ("Le son ['18' canceled] 20; son vinti cholonne laplanta"). The drawing's relationship to that in the Fossombrone sketchbook is strengthened by the section through the peristasis *e*, which is clearly a highly summary and fragmentary variant of a section found on the same page of the sketchbook. Although the door cornice in U 1631A appears heavier, the closeness of the drawing to that in the sketchbook clearly emerges through the comparison with Antonio's section (U 1216A), which is not taken through the door (see also the sections in Codex Coner, fol. 16 v.; Albertina, Egger (1903), fol. 285 v.; Windsor, Royal Library, no. 10355). All this suggests that the anonymous draftsman of the Fossombrone sketchbook and Giovanni Battista da Sangallo had access to a common model for the circular temple.

The verso of the sheet contains some rather rough drawings relating to the stage of a Roman theater of difficult attribution. In the right margin there is a drawing of a section of the corridor toward the back of the stage, which presumably would have been decorated with grotesques. Sculptures would have been displayed on the upper levels. | JN, ACF

BIBLIOGRAPHY Ferri (1885) 216, 220; Nesselrath (1993) 93 f. (for the Fossombrone sketchbook); CensusIDs 10156112, 10156113.

U 1636A *recto*

Giovanni Battista da Sangallo

Rome, Via Appia, Mausoleum of Maxentius, before 1548.

Dimensions 434 × 593 mm.
Technique Pen and ink, light brown for squaring, darker for drawing, stylus, straightedge, compass.
Paper Squared, partly yellowed, central horizontal fold, corners reinforced.

INSCRIPTION (bottom left, blue pencil, nineteenth-century hand, numbering, 1636; brown ink) *ad s[an]c[t]u[m] sebastianu[m] estra porta[m] Capena[m]*

The drawing shows a plan of the remains of the mausoleum on the Via Appia, begun by the emperor Maxentius, probably after 308, after he had defeated the immediate challengers to his rule, but left unfinished after his overthrow by Constantine in 312. The spectacular remains were a favorite subject of Renaissance architects (see Rasch 1984). Giovanni Battista's plan differs from most in not being a full-blown reconstruction. However, he did speculate on the existence of the three-bay entrance in the southwest side of the quadriporticus, for which no evidence survives. He was perhaps misled by the evidence of the foundations of earlier tombs, cleared to make way for the mausoleum complex.

Nor is there evidence for the stairs he put next to the entrance, but he scrupulously refrained from showing more bays vaulted than the evidence actually suggests, implying that he recognised the unfinished nature of the project.

Giovannoni gives the drawing to Antonio, but the handwriting is clearly Giovanni Battista's, and there is nothing in the style of drawing to suggest Antonio as the author rather than his brother. Both made drawings on squared paper, but Antonio's are of modern buildings, where the squares could help in planning according to modular schemes. Why Giovanni Battista should use squared paper to draw antiquities is less obvious; perhaps he was trying to see if the monuments conformed to modular principles. Whatever their purpose, these drawings represent a very early use of small-squared paper by architects. | IC

BIBLIOGRAPHY Ferri (1885) 155, 199; Lanciani (1902–12) III: 14; Bartoli (1914–22) IV: fig. 550, pl. 329; VI: 100; Giovannoni (1959) I: 40; II: fig. 5; Rasch (1984) 9, no. 5, p. 15; CensusID 43896.

U 1637A *recto*

Giovanni Battista da Sangallo

Rome, Forum Boarium, Temple of Portunus; mausoleum on the Via Appia near S. Sebastiano, before 1530.

Dimensions 167 × 233 mm.
Technique Squared in pen and brown ink, buildings in black ink, straightedge.
Paper Heavy, reinforced.
Drawing Scale Roman *palmi*(?).

INSCRIPTION *Santa Marja eqyptiaca*; *ad s[an]c[t]um sebastianum estra portam / capenam*

Both temples are shown in the ground plan. The conjectured Temple of Portunus deviates from the real temple in having distinctly engaged and three-quarter columns, the radius of which are corresponding to one square of the grid. The mausoleum near S. Sebastiano is illustrated by Serlio (1540, Book 3, XXXII) in perspective cross section. | HCD

BIBLIOGRAPHY Ferri (1885) 144, 163, 199; Bartoli (1914–22) III: fig. 551, pl. 329; VI: 101; CensusID 10072184.

U 1638A *recto*

Giovanni Battista da Sangallo

Rome, Via Appia, so-called "Sepolcro dei Cercennii" in the Cemetery of Praetextatus, before 1548.

Dimensions 295 × 210 mm.
Technique Pen and ink, light brown ink for squares, darker ink for drawing, stylus, straightedge, compass.
Paper Squared, partly yellowed, trimmed on four sides, corners reinforced.

INSCRIPTION (bottom left, blue pencil, nineteenth-century hand, numbering) *1638* (brown ink) *ad s[an]c[t]um sebastianum estra portam Capenam*

This is another plan of the cruciform structure, already discussed in U 575A r. The plan is accurate apart from the additions of rectangular chambers with apses to either side (that on the left has for the most part been lost by the cutting down of the sheet). This is reminiscent of a plan attributed to Fra Giocondo (U 3993A, Spera 1999, fig. 134; CensusID 10075641), which incorporates the cruciform building in a range of structures. To its immediate left is a stair, followed by an apsidal chamber similar to the one shown here, while on the right side, there is a rectangular chamber with a rectangular alcove. Since U 3933A r. includes measurements, the chamber possibly has some basis. On the squared paper, see U 1636A, which, with its virtually identical text, must be a very close contemporary of the present drawing. | IC

BIBLIOGRAPHY Ferri (1885) 163, 199; Huelsen (1910) 30; Bartoli (1914–22) IV: fig. 552, pl. 379; VI: 101; Giovannoni (1959) I: 40; Windfeld-Hansen (1969) 77–78; CensusID 48263.

U 1648A *recto*

Giovan Francesco da Sangallo

Rome, Basilica of Constantine, before 1527.

Dimensions 180 × 225 mm.
Technique Pen and brown ink, stylus, straightedge, compass.
Paper Heavy, partly yellowed.
Drawing Scale Florentine *braccia.*

INSCRIPTION (top right, dark brown ink, 16th century hand, old numbering) *368*; (bottom left, blue pencil, nineteenth-century hand, numbering) *1648*; *tenplu[m] pacis*; *questo no[n] ce*

This is a plan for reconstructing the Basilica of Constantine, the last of the great imperial basilicas of ancient Rome, which was initiated by Maxentius (306–12) and completed, to a modified design, by his successor, Constantine. The reconstruction makes the usual 16th century mistake of balancing the existing northern apse (on the right of this plan), with another on the south, where, in fact, there had been a small rectangular, four- column portico, noted by Francesco di Giorgio and probably unearthed at the same time as the remains of the colossus of Constantine, the fragments of which are now in the Palazzo dei Conservatori on the Campidoglio. The colossus stood in the west apse, and its rectangular base can be seen in the present plan. The desire for symmetry also misled Giovan Francesco into treating the northwest bay identically to the northeast, which had its upper range of windows partly filled with Constantinian tiles, in another modification from the Maxentian design. The still-buried narthex area was more difficult for him to imagine, which may explain why he left the bottom left corner of the plan unfinished, while in the other corner he put an octagonal chamber, bearing no relation to reality, as he engagingly admitted: "questo no[n] ce." | IC

BIBLIOGRAPHY Ferri (1885) 130; Bartoli (1914–22) IV: fig. 519, pl. 310; VI: 96; Buddensieg (1975) 108; Campbell (1984) I: 315, 319; CensusID 44045.

U 1650A *recto and verso*

Giovan Francesco da Sangallo and Antonio da Sangallo the Younger

Rome, Forum Romanum, Temple of Castor and Pollux, Arch of Titus, Arch of Septimius Severus; Forum of Augustus, Temple of Mars Ultor; Arch of Constantine; capital from S. Prassede (*recto*); Forum Romanum, Temple of Antoninus and Faustina (*verso*), ca. 1515–20(?).

Dimensions 346 × 481 mm.
Technique Pen and dark (Giovan Francesco) and light (Antonio) brown ink, stylus, graphite.
Paper Heavy, center fold, repairs.
Drawing Scale *Minuti.*

INSCRIPTION, Recto (left half, turned 180 degrees) (Giovan Francesco's hand) *Basa delle 3 cholonne & sono 24 canale*; *Basa dell archo di tito & vespasiano cioe delle cholone / questo piano e largo minuti 92*; *I[m]basamento dell archo di tito e vespasiano*; (right half) *in Inquesto piano e p[er] facia minuti 72 / Chapitello sotto alla cholona che e alla p[or]ta di santa p[ra]sedia*; *questo dado e p[er] facia minuti 29½ / Lutio Settimio*; (Antonio's hand) *Basa delle Cholonne dell archo da chanpidoglio / la cholona a chanali 24*; *Cio cola dopia / chorta / bacegli / Basa delle cholone di santo basilio*; *Basa delle cholone dell archo di trasi / questo piano e largo minuti 29*

Verso (left half) *sono gli [...] chosi / suo architraue / sta chosi [...]lato / Suo fregio minuti 105*; (right half) (Antonio's hand) *antonino pio e faustina / cioe gl[i] ucegli grifoni*

The various profiles of bases and a socle on the recto reappear in the same arrangement on folios 63 r. and 70 r. of the Codex Barberini. According to Huelsen, the examples by Giuliano da Sangallo are copies of a lost prototype. The drawings on the recto of this sheet are mainly concerned with profiles, while on the verso, the draughtsman was interested in ornamental detail. The entablatures are rendered in axonometric cross section. | HCD

BIBLIOGRAPHY Ferri (1885) 124, 126, 153, 165, 194, 197; Huelsen (1910) 66 f., fig. 76; Bartoli (1914–22) III: figs 569, 570, pl. 338, 339, VI: 103; Günther (1988) 125, 127 n. 144, 338; CensusIDs 62076, 10030869.

U 1652A *recto and verso*

Giovan Francesco da Sangallo

Rome, studies of profiles of ancient architecture, 1507 or 1511.

Dimensions 256 × 201 mm.
Technique Pen and brown ink, freehand.
Paper Heavy, fold marks, trimmed on four sides, stains, strip pasted on at upper edge.
Drawing Scale Florentine *braccio* (1/60 *braccio* = ca. 168 mm.).

INSCRIPTION, Recto (center left of sheet) *Chornjcie chauata nello fondametto / del foglietta doue fu sotterato eluernja / i[n] Santo pietro. e bramante la fecie sotte / rare nello fondamento*; (below) *sono sexantesimi di braccio*; (below) *E chanali della cholon[n]a di templo / i[n] pacis sono chanali 24 e sono / largi 20¹/₁ el sodo sie largo daluno / chanale alatro 5⅔ questa sie lapiu grosa cholona che siuega i[n] roma / cioe di marmo*; (in cross section of column) *chanali 24 e sottera lo terzo della cholonna*

Verso *i[n] Basamento chauato / i[n] nauona nel* MDXI

Most of the recto of the sheet is taken up by a freehand, thoroughly measured study of an antique Doric entablature: the architrave composed of two fasciae with the terminating taenia, from which hangs the regula with six guttae, as well as the frieze with the triglyph, the field of the metope left empty, are drawn in elevation. On the contrary, the cornice with cavetto and torus, the corona supported by mutuli, and the smaller as well as larger cymas are given in section. The measurements are in one-sixtieth of a *braccio*, as the draftsman notes in an inscription. The scale at the bottom edge is marked accordingly; however, the drawing itself is not drawn to scale and only adheres to the scale in a generic way.

According to the inscription, the entablature was found at St Peter's in the foundation "del foglietta," and Bramante had it reburied there. Foglietta, whose real name was Giovanantonio di Cristoforo Pallavicini, was the master mason who, beginning on the 1st of March, 1507, was responsible for the construction of the south-east cupola pier of St Peter's, which means that the entablature could have been found in this area (Frommel 2003 *L'esordio*, p. 162). However, since Foglietta was also in charge of the southern counter-pier in the nave, which was under construction in September 1511 (Frey 1910, p. 53, E 43; Frommel 1996, p. 78, no. 357a), one cannot exclude the possibility that the draughtsman was referring to this foundation. The fact that it is measured in one-sixtieth of a *braccio* suggests that our sheet is a copy of a drawing by a Florentine—perhaps Antonio the Younger—who drew the fragment in either 1507 or 1511, before Bramante had it reburied in the foundations. The same entablature fragment, with virtually the same measurements and with a reference to the location of its discovery (however, only generically indicated as the "fondamenti di San Pietro"), was drawn by Peruzzi in a perspectivally foreshortened view (U 1699A) that was then used as a model by Serlio for his *Terzo Libro*.

The cross section of the column refers to the column that was then still standing in the Basilica of Maxentius in the Roman Forum and which Paul V had moved and reerected in front of S. Maria Maggiore in 1613. It records the width of the flutings as well as the arrises in between, with measurements that are likewise given in one-sixtieth of a *braccio*, although without any relation to the scale at the bottom edge.

The verso shows a section through an antique base, which, according to the inscription, was brought to light in 1511 during excavations at Piazza Navona. The scale, as far as it is possible to determine on the basis of corresponding measurements, comes close to that on the recto. | JN

BIBLIOGRAPHY Ferri (1885) 127, 130, 206; Bartoli (1914–22) VI: 100; Giovannoni (1959) I: 24; Buddensieg (1975) 108; Günther (1988) 336, 377; CensusID 10027146, 10030886.

U 1654A *recto and verso and U 3972A recto and verso*

Giovanni Battista da Sangallo

Rome, ground plan and elevation of a rotunda (U 1654A r. and U 3972A v.), Forum Romanum, Temple of Antoninus and Faustina (U 1654A v. and U 3972A r.), ca. 1520(?).

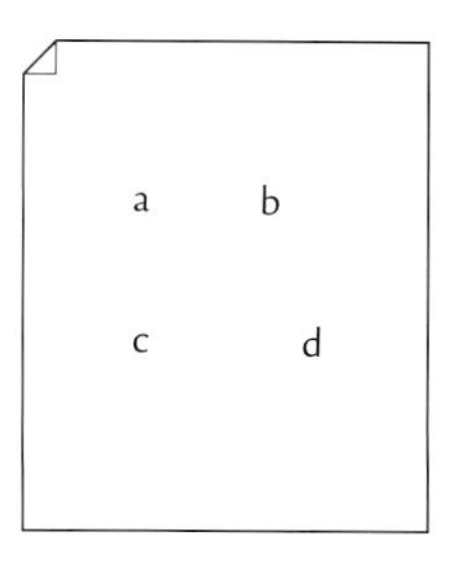

Dimensions 219 × 300 mm.
Technique Pen and brown ink, stylus, straightedge, compass (*recto*).
Paper Cut in two pieces, losses, restored.
Drawing Scale Roman *piedi*.

INSCRIPTION, Recto (all on elevation *c*) *fuor di porta maiore 2 milglia*; *45½ per lovano*; *pie 38½*; other measurements

Verso (on ground plan) *Antonino / e faustina*; (by profile of socle) *inbasamento dantonino / et faustina*; (by staircase) *scala d'antonino e faustina*; (on socle) *Sancto lorenzo delli spetiali*; (on wall) *quindici bungne*

A single sheet was cut in half and its pieces were originally catalogued separately, thus providing the double numbering system.

Drawings *a* and *b* on the recto of U 1654A (and verso of 3972A) are a plan and elevation of the tomb known as "Le Cappellette," and *c* and *d* a plan and elevation of the tomb known as the "Tor de Schiavi," both on the Via Prenestina. All four drawings have parallels on U 1270A v., but it is difficult to establish which came first. The confusion evident in the reconstruction of the portico of the Tor de Schiavi, with hatching apparently representing void, and yet extending into the entablature on the left half, may indicate the misunderstanding of 1270A v. *b* as may the differing heights of the arcade. There the left arch is shown hatched, probably to indicate that there is a portico behind, while the middle arch shows the door and the right arch a niche both set into the rear wall of the portico. The different treatment of the corner piers of the pronaos and the presence of plinths under the front columns, on the present drawing, however, suggest it is something other than a simple copy of U 1270A v. Luschi wrongly stated that Bartoli attributed the drawing to Antonio.

On the verso of the sheet Giovanni Battista reconstructs the ground plan of the temple as 85 *piedi* in length and 65–5 *piedi* in width. The profile includes the podium at its full height as well as the foot of the pilaster and the socle. The corner pilasters are given special attention. The orthogonal elevation of the flank takes into account the extant parts of the ruin and includes the exterior steps. This staircase was visible until the level of the Via Sacra was raised for the entry of Charles V in 1530. Below the elevation of the flank is the profile of a base. Measurements are given for the height of the columns, 47–6 *piedi*, the height of the capitals, 5 1/2 *piedi*, and the axis of the columns, 13–6 *piedi*. | IC, HCD

BIBLIOGRAPHY Ferri (1885) 142, 162, 194, 199–200, 209; Bartoli (1914–22) IV: figs 505, 506, pl. 308; VI: 94–95; Luschi (1984) 30–31; CensusID 60391, 10072190.

U 1656A *recto*

Giovanni Battista da Sangallo

Rome, the Baths of Caracalla, enclosure and elevation of the frigidarium.

Dimensions 427 × 235 mm.
Technique Pen and brown ink, stylus, straight-edge, compass.
Paper Stained.
Measurements: Possibly Florentine *braccia.*

This drawing is related to U 1133A and U 1381A r., both by Giovanni Battista, but in this sheet he changes the character of the restitution of some of the spaces and is more precise in some of the details. At the lower right, there is a graphic restitution of an elevation of the frigidarium with a giant order framing the minor double order and the niches enframed by windows with aedicules. In this way, a gradual crescendo of the architectural orders is attained. As Schich (2009) ascertained the sheet was conceived together with U 4117A r. as a larger drawing of the enclosure of the Baths of Caracalla. | ACF

BIBLIOGRAPHY Ferri (1885) 202; Lanciani (1902–12) II: 183; Bartoli (1914–22) IV: fig. 522, pl. 313; VI: 96; Schich (2009) 276; CensusID 10072270.

U 1657A *recto and verso*

Giovanni Battista Da Sangallo

Rome, Forum Holitorium, three temples with S. Nicola in Carcere (*recto*); plan of Baths of Caracalla, elevation and three-quarter view of "tempietti a campidoglio"; Palazzo Savelli (*verso*), ca. 1535.

Dimensions 284 × 216 mm.
Technique Pen and brown ink.
Paper Center fold, top left corner and lower right edge torn, restored.
Drawing Scale *Piedi antichi.*

INSCRIPTION, Recto *lo toscano 6–6 6–6 pie*; *lo ionico 8–11½ 8–11½*; *lo toscano acanto / asanto nicola / incharcera / lecolonne sonalte / pie 17*; *cornicione dello/ edefitio* (*do* canceled) *toscano*; *capitello deltosca/no*; *colonna e ca/pitello alta pie 18 / lecarcera / a canto asa/ncto nicola / corinto lecolo/nne sonalte pie 32½ / lecolonne grossa / 3–6*; *da colonna a / colonna da altro esei*; *cornice della / carcera*; *daldifytio disancto / nichola agnello / toscano sie pie 7½ / Santo nicola / ionicho*; *lacolonna sie alta pie* (*29½* canceled) *30½ 28¼ / senza basa esenza capitello*; *sfondato delle / intercolumni / di sancto / nicola*

Verso *Termi antoniani*; *pie 58 / a Savelli*; [...]*lonne / inalta pie / 26½ colcapitello / eben fa la tufo / della colonna / versopie 3*; *Tempietti acampidolglio*; *nelle storie di Campidaglio*

According to Günther, the recto represents one of several studies executed by the Sangallo circle of the three temples of the Forum Holitorium. It probably dates to about 1535. Giovanni Battista has used the antique foot as his unit of measure. Measured drawings such as this (see also the entries for U 1090A, 1142A, 1134A, 1174A, 1233A, 1270A) were instrumental to both Serlio's publication of his third book and Labacco's *Libro appartenente all'architettura.*

The architect has concentrated on measuring the relationship of the parts of the orders and recording the plan, disregarding the arrangement of the temples in relation to each other. The sheet has been turned several times to make notations and sketch individual details.

The temple furthest to the east is identified as "lo toscano"; its plan, a 6-by-11-*piedi* peripteral pseudodistyle, is sketched at the top of the sheet. A detail of the profile of the capital and cornice is at the right. This is the smallest of the three temples and here the architect indicated that the columns, including capitals, are 18 *piedi* high, whereas the inscription at the center of the temple states the columns are 17 *piedi*. Each column is 2½ *piedi* in diameter and the intercolumnations are 6 *piedi*, whereas the intercolumnation of the central axis is 8 *piedi*. These measurements differ slightly from Antonio the Younger's (U 1174A r.), where the intercolumnation for the central axis is noted as 9 *piedi* and the corner intercolumnation 5 *piedi* and 14 *dita*.

The plan of the central temple was sketched at the bottom of the sheet, after it had been turned 180 degrees. The cella walls correspond to the width of the nave of the medieval church of S. Nicola in Carcere, which incorporated the peripteral columns of the flanking temples; they are embedded in the exterior walls. The order, identified as Ionic in the inscription, is documented by a measured profile of the entablature and capital in the lower left corner of the sheet. The intercolumnations are 8½ *piedi* whereas the intercolumnations for the porch range from 8 to 10½ *piedi*. The length of the cella walls are 53¾ *piedi* and its width is 23 *piedi*. The height of the order is considerably taller, measuring 30½ *piedi* including base and capital. Giovanni Battista has drawn a 6-by-12-*piedi* peripteral pseudodistyle plan, whereas Antonio the Younger's plan (U 1174A r.) is 6 by 11 *piedi* and has slightly different measurements for the intercolumnations. Apparently the plan of the front porch was unclear, as suggested by Peruzzi's plan, where half of the porch is pseudotripteral and the other half is pseudodipteral (see U 478A v. and 631A r.).

The third temple, known as "the carcere," located furthest to the north, is drawn at the center of the sheet, at right angles to the "Tuscan" and "Ionic" temples. Giovanni Battista identified it as a Corinthian temple and the tallest of the three temples, with columns measuring 32½ *piedi* and diameters ranging from 3–6 *piedi*. The intercolumnations are 8½ *piedi*, which are ½ *piedi* larger than Antonio the Younger's measurements (U 1174A r.), whereas Giovanni Battista's width for the cella is 1/2 *piedi* narrower. The length of the cella walls is 46½ *piedi* while Antonio the Younger's is 48 *piedi*. The plan is a 6-by-9-*piedi* temple and is probably from the Augustan period. The back wall of the cella is articulated with engaged columns.

It seems that Giovanni Battista drew "the carcere" first and before its completion decided to add the other two temples in the remaining space on this sheet. This would explain the curious overlapping of the plans. Although it was believed at the time that the temple furthest to the south was Corinthian (see also U 1174A r.), it is now known that the temple to the north was Doric, not Tuscan, and the two temples toward the south were Ionic. The misidentification of the southernmost temple was due to its elaborate decorations, including what modern archaeologists identify as attachment holes in the architrave for metal festoons.

The verso represents three separate unrelated structures. The upper half of the sheet is a plan of the west half of the central bath complex of the Baths of Caracalla. According to Bartoli, the inscription "Termi antoniani" was added by Antonio. The central north-south axis is slightly to the west, thus the disposition of the caldarium and the contiguous rooms should be further to the east.

The lower portion of the sheet represents three structures. To the left is a plan of one of the large aule of the Palazzo Savelli built into the Theater of Marcellus. Giovanni Battista indicated that the width of the room, from pier to pier, is 58 *piedi*, approximately 4 *piedi* wider than the matching room on the south flank of the palace. The notation on the left edge of the sheet gives the height of the columns as 28½ *piedi*, including the capitals, which is 2 *piedi* taller than Antonio's measurements (U 1233A r.). This portion of the sheet relates to Giovanni Battista's plan of the Theater of Marcellus (U 626A).

To the right, Giovanni Battista penned the elevation of a temple with the note "Tempietti acampidoglio." It has been suggested that the inscription refers to the Temple of Giove of the Capitoline. Adjacent is a second temple in three-quarter view, with its porch sketched in the plan just below. This structure, still unidentified, must also be associated with the Campidoglio, as suggested by the inscription "nelle storie di Campidoglio" in the same hand as the inscription for the Baths. | MK

BIBLIOGRAPHY Jordan-Huelsen (1878–1907) I, 3: 511; Ferri (1885) 148, 193, 195, 199–200, 202; Delbrück (1903) 8; Lanciani (1902–12) II: 183; Huelsen (1906) 169, 174, 182, pl. 5; Bartoli (1914–22) IV: figs 503–04, pl. 306; VI: 94; Crozzoli Aite (1981); Günther (1988) 254, 313, 316, 377, fig. VII 50 (U 1657A r.); Campbell-Nesselrath (2006) 41, n. 70; CensusIDs 10017111, 10017548.

U 1658A *recto and verso*

Giovanni Battista da Sangallo and Antonio da Sangallo the Younger

Rome, Forum Romanum, Arch of Titus, Temple of Castor and Pollux; Quirinal, Temple of Serapis; Pantheon; Forum of Augustus, Temple of Mars Ultor; Forum Holitorium, temple near S. Nicola in Carcere; obelisks near S. Rocco and S. Sebastiano, after 1527(?).

Dimensions 284 × 425 mm.
Technique Pen and brown ink.
Paper Folded.
Drawing Scale Florentine *braccia* and *minuti*.

INSCRIPTION, Recto (center left) (Giovanni Battista's hand) *Cornicie dell arco di tito / e vespasiano*; *tre colonne*; *da colonna a colonna b[raccia] 3–55½ / La colonna e grossa infondo b[raccia] 2–31½*; *monte Cavallo* / (Antonio's hand) *Mecenato* /

(Giovanni Battista's hand) *pilastro b[raccia] 3–26 / da capo*; *Cornicie di drento della ritonda*; (top right) *el popolo*; (Antonio's hand) *Lo fregio e la cornice / i[n] parti 7 e la sima / una parte che fa otto*; *basa nell orto / di sancto basilio*

Verso *santo basilio*; *bungnie quindici conputando lo collarino*; *Cornicie de quello Tenpietto / dove stava gia el [edi] fizio acanto / a santo niccola in carciero / sta nel cortile di farnese adesso / del [e]difizio dorico*; (referring to obelisks) *A santo rocco*; *Sancto bastiano*

The sketched drawings are probably copies, with the measurements probably taken by Giovanni Battista himself. The monument shown in cross section on the recto at the upper left is unidentifiable. The three console entablatures belong to the Temple of Castor and Pollux on the Forum Romanum, the Temple of Serapis on the Quirinal, and the Pantheon (for similar surveys of the Temple of Castor and Pollux see U 1181A v.) The measurements given here are for the width of one console, 38 *minuti*, and the space between the consoles, 60 *minuti*.

The verso shows, at the left, a perspective view of the ambulatory in the Temple of Mars Ultor and beside it, at the upper right, part of a soffit with a meander. The inscription for the portal of the Doric temple on the Forum Holitorium tells us that a part of the entablature became part of the Farnese collection. The notation referring to the obelisk of S. Rocco corresponds to the obelisk from the mausoleum of Augustus erected near S. Maria Maggiore under Sixtus V. The obelisk of S. Bastiano came from the Circus of Maxentius on the Via Appia, where it lay in pieces until 1648, when Bernini gave it a brilliant new prominence as the crown of the Fontana dei Quattro Fiumi on the Piazza Navona. This obelisk was drawn and reconstructed in its original location by Giuliano da Sangallo as well.

As the notes by Antonio are in his later handwriting, the drawings might be executed after 1527. | HCD

BIBLIOGRAPHY Ferri (1885) 126, 165, 176–77, 187, 195–96, 199; Ashby (1904) no. 94; Borsari (1884) 11; Huelsen (1906) 174, 176; Jordan-Huelsen (1878–1907) I, 3: 511–12; Bartoli (1914–22) IV: figs 535–36, pl 323–24; VI: 98; Günther (1981) no. 80; Günther (1988) 257, 280, 313, 377, 378, nos 101–02, 152, 272, fig. VII 21; Viscogliosi (2000) 201–3, cat. 57 CensusID 237988, 241605.

U 1660A *recto and verso*

Antonio da Sangallo the Younger

Rome, Theater of Marcellus and other sketches, after 1527(?).

Dimensions 428 × 494 mm.
Technique Pen and black ink.
Paper Folded and restored.
Measurements: Without reference to the unit (possibly *palmi*).

INSCRIPTION, Recto (recto, at the upper left) *archi 35 con quelli che / i publicho* [...]; (next to the window jamb) *archi*[?]; (next to door) *porta / del pilo; stava fermo; nel pilo grande per casa e Savelli*; (below, along the left margin) *Savelli*; (next to the fold, to the left) *Sotto la logia ultimi sotto la loggietta(.?.)*; (at the upper right) *La chana se messe / piedi 17 e* [...] *se no 14 / dal drentro del muro 256½ / delli portici 53 / 310; – 21½ / resta 44 7 / 255 7½ / se ne cavi p[er] le* [...] */ delle misure – delle / canne quelli le tocha; alarcho 30*; (next to the sketch of the two pilasters of the arcaded corridor) *21 sotto la logia / ultimo sotto la lo / gietta del palazo / sie lo ventunesimo / di quelle van[n]o al / ce[n]tro* (at the bottom, in Giovanni Battista's hand) *lo fondamento di belvedere-fatto dal portone / del giardino inverso belvedere longo p. 105 alto / Ragualgliato p[almi]7 grosso p[almi] 4.*

Verso (set perpendicularly to the bottom of the sheet, at the upper right, between two pilasters of the arcaded corridor) *dabasso*; (further down) *dalalto; disopra; darlalto; questo si rimette questo di sopra questo di sotto; coritore di sopra*; () *Le volte allo piano di palazzo / La prima* [...] */ seconda*[?] *fenestra / fenestra* [?] / [...] */ Dipoi seguita Come / lo disegno di battista*; *piano di* [...]

On the recto, in the area to the left of the fold, above, there are two drawings of a door seen from the exterior and from the interior. At the bottom is a sketch of the plan of two arcades of the ambulatory. Set perpendicularly to the bottom of the sheet is a profile with differences in levels in the zone of the Vatican Belvedere. On the right side of the fold in the sheet above, there is half a sketch of the boy with a goose sculpture and further down is a sketch of a plan for the Theater of Marcellus with the two sale regie and the typical oval form which characterizes the drawings of ancient theaters by Antonio the Younger.

On the verso, there is a rather approximate survey of the exterior arcaded corridor of the Theater of Marcellus and the profile of the impost of the arch. | ACF

BIBLIOGRAPHY Ferri (1885) 193; Bartoli Bartoli (1914–22) III: figs 429–30, pl 248–49; VI: 79–80; CensusIDs 10073130, 10073219.

U 1661A *verso*

Giovanni Battista da Sangallo and Antonio da Sangallo the Younger

Rome, Campo Marzio, Temple of Hadrian, after 1527.

Dimensions 284 × 207 mm.
Technique Pen and dark brown ink.
Paper Reinforced in places.

INSCRIPTION (Giovanni Battista's hand) *pinostilo*; (Antonio's hand) *plastine*

Antonio seems here to have asked his brother for advice concerning the possibility that the Temple of Hadrian followed a Vitruvian type. Giovanni Battista reconstructed a peripteros with 8 by 15 columns and a pronaos similar to the opisthodomus, but with a second inner row of columns instead of antae—something like a relic of the dipteros that Vitruvius surrounds with a peristyle of 8 by 15 columns. The absence of any measurements makes it clear that this drawing is concerned only with typological questions. The interior order is conceived as freestanding.

The partial ground plan of two piers with engaged columns is unrelated. The size of the engaged columns relative to the piers suggests that the plan is not of an ancient monument. Since it deals with the problem of establishing a basic type, this sheet can be assumed to be a model for Antonio's own studies of ground plans and thus dates before U 1144A and U 1175A. | HCD

BIBLIOGRAPHY Bartoli (1914–22) IV: fig. 518, pl. 310; VI: 96; CensusID (verso) 10072284.

U 1662A *recto and verso*

Giovanni Battista da Sangallo and Antonio da Sangallo the Younger

Rome, unknown building (*recto*); Forum Romanum, Temple of Romulus (*verso*), after 1527(?).

Dimensions 335 × 166 mm.
Technique Pen and brown ink.
Paper Trimmed, vertical center fold, repair at lower left edge.
Drawing Scale Roman *palmi* and *dita*.

INSCRIPTION, Recto *Alla piaza de caualiere / dita; La sala gran[d]e resta larga / i[n] la ricorretione ricorreta p[almi] 53¼ / La capella sara p[almi] 44*; measurements

Verso *santo cosma / e damiano*; *Lo capitello e alto 53 / dita lo fuso della / colonna e alto palmi / 31–8 grossa da pie / palmi 3–10½*

The sheet shows on both sides the elevation of an entablature. While the building on the recto is not identified, the verso shows the one above one of the cipolin columns on the front of the temple of Divus Romulus facing the Via Sacra. The note on the recto and the numbers adding up the measurements of the entablatures are in Antonio's hand. | HCD

BIBLIOGRAPHY Bartoli (1914–22) III: figs 382–83, pl. 224; VI: 72; Lupi-Pettinau (1980) 62, no. 90, fig. 73; CensusID 10071566, 10071578.

U 1664A *recto*

Antonio Labacco

Unidentified arch, details, mid-16th century.

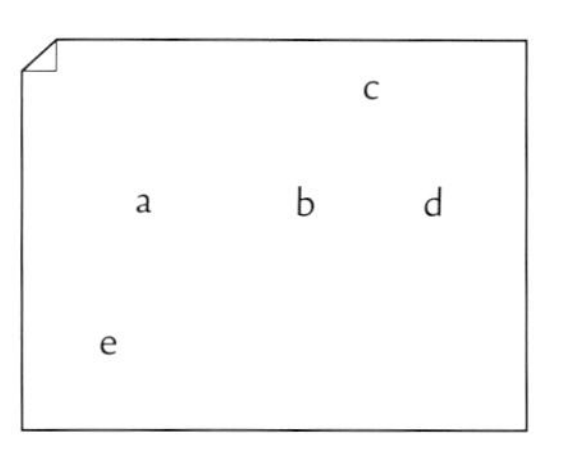

Dimensions 193 × 156 mm.
Technique Pen and brown ink, pinholes in corners.
Paper Heavy.
Drawing Scale *piede* and *dita*.

INSCRIPTION (c) *vano p[iedi] 11 D[ite] 14*; (b) *piedi* 12 D 12 1/2, (e) *archo*; (bottom edge, pencil, later hand) *Abaco*

All the drawings appear to show parts of an unidentified honorific arch. The one at the far left *a* is a sketch of a pier up to the springing of the vault. From front to back, the arch only measures 3 *piedi*. To the right (*b*) is a sketch of a column or possibly half- column, just over 12 *piedi* high. To its left (*c*), labeled *vano*, is probably a cross section of the arch proper, over 11 *piedi* wide, or, less likely, of the attic. To the far right of the sheet (*d*) is a section and part elevation of pedestal or podium, just under 8 *piedi* high. At the bottom left (*e*) is a section/elevation of an architrave, or, more likely, given the vicinity of the word *archo*, of an archivolt.

The attic of the Arch of Septimius Severus has a comparable width to that in drawing *c*, but all the other dimensions on the sheet suggest a much more modest structure, similar to the Arch of the Gavi in Verona. If one reads *c* as the void of the arch, 11 *piedi* is comparable to the Arco dei Gavi, as is the width of the pier at 3 *piedi* on drawing *a*. Also, the height of the member represented by drawing *b* is similar to that of the pilasters under the impost at Verona. None of the correspondences is close enough by itself to suggest that the Veronese arch is the subject, and the pedestal or podium of drawing *d* bears no relation at all to it, yet there are some strange points of contact. Thus, the archivolt of the Arco dei Gavi has the unusual feature of a fascia decorated with strigils, and Labacco decorates the cyma recta here with strigils. Indeed, most of the elements of the archivolt of the arch are present in the drawing but in a different order, as if Labacco was relying on a garbled verbal description, or notes, rather than a drawing.

On Antonio the Younger's drawings of the Arch of the Gavi (U 815A), the word *archo* (drawing *e*) recalls a drawing of the archivolt by Baldassarre Peruzzi on U 631A v. and 478A r., where it is similarly called *arco*. This would hardly merit mention, were it not known Labacco knew the other side of this double-sided sheet, copying with a few minor differences Peruzzi's plan of the temples at S. Nicola in Carcere in his *Libro... appartenente all'architettura*. Labacco is hardly copying Peruzzi in this case, and we cannot be even sure that the subject of any of the drawings is the Arch of the Gavi, but there could be some sort of connection. | IC

BIBLIOGRAPHY Ferri (1885) 126; Bartoli (1914–22) IV: fig. 608, pl. 351; VI: 110; CensusID 60681.

U 1667A *recto and verso*

Giovanni Battista da Sangallo

Teatro di Marcello(?), apsided *aula regia* or thermal chamber, after 1527.

Dimensions 216 × 255mm.
Technique Pen and sepia ink, stylus marks, circles drawn with a compass.
Paper Lightweight, very stained and with very obvious restoration work.
Drawing Scale and Dimensions Measurements in *braccia*.

INSCRIPTION, Recto (left, vertically) *homosara*; (center, horizontally) *homohinissimo*; (at right in descending horizontal lines) *Tubice-trombetta / Signifero: banderaro / Precor-banditore / Minister-sergente / Tergiductor – retroguardia, measurements in piedi*

Verso (in a recent hand) *mano di francesco da S.Gallo*

Three drawings, employing different scales and techniques, tackle the subject of an apsided *aula regia* or thermal chamber, subdivided into a nave and two aisles by columns with bases. In the larger plan to the right, they have been drawn partly freehand and partly with a straightedge and set square, with measurements noted in some of the intercolumniations. The columns run up to the curve of the semicircular apse. The internal perimeter wall has isolated columns, their bases on a tangent with the wall which is broken up by wide windows. The design is further explored on a small scale at the top of the page, and again very roughly at the bottom: in the latter drawing, the columns standing proud of the wall are replaced by half-columns, which would suggest that this is an attempt at a graphic reconstruction of the space.

The relationship between the columns in the central nave and two thirds of the columns projecting from the wall is well focalized; this same relationship is explored again on the right of the sheet, on an intermediate scale between the two.

The drawing can be dated to after 1527 as Giovanni Battista uses *piedi* instead of *braccia* as the unit of measurement. It can be related to others on the same subject, such as U 1233A r. as regards the dating, and U 1270A r. by Antonio da Sangallo the Younger, as mentioned by Bartoli, and U 1668A by Giovanbattista.

On the verso, there is a small decorative drawing and some numerical calculation notes. | ACF

BIBLIOGRAPHY Bartoli (1914–22) IV: fig. 517, pl. 310; VI: 96; CensusID 10072280.

U 1668A *recto*

Giovanni Battista da Sangallo

Rome, *aula regia* of Theater of Marcellus, after 1527.

Dimensions 423 × 435 mm.
Technique Pen and brown ink, stylus, compass.
Paper Folded in six, repairs at corners and along folds.
Drawing Scale Roman *piedi*.

INSCRIPTION, Recto *dal di sopra di questa / cornice al di sotto delar/chitrave del frontispitio / sono pie Quatro e mezo*

Verso (later hand, blue pencil, twice) *1668*

At the left, Giovanni Battista represented the right half of the plan of one of the two royal halls of the Theater of Marcellus. On the inside of the plan, a section is drawn at the difficult intersection between the freestanding column of the central nave linked to its corresponding element by means of an arch and half-column attached to the pilaster, which is, in turn, linked to the next pilaster by an archivolt. At the left margin, profiles of the Doric capital and of the base are drawn. At the right of the sheet is a profile of the Doric capital of the column with its trabeation with measurements in *piedi.* | ACF

BIBLIOGRAPHY Bartoli (1914–22) IV: fig. 531, pl. 320; VI: 97; Lanciani (1902–12) III: 8; Giovannoni (1959) I: 96; CensusID 242433.

U 1701A *recto*

Giovan Francesco da Sangallo

Rome, detail of Arch of Septimius Severus, before 1527.

Dimensions 163 × 195 mm.
Technique Pen and brown ink, stylus, straightedge, compass.
Paper Partly yellowed, trimmed.

INSCRIPTION *Menbretto dello archo dachanpidoglio cioe*

The drawing represents an orthogonal elevation and section of the impost of one of the side arches of the Arch of Septimius Severus. Bartoli attributed this to Giovanni Battista, but despite Buddensieg's omission of it from his list of reattributions to Giovan Francesco, the style of both the drawing and the writing strongly favor the latter as author. The label and measurements betray the likely source of the drawing to be Giuliano da Sangallo's Barberini Codex (fol. 63r.; Huelsen 1910, p. 67). The text was cut when the sheet was reduced. | IC

BIBLIOGRAPHY Ferri (1885) 171; Huelsen (1910) 67; Bartoli (1914–22) IV: fig. 572, pl. 340; VI: 104; Bober (1957) 82; Brilliant (1967) 258; CensusID 47353.

U 1702A *recto and verso*

Giovan Francesco da Sangallo

Rome, (a) profile of a modillion; (b) column of the composite order; (c) profile of a man's head (fragmented because the sheet has been torn); (d) detail of a capital belonging to the interior order of the Temple of Mars Ultor (*recto*); Rome, (a) capital in SS. Cosma e Damiano; (b) (c) capital in the basilica of S. Croce in Gerusalemme; (d) three capitals in the basilica of S. Lorenzo Fuori le Mura (*verso*), before 1510(?).

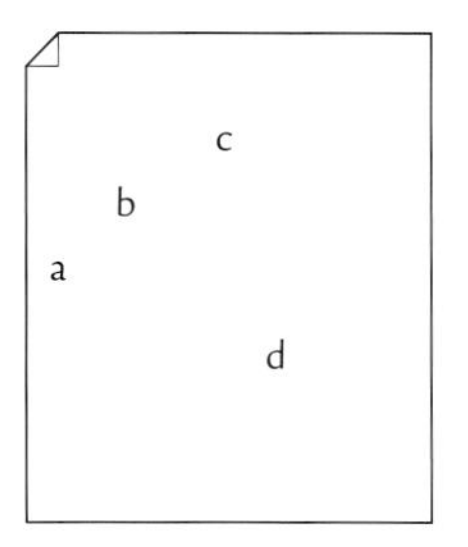

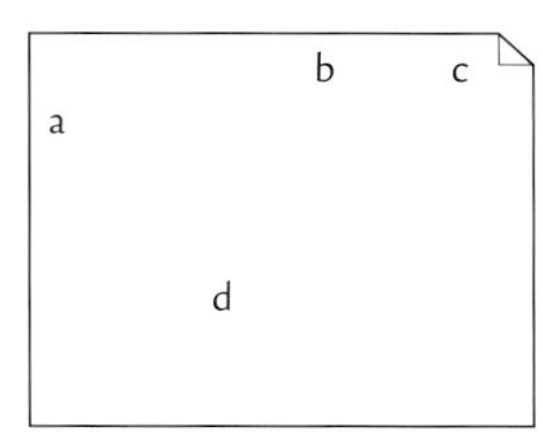

Dimensions 320 × 240 mm.
Paper Medium weight, upper central part torn out, restored.
Technique Pencil, pen and brown ink.

INSCRIPTION, Recto a *questa cholona si è a nove teste e chapitelo avatagio la cimasa cioe piu duna testa / la basa si è meza testa alta adagetto la meta che è alta le prime foglie sono alte la quarta p*[*arte*] */ del chapetello et le seconde al mezo del capitello la cholona è diritta in sino al terzo della cholona*

Verso a *in sancto chosimo e sancto damiano*; b *in sancta chroce in gie*; c d e *in sancto laurenzio fuora delle mura*

The location of the column of drawing *b* has not been specified, but it is, without doubt, a piece of ancient architecture. Giovan Francesco is trying to describe the relationship between the parts in order to determine the probable proportions of the components of the Composite column. By drawing the capital at *d* in such detail, Giovan Francesco seems to want to propose a possible variation of the column drawn next to it. This capital was also carefully drawn by Baldassarre Peruzzi (U 633A r.), and Giovan Francesco seems to be concerned not so much to reproduce the details but rather to capture the idea of the capital, and by drawing the abacus as seen from below he is showing the neck and head of the horse as a pleasing alternative to the volute of the Composite order.

The capitals on the verso seem to have been chosen for the opulence of their imaginatively decorated shapes, typical of the Roman Imperial period, and for the quality of the carving of the sculptural decoration. He also draws a side view of the volute of the Ionic capital which may have belonged to the portico in front of the basilica of S. Croce [C. Varagnoli, *S. Croce in Gerusalemme: la basilica restaurata e l'architettura del Settecento romano* (Rome 1995, p. 49, note 84). Because the sheet is torn, important parts of the two capitals at the bottom right have been lost: their locations can be can be inferred from the reference marker below which, like the one on the left-hand capital, is repeated in the caption. | AGG

BIBLIOGRAPHY Ferri (1885) 29, 137, 138, 142; Bartoli (1914–22) VI: 103; Buddensieg (1975) 108; Günther (1988) 298, n. 215; CensusID 62492.

U 1703A *recto and verso*

Giovan Francesco da Sangallo

Rome, (a) studies of profiles of mouldings; (b) measured reconstruction of an ancient cornice (*recto*); (c) (d) measured reconstructions of ancient cornices (*verso*), before 1510 (?).

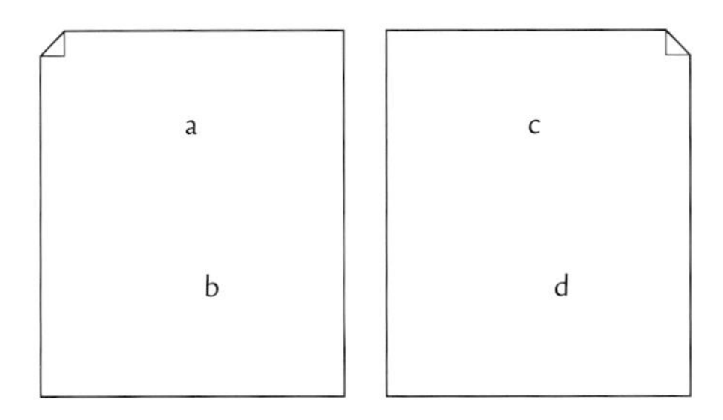

Dimensions 287 × 207 mm.
Paper Medium weight.
Technique Pencil, pen and brown ink, brush.

INSCRIPTION, Recto (A) *questo chornicione aveva rotto la gola e dera a san / basilio achanto a una osteria nella strada*; (b) *questo si è minuti 50 per ogni verso cioe di 60 minuti el bracio / fiorentino b da luna mensola a la[l]tra è minuti 20 ed è / grosa minuti 9 da luna mensola a la[l]tra si è schaglie / cioe chosì* [drawing of small Scaly leaves] / *questa chornicie in terra dallarcho di chamigliano / chavata di naouo* [meaning "di nuovo"?]

The two cyma mouldings on the recto (*a*) may be details drawn life-size despite not being identifiable with the measurements of the cornices drawn on the sheet. (*b*) The subject is a cornice which, like that on the verso of the sheet, is part of a repertory of useful models in the designing of buildings. (*c*) Despite the fact that it was found near the church of S. Basilio, and therefore near the remains of the Temple of Mars Ultor, the fragment of cornice drawn on the verso appears to have belonged to the entablature of the portico in the courtyard of the Trajan Column also surveyed by Labacco on sheet U 1211A, annotated by Antonio the Younger. The broken cyma, not drawn by Giovan Francesco, could be the cyma illustrated in Labacco's drawing. (*d*) The so-called Camillian Arch was the name given to an arch of Domitian near the Temple of Isis in the Campo Marzio, which began to be demolished in 1585; the cornice that has been drawn must have broken away from the monument during the Middle Ages, but it could well have belonged to it, not least because of the similarity of the sequence of its mouldings with that of the Arch of Titus. An axonometrical drawing by Baldassarre Peruzzi (U 486A v.) of the same cornice serves to clarify the location of the decorative detail that Giovan Francesco has drawn. | AGG

BIBLIOGRAPHY Ferri (1885) 120, 124, 160; Bartoli (1914–22) VI: 102; Buddensieg (1975) 108; CensusID 10027591, 10027606.

U 1704A *recto*

Giovan Francesco da Sangallo and Antonio da Sangallo the Younger

Rome, Forum Romanum, Temple of Venus and Roma, ca. 1512 (?).

Dimensions 212 × 230 mm.
Technique Pen and brown ink, freehand.
Paper Partly yellowed; trimmed, top edge patched.
Drawing Scale Minuti.

INSCRIPTION (Antonio's hand) *questa gola a lo regolo largo ed e bassa / p[er]che era chornicie laterale duno frontespizio; era molto bella a vederla di bona maniera*; (Giovan Francesco's hand) *19 e larga la mensola / la mensola e tanta larga quanta alta*; (Antonio's hand) *Cavata i[n] fra [i]l chuliseo e lo tenpio del solis e luna ouero / di chastore e pollucie nell orto di santa maria nova*; measurements

The principal drawing *a* is a section through the end of a pediment with part of the supporting cornice of a Corinthian entablature, drawn orthogonally with the lowest two mouldings below the modillion, shown in projection. Drawing *b*, to the right of *a*, is an elevation detail of the front of the volute of the modillion and the cyma reversa above it. Below *a* is a sketch, *c*, isolating the volute in elevation with its length measured. On the left edge is drawing *d*, a profile of the volute below the cyma reversa, fillet and corona. Three abandoned details show profiles of the cyma reversa and adjacent mouldings. Antonio's note locates the findspot of the fragment as the site of the Temple of Venus and Rome, and it may be part of one of that temple's pediments. | IC

BIBLIOGRAPHY Ferri (1885) 160; Lanciani (1891) 9; Lanciani (1902–12) II: 220; Bartoli (1914–22) IV: fig. 540, pl. 326; VI: 99; Buddensieg (1975) 108; Frommel (1994, *Introduction*) 40; CensusID 10028182.

U 1705A *recto*

Giovan Francesco da Sangallo

Rome, Doric entablature of the Theatre of Marcellus, between 1514 and 1520.

Dimensions 306 × 165 mm.
Technique Pen and brown ink, straightedge.
Paper Heavy, partly yellowed, trimmed.
Drawing Scale Florentine *braccia*.

INSCRIPTION, Recto (top, brown ink, modern hand), *Cornice dorica dell'anfiteatro/ de Savelli a Roma*; (right border, brown ink, Giovanni Franceso's hand, *Cor*[...]/ *de* [...]

The drawing is among the group attributed to Giovanni Francesco by Buddensieg (1975), having before been attributed to Giovanni Battista by Bartoli. When the right side of the sheet was trimmed the original note identifying the drawing was mostly lost but it was copied at the top of the sheet.

The drawing shows the Doric entablature and the top part of a half-column from the first storey of the Theatre of Marcellus. The entablature is drawn as an isometric section allowing the profile and the elevation to be seen to scale, but the capital and top part of the shaft of the column appear to be drawn perspectivally. It is similar in character to sections drawn by Bernardo della Volpaia, such as U 1181A r and in the Codex Coner. | CLF

BIBLIOGRAPHY Ferri (1885) 193; Bartoli (1914–22) VI: 102; Buddensieg (1975) 108; Günther (1988) 296, n. 199, 562; CensusID 10030090

U 1706A *recto and verso*

Giovan Francesco da Sangallo

Details of Doric entablature (*recto*); Rome, basement of Mausoleum of Hadrian (*verso*), before 1527.

Dimensions 275 × 156 mm.
Technique Pen and brown ink, freehand.
Paper Heavy, partly yellowed, trimmed, corner patched.
Drawing Scale Florentine *braccia*.

INSCRIPTION, Recto (bottom left, blue pencil, nineteenth-century hand, numbering) *1706*

Verso *bugni piane*; *i*[*n*] *basamento*; *anticho dichastello santo angnelo*; *nono potuto pigliare questi piani*; various measurements

The recto has two sketches of unidentified Doric entablatures, the cornices of both of which were lost when the sheet was cut down. On the verso is an elevation and section of part of the lower zones of the square basement of the Mausoleum of Hadrian, showing the plinths, dado, and the lowest course of the low-relief rustication. Although it appears as though a corner is depicted, this must be merely a device to include the section on the same drawing as the elevation, because we know that the rustication did not extend to the corners, the angles of the basement being occupied by pilasters, as can be seen in various Renaissance drawings, even if we are not sure if the pilaster sprang from the base molding, as in the Codex Escuraliensis, or from the dado, as in U 4330A v. All the surviving marble facing of the basement was removed around 1579, to be used in the building of the chapel of Gregory XIII in New St Peter's. The section, with the same measurements, is paralleled on U 1181A v., by Bernardo della Volpaia. Antonio's section on U 911A v., however, makes the lower plinth taller, and adds one or two more dimensions. | IC

BIBLIOGRAPHY Huelsen (1891) 140–45; Lanciani (1902–12) IV: 57; Egger (1906) II: fols 23 and 30 v.; Bartoli (1914–22) IV: fig. 544, pl. 327; VI: 100; Borgatti (1931) 30, fig. 12; Giovannoni (1959) I: 185; Buddensieg (1975) 108; CensusID 48009.

U 1716A *recto and verso*

Giovan Francesco da Sangallo

Rome, Forum Romanum, Basilica Aemilia, before 1527.

Dimensions 315 × 230 mm.
Technique Pen and dark brown ink.
Paper Trimmed irregularly at top.
Drawing Scale *Minuti*.

INSCRIPTION, Recto *Modanatura. del piatto. sta chosi*
Verso *chapitello dori/cho di foro i*[*n*] *bua/ro*. *i*[*n*] *roma / cioe de pilastri*; *e pilastri ano chanali*; *le cholone ano 13 chanali / e pilastri diminuischano*; *Mezo foro i*[*n*] *buarum / dichano che staua chosi*; *basa de pilastri e delle / cholonne*; *I*[*m*]*basamento di foro / i*[*n*] *buarum*

The clean drawing of a Doric entablature in elevation on the recto probably represents a synthesis of various models; it is not the result of a study of the monument in situ.

Antonio's drawing U 1413A, the measurements of which largely accord with this sheet, probably should be counted among those models. The fact that the metope ornament with its six egg-and-dart motifs is shown in cross section as it appears on the building testifies to the exactness with which the details have been observed.

On the verso, a larger capital was initially scored on the sheet, its size corresponding exactly to Giuliano da Sangallo's drawing on folio 71 v. of the Codex Barberini. This gives us the source of Giovan Francesco's drawing. The profiles of a socle are also taken over from that codex, although Giovan Francesco joined Giuliano's separate profiles and added a neck. The assumption that the building had a rectangular ground plan likewise comes from Giuliano (fol. 63 v.). | HCD

BIBLIOGRAPHY Ferri (1885) 166; Lanciani (1883, *Aula del Senato*) 30, pl. 4, fig. 8; Huelsen (1884) 326, 337, 342; Bartoli (1914–22) IV: figs 555–56, pl. 331; VI: 101; Buddensieg (1975) 108; Günther (1988) 125–27, 249, 96–7, nos 144, 199, 202, 208, 212, fig. VII 10; Zampa (2014) 211, 218, 228, fig. 4; CensusIDs 239663, 239670.

U 1720A *recto and verso*

Aristotile da Sangallo

Rome, unidentified palace, possibly on Palatine Hill (fantasy after the Basilica of Constantine?).

Dimensions 108 × 80 mm.
Technique Pen and brown ink, freehand.
Paper Yellowed, repairs, pinholes in corners.

INSCRIPTION, Recto (bottom right, blue pencil, nineteenth-century hand, numbering) *1720*; (light brown ink) *palazo maiore*

This sheet shows a plan of a structure, with vaulted nave, flanked by three bays to the left and three to the right, with apses at the ends of the nave and of the middle bays of each side. The inscription "palazo maiore" usually refers to the Palatine in the Middle Ages and Renaissance, but nothing like this has ever been found there. Krautheimer believed it could represent a lost tomb, but it is so similar, in all but proportions, to reconstructions of the Basilica of Constantine, that it seems more likely to be merely a fantasy deriving from it. Since the sheet is cut down, it is possible that the inscription, written in a paler ink than that of the drawing, is incomplete or even refers to another drawing. Ferri identified the lines at the bottom left of the sheet as part of a cornice drawn in perspective.

On the verso are two drawings, now incomplete because of the trimming of the sheet. One is the upper part of an elevation, and shows a pediment and the top of an arch below, suggesting it is a gateway or narrow entrance façade. It could perhaps correspond to the plan to its left, which has a single bay projecting from the rest of the structure. Between the two side walls of this projecting porch a coffered barrel vault is sketched in perspective. The porch opened into a vaulted arcade, which, assuming the plan was symmetrical had three bays. Beyond the arcade is a rectangular space bounded opposite the arcade by a wall with engaged columns, which almost mirrors the arcade, although the corners differ slightly. It is impossible to determine if the space is covered by a roof or is a cortile. The drawings are probably studies of some modern structure rather than records of something ancient. | IC

BIBLIOGRAPHY Ferri (1885) 172, 178; Bartoli (1914–22) IV: figs 590–91, pl. 344; VI: 106–07; Krautheimer (1961) 70, fig. 3; CensusID 44048.

U 1804A *recto and verso*

Giovan Francesco da Sangallo

Rome, reconstructions of four ancient columns with measurements (*recto*); ancient basilica of St Peter's, capital of a Composite column (*verso*), 1519–25.

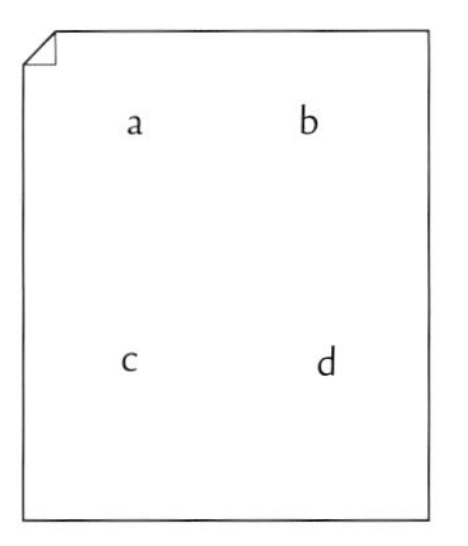

Dimensions 224 × 325 mm.
Paper Medium weight.
Technique Pen and brown ink, pencil.

INSCRIPTION, Recto (A) *Questo piano si è B 3 minuti 30 per facia / Questa basa si è in santo pagolo fuori di roma ed è tonda*; (b) *Questa basa si chauo a pie de Savegli / e furno asai e nota che chanali delle / cholone sono uno largo e uno in stretto / chome si vede in disegnio. / lo vivo da pie della cholona si è B 2 minuti 25 / cioe B 2 mj 25 lo vivo da pie*; (c) *Dalla dogana andare in nella valle / di marmo tonda*; (d) *Basa ionicha a pie del ponte a q. chapi / in tresteferi*

Verso *Dallo in gniudo* [referring to the "smooth top edge of the abacus"?] *al pionbo si è mi 76½ / lo chartocio è groso 15 dinanzi e dove posa / in sul uovolo è groso 30*; *Questo chapitello si è in sanpietro e sono / e piu begli di roma di questa sorta lo di sotto / del chartocio viene a mezo lo chapitello / a putto* [for "appunto"?]; *el fiore*; *pionbato in sul fiore*; *tutto lo chapitello alto B 2 mj 8*

As we see in other drawings, Giovan Francesco's interest, unlike that of his cousin Antonio, is in ornate and imaginatively decorated ancient architectural components.

(*a*) After giving the measurements of the faces of the plinth, Giovan Francesco specifies that this is a *round* base, which means that it belongs to a column and not to a pilaster. (*b*) Above the ornate, elegant base is a shaft which is unusual in that it has alternating grooves of two different widths. The reference to the excavations and the recovery of many ancient architectural elements around the Theatre of Marcellus, which belonged to the Savelli family at the time, agrees with Serlio's testimony [III, 69 v.] that he had seen and measured some of the items in about 1524–25 when Peruzzi reconstructed the Savelli palace (Frommel 1989, p. 39). (*c*) The base may have been recovered outside the Porta San Sebastiano near the Caffarella valley. *d* "Ionic" Base, which was also drawn by Giovan Francesco on U 2103A r.

On the verso is a reconstruction with measurements of a capital also drawn by Antonio (U 32A r.). This seems to be a fair copy, made by Giovan Francesco, of some sketches made in-situ by his cousin: a three quarter view of the capital, showing the volutes placed at 45 degrees, and the profile next to it makes it possible to study all the mouldings, and it agrees with Antonio's drawing on the verso of sheet U 32A. Giovan Francesco uses the term "chartocio" for volute. | AGG

BIBLIOGRAPHY Ferri (1885) 128, 148, 151; Frommel (1989, *Serlio*) 39; CensusIDs 205314, 66985.

U 1844A *recto and verso*

Giovanni Battista da Sangallo (?)

Section and study of an amphitheater, perhaps the Colosseum.

Dimensions 427 × 290 mm.
Technique Pen and sepia ink, freehand, black chalk, stylus, straightedge, and square.
Paper Heavy, stained.
Drawing Scale Florentine *braccia*.

INSCRIPTIONS, Recto: (at left, between section of superimposed orders and three sketches of plinths) *colonne ioniche a tutto p. 30 dita 7 / a tutto p. 29 d 2 / piedestallo piedi 40 d 5*; (upper right) *al tutto dell'altezza del'anfitheatro di Tito senza lultima cornice e palmi 182 e dita / piedi 136 dita 15*; (next to scale in *braccia fiorentine*) *braccia fiorentine 68½*

The recto of the sheet is taken up by a perspectival section of an amphitheater. It shows the two concentric rings of the radial sectors that constitute the system of artificial vaulted substructures to support the steps of the cavea. Above the steps of the cavea, the upper level of the internal ambulatory is drawn with Tuscan colonnade (cf. the arches at Antonio's early reconstruction at U 1555A v.). The access stairs are indicated at the lower level, as far as the juncture measured in *piedi*. Many parts remain undefined.

The drawing on the verso relates to the perspectival section shown on the recto of the sheet. To read it, we have to hypothesize that the observer moves his gaze upward, in accord with the height of the stories. In fact, in correspondence to the external ambulatory, which has Tuscan half-columns, the draughtsman showed the elevation of the inner circle of the innermost major and minor arcades of the upper zones. Above we see the system of the vaulted substructures and of the seven radials that support the cavea, completely raised above ground, as well as the system of stairs and corridors for circulation. | ACF

BIBLIOGRAPHY Ferri (1885) 123; Bartoli (1914–22) V: figs 888–89, pl. 486; VI: 144; CensusID 10060685.

U 1850A *recto*

Antonio Abaco and Antonio da Sangallo the Younger

Architectural fragments of Roman monuments with notes and measurements, after 1520.

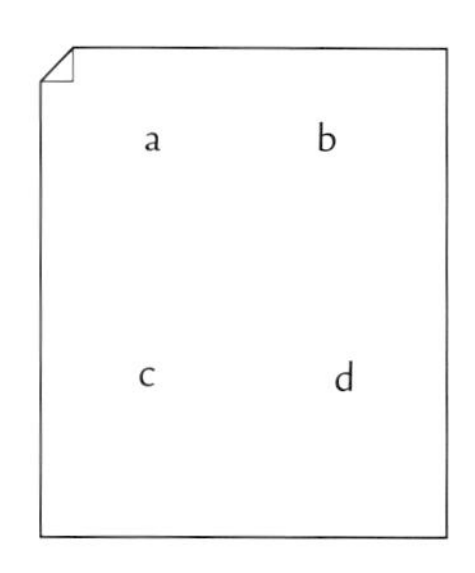

Dimensions 262 × 210 mm.
Paper White paper, sheet trimmed and reinforced, discolored or bleached at top left where the ink appears to have faded.
Technique Pen and sepia ink, freehand drawings.

INSCRIPTION, Recto (top, on a) *del popolo*; (between a and b) *A sessantesimi di braccio fiorentino*; (below a) *192*; (left of b, rotated 90 degrees anticlockwise) *45½ e alta tutta*; (above b) *a san paulo*; (at top of b) *46½ e da gietto tutta*; (above c) *apiè della croce di mo*[n]*te chauallo / sotto uno portigale*; (right of c, Antonio's hand) *jonicha bella*; (below c) *el dado e largo mi*[nuti] *72*; (at top, above d) *del pa*[n]*tano*; (centre, below c and d, rotated 90 degrees anticlockwise) addition of the measurements of the separate mouldings that make up the base to determine its total height

The sheet was probably part of a collection of surveys of antiquities. On it, in orthographic projection, are drawn the architectural details of three Corinthian columns and a base, paged in an orderly manner, all minutely measured in Florentine *braccia* of 60 *minuti* (1 *braccio* = 58.36 cm; 1 *minuto* = 0.97 cm). There was no preparation of the sheets and no auxiliary instruments were used. The freehand outlined drawings have been attributed to Antonio Abaco, a pupil and collaborator of Antonio da Sangallo the Younger, who often oversaw the work. This traditional attribution is confirmed by very recent analyses of the handwriting (Frommel 1994, *Introduction*, p. 39, p. 41), and also by the fact that the notes on the units of measurement are recognizably in Antonio the Younger's hand (*b*) as is his comment on the base "jonicha bella." The number "192" halfway up, along the left margin, in a different handwriting to those mentioned above, might relate to an attempt to impaginate a treatise in relation to the illustrations. Simpler still, it could just be the number assigned to the sheet during a reordering of the material. On this point, drawing U 1182A r., attributed to Antonio the Younger, is of a measured fragment of the same Ionic base that carries the page number "191" at the upper left, in what is recognisably the same third style of handwriting. The details that have been reproduced appear in many 16th century drawings and the drawings on this sheet are likely to be copies of surveys made by other people, rather than an autonomous survey project. The first profile on the upper left, belongs to a fragment of cornice at Porta del Popolo, probably only slightly above the door itself, as indicated in a note by Antonio the Younger on U 1195A r., where the same cornice is drawn in section and developed tridimensionally in axonometry. The dimensions of height and the overhang of the mouldings are the same in both drawings. The fragment of cornice that was also surveyed by Baldassare Peruzzi in U 409A r. (Wurm 1984, p. 447), could be the one that is still visible, in 17th and 18th century views and paintings, on the right-hand side of the Porta del Popolo, next to the new elevation, built during the second half of the Cinquecento. The cornice detail at the upper right probably corresponds to the entablature in the nave of the Roman basilica of San Paolo Fuori le Mura, which ran more or less tangentially to the top of the arches and ended above the two Ionic columns that supported the triumphal arch near the nave. An almost identical cornice (the only difference is in the bottom moulding) is shown on drawing U 1539A v., attributed to Fra Giocondo (Bartoli, I: fig. 59; VI: 15), on which the author's notes confirm the suggested identification. The third cornice has been drawn at the bottom left, which the notes say was surveyed "al pantano," i.e. in the area of the Forum of Augustus. The identification of both the site and the fragment is less positive, in this case. However, there does not seem to be any similarity between the relief and the entablatures in either the Temple of Mars Ultor or the enclosure at Nerva's Forum. The fact that the three cornices have been grouped close together means that they were intended for comparitive purposes, both in terms of proportions and dimensions, and in terms of decoration, for analysing the different patterns carved into the mouldings. The San Paolo and the Pantano cornices are of similar proportions and have a ratio of almost 1:1 between the total height and the overhang; but they are of different dimensions, (the first is ca. 45½ *braccia*, the second 71 *braccia*, equal respectively to 44.22 cm and 69.00 cm). The Porta del Popolo cornice, on the other hand, is 48½ *braccia* high and overhangs by 40½ *braccia* (equal to 47.14 cm and 39.36 cm). In all three cornices, the denticulation of the undercornice has been executed with small, separate blocks (these are the "dentils") rather than as a continuous, uniform fascia. The sequence of the mouldings in each cornice follows its own formal definition; the San Paolo and Pantano cornices, significantly placed one above the other on the right-hand side of the sheet, have almost identical components. Lastly, a finely carved base is drawn at the bottom left, made up, from top to bottom, of a torus and two scotias, the bottom one of which sits on the plinth. Each of the mouldings seem to have been carefully carved, the torus and scotias have grooves, the pairs of astragals that separate the principal mouldings have a plaited motif; the plinth features shells in relief. Beneath the drawing, rotated 90 degrees anticlockwise, a partial addition of the heights of the mouldings can be seen, which gives a total of 21 *minuti*. Finishing off the calculation by including the measurements of some of the components that are missing, achieves a total height of 38 and ⅔ *minuti* (37.57 cm). The same base, probably drawn by Antonio the Younger, appears on U 1182A, also minutely measured in Florentine *braccia*, and the identifying notes relating to the two drawings are also similar. This sheet deals with an architectural fragment found in a portico near Monte Cavallo (Quirinale). Antonio Abaco's attention to surveys of "antiques" appears to confirm his interest not only in documenting and classifying, in order to compile a treatise, but possibly a desire to analyse and understand how the individual units of the mouldings are systematically put together. The latter could also be seen as research for a project to be linked, more pragmatically, with the planning and constructive activities of the Sangallo circle. The sheet has been dated after 1520 based on the fact that it includes the cornice surveyed at the Forum of Augustus; this was a period during which Antonio the Younger and his collaborators were becoming interested in the area in question (Frommel 1994, *Introduction*, p. 39). | RB

BIBLIOGRAPHY Ferri (1885) 125, 128, 148, 165; Bartoli (1914–22) IV: fig. 614, pl. 352; VI: 110. Wurm (1984), Frommel (1994, *Introduction*); CensusID 10010273.

U 1852A *recto*

Giovan Francesco da Sangallo and Antonio da Sangallo the Younger

Rome, Forum of Augustus, before 1527.

Dimensions 270 × 427 mm.
Technique Pen and brown ink.
Paper Center fold.
Drawing Scale Florentine *braccia.*

INSCRIPTION, Recto (Giovan Francesco's hand) *pende pocho questo piano / dove e lo girare chome eudi quivi / no pende. 10 terzo diminuto*; *i[n] chasa el presidente / a monte chauallo / serviva a. S. basilio*; (on plinth) *i[n] su questo piano sie B 2. 13 / D*; (on ground plan) (Antonio's hand) *foro traiano / entrata / piaza di S[an]to basilio*; *Le base anno questo pli[n]to che andava / i[n] to[n]do e no[n] risaltata / A / C / D*; (near right profile of a base) (Giovan Francesco's hand) *B B A C*; *a sa basilio*; *basa della ch/ olonna cioe / el piano*; *e tanto si e quella del pilastro / piano*

Verso *di Sto basilio*

The ground plan and elevations of details relate to the northern exedra of the Forum of Augustus, the engaged columns of which have decorated bases with unusual round plinths. In the ground plan and a related commentary, this feature was later (after 1527) annoted by Antonio as a peculiarity. | HCD

BIBLIOGRAPHY Ferri (1885) 165, 167; Borsari (1884) 12; Ashby (1904) no. 132; Huelsen (1910) 11; Bartoli (1914–22) IV: fig. 534, pl. 322; VI: 98; Buddensieg (1975) 108; Viscogliosi (2000), 203–04, cat. no. 52; CensusID 204496.

U 1856A *recto and verso*

Giovanni Battista da Sangallo

Study of two alternative solutions for interior elevation of portico in *summa cavea* of amphitheater or theater, probably Theater of Marcellus, perhaps intended for an illustrated edition of Vitruvius' De Architectura, before.

Dimensions 184 × 171 mm.
Technique Pen and sepia ink, freehand.
Paper Lightweight, stains and repairs.

INSCRIPTION, Recto (at center) *famisol*

The drawing on the recto proposes a solution for the upper interior elevation of a theater (or amphitheater, perhaps inspired by the Colosseum). The rear wall at the top of the cavea is not only a fundamental element for assuring the proper acoustics of the spectacles but also an embellishment of the interior facade. With a giant architectural order framing two levels of apertures, the facade also serves to close the double order of superimposed internal arcades. The rough sketch of the arcades at the left of the sheet is helpful for understanding the architectural organism. At the upper level we see the crowning of the columnatio, which supports the roof sloping toward the attic of the external ambulatory.
The verso shows a different solution, somewhat less detailed than that on the recto. In particular, it seems to be a study for the reconstruction of the decoration of the bays with apertures, which were left undefined on the recto. The pediments of the windows at the first level are especially interesting. The elevation now appears more orderly, thanks to the double line of the stringcourse, which was absent from the recto.

The drawing may have been intended for the illustrated edition of Vitruvius's *De Architectura*. For earlier reconstructions of the inner facades see 1555 v. and 1844 v. | ACF

BIBLIOGRAPHY Ferri (1885) 123; Bartoli (1914–22) VI: 93; Giovannoni (1956) I: 96; CensusID 10029246.

U 1865A *recto*

Antonio da Sangallo the Younger

Schematic details of architectural components that probably belonged to the top order at the Colosseum.

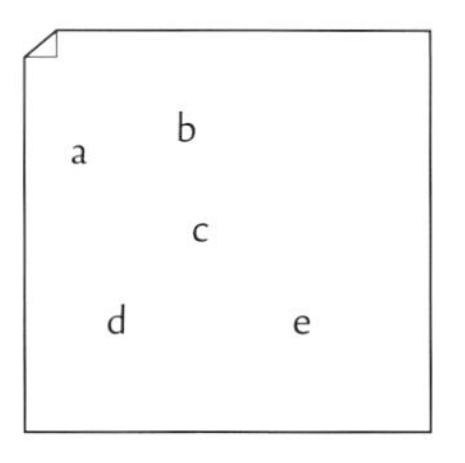

Dimensions 182 × 163 mm.
Paper trimmed.
Technique Pen and brown ink.

Drawing *a* shows the profile of the cornice of the pedestal with the base of the pilaster sitting on a double plinth. *b* depicts the elevation of the cornice of the pedestal, *c*, the plan of the pedestal underneath the base in relation to a stretch of wall, *d*, the profile of the pedestal with outlines of the mouldings and *e*, the plan showing the detail of two piers and a pedestal that belongs to a lower order, facing inwards. The sketches appear to have been executed rapidly, possibly as additions or corrections to a previous, more detailed survey. On the subject of the pedestals of the three upper orders of the Colosseum, Serlio wrote (III, 81r.) that "Tutti tre sono a un modo," in other words, that they are all the same. | AGG

BIBLIOGRAPHY Ferri (1885) 12.

U 1883A *recto and verso*

Giovanni Battista da Sangallo

Rome, Flavian Amphitheater (*recto*); Rome, Portico of Octavia and the Doric Temple in the Forum Holitorium (*verso*).

Dimensions 238 × 277 mm.
Technique Pen and brown ink, straightedge, stylus.
Paper Torn, right bottom corner missing, wrinkled.
Drawing Scale Florentine braccia.

INSCRIPTION, Recto *undici*; *undici scallini questi*; *tredici scalini*

Verso *Santangnolo dipesceria*; *pesceria*; *Tempio acanto da santo / niccolla in carciere / dorico*

The drawing at left on the recto, parallel to the base of the sheet, presents a graphic reconstruction perspective section and elevation of the porticus in *summa gradatione* of the Flavian Amphitheater. It is related to U 1856A r. and v. (two sketches in section of the Flavian Amphitheater with an arbitrary restitution of the interior), U 1136A and U 1555A v. by Antonio the Younger, in which two different solutions for the porticus are presented, the first with a colonnade with arches, the second with two orders placed one above the other, with pilasters and arches. In Giovanni Battista's version, by contrast, the internal facade is articulated in two orders of Ionic columns with architraves: at the lower level, there are windows and doors with aedicules and triangular pediments, framed in rhythmic bays of slender columns, while on the upper level which corresponds to the attic, elevated on a podium, there is an airy and open arcade with slender columns, with a slightly lower shaft, with respect to the story below, but elevated on plinths. At the lower left is a sketch of the plan of three external pilasters of the corridor with the measurements of the intercolumniations.

On the top of the verso (turned 90 degrees to the right), is a sketch of the plan of the Portico of Octavia, with several measurements for reference, and, at the center, an axonometric sketch of the reconstruction of the front and side of the same portico. At the bottom are sketches of the front of a Doric temple in the Forum Holitorium next to the church of S. Nicola in Carcere and of the side of the same temple. Note that the columns have been lined up with the elevations to allow one to draw plan and elevation together. | ACF

BIBLIOGRAPHY Ferri (1885) 190, 195, 199, 216; Bartoli (1914–22) IV: fig. 494, pl. 301; VI: 93; Jordan-Huelsen (1878–1907) I, 3: 511; Huelsen (1906) 174; CensusID 10012684, 10012656.

U 1889A *verso*

Aristotile da Sangallo

Perugia, Porta Marzia, ca. 1540.

Dimensions 216 × 141/42 mm.
Technique Pen and brown ink, stylus, straightedge, compass, pin holes.
Paper Mediumweight, trimmed.

INSCRIPTION *tetto*; *Inperugia*; (in arch) *piane le pietre / ma legono bene*

A view of the upper left part of the Porta Marzia, drawn—according to Vasori—before it was moved and incorporated into the Rocca Paolina. The drawing is accurate regarding the female bust in the spandrel, and the horse's head above the center of the arch, though the latter is now totally worn away. Inaccurate, however, is the half-length figure in the first upper panel at the left, which should have been another horse's head.

The decorative drawings above the view of the Porta Marzia are said to reproduce the designs of the floor tiles of the Sala maggiore in the Rocca Paolina (Camerieri-Palombaro 1988, 107).

Vasori notes that the inscriptions are not in Aristotile's handwriting, and Ghisetti Giavarina proposes that 1889A is one of the many sheets that should be attributed to Tommaso Boscoli. | SE

BIBLIOGRAPHY Ferri (1885) 111; Vasori (1979) 148–50; Vasori (1981) 181–82, cat. no. 137; Borsi (1986) 452; Camerieri-Palombaro (1988) 143, fig. 30; Ghisetti Giavarina (1990) 78, n. 47; CensusID 232856.

U 1966A *recto and verso*

Giovanni Battista da Sangallo

Courtyard inspired by Theater of Marcellus (recto). Theater at Ferento (verso). After 1519–20.

Dimensions 434 × 282 mm.
Technique Pen and black ink, straightedge, compass, stylus.
Paper Folds, torn, restored.
Drawing Scale Florentine *braccia* (scale from star to star measures 98 *braccia* = 77 mm).

INSCRIPTION, Recto (upper half) *membretto; cornice ultima sta cosi; capitello; zocholo e basa del sechondo hordine*; (lower half) *A basso / Credo* [...] *la misura / cioe del membretto e del primo / cornicione el chapitello primo*
Verso (upper half) (right margin) *questa sie la chornicie / dove impostava suliarchi /* [...] *le pichole / differenze* [...]; (center, above *valva hospitaliorum*) *Eldidentro; qui sorte la sala*; (left edge) *fronte*; (with arrow indicating front of *scaena*, on inside of *paraskenion*) *scoperto*; (next to stairs) [...] *da quella cornicie*; (on story marker of external view of scenic structure) *di fronte dal regolone in su aruinato non si vede niente*; (above arched doors) *di mattoni* [...]; (at ground level) *faciata dinanzi aveva inanzi cierte scale*; (lower half) *entrata*

On the recto is the elevation of one side of a courtyard with the section, to the right, of the arcade of the perpendicular side. The drawing seems to have been inspired by the external arcade of the Theater of Marcellus, as is shown by the presence of the large mask on the keystone of the arch framed by Ionic columns and by the absence of the base in the Tuscan-Doric order. (Note that the frieze with triglyphs and metopes does not appear in the drawing, perhaps because it is unfinished). There are, however, differences in the measurements and proportions, as can be determined by comparing it with U 1296A r. possibly by Pietro Rosselli for Antonio the Younger. Especially evident are the differences in the lower story and in the plinth of the Ionic columns. Recalling the work of translation and illustration of Vitruvius's *De Architectura* by Giovanni Battista, one might consider the drawing more a theoretical exercise than a project, though the presence of the measurements does allow for the latter hypothesis.

On the verso is a table in graphic form that shows how the various elements of the Theater of Ferento are put together; the theater is seen through vertical orthagonal projections (sections, profiles, and views) and horizontal projections (plans) to which are added, in order to achieve a complete representation, a perspective sketch of the *frons scaenae*, possibly the most original and interesting element of the entire complex. At the center, half of the plan of the structure is drawn; the measurements are found only for the scenic structure. Above and upside down is a reconstruction of the *postscaenium*. A perspective sketch of the *frons scaenae* of the theater is placed inside the plan, which gives an idea of the effect of the articulation of the walls and the play of projection and recession. The cornice of the projecting forward section next to the *valva regia* is marked by the letter "A": to the right, the profile of the same cornice is indicated by the same letter. At the bottom of the sheet is the reconstruction of the section of the *cavea*, which, as Vasori has pointed out, is mistaken in its proposal for the *cavea* being completely supported on foundations; beside this sketch, part of the exterior corridor is drawn, seen as if it developed along a plane rather than on a curve. The drawing by Giovanni Battista should be linked to the numerous surveys and studies by Antonio the Younger with Giovanni Battista's collaboration: U 1131A, 1132A, 1300A, and 1301A r. | ACF

BIBLIOGRAPHY Ferri (1885) 41; Galli (1911) 216 (fig. 3), 218; Bartoli (1914–22) IV: fig. 532, 321; VI: 97; Giovannoni (1958) I: 22; Vasori (1981) 174–75, cat. no. 133.

U 2043A *recto and verso*

Antonio da Sangallo the Younger

Rome, Colosseum, elevation of the exterior (*recto*); studies of details (*verso*), ca. 1504–06.

Dimensions 270 × 182 mm.
Technique Pen and ink.
Paper Parchment, probably part of a disassembled sketchbook (see U 2044–2047A).
Drawing Scale Florentine *braccia*.

INSCRIPTION, Verso (on Ionic capital) *secondo*; (on Corinthian capital) *3 + 4 chosi*; (on Doric capital) *primo capitello*; (on interior pier) *EL DI DRENTO sono a questo modo*; (on four moldings) *QUARTO, TERZO, SECONDO, PRIMO CORNICIONE DEL COLISEO*; (on cornice) *de dadoni*[?] *in da chapo tuttj sono chosi*; (on bases) *a dua chosi, base de la colonna, la prima sono chosi e la seconda*

The five parchment sheets U 2043–47A are about the same size and probably all come from a *taccuino* similar to the one put together by Antonio's uncle Giuliano. Of the twelve drawings on the recto and verso, mostly executed in pen alone, two show the Colosseum, three show details of other ancient buildings, and three show contemporary architecture. U 2045A r. is copied from Giuliano's Codex Barberini, and only U 2046A r. is his own invention. The sheets must have been made after the election of Julius II at the end of October 1503, when Antonio moved to Rome, possibly as part of Giuliano's entourage. On the other hand, the semi-perspectival method of representation, which is closely related to Giuliano's, and the archaic handwriting are evidence that they were made before Antonio entered Bramante's workshop. This points to the years between 1504 and 1506.

The recto shows an orthogonal elevation with four-and-a-half bays of the exterior of the Colosseum, and includes measurements of the total height, the height of the stories, and the heights of the socle zone, the columns, the arcades, and the three parts of the entablature. These measurements, which provided so much information for the architect, are missing in Giuliano's comparable survey on folio 6 of the *Taccuino senese* but appear on the verso of folio 68 in the Codex Barberini, where Giuliano may have taken them over from Antonio (Borsi 1985, pp. 254–59). As there, the arcades and orders are accompanied by perspective aids. But while Giuliano depicted the *voussoirs* of the arcades and windows, Antonio showed only the lateral framing stones of the windows in the fourth story. He thus seems to have enriched the survey of his uncle with this important information as well.

This is especially true of the detail studies on the verso. Like the elevation on the recto, they presupposed a physically dangerous survey of the monument, though by no means an impossible one for a trained carpenter. The entablatures of the four stories are lined up in parallel, so that the slight variations in the architrave and frieze, and the considerable differences between the two lower and the two upper moldings, immediately catch the eye. The impost moldings and bases in the two respective pairs of stories are identical. The Doric capital is the most accurately rendered and the Ionic capital is simplified, while the two Corinthian capitals are closer to quattrocento forms than to those of the Colosseum. The interior Doric order and the fragment of the adjoining arcade largely agree with Antonio's sketch on U 1576A v., where he located them in the second story but gave no measurements. These sketches and the analogous one of the interior of the first story on U 1576A r. probably preceded the parchment sheet. One can therefore assume that the ground plan and section of the Colosseum on U 1555A, which are drawn with a similar technique, have equally archaic inscriptions, and are as closely related to Giuliano's surveys, were made in the same period and may likewise have been transferred by Antonio to this presumed sketchbook.

The perspective method of representing the details on the verso was directly influenced by Giuliano, but here the perspective section made little sense. Antonio's originality expresses itself primarily in his firmer, more emphatic stroke and in the short hatched lines of his shadows. The richly decorated cornice at the upper left is not from the Colosseum. | CLF

BIBLIOGRAPHY Ferri (1885) 123; Fabriczy (1902) 111; Bartoli (1914–22) I: figs 145–46, pl 82–83; VI: 30–1.; Marchini (1942) 102; Borsi (1985) 495; Günther (1988) 112; Frommel (1994, *Introduction*) 12–18; CensusIDs 43889, 10072806.

U 2044A *recto and verso*

Antonio da Sangallo the Younger

Studies of the details of orders from ancient and contemporary buildings, ca. 1504–06.

Dimensions 270 × 182 mm.
Technique Pen and ink.
Paper Parchment.

INSCRIPTION, Recto (upper left) *in chasa jannj cjampolinj*; (center) *cornjcje della porta del palazo*; (below this) *da chapo*; (lower left) *basa della cholonna, membretto dellarco, basa doppia*; (right margin) *dellarcho, da chapo, queste sono le chornjcje dela porta del palazzo del papa*

Verso (repeatedly) *M*[*oderno*] (upper right) *A*[*ntico*]; (lower left) *ventuna*

As he was to do later in the Codex Coner, Antonio here mixes examples of details from column orders of ancient and contemporary buildings. The modern details—three undecorated cornices, an entablature, an architrave, a pier base, an impost molding, and a capital-like molding—have not been identified. They do not, however, come from any of Bramante's Roman buildings of about 1504–06, even though the profile of the capital recalls the Doric capitals in the Cortile del Belvedere. The details on the verso for the most part show the Vatican entrance portal by Baccio Pontelli. The exactitude with which Antonio captures each detail is testimony to the reputation Pontelli still had in Rome at that time. The "modern" details on the recto could therefore also be from one of Pontelli's buildings. Only the ancient cornice on the upper right of the recto is shown in perspective view. | CLF

BIBLIOGRAPHY Ferri (1885) 159, 183; Bartoli (1914–22) I: figs 147–48, pl 83–84; VI: 30–31; Marchini (1942) 102; Frommel (1983) 132; Borsi (1985) 496; CensusIDs 10071921, 65029.

U 2045A *recto and verso*

Antonio da Sangallo the Younger

Surveys of ancient centralized buildings, ca. 1504–06.

Dimensions 260/57 × 182/79 mm.
Technique Pen and ink.
Paper Parchment.

INSCRIPTION, Recto (above) *ISTUDIO DI [M]ARCHO VARONE APRESSO A SANTO GERMANO*; (center) *A CAPUA VECIA U[N] TENPIO*; (to left) *DI FORA*; (to right) *DI DENTRO*; (below) *DI FORA, lo TENPIO PRESSO A BAIA DI SIBILLA*

Verso (upper left) *FUORA DI ROMA lo MIGLIO*; (upper right) *ALLE III PERGOLE DI LA DA NAPOLI*; (lower left) *FUORA DI ROMA INVERSO MARINO III M*; (lower right) *A CHAPOVA VECHIA*

The ground plans of the four centralized buildings on the verso were copied exactly by Antonio the Younger from Giuliano da Sangallo's *Taccuino senese,* fol. 16 of the Codex Barberini (Borsi 1984, pp. 71–75, 497–99). However, the originals of the ground plans of the Temple of the Sibyls in Baia and the "studio di Marco Varone" on the recto are to be found only on fol. 8 of the Codex Barberini. Since the ground plan of the "studio" extends beyond the "Libro Piccolo" onto the enlarged page, it is evident that Antonio copied the ground plan only after Giuliano had already integrated the "Libro Piccolo" into the Codex Barberini; undoubtedly, that is after Giuliano's move to Rome at the beginning of 1504. This ground plan must be considered the nucleus of a typology of the villa that extends from the project perfected by Giuliano and Lorenzo, to the Odeion Cornaro, to the mature projects of Antonio and Serlio (Borsi 1984, p. 74).

The ground plan, perspective section, and perspective view of the exterior of the mausoleum near S. Maria in Capua Vetere cannot be found among Giuliano's drawings. The building does appear, however, in a variant representation of about 1514–15 in the Codex Coner (Günther 1988, p. 176 f.). Although there are no comparable elevations among Giuliano's drawings, it is uncertain if this is a reconstruction by Giuliano or, more likely, one by Antonio. The arches over the freestanding columns of the interior cut like lunettes into the umbrella vault, which is crowned by a lantern inspired by that of the Florentine Baptistry. The corresponding columns of the exterior are much lower and carry an encircling entablature surmounted by a high attic, articulated by blind panels and corner pilaster strips. This may well be the earliest demonstrable centralized building of the Renaissance with an attic. Between the columns, the masonry is hollowed out by semicircular shell niches, each with a door. | CLF

BIBLIOGRAPHY Ferri (1885) 16, 82, 100, 142, 172, 177, 207; Bartoli (1914–22) I: figs 153–54, pl. 86; VI: 31; Vasori (1981) 28–33, cat. nos 15–16; Frommel (1994, *Introduction*) 14; Borsi (1985) 73–74; Günther (1988), 113–14; D. Donetti in Donetti-Faietti-Frommel (2017); CensusIDs 62928, 62926.

U 2046A *recto and verso*

Antonio da Sangallo the Younger

Elevation of a centralized building, ancient moldings.

Dimensions 261 × 179 mm.
Technique Pen and ink.
Paper Parchment.

INSCRIPTION, Recto *M[oderno]*; (in the attic) *storie*

Verso (top to bottom) *andito di santo basjljo le colonne / non ano pilastro a rjnchontro / e pjlastrj sono nella testa e nei chantj*; *questo pasa i[n] sula / cholona e ffa / un quadro sfondato, quadrangulj*; (in a hand of period after 1508) *b[raccia] 3 minuti 3 / questo architrave*; *ottangolj / de templum pacis* (lower right corner) *quadri* (?)

The octagonal building on the recto, identified by the letter "M" as a contemporary invention, is reminiscent of the reconstruction of the mausoleum in Capua. Like that mausoleum, it has an attic story articulated by blank panels, a cupola, and a lantern, to which, however, pilasters and volutes have been added. The lower half is substantially wider, undoubtedly because the interior is expanded by niches. It is also markedly broader than the Temple of the Sybils in Baia (U 2045A r.). With its approximately 1:2 proportion, it is significantly steeper than most ancient centralized buildings. Antonio established a connection to the attic with a sweeping concave roof. The lower story is articulated only by a temple facade. The three-part entablature is continued around the structure but is shifted downward in perspective from the temple façade, evidence that its four slender Doric columns are meant to be freestanding. The temple facade culminates in a triangular pediment, as does the portal in the slightly wider central bay.

The entrance wall is articulated by a triumphal Serliana whose three-part entablature separates the semicircular niches of the side bays from the round niches above them. Antonio crowned the lantern with a sketch of a mounted warrior whose astonishingly assertive strokes and dynamism are reminiscent of Leonardo. A dynamic effect is also created by the hastily sketched (female?) statues on the attic entablature and by the cursory but vigorous lines of the drawing as a whole. Like U 2045A r., this is probably a reconstruction of an ancient mausoleum.

On the verso are some perspective sections of parts of an ancient entablature such as those used by Giuliano da Sangallo on folios 25 r. and 24 of the *Taccuino senese* and folios 4 v., 63 v., and 65 v. of the Codex Barberini, and which, indeed, Giuliano himself may have invented. For Antonio, what is important here is not the profile alone but its complex bending. The coffers of the Basilica of Maxentius interested him if only because of his own wooden ceilings (see U 2153A). | CLF

BIBLIOGRAPHY Ferri (1885) 130, 165, 217; Bartoli (1914–22) I: fig. 149, 150, pl. 84; VI: 31; Borsi (1985) 496–7; Frommel (1994, *Introduction*) 17; CensusID (verso) 10071744.

U 2047A *recto and verso*

Antonio da Sangallo the Younger

Studies of architectural details of ancient Temple of Antoninus and Faustina (*recto*); the bell of a Corinthian capital near SS. Cosmos and Damian (*verso*), ca. 1504–06.

Dimensions 262 × 182 mm.
Technique Pen and ink.
Paper Parchment.

INSCRIPTION, Recto *base de* [...] *cholonne / isto dado non a largo b*[*raccia*] *3–311/2* / la *cholonna* [...] *b*[*raccia*] *8 sono / chanali 24*

Verso *da luno segnjo al altro sono 11 cjmase*; vertical *9 cjmase che sono 20* [...] *del la cimasa*; *6 cjmase e mezo*

These perspective sections of the entablature of the Temple of the Dioscuri, its base, and another molding on the recto are among the most advanced drawings of the group, and prepare for Antonio's surveys of antiquity on U 1413A v. from 1507–08 as well as for the Codex Coner. The more archaic handwriting, however, suggests that the drawing was made before 1506. The contour on the verso is probably of a Corinthian capital from the Temple of SS. Cosmos and Damian, whose proportions Antonio measured using a cyma as his module. | CLF

BIBLIOGRAPHY Ferri (1885) 147; Bartoli (1914–22) I: figs 151–52, pl. 85; VI: 31; Borsi (1985) 4967; Frommel (1994, *Introduction*) 17; CensusIDs 10071752, 10071795.

U 2049A *recto and verso*

Antonio da Sangallo the Younger

Design for a tomb and a triumphal arch (recto). Rome, details of the portal of Cardinal Cesarini (verso). ca. 1504–07.

Dimensions 240 × 330 mm.
Technique Pen and ink.
Paper mediumweight, patches on the verso.

INSCRIPTION, Recto: *pianta*
Verso: (upper edge) *tuschjcj / dorjchj / djonichj / chorjntj*; (in portal frieze) *porta del chardjnale cjeserjno*; (in door opening) *larga el vano b*[*raccia*] *3⅔ / alta el vano b*[*raccia*] *6⅔*; (below) *dappie*

The two designs on the recto afford the most direct glimpse we have into Antonio's artistic formation. The tomb for a cardinal, perhaps Cardinal Cesarini, whose portal Antonio may also have designed, has its origin in the type represented by the tomb of Pius II now in Sant'Andrea della Valle. Three-story piers with niches containing the Virtues flank the sarcophagus, on which an effigy of the deceased is placed. The pedestal zone bears an inscription and a coat of arms. The projection of the abbreviated entablature over the niche piers is continued by candelabra. The attic, adorned with acanthus scrolls, culminates in a coat of arms flanked by winged putti. Antonio replaces the narrative reliefs of the tomb of Pius with a more architectonic solution: a Pantheon- like aedicula. It is crowned by a pediment whose entablature continues over the second story of niches and further glorifies the deceased. On the pediment is a statue of the Redeemer flanked by two adoring angels. The three semicircular niches framed by blind panels were probably intended to hold statues of the Madonna and the patron saints of the deceased. This ingenious bracketing of an aedicula with a quattrocentesque structure characterizes Antonio's stylistic position in 1504–06, when Bramante had not yet gained dominant influence over him. As on U 2046A r., Antonio distinguishes himself here by the sureness of his ability to characterize figural elements—unusual in an architect—a skill he may have learned from his two uncles and Filippino Lippi.

The triumphal arch on the right side of the sheet, perhaps intended for a triumphal procession of Julius II, differs from most ancient prototypes by its wholly symmetrical ground plan. Like the arch of Malborghetto near the Prima Porta, it may have been intended for a crossing. It differs from the reconstruction of the arch of Malborghetto by Giuliano (Borsi 1985, pp. 191–94) and the draftsman of the Codex Strozzi (Günther 1988, pp. 74–78, fig. 23) in the placement of a single centered column on two sides of each of the four piers. The high attic recalls Giuliano, and the terminating barrel vault, the Codex Strozzi. That the architecture was intended to be temporary rather than a triumphal arch is indicated by the candelabra on the corners of the attic. They appear to be surrounded by winged putti or geniuses and are borrowed rather from the typology of funerary monuments. The design, therefore, may be for the arch made by Antonio at the beginning of 1507 to celebrate the triumphal return of Julius II from Bologna (Frommel 1994, *Introduction*, p. 11).

On the verso, in its profile and outer frame—which is inserted between the architrave-like frame and the frieze and continued on both sides—the portal of the palace of Cardinal Cesarini is so similar to that of the *salone* of the Cancelleria that both can be said to have been designed by the same master (Letarouilly 1846, table 88). Since there is much evidence that Cardinal Riario put the Sangallos and their collaborator Bernardo della Volpaia in charge of building the Cancelleria after Pontelli's departure in the spring of 1492, it is possible that after 1503 the young Antonio also participated in the project and designed both the portal for Cesarini and that of the Cancelleria. The profile recalls the project for a chimney on U 1623A v. and U 1646A v., possibly by Bramante. | CLF

BIBLIOGRAPHY Ferri (1885) 8, 97; Giovannoni (1959) I: 383; Frommel (1994, *Introduction*) 17–18.

U 2054A *recto and verso*

Giovan Francesco da Sangallo and Antonio da Sangallo the Younger

Rome, cornice and base molding found at the Baths of Diocletian (*recto*); near Rome, tomb at Ponte Nomentano (*verso*), before 1530.

Dimensions 327 × 240 mm.
Technique Pen and brown ink, stylus, straightedge, compasses.
Paper Heavy, edges trimmed and patched.
Drawing Scale Florentine *braccia.*

INSCRIPTION, Recto *Questa chornice doricha si truovo i[n] una vignaia dirieto a termine i[n] roma*: *A*; *Questa basa si truouo cho[n] questa chornicie / Doricha* (Antonio's hand) *appresso a termine / de diocretiano*; *A*

Verso *pilastro l/l su chantoni*; *cholonna cioe meza*; *la pianta staua chosi*

The recto contains drawings of a Doric entablature and a base molding, both said to have been found near the Baths of Diocletian. Although we have no proof, other authors have suggested that the Doric order was used in the baths. The Berlin Codex Destailleur "D" (Kunstbibliothek, Hdz 4151), an album of drawings of the mid- to late sixteenth century by different hands, mainly French, makes Doric the minor order of the *caldarium* (see fols 41 r. and 46 v.). Also Bramante showed a Doric order on U 104A r. (Frommel, *Sangallo and Antiquity*, in this volume). Fréart de Chambray, in the later seventeenth century, published an ornamented Doric capital, also said to come from the baths. The infrequent use of the Doric order after Hadrian, and the richness of the ornament, suggest that the pieces come from a structure of earlier imperial date, then perhaps reused in the baths.

The verso is filled with part of the elevation of a small Doric tomb, the square plan of which appears at the bottom of the sheet. The elevation shows us part of one of the side bays, with a corner pilaster in the bottom left corner and and a half-column on the right. From its form and ornament, the tomb was probably of late Republican date. We know from other drawings, in the Codices Barberini and Coner, that the tomb was located near the Ponte Nomentano. Ashby identified it with a still-extant concrete core, on the right side of the Via Nomentana, just after the bridge as one comes from Rome.

The sheet forms part of a series of clean drawings by Giovan Francesco (cf. U 1701A r., 1705A r., 1716A r.). | IC, HCD

BIBLIOGRAPHY Ferri (1885) 127, 206; Lanciani (1902–12) II: 144; Ashby (1904) 46; Bartoli (1914–22) IV: figs 557–58, pl. 332; VI: 101–02; Berckenhagen (1970) 24; Buddensieg (1975) 108; Günther (1988) 125–27, no. 144, 296–97, no. 208, 375, 378; CensusIDs 206389 and 60675.

U 2055A *recto and verso*

Antonio da Sangallo the Younger

Rome, Arch of Septimius Severus (*recto*); Rome, Arch of Constantine (*verso*), after 1509 (?).

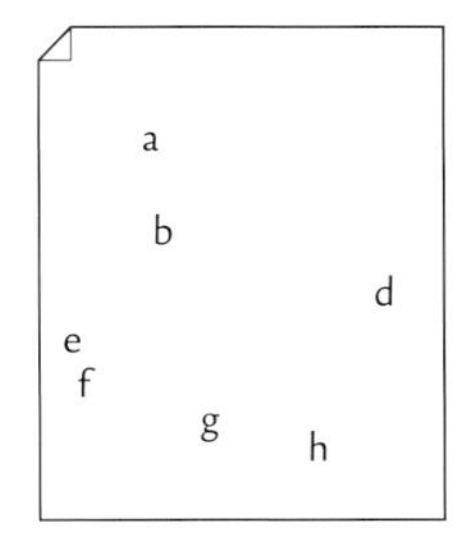

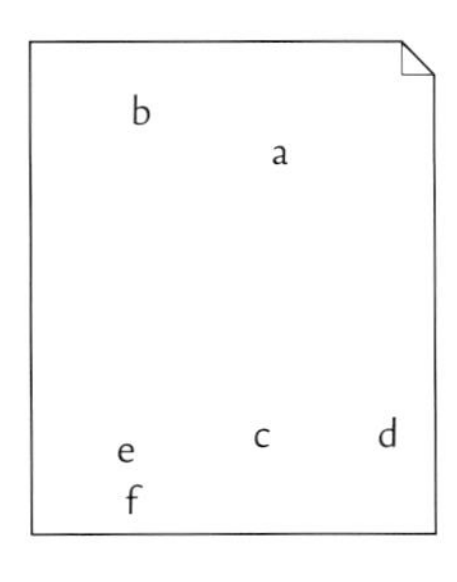

Dimensions 272 × 250 mm.
Technique Pen and brown ink, straightedge, stylus, compasses.
Paper Partly yellowed.
Drawing Scale Florentine *braccia*.

INSCRIPTION, Recto (top right, brown ink, nineteenth-century hand, old numbering) *1511*; (Antonio's hand, dark brown ink) *Larcho di Luzio Sejptimio a pie di chanpidoglio*; (brown ink) *nota che questo archo a roma a pie di chanpidoglio e de mesurato chol braco fiorentino el deto bracio eripartito. in. 20. parte e ungnuna di deti parte chiamano menuti*; (a) *questa e la pianta di questo archo a sotto*; (b) *tuto questo vano di messo b[raccia] 11 on[cie] 15 m[inuti] 4*; *A*; *F* (twice); *G*; *H*; *K*; *M* (twice); *O*; *P*; *R*; *X*; *b*; *m*; (c) *A*; *F*; *H*; *M* (twice); *O*; *P*; *R*; *X*; *b*; *m*; *4*; (d) *lo intavolato alpitafio*; (e) *architravato de larcho di mezo*; *F*; (f) *4*; (g) *architravato de larcho*; *m*; (h) *O*; measurements

Verso (bottom left, blue pencil, nineteenth-century hand, numbering) *2055*; (brown ink) *larcho di trasi fum/esurato*; *p[er] Giovanni cristofano romano*; *cholb/racio fiorentino elquale eripartito in 20 parte chiamati once euna di dite once e ripartit. in 8 parte chiamate minuti*; (a) *F*; *X*; *Z*; *tuto ilvano di mezo b[raccia] 11 on[ce] 7*; *eluano. intra la lacholona. tonda. elpilastro. on[ce] 14*; (b) *F*; (d) *X*; (f) *Z*; measurements

The recto, showing the Arch of Septimius Severus, is the more detailed, including plan *a*; an elevation of just over half the arch with the interior of the side arch shown in projection *b* and key letters referring to details depicted in the accompanying drawings; an elevation and section from the attic, through a column, to the a pedestal *c*; a section through the molding framing the inscription *d*; elevations of and sections through the archivolts of the main arch *e* and side arch *g* and similarly for the imposts of the main *f* and side *h* arches. The survey is incomplete, the principal omissions being details of the vaults and of the transverse internal arches, but more was intended, as can be seen by the key letter "M" on the elevation *b*, which should refer to a detail of the keystone.

The subject of the verso is the Arch of Constantine. Drawing *a* is again an elevation of just more than half the arch, with the interior of the main and side arches shown in projection, and key letters referring to the details in the accompanying drawings, namely: elevations and sections of the attic cornice *b*; the imposts of the side and main arches *c* and *d*, respectively); a column base and plinth (*e*); and the podium or pedestal base moulding and plinth (*f*). It can be assumed that many other details were intended to be included.

Both sides of the sheet are good examples of relatively clean studies of a single monument. The arches are shown in "abbreviated form," meaning that most ornamental features are only drawn summarily, but key letters refer the observer to details elsewhere on the page or sheet. The drawings and text can be closely linked to an album in Florence (Biblioteca Nazionale, Ms. II.I.429, fols 2r. and v.) of drawings by different sixteenth-century Italian artists. Other drawings by the same artist of the folios in the album, betray connections with the Raphael circle, including parallels in the Kassel Codex (Cod. Fol. A45; Günther 1988, 143–45). There is nothing to suggest that Antonio is copying the anonymous draftsman or vice versa, and so we must assume that they were both using earlier drawings, most probably deriving from "Giovan Cristofano Romano," who Antonio credits with measuring the Arch of Constantine (see text transcriptions above). He is almost certainly the same as Giancristoforo Romano, who is known chiefly as a sculptor, and who left Rome in 1509 for Loreto, where he died in 1512. If, as seems likely, the drawings of the Arch of Septimius Severus derive from the same source, then they are not necessarily from after 1520, as Bartoli maintained, believing that the pedestals of the Arch of Septimius Severus were first excavated in 1520, when actually they had already appeared in the Barberini Codex of Giuliano da Sangallo (BAV, Barb. lat. 4424, fol. 21v.; Huelsen 1910, 31), who died in 1515. An earlier rather than later dating of the drawing would furthermore be consistent with the style of drawing and writing on the sheet. | IC

BIBLIOGRAPHY Ferri (1885) 124, 126; Bartoli (1914–22) III: figs 487–88, pl. 298; VI: 91; Brilliant (1967) 258; Günther (1988) 143–45; CensusID 60480, 60481.

U 2056A *recto and verso*

Antonio da Sangallo the Younger and Giovan Francesco da Sangallo

Reconstructions of the basilica after Book V of Vitruvius (*recto*); studies and notes from Book III of Vitruvius (plans for different types of temple and an Ionic cornice); lists of ancient pieces of architecture (*verso*), before 1527.

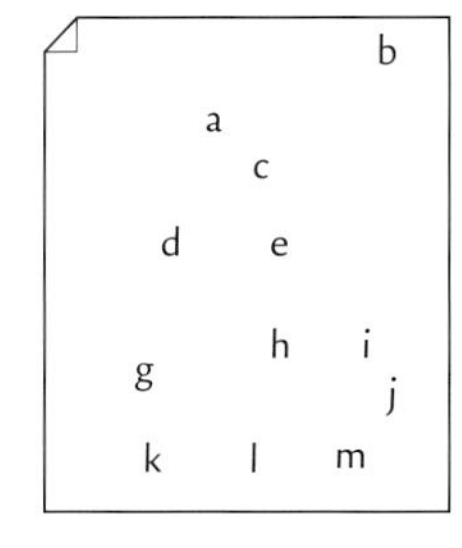

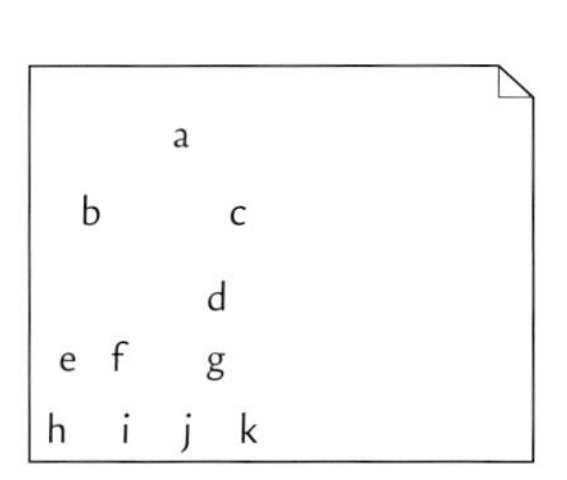

Dimensions 335 × 236.
Technique Pen and brown inks.
Paper Mediumweight, all sides trimmed, central horizontal fold, repaired.
Drawing Scale and Measurements: Roman *piedi*.

INSCRIPTION, Recto (Old marks: top, near the left-hand corner, in pen, in 18th century hand) *121*; (next to this in 19th century hand) *1312*; Antonio's notes are written in two different inks: a brown one (A), which is the same as that used for the drawings, and a paler one (B), used at a later stage for rewriting some of the notes written in (A) that had been abraded; the handwriting is slightly different, but it is still Antonio's hand. (From top, to the left of drawing *1*; ink A) *L V*, (below) *foro* (on the same drawing) *basilicha*; (below, to the left of plan *g*) (ink B) *non sia piu streta che la tertia parte che lle longa*, (cancelled) *ne minore che un quadro e mezo*; (to the right of the latter; ink A) *larga che lameta / che lle longa* (De Architectura v, 1, 4); (ink A, cancelled) *ne piu che dua quadri*; (on drawing *i*) *questa sta bene*; (to the right of *k*), *questa / sta bene*; (on drawing *m*) *caprioli, trasti, canterii, muro, questo sta bene*

Verso (Left half, in left margin) (Antonio's hand) *Lo porticho di Santa maria / in porticho era di metello. li tre / thenpli li achanto sono questi se/condo vetruvio nello libro tertio / capitolo primo nel peritteros: / lo doricho achanto Santo nichola / era di Jove Statoris; Lo ionicho dove / e / Santo nichola / proprio edificato si era di Hermodi*; *lo dove era le Carciere pure ionicho / senza posticho si era di mariana onore e virtute facto da mutio e non aveva / lo posticho perche lo logie della sciena / dello teatro di marcello le toglieva / lo locho che non / ciera tanto spa/tio che si potessi / fare. / questi* [*cinq quatro* canceled] *sei / edifitii sono / insieme chell/uno tocha quasi / laltro cioe / lo porticho di metello si e di verso mezoidi* [*sic*] *lo tenpio di giove statore achanto aldetto porticho diverso settentrione e di poi e quello di ermodi e di poi e quello di marianna* [*sic*] */ e di poi e lo teatro di marciello e di poi e lo porticho overo iano dove Santo agniolo in pescina, che sono sei edifitij / chelluno tocha quasi laltro.* (To left of plan *b*) *anfiprostilo*; (in plan *e*) *naos en parasta/tis*; (next to it, in plan *f*) *porta, naos en parastatis*; (at top in cella of temple (*a*) *Diana efesia*; (in left margin of same) *128.*; (to right margin of this) *126*; (on right, vertically) *a volere che sacorti con plinio / bisognia stia cosi perche dicie / che aveva 127 colonne cioe delli / dua modi luno*; a sum. (In partial plan of prostyle *d*, right) *prostilo cioe colo/nna contra a cholonna / e contra alle ante anchora*; (below) *L iij* (left half of sheet, laid out vertically) (Giovan Francesco da Sangallo's hand) *Vole chello architrave sia lodisotto quanto / la cholona nella diminuzione cioe nello / piu sottile da chapo e lodisopra dello ditto / architrave cioe nello agetto della gola / abia dagetto quanto la chontratura della cholona / insieme chollo agetto della champana dapie / di detta cholonna. Circha allo / partimento della altеza che vole sia / lo cimazio la settima parte della al /* [*teza* canceled] *della alteza e intende lo cima/zio senzo* [*sic*] *lo suo piano perche vole / sintenda senpre chello ditto regolo / ci sia*[?] *da vantagio e parte la sua al/teza in parte xv euna parte sia / Lo regolo dello cimazio ello cima/zio sia 2 e lo piano achanto / allo cimazio sia V e lo piano di mezo / sia parte 4 e lo utimo*[?] *sia parte 3 cioe / parte iii e questo afronta cogli antichi / che sono begli che si vegano in roma*; (below) *Nota che vole che sello fregio e lisio / cioe sanza intagli sia largo quanto larchitrave / e se glia intagli vuole sia piu la quarta parte*; (below) *vetruvjo non fa mai inmezione dello piano / dello cimazio delarcritrave e pure gli an/tichi lanno tuttj*; (right, next to a section of cornice) *architrave*; *chosi*; *chanpana*; (next to this, with sheet turned 90 degrees) *El marmo* [*porparos* canceled] *lunesi cioe dichiarava e piu /* [...] *biancho che quello di paros / In paros inspachando usaso si trovo la immagine di Sileno*; (below) *Alberinti 4 uno in negitto / uno in chreta fatto da dedalo / Latro in isula lemno*[?] *in questo ciera C. L. cholonne bilichate nel voltarle le voltano* [...] */ Latro in italia nella sepultura di porsena a chjusi. / Li sette miracholi del mondo / Le piramide degipo / Le mura di banbilonja / lo pritaneo egizecho / lo mausuleo / Lo tenplo dapoline in chandia / lo chapidolio / Diana efesia / Lo farro in alisadria*

On this sheet, at the top of which he has made a note of the reference to Book v of *De Architectura*, Antonio the Younger is attempting a graphic interpretation of Vitruvius' passage on the basilica (v, 1, 4–10) by means of 13 drawings set out as follows:

(*a*) Section of a basilica, the left side clearly delineated, showing a central space flanked by two superimposed colonnades and three external tiers of porticoes and loggias; (*b*) perspectival section of a basilica showing the roof structure and the barrel-vaulted central space onto which porticoes and galleries open, arranged in three tiers on the left – the two lower ones are arcuated – but only two tiers on the right; (*c*) plan of a square pilaster (each side measuring 10 *piedi*) with a column attached, an enlarged detail from (*d*) and (*c*); (*d*) plan of a basilica with a nave and two aisles, the perimeter walls enclosed by rows of columns, the piers to which they are attached can just be made out; (*e*) an enlarged detail from the previous plan showing columns attached to smaller square piers; (*f*) plan of a basilica with a nave and two aisles, surrounded on all 4 sides by porticoes; (*g*) fragment of a plan showing a side portico that is as wide as the intercolumniation; (*h*) plan of a basilica with a perimeter of square pillars; (*i*) perspectival section of a basilica with a nave and 2 aisles, with a row of columns of unbroken height right along the central space, flanked by two tiers of porticoes and detailed roof structure; (*j*) partial section with columns as in drawing *i* and three tiers of side porticoes; (*k*) elevation of a basilica with a *chalcidicus* on the short side; (*l*) plan of a colonnade which may belong to drawing *h* (in which case *chalcidicus*?); (*m*) details of the components of the roof structure.

Antonio seems to be especially keen to interpret the description of the Basilica built by Vitruvius at Fano, as well as the general rules for basilicas that tally with it. On plans *d* and *e*, the side porticoes are one third of the width of the medium spatium as established by Vitruvius and the measurements in *piedi* replicate those of the basilica at Fano. In section *a* the upper tier is ¾ of the height of the lower one, the ratio indicated in the treatise for the superimposed tiers of porticoes in forums (V, 1,3) having been applied to achieve the reduction prescribed in *De Architectura* (V, 1,5). Most of the other indications that he has followed come from the lengthy passage that Vitruvius dedicated to the only piece of his own architecture that he mentions in his treatise (V, 1,6–10). This was the source of the central space measuring 60 × 120 *piedi*, with porticoes 20 *piedi* wide (plans *d* and *h*), enclosed by columns soaring directly up to the roof in section *i* and consequent omission of the plutei (v, 1,10), which as a general rule Vitruvius directed should be inserted between the lower and the upper orders of columns. Of the two solutions discussed in the treatise, Sangallo has therefore chosen the one that, according to its author, adds an air of sumptuousness and dignity to the work, as well as rendering it more practical and cost-effective. The Fano basilica was also the inspiration for the pilasters attached to the columns in the same section, in plan *e*, which Sangallo also applied to the external columns in plans *d* and *f*, the eight columns along the long sides (v, 1,7), as well as, in perspectival section *i*, the windows at the top of the intercolumniations between the beams supported by the pilasters and the columns (v, 1, 6–7). Antonio has also faithfully reproduced the exedra of the Tribunal with a smaller plan of a semicircle, its front measuring 46 *piedi* and its depth 15 *piedi* (v, 1,8), but he mistakenly locates it against the short back end in plans *d*, *e* and *f*, as did Fra Giocondo before him and as shown in the set of drawings for the edition of De Architectura translated by Fabio Calvo. Cesariano and Vitruvius "Ferrarese," however, placed it correctly in the center of the long side opposite the forum. Lastly, section *m* carefully replicates the longitudinal beams made up of three pilasters 2 *piedi* wide, and provides the Vitruvian terms for the wooden framework of the roof (v, 1, 8), demonstrating that Antonio had clearly understood that the most appropriate columns for basilicas were Ionic or Corinthian. Antonio has, however, misunderstood the meaning of the term testudo which Vitruvius uses repeatedly in his paragraph on the basilica (v, 1,6; v, 1,7 and v, 1,10) to indicate the entire four gable roof over the central space, which has caused him to produce an extremely high barrel vault on a slender structure in section *b*, which must of necessity have been flimsy and non load-bearing. Although dismissed by many Latin sources, the shape of the "testuggine" must have had a bearing on Antonio's interpretation, but again Fra Giocondo before him had depicted a cavedium testudinatum surrounded by porticoes covered by cross vaults in (fol. 62r.) Book vi of his edition of *De Architectura*. Presumably Antonio realized his mistake quite early on because in section *i* he has drawn a medium spatium covered with an unvaulted roof, adding the comment "questo sta bene." Even Giovan Battista da Sangallo, who had drawn several basilicas covered with vaults in his own copy of *De Architectura*, was to put this right, adding the note "none sta bene, è solaro e non volta" (Rome, Bibl. Corsiniana, incun. 50 F 1, fol. 54r.).

U 2056A r provides useful documentation as to when and how Antonio's Vitruvian studies progressed and what exchanges of ideas and discussions he might have had, both on the subject of basilicas and on other questions relating to *De Architectura* and to antique architecture in general, not just with his brother but also with his cousin Giovan Francesco. The arrangement of the drawings on the recto is unrelated to the fold that divides the sheet in two, which was presumably made later. Subsequently Antonio used the verso of the left side of the sheet, by then already folded, for drawings and notes from Book III of Vitruvius. The sheet then passed into Giovan Francesco's hands and he filled the right-hand side of it with other notes, also taken from Book III, at some point before his death in 1530. The drawings and notes by each of them were most probably made before 1527, the year in which Antonio's cousin left Rome and the communal Sangallo house to return to Florence for good. A dating of the early 1520s for Antonio's notes is confirmed by the way in which the "ch" flows, which was not characteristic of his later handwriting. (Frommel 1994, *Introduction*, p. 36). Giovan Francesco later replicated (or perhaps had been the first to draw?) on sheet U 1378A v. (cf. entry) an almost identical illustration of the structural details of the basilica roof shown in drawing *m* on U 2056A r.

The verso shows: (*a*) Reconstruction in plan of the Temple of Diana at Ephesus; (*b*) plan of an amphiprostyle temple; (*c*) the beginnings of an unrecognizable temple; (*d*) plan of a prostyle temple; (*e*) and (*f*) reconstruction of a temple in antis with corrections; (*g*) a truncated sketch of a colonnade; (*h*) a circle divided into eight segments; (*i*) the beginnings of the pediment of a temple(?); (*j*) partial perspectival sketch of a prostyle or peripteral temple; (*k*) beginnings of a plan of an unrecognizable temple On the left half of the verso of the sheet, which is likely to have been folded after the drawings on the recto had already been made, Antonio the Younger has used the same ink as on the recto to make drawings and notes from *De Architectura* (III, 2, 1–7) relating to the various types of plans for temples and has made arbitrary identifications of Roman temples cited by Vitruvius (III, 2, 5). On the right half, Giovan Francesco has added rules on the articulation of Ionic cornices and friezes, also taken from Book III (5, 9–10) of the treatise, with comments, and has also made a list of ancient pieces of architecture, taken from Pliny the Elder in particular, including labyrinths and the seven (here there are in fact eight) Wonders of the World.

The architect had drawn plans (*a, b, d*) and probably also the other drawings, before writing the longer note, which therefore had to be confined to the area above the colonnades in plan (*b*). Antonio has completed the simplest of the different types of plans; he has drawn the temple in antis more or less correctly (*f*), but he has inserted a pair of columns between the antae of amphiprostyle (*b*) and prostyle (*d*). It should be borne in mind, however, that the corresponding schemes by Fra Giocondo, and even those in Daniele Barbaro's edition, reveal an even greater lack of comprehension. For the Temple of Diana at Ephesus (III, 2, 7), Antonio has proposed a plan that is divided in two, illustrating two different alternatives, one with 128 columns and the other with 126, on the basis of 127 columns that he refers back to Pliny as being the ideal. In a more note in an edition of Vitruvius, which had belonged to him, in an annotation Antonio proposed to solve the problem of the odd column by placing it underneath the statue of the goddess (cf. U 1039A).

In his note on U 2056A v., Antonio arbitrarily identifies some of the examples of Roman temples cited by Vitruvius (III, 2, 5) with the temples at the Forum Olitorium. The fact that both the Doric temple and the Ionic temple to the north of S. Nicola in Carcere were peripteral (despite the lack of a rear colonnade in the latter), was grounds enough for Antonio to recognize the former as the Temple of Jupiter Stator and the latter as the Temple of Honor and Virtue, without stopping to think about the fact that Vitruvius had sited the two temples in different places. The group of temples that were part of the Forum Olitorium was one of the most famous and most studied at that time, and Antonio has drawn various reconstructions, using *De Architectura* to help him fill in the gaps left among the ruins. The identifications that he puts forward with conviction and reiterates in numerous drawings were not, however, shared by the many architects who were his contemporaries and who also made reconstructions of the same temples.

Giovan Francesco's additions, on the right half of the verso, connect up with Antonio's contributions in many ways, to such an extent that it seems likely that these studies were made contemporaneously, and that there was a certain amount of collaboration between the two men. Giovan Francesco also deals with another subject in Book III, the articulation of the cornice and frieze in Ionic entablatures (5, 9–10), the rules for which could be put into immediate practice. Both cousins devoted several studies to this subject: Antonio on U 1187A r. and v., an extensive verification of the ratios between the height of columns and those of architraves, which he applied to various monuments in Rome; and later on U 1211A v., studying the proportions of cornices and under-cornices, and Giovan Francesco on U 1388A r., with a drawing and text based on the same theme as the one dealt with here. Furthermore, Antonio had consulted the text from Pliny the Elder that had provided Giovan Francesco with his lists of the seven Wonders and labyrinths and the legend on the image of Silenus, used in his reconstruction in plan of one of the Wonders—the Temple of Diana at Ephesus—on the left half of the page.

With regard to the Ionic entablature, Giovan Francesco has corrected the slip on U 1388A r., which states that the cornice should be as "high" as the diameter of the top of the column rather than as "wide" as that of the lower fascia, as prescribed by Vitruvius, but he makes another, stating that a flat frieze should be as high as the cornice, rather than as high as the cornice minus one quarter. The only addition to the Latin text concerns the *regolo* above the cyma of the cornice, omitted by Vitruvius, to which Giovan Francesco attributes a height equal to half the cyma. He therefore works up the passage from *De Architectura* again, substituting a division of the total height into 15 parts [1 part (*regolo*) + 2 (cymatium) + 5 (3r.d fascia) + 4 (2nd fascia) + 3 (1st fascia) = 15 m] for Vitruvius's division of the cornice as a whole, first into 7 parts and then into 12 of the 6 parts that remained after the cyma had been subtracted.

Giovan Francesco has inverted the order of layout, going from top to bottom, and simplified the calculations for the benefit of those who have to carry them out in practice. The odd slip and misunderstanding aside, he remains largely faithful to the precepts in *De Architectura*, while not reproducing them literally, and he integrates these with the conclusions he has reached through his studies of the antique. | PNP

BIBLIOGRAPHY Ferri (1885) 13 (recto only); Giovannoni (1959) I: 23; Buddensieg (1975) 108; Günther (1988) 296 n. 199, 297 n. 201, 206, 298 n. 220, 313 n. 269, 314, 315–16; Pagliara (1988) 186; Zavatta (2008) 44; Engel (2014) 110, 114, fig. 6; Fane-Saunders (2016) 255–56, 258–59; CensusIDs 10017657.

U 2057A *recto and verso*

Giovan Francesco da Sangallo

Ravenna, Porta Aurea, elevation, plan, and details (*recto*); Plan and elevantion of belvedere(?); palace, plan, and detail of palace; plan and view of bastion, hydraulic engine (*verso*), 1526.

Dimensions 440 × 285 mm.
Technique Pen and brown ink, freehand.
Paper lightweight, old glue on verso.
Drawing Scale *Piedi* and *dita*.

INSCRIPTION, Recto *porta aurea anticha nelle mura di rauenna / di pietra i[n]striata; questi agietti / si tochano; T. I. CLAVDIVS. DRVSI* [...] *CAESAR. AUG. GERMANICVS. PONT. MAX. TR. POT. II. COS. DESIG. III. P.P. DEDIT; nel disotto del archo sono seagoli* [*esagoni*] */ e mandorle e sono i[n] archo lo / 17 seangoli; fogliette i[n]torno; le sottoterra i[n]sino a que/ sto segno e sotto aqua / de fosi a questo* [*segno*]; *Achalante; questo sie mezo; diverso la terra*[?]; *diverso la chanpagnja; piedi 8 dita 12; piedi 29; lo mezo sie piedi 31 dita otto; piedi 11 dira 8; lo tutto sie piedi 63; i[n]torno al tondo; schaudra; de Tabernacholi; Sopra larcho; Lo ciello dell archatura / era i[n] tagliato; meza*

Verso *pie 60; pie 16; pie 8; pie 10; foso pasi 20 / murato; chateratta alza cholarnganello(?)*

The Porta Aurea in Ravenna, built during the reign of Emperor Claudius, remained mostly intact until 1582, when it was completely demolished for its decorative elements by Cardinal Guido Ferreri (Kähler 1953, pp. 172–74). The gate, part of the southern Roman city wall, was flanked by two circular towers, which were destroyed by the Turks at the end of the fifteenth century. With the drawing on U 2057A r. Giovan Francesco concentrated on the remaining twin openings of the arch, adding its plan underneath. From the latter's inscription, it becomes clear that he drew the facade toward the open countryside. The right side of the porch is only half drawn. A wavy line indicates the actual level of the earth, the lower parts being sketched only roughly, perhaps even with speculative outlines. As an annotation explains, the arch was also partly flooded by the waters of the surrounding trench. It was, in fact, excavated in 1541, which is *terminus ante quem* for our drawing (Kähler 1953, p. 174), which however most likely was drawn during the trip to northern Italy in 1526. The openings are flanked by paired columns that form narrow outer bays and carry an entablature that projects over the openings. With letters from A to F, Giovan Francesco marked ornamental parts that he repeated in detailed rendering underneath the plan. The measures are given in *piedi* and *dita*.

Giovan Francesco showed no trace of an upper story or even pediments, as can be seen in some other renderings of the Porta Aurea (Codex Destailleur, fol. 28 v. and fol. 39 r.; Turin, Archivio dello Stato, R 15; Berlin, Kunstbibliothek, inv. no. 3306; see Kähler 1953, pp. 179–89). It is unlikely, however, that the architect, who obviously recorded the status quo, would have omitted such important parts, which thus appear to be mere reconstructions.

The lower half of 2057A v. shows parts of fortifications in plan and view with special interest in the shape and position of the different loopholes. The numerous measures in *piedi* suggest that the drawing was made in situ. As the recto shows the Porta Aurea in Ravenna, the sketches on the verso may refer to the Rocca Brancaleone, where similar round bastions can be found. The sketches in the upper half remain somehow enigmatic. A small building is shown in plan, and, as the position of the asterisk indicates, in elevation. Two colonnades separate its only hall in three aisles. The front, as can be seen in plan and elevation, is adorned with six freestanding columns, which rise upon high, rusticated bases. The fanciful cupola and the festive loggia-like opening crowned by an inscription(?) recall a belvedere. The upper middle sketch suggests the building to be integrated within the fortified structures.

Below is a Sangallesque plan of an unidentified palace with *andito*, courtyard with loggia, and staircase, and, at the left, a corner of a palace that resembles the Roman Palazzo Farnese. The asterisk suggests that this detail and the plan belong to the same palace. At the lower bottom, Giovan Francesco drew an engine to raise water, displaying his never-ceasing interest in technical matters. | GMa

BIBLIOGRAPHY Ferri (1885) 39, 120; Kähler (1953) 176–78; Giovannoni (1959) I: 22, 77; Vasori (1981) 175–8, cat. no. 134; Zavatta (2008) 125–26, 194; CensusID (recto) 10010367.

U 2084A *recto and verso*

Antonio da Sangallo the Younger

Rome, cippus marking the boundary of the pomerium (recto); inscription tablet for the Vinea Publica, between 1537 and 1542.

Dimensions 288 × 212 mm.
Technique Pen and brown ink.
Paper Trimmed, patched tear.

INSCRIPTION, Recto (brown ink; top: *34*; left side of cippus), *XXXI / Largo per questo verso / piu di* [*blank*] *Dita* [*blank; front of cippus, IMPERATOR / CAESAR.AVGVS / VESPASIANVS IMP VI POT / TRIB POT IV CENSOR COS / IV.DESIG.V.AVCTIS.P.R.FINIB / POMERIVM AMPLIAVERVN / TERMINAVERN Q/ Largo per questo verso piedi* [*blank*] *Dita; to right of drawing. AVCTIS. P R / autoritatis populi Romani; Questo si e uno Cippo i[n] lavigna di mastro al/fonso Ceciliano Cerusigo dipapa pagolo / tertio farnesiano quale cippo si e i[n] ditta vigna fuora di porta pinciana a man mancha / uscendo fuora della porta fuora della stra/da maestra piedi ... aca[n]to auno vicolo tra[n]sversale / Loquale cippo si e lo[n]tano dalla muraglia passi /*[*blank*] *quali sono piedi* [*blank*] *& tanto era lo po/merio fuora della muragla dove non era / lecito edificare edifitio nesuno di muro & / da questa parte delle lettere che voltava ame/zogiorno everso la muragla e Co[n]sumato che / afaticha si discerne le lettere dallaltre parti / sie sencero e sie di pietra di tevertino*

Verso *IMP... CAESAR / VESPASINVS AVG / PONTIF / MAX TRIBVNIC / POTEST VI IMP XIIII.P.P. / COS.VI.DESIG.VII.CENSOR / LOCVM. VINIAE PVBLICAE / OCCVPATVM APRIVATIS / PER.COLLEGIVM. PONTIFICVM / RESTITVIT; Questo Epitaffio sie in frallamuragla di / roma ello fiume detto travicella al bastione nuovo chefatto & fralla porta / asanbastiano e porta S(an)to pagolo chevedera/porte una inclusa in detto bastione detta / porta ... / Laltra efuora di ditto bastione inverso po/rta S(an)to bastiano adirittura della via / appia e tengo sia porta apia & san bast/iano sia porta trigemina per gra/ni e ne laqua vergine / come dice frontino*

At the top of the recto, the number 34 belongs to a numbering sequence found on other sheets with inscriptions, including U 2083A r (37), U 2083A v (32) and U 2085A r (19) all catalogued in Frommel-Adams 2000.

The recto shows a cippus marking the boundary of the pomerium of Rome erected by Vespasian in AD 75. It is one of four recorded examples (CIL VI, 31538a-c and 40854), and, as Antonio's note says, seen by him outside the Porta Pinciana in a vigna belonging to Paul III's surgeon. 'Alfonso Ceciliano' who must be the famous Neapolitan surgeon Alfonso Ferri, called to Rome to cure the pope in 1535 (Pagano 1997), who gave him a vigna in just this location (Pandolfi 2018, pp. 52–53) He draws it again in slightly more detail on U 2085A r with an almost identical note. Pier Nicola Pagliara speculates that Antonio saw it around 1537–9 when working on the project to strengthen the walls of Rome. Antonio gives no indication whether the cippus was on its original findspot or had been transported to Ferri's vigna as a garden ornament. Its current location is unknown.

The verso has a transcription of an inscription on a tablet (CIL VI *933*), which provides the only evidence for the existence of the Vinea Publica of Rome (Coarelli 2016). Antonio omitted a letter from Vespasian's name which may be why it is copied again, more accurately, on U 2087A r, with a note giving more precise information on its location at an ancient building incorporated into the Bastione Ardeatino (1537–42), where it had been in use as a dining table. The building is marked with a star on Nolli's 1748 map and a door survives (Lanciani 1902–3, II, 100). The inscription is now in the Capitoline Museums. The latter part of the note, referring to the Porta S. Sebastiano/ originally Porta Appia and the Porta S. Paolo/ originally Porta Ostiensis, both in the Aurelian Walls, confuses the latter with the Porta Trigemina, which was in the older Servian Wall where it reached the Tiber near the Forum Boarium, a common mistake among Renaissance topographers. In his reference to Frontinus (*De Aquis*, I.5) Antonio compounds the error by substituting the Aqua Virgo for the Aqua Appia. | IC

BIBLIOGRAPHY CIL VI 933/31208 and 31538a; Ferri (1885) 169; Lanciani, (1902–03) II, 100 and 105; Giovannoni (1959) I: 25; Coarelli (1974): CensusIDs 10022098; 10082377.

U 2086A *recto and verso*

Antonio da Sangallo the Younger

Formia, epigraph regarding the gens Vitruvia.

Dimensions 64 × 130 mm.
Technique Pen and brown ink, freehand, stylus.
Paper Lightweight, trimmed on four sides, reinforcements to hole at top and in corner.

INSCRIPTION, Recto *EX* (correcting XE) *TESTAMENTO / M. VITRUVI.M.L. APELLAE ET / HOC MONUMENTUM. HERE*; (two different hands) *201/11*

Verso (Antonio's hand) *E de uno liberto di vetruvio*; (19th-century hand, black pencil, Ferri?) *Formia*; (blue pencil) *2086.*

The text is in the lapidary characters of the epigraph. The epigraph—EX TESTAMENTO / M. VITRUVI.M.L. APELLAE ET / HOC MONUMENTUM. HERE (CIL, X, no. 6190)—is often cited in the Renaissance, among others by Antonio Panormita, Fra Giocondo, who stated it was found *apud Castellonem* (Formia), and Gesualdo, who located it in *ingresso Castellonis sub ponte Rialti*. Paul Thielscher, misinterpreting Gesualdo's indication, had supposed that the epigraph had been brought to Venice, near the Rialto bridge. As a matter of fact, it is still in Formia, no longer at the foot of the Roman bridge over the Rialto but in an epigraphic collection located in the garden of Villa Rubino. The forename Marcus, attributed to Vitruvius in the Renaissance editions of *De Architectura*, derives from this epigraph. | PNP

BIBLIOGRAPHY Ferri (1885) 84; Thielscher (1961) 420–21; Giovannoni (1959) I: 25; Pagliara (1988) 186; CensusID 10078048.

U 2087A *recto*

Antonio da Sangallo the Younger

Epigraph on *Vinea Publica*, close to Ardeatine Bastion (*recto*); Pedestal of an ancient edifice at house of Gregorio de Serlupi (*verso*), after 1537.

Dimensions 198 × 146 mm.
Technique Pen and ink, freehand.
Paper Lightweight, crumpled and folded, trimmed on four sides, paper and transparent reinforcements to holes made by acid ink.
Drawing Scale Roman *palmi (verso).*

INSCRIPTION, Recto (at top) (19th-century hand, black pencil, Ferri) 21/12; (Antonio's hand) (IMP CAES canceled) *IMP CAESARI / VESPASIANVS AVG / PONTIF MAX · TRIBVNI / POTEST VI IMP XIIII · P · P / COS VI DESIG VII CENSOR / LOCVM VINIAE PVBLICAE / OCCUPATVM · A– PRIVATIS / PER COLLEGIVM PONTIFICVM RESTITVIT Questo epitaffio si e in quello edifitio quale si e / in quello colle sotto al baluardo ch e inanzi alla terme antoniane cio e inanzi a ditto balua/rdo circha 400 piedi e serve adesso per tavo/la de uno stazo di vignia da mangiarvi / suso ditto edifitio e in ditto colle e soprasta a que/l piano dove passa el fiume ditto travicella / e ancor se li dice aquadaccia ed era / uno grande edifitio e in bello loco volto a mezogiorno*

Verso (bottom, in blue pencil) 2087; (top) (Antonio's hand) *Inchasa di Messer gregorio di serlupis / presso alla torre de lmelangolo se trovato uno / inbasamento deuno edifitio che sta come qui / sotto e disegniato*; (vertically up pedestal) *in palmi moderni*

Antonio the Younger also transcribed this epitaph from the *Vinea publica* (CIL. VI, no. 933) onto U 2084A r., where he gives its location as "sotto il bastione nuovo che è fatto fra lla porta San sebastiano e porta santo pagolo," that is to say, the Ardeatine Bastion (see U 892A r. in vol. I), possibly but not necessarily after work on the bastion commenced, from 1537 onward. The sheet could, therefore, also be from after 1541–42, when work was completed. The Travicella River, as it is also named on U 2084A, or *aquadaccia*, is the Almone, which runs through the Caffarella valley.

Given the reference to the Ardeatine Bastion on the recto, it is most likely that the drawing was made after 1537. The Melangolo Tower mentioned in the note appears on the major 16th century maps of Rome in a block situated in the Sant'Angelo district, bounded by Via Cavalletti, Via dei Delfini, Via dei Funari, and Piazza S. Caterina, now occupied by Palazzo Patrizi, to the south of which the Serlupi family houses were located. Remains of the northern side of the Porticus Octaviae were discovered under the cellars of the Palazzo Patrizi, near which, as attested to by a fragment of the Forma Urbis, the Temple of Juno Regina stood. Bartoli has attributed this survey to the podium of the latter. Antonio the Younger's drawing shows the podium standing on a base with three steps, supporting an Attic base, with a torus above it, surmounted by a *tondino*. Added together, the individual heights make up an overall height of 19⅓ *palmi* up to the top edge of the Attic base, equal to 4.31 meters. | PNP

BIBLIOGRAPHY Ferri (1885) 127, 169, 230; Lanciani (1897) 454; Lanciani (1902–12) II: 65, 97; Jordan-Huelsen (1878–1907) IV: 540, 551; Bartoli (1914–22) III: fig. 350, pl. 209; VI: 67; Giovannoni (1959) I: 25; Günther (1988) 255; CensusIDs 10072885, 10072875.

U 2095A *recto and verso*

Antonio da Sangallo the Younger

Rome, inscribed cippus, 1544.

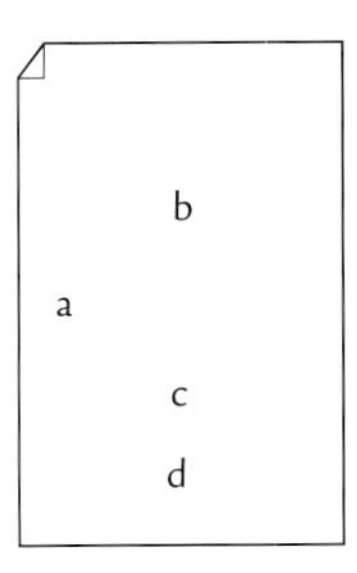

Dimensions 284 × 141 mm.
Technique Pen and brown ink.
Paper Heavy, laid down, with window cut out to reveal inscription on verso.

INSCRIPTION, Recto (a) *spatio gra[n]de*; (b, inscription on cippus): *POSI TITVLO / QVOQVO VERS P III / DIS MANIBVS / SACRVM / L. VALERIO INFANTI / RAPTVS QVI EST SVBITU / QVO FATO NON SCITVR / NATVS NOCTIS H VI / VIXIT DIEBVS LXXI / ABIT NOCTIS AB H VI / QVIS QVIS EVM LAESIT / SIC CVM SVIS VALEAT / INFRONTES DVO P TER / ET INLATERA / DVO P TER*; (c) *Trouato al bastione delli Spinelli / ouero di beluedere questo dì 24 / di sette[n]bre 1544*; (d) *Latere; fro[n]te; Latere; fro[n]te*

Verso *Epitaffio anticho / Trouato albastio / nelo di beluedere*

The inscribed cippus depicted on this sheet was found near the Belvedere bastion. | JN

BIBLIOGRAPHY Ferri (1885) 109; Giovannoni (1959) I: 25; CensusID 10082440.

U 2096A *recto and verso*

Antonio da Sangallo the Younger

Narni, plan of an ancient cistern and Latin inscription.

Dimensions 210 × 131 mm.
Technique Pen and ink, freehand.
Paper Lightweight, trimmed on four sides, reinforcements along top and part of left margin.

INSCRIPTION, Recto (top) (19th century hand, Ferri) *39*; (bottom) (Antonio's hand) *inarni*; *IULIANII / PUBLIO CAFIONIO / IULIANO / CORRECTORI TUSCIAE ET UMBRIAE / OB INSIGNI EIUS GIESTA ET INLUS / TRE ADMINISTR* (*R* written above line) *ATIONIS MERITUM / ORDO NARNIENSIUM UNA CUM / CIVIBUS CON* (*N* corrected) *LOCAVE / RUNT PATRONO DIGNISSIMO*

Antonio the Younger must have transcribed the inscription on location during one of his countless journeys in Umbria or to the Marche. He would have seen the inscription on the corner of Narni's ancient city gate, which was integrated later in the bishop's palace. The inscpription was transported to the town hall in 1886. His transcription differs from those found in several Renaissance epigraphic sylloges in the *Corpus Inscriptionum Latinarum* (CIL). For instance, Antonio misreads one of the worn letters and writes "CAFIONIO" instead of "CAEONIO." Nothing is known about the water cistern with three rows of piers supporting a cross vault, which Antonio presumably saw and rapidly sketched during this same journey. | PNP

BIBLIOGRAPHY Ferri (1885) 100–01; CIL XI: pars II, 4118; Giovannoni (1959) I: 25; Vasori (1981) 155–56, cat. no. 121; CensusID 10076366.

U 2098A *recto*

Antonio da Sangallo the Younger

Rome, Studies related to Tomb of Statilius Aper, with measuring instruments, tomb inscription, and sketch of tomb, after 1527.

Dimensions 330 × 210 mm.
Technique Pen and brown ink.
Paper Heavy, folded twice, cut on four sides.

INSCRIPTION (right half, upper part) *queste 14 Dita sono minuti 67 di 5 p. dito de nostri / che a 5 p. dito del mio piede; arieno a esere 70 / questo dito a ma macha sie Minuti 7 e questo da man / ritta ultimo sie 5½ che i tucto lo piede sie minuti / 79½ elli arieno a essere 80 a cique p ditto; Lo tucto sie minuti 257 quali sono delle nostre / Dita 51 minuti 2*; (right half, lower part) *INNOCVVS · APER ECCE · IACES · NON VIRGINIS · IRA NEC MELEACER / ATROX PERFODITVIS CERA FERRO MORS TACITA OBREPSIT SVBITO FECI O / RVINAM QVE TIBI CRESCENTI RAPVIT IVVENILE FIGVRAM; T · STATILIO · VOL APROMENSORI / AEDIFICIOR · VIXIT · ANN · XXii · M · VIII · D X V / T · STATILIVS · VOL · PRO CVLVS / ACCINSVS VELATVS · ET · ARGENTARIA / EVTYCHIA · PARENTES · FILIO OPTIMO ET / ORCIVIAE ANTHIDI · VXORI EIVS SIBI · Q · ET · SVIS / LIBERTIS LIBERTABVS POSTERIS QVE EORVM*

On the right half of the sheet is a sketch of the tomb of the *mensor aedificiorum* Statilius Aper, turned at a 90 degrees angle to the other representations, showing the socle with its two inscriptions, the main panel with a relief of the deceased and a naked youth, and the pediment with a female bust in a shell. The tombstone, which was presumably found on the Gianicolo, was placed in the Belvedere of the Vatican in 1542 under Pope Paul III. Benedict XIV presented it to the Capitoline Museums in 1743, where it has remained until today.

The draftsman was particularly interested in the measuring instruments (a foot measure and *pertica*) depicted on the narrow left side of the stone, to which the studies in the upper left quarter of the sheet refer. Attention to the exact length of the Roman foot was given relatively late in early modern studies of antiquity. An important source for its reconstruction was the Tomb of Gnaeus Cossutius Agantangelus, known since the late fifteenth century, which included a rough representation of a bar with a foot measure. It was not until the middle of the 16th century that reliable archaeological evidence of its length began to accumulate. In this connection, the monument of Statilius Aper can be considered the most important find. In keeping with the high social status of the deceased, its representation of the instruments of measurement are more precisely and finely carved than are those on the monument for Cossutius. Another early drawing of the Tomb of Statilius Aper, with the instruments depicted on the side, may be found on folio 145 of the Codex Pighianus (Staatsbibliothek, Berlin). | HR

BIBLIOGRAPHY Ferri (1885) 84, 169; Jones (1912) 76 f.; Günther (1988) 225 ff.; Günther (1998) 373–93; CensusID 10081659.

U 2099A *recto*

Antonio da Sangallo the Younger

Ancona, funerary tablet, ca. 1532–35.

Dimensions 132 × 151 mm.
Technique Pen and ink.
Paper Lightweight.

INSCRIPTION (top right, black pencil, old numbering) *33*; (Antonio's hand, brown ink) *B M / FLAVIO AVRELIANO / VETERANO QVI VIXIT / ANNIS LXII MESES · V / DIES · VI VALERIA / VIATORINA · CONIVCI* [*sic*] / *DVLCISSIMO · ET · FLA / VIVS · CALLIDIVS PATRI / BENE · MERENTI · POSVERVNT*; (below tablet) *fuora D'anchona i*[*n*] *santo stefano vechio ruinato*

The inscription is only known from this drawing. As Antonio noted, the church was already in ruins when he saw it, probably while engaged in fortification works in Ancona between 1532 and 1535 (see U 1071A r.) and the tablet has not been recorded since. | IC

BIBLIOGRAPHY Ferri (1885) 6; CIL IX. 6386.

U 2103A *recto*

GIOVAN FRANCESCO DA SANGALLO

Ionic base and two Latin inscriptions, before 1527.

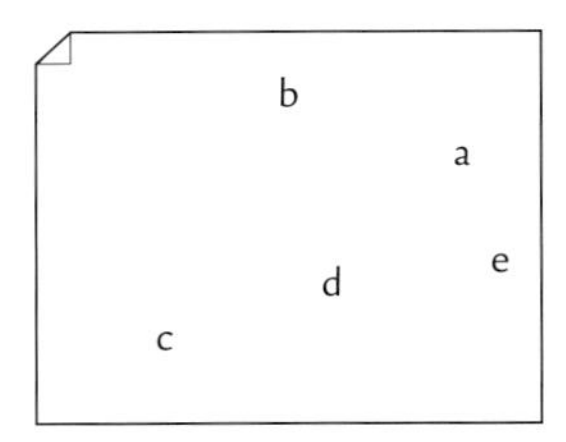

Dimensions 292 × 381mm.
Paper Lightweight, trimmed on all four edges, with a central vertical fold and one horizontal fold only visible in the left half.
Technique Pen and brown ink, freehand.
Drawing scale: Presumably in *once* or, more likely, in *dita*.

INSCRIPTION (old numbering: bottom right, ink, 16th-century hand) *38*. (Texts of the inscriptions and notes all in Giovan Francesco's hand) (a),(rotated at 90 degrees in relation to other inscriptions, to match orientation of drawing) *Basa ionjcha apie del ponte a 4 chapjora/ in tresteveri di roma*; (b), EXAVRTOR; (c), (upside down) *EXAVCTORITATE / IMP CAESARIS DIVI / TRAIANI PARTHICII · F · / DIVI · NERVAE · NEPOTIS · / TRAIANI HADRIANI · / AVG PONTIF MAX TRIB · / POTEST V IM · P. I · I · I · I COS I · I · I / IMESSIVS RVSTICVS CVRATOR · /ALVEI ET RIPARVM TIBERIS · ET · /CLOACA · RVM VRBIS R · R RESTITVIT / SECVNDVM PRAE CEDENTEM · / TERMINATIONEM PROXIM CI · pp · / PED · CXVS-*; (d), *MAGNIVM · DOMVS / AGV · CVLTORIB · SIGNVM / LIBERTATIS · RESTITVTAE / SER · GALBAE · INPERATORIS · AGV / CVRATORES · ANNI · SECVNDI · / G · TVRRANIVS · PODYBIVS / L · CALPVRNIVS · ZENA · / C · MVRDIVS · · LALVS · / C · TVRRANIVS · FLORVS · / C · MVRDINVS · DEMOSTHENES · / S·P·P·D·*, (below) *dalla banda dinanzi in sulla piaza marani*; (e), *DEDIC · IDIB · OTOBR · / C · BELLICO · NATALE · / P · CORNELIO · SIPIONE · ASIATICO · COS ·* (below) *banda laterale in sulla piaza di mesere/ damjano marani achanto alla regula/ damiano*

The sheet contains one drawing and transcriptions of two Latin inscriptions.

Drawing *a* is a part elevation of an unusual Ionic base, of the type developed in Asia Minor. It has a single *scozia*, carved with ornament, the two fillets with convergent cable moulding, and three upper mouldings carved with foliage. The inscription says it was found by the "Ponte a Quattro Capi" i.e. the Ponte Fabricio, the bridge connecting the Tiber Island to the left bank of the Tiber near the Theatre of Marcellus. In U 1804A r. (Bartoli, fig. 559), Giovan Francesco draws the same base in a highly finished measured drawing along with three other bases, one of which belonged to the Temple of Apollo *in Circo* which was excavated *a piè de Savegli*, i.e. the Theatre of Marcellus in the early 1520s. Around Rome, examples of the Asiatic Ionic base of the type described by Vitruvius, are rare (cf. U 1182A r., the lower part of which up to the scozia is very similar to this and U 1184A r.) and it is likely that Giovan Francesco has classified it as Ionic for this reason, even though it does not full corrrespond with Vitruvius's description.

The inscription, *b*, appears to be an abandoned attempt for that transcribed fully at *c*, CIL VI. 1240a/ VI. 31552a, which is on one of a group of four *cippi* found on the banks of the Tiber near the Ospedale di S. Spirito, and subsequently moved to the house of the Rustici family (Ligorio 2016, p. 299). The transcriptions *d* and *e* form part of a single inscription (CIL VI. 471) on the front and left sides, respectively, of a marble base which Giovan Francesco and others agree was visible in a piazza in the Regula *rione*. | PNP, IC

BIBLIOGRAPHY Ferri (1885) 128, 169, 230; Giovannoni (1959) I: 25; Buddensieg (1975) 108: CensusID 10030847.

U 2114A *recto*

GIOVAN FRANCESCO DA SANGALLO (?)

Verona, Porta dei Borsari, inscription, 1526.

Dimensions 207 × 206 mm.
Technique Pen and brown ink, traces of black chalk, straightedge.
Paper Medium weight, trimmed.

INSCRIPTION *VERONAE IN EXTERIOR [CON]SPECTV PORTE BVRSARIOR[UM]; COLONIA AVGUSTA VERONA NOVA / GALLIENIANA VALERIANO II ET / LVCILLO COSS MVRI VERONENSIVM / FABRICATI EX DIE III NON APRILIVM; DEDICATI PR NON DECEMBR / IVBENTE SANCTISSIMO GALLIENO / AVG N INSISTENTE AVR MARCELLINO / V P DVC DVC CVRANTE IVL MARCELLINO; IN MOENIB[US] OPPIDI VETERI[S] / WPA / KAI / TYXH*

On this sheet, Giovanni Battista neatly transcribed the inscription displayed above the two arches of the Porta dei Borsari in Verona. The elegant rubric above the proper inscription can be interpreted as referring to the location of the inscription on the Porta dei Borsari, that is, the external facade. The other rubric at the bottom, above the three-line Greek inscription, states that the auspicious Greek phrase was to be seen in the ancient town walls.

In his published catalogue, Ferri attributed U 2114A to Antonio the Younger, but in the card index, he crossed out Antonio's name and replaced it with that of Giovanni

Battista. Since it is not documented that Giovanni Battista joined on the trip to northern Italy, the drawing might rather be attributed to Giovanni Francesco. | SE

BIBLIOGRAPHY Ferri (1885) 225.

U 2134A *recto and verso*

Antonio da Sangallo the Younger (?)

Rome, Baths of Diocletian, before 1518.

Dimensions 573 × 595 mm.
Technique Pen and brown ink, stylus, straightedge, compass.
Paper Folds, restored in many places.
Drawing Scale Florentine *braccia.*

INSCRIPTION, Recto *Salone*; *Salone*; *Schizi di Termine*; *p[er] questo V b[raccia] 86 / Innanzi b[raccia] 93 [braccia] 2 3*

The recto of the sheet is almost completely taken up by a plan, with some measurements, of part of the central body of the Baths of Diocletian. The plan seems to precede and to influence the plan by Francesco da Sangallo (U 284A r.), from which it differs only in the number of columns of the short side of the portico of the gymnasium and in the exterior spaces adjacent to the *calidarium*. Therefore, it would have been executed shortely before 1518 and it would prove that Francesco elaborated a plan for Antonio the Younger. The interest in the Baths of Diocletian is already revealed in drawings by Giuliano da Sangallo (1546A), by Bramante (U 104A, U 2162A), and by Baldassare Peruzzi (U 476A, 622A); these sheets should be compared with the present drawing by Antonio and the one by Giovanni Battista da Sangallo (U 2163A r.), which is quite similar to that by Francesco (U 284A r.). At the right, in the margin, there is a small sketch of the hemicycle of the enclosure of the Baths of Diocletian. Below, between the short side of the portico of the gymnasium and the space with *exedrae*, there is a sketch of the side of an Ionic capital.

In the lower part of the verso is a sketch of a measured plan of part of the central body of the Baths of Diocletian. At the left is a sketch of an octagonal room with semicircular niches. Above is a measured profile of a cornice, drawn with the sheet turned 180 degrees. | ACF

BIBLIOGRAPHY Ferri (1885) 203; Guidi-Paribeni (1911) fig. 9; Bartoli (1914–22) IV: figs 179–80, pl 99–100; VI: 35; CensusIDs 10084066, 10084075.

U 2143A *recto and verso*

Giovan Francesco da Sangallo

Rome, Forum Romanum, Basilica Aemilia (*recto*); sketch of an oval (*verso*), ca. 1520(?).

Dimensions 343 × 268 mm.
Technique Pen and brown ink, stylus.
Paper Right half of sheet cut off.

INSCRIPTION, Recto *FORO·I*

The recto drawing copies Giuliano da Sangallo's well-known full view of the Basilica Aemilia in the Codex Barberini (Huelsen 1910, fol. 26 r.). Only half the sheet, showing one-and-a-half bays of the left part of the facade, has been preserved.

Following Giuliano even to some of the details, Giovan Francesco placed the engaged columns and the corner pilaster on pedestals. The *bucrania* that fill the metopes misled those members of the Sangallo circle who studied the monument into thinking that it was on the Forum Boarium. The partly preserved, fabricated inscription over the attic of the central door reading "FORO·I," whose full inscription in Giuliano's model reads "FORO·IN·BOVARIO," has its origin in this misunderstanding. The expressive ruins in the portals are also borrowed from Giuliano; they are a characteristic feature of a whole series of reconstructions in the Codex Barberini.

Contrary to Huelsen's belief, Giuliano probably did not transmit an accurate picture of the basilica. The attic inscription, the continuation of which was taken from the Arch of Septimius Severus (see Huelsen 1910), is in itself an indication that this is merely a fantasy. But the architecture also appears to be largely inaccurate. The entablature is treated summarily, as is shown by the detail drawings discussed below. At least on the main facade, the existence of pedestals is disproved by the ruins still in situ. The suspicion arises that Giuliano gave the columns proportions in keeping with the growing notion of "orders"; the columns standing on what are probably invented pedestals have a ratio to their entablature of about 4²/₅:1. The oval on the verso is unidentifiable.

The drawing is an insecure, pedantic work, probably from the beginning of Giovan Francesco's career. | HCD

BIBLIOGRAPHY Ferri (1885) 166; Bartoli (1914–22) I: fig. 98, pl. 63; VI: 23; Günther (1988) 115, no. 104., Ghisetti Giavarina (1983) 22; Zampa (2014) 229–31, fig. 199; CensusID 45019.

U 2147A *recto*

Collaborator of Giovanni Battista da Sangallo (?)

Preparatory schema for a 24h circuit.

Dimensions 387 × 205 mm.
Technique Pen and brown ink, compass.
Paper Two leaves joined and laid down on secondary support.

INSCRIPTION (modern hand) *51*

The drawing is probably connected with U 3945A v., U 3944A r. and v., and was prepared by one of Giovanni Battista da Sangallo's collaborators. | CLF

BIBLIOGRAPHY Ferri (1885) 81.

U 2162A *recto*

Antonio da Sangallo the Younger (?)

Detail of the of Baths of Diocletian, ca. 1505–06.

Dimensions 281 × 350 mm.
Technique Pen and brown ink, straightedge, compass.
Paper White paper.
Drawing Scale Florentine *braccia.*

INSCRIPTION (Antonio's hand) *delle terme diocleziane*; measurements

Bramante appoints the Baths of Diocletian to around 1505, probably in close connection with the planning of St Peter's. Back at his drawing table, he drew the first results of his survey, freehand, on U 104A. It is possible that Giuliano da Sangallo helped him, since his handwriting can be identified in the addition of two of the measurements. Up to now we know of no earlier survey of an ancient monument that is as precise, although not much time passed before Antonio would attempt, on U 2134A, to surpass Bramante. The detail on the present sheet, U 2162A r., is measured in *braccia* and thus drawn by Antonio da Sangallo or copied by Bramante from a florentine draughtsman.

Unlike Bramante, Antonio is not satisfied with measurements that are rounded off but he also uses a third and a quarter of the *braccio fiorentino*. Also unlike Bramante, who was most interested in the interrelationship of the individual spaces and the complex form of the dividing walls, Antonio aims to produce a finished drawing of the reconstruction. His survey comes a step closer to documenting the extant remains and may have served as the basis for even later plans by members of the Sangallo circle. On U 528A, a sketch of the ground plan dated 1507, Baldassare Peruzzi, working independently of Antonio, measured the enclosing walls of the Baths of Diocletian, likewise with disruptions, but in *palmi romani* (Frommel 2003, *L'esordio*, pp. 158–59). Clearly Bramante had known how to turn the Baths of Diocletian into a learning experience for his students. | CLF

BIBLIOGRAPHY Ferri (1885) 203; Bartoli (1914–22) I: fig. 178, pl. 98; VI: 35; Frommel (1994, *Introduction*) 9–10, Frommel (2008, *proposte*) 44, fig. 57; CensusID 10071929.

U 2163A *recto and verso*

Giovanni Battista da Sangallo

Rome, Baths of Diocletian, plan.

Dimensions 824 × 536 mm.
Technique Pen and brown ink.
Paper Stains.
Drawing Scale Roman *palmi* (10 Roman *palmi* = 48 mm).

INSCRIPTION, Recto (Giovanni Battista's hand) *queste sono chane romane fatte la chana sia palmi 10* (= 48 mm); *Da una croce alatra sia uno palmo* [...] *romano fatto* (= 223 mm) *questi palmi sia misurato termine* [...]

Verso (Antonio's hand) *terme*

The drawing on the recto is a graphic reconstruction of half of the plan of the Baths of Diocletian and is identical to one by Francesco da Sangallo (284 r.). Since the measurements are in *palmi* which the brothers Antonio and Giovanni Battista never used for their surveys of antiquities (cf. U 2134A r. and v. which is in *braccia*), the drawing is probably copied from Peruzzi or some other artist. | ACF

BIBLIOGRAPHY Ferri (1885) 203; Bartoli (1914–22) IV: fig. 525, pl. 315; VI: 97; Günther (1988) 199, 378; CensusID 10027604.

U 3944A *recto*

Giovanni Battista da Sangallo

Globe with circuit.

Dimensions 341 × 216 mm.
Technique Pen and brown ink, freehand.
Paper Medium weight.
Drawing Scale *braccia.*

INSCRIPTION (Giovanni Battista's hand) *ogni ora e partita in sei parte / cosi quelle del verno come quelle / dellastate / La luna e oggi alli 25 G[radi?] (segue il segno del sagittario) e siamo alli sedice di gennaio*

See U 3945A r. | CLF

BIBLIOGRAPHY Ferri (1885) 34.

U 3945A *recto and verso*

Giovanni Battista da Sangallo

Quarter of a globe with circuit.

Dimensions 273 × 275 mm.
Technique Pen and brown ink, compass, straightedge.
Paper Medium weight.

INSCRIPTION, Recto *Mobile distate*

On the recto of U 3944A, as on the recto and verso of U 3945A, Giovanni Battista drew a quarter circle with the hours, degrees, and zodiac signs of the six hours of what appears to be a 24h circuit. He draws the position of the moon on January 16th, and although he does not indicate the year, it could be calculated astronomically. These drawings may have been done in connection with his illustrations of the constellations and zodiac signs for Vitruvius (Rowland 2003, pp. 187–90). | CLF

BIBLIOGRAPHY Ferri (1885) 34.

U 3965A *recto and verso*

Antonio Labacco and Antonio da Sangallo the Younger

Rome, perspectival drawing of a portal of the Doric Temple of the Forum Holitorium (*recto*); plan of the porch of the Doric Temple of the Forum Holitorium with view of the lateral arcade (*verso*).

Dimensions 226 × 168 mm.
Technique Pen and brown ink.
Paper Trimmed on four sides.
Drawing Scale Florentine *braccia.*

INSCRIPTION, Recto *laporta e largha b. 5 mi. 12; b.i mi. 42; Doric*
Verso *b. 5 mi.8; b. 2 mi.6*

Bartoli first identified this portal as from the Doric temple of the Forum Holitorium, clearly indicated by the inscription "Doric" at the base of the sheet. The perspectival profile corresponds exactly to Serlio's woodcut of this temple in his third book and Peruzzi's profile on U 477 r. Serlio did not include measurements for this detail and there are slight differences between Labacco's and Peruzzi's dimensions. Labacco has marked off the height of each molding with corresponding measurements noted on the adjacent plumb line. The width of the portal opening is 5 *braccia* and 12 *minuti*, slightly larger than Peruzzi's (4 *braccia*; 14 1/2 *minuti*), as well as the distance, 1 *braccie* 42 *minuti*, from the outer edge of the jamb molding to the corner pilaster of the exterior cella wall.

The verso is a sketch of the porch of the Doric temple of the Forum Holitorium with a small perspectival view of the porch columns below. Labacco noted the variation of the intercolumnations between the first and second of the corner columns, 3 *braccia* 8 *minuti* versus 2 *braccia* 6 *minuti*. At the top right corner is a profile of a molding; its origin is not yet identified. | MK

BIBLIOGRAPHY Bartoli (1914–22) IV: figs 603–04, pl. 350; VI: 109; CensusID 10015535.

U 3966A *recto and verso*

Bernardo della Volpaia

Rome, partial elevation of so-called Frontispiece of Nero (*recto*); a series of calculations (*verso*), 1512–15.

Dimensions 222 × 167 mm.
Technique Pen and brown ink, over scored lines using straightedge, compass, freehand.
Paper Heavy, yellowed, trimmed, reinforcements at four corners and elsewhere on verso.
Drawing Scale *braccio fiorentino* of 60 *minuti.*

INSCRIPTION, Recto (lower left) *la meta e bracia 50 e minutj 5*; (right, turned 90 degrees) *insino alarchitraue sono b[racci]a 21⅔ / il pilastro di drento se alto b[racci] a 36*; (left of entablature) *b[racci]a 3 14*; (in tympanum, turned 90 degrees) *b[racci]a 2 minuti 45*; (in entablature)

(cornice, frieze, architrave) *2 20*; *2 30*; *2 36*; (in raking cornice) '*b*[*racci*]*a 3 14*; (another, later hand) (bottom) *42*; *84*; *84*[+]84[+]84[=]*253* (final digits corrected as *85*[+]85[+]85[=]*255*); (right, in pencil, later hand) *3966*

Verso (pen and ink, partly covered by reinforcement patches, written 180 degrees with respect to drawing on recto) *1020*[+] *1000*[=] (not completed; digits were corrected in pen and ink as 1120 and 1100); *80*[+]80[+]80[+]40[=]280[+]*512*[+]200½ [=] *992½*; *238*[+]*50*[+]*9½* [=] *297½* [+]*15*[+]30[+]30[+]40[=]*412½*; (another, later hand, left side) 3966

The drawing in elevation represents the reconstruction of the facade of the cella of a temple, identified in recent times as that dedicated to Jove Serapis on the Quirinal during the reign of Caracalla. Also known as the Palace of Maecenas, the building was located within the Colonna properties, its vast surface area (about 16,800 square meter) extending approximately from Piazza della Pilotta to Piazza del Quirinale. A complex system of stairs linked the lower level to the summit of the hill, where a spacious plateau with the structures serving the cult looked out over the city. Because of its significant size and the substantial parts that had survived, it was often studied, drawn, and surveyed during the Renaissance. Giuliano da Sangallo was the first of the Sangallo circle to deal with it thoroughly, as is demonstrated by various sheets in Barb. lat. 4424 (Vatican Library), most of which are dated between 1513 and 1514. U 3966A is one of the earliest attempts to reconstruct the short front of the building, beginning with the impressive fragment of the southwest corner of the cella, known since the Middle Ages as the Frontispiece of Nero. Although it was not directly used by Giuliano, the sheet seems to belong to the Roman milieu most closely connected to him about 1514, the last year of his sojourn in Rome before returning to Florence.

Originally attributed with some doubt to Antonio Labacco, the sheet was recently given to Bernardo della Volpaia, expert draftsman and Giuliano's collaborator, and the probable author of the Codex Coner. The drawing's closeness to Giuliano da Sangallo also seems to be confirmed by the series of numbers and calculations appearing in the lower part of the recto and on the verso. In all cases but one, they are additions, sometimes with corrections of the digits and totals, done by a hand different from that of the drawing. Analyzing the handwriting, Huelsen was able to attribute the calculations to Giuliano and to hypothesize their relationship to the urban layout of the Borgo Vecchio, on which Giuliano was working in 1514.

A few further observations are needed to clarify why and when the drawing on U 3966A r. was made. Details in U 3966A distinguish it from other known drawings of the same subject, such as that of Giuliano da Sangallo in Barb. Lat. 4424 (fol. 65), and that of Bernardo della Volpaia in the Codex Coner (fol. 52 v.) (see Huelsen 1910, II, esp. fols 65 and 65 v.; Ashby 1904, II, esp. pl. 64 (fol. 52 v.) and pl. 81 (fol. 63 v.)). Giuliano never drew the short front of the temple and in the notes he identified it as the Palace of Maecenas. However, he provided general measurements by way of a plan of the whole complex (fol. 65 v.), the reconstructed elevation of the left side (fol. 65), and the details of the entablature and the column bases (fol. 10, fol. 63 v., fol. 15).

On folio 52 v. of the Codex Coner we see the west elevation of the cella, fully reconstructed and liberally interpreted by Bernardo, also here identified as the Palace of Maecenas. The substantial correspondence of the dimensions and the pictorial and three-dimensional character of the elevations of the building demonstrate Giuliano's and Bernardo's contemporaneous interest in the monument and the close connection between the drawings in their manuscripts. Giuliano elaborates the elevation of the side, drawn in orthogonal projection, with a substantially coherent shadow cast by the columns on the rear wall of the portico; in the facade drawn by Bernardo we see the depth of the pilasters and the corner of the right flank, represented axonometrically. In his version of the hypothetical reconstruction of the monument, Bernardo is less analytical and less critical than Giuliano. Instead of adhering to the evidence of the visible ruins, he seems to want to combine the wall as is (composed simply of rows of blocks of *peperino*) with a Corinthian pilaster at the right corner of the cella (still visible, but structurally and formally belonging to the side elevation) and the colonnaded elevation of the temple toward the peristyle (as reconstructed by Giuliano on fol. 65 of Barb. Lat. 4424). All the same, Bernardo draws only the left part of the elevation, following his own interpretation. In the right half he represented, instead, the actual state of the monument in the years around 1512–15, the probable date of the drawings in the Codex Coner. On this side, the wall is drawn simply with blocks of stone with a large rectangular lacuna at the bottom, corresponding to the surface of the wall of the cella in connection with the structure of the monumental access stair, a detail clearly shown in the section of Giuliano's reconstruction (Barb. Lat. 4424, fol. 65).

Compared with the representations of the Frontispiece of Nero discussed above, U 3966A r. is both more simplified and drawn with greater technical rigor. The elevation, in orthogonal projection, is restricted to the left half; the stone blocks are drawn freehand only at the left corner. Above, the majestic entablature is indicated in outline, without any of its decoration; at the bottom, the elevation appears unfinished, since the part of the construction related to the access stair is left undefined. However, the drawing is quite accurate. The horizontal, vertical, and oblique lines were scored with a stylus, using a straightedge and a series of pricks. These were done with a compass point, making it possible that they were intended for preparing a copy from an already executed drawing, which would have been done by placing a sheet of blank paper beneath the drawing to be copied. The location of the pricks in fact suggests that they were to serve more as a guide for the lines to be drawn than as a scale of measurement for the individual parts of the building.

There is no written scale on the sheet, but a comparison of the inscribed dimensions and the relative measurements made it possible to confirm that each *braccio fiorentino* (of 60 *minuti*) corresponded to one third of a *minuto* of the same *braccio* (1 *minuto* = 0.972 cm; ⅓ *minuti* = 0.324 cm). The scale is therefore about 1:180 (⅓ × 1/60 = 1/180).

All the same, the dimensions inscribed on the drawing do not always coincide with the measurements obtained with reference to the scale. This supports the hypothesis that Bernardo used a preexisting drawing—from a Florentine source to judge by the unit of measurement—to which he would have added notes and dimensions obtained either directly from a survey or from second-hand information considered more up-to-date and reliable than the source of the drawing that he copied. The fact that he did not simply repeat dimensions already used in the drawing on fol. 52v. of the Codex Coner, and the precision of some of the measurements using submultiples of the *braccio*, even of a few *minuti*, lead one to think that the drawing on U 3966A r. is the result of an in-depth study of the building, carried out after the drawing on fol. 52v., but still in the same time period of 1512–15, probably when contact with Antonio the Younger intensified.

The closeness, also chronological, of U 3966A r. to the drawings in the Codex Coner seems to be confirmed by a comparison of the size of the sheets, which measure, respectively, 222 by 167 mm and 231 by 168 mm. In the Uffizi drawing, the objective analysis of the surviving fragments of the temple, the proposed reconstruction adhering more closely to the evidence still in situ, and the representation limited to half the elevation (implying symmetry) are all elements that one can connect with the contemporary working method of Antonio the Younger. | RB

BIBLIOGRAPHY Ferri (1885) 39; Huelsen (1910) I: 2–3; Bartoli (1914–22) IV: fig. 602, pl. 350; VI 109; Buddensieg (1975) 98; Borsi (1989, *Frontispiece*) 395; Frommel (1994, *Introduction*) 55 n. 216; CensusID 10006928.

U 3969A *recto and verso*

Giovanni Battista da Sangallo

Rome, Flavian Amphitheater, longitudinal section (*recto*); plan of half of amphitheater (*verso*).

Dimensions 249 × 425 mm.
Technique Pen and brown ink, straightedge, stylus, compass.
Paper Center fold, stains.
Drawing Scale Florentine *braccia*.

INSCRIPTION, Recto *qui è una morsa*

Verso (at upper left) *pluteo / del secondo piano / del Culiseo / la parape*[...]; *scala del culiseo / minuti nella / 60 al braccio fiore/ ntino*; (in external arcaded corridor) *la pianta sopra la prima volta questo quarto*; (right) *la pianta primo piano terreno*

The recto shows the linear development of the internal longitudinal section of the Flavian Amphitheater along the external arcaded corridor, with some inscribed measurements.

The construction system and the various materials, the vaulted ceilings, and the articulation of the stairs up to the sustaining stays of the *velum* are shown.

The plan on the verso is an attempt at the graphic reconstruction of a little more than half of the Flavian Amphitheater: it is divided in two quarters cut at two different heights. The higher zone, the area under the vaults, is shown at the left; to the right is the section of the ground floor. The difference is evident in the system of the ascending ramps, which become wider in the lower part. | ACF

BIBLIOGRAPHY Ferri (1885) 123; Bartoli (1914–22) IV: figs 526–27, pl 316–17; VI: 97; CensusID 10072252.

U 3973A *recto*

Giovan Francesco da Sangallo?

Roma, Terme di Agrippa, part of a coffered ceiling.

Dimensions 58 × 122 mm.
Technique Pen, brown ink, freehand.
Paper Light, trimmed, added.

INSCRIPTION *in ruina meza trebuna della ciambella dirie*[*t*]*ro*

The drawing, already attributed by Ferri (1885 p. 201) to Giovanni Battista da Sangallo, refers to a lacunar that the architect saw in some part of the baths of Agrippa restored by Hadrian of which a large portion in the ancient toponymy—still preserved—was called the "ciambella." However, the specification that reads "dirie(t)ro" leads to refer the ceiling to another part of the building, probably the closest to the Pantheon and documented virtual exposure by Piranesi (Campus Martius, tav. XXXV). The same motif appears in U 6772 r., probably also by Giovan Francesco da Sangallo, accompanied by an arch of a circle. | EB

BIBLIOGRAPHY Ferri (1885) 201, Bartoli (1914–22) VI: 95; Buddensieg (1975) 108; CensusID 10030115.

U 3974A *recto*

Giovanni Battista da Sangallo

Verona, partial elevation of facade of amphitheater, 1526.

Dimensions 318 × 233 mm.
Paper Lightweight, patches on verso.
Technique Black chalk, pen and brown ink.

INSCRIPTION *cornice di sopra / cioe terzo*; *capitello*; *cosi stanno fatte le cornice*; *cornice seconda grande*; *capitello / secondo*; *cornicione primo*; *capitello / primo*; *menbre / tto* [impost of the arch]; *vano p. 13*; key letters

The draftsman drew details of the profiles of the moldings on the surviving exterior ring of the amphitheater. Included are the entablatures of the three orders, labeled with the key letters 'E', 'C', 'A', the impost of the ground level arch 'G', and the pilaster capitals of the first 'F', second 'D', and third orders 'B'. The partial elevation of the monument is seen in perspective from a low viewing point. With quick strokes, Giovanni Battista indicated the rustication, the point to which the lower pilasters are sunk into the ground, and the depth of the arches. The drawing may have been done during the journey through Romagna and the Veneto that Giovanni Battista probably undertook in 1526 in the company of his brother. | AGG

BIBLIOGRAPHY Ferri (1885) 225; Giovannoni (1959) I: 21; Franzoni (1980) 67 (with an erroneous attribution to Antonio da Sangallo the Younger); Vasori (1981) 179, cat. no. 135; Zavatta (2008) 188. CensusID 10030826.

U 4003A *recto*

Bartolomeo Baronino

Rome, details of Quirinal temple and of Trajan's Column, before 1554.

Dimensions 209 × 119 mm
Technique Pen and brown ink.
Paper Partly yellowed, trimmed, laid down.
Drawing Scale Roman *palmi*.

INSCRIPTION (bottom left, blue pencil, nineteenth-century hand) *4003*; (brown ink) measurements

This sheet contains the only known drawings of antiquities by Baronino. On the upper part is a profile of the cornice of the huge temple on the Quirinal, probably relying on Antonio the Younger's sketch projection of the whole entablature (U 1253A), although there are not enough measurements provided to be certain.

The lower part of the sheet is filled out with sketches of the capital, the bottom of the shaft, the base, and the plinth of a Tuscan column. The dimensions of the plinth, 22 *palmi* 10 *dita*, and the abacus of the capital, 19 *palmi* 4 *dita*, indicate that this represents Trajan's Column, at the foot of the Quirinal. | IC

BIBLIOGRAPHY Ferri (1885) 197; Bartoli (1914–22) IV: fig. 600, 368; VI: 108; CensusID 10083552.

U 4039A *recto*

Antonio da Sangallo the Younger

Elevation and section of longitudinal facade of a project for a temple-like building, ca. 1538–40.

Dimensions 417 × 570 mm.
Technique Pen and ink, straightedge.
Paper Center fold, tears and corners reinforced on verso.

Antonio's design for an Ionic temple is much more mature than the the Tuscan Doric temple on U 1271A, which is certainly contemporaneous with it. Although a scale of measurement is missing, the shaft width of the columns corresponds approximately to the height of the socle. This comprises about seven steps and is thus approximately 5 feet high, the same dimension as the shaft widths of the Tuscan Doric temple. The columns are again given an 8:1 proportion and are thus even closer to the Vitruvian norm. The total length of the colonnade is about 300 feet (89.40

m). The columns possess Attic bases, and the convex frieze of the tripartite entablature is the same height as the architrave. On the outer walls of the cella, arcade-like niches alternate with rectangular niches, the two rows of which rest on cornices. Since the long sides comprise twenty-two columns, the two narrow sides were probably intended to have ten columns and the entrance bay again to be somewhat broader.

Only in the longitudinal section does the temple reveal itself to be a complex vaulted building. Above the peripteros rises a second, higher story, similarly articulated by Ionic pilasters and crowned on the narrow sides by pediments; the total height is about 120 feet (35.76 m). The pedestals over the columns of the forehall seem to prepare for two upper rows of columns on the narrow sides. The third row of columns in the forehall opens onto the barrel-vaulted atrium, which is flanked by low exedras with shell calottes and lighted by lunette windows directly recalling those of the Sala Regia of 1538–39 (U 712A, 1234A). The long cella terminates in a smaller apse. The width of the apparently single-aisled room would have corresponded to approximately the distance between the second and ninth columns of the temple facade, that is, about 90 feet. With its depth (without apse) of about 135 feet (26.82 × 40.23 m) the plan would have had a proportion of about 2:3, and with its large exedra it would have resembled more the Roman Curia than a Christian church. This was already true for Pontelli's interior of San Lorenzo in Damaso in Rome (Frommel 2005, *San Lorenzo in Damaso*). It is articulated by two orders of Ionic half-columns, the lower of which is continued into the apse and frames aedicules with niches for statues and panels with round niches.

It is more difficult to understand Antonio's intentions for the zone above the second order, since its rear wall has no support. Probably he first thought of repeating the atrium on the rear side and later added the apse, which necessarily led to the shifting of the upper part of the rear wall. This, however, is indicated only by a scoring. He used the space between the apse and the opisthodomos for the entrance to a small staircase that leads to the roof area. Antonio had in mind a flat wooden ceiling. The resulting room would have been about 112 feet high (32.85 m)—higher than wide, as were some of the Roman temples. The rear facade is designed like the one in front. The tondos in the blank panels above the statue niches were conceivably pierced by windows, and it is likely that windows were provided between the pilasters of the upper story. The temple's stylistic relationship to the Sala Regia puts it in the period from 1538 to 1540. | CLF

BIBLIOGRAPHY Ferri (1885) 217.

U 4099A *recto*

Antonio da Sangallo the Younger

Profile of moldings of richly carved Corinthian base of a column from Roman imperial era.

Dimensions 204 × 177 mm.
Technique Pen and ink, freehand.
Paper Lightweight, laid down, trimmed.

According to Serlio (1537, IV: 184), the profile of the two "delicately" carved scotias separated by two astragals would identify the base as Corinthian, which is confirmed by the plinth. Among the examples from ancient Rome, Antonio must also have known the bases of the portico of the Pantheon and those of the surviving columns of the Temple of Castor and Pollux, and the "well carved" base at the foot of a cross on Monte Cavallo—but originally from the Temple of Mars Ultor—which he drew on U 1182A r. As far as the present drawing is concerned, his interest in the decoration of architectural elements from the Roman imperial era is connected to his studies on variations of the Corinthian base. The profile is also similar to that of the base designed for the giant order of the interior the new St Peter's (U 7976A r., see vol. II). | AGG

BIBLIOGRAPHY Bartoli (1914–22) I: fig. 46, pl. 22; VI: 11.; CensusID 59628.

U 4114A *recto*

Antonio da Sangallo the Younger (?)

Rome, Temple of Venus and Roma, partial ground plan.

Dimensions 370 × 283 mm.
Paper Upper right corner missing.
Technique Pen, and brown ink, straightedge, compass.

INSCRIPTION, Recto lower left corner: *fa dentro* [?]

The drawings show the ground plan of one half of the double temple of Venus and Roma in Rome together with the corresponding apse of the other half. The half shown here can be determined as the temple of Venus which is situated towards the south, because of the completeness of the ground plan; the other half has not been fully visible in the 16th century. Though the author gives a short scale (maybe of Roman *palmi*) in the middle axe of the building, the drawing itself does not contain any measurements and seems to be rather structurally regularized than an exact representation of the building. The proportions of apse and cella do not fit the real building dimensions, because the apse is too wide compared to the cella. Other parts of the building are also shown in a simplified way; there are no hints on the decoration of the niches, and the staircase besides the apse in the upper right corner does not show the correct size and form. In addition, with the few hints on the extension of the building, the second apse is given in an even more schematic representation. The drawing suggests an exact symmetry of the entire building, which in fact does not exist. Therefore, it seems possible that the drawing was not created on site but was instead copied from an earlier drawing. On the other hand, it could have been intended to serve as a map for measurings to be taken on site later. The problems deriving from the differences between drawing and building may have then been the reason why it was not used for the measuring of the building and therefore does not contain measurements and other traces of the building's examination. | BK

BIBLIOGRAPHY Ferri (1885) 197; Kulawik (2002) II: 53–8; CensusID 10071268.

U 4117A *recto*

Giovanni Battista da Sangallo

Rome, Baths of Caracalla, plan
of part of the enclosure.

Dimensions 435 × 98 mm.
Technique Pen and black ink, straightedge, compass, stylus.
Paper Glued onto modern paper.
Drawing Scale *canne.*

INSCRIPTION (in pencil) *Terme di Caracalla*

On the left side of the sheet is a plan of a part of the *peribolus* of the Baths of Caracalla, in relation to the central exedra. The drawing is linked to many other drawings by the Sangallo circle dealing with the definition and graphic restitution of the enclosure of the Antonine baths. Notably, this sheet should be compared with U 1093A r. by Labacco and to the drawings cited in the entry for that sheet, as well as to the quite accurate drawings of the north exedra of the enclosure in the Albertina (Egger 1903, n. 12 v. and 170 v.). At the right side is a sketch of the perspective section of the octagonal room. As Schich (2009) ascertained the sheet was conceived together with U 1656A r. as a larger drawing of the enclosure of the Baths of Caracalla. | ACF

BIBLIOGRAPHY Ferri (1885) 202; Egger (1903) n. 12v.; Bartoli (1914–22) III: fig. 523, pl. 313; VI: 97; Valori (1985) 135–36; Schich (2009), 276; CensusID 10072275.

U 4119A *recto*

Giovanni Battista da Sangallo

Project to re-use an ancient arcophagus or bathtub.

Dimensions 255 × 340 mm.
Paper Lightweight, whole sheet backed; off-centre horizontal fold.
Technique Pen and brown ink, freehand.

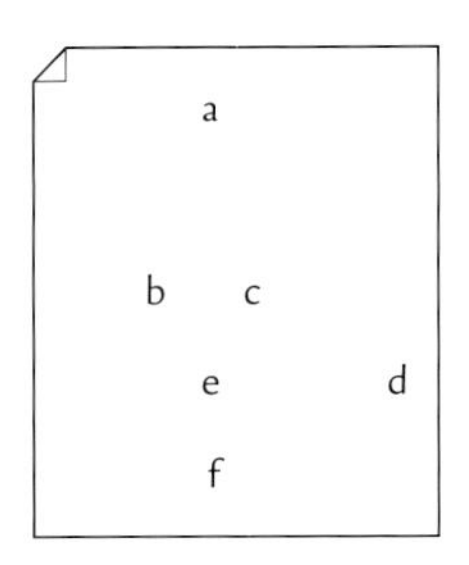

INSCRIPTION (top centre, old numbering, brown ink, sixteenth-century hand) *23*: (top left, current inventory number, blue ink, nineteenth century hand) *4119*; on drawings (a)–(e), measurements

All the drawings on the sheet appear connected to the reuse of an ancient bathtub or sarcophagus by creating a new lid for it.

At the top of the sheet, is a perspectival sketch *a* of a what appears to be a possibly ancient bathtub. If the unit of measurement is the *piede*, then the dimensions are similar to the tub drawn by Giovan Battista on U 185A v., said to be at S. Salvatore (in Lauro) and now in the Boboli Gardens in Florence (Ambrogi 1995, pp. 128–29, cat. B.I.51). It was drawn in connection with a project for a funerary monument for Pope Clement VII. The tub drawn here differs in having one curved and one straight end, a style which is known from bronze examples from the vicinity of Pompei, such as the one in the Casa dei Cervi at Herculaneum, and also from Greece, made from terracotta, concrete and marble (Ambrogi 1993, p. 105). However, the form was sometimes also used for sarcophagi made in Egypt from granite, some examples of which are extant in Rome (Ambrogi 1993, pp. 103–04). It is furthermore possible that Sangallo was drawing a similar one with the intention of reusing it, by creating a new lid.

Below the horizontal fold in the sheet, is a sketch *b*, rotated by 90 degrees to *a*, of a section of the lid slightly wider than the adjacent plan *c* of the tub, apparently to the same scale. To its right is a larger scale elevation *d*, again rotated by 90 degrees to *a*, of the straight end of the lid, in the form of a segmental pediment with two projections like acroteria on top. Their presence is explained by drawing *e*, a longitudinal elevation of the lid showing two lugs, set back from either end, which would aid the lifting of the lid when needed to insert one or more corpses. The final drawing *f*, the only one without measurements, is probably an abandoned attempt at the longitudinal elevation *e*. | AGG, IC

BIBLIOGRAPHY Ferri (1885) 101.

U 4128A *recto and verso*

GIOVANNI BATTISTA SANGALLO

Rome, Basilica of Constantine, before 1548.

Dimensions 440 × 598 mm.
Technique Pen and light brown ink for squaring, pen and dark brown ink, brown wash, heightened with black, black chalk underdrawing, stylus, straightedge, compasses, pinholes in corners.
Paper Partly yellowed, central vertical fold, patched, corners repaired.

INSCRIPTION, Verso (brown ink) calculations

The plan on the recto is a reconstruction of the Basilica of Constantine (see U 1648A r.). It is one of a small group of drawings on squared paper discussed earlier (see U 1636A r.). The total lack of written information suggests it is a theoretical drawing. Like most 16th century reconstructions, it wrongly adds an apse on the southern-left side. No attempt was made to show the narthex or the windows in the corner bays. Instead, Giovanni Battista screened these bays from the nave with lines of columns. The effect is to make the middle bays read like the transepts of a cruciform church. The columnar screens were possibly inspired by those in the side bays of the caldarium of the Baths of Diocletian, which had a similar plan. The niches are delineated only in black chalk. On the verso are what appear to be a sexfoil ornament and a "plan" of a single column flute. | IC

BIBLIOGRAPHY Ferri (1885) 129; Bartoli (1914–22) IV: fig. 549, pl. 329; VI: 100; Giovannoni (1959) I: 40n; Campbell (1984) I: 323, CensusID 44047.

U 4151A *recto and verso*

ANTONIO DA SANGALLO THE YOUNGER

Study of ionic volutes, after 1532.

Dimensions 288 × 427 mm.
Technique Pen and brown ink; stylus with punctures on the tracing of lines.
Paper Yellowish, patches.

In two drawings, on the recto and the verso, Antonio da Sangallo intends to look for a way to draw a spiral, the ornamental motive characteristic of an Ionic capital. More often, Antonio is interested in constructing the curve by points, which is a concept inspired by Albrecht Dürer's *Instituciones geometricae* (ch. 4 and 5), a treatise known to Giovanni Battista da Sangallo. To obtain an elegant decrease of the distance between the turnings while going inwards the spiral, Dürer proposes a geometric construction of 24 or 36 points of the spiral (2 or 3 turns of twelve points each), which in modern terms involves several trigonometric functions.

On the contrary, another possible font of Sangallo, that is the *De spiralibus* by Archimedes, follows the spiral concept attributed to Conon of Samos (Archimedes, ms., Prop. XVIII, lib. IV). Here, a spiral is obtained by the movement of a vector (ab), which gets longer by a constant value with each rotation by a given angle; thus the radial distance between turnings is constant. Looking at a graph representing the distance (*r*) of a spiral point to the center as a function of the polar angle, it is evident that the Archimedean spiral will be represented by a straight line on that graph, while the Dürer construction will be represented by a curved line.

Sangallo may have learned about Archimedean spirals from Leonardo da Vinci and his works on vortexes and mechanics. The Archimedean spiral is shown in chapter 15 v of cod. Vat. Ott. Lat. (1850), owned by Andreas Coner, who corrected the Latin translation by Guglielmo di Moerbeke and was probably in contact with Dürer during his trip to Venice in 1505–07. Dürer could also, however, be familiar with the Archimedean spirals found in *De arte mensurandi* by Johannes de Muris, where the first part of chapter 5 contains a description of spirals taken from the Moerbeke's translation concerning Archimedean spiral lines. Together with the Archimedean construction from c. 10, in his treatise, Dürer also introduces in fol. 4v. and 5r. a variant which is close to one used by Antonio the Younger in his U 4151A r. Since Dürer's spiral design is similar to that of Ionic capitals of the Theatre of Marcellus, the latter could have been a direct source as well.

Antonio marks twelve points per turn of the spiral, each with equal angular spacing (30 degree angles). It is evident that the U 4151A r. spirals do not follow an Archimedean spiral, but they can be fitted with good accuracy respectively by the formulas:

a) $r = 8.141 - 0{,}248\, n + 0.00180\, n^2$

b) $r = 8.366 - 0.479\, n + 0.006402\, n^2$

c) $r = 7.327 - 0.579n + 0.1104\, n^2$

where (n) is the progressive number of the marked points, going inward into the spiral, and (r) is the distance in centimeters of each point from the center. Dürer's design in c. 4v. and 5r. will instead translate to a formula

$r = m_1 \tan((48\text{-}n)\, m_2)$

with m_1 and m_2 fit parameters, but this gives a less accurate fitting of Antonio's drawings *a*, *b* and *c*. Thus the shape of the curves forming the spirals from U 4151A r. is of parabolic character and the increase of the distance between turnings is then an arithmetic progression, as in the volute from U 619A v. (vol. IV) and in U 983A r. Indeed, the course of the graph reflects the mathematical law of the construction of a spiral, and immediately renders visible the diversified types of the volutes. | ML

BIBLIOGRAPHY Archimedes, *De Spiralibus* (Biblioteca Apostolica Vaticana cod. Ott. Lat. 1850); Dürer (1532) 4v., 5r., 10r.; Stevens (1931) 135–44; Wurm (1984) 283–84; Losito (1993, *Il capitello*) I: 132–35; Losito (1997) II: 1409–28; Losito (2008) 164–71.

U 4152A *recto*

Antonio da Sangallo the Younger

Study of an ionic volute, 1540–46.

Dimensions 239 × 215 mm.
Technique Pen and brown ink, stylus with perforations on the tracing of the lines.
Paper Yellowish, trimmed at upper right corner.

The precise studies of construction of the spirals from U 4152A r. and U 4153A r. intend to find a procedure to trace spirals by points. They reveal an accurate analysis of the geometrical problem in constructing the Ionic volute. Indeed, if we carefully measure the drawings of the spirals, we note that the shape of the curve representing the distance (r) from the center is not parabolic as in U 4151A r. and v., in U 619A v. (vol. IV) and in U 4154A r. (all of which follow the same model), but that the shape shows a superimposed sinusoidal waving. That could be due to the irregular placement of the marked or presumed center of the drawing. In such case the mathematical rule would be of the following type:

$r = m_1 + m_2 n + m_3 n^2 + m_4 \cos((\pi/6)\, n - m_5)$

where (n) is the successive number of points spaced by 30 degree angles around the center (n increases going inward into the spiral), (r) is the distance from the center, and $m_1, \ldots, m_5$ are fitting parameters; m_4 is the distance of the center of the spiral from the center of the drawing and m_5 a given angle. For the sheet U 4152A r. we have:

$m_1 = 9.9025$ cm; $m_2 = -0.456$ cm; $m_3 = 0.00548$ cm; $m_4 = 0.265$ cm; $m_5 = 301.6$ degrees.

On U 4153A r., more spiral turns are visible than U 4152A, and so we obtain a more precise fit:

$m_1 = 8.916$ cm; $m_2 = -0.120$ cm; $m_3 = 0.000341$ cm; $m_4 = -0.0948$ cm; $m_5 = 106.9$ degrees.

The existence of the mentioned sinusoidal oscillation may pose an interesting question: is it an intentional special feature of the spiral, an inherent deviation of the used graphic construct, or is it a characteristic trait of a mechanical construction? | ML

BIBLIOGRAPHY Losito (1993, *Il capitello*) I: 138–40.

U 4153A *recto*

Antonio da Sangallo the Younger

Study of a spiral, 1540–46.

Dimensions 285 × 251 mm.
Technique Pen and brown ink; stylus with perforations on the tracing of the lines.
Paper Medium weight, patches.

This drawing closely follows U 4152A r., although more turns (nine) of the spiral are visible. Using the same fit formula, we get the parameters: $m_1 = 8.916$ cm, $m_2 = -0.12$ cm, $m_3 = 0.000341$ cm, $m_4 = -0.0948$ cm, $m_5 = 106.9$ degree.

The fact that sinusoidal oscillation m_4 is here smaller than on U 4152A r. may indicate that the U 4153A r. spiral is a second and more accurate version of the same mechanical construction; both drawings may be seen as preparatory for further drawings. | ML

BIBLIOGRAPHY Losito (1993, *Il capitello*) I: 138–40.

U 4154A *recto*

Antonio da Sangallo the Younger

Study of an ionic volute, 1540–46.

Dimensions 247 × 267 mm.
Technique Pen and brown ink, traces of charcoal, holes along the line.
Paper Medium weight, yellowish.

In U 4154A r., Antonio da Sangallo demonstrates a method for tracing a spiral of an Ionic capital constructed by points, which become progressively wider from a fixed center. It seems closer in spirit to U 4151A r. drawings since the point of origin of the drawing is in the center of the spiral. The five turns of the volute reveal precise study of the geometry of a spiral, not necessarily related to the task of construction of an ionic volute.

Furthermore, if we apply the graphic procedure that reproduces the unwinding of a spiral, just as in the case of U 4151A r. and of U 619A v. we note that the progression of the curve of the distances (r) from the center is still the same as the parabolic curve.

In the volute shown in U 4151A r., the distance from the center (r) in centimeters follows a quadratic progression, as evident from the fitted equation

$$r = 8.589 - 0.218\, n + 0.00130\, n^2$$

where (n) is a progressive number of points spaced by 30 degree angles around the center (n increases going inward into the spiral). Finally, the excellent precision of the tracing (somewhat difficult to obtain with a realization by points) and the large number of turns used for this volute allows one to imagine that the use of a specialized instrument might be involved. | ML

BIBLIOGRAPHY Losito (1993, *Il capitello*) I: 137–38.

U 6771A *recto and verso*

Antonio da Sangallo the Younger

Design for a coffered ceiling, probably before 1514.

Dimensions 76 × 477 mm.
Technique Pen and ink, wash, pencil.
Paper Trimmed and restored.

The design appears to be for a coffered ceiling either of considerable size or, more likely, with relatively small coffers, as in Peruzzi's Sala delle Prospettive, where ten rows of coffers correspond to a length of approximately 15.60 m. The wide rows of large octagons are separated by narrower rows, where squares alternate with flat rhombuses. On the left side, the round discs of simulated nails between the corners of the coffers are indicated, and on the left half, the narrow edge strips of the coffers are shown. The rectangular grid on which the system is based can also be seen. The not very convincing fragmentation of the rhombuses at the sides, the manner in which the wash is applied, and some insecurities indicate a relatively early date, probably before 1514. | CLF

BIBLIOGRAPHY unpublished.

U 6772A *recto*

Giovan Francesco da Sangallo?

Roma, Terme di Agrippa, part of a coffered vault.

Dimensions 134 × 144.
Technique Pen, brown ink, freehand.
Paper Light, trimmed.

Not mentioned by Ferri, the drawing is similar in graphic expression to U 3973 r., which shows the same motif of a lacunar. Accompanied by an arc, one can assume that the lacunar was part of an arch or vaulting. | EB

BIBLIOGRAPHY unpublished.

U 6803A *recto and verso*

Giovan Francesco da Sangallo

Survey of ancient hieroglyph frieze in San Lorenzo Fuori le Mura (*recto*); Doric capital (from Theatre of Marcellus?) (*verso*), ca. 1520–27.

Dimensions 345 × 225.
Technique Pen and ink, stylus, straitedge and freehand.
Paper Lightweight, partially glued on verso.
Drawing Scale (*verso*) *braccia, 60 minuti.*

INSCRIPTION, Recto *i[n] santo lorenzo fuora le mura*
Verso *i[n] questo piano e braccia i[n] e minuti 55*

The representations on the recto and verso once again confirm Giovan Francesco's great drawing ability for both architecture and figural details. The deciphering and imitation of ancient hieroglyphics enjoyed great popularity even before Bramante's failed attempt to decorate the frieze of the great interior order of St Peter's with hieroglyphs. Earlier drawings of the same piece are known by the author of the Codex Escurialensis (fol. 43v.) and Francesco di Giorgio (Turin, Cod. Saluzziano 148, fols 96, 97).

On the verso, Giovan Francesco drew a very precise elevation of a Doric capital, probably from the Theatre of Marcellus, with measurements even in the smallest parts in *braccia* und *minuti.* | CLF

BIBLIOGRAPHY Bartoli (1914–22) II: figs 186–87, pl. 103; VI: 36; Günther (1988) 107; Waters (2014) 41; CensusID 62355.

Codex Rootstein Hopkins

In spring 2005, an album of drawings of ancient Roman buildings was discovered at Pallinsburn House, in Northumberland, near the Anglo-Scottish border. It was quickly established that the drawings were by Giovanni Battista da Sangallo, but, even more interesting was the presence of drawings of the Temple of Hercules at Cori. These exactly fitted the description given by Johann Joachim Winckelmann (1717–68), in the 1760s, when he had seen them in an album of 'twenty something folios', among the great antiquarian collections of Baron Philipp von Stosch (1691–1757) in Florence. Winckelmann identified the drawings with Raphael's lost reconstruction of ancient Rome (Winckelmann 1825–9, vol. 2, pp. 392–5; Winckelmann 1952, vol. 2, pp. 99–101, no. 374; Campbell 2005, p. 5; Campbell-Nesselrath 2006, pp. 14 f.). Accompanying the drawings was a loose sheet of eighteenth-century paper with an extract copied in von Stosch's handwriting from a published letter of Celio Calcagnini (1479–1541) about Raphael's reconstruction and his collaboration with Fabio Calvo on translating Vitruvius (Campbell 2005, p. 61; Campbell-Nesselrath 2006, p. 12). The album was named the 'Codex Stosch' for its sale at auction, which took place in July 2005. The successful bidder was foreign but the granting of an export licence was deferred to allow a British institution the chance to acquire it. In May 2006, the RIBA British Architectural Library announced it had bought it. Since then the Rootstein Hopkins Foundation have pledged funds to conserve the album which is now to bear its name.

How the album reached Northumberland is not clear. After Stosch's death, his collections passed to his nephew, Wilhelm Muzell (1723–82), on condition he assumed his uncle's surname. The album does not appear in Winckelmann's list of the contents of the 'Atlas', Stosch's 324 volumes of topographical and architectural drawings and prints which was acquired en bloc by the Hofbibliothek in Vienna, nor does it appear in the sale catalogue of his printed books and manuscripts, which were bought by the Vatican Library (Bibliotheca Stoschiana 1758; Winckelmann 1760, pp. 571–96; Campbell 2005, 6; Campbell-Nesselrath 2006, pp. 14 f.). Muzell-Stosch (as we will call him) appears to have held the album back for some reason, and, most probably, sold it to Anthony Askew (1722–74), during his visit to England in 1761–2. Askew amassed a great classical library at his house in Hampstead, which was dispersed in a sale in 1775, but the album fails to appear in the sale catalogue and so we must assume it passed to his heirs who took it to the Askews' country seat, Pallinsburn, where it remained unnoticed until 2005.

In its present state, the album consists of 23 folios, ca. 278 × 210 mm, bound between endpapers with a watermark dating ca. 1760 and in plain vellum. Except for fol. 17, all the folios comprised bifolia and fols 18–21 make a small gathering (Campbell-Nesselrath 2006, p. 7). There is evidence of a second set of sewing holes besides those for the present binding, although the poor condition of the folio edges in general and of the verso of fol. 23, suggests that the sixteenth-century folios were not protected before the ca. 1760 binding. Ink page numbers, from 1–46, running in reverse, indicate that no folios have been lost since they were added but, on stylistic grounds, that might be as late as the eighteenth century. Graphite folio numbers, instead, run from 4–23, and make clear that at least three folios are missing. Graphite comes into use in the late sixteenth century and the style of the figures suggests they could date from then or the early seventeenth century.

Of the 46 pages, 43 carry drawings, all executed in brown ink by Giovanni Battista, with signs of the use of stylus, straightedge and compass. Black chalk only appears to be used for underdrawing in one case (fol. 10 r.) and for corrections in inscriptions (fols 1 r., 9 v. and 14 r.). The drawings are all reconstructions of temples and arches in Rome, apart from two temples in Cori. Plans, elevations, sections and details are all drawn in orthogonal projection, apart from one detail (fol. 3 r.) represented axonometrically. All are measured using the ancient Roman foot apart the two Cori temples where Roman palms are employed.

The paper is thin and poor quality but the drawings are highly finished and often accompanied by formulaic inscriptions, which are sometimes written with a thicker or darker ink suggesting Giovanni Battista added them later. The black chalk corrections seem to be even later, but again by him.

Everything about the drawings suggests that they were preparatory material for some presentation or publication project, and it is easy to see why Stosch and Winckelmann connected them with Raphael's reconstruction of ancient Rome (Campbell-Nesselrath 2006, pp. 26–32). However, some pages have headings indicating that the buildings were to be ordered by types or parts ('Temples', 'Triumphal Arches', and 'Doors': fols 3 r. and v., 4 v. and 23 r.), although their placing demonstrates that the intended original order has not been achieved or preserved. The fact that we have only two arches and one door, as opposed to thirteen temples also points to the present fragmentary state of the album.

The drawings are very close in character to those Giovanni Battista added to his copy of the first edition of Vitruvius, known as the 'Corsini Incunabulum', because it is in the library of the Accademia dei Lincei in Rome (Rowland 2003). The earliest of the Corsini drawings are conventionally dated to the late 1520s, but the evidence suggests that the Rootstein Hopkins drawings are earlier. Firstly, the handwriting of the first phase of the inscriptions, contemporary with the drawings, is close to Giovanni Battista's hand around 1521–4, and to that on three sheets of parallel drawings by Antonio the Younger (U 1140A, U 1165A and U 1166A; Campbell-Nesselrath 2006, pp. 18 and 23). Secondly, the anchor watermark, found on several sheets, is close to examples dated 1517–22 (Campbell-Nesselrath 2006, p. 7). Thirdly, the names given to the three temples at S. Nicola in Carcere (fols 11 r. – 15 r.) betray such a profound misreading of the Latin of Vitruvius 3.2.5, that one must conclude Giovanni Battista had not consulted an Italian translation. Antonio the Younger owned Durantino's 1524 Vitruvius, combining Fra Giocondo's illustrations with Cesariano's translation. While we do not know when Antonio acquired it, it is unlikely to be later than the mid-1520s. Inscriptions on some of his drawings of the S. Nicola temples, corresponding closely with the Rootstein Hopkins drawings, reveal a correct understanding of Vitruvius and therefore must post-date the latter (Campbell-Nesselrath 2006, pp. 17 f.).

CODEX ROOTSTEIN HOPKINS fol. 1 *recto*

GIOVANNI BATTISTA DA SANGALLO

Rome, Arch of Titus, front elevation

Dimensions 273 × 209 mm
Technique Pen and brown ink, partly with stylus, straightedge, and compass and partly freehand.
Paper double folio with fol. 2; rectangular patch in middle left edge connecting with fol. 2v.; four water stains on or near right edge.
Watermark: anchor (cut).

INSCRIPTION (on drawing, thick brown ink with black chalk) ·· *SENATVS/POPVLVS·QVE ROMANVS/DIVO TITO DIVI VESPASIANI F/VESPASINO· AVGVSTO*; Numbering: (bottom right, graphite) *4*; (bottom centre, upside down, brown ink) *4*[*6*] (cut)

The Arch of Titus is the earliest extant triumphal arch in Rome, dedicated shortly after the emperor Titus' death in AD 81. What we see today is a rebuilding by the architects Raffaele Stern and Giuseppe Valadier from 1817–24, sensitively using travertine to distinguish reconstructed features from the original marble elements (Pfanner 1983; LTUR, I. 109–11 [J. Arce]); Claridge 1998, pp. 116–18).

The reconstruction was undertaken because, while serving as a fortification for the Frangipane family during the Middle Ages, it suffered major damage to the piers and attic. By the Renaissance, it was also partly encased in later buildings and was in a sorry state. Nevertheless it remained an object of great interest because it was erected to celebrate the victory of Titus in the Jewish War, which led to the destruction of the Temple of Jerusalem (see next folio).

The drawing is an elevation, reconstructing probably the east front of the arch, which was better preserved than the west, and retained its inscription (CIL VI. 945) which is transcribed accurately here apart from one slip in the penultimate word, and a black chalk dot added between the *S* and *E* of SENATVS. The reconstruction is generally excellent, matching in accuracy, except in two respects, that in the sketchbook (fol. 2r.) of 'Master C of 1519' in the Albertina (part of Stosch's 'Atlas'), generally accepted as unsurpassed until modern studies (Nesselrath 1986, *Archaeolgical Method*, pp. 366–8). Master C was a member of the Raphael circle and his drawings, are regarded as the best reflection of Raphael's archaeological method of recording and reconstruction.

The respects in which it is inaccurate are the pedimented roof and the open aedicules, both features almost certainly copied from Giuliano da Sangallo's (Giovanni Battista's uncle), 'Barberini Codex' (fol. 23r.; Huelsen 1910, I, p. 32) the only case of such borrowing in the present drawings. The Arch of Titus is also one of only two subjects where we find no parallels among the drawings of the Sangallo circle, only drawings of details, which are not related (U 1231A r. and U 1255A r.). | IC

BIBLIOGRAPHY Campbell (2005) 46; Campbell-Nesselrath (2006) 27 and 41; CensusID 10000257.

CODEX ROOTSTEIN HOPKINS fol. 1 *verso*

GIOVANNI BATTISTA DA SANGALLO

Rome, Arch of Titus, section and details.

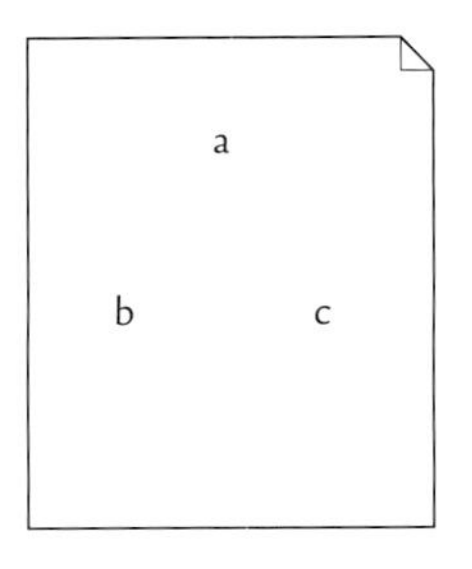

Dimensions see recto.
Technique Pen and brown ink, drawing *a* partly with stylus, straightedge, and compass and partly freehand; drawings *b* and *c* freehand.
Paper see recto.

INSCRIPTION (below drawing *a*, thick brown ink) *Profilo delarcho ditito*; (below drawing *c*, brown ink) *archam federis*; Numbering: (bottom right, upside down, brown ink, cut) *45*

The main drawing, *a*, is a section through the arch, the only one known from the Renaissance. It is accurate apart from the roof copied from Giuliano da Sangallo (see fol. 1r.), which makes the vaulted chamber inside the attic too high. The drawing of the relief, showing the booty from the Temple of Jerusalem being carried in triumph, indicates that we are looking at the north pier. Drawings *b* and *c* show two details from the relief, *b* the *menorah*, the great seven-branched candelabrum, and *c*, the Table of the Shewbread, here misidentified as the Ark of the Covenant, following medieval tradition.

Both treasures were housed in Vespasian's Temple of Peace, which stood just north of the present church of SS. Cosmas and Damian, which occupies one of its ancillary buildings. The temple was built, like the arch, to commemorate Titus' victory over the Jews (LTUR, IV, 67–70 [F. Coarelli]). An inscription thought to date to Pope Nicholas IV (r. 1288–92) in St John Lateran testifies to the widespread belief that the treasures were buried under the high altar of the church, although an alternative tradition claims they were stolen by the Vandals in AD 455 (Lauer 1911, pp. 50 f. and 293–5). | IC

BIBLIOGRAPHY Campbell (2005) 46; Campbell-Nesselrath (2006) 42.

CODEX ROOTSTEIN HOPKINS fol. 2 *recto*

Giovanni Battista da Sangallo

Rome, Janus Quadrifrons, plan and detail.

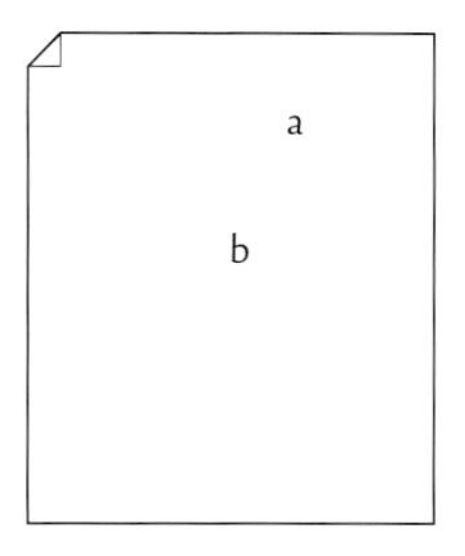

Dimensions 275 × 209 mm.
Technique Pen and brown ink, partly with stylus, straightedge, and partly freehand.
Paper double folio with fol. 1.
Watermark: anchor (cut).

INSCRIPTION (to right of drawing *a*, upwards, brown ink) *in basamento delarcho/ Quadro*; (below drawing *b*) *la pianta delarcho quadro/ diroma*; Numbering: (bottom right, graphite) *5*; (bottom centre, upside down, brown ink) *44*

Little is known about this substantial 16m wide and 12 high four-way arch, and no identification is hazarded by Giovanni Battista. It may be the Arch of the Deified Constantine, which is listed in this area in the Regionary catalogues, two versions of a list of the most significant buildings and sights in the fourteen regions of ancient Rome. It does not resemble a triumphal arch, and is probably a *Janus*, a gateway marking a significant boundary. Much of the marble, which clad the concrete core appears to be *spolia*, i.e. re-used from earlier monuments, a practice which became increasingly common from the early fourth century AD. All the colonnettes, which originally stood between the two tiers of shell-headed niches, were removed as *spolia* themselves in the Middle Ages. Whether statues ever occupied the niches is unknown. The upper part is missing, but was probably a rectangular attic, although some believe it had a pyramidal roof. The keystones of the north and east arches are decorated with figures of Minerva and Roma respectively (LTUR, III, 94 [F. Coarelli]; Claridge 1998, pp. 256 f.)

The two drawings represent the plan of the arch (*b*) and the profile of the base moulding of its podium (*a*). The presence of the colonnettes indicates that the plan is a reconstruction. Both drawings have parallels on a sheet of similar size (218 × 275/80 mm) by Antonio da Sangallo the Younger, U 1046A r., which also has the elevation (see fol. 2v.) and a sketch of the cross vault. Antonio's plan only consists of one pier but the relationship between it and his profile of the base moulding strongly suggests he was tracing the present drawings or that both were copying a common source. The only differences are lines extending from the pier to indicate the groin vault at the centre. | IC

BIBLIOGRAPHY Campbell (2005) 46 f.; Campbell-Nesselrath (2006) 22 and 43.

CODEX ROOTSTEIN HOPKINS fol. 2 *verso*

Giovanni Battista da Sangallo

Rome, Janus Quadrifrons, elevation and part-section.

Dimensions see recto.
Technique Pen and brown ink, partly with stylus, straightedge, and compass and partly freehand.
Paper see recto.

INSCRIPTION (on drawing, thick brown ink and black chalk) *IMP·CAES · DITICO/ DIABENCO/ SPQR/ M·F· PP*; (below drawing, thick brown ink) *larcho quadro diroma*; Numbering: (bottom left, upside down, brown ink) *43*

The drawing combines an elevation and section of the arch, adding colonnettes to the two tiers of niches, and statues in the niches of the left pier. The attic storey has colonnettes but no niches over the left pier, and part of an inscription fills the attic over the left half of the arch. The right half of the attic is represented in section, with vaulted chambers over the arch and pier, all capped by a low-pitched roof.

The lettering of the part inscription makes no sense but a late fifteenth-century reconstruction by an unknown Lombard draughtsman (Salzburg, Universitätsbibliothek, 'Monumenta Antiqua Romana', fol. 17r.) reconstructed the arch very similarly and borrowed the inscription of the nearby Arch of the Silversmiths (CIL VI. 1035), which has some echoes here and may be Giovanni Battista's inspiration. A black chalk dot has been added between *Q* and *R* of SPQR.

Antonio's drawing, U 1046A r., which only includes the left half of the arch, reproduces Giovanni Battista's mock inscription, and the lower, extant parts of the arch parallel that here, including the measurements (note that the width of the niches is given as slightly less than on the plan), but minus the statues. Antonio, however, reconstructs the rest of the attic very differently, with pilasters instead of colonnettes, in front of which stand statues, with relief panels in between. Over the whole width of the arch stretches a pediment. This perhaps weakens the idea that they were copying a common source, since one would not expect then differing reconstructions. Antonio's sheet also includes a perspectival sketch of the groin vault missing from our drawings.

A reconstruction dating after 1525 by the Anonymous Mantuan *a* (Kassel, Staatlichen Kunstsammlungen, Cod. A. 45, fol. 46v.; Günther 1988, pl. 122a) follows Giovanni Battista in putting colonnettes on the attic over the piers, but replaces the inscription with an arch. It is worth remarking that some fragments of a large inscription preserved in the nearby church of S. Giorgio al Velabro are suspected by some to be come from the arch (LTUR, III, 94 [F. Coarelli]). | IC

BIBLIOGRAPHY Campbell (2005) 47; Campbell-Nesselrath (2006) 44.

CODEX ROOTSTEIN HOPKINS fol. 3 *recto*

Giovanni Battista da Sangallo

Cori, door of the Temple of Hercules, elevation and details.

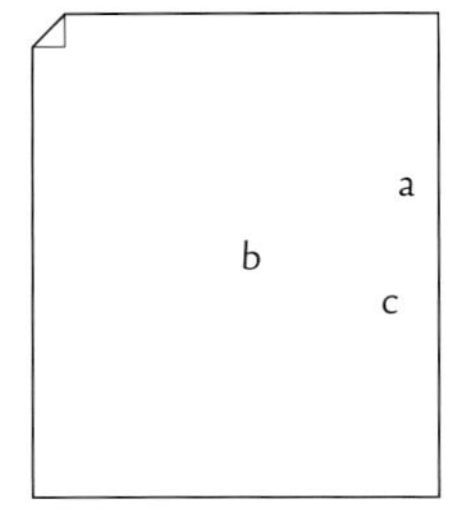

Dimensions 275 × 207 mm.
Technique Pen and brown ink; drawing *a* freehand, drawing *b* with straightedge.
Paper guard strip on right edge connects with fol. 4 left edge.

INSCRIPTION all in brown ink (top centre) *PORTE* ('Doors'); (above drawing *a*, brown ink) *Lacornice della porta/ sta cosi e la suo mensola* =; (on drawing *b*) *M·MANILIVS·M·F·I· TVRPILIVS·LA·DVOM·VIRES DESENATVS/ SENTENTIA AEDEM. FACIENDAM COERAVERVNT EISDEM·QVE··PROIAVERE*; *larga·louano pp. 10–1*; *p. 10⅔ louano*; (reading upwards, brown ink) *Alta louano palmi 22*; (left of drawing *b*, reading downwards, brown ink) *5¾ longa·lamensola*; (below drawing *b*, brown ink) *Porta·dun tempio toscano A chori in canpangna*; (right of drawing *c*, brown ink) *modano/ della mensola*; Numbering: (bottom right, graphite) *6*; (bottom centre, upside down, brown ink) *42*

The Temple of Hercules at Cori is a Doric tetrastyle prostyle, standing on a podium and having a pronaos, or front porch, four columns wide by three deep columns deep, behind which was an almost square cella, decorated with applied pilasters to the exterior walls (Brandizzi Vittucci 1968, pp. 77–96, no. 67). It was converted into the church of St Peter at some unknown date and most of the rear part of the cella had disappeared by the time of these drawings. The pronaos is constructed of travertine, slabs of which were also used to clad the rubble core of the cella walls, while the podium was faced with tufa blocks. The Doric order of the temple departs in several respects from that prescribed by Vitruvius (Brandizzi Vittucci 1968, p. 82), most obviously in the columns being more attenuated (nine diameters high rather than seven) and having bases, consisting of a round torus (a convex moulding) on square plinth. Stylistically, the temple can be dated to the early first century BC (Brandizzi Vittuci 1968, p. 95).

The cella doorway is one of the best preserved ancient Roman doorways, yet, probably because of Cori's relative remoteness, it only seems to have attracted the attention of the Sangallo brothers among architectural draughtsmen. Their interest may also have been inspired by the humanist Giovanni Battista Veralli, who is said to have encouraged Cardinal Alessandro Farnese (later Pope Paul III) to model the doors and windows of his new palace on the doorway here (Frommel 1981 *Sangallo et Michel-Ange*, p. 168, n. 218; Pagliara 1986 *Vitruvio*, p. 51).

The drawings of the Cori temples (here and fols 4r.–5v.) stand out from the rest of the drawings of the codex, not only because they are the only subjects from outside Rome, but also because they are measured in Roman palms rather than the antique Roman foot. It seems unlikely, therefore that they were part of the same project, even though the style of all the Cori drawings but one closely matches those of the Roman subjects. The exception is drawing *a* here, which shows a detail of the upper left corner of the doorway axonometrically, as opposed to the orthogonal projection used for all the rest.

All three drawings find parallels on a sheet of Antonio the Younger's (U 1165A v.), which also includes the parallels of the rest of the drawings of the temples at Cori (fols 4r.–5v.) and of some of the Hadrianeum in Rome (fols 6 r and v). Antonio only draws the left half of the doorway but transcribes the whole inscription (Brandizzi Vittucci 1968, p. 81; CIL, X. 651) with only minor errors.

BIBLIOGRAPHY Campbell (2005) 47 f.; Campbell-Nesselrath (2006) 9, 14 and 45; Winckelmann (1825–9), vol. 2, 393 f.; Winckelmann (1952–7), vol. 2, 101.

CODEX ROOTSTEIN HOPKINS fol. 3 *verso*

GIOVANNI BATTISTA DA SANGALLO

'Archi triophali'.

Dimensions see recto.
Paper see recto.

INSCRIPTION (top centre, brown ink) *Archi triophali*; Numbering: (bottom centre, upside down, brown ink) *41*

The heading confirms that the codex was at least intended to contain drawings of other arches, and the likelihood is that they filled the three missing folios. Besides other details of the Arches of Titus and Janus, the Arches of Septimius Severus and Constantine are the most likely candidates for inclusion. | IC

BIBLIOGRAPHY Campbell (2005) 8 and 48; Campbell-Nesselrath (2006) 12 and 46.

CODEX ROOTSTEIN HOPKINS fol. 4 *recto*

GIOVANNI BATTISTA DA SANGALLO

Cori, Temple of Hercules, side elevation.

Dimensions 275 × 205 mm.
Technique Pen and brown ink, partly with straightedge and partly freehand.
Watermark: anchor (cut).

INSCRIPTION (on drawing, brown ink) *mancha·ancora/ unpilastro qua·adrieto*; *Veduta p[er] fiancho ·diquel tempio toschano ·/ che: a chori in campagna*; *La cornice· no[n] Risalta·dalla/ Colonna · alpilastro*; *Palmi di roma*

The single drawing on the sheet shows the reconstructed side elevation of the Temple of Hercules. Space did not permit Giovanni Battista to show the last bay to the left, as his annotation explains. Antonio's parallel on U 1165A r. does include it and his accompanying annotation makes it clear that the rear parts are reconstructed. The height given for the podium (9⅔ palms = 2.7 m) is also higher than in reality (1.55 m) showing that the drawing of the lower parts of the podium is conjectural. No trace of the base moulding survives.

The extra information provided by Antonio suggests that in this case his drawings are the source for Giovanni Battista's, rather than the other way round. Both share the idiosyncrasy of showing the steps of the temple in section, seen through the flanking side wall extending from the podium. This is a characteristic of all the side elevations of temples on podia in the codex (fols 8r., 10r., 13v., 14v., 16v. and 22v.).

The description of the temple as Tuscan rather than Doric is probably because the columns have bases of a single torus as Vitruvius prescribed for Tuscan columns (Vitruvius 4.7.3), whereas Doric columns should have no base. | IC

BIBLIOGRAPHY Campbell (2005) 48; Campbell-Nesselrath (2006) 21 and 47.

CODEX ROOTSTEIN HOPKINS fol. 4 *verso*

GIOVANNI BATTISTA DA SANGALLO

Cori, Temple of Hercules, plan and details.

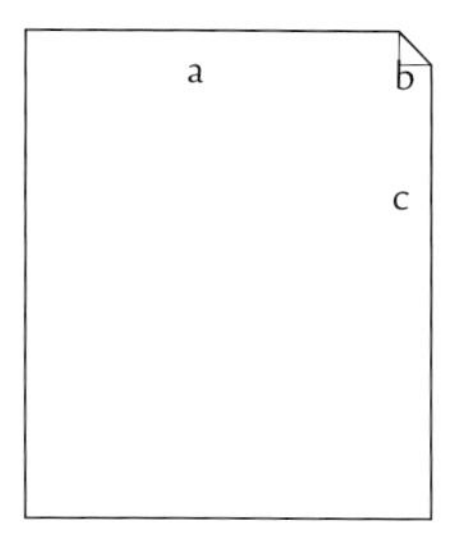

Dimensions see recto.
Technique Pen and brown ink; drawing *a* with straightedge and compass; drawings *b* and *c* freehand.
Paper see recto.

INSCRIPTION (top centre, brown ink) *TEMPLI*; (on drawing *a*, brown ink) *Pianta ·de· undif* (cancelled) *Un tempio Toscano/ a corj incampangna di roma ·fatto/ almodo ·grecho fatto e ordinato*; (on drawing *c*) *modano del/ capitello del/ pilastro*; *pilastr[o]*; (below drawing *c*, brown ink) *Lo modano d[el ca]/ pitello del pila[stro] comeuedi edi [verso]/ da quello della co[lonna]/ Come uedi qui*; Numbering: (bottom centre, upside down, brown ink) *39*

The three drawings show the plan of the temple (*a*), a section through the entablature and a column capital, which continues across the fold to fol. 5r. (*b*) and a section through the pilaster capital (*c*).

Antonio's parallel plan on U 1165A r. omits the podium, and his parallel to *b* adds information on the lower part of the column, which Giovanni Battista is able to show elsewhere (fol. 5 r *c*). | IC

BIBLIOGRAPHY Campbell (2005) 48; Campbell-Nesselrath (2006) 12, 14 and 48.

CODEX ROOTSTEIN HOPKINS fol. 5 *recto*

Giovanni Battista da Sangallo

Cori, Temple of Hercules, front elevation and details.

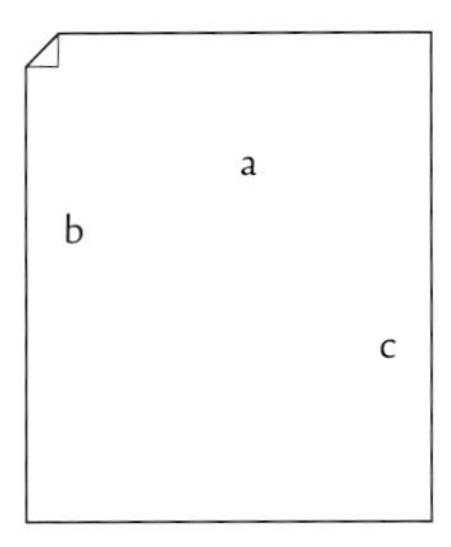

Dimensions 278 × 201 mm.
Technique Pen and brown ink; drawing *a*, partly with straightedge and partly freehand; drawings *b* and *c* freehand.
Paper double folio with fol. 6—guard strip down centrefold between fol. 5v. and fol. 6r.

INSCRIPTION (on drawing *a*, brown ink) *lo uano p[almi] 10–1*; *larga p[almi] 10⅔/ lo uano* (reading upwards) *la porta alta lo uano p[almi] 22*; *la mensola*; *M·M... LIVS·M·F·I TVRPILIU... ENVS/ SENT... AEDEM·FACIEDAM COE... VERE*; (below drawing *a*, brown ink) *La faciata ·di questo tempio che· achori/ in campagna*; (on drawing *b*, brown ink) *Buca p[er] li trauj/ Del tetto*; (right of drawing *c*, reading upwards, brown ink) *Colonna basa · con un collarino/pie* [...]; Numbering: (bottom right, graphite) *8*; (bottom centre, upside down, brown ink) *38*

The main drawing *a* of the front elevation of the temple is accompanied by a detailed section through the entablature and elevation of the top of a column, *b* which continues across from fol. 4v. Another detail, *c*, is a sketch of part of the foot of a column. This last has an annotation referring to the column base as a 'collarino', is a term usually reserved for a thin convex moulding. The thicker convex moulding of a column base is more often known as a torus from Vitruvius (4.7.3), suggesting Giovanni Battista was not yet so well acquainted with Vitruvian terminology.

The parts of the inscription on the architrave over the doorway seen between the columns are recorded far less accurately than on fol. 3r. A very strange feature is the hatching over the architrave, used everywhere else to indicate a void as in the doorway below.

While Antonio took great with his parallel of drawing *b* on U 1165A r., his version of the front elevation is a very schematic freehand sketch omitting details such as the fluting of the columns. | IC

BIBLIOGRAPHY Campbell (2005) 48 f.; Campbell-Nesselrath (2006) 49; Winckelmann (1825–9), vol. 2, 393 f.; Winckelmann (1952–7), vol. 2, p. 101.

CODEX ROOTSTEIN HOPKINS fol. 5 *verso*

Giovanni Battista da Sangallo

Cori, Temple of Castor and Pollux, plan.

Dimensions see recto.
Technique Pen and brown ink with straightedge and compass, and partly freehand.
Paper see recto.

INSCRIPTION (on drawing, brown ink) *TENpio ·dichastore epolluce/ Corintio lisuo capitelli sonalti 4/ palmj le colonne grosse 4 palmj/ Le cholonne ·infaccia son piu larghe/ Luna ·dalaltro ·piu che p[er] fiancho/ Come uedi qui ·equesto sie in chori/ Di canpangna ·hordine ·Corintio/ nelsuo ·fregio son Queste littere/ TENLV ·CASTORIS· EPOLVCI*; Numbering: (bottom left, upside down, brown ink) *37*

The Temple of Castor and Pollux is like that of Hercules datable to the early first century BC (Brandizzi Vittucci 1968, pp. 58–66) Very little survives but excavations have established that it was of the Etruscan type (Vitruvius 4.7. 1–5). A short cella divided into three compartments, which opened onto the pronaos, which was six columns wide and two deep. Two of these columns, of travertine, still stand with Corinthian capitals, marked by the distinctive intertwined central pair of volutes, found also on the temples of Castor and Pollux in Rome and in Naples. The architrave the columns support has a fragment of the inscription giving the dedication. Another fragment is preserved elsewhere in Cori (CIL X. 6506; Brandizzi Vittucci 1968, p. 59)

Giovanni Battista's plan accurately reconstructs the pronaos but the cella is far from reality and certainly had no rear wall since it abuts the rock face behind (Brandizzi Vittucci 1968, p. 63). The annotation gives measurements for the columns and capitals, but no details or drawn. This strengthens the suggestion that he was relying on Antonio for information. On the latter's parallel plan (U 1165A r.), the cella is drawn with a single line apart from the front left corner, perhaps indicating the rest was conjectural. Antonio's annotation says that he saw four columns *in situ*, which may be true but cannot be corroborated from other sources. | IC

BIBLIOGRAPHY Campbell (2005) 49; Campbell-Nesselrath (2006) 50.

CODEX ROOTSTEIN HOPKINS fol. 6 *recto*

GIOVANNI BATTISTA DA SANGALLO

Rome, Hadrianeum, plan.

Dimensions 278 × 210 mm.
Technique Pen and brown ink with straightedge and compass and partly freehand.
Paper tears top and bottom edges.
Watermark: anchor (cut).

INSCRIPTION (above drawing, upside down, brown ink) *oPera ·Corintia ·fatto secondo lordine/ Pinostilo li inter culu[m]nij*; (on drawing) *TEMLVM · MINERVA · IROMA/ ALA·PIAZA·DEPRETI*; (upside down, brown ink) *Louoto*; (left margin, reading downwards, brown ink) *Piedi 10 da stella a stella* (drawing scale); Numbering: (bottom left, upside down, brown ink) *36*

The Hadrianeum was the Temple of the Deified Hadrian, who died in AD 138. Eleven marble columns and the cella wall of the north side of the temple survive, incorporated into the nineteenth-century stock exchange of Rome. Excavations have revealed enough to establish that it was probably originally thirteen columns long and eight wide and faced east. It stood on a high podium of blocks of tufa, originally clad in marble and possibly decorated with the relief panels of Roman provinces, which have been excavated in the immediate vicinity (Claridge 1999). The columns are 50 Roman feet (14.8 m) high. Part of the coffered barrel vault of the cella survives but none of the engaged order of columns 36 Roman feet high, which originally lined its walls (Cozza 1982; LTUR, III, 9 f. [F. Coarelli]; Claridge 1998, pp. 199–201).

Giovanni Battista identifies as it the Temple of Minerva, probably after the 'Minerva Chalcidia', which is listed in the area in the Regionary catalogues, and whose name is preserved in the church of S. Maria sopra Minerva, a little distance south of the Hadrianeum. 'Piazza de' Preti' is a variant of Piazza di Pietra as the square in front of the temple is still called today.

He reconstructs it with eight by fifteen columns, following Vitruvius' description of the dipteral and pseudodipteral temples (Vit. 3.2.6–7). The term 'pinostilo' (pycnostyle) is that used by Vitruvius (3.3.1) for the narrowest gap between columns (1½ column widths). Vitruvius probably also accounts for the presence of a Greek-style stylobate (steps on all four sides), which he favored for temples, rather than the Roman preference for a podium with steps only at the front. Indeed, the plan recalls that which Giovanni Battista drew in his 'Corsini Incunabulum to illustrate the pseudodipteral (Rome Biblioteca Corsiniana, Inc.50.F.1, fol. 31v.; Rowland 2003, pl. 62)

Having the cella open at both ends is also erroneous. It is a feature of the plans of the peripteral and larger temples in Fra Giocondo's 1511 edition of Vitruvius, the first illustrated, on which the Sangallo brothers were almost certainly relying at the time of these drawings.

Antonio has four plans of the Hadrianeum, all calling it 'Le Plastine', the medieval name for the ruins. The first, on the same sheet as the Cori and other Hadrianeum parallels (U 1165A v.), is a part plan with the same measurements. The second (U 1661A v,) reproduces most of the present plan but omits the stylobate and measurements. Giovanni Battista has written 'pinostilo' on it, showing it to be closely related. The third (U 1175A r.) is less close; it includes notes about the materials and more measurements, suggesting firsthand observation, although other drawings on the sheet, namely a section of the temple and one of a column base relate to those on fol. 6v. The last (U 1144A r.) makes clear which columns are hypothetical reconstructions by representing them with dotted outlines, and yet show flights of steps at the end of the cella, for which we have no other evidence.

The drawing scale on the left edge is the first of several (fols 14r., 17r., 19v. and 21v.) but is the only one with an accompanying explanatory note, suggesting that the present ordering of folios reflects that intended by Giovanni Battista. | IC

BIBLIOGRAPHY Campbell (2005) 49; Campbell-Nesselrath (2006) 51.

CODEX ROOTSTEIN HOPKINS fol. 6 *verso*

GIOVANNI BATTISTA DA SANGALLO

Rome, Hadrianeum, side elevation and detail.

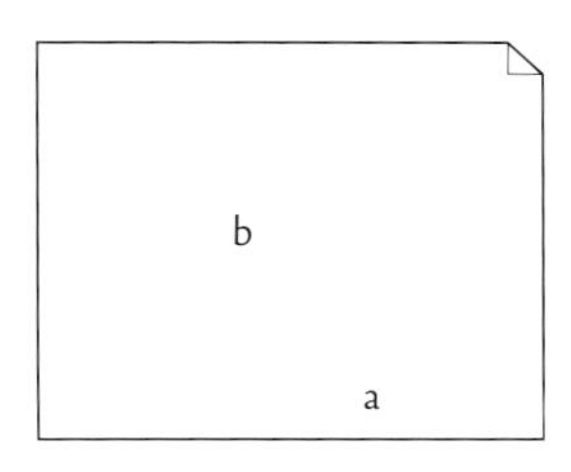

Dimensions see recto.
Technique Pen and brown ink with straightedge and freehand.
Paper see recto.

INSCRIPTION (below drawing *a* thick brown ink) *La suo basa*; (right of drawing *b*, reading upwards, thick brown ink) *Prophilo · del tempio · diminerua/ · Jn roma · alla piazza · elepreti/ Quelle · fiurine son grande de Qua/ nto naturale*; Numbering: (bottom centre, upside down, brown ink) *35*

The main drawing, *b*, is a side elevation (wrongly called a profile here, which means section) of the Hadrianeum, reconstructed according to the plan on fol. 6r. Drawing *a* is a section through one of its column bases. An annotation explains that the figures are there to give a sense of scale rather than extraneous ornament. As such they are extremely useful in a series of buildings of varying size drawn to differing scales.

Antonio sketched a parallel of *b* on U 1165A v., but only includes the first five bays from the left. He erroneously adds statues on top of the entablature over each of the columns. His parallel to *a* on the same sheet has the same measurements but also includes the foot of the column shaft with measurements of the flutes, something not found on Giovanni Battista's drawing. | IC

BIBLIOGRAPHY Campbell (2005) 49 f.; Campbell-Nesselrath (2006) 15 and 52.

CODEX ROOTSTEIN HOPKINS fol. 7 *recto*

Giovanni Battista da Sangallo

Rome, Hadrianeum, front, half-elevation and half-section.

Dimensions 278 × 210 mm.
Technique Pen and brown ink with straightedge and freehand.
Paper double folio with fol. 8; bottom left corner torn.

INSCRIPTION (below drawing, thick brown ink) *facciata del tempio di minerua iroma alla piazza/ Depreti meza la facciata ·sana e meza Rotta/ Le suo Colonne tutte a chanalate da basso:a·· alto*; Numbering: (bottom right, graphite) *15*; (bottom centre, upside down, brown ink) *34*

The single drawing combines an elevation of the front of the Hadrianeum in the right half with a section through the temple in the left half. The latter reveals the vault between the outer colonnade and the wall of the cella and the internal engaged order of columns and coffered barrel vault of the cella.

The half-section is paralleled in a very schematic sketch on Antonio's U 1165A v. However another section by Antonio on U 1175A r. is more faithful to the remains in two respects; one is that the temple appears to stand on a podium rather than a stylobate (see fol. 6r.) and the other that the frieze of the main external entablature is shown as pulvinated, something that Giovanni Battista does not make clear in any of his drawings, although he may have intended there to be a detail of the entablature. U 1175A r. also includes a detail sketch of the internal entablature, again showing a pulvinated frieze, a feature for which we have no independent corroboration. | IC

BIBLIOGRAPHY Campbell (2005) 50; Campbell-Nesselrath (2006) 9 and 53.

CODEX ROOTSTEIN HOPKINS fol. 7 *verso*

Giovanni Battista da Sangallo

Rome, Temple of Portunus, plan.

Dimensions see recto.
Technique Pen and brown ink with straightedge and compass, and partly freehand.
Paper see recto.

INSCRIPTION (on drawing, brown ink) *Volta ·sopra ·a questo ·porticho/ aschifo*; (reading downwards) *Bungne di stuchi*; Numbering: (bottom centre, upside down, brown ink) *33*

The Temple of Portunus, a god of ports, stands by the Tiber. The original late fourth- or early third-century BC temple was replaced by the present one about 80–70 BC. It owes its survival to conversion into a church around AD 872, while still in good condition. The podium and the columns of the porch are of travertine, while the cella walls and engaged columns are made from tufa. All were decorated with stucco, to make the fluting on the column shafts to give the appearance of rustication on the cella walls, and to sharpen the mouldings of the capitals and bases; and to decorate the frieze on the entablature. In the 1930s the temple was stripped of later accretions (apart from some early medieval frescoes) and left in its present (Adam 1994; LTUR IV, 153 f. [C. Buzzetti]; Claridge 1998, pp. 253 f.).

As one would expect for a building so well preserved, the plan is very accurate. One idiosyncrasy is that the plans of all the capitals are included except for the middle pair at the front, possibly because they were immured in the walls of the later church. although, Antonio, on U 1166A r, felt able to show the plan of the inner right capital in a sketch showing the three columns at the front right corner. This sketch is an enlarged detail of a part plan, which parallels the one here in all other respects. Giovanni Battista's observation that the porch had a pavilion vault is valuable additional support to the evidence of the 'Fossombrone Sketchbook' (Biblioteca Civica Passionei, inv. Disegni vol. 3, fol. 13v.; Nesselrath 1993, pp. 115–7, pl. 24). | IC

BIBLIOGRAPHY Campbell (2005) 50; Campbell-Nesselrath (2006) 54.

CODEX ROOTSTEIN HOPKINS fol. 8 *recto*

GIOVANNI BATTISTA DA SANGALLO

Rome, Temple of Portunus, side elevation.

Dimensions 276 × 210 mm.
Technique Pen and brown ink with straightedge and freehand.
Paper tear at bottom left corner matching fol. 7r.; top right corner folded.

INSCRIPTION (below drawing, brown ink) *fiancho diquel tempio iochinicho/ a ponte ·S[an]ta maria*; Numbering: (bottom right, graphite) *11*; (bottom centre, upside down, brown ink) *32*

This side elevation reconstructs the cella, rightly ignoring the window inserted after it became a church (compare the drawing by Pirro Ligorio at Windsor, RL 19258; Campbell 2004, I, p. 216, no. 65), but wrongly articulating the podium so that it projects like a pedestal under each column and half-column, possibly reflecting a misunderstanding of Vitruvian *scamilli inpares* (see fol. 10r. and Campbell 1980, p. 20). The stucco frieze decoration is reconstructed not quite accurately, including ox-skulls, garlands, candelabra, but omitting *putti*, which, however, do appear on the front elevation (see next folio)). What is not made clear is whether the three half-columns on the right are meant to be read as unfluted. They may have been left so to allow the inclusion of measurements but no clues are given to the viewer. Antonio's parallel on U 1166A r. shows only the front column as fluted. It also errs in extending the dado of the cella into the portico.

The inscription below the drawing does not hazard an identification but merely locates the building near the Ponte Santa Maria, better known as the Ponte Rotto, the 'Broken Bridge', which was the ancient Roman Pons Aemilius. | IC

BIBLIOGRAPHY Campbell (2005) 50; Campbell-Nesselrath (2006) 55.

CODEX ROOTSTEIN HOPKINS fol. 8 *verso*

GIOVANNI BATTISTA DA SANGALLO

Rome, Temple of Portunus. front elevation.

Dimensions see recto.
Technique Pen and brown ink with straightedge and freehand.
Paper see recto.

INSCRIPTION (below drawing, brown ink) *facciata dequel tempio/ jonicho aponte · S[an]ta maria*; *La suo porta elarga pie ·10½ alta/ pie 22 apunto louano*; Numbering:: (bottom centre, upside down, brown ink) *31*

The front elevation is accurately reconstructed but again it is not made clear that we are meant to read the two outer columns as fluted, which was surely intended since the far right column here is the same as the far left one on fol. 8r., which is shown fluted. This is supported by the parallel on U 1166A r., where, on a half-elevation, Antonio puts flutes on the outer column and leaves the inner one unfluted.

As already said on fol. 8r., the frieze is accurately recorded here—ox skulls, candelabra and *putti* linked by garlands (Adam 1994, p. 67). | IC

BIBLIOGRAPHY Campbell (2005) 51; Campbell-Nesselrath (2006) 56.

CODEX ROOTSTEIN HOPKINS fol. 9 *recto*

GIOVANNI BATTISTA DA SANGALLO

Rome, Temple of Antoninus and Faustina, plan and detail.

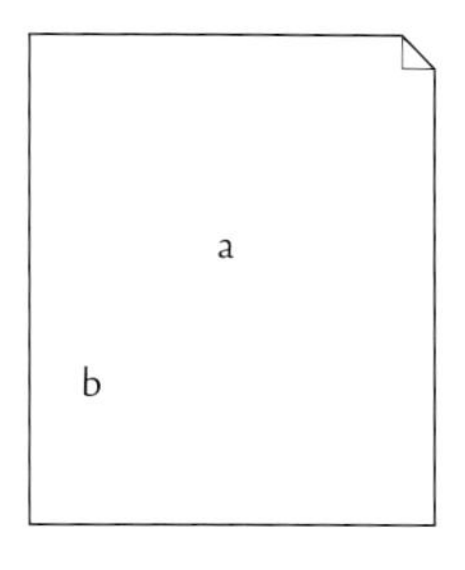

Dimensions 278 × 210 mm.
Technique Pen and brown ink with straightedge and compass.
Paper double folio with fol. 10; water stain in bottom right corner.
Watermark: anchor (cut).

INSCRIPTION (on drawing *a*, thick brown ink) *TENPIO DE ANTONINO/ ET FAVSTINA/ ROME*; (on drawing *b*, reading upwards) *Prophilo dello imbasamento/ Di questo tempio dantonino*; Numbering: (bottom right, graphite) *12*; (bottom left, upside down, brown ink) *30*

The Temple of the Deified Antoninus and Faustina was built by the emperor Antoninus Pius after his wife Faustina's death in AD 140. His name was added above hers on the frieze after he died twenty years later. The temple stands on a tall podium and consists of a portico six columns wide by three deep which are 48 Roman feet high (with shafts of beautiful Carystian green marble, 40 Roman feet high), and the cella behind. It has been the church of S. Lorenzo in Miranda since the seventh or eighth centuries, but, nevertheless, the rear wall of the cella, the original roof and most of the upper cornice have been lost. The podium was also originally faced with marble slabs which probably extended part way up the cella walls before turning to stucco, but all have been lost leaving the grey *peperino* tufa blocks exposed (LTUR, I, 46f [A. Cassatella]; Claridge 1998, pp. 107–9).

The first drawing in Giovanni Battista's sequence is the plan *a*, accompanied by a section or profile, *b* through the podium up to the first two courses of rustication above the dado on the cella. Both drawings include a wealth of measurements and both find parallels on Antonio's U 1166A v., with a pattern emerging that the plan is drawn to a smaller scale and rather schematically, while more attention is given to the detail. | IC

BIBLIOGRAPHY Campbell (2005) 51; Campbell-Nesselrath (2006) 57.

CODEX ROOTSTEIN HOPKINS fol. 9 *verso*

Giovanni Battista da Sangallo

Rome, Temple of Antoninus and Faustina, front elevation.

Dimensions see recto.
Technique Pen and brown ink with straightedge and freehand.
Paper see recto.

INSCRIPTION (on drawing, thick brown ink, with traces of black chalk) *DIVO·ANTONINO·ET·/ DIVAE · FAVSTIN AE*; (reading upwards, brown ink) *Lo fuso della colonna/ senza capitello ebasa pie 39½*; Numbering: (bottom centre, upside down, brown ink) *29*

The front elevation is shown reconstructed with a pediment. The transcription of the inscription adds the word 'et' on the first line and omits EX S.C ('by decree of the Senate' on the second line). The inscription seems to have been traced out in black chalk before it was written in ink. The first three letters of FAVSTINA appear to have been written slightly to the left originally, but then erased. The letters '*E*' at the end of *Divae* and *Faustinae* are both in black chalk and appear to be later corrections. Neither appears on Antonio the Younger's parallel on U 1166A v.

The latter is a half-elevation drawn freehand and its proportions are made much squatter to fit on the page, so that the statue in front of the far left column looks much bigger than it should. Antonio includes more measurements but most are repeated from the section of the podium and cella discussed on fol. 9r.). | IC

BIBLIOGRAPHY Campbell (2005) 10 and 51; Campbell-Nesselrath (2006) 7, 9, 12 and 58.

CODEX ROOTSTEIN HOPKINS fol. 10 *recto*

Giovanni Battista da Sangallo

Rome, Temple of Antoninus and Faustina, side elevation.

Dimensions 278 × 210 mm.
Technique Pen and brown ink with straightedge and freehand.
Paper double folio with fol. 9; bottom right corner torn.
Watermark: anchor (cut).

INSCRIPTION (below drawing, thick brown ink) *Veduta · per fiancho/ deltempio dantonino/ et· faustina*; (on drawing, reading upwards, brown ink) *lo fuso della colonna senza/ capitello e senza labasa alto pie 39½*; Numbering: (bottom right, graphite) *13*; (bottom centre, upside down, brown ink) *28*

The side elevation again includes a wealth of measurements. The latticed parapets between the columns of the porch are almost certainly taken from Roman coins depicting this temple, which show a fence in front (compare Mattingly 1923–50, IV, Antoninus Pius 339, 383 and 1562; see also Claridge 1998, fig. 43). Giovanni Battista includes the fences on the side elevation of an Ionic temple in his illustrations to the 'Corsini Incunabulum' (Rome, Biblioteca Corsiniana, Inc. 50.F.1, fol. 38v.; Rowland 2003, pl. 76) which he uses to demonstrate the mysterious *scamilli inpares* (Vit. 3.4.5). It is so similar to the present drawing that he must surely have had it in mind, especially since he cites the Temple of Antoninus and Faustina as an example of *scamilli inpares*, despite the fact that its podium does not break forward beneath each column as that in the Vitruvius illustration does. Campbell (1980, p. 21) speculated that Giovanni Battista was confusing the Temple of Antoninus and Faustina with the Hadrianeum, which at the time was often thought to be the Temple (or Basilica) of Antoninus Pius, and did have such an articulated podium. However, the present drawing would appear to weaken that suggestion.

Antonio's parallel on U 1166A r. only includes the front half of the temple. As with the front elevation, he has made the proportions much squatter to fit the drawing on to the page. However, by retaining the figures inside the portico he has completely lost the sense of scale. This again suggests that Antonio was copying the present drawings rather than vice versa. | IC

BIBLIOGRAPHY Campbell (2005) 10 and 51; Campbell-Nesselrath (2006) 17 and 59.

CODEX ROOTSTEIN HOPKINS fol. 10 *verso*

Giovanni Battista da Sangallo

Rome, Temple of Antoninus and Faustina, details.

Dimensions see recto.
Technique Pen and brown ink with straightedge and freehand, with traces of black chalk.
Paper see recto.

INSCRIPTION (on drawing *a*, brown ink) *Cornicione · del tempio/ Dantonino der faustina*; (on drawing *b*, reading upwards, brown ink) *Lo f[?]atto? del capitello/ alto pie 5–11*

The two drawings on the page represent the entablature, *a*, and the column capital and top of the shaft, *b*, both with ample measurements. Enough of the former is drawn to represent the full range of motifs in the frieze, which are underdrawn in black chalk. A short stretch of the ornaments of the cornice is also fully drawn, the rest being shown in outline.

Only the entablature appears on U 1166A r., and not the capital. | IC

BIBLIOGRAPHY Campbell (2005) 52; Campbell-Nesselrath (2006) 7 and 60.

CODEX ROOTSTEIN HOPKINS fol. 11 *recto*

Giovanni Battista da Sangallo

Rome, Middle temple, Forum Holitorium, plan.

Dimensions 277 × 210 mm.
Technique Pen and brown ink with straightedge and compass.
Paper was double folio with fol. 12, now linked by three strips of paper.

INSCRIPTION (on drawing, thick brown ink, except final *E*, which is in black chalk) *OLIM/ TEMPLVM MARIANAE/ nuc ·S·to nichola incarcere/ ·Jonicho*; Numbering: (bottom right, graphite) *14*

The church of S. Nicola in Carcere, reconsecrated after enlargement in 1128, incorporates remains of three temples, which stood together on the west side of the Forum Holitorium (Crozzoli Aite 1981; Claridge 1998, pp. 247–50, Campbell 2004, I, pp. 138–41). The church included the whole of the middle temple, an Ionic peripteral, six columns wide by eleven deep built from *peperino* tufa, and finished in stucco, as were the cella walls, all standing on a podium of travertine. It extended south to incorporate the north colonnade of its smaller southern neighbour, again a peripteral temple with six by eleven columns on a podium, but of the Doric order and all constructed of travertine, decorated with stucco. The church also incorporated the south colonnade of the northern temple, of similar size and materials to the middle temple, and also an Ionic peripteral but *sine postico* (meaning that the colonnade did not extend round the rear), six columns wide and nine columns plus an anta deep. Most scholars agree that the north temple is likely to be dedicated to Janus, vowed in 260 BC and rededicated in AD 17 (LTUR, III, 90 f. [F. Coarelli]). The other two must be those of Spes (Hope), vowed between 258 and 249 BC, again rededicated in AD 17 (LTUR, V, 336 f. [F. Coarelli]), and Juno Sospita, vowed in 197 BC, dedicated in 194 and rebuilt in 90 BC (LTUR, III, 128 f. [F. Coarelli]). Scholars disagree which is which: Claridge (1998, p. 249) gives Juno Sospita the middle temple and Spes the south, while Campbell (2004, I, p. 138) argues the contrary. For clarity, they are referred to here as the northern, middle and Doric temples.

The identification 'Templum Marianae' derives from Vitruvius 3.2.5 '… quemadmodum est in portico Metelli Iovis Statoris Hermodori et ad Mariana Honoris et Virtutis sine postico a Mucio facta', which can be translated as 'just as there is in Hermodorus' Temple of Jove Stator in the Porticus of Metellus and in the Temple of Honour and Virtue, made by Mucius, without a rear porch, near the Monuments of Marius'. Giovanni has misunderstood the Latin and split the Temple of Honour and Virtue (which was actually on the slopes of the Capitoline nearby) into two temples and made 'Mariana' into a third. He compounded his error on fol. 11 v., by referring to the middle temple as 'Dermodi', linking it to Hermodorus rather than to the Temple of Jove Stator.

The letter *E* in black chalk at the end of MARIANAE appears to be a later correction. The plan correctly makes the middle temple six columns by eleven, and gives the cella projecting antae at the four corners. It errs by giving the cella two entrances (probaby following Fra Giocondo's plan of the Vitruvian peripteral temple). Giovanni Battista is also mistaken in showing front and rear porches both three columns deep whereas in reality there was only a front porch four columns deep. Finally he puts it on a stylobate rather than a podium, which would have been impossible given the proximity of its neighbours (see fol. 14r.).

Among Sangallo Circle studies, the plan on U 1134A r. by Pietro Rosselli comes closest in form and major measurements. Giovanni Battista's own U 1657A r. with sketch plans of all three temples, is also close although it is twelve columns long and not every measurement corresponds. Antonio's sketch plan on U 1090A r.+1230A v., follows the form and gives the same measurements for the cella and its entrances but those of the intercolumniations differ. Another sketch plan of Antonio's, U 1174A r., has the same width for the cella, but correctly shows it with only one entrance, slightly narrower, while the intercolumniations match those on U 1090A r.+1230A v. | IC

BIBLIOGRAPHY Campbell (2005) 8, 52 and 57; Campbell-Nesselrath (2006) 18 and 61.

CODEX ROOTSTEIN HOPKINS fol. 11 *verso*

Giovanni Battista da Sangallo

Rome, Middle temple, Forum Holitorium, side elevation.

Dimensions see recto.
Technique Pen and brown ink with straightedge and freehand.
Paper see recto.

INSCRIPTION (below drawing, brown ink) *Veduta per fiancho ·del tempio Dermodi/ Oggi si chiama s^to^· nichola in charcere/ le colonne fatte· scanalate · da capo· apie/ Li sua · lacunarij son dua architrave/ luno sopra laltro dipaperingno 33*; (on drawing, reading upwards, brown ink) *la colonna senza capitello ebasa/ ·e· alta · pie 30¼*; *la colonna ·col capitello ebasa/ ·e· alta pie 33*; Numbering: (bottom centre, upside down, brown ink) *25*

The side elevation corresponds to the plan. Only the second column from the left is shown fluted, but the inscription makes clear that they all were. The inscriptions to 'lacunarii' refer to drawing *b* on fol. 12 recto.

The meaning of 'Dermodi' is discussed in the entry on fol. 11 r. Antonio's U 1090A v.+1230A r. calls the middle temple 'Santo Nicola di Ermodi' but it was subsequently crossed out. No other Sangallo Circle drawing reconstructs the side elevation. | IC

BIBLIOGRAPHY Campbell (2005) 52; Campbell-Nesselrath (2006) 62.

CODEX ROOTSTEIN HOPKINS fol. 12 *recto*

Giovanni Battista da Sangallo

Rome, Middle temple, Forum Holitorium, front elevation and detail.

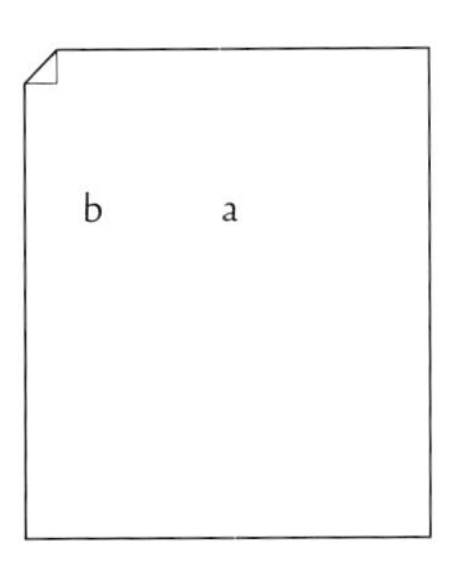

Dimensions 277 × 211 mm.
Technique Drawing *a*, pen and brown ink with straightedge and freehand; drawing *b*, freehand.
Paper was double folio with fol. 11; tear on top edge; patch at upper right.

INSCRIPTION (below drawing 'A, thicker brown ink') *facciata del tenpio ·iochinicho/ Di S^to^ nichola in carcere e nota/ che le colonne della· facciata mostra/ no · alli capitelli dinanzi li fastellinj/ ·e· non· licarto cci Come ·fanno/ li altri ionichi Cosa Rara come/ uedi indisegno Qui sopra*; (on drawing, reading upwards, brown ink) *la colonna senza capitello· ebasa pie 30¼*; (on drawing *b*) *lacunari*; Numbering: (bottom right, graphite) *15*; (bottom right, upside down, brown ink) *24*

The reconstruction of the front elevation bizarrely shows the Ionic capitals turned sideways. The explanation is that no remains of the front row of columns were visible and Giovanni Battista and others assumed that the three extant columns of the second row of columns were actually at the front (adding an extra row of columns at the rear to keep to the Vitruvian ideal of eleven along the sides). Since the capitals of this second row faced towards the side elevations, as is apparent on Antonio's part-elevation/part-section of the tops of the two columns and the entablature of the temple on U 1090A v.+1230A r., Giovanni Battista drew a completely false inference. Although no one until the twentieth century realised that the front row was missing, no other reconstruction followed Giovanni Battista's literal interpretation of the apparent evidence.

The detail, *b*, of the ceiling coffers, is paralleled with measurements, on Giovanni Battista's U 1657A r., which also has an inscription 'la colonna pie 30 1/4 alta senza basa e senza capitello', almost identical to that here. Antonio also has a perspectival view of the same detail with identical measurements on U 1090A v.+1230A r. | IC

BIBLIOGRAPHY Campbell (2005) 53; Campbell-Nesselrath (2006) 9, 18, 25 and 63.

CODEX ROOTSTEIN HOPKINS fol. 12 *verso*

Giovanni Battista da Sangallo

Rome, North temple, Forum Holitorium, plan.

Dimensions see recto.
Technique Pen and brown ink with straightedge and compass.
Paper see recto.

INSCRIPTION (above drawing, brown ink) *Dameza Colonna ameza colonna/ sie pie otto e mezzo:· le colonne / songrosse· pie tre· emezo/ Alte senza capitello/ et senza basa ·pie/ Venti noue et ¾ / perquanto*; (on drawing, brown ink) *Olim/ TENPLVM ·VIRTVTIS/ NVNC/ LE CARCERE/ Corintio ·colonne ··/ son senza canalj*; Numbering: (bottom centre, upside down, brown ink) *23*

The identification 'Temple of Virtue' is discussed in the entry to fol. 11 r. The temple had its intercolumniations walled up and was turned into a prison in the Dark Ages, from which the neighbouring church of S. Nicola (patron of prisoners) took its name. Antonio Labacco says in his *Libro d'Architettura*, first published in 1552, that it was destroyed 'in our times' by being converted into houses (Labacco 1559, pp. 23 f.).

The plan correctly places the temple on a podium rather than a stylobate, but errs in giving it only eight columns along the sides rather than nine, because, as with the middle temple, no evidence of the front row was visible. Another defect is the omission of pilasters from the outer walls of the cella, the presence of which is attested by a plan by Giovanni Francesco (U 1373A r.) and one by Antonio the Younger (U 1142A v.) backed up by the independent plan of Baldassare Peruzzi (1481–1536) made around 1525 (U 478A v.+631A r.; Bartoli 1914–22, III, fig. 320, VI, p. 59), when he was converting the adjacent Theatre of Marcellus into the Palazzo Savelli (Tessari 1995, 124 f.).

Antonio's theoretical study on U 1090A r.+1230A v. seems the closest drawing to the present plan, but his incomplete plan on U 1090A v.+1230A r. has some different measurements, such as the width of the door, suggesting it was based on actual observation. Giovanni Battista's own plan on U 1657A r. corresponds in most of the measurements but has ten columns along the side. | IC

BIBLIOGRAPHY Campbell (2005) 53; Campbell-Nesselrath (2006) 64.

CODEX ROOTSTEIN HOPKINS fol. 13 *recto*

Giovanni Battista da Sangallo

Rome, North temple, Forum Holitorium, front elevation and section, and details.

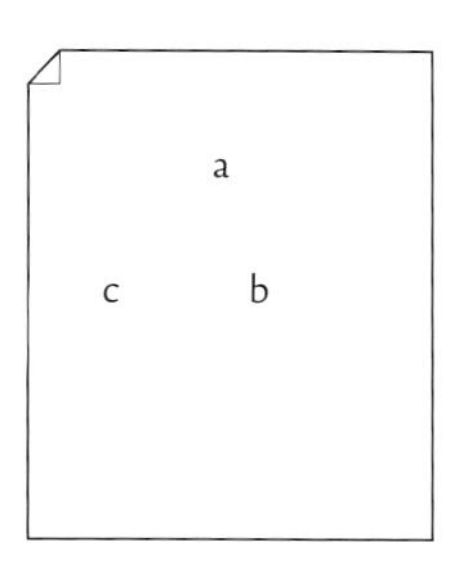

Dimensions 277 × 210 mm.
Technique Pen and brown ink with straightedge and freehand.
Paper was double folio with fol. 14; ragged top edge with some loss at top right corner.
Watermark: anchor (cut).

INSCRIPTION (on drawing *a*, upside down, brown ink) *pie 1–13/ fregio architraue/* [*.pie?. 2*] *pie 6 ongnicosa*; (to left of drawing *a*, reading upwards, brown ink) *Porta· diquesto tenpio*; (on drawing *b*) *13¾ lo uano*; (reading upwards) *alta louano pie XXV ¼*; (below drawing *b*, brown ink) *facciata· diquesto tempio · coe · le · carcere/ Li sua ·lacunarij · sono · dua architrauij luno/ sopra · laltro*; Numbering: (bottom right, graphite) *16*; (bottom centre, upside down, brown ink) *22*

Giovanni Battista draws a half-elevation/half-section of the front, *b*, because enough of the cella survived to make it worthwhile, unlike the middle temple. Most striking is that he reconstructs the temple with Corinthian capitals instead of Ionic, probably because he believed at the time that it formed a series with the Doric southern temple, and the Ionic middle temple. He appears to be supported by two of Antonio's drawings (U 1090A v.+1230A r. and U 1174A r.), which have accurately-drawn sections of the entablature with the same measurements as here, resting on Corinthian capitals. Accepting that the brothers were not deliberately ignoring the evidence, one must assume that the capitals were hidden by later accretions to the temple. However, one at least must have been visible long enough to have been seen by Baldassare Peruzzi, who notes on his plan (U 478A v.+631A r.) that the temple was Ionic, and Labacco's reconstructional elevation drawings and engraving make it so (Labacco 1559, pp. 23 f.).

Although the half-section allowed the *lacunarii* (ceiling coffers) to be illustrated without the need for separate detail drawing as in the case of the middle temple, whose coffers were the same type, Giovanni Battista still provides one, *c*. The third drawing at the top of the sheet, *a*, shows the top left corner of the cella door, which appears to have been of marble. Antonio the Younger drew the same detail (U 1174A v.) but it differs in showing the frieze as pulvinated and decorated with acanthus scroll. His measurements are independent of Giovanni Battista's but add up to the same overall height for the entablature. However, Antonio's two other studies of the door (U 1090A v.+1230A r. and U 1270A v.) both show the frieze to be vertical with no sign of decoration. On balance therefore, the present drawing can probably be trusted. The use of Roman numerals to express the height of the door is an idiosyncrasy shared by several of the Codex Rootstein Hopkins drawings (see fols 17 v., 18 v. and 19 v.) as well as some in the 'Corsini Incunabulum' (Rowland 2003, pl. 269).

One last drawing should be mentioned, U 1112A r., a freehand schematic sketch by Giovanni Battista of one column (with Corinthian capital) and of the door. All the measurements match those of the present drawing, and the phrasing of the annotation 'la colonna capitello e basa e alo pie 31–13' echoes those on other Codex Rootstein Hopkins drawings, suggesting a very close relationship. | IC

BIBLIOGRAPHY Campbell (2005) 53 f.; Campbell-Nesselrath (2006) 17 and 65.

CODEX ROOTSTEIN HOPKINS fol. 13 *verso*

GIOVANNI BATTISTA DA SANGALLO

Rome, North temple, Forum Holitorium, side elevation.

Dimensions see recto.
Technique Pen and brown ink with straightedge and freehand.
Paper see recto.

INSCRIPTION (below drawing, brown ink) *Ve[du]ta· perfiancho ·deltempio/ della· uirto adesso ditto lecar/ cere ·acanto · S·^{to}/ nichola*; Numbering: (bottom left, upside down, brown ink) *21*

The side elevation calls for little comment except to remark on the rustication of the cella walls, which Labacco (1559, 24) noted was of marble rather than stucco. Since he even says how thick the marble slabs were, he can probably be relied upon.

Giovanni Battista's schematic section of the entablature on U 1657A r., and Antonio's section of the entablature and colonnade on U 1174A r. have identical measurements. | IC

BIBLIOGRAPHY Campbell (2005) 54; Campbell-Nesselrath (2006) 66.

CODEX ROOTSTEIN HOPKINS fol. 14 *recto*

GIOVANNI BATTISTA DA SANGALLO

Rome, Doric temple, Forum Holitorium, plan.

Dimensions 275 × 210 mm.
Technique Pen and brown ink with straightedge and compass.
Paper was double folio with fol. 13; top right corner torn off; tear at bottom left corner.
Watermark: anchor (cut).

INSCRIPTION (on drawing, brown ink, except for last letters of 'aliquod' and 'nomen', which are black chalk) *OLIM/ TENPVM· HONORIS/ NUNC ·NON HABET/ ·ALIQUOD NOMEN/ ·e· acanto a sancto nichola/ in care ·ede toscano* (to right of drawing, reading upwards, dark brown ink) *Questa scalea· non ci poteua/ essere tutta ·p[er]che· le scale du/ naltro · tempio le impediuano*); Numbering: (bottom right, graphite) *17*; (bottom right, upside down, brown ink) *20*

The identification is discussed in the entry for fol. 11 r. The Doric temple was the subject of more drawings than its two neighbours, because examples of the Doric order were very rare in and around Rome, and the temple seems to have been well preserved until around 1520. Why it was demolished, apart from the short stretch of its northern colonnade incorporated in S. Nicola, is not known. It seems latterly to have been used to store hay (Crozzoli Aite 1981, p. 27), and may have been regarded as expendable. The canons of S. Nicola were granted a licence in 1506 to remove marble and travertine from the ruins around the church in order to widen the road in front (Lanciani 1902–12, I, p. 139), which they may not have acted on immediately. It may also have been used as a quarry for the building of the Palazzo Farnese since a note accompanying a drawing of part of the entablature of the door of the Doric temple on U 1658A v. says that it was then in the courtyard of that palace, where building began around 1514.

With the present plan, Giovanni Battista was more concerned in conforming to Vitruvius' precepts than recording it accurately. He admits that it could stand not on the stylobate he shows, because the middle temple is too near (the darker ink suggests this comment was added later), and the two elevation drawings (fols 14v. and 15r.) put it correctly on a podium. The cella, like that of the plan of the middle temple is open front and back, and has back and rear porches of equal size, with the walls of the cella extending out a full intercolumniation beyond the entrances at either end to make shallow pronaoses, following the illustrations in Fra Giocondo's Vitruvius of 1511.

No surviving Sangallo circle drawings provide exact parallels: Giovanni Battista's plan on U 1657A r. is close but it is not clear whether both ends are intended to be open and the cella walls extending only an anta beyond the entrances. Antonio's two theoretical studies on U 1090A r.+1230A v. and U 1174A r., both have only one entrance to the cella, although the cella walls do extend further. None has measurements which correspond closely. Two plans, one a survey of the pronaos and front part of the cella by Giovanni Francesco da Sangallo (U 1376A r.), and a schematic but measured one by Giovanni Battista (U 1377A r.) demonstrate that there was knowledge within the Sangallo circle that the pronaos was four columns deep and that behind the cella there was only a single intercolumniation.

On the left edge appears a scale in feet like that on fol. 6r., but in this case without any explanation. The two letters written in black chalk on the annotation in the cella appear to be later corrections (compare, fols 9v. and 11r.). | IC

BIBLIOGRAPHY Campbell (2005) 54; Campbell-Nesselrath (2006) 67.

CODEX ROOTSTEIN HOPKINS fol. 14 *verso*

GIOVANNI BATTISTA DA SANGALLO

Rome, Doric temple, Forum Holitorium,
side elevation and detail.

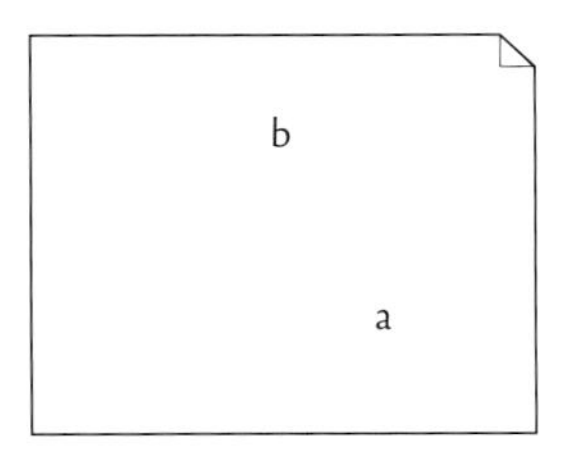

Dimensions see recto.
Technique Pen and brown ink with straightedge, compass and freehand.
Paper see recto.

INSCRIPTION (on drawing *a*, brown ink) *La colonna ·ecapitello/ alta*; *La colonna elcapitello ·alta ·pie 17½*; (on drawing *b*, brown ink) *Veduta per fiancho ·del tenpio canto Sto ·nichola incarcere*; (right of drawing, reading upwards, brown ink) *Da questa Banda ·non ·poteua/ essere· scalee p[er] che lo tempio di Sto/ nichola incarcere liera ·presso/ a sette ·piedi emezo*; Numbering: (bottom centre, upside down, brown ink) *19*

The side elevation, *b*, follows the plan except for correctly replacing the stylobate with a podium. Measured drawings by Giovanni Battista (U 1883A v.) and Giovanni Francesco da Sangallo with Antonio the Younger (U 1372A r.) reveal that the podium was visible at some time, although Baldassare Peruzzi shows the temple on a stylobate on his otherwise exemplary view (U 477A r.; Bartoli 1914–22, III, fig. 321, VI, p. 59).

The detail *a* shows a side intercolumniation with two columns of the pronaos in elevation and the entablature and roof in section. Instead of the ceiling coffers of the two Ionic temples, here there is a narrow barrel vault, which, one assumes, extended the length of the peristyle.

Giovanni Battista's U 1657A r. and Antonio the Younger's U 1090A r.+1230A v., U 1233A v. and 1270A r. all have parallels of the entablature section with the same measurements and the vault. Antonio's U 1174A v. has a section of the opposite corner, also hinting at a vault. However, on the recto of the same sheet, another section, despite having the same measurements for the entablature shows a coffer over the intercolumniation, like those of its neighbour. It must be dismissed a theoretical aberration, rather than a record. Another section of the same detail on U 1377A v., by Giovanni Battista, again shows the vault. It is measured with the Florentine *braccio* and hence is not dependent on the present drawings and perhaps can be regarded as more reliable.

Perhaps an even more interesting feature of this detail is the treatment of the capital as an enriched Doric, with the echinus decorated with egg-and-dart over two beaded astragals. It is only paralleled on the profile on Giovanni Battista's own U 1883A v. No other draughtsman depicts it so, making one doubt his veracity, even allowing it to be a reconstruction of a stucco detail. Measured drawings by Giovanni Francesco da Sangallo (U 1376A v.), Bernardo della Volpaia (London, Sir John Soane's Museum, 'Codex Coner', fol. 81r.; Ashby 1904, no. 106) agree in showing a more complex profile. The details of the frieze are similarly a reconstruction, and no drawings appear to record extant fragments. | IC

BIBLIOGRAPHY Campbell (2005) 55; Campbell-Nesselrath (2006) 17 and 68.

CODEX ROOTSTEIN HOPKINS fol. 15 *recto*

Giovanni Battista da Sangallo

Rome, Doric temple, Forum Holitorium, front elevation and door.

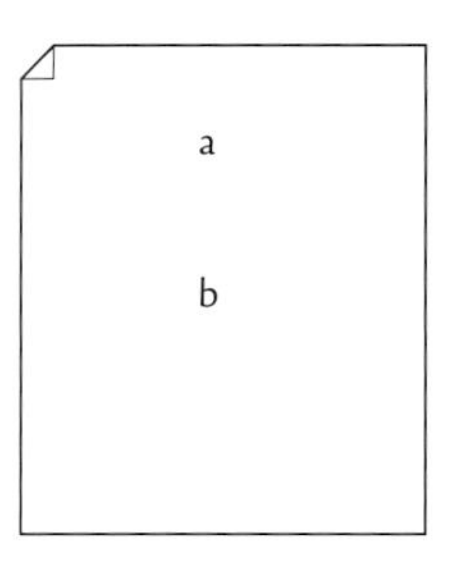

Dimensions 277 × 210 mm.
Technique Pen and brown ink with straightedge and freehand.
Paper was double folio with fol. 16; tear top left; top right corner torn and ragged; tears on right edge; bottom left corner tear; repair strip on left edge.

INSCRIPTION (on drawing *a*, upside down, brown ink) *alta·louano pie 13¾*; (reading upwards) *la pie larga louano pie 6–6*; (right of drawing *a*, reading upwards, brown ink) *Porta ·doricha Diquesto tempio sta cosi*; (below drawing *b*, brown ink) *facciata · deltempio doricho ·canto S*[to]*/ nichola · incarcere*; Numbering: (bottom right, graphite) *18*; (bottom right, upside down, brown ink) *18*

The front elevation, shown correctly on a podium, is subordinate to drawing 'A, an elevation of the cella door. The many measurements on drawing *a* suggest it is the result of careful survey, and they are repeated on details of the door on Antonio the Younger's U 1174A r. and v. However the latter makes the ovolo moulding, where the cornice meets the architrave, project much further laterally, and the same detail is even more pronounced on Peruzzi's U 477A r. (Bartoli 1914–22, III, fig. 321, VI, p. 59), which can probably be relied upon. Peruzzi says the doorframe was marble. | IC

BIBLIOGRAPHY Campbell (2005) 54 f.; Campbell-Nesselrath (2006) 17 and 69.

CODEX ROOTSTEIN HOPKINS fol. 15 *verso*

Giovanni Battista da Sangallo

Rome, Temple of Vespasian, plan.

Dimensions see recto.
Technique Pen and brown ink with straightedge and compass.
Paper see recto.

INSCRIPTION (on drawing, brown ink, some black chalk) *TENPIO SOTTO CA[M]PITOLGIO/ DOVE SON QVELLE TRE/ COLONNE INTERZO/ HOPERA ·CORINTIA*

The plan is a reconstruction of the Temple of the Deified Vespasian and Titus, begun in AD 79 and restored in the third century Septimius Severus and Caracalla (De Angeli 1992; LTUR, V, 124 f.[S. De Angeli]; Claridge 1998, p. 79). It occupied a tight site at the west end of the Forum Romanum hard up against the Capitoline Hill, The pronaos was six columns wide by three deep with a short cella behind extending the whole width of the prostyle temple. The lack of space probably accounts for the interruption of the steps at the front by the pedestals of the Corinthian columns. By the Renaissance, only three columns at the front right corner supporting a fragment of entablature were extant. Although they frequently appear half-buried or more in views of the Forum, drawings by Bernardo della Volpaia in the Codex Coner (Ashby 1904, no. 67) and by an anonymous draughtsman in the Codex Escuraliensis (Egger 1906, I, p. 79, II, pl. XX) demonstrate that they were fully exposed at some point in the early sixteenth century.

Giovanni Battista's plan wrongly reconstructs the temple as a peripteral *sine postico*, very similar to the north temple of the Forum Holitorium (fol. 12v.). This means we cannot place any credence in the measurements other than those that can be extrapolated from the three surviving columns. The plan also errs in assuming that the steps stopped in front of the columns, which is strange, since the drawing of the column base on the next folio (fol. 16r. *b*) demonstrates some knowledge of the lower parts of the temple. The annotation shows some black chalk, apparently correcting the spelling of Campidoglio.

Antonio the Younger drew a part plan, strictly paralleling every detail and measurement here, on U 1140A r., but he does not merely copy his brother. He adds information such as the distance from the front of the temple to the Tabularium built into the Capitoline Hill behind. He includes another plan of the three extant columns, locating them again in relation to the Tabularium. | IC

BIBLIOGRAPHY Campbell (2005) 8, 10 and 56; Campbell-Nesselrath (2006) 33, n. 4 and 70.

CODEX ROOTSTEIN HOPKINS fol. 16 *recto*

GIOVANNI BATTISTA DA SANGALLO

Rome, Temple of Vespasian, front elevation and detail.

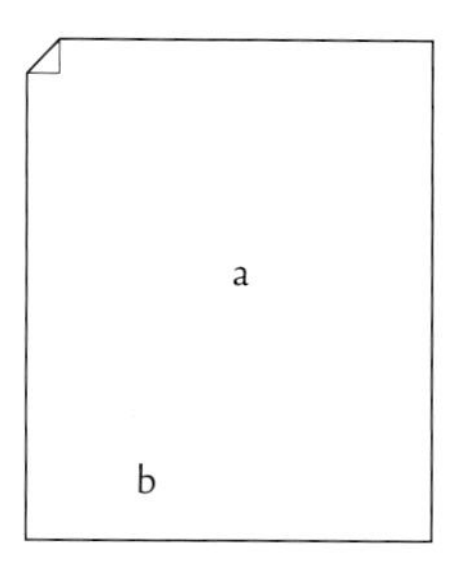

Dimensions 277 × 210 mm.
Technique Pen and brown ink with straightedge and freehand.
Paper was double folio with fol. 15; loss from tears in middle of top edge and top right corner, repair strip on right edge; tear in middle of bottom edge.

INSCRIPTION (on drawing 'a.', brown ink) *IMP ·CAES ·L ·PATE SEVE P CVES CA S III COS/ SE ·S·BE CAES· AN·TO·M · DE SIC · CAS ·CAG IIII CA SI*; (darker brown ink) STITVER; (reading upwards) *lo fuso della colonna senza basa/ senza ·capitello sie pie 39–10*; (below drawing *a*, darker brown ink) *FACIATA·DIQVESTA PIANTA QVI/ DACANTO ·CHESONO ·QVELLE ·TRE/ COLONE SOTO ·CAMPIDOLGLIO*; Numbering: (bottom right, graphite) *19*; (bottom right, upside down, brown ink) *16*

The front elevation appears strange at first sight in that the side intercolumniations are shown both with diagonal hatching to represent voids and with rustication, which must belong to the rear wall of the temple, unlike the elevation of the north temple of the Forum Holitorium (fol. 12r.), which had a similar plan, but which only has the hatching. The heights given for the base, shaft and capital correspond well to the actual 48 Roman feet (14.2 m).

Only the final word, STITVER ('restored') was actually extant from the inscription on the entablature. A vertical line to the left of STITUER marks the break. The complete inscription CIL VI. 938), was seen by a ninth-century monk in the 'Einsideln Itinerary' when it was still intact, who transcribed it thus: *divo Vespasiano Augusto* SPQR/ *Im Caes. Severus et Antoninus Pii felices Augg. restituerunt.* Giovanni Battista's attempt at reconstruction is very garbled but the words IMP.CAES ... SEVE and ANTOM appear to echo Severus and 'Antoninus' in the original. Antonio's drawing of just the entablature and pediment on U 1140A r. says that the inscription was taken from a 'Libro delli epitaffij', indicating they had access to some so far unidentified sylloge of epigraphic material (Giovannoni 1959, p. 25).

The detail of the base, *b*, is accurately drawn and measured, and has an exact parallel on Antonio's U 1140A v., which adds an annotation about the heights of the base, shaft and capital all corresponding to the present drawing. | IC

BIBLIOGRAPHY Campbell (2005) 56; Campbell-Nesselrath (2006) 71.

CODEX ROOTSTEIN HOPKINS fol. 16 *verso*

GIOVANNI BATTISTA DA SANGALLO

Rome, Temple of Vespasian, side elevation.

Dimensions see recto.
Technique Pen and brown ink with straightedge and freehand.
Paper see recto.

INSCRIPTION (on drawing, thick brown ink) *Veduta perfiancho ·deltempio/ diquelle ·tre colonne sotto cam/ pitolglio doue scritto entro stituer*); Numbering: (bottom left, upside down, brown ink) *15*

The side elevation is a conjectural and inaccurate reconstruction apart from the two columns of the pronaos of the front portico on the left and the entablature over. The decoration of the frieze is based on the extant fragment.

There are no related drawings. | IC

BIBLIOGRAPHY Campbell (2005) 56; Campbell-Nesselrath (2006) 72.

CODEX ROOTSTEIN HOPKINS fol. 17 *recto*

GIOVANNI BATTISTA DA SANGALLO

Rome, Temple of Vespasian, details.

Dimensions 277 × 210 mm.
Technique Pen and brown ink with straightedge and freehand.
Paper loose; top right corner torn; patch bottom left corner.

INSCRIPTION (on drawing, thick brown ink) *Cornice· diquesto tempio ·disopra/ chedi sotto a campidolglio*; (brown ink) *Questa cosa sfonda quanta/ dagetto Questo intauolato piu/ chel uiuo*; (thick brown ink) STITVER; (right of drawing, reading upwards, brown ink) *Lo capitello alto/ pie 5½*; (to right of drawing, brown ink) drawing scale showing four Roman feet, subdivided into halves, quarters and 16 *dita*; Numbering: (bottom right, graphite) *20*; (bottom centre, upside down, brown ink) *14*

The drawing is a beautifully-drawn detail of the extant part of the front entablature and the upper parts of the two Corinthian capitals. It is paralleled on U 1140A v. by Antonio, who omits the capitals but provides an adjacent detail of the abacus of a capital including the decoration omitted by Giovanni Battista. Antonio's entablature also differs in drawing the dripstone moulding partly in section rather than elevation, permitting him to show the coffers between the modillions. Again this demonstrates that Antonio was not relying entirely on the Codex Rootstein Hopkins. | IC

BIBLIOGRAPHY Campbell (2005) 56 f.; Campbell-Nesselrath (2006) 22 and 73.

CODEX ROOTSTEIN HOPKINS fol. 17 *verso*

Giovanni Battista da Sangallo

Rome, Temple A, Largo Argentina, plan.

Dimensions see recto.
Technique Pen and brown ink with straightedge and compass.
Paper see recto.

INSCRIPTION (on drawing) *TEMPIO DOPERA CORINTIA/ EDE DI TVFO COPERTO DI/STVCHI ·DRIETO ·ALLA/CASA DE CESERINI/EDE ·ADESO VNA/CHIESA CHIA/·MASI/S^to^ NICCOLA*; Numbering: (bottom left, upside down, brown ink) *13*

The plan depicts the northernmost of four temples built in a row in the middle of what is now the Largo Argentina. They all date from pre-imperial times, and, even more than the comparable Forum Holitorium temples, there is debate over identifying which temple belonged to which god. Temple A is possibly dedicated to Juturna (LTUR, III, 162 f. [F. Coarelli]]; Claridge 1998, pp. 215–8). It was a peripteral temple, six columns wide by nine long with the front porch three columns deep, and no rear porch. The tufa podium and columns, all originally covered in stucco appear to date from the mid-late 1st century BC. Two travertine columns at front right probably date from restoration after a great fire in AD 80. It survived better than its neighbours because the church of S. Nicola dei Cesarini was established in it in 1132, but it was little regarded during the Renaissance and the present drawing and the parallel by Antonio on U 1140A r. are the only ones known. It may have come to Antonio's attention as early as 1506 when he drew the door of the house of Cardinal Giulio Cesarini (U 2049Ar.; Frommel 1994, *Introduction*, p. 18), which was part of his family's residential complex at this site.

Giovanni Battista makes it conform to the ideal Vitruvian peripteral, six by eleven columns on a stylobate, with a cella open at both ends, as interpreted by Fra Giocondo. It is almost identical apart from the measurements to the plan of the middle Forum Holitorium temple (fol. 11r.). Antonio's version of the plan on U 1140A r., has the same measurements but is much more cautious, in only showing the six columns at the front, extending two back on the south side, and the left corner of the cella. The accompanying annotation does not describe the overall form of the temple. One suspects that Antonio's drawing represents what was to be seen, from which Giovanni Battista has reconstructed the whole rather cavalierly. It is notable that no reconstruction elevation accompanies the plan. | IC

BIBLIOGRAPHY Campbell (2005) 57; Campbell-Nesselrath (2006) 17 and 74.

CODEX ROOTSTEIN HOPKINS fol. 18 *recto*

Blank.

Dimensions 278 × 211 mm.

Paper double folio with fol. 21.

INSCRIPTION Numbering (bottom right, graphite) *21*; (bottom right, upside down, brown ink) *12*

BIBLIOGRAPHY Campbell (2005) 57; Campbell-Nesselrath (2006) 75. | IC

CODEX ROOTSTEIN HOPKINS fol. 18 *verso*

Giovanni Battista da Sangallo

Rome, Temple of Saturn, plan.

Dimensions see recto.
Technique Pen and brown ink with straightedge and compass.
Paper see recto.

INSCRIPTION (on drawing, brown ink) *TENPIO APRESO A CA[M]PITOLGLIO/FATTO DISPOGLIE NEIONI· CHO NECORINTIO CHIA/MATO LO INCENDIO/COSA DA FARNE/ POCHO CONTO/SOLO LOFA/TTO PER/MOSTRATI PIU COSE CHE/SIA ·POSSIBILE*; Numbering: (bottom left, upside down, brown ink) *11*

The Temple of Saturn was a very old foundation, perhaps as early as 497 BC, but the present remains only date back to a restoration about AD 360–80, after a fire (LTUR, V, 234–6

[F. Coarelli]; Claridge 1998, pp. 80 f.) It was a prostyle temple, consisting of a pronaos six columns wide by two deep with the cella behind, all standing on a podium. All that survives are the columns of the pronaos and the entablature over. Poggio Bracciolini in his *De Varietate Fortunae* (Valentini-Zucchetti 1940–53, IV, p.235) reported that the cella had been virtually intact when he first came to Rome around 1403, but by the time he was writing (ca. 1448), it was reduced to its present state with only the pronaos standing. Apart from the Ionic capitals, carved from new marble, all the materials are *spolia*, re-used from earlier buildings. The architrave blocks and four of the column bases are datable to about 30 BC and may have been salvaged from the previous temple. The other four bases are of mixed date and origin. The column shafts, six grey granite shafts at the front and two pink to the sides come from several different colonnades.

Giovanni Battista's plan draws the pronaos accurately and reconstructs the cella as almost square, on the basis of the podium. In his annotation he calls it the 'Fire', having misunderstood the inscription (see fol. 19 r.). He recognises that it is made up of various *spolia* and includes it more for curiosity value than as an exemplar to be imitated.

Antonio's parallel plan on U 1140A v. only includes the pronaos and part of the front wall of the cella but he includes the same dimensions of the cella as his brother, allowing it to be fully reconstructed. | IC

BIBLIOGRAPHY Campbell (2005) 57; Campbell-Nesselrath (2006) 17 and 76.

CODEX ROOTSTEIN HOPKINS fol. 19 *recto*

Giovanni Battista da Sangallo

Rome, Temple of Saturn, front elevation and details.

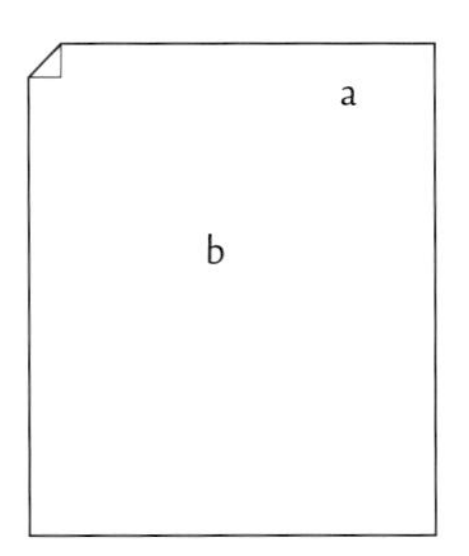

Dimensions 278 × 211 mm.
Technique Pen and brown ink with straightedge and freehand.
Paper was double folio with fol. 20; top right corner torn.
Watermark: anchor (cut).

INSCRIPTION (right of drawing *a*, reading upwards, brown ink) *La suo basa di questo/ tenpio benche· tutte e di spolg[lie*; (on drawing *b*) *SENATVS · POPOLVS·Q·ROMANVS/ INCENDIO · CONSVMPTVM · RESTITVIT*; Numbering: (bottom right, graphite) *22*; (bottom right, upside down, brown ink) *10*

The principal drawing, *b*, reconstructs the front elevation. The inscription is accurately transcribed (CIL, VI. 937). The note that the dado of the cella wall was of stucco suggests that some fragments were still *in situ*.

Drawing *a* is the profile of one of the four column bases dating from about 30 BC, probably salvaged from the earlier temple as discussed on fol. 18v. (on these bases see Pensabene 1984, 115 f., nos 56–8 and 60).

On U 1140A v., Antonio conflates and adds to the information from the two drawings here into a single drawing. It has a measured base, a very squat shaft, but with the same measurement as on our present drawing, the capital drawn in more detail, and the entablature with measurements, including a profile of the architrave at the side. Again this may suggest Antonio was not dependent on the present drawing, but it is possible that a lost folio from the codex contained drawings of the capital and probably of the side elevation. | IC

BIBLIOGRAPHY Campbell (2005) 58; Campbell-Nesselrath (2006) 22 and 77.

CODEX ROOTSTEIN HOPKINS fol. 19 *verso*

Giovanni Battista da Sangallo

Rome, Temple of Castor and Pollux, plan.

Dimensions see recto.
Technique Pen and brown ink with straightedge and compass.
Paper see recto.

INSCRIPTION (on drawing, brown ink) *OPERA CORINTIA*; *Tempio anticho ·scontro/ altempio dantonino et/ faustina ditto adesso letre/ Colonne ··Antichamente/ sidomandaua lotempio*; *XXXXIIIJ½/ pie larga*; (right of drawing, brown ink) two drawing scales in units of ten feet, some subdivided; Numbering: (bottom left, upside down, brown ink) *9*

The Temple of Castor and Pollux was one of the oldest in Rome, founded in 484 BC. The present remains date back to a rebuilding by Augustus, dedicated in AD 6. The podium was originally 32m wide, 50m long and 7m high. On it stood the peripteral temple, eight columns wide by eleven long, the Corinthian columns 50 Roman feet (14.8m) high. It was already in a ruinous state by the fourth century and by the fifteenth only the present three columns and their entablature were extant (LTUR, I, 242–5 [I. Nielsen]; Claridge 1998, pp. 91 f.).

The plan reconstructs the temple as an ideal Vitruvian peripteral, eleven columns long by six wide, on a stylobate, with the Fra Giocondo-type cella, open at both ends. Although the front wall of the cella is measured it cannot be relied upon since the door would have been aligned on the middle of the octastyle façade. The longer of the two drawing scales appears less complete and was probably abandoned in favor of the shorter one.

There are no other plans of the temple in the Sangallo circle. Enough evidence was available for Andrea Palladio (1508–80) to reconstruct it as octastyle in his *Four Books* (1570, Bk. IV, 68), albeit with fifteen columns along the sides. | IC

BIBLIOGRAPHY Campbell (2005) 58; Campbell-Nesselrath (2006) 17 and 78.

CODEX ROOTSTEIN HOPKINS fol. 20 *recto*

Giovanni Battista da Sangallo

Rome, Temple of Castor and Pollux,
front elevation and detail.

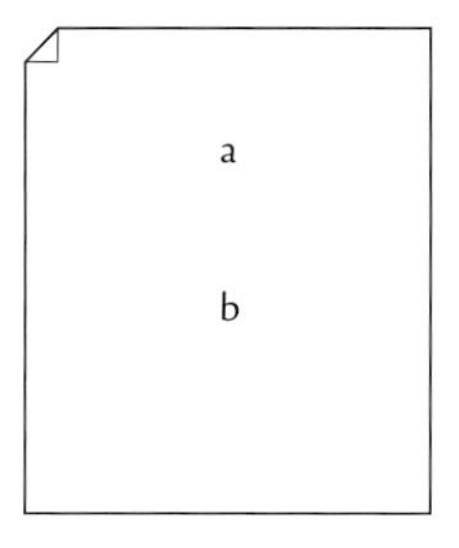

Dimensions 278 × 210 mm.
Technique Pen and brown ink with straightedge and freehand.
Paper was double folio with fol. 19; top right corner torn. *Watermark*: anchor (cut).

INSCRIPTION (right of drawing *a*, reading upwards, brown ink) *La basa ·delle ·tre colonne ·diquesto tempio*; (below drawing *b*, thick brown ink) *Questa facciata ·sie di questa pianta da canto/ oggi sidomanda letre colonne elnome/ anticho I nolloso chome si chiamaua) / Le colonne sono scanalate ·da imo a som*[*m*]*o*; Numbering: (bottom right, graphite) [2]*3*; (bottom right, upside down, brown ink)

The front elevation, *b* corresponds to the plan in placing the temple on a stylobate. Antonio Labacco reconstructed the temple in a very similar manner, both drawn and engraved (Windsor Royal Library, inv. 19278; Campbell 2004, I, pp. 114 f., no. 21; and Labacco 1559, p. 20).

Drawing *a* is a carefully-drawn measured section of a column base from the temple. A similar section is drawn by Giovanni Francesco da Sangallo on U 1650A r. but it is copied from Giuliano da Sangallo's Barberini Codex (BAV, Barb. lat. 4424, fol. 63r.; Huelsen 1910, p. 66) and is measured in Florentine *minuti.* | IC

BIBLIOGRAPHY Campbell (2005) 58; Campbell-Nesselrath (2006) 79.

CODEX ROOTSTEIN HOPKINS fol. 20 *verso*

Giovanni Battista da Sangallo

Rome, Temple of Castor and Pollux, side elevation.

Dimensions see recto.
Technique Pen and brown ink with straightedge and freehand.
Paper see recto; ink marks, some matching those on fol. 21r.

INSCRIPTION (below drawing) *La veduta ·Per fiancho ·del tempio ditto ·oggi letre colonne / Dirinpeto ·a· antonino ·et faustina Rome*; Numbering: (bottom left, upside down, brown ink) *7*

The side elevation is in the standard manner for the codex. Although not drawn in detail, the capitals here and on the previous folio are large enough to see that they do not have the characteristic interlinked volutes, which make the temple's capitals so distinctive. It must surely have been originally intended to include drawings of the capitals and the very handsome entablature. It is worth remarking that Giovanni Battista's earliest known work is an intervention to a Sangallo circle drawing of the profile of the entablature on U 1181A v., datable to ca. 1513–15. | IC

BIBLIOGRAPHY Campbell (2005) 58; Campbell-Nesselrath (2006) 24, 38, n. 64, and 80; Fane-Saunders (2016) 277.

CODEX ROOTSTEIN HOPKINS fol. 21 *recto*

Ink marks.

Dimensions 277 × 210 mm.

Paper was double folio with fol. 18; top right corner torn.
INSCRIPTION Numbering: (bottom right, graphite) *24*; (bottom right, upside down, brown ink) *6*

BIBLIOGRAPHY Campbell (2005) 59; Campbell-Nesselrath (2006) 81. | IC

CODEX ROOTSTEIN HOPKINS fol. 21 *verso*

Giovanni Battista da Sangallo

Rome, Temple of Minerva: Forum of Nerva, plan.

Dimensions see recto.
Technique Pen and brown ink with straightedge and compass.
Paper see recto; some ink marks have soaked through from recto.

INSCRIPTION (on drawing, brown ink) *Tenpio ·di nerua ·fatto/ nel foro transitorio*; *A nerua traiano*; (right of drawing, brown ink) *Piaza di foro/ transitorio ·con/ quel· procinto ·di/ colonne intorno*; drawing scale in units of ten feet, some subdivided; Numbering: (bottom left, upside down, brown ink) *5*

The emperor Domitian began building the temple to his favorite goddess Minerva, but it was finished and dedicated by his successor Nerva in AD 97, who gave his name to the surrounding forum, which filled the narrow space between the Forum of Augustus to the north west and Vespasian's Forum of Peace to the south-east (Meneghini 1991; LTUR, II, 307–11 [H. Bauer/C. Morselli]; Claridge 1998, pp. 156 f.). An existing thoroughfare ran through it from the Roman Forum to the densely-populated Suburra, hence its alternative name 'Forum Transitorium'. The temple was a prostyle, six columns wide by three deep, with an unusual pattern of different widths of intercolumniations to the front, and restricted space for the cella behind. It was flanked by arches leading through to the Suburra, and the lateral walls of the forum were embellished with about twenty bays of Corinthian columns, linked by projecting entablatures to the enclosing wall. Extensive remains of the temple survived until its complete destruction by Pope Paul V in 1606.

The present plan depicts the temple accurately, even the unusual rectangular recess at the back of the cella, often reconstructed as an apse. The flanking arches of the forum are included as far as the width of the folio allows, and, to the left of the cella, part of the south-east exedra of the Forum of Augustus.

Various plans of the temple and forum do survive from the Sangallo circle do survive but none appear to be closely related. | IC

BIBLIOGRAPHY Campbell (2005) 59; Campbell-Nesselrath (2006) 82.

CODEX ROOTSTEIN HOPKINS fol. 22 *recto*

Giovanni Battista da Sangallo

Rome, Temple of Minerva: Forum of Nerva, front elevation and details.

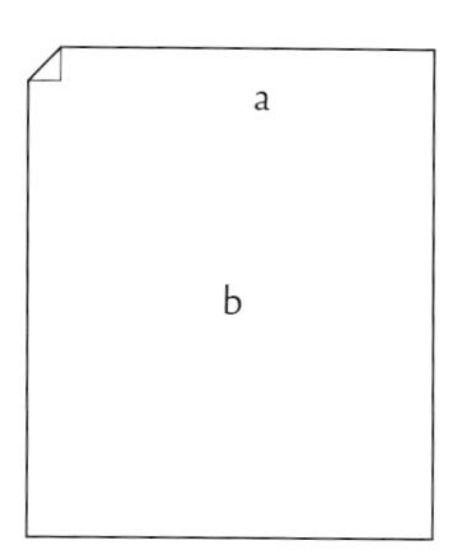

Dimensions 278 × 210 mm.
Technique Drawing *a*, pen and brown ink with straightedge and freehand; drawing *b*, Pen and brown ink with straightedge and compass.
Paper was double folio with fol. 23; loose; top right corner torn/worn; tear at top left; rectangular loss and tear at bottom left corner.

INSCRIPTION (on drawing *b*, thick brown ink) *IMP·NERVA·CAESAR·AVG·GERMANICO ·DATICO COS XII/ TRIB·POTEST· II·IMP·II ANT DII CVR SPQR·*; (brown ink) *una cornice gira/ intorno alarcho/ no[n]ne architraue/ tutta dentro allarcho*; (reading upwards, brown ink) *La colonna ecapitello ebasa 36*; *la colonna senza basa senza/ capitello alta pie XXXViiii-6*; *lacolonna ecapitello ebasa/ sie pie XXXVI*; (below drawing) *La facciata · di questa ·pianta ·qui dacanto ·del tempio/ Di nerua traiano et ·una particella ·del procinto della/ Piaza come uedi ·Qui staua ·apresso ·le colonne deltem/ Pio ·e· quelle · delpro cinto ·son tutte scanalate benche ibo/ nollo· mostri ·col disengno · Presente nelle Resto si uedea*

The front elevation of the temple and flanking arches of the forum are reconstructed in great detail in drawing *b*, all apparently carefully measured. However, there is no evidence that the archways to either side were flanked by columns. It is likely that Giovanni Battista is taking his cue from the one surviving lateral bay of the forum, the Colonnacce. The inscription is correctly transcribed over the three columns on the left, where it was extant (CIL VI. 953). A thick vertical line shows the break. The rest is invented.

The detail *a* represents the attic of the enclosing wall and the cornice of the entablature below. The attic cornice and base moulding are paralleled on Antonio the Younger's U 1140A r. with the same measurements. | IC

BIBLIOGRAPHY Campbell (2005) 59; Campbell-Nesselrath (2006) 22 and 83.

CODEX ROOTSTEIN HOPKINS fol. 22 *verso*

Giovanni Battista da Sangallo

Rome, Temple of Minerva: Forum of Nerva, side elevation and details.

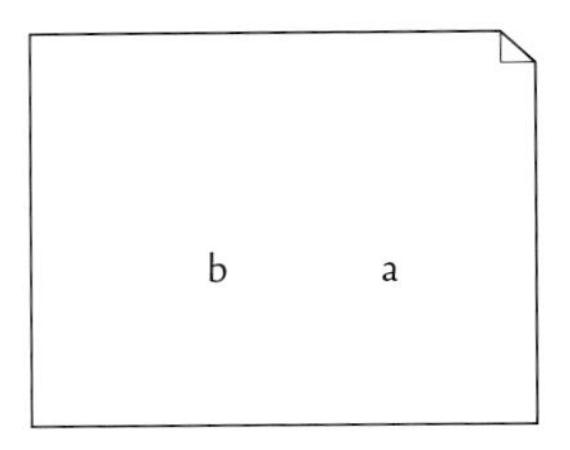

Dimensions see recto.
Technique Pen and brown ink with straightedge and freehand.
Paper see recto.

INSCRIPTION (on drawing *a*, reading upwards, brown ink) *canali del pilastro/ son sette*; (on drawing *b*, reading upwards, brown ink) *Basa · di queste colonne di sopra / Di nerua traiano*; (on drawing *c*, key letters, brown ink) *A, B*; (reading upwards) *la colonna · senza basa senza · capitello alta pie 39–9*; (below drawing *c*, brown ink) *Veduta p[er] fiancho del tempio · di nerua traiano/ nelforo transitorio cioe · quello direto qui*; Numbering: (bottom left, upside down, brown ink) *3*

The side elevation, drawing *c*, only incorporates the pronaos, ignoring the cella wall, which stood outside the forum. The section through the wall and flanking arch is accompanied by a wealth of measurements (not all of which can be believed if the arches were not flanked by columns as discussed on fol. 22r.). Key letters *A* and *B* refer to the drawings on fols 23r. and v.

Drawings *a* and *b* are sections through the bases of the pilaster and column of the temple respectively, with part elevations of the bottom of the shafts. Although the bases have the same measurements, the fluting of the shafts differs, hence the need for two drawings. | IC

BIBLIOGRAPHY Campbell (2005) 59 f.; Campbell-Nesselrath (2006) 84.

CODEX ROOTSTEIN HOPKINS fol. 23 *recto*

Giovanni Battista da Sangallo

Rome, Forum of Nerva, details of the 'Colonnacce'.

Dimensions ca. 268 × 210 mm.
Technique Pen and brown ink with straightedge and freehand.
Paper was double folio with fol. 22; top edge partly lost through wear; tears on lower right edge and bottom left corner; water stain at bottom left.

INSCRIPTION (top margin) TENPII; (below drawing, brown ink) · *La cornice · delle colonne delprocinto/ · di foro transitorio · dinerua traiano / Segnata · B · ·nella carta · doue lo tempio/ in faccia et · lo procinto lobi sengnato/ nel fregio · elqua fregio · e· intalgliato/ TVTTO a fiure*; Numbering: (bottom right, graphite) 26 (bottom right, upside down, brown ink) 2

The drawing combines an elevation and a section detailing the capital and entablature of the 'Colonnacce', including the reliefs of the frieze, with the attic above. Although the key letter 'B' relates to the bay with the arch flanking the temple, the reliefs are probably those of the 'Colonnacce'. | IC

BIBLIOGRAPHY Campbell (2005) 60; Campbell-Nesselrath (2006) 12 and 85.

CODEX ROOTSTEIN HOPKINS fol. 23 *verso*

Giovanni Battista da Sangallo

Rome, Forum of Nerva, details of the Temple of Minerva.

Dimensions see recto.
Technique Pen and brown ink with straightedge and freehand.
Paper see recto; repair patch at bottom right corner.

INSCRIPTION (on drawing, brown ink) *Cornicione · grande · del tempio · chede/ nel foro dinerua traiano chi uedi Qui/ Disopra segnato · A · e de tutta intalglia/ ta · Come · uedi*; *Questo · e · lo risalto · chefa/ La cornice apartirssi · da e/ pilastri edi sopra · le colonne/ Risalta tutta ·ladiminuitione/ Della colon[n]a*; (bottom right on patch) = *fin*[e]; Numbering: (bottom right corner on patch, upside down, brown ink) > *1* <

The drawing combines an elevation and section of the main entablature and capitals of the temple, corresponding to the key letter 'A' on fol. 22v. | IC

BIBLIOGRAPHY Campbell (2005) 60; Campbell-Nesselrath (2006) 86.

Bibliography

Ackerman (1954)
Ackerman, James S. *The Cortile del Belvedere* (Rome).

Adam (1994)
Adam, Jean-Pierre. *Le Temple de Portunus au Forum Boarium* (Collection de l'École Française de Rome, 199) (Rome).

Adams-Pepper (1994)
Adams, Nicholas, and Simon Pepper "The Fortification Drawings," in *The Architectural Drawings of Antonio da Sangallo the Younger and His Circle*, vol. 1, *Fortifications, Machines, and Festival Architecture*, ed. C.L. Frommel and N. Adams (Cambridge, Mass., London): 61–74.

Alfieri (1936)
Alfieri, Nereo. "Ricina," *Atti e Memorie della Reale Deputazione di Storia Patria per le Marche* 5: 1–21.

Ambrogi (1993)
Ambrogi, Annarena. "Sarcofagi in granito di produzione egiziana," *Xenia Antiqua*, 2: 103–10.

Ambrogi (1995)
Ambrogi, Annarena. *Vasche di età romana in marmi bianchi e colorati* (Rome).

Antonucci (2008)
Antonucci, Micaela. *Palazzo della Zecca in Banchi* (Rome).

Ashby (1904)
Ashby, Thomas. "Sixteenth-Century Drawings of Roman Buildings Attributed to Andreas Coner," *Papers of the British School at Rome* 2: 1–96.

Bacile di Castiglione (1903)
Bacile di Castiglione, Gennaro. "La Rocca Paolina," *L'Arte* 6: 347–67.

Bartoli (1914–22)
Bartoli, Alfonso. *I monumenti antichi di Roma nei disegni degli Uffizi*, 6 vols (Rome).

Bartsch (2019)
Bartsch, Tatjana. *Maarten van Heemskerck. Römische Studien zwischen Sachlichkeit und Imagination* (Munich).

Beltrami (1902)
Beltrami, Luca. *Relazione sullo stato delle rocche di Romagna stesa nel per ordine di Clemente VII da Antonio da Sangallo il Giovane e Michele Sanmicheli* (Milan).

Benelli (2014, *Tempio*)
Benelli, Francesco. "L'interpretazione di Antonio da Sangallo il Giovane del tempio 'in antis' dedotta da Vitruvio e dalle rovine," in eds. M. Basso, J. Gritti, and O. Lanzarini, *The Gordian Knot* (Rome) 175–84.

Benelli (2014, *Fra Giocondo*)
Benelli, Francesco: "Secondo fra Giocondo. Antonio da Sangallo il Giovane e l'edizione di Giocondo del 1513 del Metropolitan Museum of Art di New York," in eds. Gros e P.N. Pagliara, *Giovanni Giocondo/umanista, architetto e antiquario* (Vicenza, Venica) 54–55.

Benelli (2018, *Vitruvian Pantheon*)
Benelli, Francesco, "Antonio da Sangallo the Younger and a Vitruvian Pantheon for Leo X," *Pegasus* 18/19: 73–114.

Benelli (2018 *Sostegno e adornamento*)
Benelli, Francesco. "'Sostegno e adornamento'. La versione di Antonio." in eds. M. Beltramini and C. Conti, *Antonio da Sangallo il Giovane: architettura e decorazione da Leone X a Paolo III* (Milan): 43–54.

Bentivoglio (1972)
Bentivoglio, Enzo. "Il progetto per Palazzo Medici in Piazza Navona di Giuliano da Sangallo," *L'architettura cronache e storia* 18: 196–204.

Bentivoglio (1987)
Bentivoglio, Enzo. "Vestigia romane nella porta del Popolo integrate nell'ornamentazione di Nanni di Baccio Bigio," *Saggi in onore di Guglielmo de Angelis d'Ossat. Quaderni dell'Istituto di Storia dell'Architettura* n.s. 1–10: 261–72.

Benzi (2000)
Benzi, Fabio. "Baccio Pontelli a Roma e il Codex Escurialensis," in ed. F. Benzi, *Sisto IV Le Arti a Roma nel Primo Rinascimento* (Rome), 475–96.

Berckenhagen (1970)
Berckenhagen, Ekhart. *Die französischen Zeichnungen der Kunstbibliothek Berlin* (Berlin).

Biermann (1970)
Biermann, Hartmut. "Das Palastmodell Giuliano da Sangallos für Ferdinand I. König von Neapel," *Wiener Jahrbuch für Kunstgeschichte* 23: 154–95.

Bober (1957)
Bober, Phyllis Pray. *Drawings after the antique by Amico Aspertini: sketchbooks in the British Museum* (London).

Bober and Rubinstein (1986)
Bober, Phyllis Pray, and Ruth Rubinstein. *Renaissance artists & antique sculpture: a handbook of sources* (London).

Borgatti (1931)
Borgatti, Mariano. *Castel Sant'Angelo in Roma: storia e descrizione* (Rome).

Borsari (1884)
Borsari, Luigi. "Il Foro di Augusto e il tempio di Marte Ultore," *Atti della Reale Accademia d'Italia, Mem. della classe di scienze morali e storiche*, ser 3, 13: 400–15.
Borsi (1985)
Borsi, Stefano. *Giuliano da Sangallo: I disegni di architettura e dell'antico* (Rome).
Borsi (1986)
Borsi, Stefano. "Disegni dell'antico di Antonio da Sangallo: Le antichità etrusche," in ed. G. Spagnesi, *Antonio da Sangallo il Giovane: La vita e l'opera*, conference proceedings (Rome): 445–54.
Borsi (1989 *Frontespizio*)
Borsi, Stefano. "La fortuna del 'Frontespizio di Nerone' nel Rinascimento," in ed. S. Danesi Squarzina, *Roma, centro ideale della cattura dell'antico nei secoli XV e XVI*, conference proceedings, (Milan): 390–400.
Borst (1994)
Borst, Arno. *Das Buch der Naturgeschichte. Plinius und seine Leser im Zeitalter des Pergaments* (Heidelberg).
Brandizzi Vittucci (1968)
Brandizzi Vittucci, Paola. *Cora* (Forma Italiae, vol. 1.5) (Rome): 58–66.
Brands (1988)
Brands, Gunnar "Der Augustusbogen von Fano und der Beginn des Architekturstudiums in der Renaissance,": *Jahrbuch des Deutschen Archäologischen Instituts* 103: 489–513.
Brilliant (1967)
Brilliant, Richard. *The Arch of Septimius Severus in the Roman Forum* (Rome).
Bruschi (1983)
Bruschi, Arnaldo. "Cordini (Cordiani?) Antonio, detto Antonio da Sangallo il Giovane," in *Dizionario Biografico degli Italiani* 29 (Rome): 3–23.
Bruschi (1992)
Bruschi, Arnaldo. "L'antico e il processo di identificazione degli ordini nella seconda metà del Quattrocento," in ed. J. Guillaume, *L'emploi des ordres à la Renaissance* (Paris): 11–57.
Bruschi (1998)
Bruschi, Arnaldo. "Brunelleschi e la nuova architettura fiorentina," in ed. F.P. Fiore, *Storia dell'architettura italiana*, vol. 1, *Il Quattrocento* (Milan): 38–113.
Bruschi (2003)
Bruschi, Arnaldo. "Dopo Alessandro VI. Gli interventi di Giulio II nella fortezza di Civita Castellana," in eds. M. Chiabò, M. Gargano, *Le Rocche Alessandrine e la Rocca di Civita Castellana*, conference proceedings (Rome): 129–41.
Buchowiecki-Kuhn (1967–97)
Buchowiecki, Walter, and Brigitte Kuhn. *Handbuch der Kirchen Roms*, 4 vols (Vienna).
Buddensieg (1975)
Buddensieg, Tilmann. "Bernardo della Volpaia und Giovanni Francesco da Sangallo: Der Autor des Codex Coner und seine Stellung im Sangallokreis," *Römisches Jahrbuch für Kunstgeschichte* 15: 89–105.
Bulgarelli-Calzona-Ceriana-Fiore (2006)
Bulgarelli, Massimo; Calzona, Arturo; Ceriana, Matteo; and Francesco Paolo Fiore (eds), *Leon Battista Alberti e l'architettura*, exhibition catalogue of the exhibition Mantua 2006/07 (Milan).
Buranelli (2010)
Buranelli Francesco. *Palazzo Farnèse: dalle collezioni rinascimentali ad ambasciata di Francia* (Florence).
Burns (1965–66)
Burns, Howard. "A Peruzzi Drawing in Ferrara,"*Mitteilungen des Kunsthistorischen Instituts in Florenz* 12: 245–70.
Burns (1984)
Burns, Howard. "Giulio Romano. Veduta del Mausoleo di Adriano del ponte Elio e del Campo Marzio," in eds. C.L. Frommel, S. Ray and M. Tafuri, *Raffaello architetto* (Milan): 448–49.
Burns (1998)
Burns, Howard. "Leon Battista Alberti," in ed. F.P. Fiore, *Storia dell'architettura italiana*, vol. 1, *Il Quattrocento*, (Milan): 114–65.
Burns (2017)
Burns, Howard. "Giuliano da Sangallo and the renewal of residential architecture," in eds. A. Belluzzi, C. Elam, and F- P. Fiore, *Giuliano da Sangallo* (Milan): 95–119.
Burns-Oberhuber (1984)
Oberhuber, Konrad, and Howard Burns. "La citazione dell'antico: Il progetto per il monumento funebre al marchese Francesco Gonzaga," in eds. C.L. Frommel, S. Ray and M. Tafuri, *Raffaello architetto* (Milan): 429–32.
Camerieri-Palombaro (1988)
Camerieri, Paolo, and Fabio Palombaro. *La "Rocca Paolina" un falso d'autore: Dal mancato compimento alla radicale alterazione del progetto di Antonio da Sangallo il Giovane per il Forte di S. Cataldo* (Perugia).
Campbell (1980)
Campbell, Ian. "'Scamilli Inpares': a problem in Vitruvius," *Papers of the British School at Rome* XLVIII: 17–22.
Campbell (1984)
Campbell, Ian. *Reconstruction of Roman Temples Made in Italy between 1400–1600* (Ph.D. diss., Oxford University).
Campbell (2004 *Paper Museum*)
Campbell, Ian. *The Paper Museum of Cassiano dal Pozzo: A Catalogue Raisonné: Roman Topography and Architecture*, 3 vols, *Series A – Antiquities And Architecture*, IX/1–3 (London).
Campbell (2005)
Campbell, Ian. *The Codex Stosch to be included in the sale of Books and Manuscripts: Tuesday 12th July 2005 12 noon* (Edinburgh).

Campbell-Nesselrath (2006)
Campbell, Ian and Arnold Nesselrath. "The Codex Stosch: Surveys of Ancient Buildings by Giovanni Battista da Sangallo," *Pegasus* 8: 7–86.
Cellini-Milanesi (1893)
Cellini, Benvenuto. *I trattati dell'oreficeria e della scultura di Benvenuto Cellini. Novamente messi alle stampe secondo la originale dettatura del Codice Marciano*, ed. C. Milanesi (Florence).
CensusID
Open access research database of the Census of Antique Works of Art and Architecture Known in the Renaissance, Humboldt-Universität zu Berlin (www.census.de).
Cerutti Fusco (1986)
Cerutti Fusco, Annarosa. "Teatro all'antica e teatro vitruviano nell'interpretazione di Antonio da Sangallo il Giovane," in ed. G. Spagnesi, *Antonio da Sangallo il Giovane: La vita e l'opera*, conference proceedings (Rome): 455–69.
Cerutti Fusco (1987)
Cerutti Fusco, Annarosa. "La restituzione grafica dei teatri antichi nei primi decenni del Cinquecento: Interesse antiquario, studi vitruviani e 'inventioni'," *Quaderni dell'Istituto di Storia dell'Architettura* 10: 301–12.
Chatzidakis (2017)
Chatzidakis, Michail. *Ciriaco d'Ancona und die Wiederentdeckung Griechenlands im 15. Jahrhundert* (Petersberg).
Christern-Thiersch (1969)
Christern, Jürgen, and Katharina Thiersch. "Der Aufriß von Alt-St Peter 2. Teil (Ergänzungen zum Langhaus; Querschiffshöhe)," *Römische Quartalschrift* 64: 3–34.
CIL
Corpus Inscriptionum Latinarum, 1–, Berlin 1862– (in progress)
Claridge (1998)
Claridge, Amanda. *Rome. An Oxford Archaeological Guide* (Oxford).
Claridge (1999)
Claridge, Amanda. Rome, "L'Hadrianeum in Campo Marzio: storia dei rinvenimenti e topografia antica nell'area di piazza di Pietra," in ed. M. Sapelli, *Provinciae fideles: il fregio del Tempio di Adriano in Campo Marzio* (Rome): 117–27.
Coarelli (1974)
Coarelli, Filippo. *Guida archeologica di Roma* (Verona).
Coarelli (1980)
Coarelli, Filippo. *Roma* (Rome, Bari).
Coarelli (1982)
Coarelli, Filippo. *Lazio* (Rome, Bari).
Collobi Ragghianti (1973)
Collobi Ragghianti, Licia. "Nuove precisazioni sui disegni di architettura del 'Libro' del Vasari," *Critica d'arte* N.S. 20: 31–54.
Collobi Ragghianti (1974)
Collobi Ragghianti, Licia. *Il libro de' disegni del Vasari*, 2 vols (Florence).
Contardi-Lilius (1984)
Contardi, Bruno, and Henrik Lilius ed. *Quando gli dei si spogliano: Il bagno di Clemente VII a Castel Sant'Angelo e le altre stufe romane del primo Cinquecento*, catalogue of the exhibition, Rome.
Cozza (1982)
Cozza, Lucos, ed., *Tempio di Adriano* (Lavori e studi di archeologia pubblicati dalla Soprintendenza Archeologica di Roma 1) (Rome).
Cozzo (1971)
Cozzo, Giuseppe. *Il Colosseo: l'Anfiteatro Flavio nella tecnica edilizia, nella storia delle strutture, nel concetto escecutivo dei lavori* (Rome).
Crozzoli Aite (1981)
Crozzoli Aite, Livia. *I tre templi del Foro Olitorio* (Lavori e studi di archeologia pubblicati dalla Soprintendenza Archeologica di Roma 18) (Rome).
D'Onofrio (1957)
D'Onofrio, Cesare. *Le fontane di Roma* (Rome).
D'Onofrio (1967)
D'Onofrio, Cesare. *Gli obelischi di Roma* (Rome), 2nd revised edition.
D'Onofrio (1976)
D'Onofrio, Cesare. *Roma val bene un'abiura* (Rome).
Di Teodoro (1994)
Di Teodoro, Francesco P. *Raffaello, Baldassar Castiglione e la Lettera a Leone X* (Bologna)
Dacos (1969)
Dacos, Nicole. *La découverte de la Domus Aurea et la formation des grotesques à la Renaissance* (London).
De Angeli (1992)
De Angeli, Stefano. *Templum Divi Vespasiani* (Lavori e studi di archeologia pubblicati dalla Soprintendenza Archeologica di Roma 18) (Rome).
De Angelis D'Ossat (1959–61)
De Angelis D'Ossat, Guglielmo. "Un enigma risolto, il completamento del Mausoleo Teodoriciano," *Quaderni dell'Istituto di Storia dell'Architettura* 31/48: 67–82.
De Maria (1988)
De Maria, Sandro. *Gli archi onorari di Roma e dell'Italia romana* (Rome).
Del Pesco (2002)
Del Pesco, Daniela. "Oliviero Carafa e il Succorpo di San Gennaro nel Duomo di Napoli," in *Donato Bramante ricerche, proposte, riletture*, ed. F.P. Di Teodoro (Milan) 143–205.
Delbrück (1903)
Delbrück, Richard. *Die drei Tempel am Forum holitorium in Rom* (Rome).
Delbrück (1907–12)
Delbrück, Richard. *Hellenistische Bauten in Latium*. 2 vols (Strassburg).

Denker- Nesselrath (1990)
Denker-Nesselrath, Christiane. *Die Säulenordnungen bei Bramante* (Worms).
Denker- Nesselrath (1996)
Denker-Nesselrath, Christiane. *Bramante's spiral staircase* (Vatican City).
Donetti-Faietti-Frommel (2017)
Donetti, Dario; Faietti, Marzia, and Sabine Frommel (eds). Giuliano da Sangallo. Disegni degli Uffizi (2017).
Egger (1903)
Egger, Hermann. *Kritisches Verzeichnis der Sammlung architektonischer Handzeichnungen der K.K. Hof-Bibliothek* (Wien).
Egger (1906)
Egger, Hermann, *Codex Escurialensis: Ein Skizzenbuch aus der Werkstatt Domenico Ghirlandaios*, 2 vols (Vienna).
Eisner (1986)
Eisner, Michael. *Zur Typologie der Grabbauten im Suburbium Roms* (Wiesbaden).
Engel (2014)
Engel, Franz. "Dorisch, ionisch, korinthisch? Anmerkungen zu einigen Zeichnungen der drei Tempel des Forum Holitorium aus dem Sangallo-Kreis," *Pegasus* 16: 103–22.
Fabriczy (1902)
Fabriczy, Cornel von. *Die Handzeichnungen Giuliano's da Sangallo* (Stuttgart).
Falb (1902)
Falb, Rodolfo. *Il Taccuino senese. 50 facsimili di disegni d'architettura, scultura ed arte applicata di Giuliano da Sangallo* (Siena).
Fane-Saunders (2016)
Fane-Saunders, Peter *Pliny the Elder and the Emergence of Renaissance Architecture* (Cambridge).
Fernández (2009)
Fernández, Henry Dietrich. "A temporary home: Bramante's Conclave Hall for Julius II.," in eds. S. Cavallo and S. Evangelisti, *Domestic institutional interiors in early modern Europe* (Farnham): 27–49.
Ferri (1885)
Ferri, Pasquale Nerino. *Indice geografico-analitico dei disegni di architettura civile e militare esistenti nella Reale Galleria degli Uffizi in Firenze* (Rome).
Fiechter (1906)
Fiechter, Ernst Robert. "Der ionische Tempel am Ponte Rotto in Rom." *Mitteilungen des Kaiserlich Deutschen Archäologischen Instituts* 21: 221–79.
Fiore (2001)
Fiore, Francesco Paolo (ed.). *Sebstiano Serlio, L'architettura: I libri I–VII e l'Extraordinario nelle prime edizioni* 2 vols (Milan).
Fiore (2002, *Roma*)
Fiore, Francesco Paolo. "Roma, le diverse maniere," in ed. A. Bruschi, *Storia dell'architettura italiana*, vol. 2, *Il primo Cinquecento* (Milan): 132–59.
Fiore (2002, *Trattati*)
Fiore, Francesco Paolo. "Trattati e teorie d'architettura del primo Cinquecento," in ed. A. Bruschi, *Storia dell'architettura italiana*, vol. 2, *Il primo Cinquecento* (Milan): 504–21.
Fiore-Tafuri (1994)
Fiore, Francesco Paolo, and Manfredo Tafuri, eds., *Francesco di Giorgio architetto* (Milan). Revised edition of catalogue of 1993 exhibition.
Fontana-Morachiello (1975)
Fontana, Vincenzo, and Paolo Morachiello, eds., *Vitruvio e Raffaello. Il "De architettura" di Vitruvio nella traduzione inedita di Fabio Calvo Ravennate* (Rome).
Franzoni (1980)
Franzoni, Lanfranco "L'anfiteatro," in ed. P. Marini, *Palladio e Verona* (Verona): 63–67.
Frey (1910)
Frey, Karl. "Zur Baugeschichte des St Peter," *Jahrbuch der Königlich Preussischen Kunstsammlungen* 31: 1–95 (Supplement).
Frey (1922–23)
Frey, Dagobert. "Eine unbeachtete Zeichnung nach dem Modell Michelangelos für die Fassade von San Lorenzo," *Kunstchronik und Kunstmarkt* n.s. 33: 221–28.
Frommel (1973)
Frommel, Christoph Luitpold. *Der römische Palastbau der Hochrenaissance*, 3 vols (Tübingen).
Frommel (1974)
Frommel, Christoph Luitpold. "Raffaello e il teatro alla corte di Leone X," *Bollettino del Centro Internazionale di Studi di Architettura Andrea Palladio* 16: 173–87.
Frommel (1981)
Frommel, Christoph Luitpold. "Sangallo et Michel-Ange (1513–1550)," in *Le Palais Farnèse* (Rome) 1, 1: 127–225.
Frommel (1983)
Frommel, Christoph Luitpold. "Francesco del Borgo. Architekt Pius' II. und Pauls II. I. Der Petersplatz und weitere römische Bauten Pius' II. Piccolomini," *Römisches Jahrbuch für Kunstgeschichte* 20: 107–54.
Frommel (1984, *Raffaello*)
Frommel, Christoph Luitpold. "Raffaello e la sua carriera architettonica," in eds. C.L. Frommel, S. Ray, and M. Tafuri, *Raffaello architetto* (Milan): 13–46.
Frommel (1984, *San Pietro*)
Frommel, Christoph Luitpold. "San Pietro, Storia della sua costruzione," in eds. C.L. Frommel, S. Ray, and M. Tafuri, *Raffaello architetto* (Milan): 241–310.
Frommel (1984, *Villa Madama*)
Frommel, Christoph Luitpold. "Villa Madama," in eds. C.L. Frommel, S. Ray, and M. Tafuri, *Raffaello architetto*, (Milan): 311–42.
Frommel (1986)
Frommel, Christoph Luitpold. "Giovanfrancesco da Sangallo, architetto di Palazzo Balami-Galitzin," in ed. G. Spagnesi, *Antonio da Sangallo il Giovane: La vita e l'opera* (Rome): 63–69.

Frommel (1987)
Frommel, Christoph Luitpold. "S. Luigi dei Francesi: Das Meisterwerk des Jean de Chenevières," in *"Il se rendit en Italie": Etudes offertes à André Chastel* (Rome).
Frommel (1989, *Bramante*)
Frommel, Christoph Luitpold. "Bramante e il disegno 104A degli Uffizi," in eds. P. Carpeggiani and L. Patetta, *Disegno di architettura*, conference proceedings (Milan): 161–68.
Frommel (1989, *Serlio*)
Frommel, Christoph Luitpold. "Serlio e la scuola romana," in ed. C. Thoenes, *Sebastiano Serlio* (Milan): 39–49.
Frommel (1990)
Frommel, Christoph Luitpold. "Roma e la formazione architettonica del Palladio," in eds. A. Chastel and R. Cevese, *Andrea Palladio: Nuovi contributi*, conference proceedings (Milan): 146–65.
Frommel (1991)
Frommel, Christoph Luitpold. "Il Cantiere di S. Pietro prima di Michelangelo," in ed. J. Guillaume, *Les Chantiers de la Renaissance*, conference proceedings, (Paris): 175–83.
Frommel (1994, *Introduction*)
Frommel, Christoph Luitpold. "Introduction. The Drawings of Antonio da Sangallo the Younger: History, Evolution, Method, Function," in eds. C.L. Frommel and N. Adams, *The Architectural Drawings of Antonio da Sangallo the Younger and his Circle*, vol. 1, *Fortifications, Machines, and Festival Architecture* (Cambridge, Mass., London): 1–60.
Frommel (1994, *Saint Peter's*)
Frommel, Christoph Luitpold. "Saint Peter's. The Early History," in eds. H.A. Millon and V Magnano Lampugnani, *The Renaissance from Brunelleschi to Michelangelo: The representation of architecture* (Milan): 398–423.
Frommel (1994, *Reflections*)
Frommel, Christoph Luitpold. "Reflections on the early achitectural drawings," in eds. H.A. Millon and V. Magnano Lampugnani, *The Renaissance from Brunelleschi to Michelangelo: The representation of architecture* (Milan): 101–21.
Frommel (1995, *Palazzo Farnese*)
Frommel, Christoph Luitpold. "Palazzo Farnese a Roma: L'architetto e il suo committente," *Annali di Architettura* 7: 7–18.
Frommel (1995, *Sanmicheli*)
Frommel, Christoph Luitpold. "Roma e l'opera giovanile di Sanmicheli," in eds. H. Burns, C.L. Frommel, L. Puppi, and M. Tafuri, *Michele Sanmicheli: Architettura, linguaggio e cultura artistica nel Cinquecento* (Milan): 14–31.
Frommel (1996, *La chiesa di San Pietro*)
Frommel, Christoph Luitpold. "La chiesa di San Pietro sotto papa Giulio II alla luce di nuovi documenti," in ed. C. Tessari, *San Pietro che non c'è da Bramante a Sangallo il Giovane* (Milan): 23–84.
Frommel (1996, *San Pietro*)
Frommel, Christoph Luitpold. "San Pietro," in ed. C. Tessari, *San Pietro che non c'è da Bramante a Sangallo il Giovane*, (Milan): 249–80.
Frommel (1999)
Frommel, Christoph Luitpold. "Raffaele Riario, la Cancelleria, il teatro e il 'Bacco' di Michelangelo," in ed. K. Weil-Garris Brandt, *Giovinezza di Michelangelo*, catalogue of the exhibition (Florence): 143–48.
Frommel (2001)
Frommel, Christoph Luitpold. "Sant'Egidio a Cellere: Funzione, tipologia e forma," in *All'ombra di "sa' gilio a celeri di farnesi,"* conference proceedings, ed. E. Galdieri (Cellere): 79–110.
Frommel (2002, *Bramante e Raffaello*)
Frommel, Christoph Luitpold. "La città come opera d'arte: Bramante e Raffaello (1500–20)," in ed. A. Bruschi, *Storia dell'architettura italiana*, vol. 2, *Il primo Cinquecento* (Milan): 76–131.
Frommel (2002, *Lombardia*)
Frommel, Christoph Luitpold. "Lombardia," in eds. C.L. Frommel, L. Giordano, and R Schofield, *Bramante milanese e l'architettura del Rinascimento lombardo* (Milan): 22–23.
Frommel (2002, *Progetto di Sangallo*)
Frommel, Christoph Luitpold. "Il progetto di Sangallo per Piazza Nicosia e una torre di Raffaello," *Strenna dei Romanisti* 63: 265–93.
Frommel (2002, *Villa Giulia*)
Frommel, Christoph Luitpold. "Villa Giulia a Roma," in eds. B. Adorni, C.L. Frommel, C. Thoenes, and RJ. Tuttle, *Jacopo Barozzi da Vignola* (Milan): 163–66.
Frommel (2003, *L'architettura*)
Frommel, Christoph Luitpold. "L'architettura," in ed. S. Schütze, *Palazzo Sacchetti* (Rome): 44–75.
Frommel (2003, *Cappella Paolina*)
Frommel, Christoph Luitpold. "La Cappella Paolina di Antonio da Sangallo: Un contributo alla storia edilizia del Palazzo Vaticano," in *Architettura alla corte papale nel Rinascimento* (Milan): 359–91 (first published in1964).
Frommel (2003, *Civita Castellana*)
Frommel, Christoph Luitpold. "La Rocca di Civita Castellana: funzione e forma," in eds. M. Chiamò and M. Gargano, *Le Rocche Alessandrine e la Rocca di Civita Castellana*, conference proceedings, Civita Castellana (Rome): 89–100.
Frommel (2003, *L'esordio*)
Frommel, Christoph Luitpold. "L'esordio romano di Peruzzi: dal gruppo dei disegni del Pseudo-Cronaca a Bramante," in *Architettura alla corte papale nel Rinascimento* (Milan): 157–91 (first published in 1991).

Frommel (2003, *Farnesina*)
Frommel, Christoph Luitpold, ed., *La Villa Farnesina a Roma. The Villa Farnesina in Rome* (Modena).
Frommel (2003, *Porta ionica*)
Frommel, Christoph Luitpold. "La porta ionica nel Rinascimento," in *Architettura alla corte papale nel Rinascimento* (Milan): 35–87 (first published in 2000).
Frommel (2003, *Raffaello e Sangallo*)
Frommel, Christoph Luitpold. "Raffaello e Antonio da Sangallo il Giovane (1511–20)," in *Architettura alla corte papale nel Rinascimento* (Milan): 257–315 (first published in 1986).
Frommel (2003, *Tre progetti*)
Frommel, Christoph Luitpold. "I tre progetti bramanteschi per il cortile del Belvedere," in *Architettura alla corte papale nel Rinascimento* (Milan): 89–155 (first published in 1998).
Frommel (2003, *Disegni sconosciuti*)
Frommel, Christoph Luitpold, "Disegni sconosciuti di Sangallo per le tombe di Leone X e Clemente VII": in *Architettura alla corte papale nel Rinascimento* (Milan): 335-357 (first published in German in 2001).
Frommel (2005)
Frommel, Christoph Luitpold. "'Ala maniera e uso delj bonj antiquj': Baldassarre Peruzzi e i quarant'anni della sua conqueista dell'antico," in eds. C.L. Frommel, A. Bruschi, and H. Burns, *Baldassarre Peruzzi*, conference proceedings (Vicenza): 3–82.
Frommel (2006, *Villa Medici a Fiesole*)
Frommel, Christoph Luitpold. "Villa Medici a Fiesole e la nascita della villa rinascimentale," in C.L. Frommel, *Architettura e committenza da Alberti a Bramante* (Florence): 43–78.
Frommel (2006, *Tavole*)
Frommel, Christoph Luitpold. "Le tavole di Berlino, di Urbino e di Baltimora," in C.L. Frommel, *Architettura e committenza da Alberti a Bramante* (Florence): 337–66.
Frommel (2007, *Architecture*)
Frommel, Christoph Luitpold. *The Architecture of the Italian Renaissance* (London/Boston), revised edition and translation: *Architettura del Rinascimento italiano* (Milan).
Frommel (2007, *Colonna*)
Frommel, Christoph Luitpold. "La colonna nella teoria e nelle architetture di Alberti," in eds. A. Calzona, F.P. Fiore, A. Tenenti, C. Vasoli, *Leon Battista Alberti teorico delle arti e gli impegni civili del "De re aedificatoria"* (Florence): 695–725.
Frommel (2008, *Castel Nuovo*)
Frommel, Christoph Luitpold. "Alberti e l'arco trionfale di Castel Nuovo," in *Annali di Architettura* 20: 13–36.
Frommel (2008, *Proposte*)
Frommel, Christoph Luitpold. "Proposte per una revisione del corpus dei disegni di Bramante," in *Opus Incertum* 3: 38–55.
Frommel (2009, *Palazzo Alberini*)
Frommel, Christoph Luitpold, *Palazzo Alberini a Roma*, (Rome).
Frommel (2009, *Progetto*)
Frommel, Christoph Luitpold. "Il progetto per l'altare di San Lorenzo in Damaso attribuibile a Leon Battista Alberti," in eds. C.L. Frommel and M. Pentiricci, (*L'antica basilica di San Lorenzo in Damaso indagini archeologiche nel Palazzo della Cancelleria (1988–1993)*, Vatican City) I: 428–30.
Frommel (2009, *San Lorenzo in Damaso*)
Frommel, Christoph Lutipold, "San Lorenzo in Damaso e l'attiguo palazzo cardinalizio tra il tardo Quattrocento e il primo Cinquecento," in eds. Christoph Luitpold Frommel, and Massimo Pentiricci, (*Gli scavi di San Lorenzo in Damaso*, Vatican City): 411–30.
Frommel (2010, *Mantegna*)
Frommel, "Mantenga architetto," in eds. R. Signorini, V. Rebonato, S. Tasmmaccaro, *Andrea Mantegna impronta del genio Acts of the international conference Padua and Verona* 2007 (Florence): 181–8.
Frommel (2010, *Fabbrica*)
Frommel, Christoph Luitpold, "La fabbrica," in ed. Francesco Buranelli, *Palazzo Farnèse: dalle collezioni rinascimentali ad ambasciata di Francia* (Rome): 49–61.
Frommel (2011, *Palazzo Farnese*)
Frommel, Christoph Luitpold. "Antonio da Sangallo il Giovane e i primi cinque anni della progettazione di palazzo Farnese," *Annali di Architettura* 23: 37–58.
Frommel (2012, *Presbytère*)
Frommel, Christoph Luitpold. "Presbytère et choeur de Saint-Pierre de Rome de Nicolas V à Jules II," in ed. S. Frommel, *La place du choeur* (Paris): 113–30.
Frommel (2012, *Presbiterio*)
Frommel, Christoph Luitpold. "La progettazione del presbiterio di San Pietro da Niccolò V a Giulio II," in ed. Giovanni Morello, *La basilica di San Pietro* (Rome): 171–96.
Frommel (2017, *Tempietto*)
Frommel, Christoph Luitpold. "Bramante, il Tempietto e il convento di San Pietro in Montorio," *Römisches Jahrbuch der Bibliotheca Hertziana* 41 (2013/14): 111–64.
Frommel (2018, *Granada*)
Frommel Christoph Luitpold, "Il palazzo di Carlo V a Granada e Pedro Machuca," in eds. P.A. Galera and S. Frommel, *El patio circular en la arquitectura del Rinacimiento* (Sevilla): 77–119.
Frommel (2018, *Loreto*)
Frommel, Christoph Luitpold. *L'architettura del santuario e del palazzo apostolico di Loreto da Paolo II a Paolo III*, con un regesto di Marco Calafati (Loreto).
Frommel (2019, *Metodo progettuale*)
Frommel, Christoph Luitpold, "Sul metodo progettuale nei disegni di Bramante, Raffaello e Antonio da Sangallo il Giovane per San Pietro," *Annali di architettura* 30: 37–58.

Frommel-Adams (1994)
Frommel, Christoph Luitpold, and Nicholas Adams, eds., *The Architectural Drawings of Antonio da Sangallo the Younger and his Circle*, vol. 1, *Fortifications, Machines, and Festival Architecture* (Cambridge, Mass., London) (= vol. I).
Frommel-Adams (2000)
Frommel, Christoph Luitpold, and Nicholas Adams, eds., *The Architectural Drawings of Antonio da Sangallo the Younger and his Circle*, vol. 2, *Churches, Villas, The Pantheon, Tombs, Ancient Inscriptions* (Cambridge, Mass., London) (= vol. II).
Frommel-Pentricci (2009)
Frommel, Christoph Luitpold, and Massimo Pentricci, eds., *L'antica basilica di San Lorenzo in Damaso indagini archeologiche nel Palazzo della Cancelleria (1988–1993)*, 2 vols (Vatican City).
Frommel-Ray-Tafuri (1984)
Frommel, Christoph Luitpold, Stefano Ray, and Manfredo Tafuri, eds., *Raffaello architetto*, catalogue of the exhibition (Milan).
Frommel S. (2002)
Frommel, Sabine. "Vitruvio De architectura," in ed. A. Cadei, *Il trionfo sul tempo: Manoscritti illustrati dell'Accademia Nazionale dei Lincei*, catalogue of the exhibition (Rome): 294–301.
Frommel S. (2008)
Frommel, Sabine. "I disegni di Giuliano da Sangallo: relazioni tra studio dell'antico e progettazione," *Opus Incertum* 3: 13–37.
Frommel S. (2014)
Frommel, Sabine. *Giuliano da Sangallo* (Florence).
Galli (1911)
Galli, Edoardo. "I primi risultati degli scavi governativi nel teatro Romano di Ferento," *Bollettino d'arte del Ministero della Pubblica Istruzione* 5, 6: 213–26.
Gaudioso (1976)
Gaudioso, Eraldo. "I lavori farnesiani a Castel Sant'Angelo. Precisazioni ed ipostesi," *Bollettino d'Arte* 61: 21–42.
Gazzola (1963)
Gazzola, Piero. *Ponti romani: contributo ad un indice sistematico con studio critico bibliografico* (Florence).
Ghini (1988)
Ghini, Giuseppina. *Le Terme Alessandrine nel Campo Marzio* (Rome).
Ghini (2000)
Ghini, Giuseppina. s.v "Thermae Neronianae/ Alexandrinae," in ed. E.M. Steinby, *Lexicon topographicum urbis Romae (1993–2000)*, vol. V (Rome): 60–62.
Ghisetti Giavarina (1983)
Ghisetti Giavarina, Adriano. "La Basilica Emilia e la rivalutazione del Dorico nel Rinascimento." *Bollettino del Centro di Studi per la Storia dell'Architettura* 29: 7–36.
Ghisetti Giavarina (1990)
Ghisetti Giavarina, Adriano. *Aristotele da Sangallo. Architettura, scenografia e pittura tra Roma e Firenze nella prima metà del Cinquecento. Ipotesi di attribuizione dei disegni raccolti agli Uffizi* (Rome).
Giess (1981)
Giess, Hildegard. "Die Stadt Castro und die Pläne von Antonio da Sangallo dem Jüngeren (Teil II)," *Römisches Jahrbuch für Kunstgeschichte* 19: 85–140.
Giess (1994)
Giess, Hildegard. "Castro and Nepi," in eds. C.L. Frommel and N. Adams, *The Architectural Drawings of Antonio da Sangallo the Younger and His Circle*, vol. 1, *Fortifications, Machines, and Festival Architecture* (Cambridge, Mass., London): 75–80.
Giovannoni (1959)
Giovannoni, Gustavo. *Antonio da Sangallo il Giovane*, 2 vols (Rome).
Giuliani (1970)
Giuliani, Cairoli Fulvio. *Tibur: Pars prima* (Forma Italiae, vol. I) (Rome).
Glass (1980)
Glass, Dorothy F. *Studies on Cosmatesque Pavements* (Oxford).
Golvin (1988)
Golvin, Jean-Claude. *L'Amphithéatre romain* (Paris).
Grohmann (1981*Perugia*)
Grohmann, Alberto. *Perugia* (Rome, Bari).
Gros (1992)
Gros, Pierre. *Vitruve, De l'Architecture, Livre IV* (Paris).
Gros (2005)
Gros, Pierre. "Baldassarre Peruzzi, architetto e archeologo: i fogli al Gabinetto Disegni e Stampe degli Uffizi A 632–33," in *Baldassarre Peruzzi, 1481–1536* (Venice): 225–29.
Guidi – Paribeni (1911)
Guidi, Pietro, and Roberto Paribeni. "Lavori d'isolamento delle Terme Diocleziane," *Bollettino d'arte del Ministero della Pubblica Istruzione* 5, 9: 347–61.
Günther (1981)
Günther, Hubertus. "Porticus Pompeji: zur archäologischen Erforschung eines antiken Bauwerkes in der Renaissance und seiner Rekonstruktion im dritten Buch des Sebastiano Serlio," *Zeitschrift für Kunstgeschichte* 44: 358–98.
Günther (1982)
Günther, Hubertus. "Werke Bramantes im Spiegel einer Gruppe von Zeichnungen der Uffizien in Florenz," *Münchner Jahrbuch der bildenden Kunst* III/33: 77–108.
Günther (1985)
Günther, Hubertus. "Die Strassenplanung unter den Medici Päpsten in Rom (1513–1534)," *Jahrbuch des Zentralinstituts für Kunstgeschichte* 1: 237–93.
Günther (1988)
Günther, Hubertus. *Das Studium der antiken Architektur in den Zeichnungen der Hochrenaissance* (Tübingen).

Günther (1990)
Günther, Hubertus. "Ein Entwurf Baldassare Peruzzis für ein Architekturtraktat," *Römisches Jahrbuch der Bibliotheca Hertziana* 26: 135–70.

Günther (1994, *Insana aedificia*)
Günther, Hubertus. *"Insana aedificia thermarum nomine extructa." Die Diokletiansthermen in der Sicht der Renaissance* (Weimar).

Günther (1994, *Urban planning*)
Günther, Hubertus. "Urban planning in Rome under the Medici Popes," in eds. H.A. Millon and V. Magnago Lampugnani, *The Renaissance from Brunelleschi to Michelangelo. The Representation of Architecture*, catalogue of the exhibition (Milan): 545–50

Günther (1998)
Günther, Hubertus. "Die Rekonstruktion des antiken Fussmasses in der Renaissance: Geschichte und Methode," in *Ordo et mensura 4*, conference proceedings, ed. D. Ahrens (St Katharinen): 373–93.

Günther (2001, *L'opera tuscanica*)
Günther, Hubertus. "L'opera tuscanica di Antonio da Sangallo e di Andrea Palladio," *Annali di Architettura* 29: 91–100.

Günther (2001, *Palazzo di Mecenate*)
Günther, Hubertus. "Dal Palazzo di Mecenate al Palazzo Farnese: La concezione rinascimentale della casa antica," in *Aspetti dell'abitare in Italia tra XV e XVI secolo*, ed. A. Scotti (Milan): 219–39.

Haskell-Penny (1981)
Haskell, Francis, and Nicholas Penny. *Taste and the Antique: The Lure of Classical Sculpture 1500–1900* (New Haven, London).

Heidenreich-Johannes (1971)
Heidenreich, Robert, and Heinz Johannes. *Das Grabmal Theoderichs zu Ravenna* (Wiesbaden).

Heikamp (1966)
Heikamp, Detlef. "Die Entwurfszeichnungen für die Grabmäler der Mediceer-Päpste Leo X. und Clemens VII.," *Albertina-Studien* 4: 134–54.

Hemsoll (2014)
Hemsoll, David. "Drawings by Palladio and others of the Porta dei Leoni in Verona," in *Pegasus* 16: 263–94

Hibbard (1961)
Hibbard, Howard. "The early history of Sant'Andrea della Valle," *The Art Bulletin* 43: 289–318.

Hubert (2008)
Hubert, Hans W. "Lineamenta und pulchritudo—Anmerkungen zu Albertis Architekturentwurf," in eds. J. Poeschke and C. Syndikus, *Leon Battista Alberti Humanist, Architekt, Kunsttheoretiker* (Münster): 209–26.

Huelsen (1884)
Huelsen, Christian."Sopra un edificio antico già esistente presso la chiesa di S. Adriano al Foro Romano." *Annali dell'Istituto di Corrispondenza Acheologica* 56: 332–56.

Huelsen (1891)
Huelsen, Christian. "Jahresbericht ueber neue Funde und Forschungen zur Topographie der Stadt Rom 1889–1890," *Mittheilungen des K. Deutschen Archäologischen Instituts, Römische Abtheilung* 6,1: 74–150.

Huelsen (1906)
Huelsen, Christian. "Der dorische Tempel bei S. Nicola in Carcere," *Römische Mitteilungen des Deutschen Archäologischen Instituts* 21: 169–92.

Huelsen (1910)
Huelsen, Christian. *Il libro di Giuliano da Sangallo. Codice Vaticano Barberiniano Latino 4424*, 2 vols (Leipzig).

Huelsen (1927)
Huelsen, Christian. *Le chiese di Roma nel medioevo* (Florence).

Huelsen-Egger (1913–16)
Huelsen, Christian, and Hermann Egger *Die römischen Skizzenbücher von Marten van Heemskerk im Königlichen Kupferstichkabinett zu Berlin*, 4 vols (Berlin).

Huppert (2001)
Huppert, Ann C. *The Archaeology of Baldassarre Peruzzi's Architectural Drawings* (Ph.D. diss., University of Virginia) (Ann Arbor, Michigan).

Huppert (2015)
Huppert, Ann C. *Becoming an architect in Renaissance Italy. Art, Science, and the Career of Baldassarre Peruzzi* (New Haven and London).

Huth (2014)
Huth, Andreas. "Antike Rundgräber in der Vigna Cavalieri. Drei Zeichnungen des Sangallo-Kreises und die archäologischen Befunde am Bastione Ardeatino in Rom,"*Pegasus* 16. 151–66.

Inglieri (1939)
Inglieri, RV "Il teatro Romano di Helvia Ricina," *Dionysos* 7: 104–9.

Jäggi (1998)
Jäggi, Carola. *San Salvatore in Spoleto. Studien zur spätantiken und frühmittelalterlichen Architektur Italiens* (Wiesbaden).

Jeppesen (1981–)
Jeppesen, Kristian. *The Mausolleion at Halikarnassos*, 7 vols (Aarhus).

Jobst (1990)
Jobst, Christoph. "Die kritischen Studien nach antiken Triumphbogen von Antonio da Sangallo dem Jüngeren: Das Verhältnis von Säulenordnung und Mauerwerk," *Annali di Architettura* 2: 43–52.

Jobst (1992)
Jobst, Christoph. *Die Planungen Antonios da Sangallo des Jüngeren für die Kirche S. Maria di Loreto in Rom* (Worms).

Jobst (1994)
Jobst, Christoph. "La riconstruzione dell'Arco di Tito a Roma nei disegni del primo Cinquecento. Il Codex Coner e Antonio da Sangallo il Giovane," in eds. G. Alisio, G. Cantone, and C. de Seta, *I disegni d'archivio negli studi di storia del'architettura* (Naples): 31–37.

Jones (1912)
Jones, Stuart Henry, ed. *A Catalogue of the Ancient Sculptures Preserved in the Municipal Collections of Rome. The Sculptures of the Museo Capitolino* (Oxford).

Jordan-Huelsen (1878–1907)
Jordan, Heinrich, and Christian Huelsen. *Topographie der Stadt Rom im Alterthum*, 4 vols (Berlin).

Juren (2004)
Juren, Vladimir "Neznámý výtisk Vitruvia s poznámkami a kresbami Antonia da Sangallo il Giovane (Un exemplaire inconnu de Vitruve avec des notes et des dessins d'Antonio da Sangallo il Giovane)," *Bibliotheca Strahoviensis* 6: 157–68.

Juren (2006)
Juren, Vladimir "Un Vitruve inconnu d'Antonio da Sangallo il Giovanne." *Revue d'Histoire des Textes* 1: 335–41.

Kähler (1953)
Kähler, Heinz. *Die Gebälke des Konstantinsbogens* (Heidelberg).

Kammerer-Grothaus (1974)
Kammerer-Grothaus, Helke. "Der Deus Rediculus im Triopion des Herodes Atticus: Untersuchung am Bau und zu polychromer Ziegelarchitektur des 2. Jahrhunderts n. Chr in Latium," *Mitteilungen des deutschen archäologischen Instituts: Römische Abteilung* 81: 131–252.

Keller (1996)
Keller, Fritz-Eugen. "Ricostruire l'antico. Ville rinascimentali su ville antiche," in ed. E.M. Steinby, *Ianiculum – Gianicolo. Storia, topografia, monumenti, leggende dall'anichità al rinascimento* (Acta Instituti Romani Finlandiae, 16) (Rome): 101–07, 111–17.

Krautheimer (1994)
Krautheimer, Richard. "Le tavole di Urbino, Berlino e Baltimora riesaminate," in eds. H.A. Millon and V Magnago Lampugnani, *Il Rinascimento da Brunelleschi a Michelangelo: La rappresentazione dell'architettura*, catalogue of the exhibition (Milan): 233–57.

Krautheimer-Corbett-Frankl (1937–77)
Krautheimer, Richard, Spencer Corbett, and Wolfgang Frankl, eds., *Corpus Basilicarum Christianarum Romae*, 7 vols (Vatican City).

Krencker-Krüger (1929)
Krencker, Daniel and Emil Krüger *Die Trierer Kaiserthermen. Abteilung I. Ausgrabungsbericht und grundsätzliche Untersuchungen römischer Thermen* (Augsburg).

Kulawik (2002)
Kulawik, Bernd. *Die Zeichnungen im Codex Destailleur D (HDZ 4151) der Berliner Kunstbibliothek Preußischer Kulturbesitz zum letzten Projekt Antonio da Sangallos des Jüngeren für den Neubau von St Peter in Rom*, vol. I, *Text und Quellen*, vol. II, *Katalog der Zeichnungen* (Ph.D. diss., Technische Universität Berlin). (DOI: 10.14279/depositonce-499).

La Rocca (1986)
La Rocca, Eugenio. *Rilievi storici capitolini: Il restauro dei pannelli di Adriano e di Marco Aurelio nel Palazzo dei Conservatori* (Rome).

Labacco (1552)
Labacco, Antonio. *Libro d'Antonio Labacco appartenente all'architettura nel qual si figurano alcune notabili antiquità di Roma* (Rome).

Labacco (1559)
Labacco, Antonio. *Libro appartenente appartenente all'architettura nel qual si figurano alcune notabili antiquità di Roma* (Rome).

Lanciani (1883, *Aula del Senato*)
Lanciani, Rodolfo. *L'aula e gli uffici del Senato Romano* (Rome).

Lanciani (1883, *Basilica*)
Lanciani, Rodolfo. "La Basilica Matidies et Marcianes dei cataloghi," *Bulletino della Commissione Archeologica Comunale di Roma* 11: 5–16.

Lanciani (1883, *Portici*)
Lanciani, Rodolfo. "I portici della Regione IX, discorso letto dal sig. comm. R Lanciani nella seduta solenne intitolata alla fondazione di Roma il 20 Aprile 1883" *Annali del'Instituto di Corrispondenza Archeologica* (1883): 3–20.

Lanciani (1891)
Lanciani, Rodolfo. "Miscellanea topografica," *Bullettino della Commissione Archeologica Comunale di Roma* 19: 141–43.

Lanciani (1893–1901)
Lanciani, Rodolfo. *Forma Urbis Romae consilio et auctoritate Regiae Academiae Lyncaeorum formam dimensus est et ad modulum 1:1000*, 9 vols (Milan). Reissued in 1 vol., Rome, 1988.

Lanciani (1897)
Lanciani, Rodolfo. *The Ruins and Excavations of Ancient Rome: A Companion Book for Students and Travelers* (Boston).

Lanciani (1902–12)
Lanciani, Rodolfo. *Storia degli scavi di Roma e delle collezioni romane di antichità*, 3 vols (Rome).

Lemerle, Frédérique (ed.). *Les 'Annotations' de Guillaume Philandrier sur le 'De architectura' de Vitruve. Livres I à IV* (Paris).

Letarouilly (1849–86)
Letarouilly, Paul Marie. *Édifices de Rome moderne ou Recueil des palais, maisons, églises, couvents et autres monuments publics et particuliers les plus remarquables de la Ville de Rome*, 6 vols (Liège).

Losito (1993 *Il capitello*)
Losito, Maria. *Il capitello ionico nel Rinascimento italiano toscano, romano e Veneto (1423–1570)*, PhD thesis, Scuola Normale Superiore, supervisor S. Settis, advisors P. Gros and P.N. Pagliara (Pisa)

Losito (1997 *La ricostruzione*)
Losito, Maria. "La ricostruzione della voluta del capitello ionico vitruviano nel Rinascimento italiano (1450–1570)," in Vitruvio, *De architectura*, ed. P. Gros, trans. and commentary by A. Corso and E. Romano, vol. 2 (Turin): 1409–28.

Losito (2008)
Losito, Maria, "Symétrie de la nature dans le dessin de la volute ionique vitruvienne-archimédienne," in ed. R Gargiani, *La colonne. Nouvelle histoire de la construction*, (Lausanne): 164–71.

Lotz (1956)
Lotz, Wolfgang. "Die ovalen Kirchenräume des Cinquecento," *Römisches Jahrbuch für Kunstgeschichte* 7: 7–99.

LTUR
Lexicon Topographicum Urbis Romae, E.M. Steinby (ed.), 6 vols, Rome 1993–2000.

Luchterhandt (1999)
Luchterhandt, Manfred. "Päpstlicher Palastbau und höfisches Zeremoniell unter Leo III.," in eds. M. Stiegemann and M. Wemhoff, *799. Karl der Grosse und Leo III. in Paderborn. Kunst und Kultur der Karolingerzeit*, vol. 3, catalogue of the exhibition (Paderborn): 109–22.

Lugli (1926)
Lugli, Giuseppe. *Anxur-Terracina* (Forma Italiae, vol. 1) (Rome).

Lupi-Pettinau (1980)
Lupi, Loretta, and Barbara Pettinau. "Disegni e stampe. Il Tempio di Romolo al Foro Romano," *Quaderni dell'Istituto di Storia dell'Architettura* 26: 35–62.

Luschi (1984)
Luschi, Licia. "Un edificio funerario della via Prenestina nei disegni degli Uffizi," *Prospettiva* 39: 30–37.

Madonna (1980)
Madonna, Maria Luisa. "L'ingresso di Carlo V a Roma," in ed. M. Fagiolo, *La città effimera e l'universo artificiale del giardino: La Firenze dei Medici e l'Italia dell '500* (Rome): 63–68.

Magagnato (1992)
Magagnato, Licisco. *Il Teatro Olimpico* (Milan).

Manetti-Saalman (1970)
Manetti, Antonio. *The Life of Brunelleschi*, ed. H. Saalman (University Park, London).

Mansuelli (1941)
Mansuelli, Guido Achille. *Ariminum (Rimini): regio VIII – Aemilia* (Rome).

Marchini **(1**942)
Marchini, Giuseppe. *Giuliano da Sangallo* (Florence).

Marias (1992)
Marias, Fernando "Sobre el Castello de la Calahorra y el Codex Escurialensis," in *Saggi in onore di Renato Bonelli*, eds. C. Bozzoni, G. Carbonara, G. Villetti (Rome): 539–53.

Mattingly (1923–50)
Mattingly, Harold. *Coins of the Roman Empire in the British Museum*, 5 vols, (London) 1923–50.

Meneghini (1991)
Meneghini, Roberto. *Il Foro di Nerva* (Rome).

Millon (1988)
Millon, Henry. "The Facade of San Lorenzo," in eds. H.A. Millon and C.H. Smyth, *Michelangelo Architect: The Facade of San Lorenzo and the Drum and Dome of St Peter's* (Milan): 1–89.

Minnich-Pfeiffer (1981)
Minnich, Nelson H., and Heinrich W. Pfeiffer "De Grassi's 'Conciliabulum' at Lateran V: The De Gargiis Woodcut of Lateran V Re-examined," *Archivium Historicae Pontificiae* 19: 147–72.

Modonutti (2014)
Cristina Modonutti, "Bussola e rilievo architettonico nei disegni di Antonio da Sangallo il Giovane e Baldassarre Peruzzi," *Annali di Architettura* 26: 7–28.

Moneti (1993)
Moneti, Andrea. "Forma e posizione della villa degli horti Lucullani secondo i rilievi rinascimentali. La loro influenza sui progetti del Belvedere e delle ville Madama, Barbaro e Aldobrandini" *Palladio* 6.12: 5–24.

Nash (1961–62)
Nash, Ernest, *Bildlexikon zur Topographie des antiken Rom*. 2 vols (Tübingen).

Nesselrath (1986 *Archaeological method*)
Nesselrath, Arnold. "Raphael's archaeological method," in *Raffaello a Roma, il convegno di 1983* (Rome): 357–72.

Nesselrath (1986 *I Libri*)
Nesselrath, Arnold. "I libri di disegni di antichità. Tentativo di una tipologia," in ed. S. Settis, *Memoria dell'antico nell'arte italiana* III: *Dalla tradizione all'archeologia*, (Turin): 87–147.

Nesselrath (1989 *Monumenta Antiqua*)
Nesselrath, Arnold. "'Monumenta Antiqua Romana': Ein illustrierter Rom-Traktat des Quattrocento," in eds. R. Harprath and H. Wrede, *Antikenzeichnung und Antikenstudium in Renaissance und Frühbarock* (Mainz): 21-37.

Nesselrath (1989 *Review Giuliano*)
Nesselrath, Arnold. "Review of reprint of Christian Hülsen, *Il Libro di Giuliano da Sangallo*," in *Zeitschrift für Kunstgeschichte* 2: 281–92.

Nesselrath (1992)
Nesselrath, Arnold. "The Codex Coner—85 Years On," in *Cassiano Del Pozzo's Paper Museum – Quaderni Puteani III* (Milan): 145–67 [some kind of a periodical].

Nesselrath (1993)
Nesselrath, Arnold. *Das Fossombroner Skizzenbuch* (London).

Nesselrath (1996)
Nesselrath, Arnold. "Il 'Codice Escurialense'," in eds. W. Prinz and M. Seidel, *Domenico Ghirlandaio* (Florence): 175–98.
Nesselrath (2005)
Nesselrath, Arnold. "Disegnare Roma," in ed. F.P. Fiore, *La Roma di Leon Battista Alberti umanisti, architetti e artisti alla scoperta dell'antico nella città del Quattrocento* (Milan): 44–55.
Nesselrath (2008)
Nesselrath, Arnold. "Impressionen zum Pantheon in der Renaissance," *Pegasus* 10: 37–84.
Niebaum (2008)
Niebaum, Jens. "Zur Planungs- und Baugeschichte der Peterskirche zwischen 1506 und 1513," in eds. G. Satzinger and S. Schütze, *Sankt Peter in Rom 1506–2006*. (Munich): 49–82.
Pacciani (1998)
Pacciani, Riccardo. "Firenze nella seconda metà del secolo," in ed. F.P. Fiore, *Storia dell'architettura italiana*, vol. 1, *Il Quattrocento*, (Milan): 330–73.
Pacciani (2008)
Pacciani, Riccardo. "Disegni di Cronaca," *Opus Incertum* 5 (2008): 29–37.
Pagano (1997)
Pagano, Antonella. "Ferri, Alfonso," *Dizionario Biografico degli Italiani* (1925–2020), 47: 111–114.
Pagliara (1972)
Pagliara, Pier Nicola. "L'attività edilizia di Antonio da Sangallo il Giovane: Il confronto tra gli studi sull'antico e la letteratura vitruviana," *Controspazio* 7: 19–55.
Pagliara (1984, *Cripta Balbi*)
Pier Nicola Pagliara. "Giuliano da Sangallo. Alzato della Cripta Balbi," in eds. C.L. Frommel, S. Ray, and M. Tafuri, *Raffaello architetto* (Milan): 417.
Pagliara (1984, *Palazzo Alberini*)
Pagliara, Pier Nicola. "Palazzo Alberini," in eds. C.L. Frommel, S. Ray, and M. Tafuri, *Raffaello architetto* (Milan): 171–88.
Pagliara (1984, *Palazzo Branconio*)
Pagliara, Pier Nicola. "Palazzo Branconio," in eds. C.L. Frommel, S. Ray, and M. Tafuri, *Raffaello architetto*, (Milan): 197–216.
Pagliara (1986 *Vitruvio*)
Pagliara, Pier Nicola. "Vitruvio da testo a canone," in *Memoria dell'antico nell'arte italiana* 3; *Dalla tradizione all'archeologia*, ed. S. Settis (Turin): 5–85.
Pagliara (1988)
Pagliara, Pier Nicola. "Studi e pratica vitruviana di Antonio da Sangallo e di suo fratello Giovanni Battista," in ed. J. Guillaume, *Les Traités d'architecture de la Renaissance*, conference proceedings (Paris): 179–206.
Pagliara (1992, *Ordini*)
Pagliara, Pier Nicola. "Antonio da Sangallo il Giovane e gli ordini," in ed. J. Guillaume, *L'emploi des ordres dans l'architecture de la Renaissance*, conference proceedings (Tours): 137–56.
Pagliara (1992, *Battista Sangallo*)
Pagliara. Pier Nicola. "Sangallo, (Giovanni) Battista," *The Dictionary of Art*, vol. 27 (New York): 747–49.
Pagliara (1995)
Pagliara, Pier Nicola. "Sanmicheli e gli ordini," in ed. S. Foschi, *Michele Sanmicheli*, conference proceedings (Milan): 134–53.
Pagliara (forthcoming, *Domestic Architecture*)
Pagliara, Pier Nicola. "Domestic Architecture in the Project Drawings of Antonio da Sangallo the Younger," in eds. C.L. Frommel, G. Schelbert, *The Architectural Drawings of Antonio da Sangallo the Younger, Vol. IV, Palaces and Houses* (London-Turnhout).
Palladio (1570)
Palladio, Andrea. *I quattro libri dell'architettura: Ne'quali, dopo un breve trattato de'cinque ordini, et di quelli avertimenti, che sono più necessarij nel fabricare; si tratta delle case private, delle vie, de i ponti, delle piazze, de i xisti, et de'tempij*, 4 vols (Venice).
Pandolfi (2018)
Pandolfi, Simone. *Corti al vetriolo: Veleni e medici nel rinascimento italiano*, (Zanica).
Pasini (1974)
Pasini, Pier Giorgio. *L'arco di Augusto* (Rimini).
Pastor (1891–1933)
Pastor, Ludwig von. *Geschichte der Päpste seit dem Ausgang des Mittelalters*. 1st edition. 16 vols (Freiburg).
Pellecchia (1992)
Pellecchia, Linda. "Architects Read Vitruvius: Renaissance Interpretation of the Antique House," *Journal of the Society of Architectural Historians* 51: 377–416.
Pellecchia (1993)
Pellecchia, Linda. "Reconstructing the Greek House: Giuliano da Sangallo's Villa for the Medici in Florence," *Journal of the Society of Architectural Historians* 52: 323–38.
Pensabene (1984)
Pensabene, Patrizio. *Tempio di Saturno* (Lavori e studi di archeologia pubblicati dalla Soprintendenza Archeologica di Roma, 5) (Rome).
Pfanner (1983)
Pfanner, Michael. *Der Titusbogen* (Mainz).
Pietrangeli (1939)
Carlo Pietrangeli, Spoletium (Spoleto). Regio VI, Umbria, Istituto di studi romani (Rome).
Pochat (1990)
Pochat, Götz. *Theater* und *bildende Kunst im Mittelalter und in der Renaissance in Italien* (Graz).
Poeschke (1990)
Poeschke, J. *Die Skulptur der Renaissance in Italien*, vol. 1. *Donatello und seine Zeit* (Munich).
Puppi (1973)
Puppi, Lionello. *Andrea Palladio*, 2 vols (Milan).

Puppi (1986)
Puppi, Lionello. "Un viaggio per il Veneto di Antonio da Sangallo e di Michele Sanmicheli nella primavera del 1526, un progetto per i Griman, e qualche riflessione a margine," in ed. G. Spagnesi, *Antonio da Sangallo il Giovane: La vita e l'opera* (Rome): 101–7.
Rasch (1984)
Rasch, Jürgen J. *Das Maxentius-Mausoleum an der Via Appia in Rom* (Mainz).
Raub (2014)
Raub, Andreas. "Das Mausoleum von Halikarnassos in den Zeichnungen Antonio da Sangallos des Jüngeren. Ein zerstörtes Weltwunder und der Beginn seiner Rekonstrukion,"*Pegasus* 16: 167–206.
Rausa (1997)
Rausa, Federico. *Pirro Ligorio: tombe e mausolei dei Romani* (Rome).
Rickman (1971)
Rickman, Geoffrey, *Roman Granaries and Store Buildings* (Cambridge).
Riegel (1998)
Riegel, Nicole. *Santa Maria presso San Celso in Mailand. Der Kirchenbau und seine Innendekoration* (Worms).
Righetti (1833–36)
Righetti, Pietro. *Descrizione del Campidoglio*, 2 vols (Rome).
Rowland (2003)
Rowland, Ingrid (ed.). *Vitruvius: Ten books on architecture. The Corsini incunabulum. With the annotations and autograph drawings of Giovanni Battista da Sangallo* (Rome).
Russo (1992)
Russo, Eugenio. "Su S. Salvatore di Spoleto sul tempietto del Clitumno," *Acta ad archaeologiam et artium historiam pertinentia* 8: 87–143.
Salmi (1951)
Salmi, Mario. *La Basilica di San Salvatore di Spoleto* (Florence).
Santoni (1887)
Santoni, Milziade. *Il teatro dell'antica Ricina* (Camerino).
Sanudo (1969–70)
Sanudo, Marin. *I Diarii di Marino Sanuto: 1496–1533*, 58 vols (Bologna).
Satzinger (1991)
Satzinger, Georg. *Antonio da Sangallo der Ältere und die Madonna di San Biagio bei Montepulciano* (Tübingen).
Scaglia (1991–92)
Scaglia, Giustina. "Drawings of 'Roma Antica' in a Vitruvius edition of the Metropolitan Museum of Art," *Römisches Jahrbuch der Bibliotheca Hertziana* 27–28: 59–136.
Scaglia (1994)
Scaglia, Giustina. "Antonio del Tanghero in Rome in 1518 with Pietro Rosselli, Michelangelo Buonarroti, and Antonio da Sangallo il Giovane," *Mitteilungen des Kunsthistorischen Instituts in Florenz* 38: 218–45.
Scaglia (1995)
Scaglia, Giustina. "Drawings of 'Roma antica' in a Vitruvius Edition of the Metropolitan Museum of Art: Part. III," *Römisches Jahrbuch der Bibliotheca Hertziana* 30: 249–305.
Schich (2009)
Schich, Maximilian: *Rezeption und Tradierung als komplexes Netzwerk. Der Census und visuelle Dokumente zu den Thermen in Rom* (Munich).
Schweikhart (1977)
Schweikhart, Gunter *Le antichità di Verona di Giovanni Caroto* (Verona).
Serlio (1537)
Serlio, Sebastiano. *Regole generali di architettura di Sebastiano Serlio sopra le cinque maniere degli edifici, cioè, Thoscano, Dorico, Ionico, Corinthico, e composito: con gli essempi de l'antiquita* (Venice).
Serlio (1540)
Serlio, Sebastiano. *Il terzo libro di Sebastiano Serlio nel qual si figurano e descrivono le antiquita di Roma, e le altre che sono in Italia, e fuori d'Italia* (Venice).
Serlio (1619)
Serlio, Sebastiano. *Il terzo libro di Sebastiano Serlio nel qual si figurano e descrivono le antiquita di Roma, e le altre che sono in Italia, e fuori d'Italia* (Venice).
Shearman (2003)
Shearman, John K. *Raphael in early modern sources (1483–1602)*, 2 vols (New Haven).
Spera (1999)
Spera, Lucrezia. *Il paesaggio suburbano di Roma dall'antichità al medioevo: il comprensorio tra le vie latina e ardeatina dalle Mura Aureliane al III miglio* (Rome)
Stevens (1931)
Stevens, Gorham P, "The volute of the capital of the temple of Athena at Priene," *Memoirs of the American Academy in Rome*, IX (1931): 135–44.
Tafuri (1984, *Obelisco*)
Tafuri, Manfredo. "Obelisco," in *Raffaello architetto*, eds. C.L. Frommel, S. Ray, and M. Tafuri (Milan): 229–30.
Tafuri (1984, *Roma instaurata*)
Tafuri, Manfredo. "Roma instaurata: Strategie urbane e politiche pontificie nella Roma del primo '500," in eds. C.L. Frommel, S. Ray, and M. Tafuri, *Raffaello architetto* (Milan): 59–107.
Tafuri (1992)
Tafuri, Manfredo. *Ricerca del Rinascimento principi, città, architetti* (Turin). English edition 2006 *Interpreting the Renaissance. Princes, Cities, Architects* (New Haven and London).
Tessari (1995)
Tessari, Cristiano. *Baldassarre Peruzzi: Il progetto dell'antico* (Milan).
Thielscher (1961)
Thielscher, Paul. "Vitruvius," in *Realenzyclopaedie, Pauly Wissova*, IX.A, I: 420–21.

Tolnai (1934)
Tolnai, Karl. "Michelange e la façade de San Lorenzo," *Gazette des Beaux-Arts* ser 6, 11: 24–42.
Tolnay (1972)
De Tolnay, Charles. "I progetti di Michelangelo per la facciata di S. Lorenzo a Firenze: Nuove ricerche," *Commentari* 12: 53–71.
Tolnay (1975–80)
De Tolnay, Charles, ed. *Corpus dei disegni di Michelangelo*, 4 vols (Novara).
Tosi (1980)
Tosi, Giovanna. "L'arco dei Gavi," in ed. P. Marini, *Palladio e Verona* (Verona): 34–49.
Tosi (1983)
Tosi, Giovanna. *L'Arco dei Gavi* (Rome).
Uginet-Fossier (1980–94)
Uginet, François-Charles, and F. Fossier, eds., *Le Palais Farnèse*. 3 vols (Rome).
Valentini-Zucchetti (1940–53)
Valentini, Roberto, and Giuseppe Zucchetti. *Codice topografico della città di Roma*, 4 vols, (Rome).
Valori (1985)
Valori, Susanna. *Disegni di antichità dell'Albertina di Vienna* (Xenia Quaderni 6) (Rome).
Valtieri (1983)
Valtieri, Simonetta. "La fabbrica del Palazzo del Cardinale Raffaele Riario (La Cancelleria)," *Quaderni dell'Istituto di Storia dell'Architettura* 27: 3–25.
Valtieri (1984 *Sant'Eligio*)
Valtieri, Simonetta. "Sant'Eligio degli Orefici," in *Raffaello architetto*, eds. C.L. Frommel, S. Ray, and M. Tafuri (Milan): 148–49.
Valtieri (1986)
Valtieri, Simonetta. "Sistemazioni absidiali di chiese in funzione di 'Mausoleo' in progetti di Antonio da Sangallo il Giovane," in ed. G. Spagnesi, *Antonio da Sangallo il Giovane: La vita e l'opera* (Rome): 109–18.
Vasari-Milanesi (1878–85)
Vasari, Giorgio. *Le vite de' più eccellenti pittori scultori e architettori italiani, da Cimabue insino a' tempi nostri*, 9 vols, ed. G. Milanesi (Florence).
Vasari-Milanesi (1906)
Vasari, Giorgio. *Le vite de' più eccellenti pittori scultori e architettori italiani, da Cimabue insino a' tempi nostri*, ed. G. Milanesi, 9 vols (Florence).
Vasori (1979)
Vasori, Orietta. *Disegni di antichità etrusche agli Uffizi* (Florence).
Vasori (1981)
Vasori, Orietta, and Antonio Giuliano. *I monumenti antichi in Italia nei disegni degli Uffizi* (Rome).
Viscogliosi (2000)
Viscogliosi, Alessandro. *I Fori Imperiali nei disegni d'architettura del primo Cinquecento: Ricerche sull'architettura e l'urbanistica di Roma* (Rome).
Viscogliosi (2017)
Viscogliosi, Alessandro. "Antonio da Sangallo e Palladio tra foro di Augusto e foro di Nerva. Diverse maniere di osservare l'Antico, tra la pianta di Roma di Raffaello e il Teatro Olimpico," *Annali di Architettura* 29: 101–16.
Vitruvius-Barbaro (1567)
Vitruvius. *I dieci libri dell'architettura di M. Vitruvio*, trans. and annotated, D. Barbaro (Venice).
Vitruvius-Barbaro-Carunchio (1999)
Vitruvius. *I dieci libri dell'architettura di M. Vitruvio*, trans. and annotated, D. Barbaro. Reprint ed. D. Carunchio (Rome).
Vitruvius-Cesariano (1521)
Vitruvius. *Di Lucio Vitruvio Pollione de Architectura Libri Dece traducti de latino in Vulgare affigurati, comentati et con mirando ordine insigniti*, ed. and tr C. Cesariano, B. Giovio and B. Mauro (Como).
Vitruvius-Durantino (1524)
Vitruvius. M. L. Vitruvio Pollione de Architectura traducto de Latino in Vulgare dal vero exemplare, ed. and tr. F. Lutio Durantino (Venice).
Vitruvius-Fra Giocondo (1511)
Fra Giocondo. *M. Vitruvius per Iocundum solito castigatior factus: cum figuris et tabula, ut iam legi et intelligi possit* (Venice).
Vitruvius-Fra Giocondo (1513)
Fra Giocondo. *Vitruvius iterum et Frontinus à Iocundo revisi repurgatique quantum ex collatione licuit* (Florence).
Vitruvius-Philandrier (1544)
Philandrier, Guillaume. *In decem libros M. Vitruvij Pollionis De archetectura annotationes* (Rome).
Von Heilmeyer (1970)
von Heilmeyer, Wolf-Dieter "Korinthische Normalkapitelle, Studien zur Geschichte der Roemischen Architeckturdekoration," in *Mitteilungen des Deutschen Archaeologischen Instituts. Roemische Abteilung*. Sechzehntes Ergaenzungsheft (Heidelberg).
Ward-Perkins (1949)
Ward-Perkins, John Bryan. "The Church of San Salvatore at Spoleto: some structural notes," *Papers of the British School at Rome* 17: 72–86.
Waters (2014)
Waters, Micheal J. "Francesco di Giorgio and the Reconstruction of Antiquity. Epigraphy, Archeology, and Newly Discovered Drawings," *Pegasus* 16: 9–102.
Winckelmann (1760)
Winckelmann, Johann Joachim. *Description des pierres gravées du feu baron de Stosch* (Florence).
Winckelmann (1762)
Winckelmann, Johann Joachim. *Anmerkungen über der Baukunst der Alten* (Leipzig).
Winckelmann (1825–9)
Winckelmann, Johann Joachim. *Sämtliche Werke*, ed. Joseph Eiselein, 12 vols, (Donaueschingen).
Winckelmann (1952–7)
Winckelmann, Johann Joachim. *Briefe*, ed. W. Rehm with H. Diepolder, 4 vols, (Berlin) 1952–7.

Windfeld-Hansen (1969)
Windfeld-Hansen, Hemming. "La rotonde paléochrétienne du cimetière de Prétextat à Rome et sa comparaison avec les églises en forme d'hexaconque de Dalmatie,"*Bulletin du CIHA* 4: 18–19.
Wolff Metternich (1972)
Wolff Metternich, Franz Graf. *Die Erbauung der Peterskirche zu Rom im 16. Jahrhundert* (Vienna, Munich).
Wolff Metternich–Thoenes (1987)
Wolff Metternich, Franz Graf. *Die frühen St Peter-Entwürfe 1505–1514. Aus dem Nachlass herausgegeben*, ed. C. Thoenes (Tübingen).
Wurm (1965)
Wurm, Heinrich. *Der Palazzo Massimo alle Colonne* (Berlin)
Wurm (1984)
Wurm, Heinrich. *Baldassarre Peruzzi: Architekturzeichnungen* (Tübingen).
Yegül (1992)
Yegül, Fikret. *Baths and Bathing in Classical Antiquity* (Cambridge, Mass., London).
Zampa (2008)
Zampa, Paola. "Codice Strozzi: alcune considerazioni," *Opus Incertum* 5 (2008): 65–75.
Zampa (2014)
Zampa, Paola. "La basilica Emilia – architettura, lessico, costruzione." *Pegasus* 16. 207–40.
Zampa (2017)
Zampa, Paola. "«Questo tempio è di opera dorica»: il dorico, da Antonio da Sangallo il Giovane a Palladio," Annali di architettura, 29, 2017. 127–34.
Zampa (2019)
Zampa, Paola. "«una bella discrezione da esser considerata." L'angolo della basilica Emilia," 2019 (Roma).
Zanchettin (2003–4)
Zanchettin, Vitale. "Via di Ripetta e la genesi del Tridente. Strategie di riforma urbana tra volontà papali e istituzioni laiche" *Römisches Jahrbuch der Bibliotheca Hertziana* 35: 209–86.
Zavatta (2008)
Zavatta, Giulio. *1526. Antonio da Sangallo il Giovane in Romagna. Rilievi di fortificazioni e monumenti antichi romagnoli di Antonio da Sangallo il Giovane e della sua cerchia al Gabinetto Disegni e Stampe degli Uffizi* (Imola).
Zorzi (1956)
Zorzi, Giangiorgio. "Altri disegni di vari artisti riguardanti monumenti antichi nelle raccolte palladiane di Vicenza e di Londra." *Palladio* N.S. 6: 54–67.
Zorzi (1957)
Zorzi, Giangiorgio. "La 'Villa di Mecenate' e il tempio di Ercole Vincitore a Tivoli nei disegni di Andrea Palladio," *Palladio* n.s. 8: 149–71.

Index of Places and Buildings

The places and buildings index refers only to the catalogue. It is a compilation of identifications from information written on the sheets themselves and identifications made by scholars. Monuments in and around Rome, as well as today's Vatican state are generally subsumed under Rome.

Index of Proper Names

This index provides the names of persons cited in the entries and in the inscriptions.

List of Sheets Included in Volume III

Florence, Le Gallerie degli Uffizi, Gabinetto dei Disegni e delle Stampe

U 32A *recto and verso*
U 184A *recto and verso*
U 284A *recto and verso*
U 508A *recto and verso*
U 562A *recto and verso*
U 575A *recto and verso*
U 606A *recto*
U 716A *recto*
U 626A *recto and verso*
U 788A *verso*
U 790A *recto and verso*
U 815A *recto and verso*
U 834A *recto and verso*
U 844A *recto*
U 853A *recto and verso*
U 854A *verso*
U 859A *recto*
U 888A *recto and verso*
U 894A *recto*
U 896A *recto*
U 900A *recto*
U 903A *recto*
U 911A *recto*
U 913A *recto and verso*
U 915A *recto and verso*
U 917A *recto and verso*
U 919A *recto and verso*
U 930A *recto and verso*
U 932A *recto and verso*
U 949A *recto*
U 992A *recto*
U 1037A *recto and verso*
U 1038A *recto*
U 1039A *recto and verso*
U 1040A *recto*
U 1042A *recto*
U 1043A *recto*
U 1044A *recto and verso*
U 1046A *recto*
U 1057A *recto and verso*
U 1064A *recto and verso*
U 1065A *recto*
U 1066A *recto and verso*
U 1067A *recto and verso*
U 1068A *recto and verso*
U 1069A *recto and verso*
U 1071A *recto and verso*
U 1072A *recto and verso*
U 1088A *recto*
U 1089A *recto and verso*
U 1090A *recto and* U 1230A *verso and* U 1090A *verso and* U 1230A *recto*
U 1093A *recto*
U 1095A *recto and verso*
U 1099A *recto*
U 1107A *recto and verso*
U 1112A *recto*
U 1115A *recto*
U 1117A *recto and verso*
U 1119A *recto and verso*
U 1120A *recto and verso*
U 1121A *recto*
U 1122A *recto and verso*
U 1123A *recto*
U 1124A *recto and verso*
U 1126A *recto*
U 1127A *recto*
U 1128A *recto*
U 1131A *recto*
U 1132A *recto*
U 1133A *recto*
U 1134A *recto and verso*
U 1135A *recto*
U 1136A *recto*
U 1137A *recto*
U 1138A *recto and verso*
U 1139A *recto*
U 1140A *recto and verso*
U 1141A *recto and verso*
U 1142A *recto and verso*
U 1143A *recto and verso*
U 1144A *recto*
U 1147A *recto*
U 1150A *recto*
U 1152A *recto and verso*
U 1153A *recto and verso*
U 1154A *recto and verso*
U 1156A *recto and verso*
U 1159A *recto and verso*
U 1161A *recto and verso*
U 1162A *recto and verso*
U 1163A *recto*
U 1165A *recto and verso*
U 1166A *recto and verso*
U 1167A *recto*
U 1168A *recto and verso*
U 1171A *recto and verso*
U 1172A *recto*
U 1174A *recto and verso*
U 1175A *recto*
U 1176A *recto*
U 1177A *recto*
U 1178A *recto*
U 1179A *recto*
U 1180A *recto*
U 1181A *recto and verso*
U 1182A *recto*
U 1183A *recto*
U 1184A *recto*
U 1186A *recto*
U 1187A *recto and verso*
U 1188A *recto*
U 1189A *recto and verso*
U 1190A *recto*
U 1192A *recto and verso*
U 1193A *recto*
U 1195A *recto*
U 1197A *recto*
U 1200A *recto*
U 1201A *recto*
U 1202A *recto*
U 1203A *recto and verso*
U 1204A *recto and verso*
U 1206A *recto and verso*
U 1207A *recto and verso*
U 1208A *recto and verso*
U 1209A *recto*
U 1210A *recto and verso*
U 1211A *recto and verso*
U 1213A *recto and verso*
U 1214A *recto*
U 1216A *recto and verso*
U 1218A *recto*
U 1220A *recto*
U 1221A *recto and verso*
U 1223A *recto and verso*
U 1225A *recto*
U 1226A *recto*
U 1227A *recto*
U 1229A *recto and verso*
U 1231A *recto*
U 1232A *recto*
U 1233A *recto and verso*
U 1240A *recto and verso*
U 1243A *recto*
U 1249A *recto and verso*
U 1253A *recto and verso*
U 1255A *recto and verso*
U 1270A *recto and verso*
U 1271A *recto*
U 1273A *recto and verso*
U 1283A *recto and verso*
U 1287A *recto*
U 1296A *recto and verso*
U 1299A *recto*
U 1300A *recto*
U 1301A *recto and verso*
U 1305A *recto*
U 1306A *recto*

U 1318A *recto and verso*
U 1319A *recto*
U 1325A *recto*
U 1327A *recto and verso*
U 1329A *recto*
U 1335A *recto*
U 1336A *recto and verso*
U 1337A *recto*
U 1338A *recto and verso*
U 1351A *recto*
U 1357A *recto*
U 1366A *recto*
U 1369A *recto and verso*
U 1372A *recto*
U 1373A *recto and verso*
U 1374A *recto*
U 1375A *verso*
U 1376A *recto*
U 1377A *recto and verso*
U 1378A *recto and verso*
U 1381A *recto and verso*
U 1382A *recto*
U 1383A *recto*
U 1384A *recto*
U 1385A *recto and verso*
U 1386A *recto and verso*
U 1387A *verso*
U 1388A *recto*
U 1393A *recto*
U 1394A *recto and verso*
U 1402A *recto and verso*
U 1404A *recto*
U 1407A *recto*
U 1409A *recto*
U 1410A *recto*
U 1413A *recto and verso*
U 1414A *recto and verso*
U 1427A *recto and verso*
U 1428A *recto*
U 1430A *recto*
U 1453A *recto*
U 1465A *recto and verso*
U 1489A *recto and verso*
U 1544A *recto*
U 1545A *recto and verso*
U 1547A *recto and verso*
U 1553A *recto and verso*
U 1555A *recto and verso*
U 1565A *recto*
U 1576A *recto and verso*
U 1578A *recto*
U 1579A *recto*
U 1627A *recto and verso*
U 1630A *recto and verso*
U 1631A *recto and verso*
U 1636A *recto*
U 1637A *recto*
U 1638A *recto*
U 1648A *recto*
U 1650A *recto and verso*
U 1652A *recto and verso*
U 1654A *recto and verso*
and U 3972A *recto and verso*
U 1656A *recto*
U 1657A *recto and verso*
U 1658A *recto and verso*
U 1660A *recto and verso*
U 1661A *verso*
U 1662A *recto and verso*
U 1664A *recto*
U 1667A *recto and verso*
U 1668A *recto*
U 1701A *recto*
U 1702A *recto and verso*
U 1703A *recto and verso*
U 1704A *recto*
U 1705A *recto*
U 1706A *recto and verso*
U 1716A *recto and verso*
U 1720A *recto and verso*
U 1804A *recto and verso*
U 1844A *recto and verso*
U 1850A *recto*
U 1852A *recto*
U 1856A *recto and verso*
U 1865A *recto*
U 1883A *recto*
U 1889A *verso*
U 1966A *recto and verso*
U 2043A *recto and verso*
U 2044A *recto and verso*
U 2045A *recto and verso*
U 2046A *recto and verso*
U 2047A *recto and verso*
U 2054A *recto and verso*
U 2055A *recto and verso*
U 2056A *recto and verso*
U 2057A *recto and verso*
U 2084A *recto and verso*
U 2086A *recto and verso*
U 2087A *recto*
U 2095A *recto and verso*
U 2096A *recto and verso*
U 2098A *recto*
U 2099A *recto*
U 2103A *recto*
U 2114A *recto*
U 2134A *recto and verso*
U 2143A *recto and verso*
U 2147A *recto*
U 2162A *recto*
U 2163A *recto and verso*
U 3944A *recto*
U 3945A *recto and verso*
U 3965A *recto and verso*
U 3966A *recto and verso*
U 3969A *recto and verso*
U 3973A *recto*
U 3974A *recto*
U 4003A *recto*
U 4039A *recto*
U 4099A *recto*
U 4114A *recto*
U 4117A *recto*
U 4119A *recto*
U 4128A *recto and verso*
U 4151A *recto and verso*
U 4152A *recto*
U 4153A *recto*
U 4154A *recto*
U 6771A *recto and verso*
U 6772A *recto*
U 6803A *recto and verso*

Codex Rootstein Hopkins (London, Royal Institute of British Architects)

fol. 1r.
fol. 1v.
fol. 2r.
fol. 2v.
fol. 3r.
fol. 3v.
fol. 4r.
fol. 4v.
fol. 5r.
fol. 5v.
fol. 6r.
fol. 6v.
fol. 7r.
fol. 7v.
fol. 8r.
fol. 8v.
fol. 9r.
fol. 9v.
fol. 10r.
fol. 10v.
fol. 11r.
fol. 11v.
fol. 12r.
fol. 12v.
fol. 13r.
fol. 13v.
fol. 14r.
fol. 14v.
fol. 15r.
fol. 15v.
fol. 16r.
fol. 16v.
fol. 17r.
fol. 17v.
fol. 18r.
fol. 18v.
fol. 19r.
fol. 19v.
fol. 20r.
fol. 20v.
fol. 21r.
fol. 21v.
fol. 22r.
fol. 22v.
fol. 23r.
fol. 23v.